The Descent of Mind

The Descent of Mind

Psychological Perspectives on Hominid Evolution

Edited by

Michael C. Corballis

Department of Psychology,
University of Auckland

and

Stephen E. G. Lea

Department of Psychology,
University of Exeter

OXFORD

UNIVERSITY PRESS

Great Clarendon Street, Oxford OX2 6DP
Oxford University Press is a department of the University of Oxford.
It furthers the University's objective of excellence in research, scholarship,
and education by publishing worldwide in

Oxford   New York

Athens   Auckland   Bangkok   Bogotá   Bombay   Buenos Aires   Calcutta
Cape Town   Chennai   Dar es Salaam   Delhi   Florence   Hong Kong   Istanbul
Karachi   Kuala Lumpur   Madrid   Melbourne   Mexico City   Mumbai
Nairobi   Paris   São Paulo   Singapore   Taipei   Tokyo   Toronto   Warsaw

with associated companies in Berlin Ibadan

Published in the United States
by Oxford University Press Inc., New York

First published 1999

A catalogue record for this book is available from the British Library

Library of Congress Cataloging in Publication Data
(Data available)

ISBN 0 19 852419 6 (Hbk)

Typeset by Technical Typesetting Ireland, Belfast
Printed and bound in Great Britain by
Biddles Ltd, Guildford and King's Lynn.

Preface

To most people, it seems obvious that there is a profound mental discontinuity between us and all other species. This is a belief that we should naturally view with suspicion, because there are clear benefits to be gained from holding it even if it is untrue. Humans have long exploited other animals; we breed them, eat them, milk them, skin them, fleece them, ride them, steal their eggs, shoot them for sport, take them apart to see how they work, wittingly and unwittingly give them diseases, keep them in captivity as objects of curiosity or ridicule, and make them work for us. We can be relieved of at least some of our guilt by believing them to be mentally inferior to ourselves, perhaps to the point of being unable to experience pain, shame, humiliation, or self-awareness. It is sometimes assumed that only humans are capable of consciousness itself. Of course, one might equally turn the tables and argue that we are able to exploit animals in the ways we do precisely because they *are* our mental inferiors.

The question of how we might differ mentally from other animals is not just a matter of folk psychology. There has been considerable academic speculation on the topic, much of it from specialists in fields other than psychology. In a recent book, for example, the archaeologist Stephen Mithen (1996) asks, "Why ask an archaeologist about the human mind?" (p. 9). It is a reasonable question, and Mithen provides fair and insightful answers. Archaeologists have provided much of the material from which we can make inferences about the minds of our ancestors, and Mithen makes an eloquent plea for 'cognitive archaeology', a phrase originally coined by his fellow archaeologist Colin Renfrew (1983). Mithen's own speculations are interesting, and feature in several of the chapters of this book.

Our aim, though, has been to show what psychologists themselves have to say on the evolution of mind. At the end of *Origin of Species* Charles Darwin predicted that "Psychology will be based on a new foundation", but psychologists have on the whole been curiously reluctant to embrace the theory of evolution. Over the past decade, with the surge of general interest in evolution, and more particularly human evolution, this has begun to change. About a decade ago, there emerged a discipline called 'evolutionary psychology', stemming largely from the work of John Tooby and Leda Cosmides. The seminal publication in this field is the edited volume by Barkow *et al.* (1992), but Steven Pinker's (1997) popular book *How the Mind Works* will undoubtedly place evolutionary psychology on a wider intellectual map, and perhaps even radically alter the public perception of what psychology itself is all about. As Pinker summarizes it, evolutionary psychology takes the view that the mind is made up of specialized modules, and attempts the 'reverse-engineering' enterprise of determining how these modules might have emerged as adaptations in the course of hominid evolution, with a primary focus on the hunter–gatherer phase which, according to Pinker, makes up 99 percent of our evolutionary heritage.[1]

This book is about evolutionary psychology in a wider sense, although Pinker's more specific concept of evolutionary psychology naturally features in several of the chapters that follow. But not all the authors of the chapters accept the idea that the mind is composed of special-purpose modules, and not all of them consider the hunter–gatherer phase to have been the critical one. Some of them come from a background of comparative psychology, some from developmental psychology, some from the psychology of language—but they are all primarily *psychologists*. We simply asked them to give us their perspectives on the human mind, how it differs from the minds of other animals, how and when it might have evolved.

We are delighted with their responses, and with the sheer variety of ideas that have emerged. The first three chapters are intended primarily as background to those that follow. Chapter 1 is historical; although psychologists have seldom explicitly imported natural selection into their theories, a good deal of psychological theory involves at least implicit assumptions about the similarities or differences between humans and other species. The chapter traces these assumptions through the history of scientific psychology. Chapter 2 summarizes a little of what is known about mind, or mind-like phenomena, in animals other than primates, to provide a perspective on what the evolution of mind had to build upon, while Chapter 3 provides an overview of primate and hominid evolution, to bring the reader up to date with the various species that carried the evolving mind from that pre-primate level to its modern state. The remaining chapters are then arranged in a rough temporal sequence, in terms of the stage of human evolution they are discussing. So we begin with chapters that focus on pre-hominid primates, whose mental commonalities with modern humans are assumed to date back twenty million years or so, and end with a focus on contemporary human behaviour.

Auckland   M.C.C.
Exeter   S.E.G.L.
June 1998

References

Barkow, J., Cosmides, L., and Tooby, J. (eds.) (1992). *The adapted mind: evolutionary psychology and the generation of culture*. Oxford University Press, New York.

Darwin, C. (1859). *The origin of species by means of natural selection*. John Murray, London.

Jones, S. (1997). The set within the skull. *New York Review of Books*, **44** (17), 13–16.

Mithen, S. (1996). *The prehistory of the mind: the cognitive origins of art, religion and science*. Thames and Hudson, London.

Pinker, S. (1997). *How the mind works*. W. W. Norton, New York.

Renfrew, C. (1983). *Towards an archaeology of mind*. Cambridge University Press.

---

[1] This is of course a debatable claim. At one point in the book, Pinker recounts how a lecture on the evolutionary psychology of sexual behaviour was interrupted by a young woman who claimed to have an alternative theory. When asked what it was, she said "Men are slime". Reviewing Pinker's book in the *New York Review of Books*, the geneticist Steve Jones (1997) notes that she was right. For 99 percent of their evolutionary history, men *were* slime—and so were women, along with everything else that lives. It all depends where you date our evolution from.

Acknowledgements

We thank the Department of Psychology at the University of Exeter for kindly providing support for M. C. C. to visit S. E. G. L. in Exeter for the month of May, 1997, when much of the editing work on the book was accomplished. We are also undyingly grateful to our wives, Barbara Corballis and Bronwen Lea, for their patience, support, and encouragement throughout.

Contents

Contributors

Simon Baron-Cohen
Departments of Experimental Psychology and Psychiatry, University of Cambridge, Downing Street, Cambridge CB2 3EB, UK.

Michael J. Beran
3401 Panthersville Road, Decatur, GA 30034, USA.

Paul Bloom
Department of Psychology, University of Arizona, Tucson, AZ 85721, USA.

Richard W. Byrne
School of Psychology, University of St Andrews, St Andrews, Fife KY16 9JU, UK.

Michael C. Corballis
Department of Psychology, University of Auckland, Private Bag 92019, Auckland, New Zealand.

Merlin Donald
Department of Psychology, Queens University, Kingston, Ontario, Canada K7L 3N6.

Kathleen R. Gibson
Department of Anatomical Sciences, University of Texas Health Services Center, P.O. Box 20068, Houston, TX 77225, USA.

Susan Goldin-Meadow
Department of Psychology, University of Chicago, 5730 South Woodlawn Avenue, Chicago, IL 60637, USA.

Deborah Kelemen
Department of Psychology, The Pennsylvania State University, 417 Bruce V. Moore Building, University Park, PA16802, USA.

James E. King
Department of Psychology, University of Arizona, Tucson, AZ 85721, USA.

Stephen E. G. Lea
Department of Psychology, University of Exeter, Washington Singer Laboratories, Exeter EX4 4QG, UK.

Andrew Lock
Department of Psychology, Massey University, Palmerston North, New Zealand.

Peter F. MacNeilage
Department of Psychology, University of Texas, Austin, TX 78712, USA.

I. C. McManus
Department of Psychology, University College London, Gower Street, London WC1E 6BT, UK.

David McNeill
Department of Psychology, University of Chicago, 5730 South Woodlawn Avenue, Chicago, IL 60637, USA.

Duane M. Rumbaugh
Department of Psychology, Georgia State University, University Plaza, Atlanta, GA 30303, USA.

E. Sue Savage-Rumbaugh
Department of Biology, Georgia State University, Atlanta, GA 30303, USA.

Thomas Suddendorf
Department of Psychology, University of Auckland, Private Bag 92019, Auckland, New Zealand.

Del Thiessen
Department of Psychology, University of Texas at Austin, Mezes Hall 330, Austin, TX 78712, USA.

Andrew Whiten
School of Psychology, University of St Andrews, St Andrews, Fife KY16 9JU, UK.

Are humans special? A history of psychological perspectives

Michael C. Corballis and Stephen E. G. Lea

Introduction

Until the emergence of 'evolutionary psychology' in the late 1980s (e.g. Cosmides and Tooby 1987), the theory of evolution has never been systematically incorporated into psychological theory. Even in the context of animal behaviour psychologists have generally sought behavioural principles common to different animals, leaving the study of inter-species variation to the ethologists. To be sure, there have been some exceptions, some of which are discussed in the next chapter, but for much of our history psychology and ethology have been complementary; ethologists have focused on instinct, psychologists on learning, often with the assumption that the principles of learning are essentially the same across all species. Yet, whether one is a behaviourist or a cognitivist, there is one question that is at least implicit in all attempts to develop psychological theory: Are humans special? Is there some special quality of mind or behaviour that sets us apart from other creatures, or can the principles of behaviour that are derived from, say, rats or pigeons be safely applied to our own species?

In this introductory chapter, then, we briefly review the history of psychological attitudes toward the question of continuity versus discontinuity between ourselves and other species. Although these attitudes are often implicit rather than explicit, we shall see that the pendulum has tended to swing from one extreme to the other.

Intellectual precursors

Intellectually, the two extreme positions were established well before the emergence of psychology as an experimental science in the latter half of the nineteenth century. More than anyone else, it was probably Descartes (1647/1985) who gave scientific and philosophical respectability to the idea of a fundamental discontinuity between us and other creatures. Intrigued by mechanical toys that were popular at the time, he concluded that it should be possible, at least in principle, to make a mechanical replica of an animal, even an ape. But the freedom of action enjoyed by humans implied some non-material influence that could never be captured by mechanical principles. Descartes was especially impressed with the unbounded nature of language, enjoyed even by human imbeciles, but apparently unattainable by any non-human animal. He suggested that the antenna for this God-given freedom of speech and action was the pineal gland, an organ that has sadly failed to live up to this exalted role. Russell (1961) raised the suspicion that Descartes was motivated in part by a wish not to offend the Christian Church, which had traditionally placed humans on a pedestal somewhere between the animals and the angels.

The comfortable idea that we are mentally and morally superior to other animals was rudely shaken with the publication, in 1859, of Darwin's book *The Origin of Species by Means of Natural Selection*. Darwin was at first reluctant to spell out the implications for human evolution, but in his later (1872) book *The Expression of the Emotions in Man and Animals* he made the explicit suggestion that humans are descended from African apes. This implies a basic continuity between ourselves and other species, an idea that was opposed from the outset by the established church, and is still at the centre of debate and controversy.

The dualistic beginnings of psychology

Historically, academic psychology has wavered between the two extremes of continuity and discontinuity. We may begin the story with the foundation of the first laboratory of experimental psychology by Wilhelm Wundt in Leipzig in 1879. Despite the widespread influence of Darwin's ideas at the time, Wundt was essentially a Cartesian dualist, and sought to develop a science of the mind that paralleled the science of the material world. He advocated *introspection* as the main technique for investigating the mind—just as a physical scientist looks outward upon the natural world to discover its secrets, so the experimental psychologist looks inwards. Wundt's introspectionism was transported from Leipzig to Cornell University in the United States by an Englishman, E. B. Titchener (1898), and came to be known there as *Titchenerism* (Boring 1969). By its very nature, introspective psychology seems to preclude investigation of other animals, although late in his career Wundt (1894) did recognize that animal introspection might be possible. Despite his prodigious output, little of his psychology remains, and we now know that introspection tells us rather little, if anything, about the way the mind works.

Toward the end of the nineteenth century there were growing doubts about the effectiveness of introspection as a method. Early in his career Alfred Binet (1886) wrote a book on reasoning, blithely assuming that reasoning was simply a play of images, but when he later came to actually study reasoning in his own two daughters he became convinced that many thoughts were not comprised of images, and therefore could not be accessed through introspection (Binet 1902). In 1894 one of Wundt's former students, Oswald Kulpe, established what became known as the Würzburg school, which challenged the notion that thoughts could be studied through introspection. Indeed, their investigations of thought processes led them to the notion of unanschauliche Bewusstheit, which was translated into English as 'imageless thought' (Boring 1929). Although Titchener (1909) tried vainly to argue that so-called imageless thought could be reduced to fleeting sensations, the battle was probably already lost, and in his textbook of 1910 he appears to have accepted that at least some forms of habitual thought were entirely unconscious:

Is meaning always conscious meaning? Surely not—meaning may be carried in purely physiological terms. In rapid reading, the skimming of pages in quick succession; in the rendering of a musical composition, without hesitation or reflection, in a particular key; in shifting from one language to another as you turn to your right- or left-hand neighbour at the dinner table; in these and similar cases meaning has, time and time again, no discoverable representation in consciousness (Titchener 1910, p. 369).

Even so, Titchener remained convinced of a mental discontinuity between humans and other animals, and in the 1913 edition of his book *A Primer of Psychology* he wrote:

...we must not lose sight of the advantage that even a little thinking gives man over the animals. There is evidence that the higher animals are, at times, actively imaginative. But it is highly significant that, although many of them have the physical means of speech, man alone has developed an articulate language, the vehicle of symbolic imagination or thought. The very fact that he can accept judgements ready made, that he can be passively attentive to groups of word-ideas, is a clear indication of his mental superiority (p. 218).

As we shall see below, 1913 proved to be a fateful year for such ideas.

Behaviourism

By early in the 20th century the situation was clearly ripe for change. Impatient with a mentalism that seemed airily disconnected from empirical observation, the behaviourists banished all mental terms from psychological theory, and replaced introspection with objective observation of overt behaviour. It was J. B. Watson's article 'Psychology as a behaviorist views it,' published in the *Psychological Review* in 1913, that served as the new manifesto, and established an era that was to last until the publication of B. F. Skinner's *Verbal Behavior* in 1957. With behaviourism, Cartesian dualism effectively gave way to the Darwinian idea of a continuity between humans and other animals. Watson (1913) put it bluntly: "The behaviorist, in his efforts to get a unitary scheme of animal response, recognizes no dividing line between man and brutes" (p. 158). Overt behaviour could be observed as readily in animals as in humans, if not more so, and rats and later pigeons moved into the laboratories of experimental psychology.

By the 1950s, behaviourism was riding high. The dominant theorist at the time was Clark L. Hull, whose general behavioural theory, presented in his 1952 book *A Behavior System*, seemed at the time to be the ultimate in theoretical sophistication. Hull saw behaviour as dependent upon associations between stimuli and responses. He did allow hypothetical constructs to intervene, but these were conceived as objectively defined mathematical entities rather than as mental processes. Hull's theories, like those of Wundt, are now largely forgotten, except perhaps in the area of motivation. The more influential theorist in the longer term was the radical behaviourist B. F. Skinner, who sought to eliminate all intervening concepts and reduce psychology to observable events. By the 1950s Skinner was ready to tackle the summit —his 1957 book *Verbal Behavior* was an ambitious attempt to explain language itself in behavioural terms. That, surely, would establish the continuity between humans and other species.

In an appendix to *Verbal Behavior*, Skinner recounted how he had dined in 1934 with the British philosopher Alfred North Whitehead, and had tried to explain to Whitehead the power and elegance of behaviourism. Whitehead, feeling obliged to offer a Cartesian challenge, thereupon uttered the sentence "No black scorpion is falling upon this table." and asked Skinner to explain, in behavioural terms, why he might have said that. The reply, in an appendix to *Verbal Behavior*, was over 20 years in the making. It has amusing Freudian overtones, because Skinner suggested in effect that the black scorpion was symbolic of behaviourism itself, and Whitehead was expressing the fear that it might take over. But what Skinner was not to know was that a black scorpion was about to fall upon his own table.

The cognitive revolution

Ironically, Skinner's *Verbal Behavior* was published in the same year (1957) as Noam Chomsky's *Syntactic Structures*, a book that was ultimately to have much the greater impact. Two years later, Chomsky (1959) published his famous review—some would say demolition—of *Verbal Behavior*, and psychological theory has never been quite the same since. Like Descartes, Chomsky stressed the open-endedness, or *generativity*, of language, and argued that language is a matter of symbols and rules, not associations. He also argued that language is uniquely human and that there is nothing remotely resembling it in the communication systems of other animals:

The unboundedness of human speech, as an expression of limitless thought, is an entirely different matter [from animal communication], because of the freedom from stimulus control and the appropriateness to new situations...Modern studies of animal communication so far offer no counter-evidence to the Cartesian assumption that human language is based on an entirely different principle. Each known animal communication system either consists of a fixed number of signals, each associated with a specific range of eliciting systems or internal states, or a fixed number of 'linguistic dimensions', each associated with a non-linguistic dimension (pp. 77–78).

Although a self-confessed Cartesian, Chomsky did not appeal to any non-material influence, let alone to God, but argued that language could be understood in terms of computational principles. This approach to language coincided with the emergence of artificial intelligence and the rise of the digital computer as the dominant metaphor for the mind. The American author Howard Gardner (1985) identifies the critical date for the so-called 'cognitive revolution' as 11 September 1956, when the speakers at a conference held at the Massachusetts Institute of Technology included Chomsky on syntactic structures, Herbert Simon and Allen Newell on the first complete proof of a theorem carried out by a computing machine, and George A. Miller on the magical number seven (see Miller 1956). British psychologists, perhaps not so caught in the tide of behaviourism, like to see the seeds of the cognitive revolution as having been sown earlier, in the work of such authors as Bartlett (1932), Craik (1943), Cherry (1953), and Broadbent (1958). In any event, as a result of the cognitive revolution, psychology became people-oriented again. It did not return to introspectionism, though, and theory was based for the most part on objective experiments. Although it was not often stated explicitly, the information-processing models that emerged in the 1960s and 70s were models of the mind, and the idea of a discontinuity from other species was at least implicit.

Another influence that led to a re-emphasis on the human mind was the publication of D. O. Hebb's book *Organization of Behavior* in 1949, which effectively revived physiological psychology. While this allowed some of the rats to remain, Hebb's book also stirred interest in the human brain, and neuropsychology was born. A dominant theme of the neuropsychology of the 1950s and 1960s was cerebral asymmetry, which seemed to lend support to the idea of a discontinuity between humans and other animals. In contrast with other animals the great majority of humans are right-handed, and it seemed natural to link this with the use and manufacture of tools—indeed, it can be argued that manufacture has the open-ended, generative character of language itself (Corballis 1989, 1991). But more critically, perhaps, the left-cerebral dominance for language displayed by most people seems to add further support to the uniqueness of language, and of the brain mechanisms that make it possible. Here is Chomsky again:

...a chimpanzee is very smart and has all kinds of sensorimotor constructions (causality, representational functions, and so forth), but one thing is missing: that little part of the left hemisphere that is responsible for the very specific functions of human language (quoted in Piattelli-Palmarini 1980, p. 182).

Yet another argument against the behavioural view of language was based on children's seemingly miraculous ability to acquire language. Chomsky argued that it was impossible in principle to extract the knowledge required for language from the information provided by the linguistic environment, because of what he called 'the poverty of the stimulus'. Because syntax, in particular, cannot be learned from the information available in speech samples, it must be innate. Indeed, he went so far as to suggest that the very idea of 'learning' might become obsolete: "It is possible" he wrote, "that the notion 'learning' might go the way of the rising and setting of the sun" (Chomsky 1980, p. 245). Provocative remarks like this effectively challenged the efforts of over 50 years of behaviourism.

This is not to say that the battle against continuity was completely won; there are always black scorpions lurking. *The Journal of the Experimental Analysis of Behavior* continues as the vehicle for hard-line behaviourists, but some animal behaviourists regrouped under the rubric of *animal cognition*, turning the tools and concepts of cognitive psychology to the study of animal learning, in some cases with the goal of showing that animals have conscious minds just as humans do. Just as behaviourism seemed to dehumanize humans, so the cognitive revolution may have been instrumental in humanizing animals, providing fuel for animal rights movements. Moreover, there is growing evidence for laterality in other animals, even though it may not have quite the consistency and strength of that in humans. For example, there is now evidence for population-level right-handedness in the other great apes (Hopkins 1996), and many examples of cerebral asymmetries in other species, including monkeys and apes (Bradshaw and Rogers 1993; Gannon *et al.* 1998). But the main arena for debates over the continuity question, as ever, was language, and a number of animal behaviourists took up the Skinnerian challenge of trying to prove that Chomsky was wrong in supposing that language was the exclusive domain of humans.

The language wars

At first it seemed that the cause was lost before it began, since attempts to teach an ape to actually talk have never been even remotely successful (Kellogg 1968). For example, a husband-and-wife team had earlier raised a chimpanzee called Viki from the age of three days until about six and a half years in their own home (Hayes 1952). They treated her as one of their own children with respect to feeding, toilet training, discipline, and play, and of course they spoke to her. Viki never learned to speak more than three or four crude words, including *mama*, *papa*, *cup*, and possibly *up*. It was soon pointed out, however, that Viki's failure to talk might have been because of deficiencies of the vocal tract rather than to the lack of any capacity for language. Greater success has been achieved in teaching a form of manual sign language, not only to our nearest relative the chimpanzee (Gardner and Gardner 1969), but also to a gorilla (Patterson 1978) and an orang-utan (Miles 1990). Chimpanzees have also proven fairly adept at using plastic tokens (lexigrams) to represent objects and actions (Rumbaugh 1977). But even the work on gestures and tokens has not been universally accepted as demonstrating true language. Terrace (1979) analysed the utterances of a trained chimpanzee, optimistically named Nim Chimpsky, and observed that they consist mainly of repetitions and simple sequencing of ideas. There was no evidence of anything approaching genuine syntax. Seidenberg and Pettito (1987) suggest that chimpanzee 'language' can be interpreted simply as conditioned responses for food reward, without the generativity and spontaneity that characterize human language.

These objections appear to be at least partly overcome in the work of Savage-Rumbaugh on two young bonobos, or pygmy chimpanzees (*Pan paniscus*), named Kanzi and Mulika, who have learned to use gestures and lexigrams spontaneously while watching their mother being taught. Most of their productions are not random sequences or meaningless repetitions, but are spontaneous comments, requests, or announcements (Savage-Rumbaugh and Lewin 1994). Kanzi even appears to have an understanding of spoken human language, with at least some regard to grammatical structure, at about the level of a two-year-old child (Savage-Rumbaugh *et al.* 1993). The common chimpanzee (*Pan troglodytes*) has also been observed to gesture spontaneously, and to teach signs spontaneously to a foster baby (Fouts *et al.* 1989). In their recent review, in stark defiance of Chomsky, Bradshaw and Rogers (1993) write of language as "having a long evolutionary tradition continuous with animal communicatory systems" (p. 383).

But even Kanzi's exploits have been treated with scorn by some cognitivists and linguists. Pinker (1994) remarks that the apes "just don't 'get it'" (p. 340). He cites an observation by Jane Goodall that every one of the signs made by Nim Chimpsky were familiar to her from her own observations in the wild, suggesting that Nim was not 'taught' any signs at all. But Pinker's main objection is that there is still no evidence of the ability to generate sentences according to grammatical rules: "The chimps' abilities at anything one would want to call grammar were next to nil" (p. 339). Bickerton (1995), although at odds with Pinker on other matters, concurs.

If apes are incapable of acquiring grammar, then it is a reasonable inference that the common ancestor of humans and chimpanzees must also have been without grammar. But even those who are united on this point disagree as to when and how language might have emerged over the past five or six million years of hominid evolution. While there has been hope that the fossil record might reveal the steps by which language evolved, the view that emerged from the Chomskyan revolution is that language must have emerged fully fledged, presumably late in hominid evolution. Piattelli-Palmarini (1989), for example, stated that the fossil record is incomplete, "not because the intermediate forms have been lost *for us*, but because they simply never existed" (p. 8; *his italics*). David Premack, a one-time behaviourist, remarked similarly that "nature provides no intermediate steps, nothing between the lowly call system and the towering human language" (Premack 1985, p. 276). He nevertheless speculated about an intermediate stage that might have been lost in antiquity. Bickerton (1986) suggested that we do not need to search in the mists of antiquity; an intermediate stage that is higher than the call systems of animals can be discerned in pidgin languages before creolization, in the best efforts of Kanzi and other trained apes or dolphins, and in the speech of the two-year-old child or of children deprived of linguistic input, such as Genie (Fromkin *et al.* 1974). Premack (1986) adds a further example—the drunken teenager. This intermediate language, which Bickerton calls *protolanguage*, is symbolic, but effectively devoid of grammar.

But even if we concede protolanguage to apes, there is still a large gap. In the view of Chomsky and his followers, it is grammar that effectively endows language with its flexibility and generativity, and places it beyond the reach of any other species. Further, it is asserted that grammar cannot have emerged incrementally, but must have evolved as a whole, presumably as the result of some adventitious mutation (Bickerton 1986; Piattelli-Palmarini 1989). This is sometimes known as the 'big bang' theory. Bickerton (1995) argues, in fact, that it was this big bang that distinguished our species from all other hominids: ".. true language, via the emergence of syntax, was a catastrophic event, occurring within the first few generations of the species *Homo sapiens sapiens*" (p. 69). If this sounds like creationism, it should be said that Bickerton's argument is based entirely on his evaluation of the evidence and of the special nature of syntax, and owes nothing to religious doctrine.

Pinker and Bloom (1990) have pointed out, though, that the argument for the all-or-none evolution of syntax is reminiscent of the 19th-century claim that the mammalian eye was too perfect to have evolved gradually through the incremental processes of natural selection, a claim long since rejected. They argue that grammar evolved gradually in the course of hominid evolution, and not suddenly as Bickerton and others have maintained. Even so, they continue to insist that language is uniquely human, and Pinker (1994) has even suggested that there may be uniquely human 'grammar genes' (p. 299).

Beyond the language wars

The language wars are still being fought, without any sign of a clear winner. As so often happens, however, the questions have changed somewhat. Some 20 years ago, Premack and Woodruff (1978) deflected some of the attention away from language by asking the intriguing question 'Does the chimpanzee have a theory of mind?' Individuals are said to have a theory of mind if they have concepts like *want*, *know*, or *see*, and can attribute them to others. For example, if one animal can imitate another, one might suppose that it is somehow able to understand that the other animal sees the world from a different perspective, and mentally adopt this perspective when performing the same actions (Whiten and Byrne 1991; Tomasello 1996). Another example is tactical deception, especially in cases where the deception manifestly involves an appreciation of what the deceived animal is thinking, or what it can see (Byrne and Whiten 1990). Again, the ability of an animal to recognize itself in a mirror might be said to require the ability to understand what it looks like from the point of view of another animal, and indeed to imply the concept of self (Gallup 1970, 1977). Theory of mind might even be a prerequisite for language itself (Premack and Premack 1994; but see also Baron-Cohen, this volume), and it has also been suggested that we may need a theory of mind to represent our own past experiences, as in episodic or autobiographical memory, or in the ability to travel mentally into the past or future (Suddendorf and Corballis 1997). In elaborating his view of episodic memory, Tulving (1993) states:

The owner of an episodic memory system is not only capable of remembering the temporal organization of otherwise unrelated events, but is also capable of mental time travel: Such a person can transport at will into the personal past, as well as into the future, a feat not possible for other kinds of memory (p. 67).

Tulving argues that episodic memory is uniquely human, a view elaborated in detail by Suddendorf and Corballis (1997). Wheeler *et al.* (1997) have argued further that the prefrontal cortex is critical to the evolution of episodic memory and mental time-travel.

There is growing evidence that the great apes can accomplish at least some of these tasks, and Byrne (this volume) argues that great apes, but not monkeys, do indeed demonstrate a theory of mind. He also concludes that the great apes, but not monkeys, are capable of symbolic representation. Byrne suggests that theory of mind and symbolic representation provide the underpinnings of language, and although he does not go so far as to claim that great apes are capable of grammatical language itself, his conclusions lend support to the claim that the real discontinuity lies, not between humans and apes, but between the great apes, including humans, and the other primates. This view has a certain popular currency, as reflected in the Great Ape Project, which was recently established by a group of lobbyists for the purpose of conferring on great apes the ethical status of humans. Needless to say, however, not all are agreed that great apes have mental state concepts, let alone a fully fledged theory of mind. Heyes (1998) has examined the evidence for theory of mind in several contexts, including imitation, self-recognition, social relationships, role-taking, deception, perspective-taking, seeing and knowing, and seeing and attending. She concludes that in most cases, the evidence can be explained by associative mechanisms that do not require the assumption of a theory of mind. Suddendorf (this volume) also examines the evidence, and suggests that what he calls 'metamind'—the ability to represent representations themselves—is uniquely human.

A related question is whether language can be distinguished from thought itself. Those who argue that animals can think necessarily argue that it can (e.g. Lea and Kiley-Worthington 1996). But others with quite different agendas agree. Pinker (1994) is adamant that the structure of thought is quite different from that of language, and indeed that it is often extremely difficult to transform our thought processes into the linear, sequential medium of spoken language. Donald (this volume) makes similar points. Bickerton (1995), though, takes the opposite view. To him, it is language that uniquely characterizes human thought, and allows us to think and even construct visual images in a symbolic, generative manner. It is language-based thought that allows humans the unique privilege of 'off-line thinking', so that our thoughts are not tied to the present location or point in time (see also Suddendorf, this volume; Suddendorf and Corballis 1997). In this view, the discontinuity is not merely between humans and apes, but between *H. sapiens* of a mere 100 000 to 150 000 years ago and all other earlier and contemporary hominids. Moreover, since off-line thinking dominates human mental life, the discontinuity must be a very considerable one indeed.

Neo-associationism

The change brought about by the cognitive revolution dominated psychology from the 1960s until well into the 1980s, but it might now be drawing to an end. The past decade has seen a revival of associationist approaches to human cognition. A critical date was 1986, with the publication of the two volumes on *Parallel Distributed Processing* (McClelland *et al.* 1986; Rumelhart *et al.* 1986). Parallel distributed processing, now more commonly known as *connectionism*, refers to models of the mind based on neural networks that can be modified as the result of experience, and the general aim is to specify how the connections might be altered by experience to produce desired outputs from given inputs. This is very different in spirit from the earlier computational models based on the digital computer and the manipulation of symbols.

Connectionists are typically quick to dismiss any notion of a return to behaviourism, but there are similarities. Indeed the most obvious comparison is not with the hard-core behaviorism of B. F. Skinner, but rather with the mediated stimulus–response (S–R) connections postulated by Hull (1952) and earlier learning theorists; the very word 'connectionism' recalls the theories of E. L. Thorndike, and Chapter 2 of Hilgard's (1958) classic *Theories of Learning* is in fact entitled 'Thorndike's Connectionism'. Just as Hull's S–R connections were modified by variations in an intervening variable known as 'habit strength', so the connections between input and output layers in a connectionist system are modified by changes in the strength of connections with a 'hidden layer' of neuron-like elements. Connectionist models are fundamentally associationistic, and so are susceptible to the critique that Chomsky

(1959) levelled against Skinner, and there have indeed been critiques of connectionist approaches to language, in particular, that echo Chomsky's famous review (Fodor and Pylyshyn 1988; Pinker and Prince 1988).

Connectionist models have for the most part been applied to *human* cognition, but the fundamental simplicity of connectionist architecture suggests that they might apply equally to the cognition of non-human animals. In their original manifesto, Rumelhart and McClelland (1986) briefly raise the question of why humans are smarter than rats (so *they* think), and their answer is rather coy: "... it seems to us quite plausible", they write, "that some of the differences between rats and people lie in the potential for forming connections that can subserve the vital functions of language and thought that humans exhibit and other animals do not" (p. 143). They draw attention particularly to the angular gyrus, which is strategically placed in the human brain between the language areas and the visual areas—a 'hidden layer', as it were, for mapping printed words onto meanings. It seems that Rumelhart and McClelland are not entirely ready to relinquish the Cartesian heritage, and the spirit of the pineal gland lives on in the angular gyrus.

Connectionism, though, has not seen an Ark-like return of animals to psychological laboratories, and theorists have sought to prove their mettle by modelling human cognition, with language again as the ultimate challenge. There is, after all, an answer to the Chomskyan attack on associations, which is that, when all is said and done, the brain *does* consist of associated elements; they are called neurons. There is no model of brain function, to our knowledge, that would suggest that the brain might produce generative language other than through networks of intercommunicating neurons. One of the missions of the connectionists has been to challenge the Chomsky-inspired notion that 'the poverty of the stimulus' makes language unlearnable. The sun might have started to rise again.

One of Chomsky's assumptions is that our ability to use language creatively means that our knowledge of linguistic structure must be essentially perfect, even though we do not always speak with perfect grammar. As Elman *et al.* (1996) point out, there is little evidence for this, and connectionist networks are now able to infer regular patterns from irregular input and generalize them to novel patterns. This goes at least a small way toward overcoming the poverty-of-the-stimulus argument, and showing that generalization—if not generativity—can be achieved without perfect knowledge. Moreover, there is increasing evidence that infants have powerful associative mechanisms that discover regularities in input that are defined only statistically. For example, two-month-old infants need only two minutes of listening to strings of nonsense syllables to discover which syllables go together to form three-syllable nonsense words (Saffran *et al.* 1996). Since the words so learned have no meaning and the context in which they are embedded has no syntax, this ability must be based on associative learning, and not on innately determined knowledge of the structure of language. It remains an open question whether this ability is specific to language, or whether it also underlies the infants' learning of other entities, such as objects or faces.

Another of Chomsky's arguments is that children seem to instinctively understand the phrase structure of language. For example, given a sentence like *My friend is coming to play*, a child might readily learn how to turn this into a question by moving the auxiliary is to the beginning of the sentence: *Is my friend coming to play?* But if this easily inferred rule is applied to a sentence with an embedded clause, such as *My friend who is staying with her aunt is coming to play*, it would yield the anomalous sentence *Is my friend who staying with her aunt is coming to play*? Crain (1991) has confirmed Chomsky's intuition that children simply do not make mistakes like this, implying that they must have an innate knowledge of phrase structure. However, Elman (1993) has shown that this problem might be solved, at least in principle, by a connectionist network that initially has a rapidly fading memory, but gradually increases its memory over time. In the early stages of learning, the network can only learn about short strings of words, but is gradually able to deal with larger strings, and to handle previously learned strings (phrases) as units. More generally, networks that grow as they learn might well be able to achieve the hierarchical learning that humans display, not only in language, but in other pursuits such as music and manufacture. Newport (1990) similarly noted that the relatively minimalist learning strategies employed by young children might actually be advantageous in learning language; as she put it, 'less is more'.

Deacon (1997) makes the further point that language is as much an adaptation to the human mind as the mind is to language. Indeed, languages adapt and change much more quickly and readily than biological structures do, so it is reasonable to suppose that most of the adapting has come from language itself, and not from the brain. Languages may be likened to viruses, competing for survival in a relatively (but not entirely) fixed mental environment. Deacon's is one of the most recent voices in what appears to be a mounting chorus against the Chomsky-inspired view that language is an innate, uniquely human endowment that is independent of other cognitive functions. Even more outspoken in his attack is the British author, Geoffrey Sampson (1997).

Conclusions

We have seen how, in the brief history of psychology as a scientific discipline, continuity and discontinuity have each in turn dominated the scene. Nineteenth-century psychology was clearly concerned with the *human* mind, and the introspective method effectively ruled other animals out of bounds. Implicitly if not explicitly, the mind effectively set humans apart. During the behaviourist era, which lasted from about 1913 to the late 1950s, the shift from subjective to objective methods removed any dividing line between humans and other animals, a point made explicit by the founder of behaviourism, J. B. Watson, from the very beginning. The cognitive revolution of the 1960s, inspired largely by Chomsky's attack on the behaviourist approach to language, produced another swing of the pendulum back toward discontinuity.

Within the past decade, however, there are clear signs that the pendulum might be swinging back to continuity, if indeed it has not already done so. While the linguistic arguments for discontinuity are still strongly expressed (e.g. Pinker 1994; Bickerton 1995), there are other signs they might be losing ground. This might be attributed partly to the rise of connectionism against the symbolic, computational models of thought that dominated the 1970s and early 1980s, partly to the sheer tenacity of some of those who worked to demonstrate language-like behaviour in the other great apes (e.g. Savage-Rumbaugh and Lewin 1994), and partly to growing evidence for lateral asymmetries in other animals that threaten our unique claim to lopsidedness (Bradshaw and Rogers 1993; Hopkins 1996; Gannon *et al*. 1998). The swing to continuity has no doubt also been profoundly influenced by the revelation that, genetically speaking, we are extraordinarily similar to the chimpanzee, with something like 98.4 DNA sequences in common (Goodman 1992)—indeed, it has even been suggested that the resemblance is close enough to make possible a human–chimpanzee hybrid (Miyamoto *et al*. 1987). Moreover, modern biochemical techniques have shown that the common ancestor of ourselves and the chimpanzee was much more recent than had been previously believed, dating from a mere five million years or so instead of the more comfortable 20 million years that was widely accepted until the early 1980s (Waddell and Penny 1996). These developments have been accompanied by ever-increasing discoveries of hominid fossils, especially from Africa, Europe, and Asia, so that the once-chimeric 'missing link' has given way to a tapestry of different hominid species whose characteristics have been quite well identified. These developments are discussed in Chapter 3.

Despite what looks like a revival of Darwinian continuity, the long view suggests that the pendulum has swung often enough for neither extreme to be totally correct. No doubt there are some respects, psychological as well as physical, in which we resemble the great apes more than the great apes resemble other primates, and other respects in which we stand alone. The evidence supporting mental continuity might well make us want to confer a higher intellectual status on the great apes than we have traditionally accorded them. Even so, those of us working on this book do not need to be troubled by the thought that there might be somewhere a chimpanzee banging away on a laptop, with the intent of proving once and for all that our long-held assumptions of human uniqueness are totally incorrect.

References

Bartlett, F. C. (1932). *Remembering: a study in experimental and social psychology*. Cambridge University Press.
Bickerton, D. (1986). More than nature needs? A reply to Premack. *Cognition*, **23**, 173–221.
Bickerton, D. (1995). *Language and human behavior*. University of Washington Press/UCL Press, Seattle.
Binet, A. (1886). *La psychologie du raisonnement*. Alcan, Paris.
Binet, A. (1902). *L'étude expérimentale de l'intelligence*. Schleicher, Paris.
Boring, E. G. (1929). *A history of experimental psychology*. Appleton–Century–Crofts, New York.
Boring, E. G. (1969). Titchener, meaning, and behaviorism. In *Schools of psychology* (ed. D. L. Krantz), pp. 21–34. Appleton–Century–Crofts, New York.
Bradshaw, J. L. and Rogers, L. J. (1993). *The evolution of lateral asymmetries, language, tool use, and intellect*. Academic Press, London.
Broadbent, D. E. (1958). *Perception and communication*. Pergamon, Oxford.
Byrne, R. W. and Whiten, A. (1990). Tactical deception in primates: the 1990 data base. *Primate Report*, **27**, 1–101.

Cherry, E. C. (1953). Some experiments on the recognition of speech with one and two ears. *Journal of the Acoustical Society of America*, **25**, 975–9.

Chomsky, N. (1957). *Syntactic structures*. Mouton, The Hague.

Chomsky, N. (1959). A review of B. F. Skinner's 'Verbal behavior'. *Language*, **35**, 26–58.

Chomsky, N. (1980). *Rules and representations*. Columbia University Press, New York.

Corballis, M. C. (1989). Laterality and human evolution. *Psychological Review*, **96**, 492–505.

Corballis, M. C. (1991). *The lopsided ape: evolution of the generative mind*. Oxford University Press, New York.

Cosmides, L. and Tooby, J. (1987). From evolution to behavior: evolutionary psychology as the missing link. In *The latest on the best: essays on evolution and optimality* (ed. J. Dupre), pp. 277–306. MIT Press, Cambridge, MA.

Craik, K. J. W. (1943). *The nature of explanation*. Cambridge University Press.

Crain, S. (1991). Language acquisition in the absence of experience. *Behavioral and Brain Sciences*, **14**, 597–611.

Darwin, C. (1859). *The origin of species by means of natural selection*. John Murray, London.

Darwin, C. (1872). *The expression of the emotions in man and animals*. John Murray, London.

Deacon, T. (1997). *The symbolic species*. Allen Lane, The Penguin Press, Harmondsworth.

Descartes, R. (1985). *The philosophical writings of Descartes* (ed. and trans. J. Cottingham, R. Stoothoff, and D. Murdock). Cambridge University Press. (Original work published in 1647).

Elman, J. L. (1993). Learning and development in neural networks: the importance of starting small. *Cognition*, **48**, 71–99.

Elman, J., Bates, E., Johnson, M., Karmiloff-Smith, A., Parisi, D., and Plunkett, K. (1996). *Rethinking innateness: a connectionist perspective on development*. MIT Press and Bradford Books, Cambridge, MA.

Fodor, J. A. and Pylyshyn, Z. W. (1988). Connectionism and cognitive architecture. *Cognition*, **28**, 3–71.

Fouts, R. S., Fouts, D. H., and Van Cantfort, T. E. (1989). The infant Loulis learns signs from cross-fostered chimpanzees. In *Teaching sign language to chimpanzees* (ed. R. A. Gardner, B. T. Gardner, and T. E. Van Cantfort), pp. 280–92. State University of New York Press.

Fromkin, V. A., Krashen, S., Curtiss, S., Rigler, D., and Rigler, M. (1974). The development of language in genie: a case of language acquisition beyond the critical period. *Brain and Language*, **1**, 81–107.

Gallup, G. G., Jr. (1970). Chimpanzees: self-recognition. *Science*, **167**, 86–7.

Gallup, G. G., Jr. (1977). Self-recognition in primates: a comparative approach to the bidirectional properties of consciousness. *American Psychologist*, **32**, 329–38.

Gannon, P. J., Holloway, R. L., Broadfield, D. C., and Braun, A. R. (1998). Asymmetry of chimpanzee planum temporale: humanlike pattern of Wernicke's brain language area homolog. *Science*, **279**, 220–2.

Gardner, H. (1985). *The mind's new science: a history of the cognitive revolution*. Basic Books, New York.

Gardner, R. A. and Gardner, B. T. (1969). Teaching sign language to a chimpanzee. Science, 165, 664–72.

Goodman, M. (1992). Reconstructing human evolution from proteins. In *The Cambridge encyclopaedia of human evolution* (ed. S. Jones, R. Martin, and D. Pilbeam), pp. 307–12. Cambridge University Press.

Hayes, C. (1952). *The ape in our house*. Gollancz, London.

Hebb, D. O. (1949). *Organization of behavior*. Wiley, New York.

Heyes, C. M. (1998). Theory of mind in nonhuman primates. *Behavioral and Brain Sciences*, **21**, 101–48.

Hilgard, E. R. (1958). *Theories of learning*, (2nd edn). Methuen, London.

Hopkins, W. D. (1996). Chimpanzee handedness revisited: 55 years since Finch (1941). *Psychonomic Bulletin and Review*, **3**, 449–57.

Hull, C. L. (1952). *A behavior system*. Yale University Press, New Haven, CT.

Kellogg, W. N. (1968). Communication and language in the home-based chimpanzee. *Science*, **162**, 423–7.

Lea, S. E. G., and Kiley-Worthington, M. (1996). Can animals think? In *Unsolved mysteries of the mind* (ed. V. Bruce), pp. 211–44. Hove: Erlbaum (UK) Taylor and Francis.

McClelland, J. L., Rumelhart, D. E., and the PDP Research Group (ed.). (1986). *Parallel distributed processing: explorations in the microstructure of cognition. Vol. 2: Psychological and biological models*. Bradford/MIT Press, Cambridge, MA.

Miles, H. L. (1990). The cognitive foundations for reference in a signing orangutan. In *'Language' and intelligence in monkeys and apes: comparative developmental perspectives* (ed. S. T. Parker and K. Gibson), pp. 511–39. Cambridge University Press, New York.

Miller, G. A. (1956). The magical number seven, plus or minus two: some limits on our capacity for processing information. *Psychological Review*, **63**, 81–97.

Miyamoto, M., Slightom, J. L., and Goodman, M. (1987). Phylogenetic relations of humans and African apes from DNA sequences in the psi–nu–globin region. *Science*, **238**, 369–73.

Newport, E. L. (1990). Maturational constraints on language learning. *Cognitive Science*, **14**, 11–28.

Patterson, F. (1978). Conversations with a gorilla. *National Geographic*, **154**, 438–65.

Piattelli-Palmarini, M. (1980). *Language and learning: the debate between Jean Piaget and Noam Chomsky*. Harvard University Press, Cambridge, MA.

Piattelli-Palmarini, M. (1989). Evolution, selection and cognition: from 'learning' to parameter setting in biology and the study of language. *Cognition*, **31**, 1–44.

Pinker, S. (1994). *The language instinct: how the mind creates language*. Morrow, New York.

Pinker, S. and Bloom, P. (1990). Natural language and natural selection. *Behavioral and Brain Sciences*, **13**, 707–84.

Pinker, S. and Prince, A. (1988). On language and connectionism: analysis of a parallel distributed processing model of language acquisition. *Cognition*, **28**, 73–193.

Premack, D. (1985). 'Gavagai!' or the future history of the animal language controversy. *Cognition*, **19**, 207–96.

Premack, D. (1986). Pangloss to Cyrano de Bergerac: 'Nonsense, it's perfect!' A reply to Bickerton. *Cognition*, **23**, 81–8.

Premack, D. and Premack, A. J. (1994). How 'theory of mind' constrains language and communication. *Discussions in Neuroscience*, **10**, 93–105.

Premack, D. and Woodruff, G. (1978). Does the chimpanzee have a theory of mind? *Behavioral and Brain Sciences*, **4**, 515–26.

Rumbaugh, D. (1977). *Language learning by a chimpanzee: the LANA project*. Academic Press, New York.

Rumelhart, D. E. and McClelland, J. L. (1986). PDP models and general issues in cognitive science. In *Parallel distributed processing: explorations in the microstructure of cognition. Vol. 1: Foundations* (ed. D. E. Rumelhart, J. L. McClelland, and the PDP Research Group), pp. 110–46. Bradford Books/MIT Press, Cambridge, MA.

Rumelhart, D. E., McClelland, J. L., and the PDP Research Group (ed.). (1986). *Parallel distributed processing: explorations in the microstructure of cognition. Vol. 1: Foundations*. Bradford Books/MIT Press, Cambridge, MA.

Russell, B. (1961). *A history of western philosophy* (2nd edn). Allen and Unwin, London.

Saffran, J. R., Aslin, R. N., and Newport, E. L. (1996). Statistical learning by 8-month-old infants. *Science*, 274, 1926–8.

Sampson, G. (1997). *Educating Eve: the 'language instinct' debate*. Cassell, London.

Savage-Rumbaugh, S. and Lewin, R. (1994). *Kanzi: an ape at the brink of the human mind*. Wiley, New York.

Savage-Rumbaugh, E. S., Murphy, J., Sevcik, R. A., Brakke, K. E., Williams, S. L., and

Rumbaugh, D. M. (1993). *Language comprehension in ape and child*. University of Chicago Press.

Seidenberg, M. S. and Pettito, L. A. (1987). Communication, symbolic communication, and language. *Journal of Experimental Psychology: General*, **116**, 279–87.

Skinner, B. F. (1957). *Verbal behavior*. Appelton–Century–Croft, New York.

Suddendorf, T. and Corballis, M. C. (1997). Mental time travel and the evolution of the human mind. *Genetic, Social, and General Psychology Monographs*, **123**, 133–67.

Terrace, H. S. (1979). Is problem solving language? *Journal of the Experimental Analysis of Behavior*, **31**, 161–75.

Titchener, E. B. (1898). The postulates of a structural psychology. *Philosophical Review*, **7**, 449–65.

Titchener, E. B. (1909). *Lectures on the experimental psychology of the thought process*. Macmillan, New York.

Titchener, E. B. (1910). *A textbook of psychology*. Macmillan, New York.

Titchener, E. B. (1913). *A primer of psychology*. Macmillan, New York.

Tomasello, M. (1996). Do apes ape? In *Social learning: The roots of culture* (ed. C. M. Heyes and B. G. Galef), pp. 319–346. Academic Press, London.

Tulving, E. (1993). What is episodic memory? *Current Directions in Psychological Science*, **2**, 67–70.

Waddell, P. J. and Penny, D. (1996). Evolutionary trees of apes and humans from DNA sequences. In *Handbook of human symbolic evolution* (ed. A. Lock and C. R. Peters), pp. 53–73. Oxford University Press.

Watson, J. B. (1913). Psychology as a behaviorist views it. *Psychological Review*, **20**, 1–14.

Wheeler, M. A., Stuss, D. T., and Tulving, E. (1997). Toward a theory of episodic memory: the frontal lobes and autonoetic consciousness. *Psychological Bulletin*, **121**, 331–54.

Whiten, A. and Byrne, R. W. (1991). The emergence of metarepresentation in human ontogeny and primate phylogeny. In *Natural theories of mind* (ed. A. Whiten). Blackwell, Oxford.

Woodruff, G. and Premack, D. (1979). Intentional communication in the chimpanzee: the development of deception. *Cognition*, **7**, 333–62.

Wundt, W. (1894). *Lectures on human and animal psychology*. Swan and Sonnenschein, London.

2

The background to hominid intelligence

Stephen E. G. Lea

Introduction

This book is chiefly concerned with the evolution of mind within the immediate ancestors of humans. That is to say, we are concerned with the history of mind from either after, or just before, that point, about 5 million years ago, when the hominid line diverged from the line leading to present-day chimpanzees and bonobos. This chapter attempts to put that history into a wider context. Before the evolution of hominids proper began, our ancestors had lived as primates for around 65 million years, as mammals for perhaps 200 million years before that, and as vertebrates for perhaps an additional 200 million years. For the perhaps 3000 million further years between the origins of life and the emergence of vertebrates, our more distant ancestors had still been subject to the same laws of evolution. Among the innumerable animal species that share some kind of common ancestor with us there are many, in addition to the four species of great ape, that apparently also share some kind of intelligence. In some cases, such shared intelligence might be due to common descent; in others it might be due to convergence—common evolutionary processes operating on a common inheritance, but independently.

The argument of this chapter is that understanding intelligence in these more remote relatives has something to contribute to our understanding of the hominid mind. The argument is in three parts. First, I shall outline a few basic principles of modern evolutionary theory that I and every other chapter author will be taking for granted. Secondly, I shall consider what might form the common cognitive inheritance of all mammals, and therefore the foundation on which the extraordinary cognitive evolution of the primates must have been built. Finally, and much more tentatively, I shall consider where else in the animal kingdom human-like intelligence can be found, so that we can consider what selective pressures might have been critical in recent hominid evolution.

Evolutionary principles

Descent

The most basic of all evolutionary principles is that of descent. The species we see today are the descendants of different species that lived in former times, and many different modern species might be descended from a single extinct ancestral species. This simple idea lies at the heart of several of the chapters in this book, because from it springs a very important hypothesis. If we believe that two or more species are descended from a common ancestor, and we observe that they share a characteristic (whether it is anatomical, physiological, behavioural, or cognitive), we can suppose that the common ancestor also shared that characteristic. If we can, from the fossil record or otherwise, date the divergence of the modern species from a common stock, we can therefore set a latest possible date on the emergence of their common traits, even when those traits are not recorded in the fossil record, as is very often the case when we are concerned with behaviour and cognition. In this chapter, therefore, what we are concerned with is the descent of hominid and hominid-like intelligence.

Natural selection

Behind every chapter of this book lies Darwinian evolutionary theory, or rather that version of it that formed the 'Modern Synthesis' of evolutionary and genetic theory (Fisher 1930), further enlightened by the elucidation of the mechanisms of inheritance by the molecular biologists of the 1960s. What is inherited is taken to be variations in DNA sequences produced by random mutation; there is no room for Lamarckism. And, whatever role might be admitted for mass extinctions, for saltation, or for rapid adaptive radiations in newly invaded environments, the main engine of evolution is seen as natural selection—the preferential survival and reproduction of some genetic forms rather than others.

But it is equally true that all the present authors have been strongly influenced by what Wilson (1975) called the 'New Synthesis' of population genetics, behavioural ecology, and ethology, a synthesis that he also dubbed 'Sociobiology'. Not all of them would describe themselves as sociobiologists—indeed, some would see themselves as opponents of sociobiology—but no one who works in evolution can ignore it. In this chapter, therefore, we must in part be concerned with a sociobiological theory of human-like intelligence.

The four spheres of the environment

What is distinctive about sociobiology can be best expressed if we first distinguish four different spheres within which species evolve.

First, there is the physical environment, a matter largely of geology and meteorology. Second, there is the biological environment, the other species with which an animal or plant interacts. The most commonly studied interactions are those between predators and prey, but they are not the only ones: an orang-utan or gibbon brachiating through a forest is using trees as literal supports for its behaviour, not preying on them. Third, there is the social environment, the other members of the same species, who might be or become parents, mates, offspring, enemies, allies, or friends. In the first formulations of sociobiology (Wilson 1975), these three were clearly if implicitly recognized, but almost immediately (Dawkins 1976, chapter 11; Lumsden and Wilson 1981, 1983) it was also recognized that there is a fourth. The cultural environment, those members of the species with whom an individual could share ideas, forms a potentially enormously important sphere within which quite new kinds of evolution may occur.

It is tempting to think of these as four levels at which the environment acts on individuals. But they are not so much four levels of the environment as four concentric spheres. The biological is also physical, the social is also biological, and the cultural is also social. But each stage adds something to what has gone before. The chief way in which they vary is in the kind of impact a change in an individual's behaviour can have, and in particular the speed at which it can occur. Let us look at each in turn.

Organisms do modify the physical environment. Photosynthesizing plants have critically altered the constitution of the atmosphere; plants can stabilize an eroding rock surface, and grazing animals can destroy it. But until the changes due to human industrialization, all these changes have been slow, and particularly so in evolutionary terms. For the most part, when we are constructing evolutionary hypotheses we can consider the physical environment as stable—we need only ask how organisms have adapted to it, and how they have colonized new environments. If a fish or a dolphin adapts to move more efficiently through the sea, we do not expect the sea to change so as to become harder to move through.

The biological environment is different. Wherever species interact, it is likely that the process is bidirectional—each adapts so as to frustrate or exploit the adaptations of the other. Of course, for some purposes we can nonetheless treat each species as fixed in analysing the behaviour of the other, at least as regards the lifetimes of individuals. In the extensive work on optimal foraging theory (Stephens and Krebs 1986), we look at how a predator can behave so as to harvest prey most efficiently, treating the distribution or behaviour of the prey as given. But over evolutionary time, this will not work. If cheetah evolve to run fast, antelope must evolve to run faster. If predators evolve to stalk, prey must evolve to be vigilant, to dodge, and perhaps to signal to predators that they have been seen (cf. Levin 1997). If thrushes evolve to eat berries, plants can evolve brightly coloured, good tasting fruit with hard indigestible seeds. If bees or birds evolve to feed on sweet substances, plants can evolve to produce nectar and place pollen near it. If plants evolve poisons to protect their leaves, browsers will evolve enzymes to destroy them. The analysis of these different kinds of inter-species interaction forms much of the business of behavioural ecology (Krebs and Davies 1993), and has given rise to some of the most interesting ideas in recent evolutionary theory (Dawkins 1981, Chapter 4).

The social environment is different again. When individuals of two different species interact, a mutation that occurs in one might change the environment for the other, and so set up a selective pressure that will ultimately lead to a change in the gene pool of the second species. But when individuals of the same species are interacting, a mutation in one might, in the next generation, be present in the successors of both. That is inherent in the conventional definition of the species as the range of gene exchange. In consequence, when we try to find the optimum behaviour in a social interaction, we cannot rely on the passive optimizing theory that is used in a foraging situation; we have to resort to game theory, and look for strategies that are not just optimal but also evolutionarily stable.

In the cultural environment, the stakes are raised yet further. In genetic evolution, changes can only come about by chance, and those that are successful are selected by the blind process of differential fecundity over the generations. In a culture, individuals can observe the innovations of others and choose to mimic those that are successful, or even those that look as though they might succeed for the observer even though they fail for the model. Innovations can thus spread throughout a population, or become extinct, within a generation.

These four concentric spheres are likely to be associated with steadily increasing speed of evolution. Adaptation to the unchanging physical environment is likely to be slow. Because the biological environment changes in response to the organism's adaptation, it is likely to accelerate it. In the social environment, evolution is speeded up further, because the interacting individuals contribute to the gene pool of each other's descendants. And in the cultural environment, evolution can take place within a generation, not just across generations. This difference of speed of action of the four environmental spheres tends to mean that the more specialized ones will dominate evolution, and in particular will be responsible for the most distinctive features of each species. All sympatric species share the same physical environment, but they can exploit many different ecological niches within it; indeed, if we accept Gause's (1934) law of competitive exclusion, we have to say that each must have its own unique niche. And although behavioural ecologists have sought to establish general correlations between niche variations and the typical social structure of a species, it is clear that there is scope for much social variation within a niche. And, finally, the evidence from the cultural variation of modern humans is that culture can radically modify the social behaviour of a species even though all members are genetically adapted to a single set of physical, biological, and social conditions—which probably no longer pertain for any cultural group.

Because human-like intelligence seems to be a recent and rare outcome of evolution, it follows that it is above all in the social and cultural spheres that we should be looking for its evolutionary origins. This conclusion reinforces the view that what we need is a sociobiology of intelligence.

The contribution of sociobiology

The distinctiveness of sociobiology has been its recognition that the social sphere is different, and poses special evolutionary challenges. The rise of sociobiology has more or less coincided with an impressive growth in interest and progress in the area of behavioural ecology. The two have undoubtedly fed off each other for both theoretical and empirical material. It is probably best, however, to separate them for the moment. They have different spheres of study—behavioural ecology dealing primarily with a species' interaction with its biological environment, sociobiology with its social environment—but also different epistemological status. Behavioural ecology is a field of empirical study; sociobiology is a body of theory. The field to which it is applied might better be described, in a term coined by Crook (1970), as 'social ethology'—the biological study of behaviour within societies. Within that field, sociobiologists stand for a radical Darwinism, as Wilson (1975) made clear at the beginning of the book that coined the word 'sociobiology':

It might not be too much to say that sociology and the other social sciences, as well as the humanities, are the last branches of biology waiting to be included in the Modern Synthesis. One of the functions of sociobiology, then, is to reformulate the foundations of the social sciences in a way that draws these subjects into the Modern Synthesis. Whether the social sciences can be truly biologicized in this fashion remains to be seen. This book makes an attempt to codify sociobiology into a branch of evolutionary biology and particularly of modern populations biology (p. 4).

The distinctive contributions of sociobiological theory can be summarized in two propositions:

(1) that despite being inherently competitive, the process of natural selection can give rise to cooperative and altruistic behaviour;
(2) nonetheless, social relationships within groups of animals of the same species, including the very close groups of sexual partners, or parents and offspring, cannot be expected to be fully harmonious.

I will expand briefly on each of these in turn.

Dawkins (1976) famously popularized sociobiology with a book entitled 'The Selfish Gene'. It might as well have been called 'The Altruistic Organism', because its fundamental point was the resolution of a paradox. A sociobiological understanding of natural selection can explain how competitive genes, under the right conditions, can produce cooperative, altruistic organisms. That explanation is enormously successful, just because of its paradoxical nature: the exception does indeed prove (in its original sense of test) the rule. Furthermore, we can specify what the conditions for genetically mediated altruism are, in terms of relatedness, relative reproductive potential, and the possibility of future repayment.

However, the other fundamental contribution of sociobiology was to recognize the limits of cooperation. When members of a species are working towards a common goal, as when male and female act together to conceive young, or when parents and offspring act together to ensure that offspring survive and thrive, they are nonetheless subject to different selective pressures that may favour behavioural conflict. Sociobiological theory shows how the exploitation of males by females and parents by young, and the abandonment of females by males and offspring by parents, are entirely to be expected under an evolutionary theory.

What these two insights have in common is the most fundamental proposition of Darwinism—that evolution has neither purpose nor direction. It does not act 'for the good of the species', still less does it have any particular tendency to produce higher or more human-like life forms. If a gene encodes biochemical processes, which in turn produce behaviour, which in turn tends to lead to more copies of that gene being found in the next generation, that gene has by that fact been naturally selected; and that is all. The behaviour concerned may be altruistic or competitive; it may be harmonious or disruptive within the social group; it may be advanced or regressive; it may tend to the survival of the species, its modification into something new, or to its extinction. None of these is relevant to the effectiveness of natural selection. In seeking the evolutionary origins of intelligence, we need to be particularly alert to implicit assumptions of directionality in evolution. Natural selection could as easily dumb a species down as wise it up—it all depends on the selection pressures operating.

The historical nature of the evolutionary process

The final major principle of evolutionary theory that we must bear in mind is that evolution is a historical process. As such, it has few general laws. To understand any particular process of evolution, we need to know where it started from, what selective pressures were acting on what kind of gene pool in what kind of ecosystem—physical, biological, social, and cultural. And because evolution has no long-term goals, to understand each stage of the process we need to understand what the gene pool and the ecosystem were like at that stage.

These facts have severe consequences for our understanding of the evolution of the hominid mind, because we know so little about its history. Although the fossil record is improving steadily, hominid evolution has left no living relics—no human relative closer than the chimpanzees survives to confirm what genetic traits were present in our ancestors of two, one or half a million years ago. And though some products of the mind fossilize, most do not. We can know about the advance of hominids' tool-making abilities, but not about the advance of their story-telling or their feelings towards their offspring—and who knows which may have been more important in our evolution?

Even more severe, however, are the consequences for the epistemological status of evolutionary hypotheses. History is made up of unique events. It follows that proposed explanations for historical events are not open to the standard processes of scientific testing, in which we attempt to falsify general propositions by repeated observations or experiments. Evolutionary hypotheses are immune from falsification for the same reason. Here, perhaps, lies the origin of that tendency to 'pan-adaptationism' (Gould and Lewontin 1979), or 'Just-So Stories', which critics of sociobiology have repeatedly pointed out. When a popular sociobiologist suggests that the human female breast evolved as a releaser of sexual attraction in men (Morris 1967), what experiments can we carry out that would potentially falsify the hypothesis?

Our knowledge of the history of the mind is inherently limited, and we cannot carry out experiments to test the hypotheses which we use to fill the gaps. We have to look elsewhere for evidence about mental evolution. Our best possibility is to try to find, if not general laws, at least regularities in the evolutionary process. If we hypothesize that a particular change in the hominid niche created a selective pressure for a particular change in cognition, can we find other, parallel niche differences, and see whether parallel differences in cognitive process accompany them? If we can find one, that will strengthen our argument; if we can find many, that will strengthen it greatly. The key to testing evolutionary hypotheses is a comparative analysis.

But because there are no living hominids, comparisons of actual behaviour, as distinct from its fossilized traces, must inevitably involve non-hominids. Not all such comparisons will be valid. Because evolution is a historical process, a niche change will not have impacted on early hominids in the same way as the same niche change would impact on non-hominid primates, other mammals, or other vertebrates. But in so far as cognitive processes are common between us and other species (and therefore also to our common ancestors), it is worth investigating how important niche changes impact on our relatives. The natural assumption then becomes that the impact on our more immediate ancestors will have been the same.

Clearly, this strategy depends on an assumption that there are important cognitive differences between different non-hominid species. It involves an explicit rejection of Macphail's (1982) null hypothesis, that the non-human vertebrates do not differ in intelligence. That hypothesis was, I believe, only ever meant as a provocative gesture, to call easy assumptions into question. Its value is to throw the burden of proof onto those who want to claim such differences exist. This chapter takes up that burden.

Evolutionary and comparative psychology

This chapter cannot provide a detailed comparative analysis to test our hypotheses about the evolution of human cognition. In one sense, the whole endeavour which started with the work of Lloyd Morgan (1894), and has been variously known as comparative psychology, biological psychology, or animal psychology, is an attempt to provide such an analysis; the new name it is beginning to bear, 'evolutionary psychology' (see Barkow *et al.* 1995), demonstrates this. It is too vast a field to review in a book, let alone one chapter. Furthermore, the right comparative analysis can be performed only when we have more precise evolutionary hypotheses about the hominid mind—at the end of the present book, perhaps, rather than the beginning.

What we can do here, though, is to review briefly two foundations on which such a comparative analysis must build. The first, which forms the subject matter of this present section, is the common cognitive inheritance that all mammals (and, I shall argue, all warm-blooded vertebrates) seem to share. This must form part of the background within which hominid evolution took place. The second, which is discussed in the final part of this chapter, is the occurrence of other 'evolutionary islands' of more or less human-like intelligence elsewhere in the animal kingdom.

The data available for comparative analysis

Research on animal cognition has not examined a random or a representative sample of species. There is an overwhelming concentration on vertebrates, within the vertebrates on mammals and birds, and within those two warm-blooded groups on particular taxa, most of them chosen simply because they are domestic, but a few chosen because of interesting behavioural or ecological traits or because of their close relationship to humans.

The choice of birds and mammals as subjects for cognitive investigation is instantly understandable. To hypothesize about another species' mind requires some minimal degree of empathy, and most people find that difficult to achieve with a snake. But in terms of an evolutionary theory, the concentration on warm-blooded vertebrates is an unfortunate choice. Birds and mammals do not form a clade. They are descended from quite different groups of reptiles, and their common ancestor (of perhaps 150 million years ago) is almost certainly also ancestral to some modern, cold-blooded reptiles. If we find behavioural laws and cognitive capacities that seem to be common to all birds and mammals that have been investigated, it would be a reasonable hypothesis that they are also shared by at least some reptiles, and maybe even by other vertebrates and some invertebrates. But given the history of evolutionary psychology, most such hypotheses have never been tested. It is also possible that some behaviours and cognitions are adaptations to warm-bloodedness per se, or that some brain processes are made possible only by a more or less constantly high brain temperature, so that commonalities between mammals and birds could be due to convergence rather than common descent.

Be all that as it may, I know of no general behavioural or cognitive principles that apply to mammals in general without also applying to birds, or vice versa. That is surprising, since perceptual capacities differ greatly between the two orders, as they do within the groups. No bird species has been shown to depend on reflective ultrasound in the way that bats or dolphins do, or even on ultrasound social communication like many small mammals such as rats or hedgehogs. No bird has been shown to have the olfactory skills that are demonstrable in dogs and widely claimed to be typical of mammals. Conversely, no mammal has been found to have the visual receptor density that is common on the bird retina, or the dual visual system that many birds have, or the asymmetries of the auditory system that facilitate night hunting in owls.

But what birds and mammals, considered as groups, can do with their perceptual information, by way of using it to guide behaviour, seems remarkably similar. In this section, we will review briefly some of the cognitive abilities that all birds and mammals seem to share. They are arranged in a rough order of apparent cognitive complexity, though in almost all cases the mechanisms underlying the behaviours concerned are controversial, and a fuller understanding might well invert the ordering used here.

Simple behaviour and learning

We start with a number of very familiar processes. All of them can be, and usually are, characterized in entirely behavioural terms. Here, though, we look at them from a cognitive perspective, which shows that they make substantial demands on the animal's mind.

First, all vertebrate species seem to have a certain number of 'instinctual' behaviour patterns. The easiest to recognize are those that conform to Lorenz's (1935/1970) concept of an instinct subserved by an innate releasing mechanism—an identifiable set of perceptual features triggers off a stereotyped, ballistic response in any member of the species whose internal environment is in the right state. The stimuli and the response vary between species, indeed can be used as markers of an individual's or a species' ancestry, as Dilger (1962) showed in his work on hybrid lovebirds, or Lorenz (1941) in his massive comparison of the behaviour of different species of ducks and geese. But the apparent mechanism is invariant. It is clear from the huge variety of such instincts that have been studied, and the critical role they often play in such evolutionarily important events as feeding, mating, and parenting, that they are readily formed and/or modified through evolution. At first sight, such instincts seem the reverse of intelligent, but they imply two advanced cognitive processes. The perceptual input must be analysed to extract the relevant features, and the response must be organized through some kind of motor programme. Further-more, all such instinctual associations seem to be subject to refinement through learning (Hailman 1969). Although most of the well-known examples of instincts come from mammals or birds, enough reptiles, amphibians, and fish have been studied, in enough detail, for us to be confident that the possession of instincts is a common vertebrate trait.

Instinctual responses wane if repeatedly evoked by the same stimulus. This process is called habituation; the derived term dishabituation refers to the reappearance of the response when a slightly different stimulus is presented. Though it is often treated as the most elementary form of learning, habituation makes heavy cognitive demands, over and above those of instinctive response—the particular stimulus that has been repeatedly presented must in some sense be remembered, and dishabituation shows that the animal can make quite fine perceptual discriminations between this remembered stimulus and other, similar stimuli. In humans, at least, dishabituation can occur when a stimulus is omitted (Sokolov 1960), and it has been argued that this requires a mental representation of the habituated stimulus, but satisfactory demonstrations of this 'omission effect' in non-human species have not been forthcoming. But with this exception, habituation and dishabituation seem to be found as widely as instincts themselves, so this too can be regarded as part of a common vertebrate cognitive inheritance.

The next stage is the learned elicitation of a response by a new stimulus. This is demonstrated in what we now call classical or Pavlovian conditioning—if we have an 'unconditional reflex' in which a stimulus elicits a response (usually such reflexes are, in fact, what we have called above 'instincts'), and we pair a new stimulus with the unconditional eliciting stimulus, then a new 'conditional reflex' will develop, in which the new stimulus elicits a new response, which is like, though not identical to, the original response. More recent research has shown that, if the conditional response is directive, it will tend to be directed at the conditional stimulus (Brown and Jenkins 1968). Furthermore, it is not the mere pairing of conditional and unconditional stimulus that is important, but a positive correlation between them (Rescorla 1968). In consequence, Pavlovian conditioning means that animals will respond to causal relationships within their environments (Dickinson 1980). In turn this means that they must have the cognitive means to detect such relationships, and use them to elaborate new stimulus-response relationships. Note that virtually all our evidence about Pavlovian conditioning comes from cases where the event that is caused is a stimulus of sufficient biological importance to the animal to elicit an instinctive response, but that restriction is due only to methodological limitations—there is at least some evidence that causal relationships between arbitrary stimuli are detected, and the animal's knowledge of them will be revealed when one of them subsequently becomes biologically significant (e.g. Rizley and Rescorla 1972). Pavlovian conditioning appears to be general to all vertebrates, and quite a range of Pavlovian phenomena have been demonstrated in various invertebrates also. Some associations are more easily learned than others, and these vary between species in ways that can be interpreted in terms of the animals' ecological niches.

Reliable correlations between an animal's own responses and biologically significant stimuli give rise to what is variously called instrumental learning or operant
conditioning. The set of stimuli that will support operant conditioning (usually called
reinforcers) is not well defined, but it overlaps strongly with those that elicit instinctual responses. Unlike Pavlovian conditioning, operant conditioning is strikingly
robust in the face of an intermittent relationship between response and reinforcer,
and both the general rule specifying which responses will be reinforced (the schedule
of reinforcement), and its quantitative parameters, have strong and highly predictable
effects on the rate and pattern of responding. While the effects of the simplest
schedules of reinforcement are well known, it is probable that much more biological
significance attaches to the laws governing compound schedules. Where two or more
schedules are in effect simultaneously or sequentially, they will in general interact,
but it is possible to predict the distribution of responses between them quantitatively
(see the review by Davison and McCarthy 1988). The exact forms of the quantitative
relationships have been the subject of endless dispute, but it is uncontroversial that in
many situations they will produce a good approximation to the optimum pattern of
choice. It is therefore no surprise that operant conditioning has been seen as the
mechanism underlying foraging behaviour, and the selective pressure to forage
optimally has been seen as the evolutionary origin of the laws of operant conditioning
(Lea 1979; Fantino and Abarca 1985). Consistent with this hypothesis is the fact that
operant conditioning seems to be found, and to follow the same laws, in all vertebrate
species that have been studied.

A particular form of instrumental learning is learning to withhold responses that
lead to damaging consequences, or to emit responses that prevent damaging consequences. Such avoidance learning has always been seen as important to the study of
animal cognition, because if it is successful the noxious stimulus is never presented. It
is therefore argued that behaviour must be controlled by a mental representation of
the noxious stimulus. A special case of avoidance learning has gained extraordinary
prominence in recent decades following a demonstration by Garcia and Koelling
(1966): animals of a variety of species have exceptional capacity to learn to avoid
novel foods that are associated, even relatively remotely, with illness. Food avoidance
learning can occur even when there are long delays between eating the food and
becoming ill. It is easy to see the selective pressure for such long-delay learning,
because some toxins are slow-acting, but its cognitive demands are considerable: it
requires the animal to be able to remember the perceptual characteristics of a food
that it ate perhaps hours earlier, at a time when it had no reason to know that that
food might become significant. Not all characteristics of food are equally well learned
as cues for food avoidance, and the particular characteristics that are readily learned
vary between species. For most mammals taste is the key feature (hence the usual
title, 'taste avoidance learning' for this area of research), but for birds visual or
olfactory cues may be more important (Wilcoxon *et al.* 1971; Roper and Marples
1997). But no vertebrate species has been found to be incapable of avoidance learning
in general, or food avoidance in particular. On the other hand, although reports of
avoidance learning in invertebrates exist, even claims that such learning can proceed
in decapitated animals (Horridge 1962), they are few in number and some at least are
open to non-associative explanations (Church and Lerner 1984).

The cognitive resources of the vertebrates

The basic processes discussed in the previous section could all have been included in a review of animal learning and behaviour written a century ago, though the amount we know about them has, of course, increased enormously since that time. In the past quarter of a century, however, the way we look at them has changed in two significant ways, both reflected in the brief survey above. First, it has been recognized that it is essential to give a coherent evolutionary account of behaviour and learning, and therefore to integrate our knowledge of both with our understanding of the general biology of each species. Secondly, it has been accepted that while we still need to describe animals' behaviour and how it changes as a result of experience in rigorously objective terms, we also need to specify the cognitive mechanisms that are required to produce them. In surveying these simple processes of learning and behaviour, we have seen that animals must be able to analyse stimuli, to programme responses, to remember stimuli and discriminate current from remembered percepts, to recognize causal relationships, to choose between sources of food, and to scan old memories. The evidence suggests that all these cognitive processes are common to all vertebrates that have been studied, though the particular stimuli or responses to which they are applied, or to which they are most easily applied, frequently vary between species.

However, the cognitive processes implied by these elementary properties of learning and behaviour do not exhaust the common cognitive resources we can attribute to the warm-blooded vertebrates. If we approach the matter from a more cognitive standpoint, as has become common in the last two decades, we can recognize a number of processes which have been demonstrated across a range of species.

First, we can consider the process of stimulus analysis. Even the simplest instinct requires some degree of analysis of the perceptual input. However, our ability to decipher the sign stimuli that trigger instinctual behaviour patterns depends on the fact that the analysis might be very crude. If a herring gull chick is more likely to beg for food from a red knitting needle with three white bands round it than from a life-size model of its parent's head (Tinbergen and Perdeck 1950), the perceptual analysis triggering the instinct must be much less sophisticated than the analysis that enables us to recognize an adult herring gull. Our everyday perceptual world is not made up of elementary perceptual features such as red, contrasty, and pointed, but of objects, such as gulls and knitting needles. Such objects typically vary in their appearance, both from moment to moment and from one instance of the object to the next. Although perceptual features are associated with such objects, they tend not to be either necessary or sufficient conditions for membership of what can be called a 'polymorphous concept' (Ryle 1951; Dennis *et al.* 1973) linked by 'family resemblances' between instances (Wittgenstein 1953; Rosch and Mervis 1975). An extensive research literature has demonstrated that animals can be trained to discriminate between stimulus sets defined in terms of polymorphous concepts (see Watanabe *et al.* 1993 for a review). Many of the experiments have followed the pioneering work of Herrnstein and Loveland (1964) and used visual stimuli and pigeons as subjects, but there seems to be no difficulty in replicating the experiments with other species (which may do better than pigeons; Ryan and Lea 1994) and other sensory modalities (e.g. audition in chinchillas; Burdick and Miller 1975). The evidence suggests that all warm-blooded vertebrates have the ability to recognize complex, variable objects and to categorize perceptual input at a variety of levels. There has been relatively little discussion of the mechanisms underlying such 'concept discriminations' (see Lea 1984; Herrnstein 1990), and in particular it is very unclear whether it is appropriate to describe the animals as possessing or forming concepts. Lea and Kiley-Worthington (1996) argue that the issue revolves around that of mental representation—a minimum condition for saying that an animal has a concept of some object or category is that it can manipulate a mental representation of that object.

The issue of representation is a recurrent one. We have encountered it already in the contexts of habituation and avoidance learning, where it has long been discussed. Somewhat more recently, the extensive modern work on Pavlovian conditioning has led many researchers to the conclusion that animals, during the conditioning process, form associations between mental representations of stimuli, and that these representations can be activated and can evoke behaviour or undergo change in the absence of the stimulus itself (Dickinson 1980; Pearce 1997, pp. 38–41). But how far can this be taken? As we saw above, the whole phenomenon of classical conditioning functions to bring animals' behaviour under the control of causal relations in the environment. But does that require the animals to recognize, and represent to themselves, causality as such? Killeen (1977) showed that pigeons could discriminate between causal and non-causal relationships between their own behaviour and stimulus changes, but in ongoing experiments with Winand Dittrich, Catriona Ryan and Martina Siemann, I have had less success in getting pigeons to discriminate causal relations between stimuli, using a version of the classic 'launch event' described by Michotte (1954/1963).

One of the most basic kinds of representation is a map. The notion of a 'cognitive map' was first introduced by Tolman (1948), reviewing studies of rats' behaviour in mazes. It has been given far more precision in modern studies of spatial memory (Olton and Samuelson 1976; Morris 1981; O'Keefe and Speakman 1987), which were initiated in rats but have been extended to many other species. The maze was introduced into psychology by Small (1900–1901) because it seemed to him a biologically appropriate task for a rat, but no species that has been studied has been found to be incapable of learning its way around a new environment. The related skill of learning time–place correlations, enabling an animal to go to a particular place at the time when food or some other desirable object is due to arrive there, also seems to be widespread (Wilkie *et al.* 1997).

Animals that can store representations of past events or stimuli can reasonably be spoken of as having memories. Much work on animal cognition has sought to probe the functioning of animal memory, using methods and concepts derived from the study of human memory. The concept of 'working memory' has been deployed particularly effectively, to interpret animals' ability to respond differentially to stimuli after a delay. In tasks where they are required to indicate whether a stimulus has been seen before, or not, macaques show the same serial-position curve as humans (Wright and Rivera 1997) under some experimental conditions. Long-term memory has been studied by testing retention of learned discriminations—the most successful methodology, as well as the most impressive results, is to be found in the work of Vaughan and Greene (1984), who taught pigeons an 'absolute' discrimination between two randomly chosen sets of pictures, and showed that they could still classify 320 stimuli correctly after a two-year interval without experimental experience.

Finally, and perhaps more contentiously in this survey of the common vertebrate heritage, we can consider problem-solving. Above, operant conditioning was introduced as a process by which the rates of emission of learned behaviours adjust to rates of reinforcement; that is the meaning that was given to the Law of Effect by Herrnstein (1970). But when Thorndike (1911) originally formulated the Law of Effect, and when he and his contemporaries, such as Small, originally studied instrumental learning, what they were interested in was the emergence of entirely new responses in response to novel or changed environments—that is, in problem-solving. The standard operant conditioning chamber, which we usually call a Skinner box, was originally conceived of as a 'puzzle box' in direct line of descent from those used by Thorndike (1898) in his experiments on cats. Köhler (1927) argued that insightful problem-solving was not part of the common vertebrate heritage, but the prerogative of a few 'intelligent' species. That claim remains contentious. What is sure is that if an experimenter, or a natural situation, arranges that early approximations to a novel response are reinforced, any vertebrate can be trained to make novel complex responses, which will in due course become new motor programmes. That is how Lloyd Morgan's terrier Tony learned to open a gate (without Lloyd Morgan intervening, incidentally; Boakes 1984, p. 36); that is how Nakajima and Sato (1993) were able to get pigeons to mimic the performances of Köhler's chimpanzees. Skinner's discovery of shaping, in other words, validated Thorndike's hypothesis that trial-and-error learning could rival insight in producing novel responses.

Islands of intelligence

Thus there is a great deal that all warm-blooded vertebrates can do. But if we are to understand the evolution of the hominid mind, what we have to explain is the existence of cognitive capacities that stand out from this common background.

There are many cognitive capacities that seem to be restricted to particular taxa. Their adaptive origin is often self-evident. The capacity to learn the familial variant of a species-specific song, months before uttering it, is characteristic of the oscine songbirds; it is easy to find sociobiological hypotheses to account for it. The capacity to learn to navigate a long-distance route by sun and/or stars is characteristic of several groups of migratory birds, and the selective pressure against any bird that failed to learn is plainly extreme. Scatter-hoarding birds (Shettleworth and Krebs 1982; Kamil and Balda 1985) and mammals (Macdonald 1997) seem to have a remarkable ability to find food weeks or months after it was buried; those that fail will not survive the winter.

Some of these taxonomically specific learning abilities are more impressive than others. Many of them are varieties of 'phase-specific learning', in which a particular species has a sensitive period for learning particular kinds of stimuli. The paradigm case is filial imprinting in poultry, but there are many others, such as the learning of natal stream odours by fish that breed inland but mature at sea (e.g. Thunberg 1971), the learning of migratory routes by birds (Matthews 1968), and the learning of the appearance of offspring by cichlid fish (Noble and Curtis 1939). Such 'imprinting' systems do not seem cognitively complex: they can be described as 'open instincts'—a response is already available, and in a certain phase of its life the animal is adapted to learn what stimulus should elicit it.

But other specialized learning capacities seem different. Only a dolphin has ever been trained to emit new responses, previously unseen by the experimenters, every day (Pryor *et al.* 1969). Only of a parrot has it been claimed that, faced with a yellow pentagon, it can vocalize 'yellow' if asked 'What colour? and 'five-corner' if asked 'What shape?' (Pepperberg 1983). We are somehow not surprised that when Powell and Kelly (1975) taught birds to pick up a stick and use it to operate a switch that was behind a wire mesh too fine for their beaks to pass through, the birds they used were crows. And, while several authors in this book claim that some kind of 'theory of mind' is present in great apes, but not Old World monkeys, no one is claiming that monkeys possess it and apes do not.

What is being claimed here, explicitly or implicitly, is that certain taxonomic groups do not just have special capacities to learn a particular kind of information at a particular time of their lives: rather, they have a greater general ability to learn—they are particularly intelligent.

Defining animal intelligence

There is scope for endless discussion about the proper definition of intelligence in animals. In particular, it could be argued that when we talk about 'animal intelligence', we are adopting an anthropocentric view, based on the kinds of performance we regard as intelligent in humans; these might not be the only kinds of intelligence in the animal kingdom, and might not even be particularly advanced when they occur in other taxa.

In this book, however, we can joyfully bypass this tedious and probably unresolvable debate. What we are interested in is, precisely, the evolution of the *hominid* mind; so in looking for analogues or homologues of that process in other taxa, it is precisely human-like intelligence that we need to find, regardless of whether that is an appropriate criterion for intelligence in an ape, or dolphin, or dog. We want to know what selective pressures produce brains that can do the things our brains do uniquely well, so it is just those things that we should be looking for.

That leaves us, of course, with the problem of defining human intelligence, a matter which has caused at least as much contention as defining animal intelligence. But as a practical matter, when we seek to measure intelligence in humans, we include a wide range of tasks, and rest our conclusions most strongly on those tasks which intercorrelate well with most others. From Lashley (1929) to Macphail (1993), comparative psychologists have argued that we should do the same when we seek to measure animal intelligence. In the same spirit, this chapter will not identify any single ability as lying at the core of animal intelligence, but will review data on several that all seem close to the heart of what we mean by intelligence.

Species-specific abilities

In this section, we consider some of the examples of human-like intelligence that have been demonstrated in animals other than humans. Because the aim is to find independent evidence of the evolutionary processes that have been responsible for human intelligence, I will for the most part not discuss data from non-human primates. This is partly because other chapters in this book deal with them more fully, but there is also a reason of principle. Within the primate group, if another species can do what humans can also do, there are two possible explanations—common descent or independent evolution. Common descent may not be a reasonable assumption when we find signs of high human-like intelligence in New World monkeys, as has, for example, been claimed for capuchins by Chevalier-Skolnikoff (1989), since the New World monkeys diverged from the Old World monkey/ape line quite early in the history of the primates, and their common ancestor may not have been very intelligent. There may even have been independent evolution of similar mental capacities in humans and other great apes, but it is difficult to be sure. When we consider the most recent common ancestors of primates and other vertebrates, however, we are looking at animals that were probably intellectually quite undistinguished, so if a human-like intellectual capacity shows up in a mammal of another order, let alone another class of vertebrate, it is a very reasonable guess that it is the result of independent evolution.

What human-like abilities are found among non-primates, and what selective pressures might have produced them?

Tool-use is one ability that has a very scattered distribution. In some animals, it seems to be highly stereotyped—woodpecker finches always use the same kind of spine in the same kind of way to extract insects from bark (Lack 1947). The use of anvils for breaking into shells of molluscs, common in thrushes and waders, is arguably an example of tool use. In these taxonomic groups, tools are used for a single, direct purpose. Other animals, though, seem to have a more general ability to learn to use new tools, for quite esoteric purposes. For the most part, reports of spontaneous tool use come from primates, with a predominance of studies of chimpanzees. However, a few studies suggest that corvids spontaneously use tools. Reid (1982) found that a rook spontaneously learned to use a stopper to retain water on its aviary floor, Powell and Kelly (1977) reported that trained tool use in common crows readily generalized to new objects, and Jones and Kamil (1973) observed captive blue jays tearing up strips of paper to use as rakes. Elephants, also, have been argued to use tools (Chevalier-Skolnikoff and Liska 1993; Hart and Hart 1994). Among the primates there are many reports of tool use by capuchin monkeys, including the use of probes (e.g. Westergaard and Suomi 1994), pestles (e.g. Westergaard *et al.* 1995), and clubs (e.g. Fernandes 1991). This has led Chevalier-Skolnikoff (1990) to argue that there has been an evolutionary process in this New World species parallel to the emergence of tool use in the great apes. However, there are sufficient, though scattered, reports of tool use in Old World monkeys, especially baboons (e.g. Petit and Thierry 1993; Westergaard 1992) but also macaques of various species (e.g. Bayart and Anderson 1985; Tokida *et al.* 1994; Zuberbuhler *et al.* 1996), mangabeys (Kyes 1988), and colobus (Starin 1990), to make it possible that tool use is a primitive monkey trait. Better evidence for Chevalier-Skolnikoff's hypothesis, perhaps, comes from the surprising observation that there seem to be no records of tool use in New World monkeys outside the Cebus genus.

Spontaneous detouring seems to be an impressive feat of intelligence. Yet the jumping spider *Portia fimbriata* achieves remarkable feats of detour (Tarsitano and Jackson 1994). The mechanism has been elucidated, but that hardly seems to devalue the cognitive ability, since the detours can be shown to depend on the correct identification of secondary goals (Tarsitano and Jackson 1997). It is striking that Portia, like both dogs and chimpanzees, is a hunting animal, so perhaps the selective pressure for detour comes from pursuit; however, Kiley-Worthington (see Lea and Kiley-Worthington 1996) claims that horses, which are entirely pursued rather than pursuers, also show spontaneous detour.

We have already mentioned the exceptional spatial memory abilities of scatter-hoarding birds and mammals. It has been claimed (e.g. Healy and Krebs 1996) that scatter-hoarding species have a larger hippocampus than congeners that do not cache food, and since the hippocampus has repeatedly been implicated in memory for place (e.g. O'Keefe and Speakman 1987), this would be consistent with a very recent adaptive specialization.

Much recent dispute has centred on imitation and observational learning (e.g. Heyes 1993). It may or may not be valid to say that rats can learn lever pressing, say, or that marmosets can learn to pull rather than push at an obstacle (Bugnyar and Huber 1997), by watching a pretrained conspecific. However, it is clear that certain groups of birds have specialized imitative abilities, which go well beyond the passive learning of a single familial song that is common in the oscines. The specialized mimics include starlings (e.g. Eens *et al.* 1992), mynah birds, mocking birds, bower birds (Frith and McGuire 1996), and various psittacids (e.g. Cruickshank *et al.* 1993). The selective pressures producing such open-ended song learning (Nottebohm and Nottebohm 1978) are not clear, but one possible function of mimicry is social, with a mated pair of birds learning and repeating each other's distinctive calls, though obviously the birds do mimic other sounds, including human ones. Maintenance of social contact is also a plausible function of vocal mimicry in the other group in which it has been widely reported, sea mammals including both dolphins (e.g. Reiss and McCowan 1993) and seals (e.g. Ralls *et al.* 1985).

The ability to respond differentially to signals, and in particular to learn new stimulus-action rules, is the key to many kinds of domestic use of animals. Human tradition holds that dogs and horses are good at this, while not very dissimilar animals such as foxes and zebra, let alone cats and cows, are not. Nonetheless, cows are more easily trained than is traditionally thought (Randle 1994, Chapter 8), and the domestication of cats has probably depended on their ability to learn the signs that humans have left food available (Todd 1978)—even when those signs were not left for their benefit. Oxen, elephants, and various camelidae can also be trained efficiently, which suggests that much domestic use involves nothing that is outside the common vertebrate cognitive inheritance discussed above. However, the more elaborate uses of animals like dogs do seem to require a more flexible, human-like response. Could simple conditioning allow a dog to control sheep? Johnston (1995) has argued that it cannot explain the performance of a guide-dog.

Learned signalling is a skill that can be seen as related either to differential response to stimuli, or to tool use. Several research projects have tried to teach language systems to animals other than primates. Muckensturm (1974) taught woodpeckers to drum different rhythms to secure different kinds of food, Pepperberg (e.g. Pepperberg 1981; Patterson and Pepperberg 1994) has taught the African grey parrot Alex a series of distinct utterances, and Herman and his colleagues (e.g. Herman *et al.* 1984, 1990) have taught bottle-nosed dolphins to respond discriminatively, and, they argue, linguistically, to a wide range of human gestures.

In these experiments, though, humans taught animals of other species what signs to make. If a species is to cross over into the world where cultural evolution could start to dominate as it does among humans, there must be learning within the social group —perhaps even teaching. Caro and Hauser (1992) have reviewed the little evidence there is of deliberate instruction among non-humans. The clearest examples, outside the primates, both come from felids, from cheetahs and domestic cats—in both species mothers seem to systematically train the young to hunt.

The above brief survey has focused in turn on a number of different examples of human-like intelligence. A more systematic approach is to use theories of human intelligence that arrange such abilities into some kind of hierarchy, and then look to see where different species appear on such a scale. The most elaborate project of this kind is the attempt to map animals' cognitive abilities into Piaget's stage theory of cognitive development. This approach has been reviewed by Doré and Dumas (1987) and Vauclair (1996, Chapter 3); a notable example of it is Chevalier-Skolnikoff's (1989) analysis of the cognitive performance of the brown capuchin monkey. Within the Piagetian framework, most attention has focused on the capacity usually referred to as 'object permanence', the apparent ability to recognize the continuing existence of an object when it has been hidden. Strong claims have been made for its occurrence in cats (Gruber *et al.* 1971), for example, and also in several species of psittacid (Pepperberg and Funk 1990).

What species are unusually intelligent?

Despite the brevity of the previous section, a few taxonomic groups recur: among birds, corvids, psittacids, and possibly sturnids (the large group that includes both starlings and mynahs); among mammals, carnivores, and toothed whales, with Cebus monkeys possibly constituting an 'island' of human-like intelligence among the New World monkeys. Some others are notable by their absence: laboratory work on dogs or horses has revealed nothing beyond routine learning abilities (e.g. Dougherty and Lewis 1991), though the literature on their practical training tells a different story (e.g. Pinney 1990), and the entire 'Clever Hans' effect (Boakes 1984, pp. 78–81) depends on horses' exquisitely fine discrimination of postural signals. A full analysis of the animal training literature might sweep in some other species, for example the raptors used in falconry (e.g. Parry-Jones 1996).

The problem for a formal analysis is that there has been no systematic sampling of species. Experimental and even anecdotal reports of animal intelligence focus on groups that are traditionally thought of as intelligent, those that are convenient to study, and those that humans frequently observe—especially those with which humans spend much time. When we go outside these magic circles we know little or nothing, one way or the other. If a zoo curator argues, as one once did to me, that hornbills seem as intelligent as parrots, there is nothing in the published literature that could enable us to support or challenge his impression. Furthermore, we tend to treat what rats and pigeons are capable of as the baseline intelligence of rodents and birds respectively, simply because so much psychological experimentation has used them as subjects, but there is no reason to think of either as a representative species. Both are highly successful parasites on humans, suggesting they might be unusually adaptable, and pigeons have a remarkable homing ability that might well be species-specific.

Any claim to identify particular groups as of greater intelligence than others must therefore be highly tentative. That even applies to the primates, certainly if we stop short of the great apes. But if we take that tentative step, and suppose that the species we have discussed really do constitute islands of evolved intelligence, what do we see?

What selective pressures produce intelligence?

The most obvious conclusion at this point is a null one. There is no apparent ecological niche that all the 'islanders' discussed in the last section share. Dogs and dolphins are social hunters, but crows are scavengers, parrots are largely fruit eaters, and horses are grazers. There is no common sociobiology: domestic cats are as solitary as parrots (if we dare generalize across a family of around 360 species) are gregarious. Equally, every one of these specialisms has other species pursuing it, for which there is no obvious evidence of high intelligence. If there are commonalities of behaviour between the supposedly intelligent species, they sound more like signs of intelligence than causes—for example, except perhaps for horses, all the groups listed are unusually attracted by and playful with objects. Evolutionary histories also vary—dolphins and seals are highly evolved and specialized among mammals, primates in some ways quite primitive.

Can anything be drawn out that might help us understand the evolution of the hominid mind? Although there seems to be no unique niche that favours human-like intelligence, there are several niche characteristics that seem to make it more likely. The 'intelligent' species include more predators than prey, more social than solitary species. If not all are object manipulators, many are; if not all are noticeably playful, many are. Several seem to have undergone recent rapid evolution—the corvids, for example, representing a recent and uncharacteristic development among the songbirds and the sea mammals a relatively recent, secondary, adaptation of land mammals to exploit a marine habitat; the psittacids' extensive radiation through a fragmented environment must also have involved repeated rapid adaptations. In other words, these 'islanders' are not a random sample of the warm-blooded vertebrates.

It is clear from the history of the primate mind that the forces of intellectual evolution were at work before the divergence of the human and chimpanzee ancestral lines. Even if no hominids had ever evolved, the great apes would still represent the most striking of islands of human-like intelligence. It is equally clear that since that divergence, mind has developed faster than ever before, and faster than anywhere else in the vertebrate taxa. From the comparative perspective, it seems that what may have happened is that a number of characteristics favouring intellectual evolution came together. Both fossil and comparative evidence suggests that early hominids were strongly social. Comparative evidence suggests they did at least some hunting, since this behaviour is shared by humans, chimpanzees (Van Lawick-Goodall 1974) and bonobos (Ihobe 1992). All the great apes are efficient tool-makers and tool-users, and therefore must be strongly oriented to object manipulation; all are highly playful. It is commonly assumed (see Corballis, this volume) that it was a sudden environmental change that isolated our ancestors in East Africa from those of the chimpanzees in the west, and this will have demanded rapid adaptation. All these forces were acting on what was already the most intelligent animal that had yet evolved. The comparative evidence suggests that none of these factors is sufficient to specialize an ape mind into a hominid mind. Taken together, however, they might be.

Even if we accept this conjunctive hypothesis, however, we cannot be sure that we have a complete list of the relevant factors. That must wait until we have much firmer evidence of which species really do show human-like intelligence. To provide such evidence will require three improvements in our present data base:

(1) we need confirmation that our islands of intelligence really exist—that is, much clearer evidence that what looks like intelligent performance in our favoured species really deserves that description;
(2) we need to know the size of those islands—whether, where one species in a taxonomic group shows human-like intelligence, its congeners are also intelligent, and how wide the tendency spreads; and
(3) we need to know what other islands might exist—to survey cognitive capacities across a much wider range of species, motivated by a genuinely comparative spirit rather than historical prejudices about the relative intelligence of different groups.

Clearly, much remains to be investigated. Even the present partial state of our knowledge, however, shows us that hominid-like intelligence is not confined to hominids. As, in the rest of this book, we enquire further into the evolution of the hominid mind, we need to remember to test our ideas by applying them also to the evolution of cebid, delphid, canid, and even psittacid minds.

References

Barkow, J. H., Cosmides, L., and Tooby, J. (ed.) (1995). *The adapted mind*. Oxford University Press, New York.

Bayart, F. and Anderson, J. R. (1985). Mirror-image reactions in a tool-using, adult male *Macaca tonkeana*. *Behavioural Processes*, **10**, 219–27.

Boakes, R. A. (1984). *From Darwin to behaviourism*. Cambridge University Press.

Brown, P. L. and Jenkins, H. M. (1968). Auto-shaping of the pigeon's key-peck. *Journal of the Experimental Analysis of Behavior*, **11**, 1–8.

Bugnyar, T. and Huber, L. (1997). Push or pull: an experimental study of imitation in marmosets. *Animal Behaviour*, **54**, 817–31.

Burdick, C. K. and Miller, J. D. (1975). Speech perception by the chinchilla: discrimination of sustained /a/ and /i/. *Journal of the Acoustical Society of America*, **58**, 415–27.

Caro, T. M. and Hauser, M. D. (1992). Is there teaching in nonhuman animals? *Quarterly Review of Biology*, **67**, 151–74.

Chevalier-Skolnikoff, S. (1989). Spontaneous tool use and sensorimotor intelligence in Cebus compared with other monkeys and apes. *The Behavioral and Brain Sciences*, **12**, 561–627.

Chevalier-Skolnikoff, S. (1990). Tool use by wild cebus monkeys at Santa Rosa National Park, Costa Rica. *Primates*, **31**, 375–83.

Chevalier-Skolnikoff, S. and Liska, J. (1993). Tool use by wild and captive elephants. *Animal Behaviour*, **46**, 209–19.

Church, R. M. and Lerner, N. D. (1976). Does the headless roach learn to avoid? *Physiological Psychology*, **4**, 439–42.

Crook, J. H. (1970). Social organization and the environment: aspects of contemporary social ethology. *Animal Behaviour*, **18**, 197–209.

Cruickshank, A. J., Gautier, J. P., and Chappuis, C. (1993). Vocal mimicry in wild African gray parrots *Psittacus erithacus*. *Ibis*, **135**, 293–9.

Davison, M. and McCarthy, D. (1988). *The matching law*. Erlbaum, Hillsdale, NJ.

Dawkins, R. (1976). *The selfish gene*. Oxford University Press.

Dawkins, R. (1981). *The extended phenotype*. Freeman, Oxford.

Dennis, I., Hampton, J. A., and Lea, S. E. G. (1973). New problem in concept formation. *Nature*, **243**, 101–2.

Dickinson, A. (1980). *Contemporary animal learning theory*. Cambridge University Press.

Dilger, W. C. (1962). The behavior of lovebirds. *Scientific American*, **206**, (1), 88–98.

Doré, F. Y. and Dumas, C. (1987). Psychology of animal cognition: Piagetian studies. *Psychological Bulletin*, **102**, 219–33.

Dougherty, D. M. and Lewis, P. (1991). Stimulus generalization, discrimination learning, and peak shift in horses. *Journal of the Experimental Analysis of Behavior*, **56**, 97–104.

Eens, M., Pinxten, R., and Verheyen, R. F. (1992). Song learning in captive European starlings, *Sturnus vulgaris*. *Animal Behaviour*, **44**, 1131–43.

Fantino, E. and Abarca, N. (1985). Choice, optimal foraging, and the delay-reduction hypothesis. *The Behavioral and Brain Sciences*, **8**, 315–62.

Fernandes, M. E. (1991). Tool use and predation of oysters (*Crassostrea rhizophorae*) by the tufted capuchin, *Cebus apella apella*, in brackish water mangrove swamps. *Primates*, **32**, 529–31.

Fisher, R. A. (1930). *The genetical theory of selection*. Clarendon Press, Oxford.

Frith, C. B. and McGuire, M. (1996). Visual evidence of vocal avian mimicry by male tooth-billed bowerbirds *Scenopoeetes dentirostris* (Ptilonorhynchidae). *Emu*, **96**, 12–16.

Garcia, J. and Koelling, R. A. (1966). Relation of cue to consequence in avoidance-learning. *Psychonomic Science*, **4**, 123–4.

Gause, G. F. (1934). *The struggle for existence*. Williams and Wilkins, Baltimore, MD.

Gould, S. J. and Lewontin, R. C. (1979). The spandrels of San Marco and the Panglossian paradigm. *Proceedings of the Royal Society, Series B*, **205**, 581–98.

Gruber, H. E., Girgus, J. S., and Banuazizi, A. (1971). The development of object permanence in the cat. *Developmental Psychology*, **4**, 9–15.

Hailman, J. P. (1969). How an instinct is learned. *Scientific American*, **221**, (6), 98–106.

Hart, B. L. and Hart, L. A. (1994). Fly switching by Asian elephants: tool use to control parasites. *Animal Behaviour*, **48**, 35–45.

Healy, S. D. and Krebs, J. R. (1996). Food storing and the hippocampus in Paridae. *Brain, Behavior and Evolution*, **47**, 195–9.

Herman, L. M., Richards, D. G., and Wolz, J. P. (1984). Comprehension of sentences by bottlenosed dolphins. *Cognition*, **16**, 129–219.

Herman, L. M., Morrel-Samuels, P., and Pack, A. A. (1990). Bottlenosed dolphin and human recognition of veridical and degraded video displays of an artificial gestural language. *Journal of Experimental Psychology: General*, **119**, 215–30.

Herrnstein, R. J. (1970). On the law of effect. *Journal of the Experimental Analysis of Behavior*, **13**, 243–66.

Herrnstein, R. J. (1990). Levels of stimulus control: a functional approach. *Cognition*, **37**, 133–66.

Herrnstein, R. J. and Loveland, D. H. (1964). Complex visual concept in the pigeon. *Science*, **146**, 549–51.

Heyes, C. M. (1993). Imitation, culture and cognition. *Animal Behaviour*, **46**, 999–1010.

Horridge, G. A. (1962). Learning of leg position by the ventral nerve cord in headless insects. *Proceedings of the Royal Society, Series B*, **157**, 33–52.

Ihobe, H. (1992). Observations on the meat-eating behavior of wild bonobos (*Pan paniscus*) at Wamba, Republic of Zaire. *Primates*, **33**, 247–50.

Johnston, B. (1995). *Harnessing thought: guide dog—a thinking animal with a skilful mind*. Lennard, Harpenden.

Jones, T. B. and Kamil, A. C. (1973). Tool-making and tool-using in the Northern blue jay. *Science*, **180**, 1076–8.

Kamil, A. C. and Balda, R. P. (1985). Cache recovery and spatial memory in Clark's nutcrackers (*Nucifraga columbiana*). *Journal of Experimental Psychology: Animal Behavior Processes*, **11**, 95–111.

Killeen, P. R. (1977). Superstition: a matter of bias, not detectability. *Science*, **199**, 88–90.

Köhler, W. (1927). *The mentality of apes* (2nd edn). Routledge and Kegan Paul, London.

Krebs, J. R. and Davies, N. B. (1993). *Introduction to behavioural ecology* (3rd edn). Blackwell, Oxford.

Kyes, R. C. (1988). Grooming with a stone in sooty mangabeys (*Cercocebus atys*). *American Journal of Primatology*, **16**, 171–5.

Lack, D. (1947). *Darwin's finches*. Cambridge University Press.

Lashley, K. S. (1929). *Brain mechanisms and intelligence*. University of Chicago Press.

Lea, S. E. G. (1979). Foraging and reinforcement schedules in the pigeon: optimal and non-optimal aspects of choice. *Animal Behaviour*, **27**, 875–86.

Lea, S. E. G. (1984). In what sense do pigeons learn concepts? In *Animal cognition* (ed. H. L. Roitblat, T. G. Bever, and H. S. Terrace), pp. 263–76. Erlbaum, Hilldale, NJ.

Lea, S. E. G. and Kiley-Worthington, M. (1996). Can animals think? In *Unsolved mysteries of the mind* (ed. V. G. Bruce), pp. 211–44. Erlbaum (UK), Taylor and Francis, Hove.

Levin, L. E. (1997). Kinetic dialogs in predator–prey recognition. *Behavioural Processes*, **40**, 113–20.

Lorenz, K. (1941). Vergleichende Bewegungsstudien an Anatinen. Supplement to *Journal für Ornithologie*, **89**, 194–294.

Lorenz, K. (1970). Companions as factors in the bird's environment. In *Studies in animal and human behaviour*, Vol. 1, (trans. R. Martin), pp. 101–258. Methuen, London (originally published 1935).

Lumsden, C. J. and Wilson, E. O. (1981). *Genes, mind and culture*. Harvard University Press, Cambridge, MA.

Lumsden, C. J. and Wilson, E. O. (1983). *Promethean Fire*. Harvard University Press, Cambridge, MA.

Macdonald, I. M. V. (1997). Field experiments on duration and precision of grey and red squirrel spatial memory. *Animal Behaviour*, **54**, 879–91.

Macphail, E. M. (1982). *Brain and intelligence in vertebrates*. Clarendon, Oxford.

Macphail, E. M. (1993). *The neuroscience of animal intelligence*. Columbia University Press, New York.

Matthews, G. V. T. (1968). *Bird navigation* (2nd edn). Cambridge University Press.

Michotte, A. (1963). *The perception of causality*. Methuen, London (originally published 1954).

Morgan, C. L. (1894). *An introduction to comparative psychology*. Scott, London.

Morris, D. (1967). *The naked ape*. Jonathan Cape, London.

Morris, R. G. M. (1981). Spatial localization does not require the presence of local cues. *Learning and Motivation*, **12**, 239–60.

Muckensturm, B. (1974). Y a-t-il utilization de signaux appris comme moyen de communication chez l'Epinoche? *Revue de Comportement Animal*, **9**, 185–207.

Nakajima, S. and Sato, M. (1993). Removal of an obstacle: problem-solving behavior in pigeons. *Journal of the Experimental Analysis of Behavior*, **59**, 131–45.

Noble, G. K. and Curtis, B. (1939). The social behavior of the jewel fish, Hemichromis bimaculatus Gill. *Bulletin of the American Museum of Natural History*, **76**, 1–46.

Nottebohm, F. and Nottebohm, M. E. (1978). Relationship between song repertoire and age in the canary *Serinus canarius*. *Zeitschrift für Tierpsychologie*, **46**, 298–305.

O'Keefe, J. and Speakman, A. (1987). Single unit activity in the rat hippocampus during a spatial memory task. *Experimental Brain Research*, **68**, 1–27.

Olton, D. S. and Samuelson, R. J. (1976). Remembrance of places past: spatial memory in rats. *Journal of Experimental Psychology: Animal Behavior Processes*, **2**, 97–116.

Parry-Jones, J. (1996). *Training birds of prey*. David and Charles, Newton Abbot.

Patterson, D. K. and Pepperberg, I. M. (1994). A comparative study of human and parrot phonation: acoustic and articulatory correlates of vowels. *Journal of the Acoustical Society of America*, **96**, 634–48.

Pearce, J. M. (1997). *Animal learning and cognition* (2nd edn). Psychology Press, Hove.

Pepperberg, I. M. (1981). Functional vocalizations by an African grey parrot (*Psittacus erithacus*). *Zeitschrift für Tierpsychologie*, **55**, 139–60.

Pepperberg, I. M. (1983). Cognition in the African grey parrot: preliminary evidence for auditory/vocal comprehension of the class concept. *Animal Learning and Behavior*, **11**, 179–85.

Pepperberg, I. M. and Funk, M. S. (1990). Object permanence in 4 species of psittacine birds—an African gray parrot (*Psittacus erithacus*), an Illiger mini macaw (*Ara maracana*), a parakeet (*Melopsittacus undulatus*), and a cockatiel (*Nymphicus hollandicus*). *Animal Learning and Behavior*, **18**, 97–108.

Petit, O. and Thierry, B. (1993). Use of stones in a captive group of Guinea baboons (*Papio papio*). *Folia Primatologica*, **61**, 160–4.

Pinney, C. (1990). Draught horses. In *Animal Training*. Universities Federation for Animal Welfare, Potters Bar.

Powell, R. W. and Kelly, W. (1975). A method for the objective study of tool-using behavior. *Journal of the Experimental Analysis of Behavior*, **24**, 249–53.

Powell, R. W. and Kelly, W. (1977). Tool use in captive crows. *Bulletin of the Psychonomic Society*, **10**, 481–3.

Pryor, K. W., Haag, R., and O'Reilly, J. (1969). The creative porpoise: training for novel behavior. *Journal of the Experimental Analysis of Behavior*, **12**, 653–61.

Ralls, K., Fiorelli, P., and Gish, S. (1985). Vocalizations and vocal mimicry in captive harbor seals, *Phoca vitulina*. *Canadian Journal of Zoology*, **63**, 1050–6.

Randle, H. D. (1994). *Adoption and personality in cattle*. Unpublished Ph.D. dissertation, University of Exeter.

Reid, J. B. (1982). Tool use by a rook (*Corvus frugilegus*), and its causation. *Animal Behaviour*, **30**, 1212–6.

Reiss, D. and McCowan, B. (1993). Spontaneous vocal mimicry and production by bottle-nosed dolphins (*Tursiops truncatus*)—evidence for vocal learning. *Journal of Comparative Psychology*, **107**, 301–12.

Rescorla, R. A. (1968). Probability of shock in the presence and absence of CS in fear conditioning. *Journal of Comparative and Physiological Psychology*, **66**, 1–5.

Rizley, R. C. and Rescorla, R. A. (1972). Associations in second-order conditioning and sensory preconditioning. *Journal of Comparative and Physiological Psychology*, **81**, 1–11.

Roper, T. J. and Marples, N. M. (1997). Odour and colour as cues for taste avoidance learning in domestic chicks. *Animal Behaviour*, **53**, 1241–50.

Rosch, E. and Mervis, C. B. (1975). Family resemblances: studies in the internal structure of categories. *Journal of Experimental Psychology: Human Perception and Performance,* **1,** 303–22.

Ryan, C. M. E. and Lea, S. E. G. (1994). Images of conspecifics as categories to be discriminated by pigeons and chickens: slides, video tapes, stuffed birds and live birds. *Behavioural Processes,* **33,** 155–75.

Ryle, G. (1951). Thinking and language. *Proceedings of the Aristotelian Society, Supplement,* **25,** 65–82.

Shettleworth, S. J. and Krebs, J. R. (1982). How marsh tits find their hoards—the roles of site preference and spatial memory. *Journal of Experimental Psychology: Animal Behavior Processes,* **8,** 354–75.

Small, W. S. (1900–1901). Experimental studies of the mental processes of the rat II. *American Journal of Psychology,* **12,** 206–39.

Sokolov, Y. N. (1960). Neuronal models and the orienting reflex. In *The central nervous system and behaviour* (ed. M. A. B. Brazier), pp. 187–276. Macy Foundation, New York.

Starin, E. D. (1990). Object manipulation by wild red colobus monkeys living in the Abuko Nature Reserve, The Gambia. *Primates,* **31,** 385–91.

Stephens, D. W. and Krebs, J. R. (1986). *Foraging theory.* Princeton University Press.

Tarsitano, M. S. and Jackson, R. R. (1994). Jumping spiders make predatory detours requiring movement away from prey. *Behaviour,* **131,** 65–73.

Tarsitano, M. S. and Jackson, R. R. (1997). Araneophagic jumping spiders discriminate between detour routes that do and do not lead to prey. *Animal Behaviour,* **53,** 257–66.

Thorndike, E. L. (1898). Animal intelligence. *Psychological Review Monographs,* **2,** (8), 1–109.

Thorndike, E. L. (1911). *Animal intelligence.* Macmillan, New York.

Thunberg, B. E. (1971). Olfaction in parent stream selection by the alewife (*Alosa pseudoharengus*). *Animal Behaviour,* **19,** 217–25.

Tinbergen, N. and Perdeck, A. C. (1950). On the stimulus situation releasing the begging response in the newly-hatched herring-gull chick (*Larus argentatus* Pont.). *Behaviour,* **3,** 1–39.

Todd, N. B. (1978). An ecological, behavioral genetic model for the domestication of the cat. *Carnivore,* **1,** 52–60.

Tokida, E., Tanaka, I., Takefushi, H., and Hagiwara, T. (1994). Tool-using in Japanese macaques: use of stones to obtain fruit from a pipe. *Animal Behaviour,* **47,** 1023–30.

Tolman, E. C. (1948). Cognitive maps in rats and men. *Psychological Review,* **55,** 189–208.

Van Lawick-Goodall, J. (1974). *In the shadow of man.* Fontana, London.

Vauclair, J. (1996). *Animal cognition.* Harvard University Press, Cambridge, MA.

Vaughan, W. and Greene, S. L. (1984). Pigeon visual memory capacity. *Journal of Experimental Psychology: Animal Behaviour Processes,* **10,** 256–71.

Watanabe, S., Lea, S. E. G., and Dittrich, W. H. (1993). What can we learn from experiments on concept recognition in pigeons? In *Vision, brain and behavior in birds* (ed. H. P. Zeigler and H.-J. Bischof), pp. 351–76. MIT Press, Cambridge, MA.

Westergaard, G. C. (1992). Object manipulation and the use of tools by infant baboons (*Papio cynocephalus anubis*). *Journal of Comparative Psychology,* **106,** 398–403.

Westergaard, G. C. and Suomi, S. J. (1994). Asymmetrical manipulation in the use of tools by tufted capuchin monkeys (*Cebus apella*). *Folia Primatologica,* **63,** 96–8.

Westergaard, G. C., Greene, J. A., Babitz, M. A., and Suomi, S. J. (1995). Pestle use and modification by tufted capuchins (*Cebus apella*). *International Journal of Primatology,* **16,** 643–51.

Wilcoxon, H. C., Dragoin, W. B., and Kral, P. A. (1971). Illness-induced aversions in rat and quail: relative salience of visual and gustatory cues. *Science,* **171,** 826–8.

Wilkie, D. M., Carr, J. A. R., Galloway, J., Parker, K. J., and Yamamoto, A. (1997). Conditional time–place learning. *Behavioural Processes,* **40,** 165–70.

Wilson, E. O. (1975). *Sociobiology*. Harvard University Press, Cambridge, MA.

Wittgenstein, L. (1953). *Philosophical investigations*. Blackwell, Oxford.

Wright, A. A. and Rivera, J. J. (1997). Memory of auditory lists by rhesus monkeys (*Macaca mulatta*). *Journal of Experimental Psychology: Animal Behavior Processes*, **23**, 441–9.

Zuberbuhler, K., Gygax, L., Harley, N., and Kummer, H. (1996). Stimulus enhancement and spread of a spontaneous tool use in a colony of long-tailed macaques. *Primates*, 37, 1–12.

3

Phylogeny from apes to humans

Michael C. Corballis

Introduction

In 1871 Darwin made the remarkable suggestion that humans are descended from African apes. The discoveries of the last 70 years leave little doubt that he was correct. Until as recently as the 1960s, though, it was supposed that the common ancestor of humans and our closest relative, the chimpanzee, dated from some 20 or 30 million years ago, allowing plenty of time for physical and mental divergence. The analysis of molecular data, beginning with the work of Sarich and Wilson (1967) comparing the albumens of living primate species, has forced a radical reappraisal of our similarities to other apes, and of the dates of divergence between the different species. Analysis of DNA sequences has confirmed the major conclusions of this earlier work, showing that humans are much closer to the chimpanzee than was previously suspected, the hominid clade having diverged only five or six million years ago (Cann *et al.* 1987; Waddell and Penny 1996). By one estimate, the chimpanzee has about 99.6 percent of its amino acid sequences and 98.4 percent of its DNA nucleotide sequences in common with our own species (Goodman 1992).

After initial scepticism, palaeontologists now generally see the fossil evidence as consistent with that from molecular biology (Stringer and Andrews 1988). Recently discovered hominid fossils have been dated at over four million years ago, very close to the common ancestor of humans and chimpanzees. Some psychologists have also interpreted recent behavioural evidence as indicating a greater similarity between ourselves and the great apes than was hitherto suspected. For example, Byrne (this volume) argues that the great apes even possess what has been called 'theory of mind' (Premack and Woodruff 1978; Premack 1988), and that this, along with a capacity for symbolic representation, provides the underpinnings for language. Although this conclusion is disputed (Heyes 1993, 1998; Baron-Cohen, this volume), evidence like this has suggested to some that any discontinuity might lie, not between humans and the other great apes, but between the great apes and the other primates (e.g. Savage-Rumbaugh and Lewin 1994). It has even been recently proposed that the term *hominid*, previously applied only to human ancestry subsequent to the split from the chimpanzee clade, be extended to include chimpanzees and gorillas, and that humans and their precursors be known as *hominines* (Groves 1989; Martin 1990, 1992; Andrews 1995). It would be premature for us to adopt this terminology in this book, but it might be a sign of what is to come.

Although the estimate of the period of hominid evolution has been dramatically reduced by these developments, the many discoveries over the past 70 years of hominid fossils, dating from about 4.4 million years ago, have provided fuel for increasingly detailed theories as to the nature and time course of hominid evolution. Nevertheless, this proliferation of hominid fossils is in marked contrast to the lack of fossils for the period from about eight million to 4.4 million years ago, so the common ancestor itself has remained elusive. Information about the common ancestor has to be inferred either by extrapolating back from the early hominids, or by seeking characteristics that are shared by humans and present-day apes. All of the known hominid species originated in Africa, in triumphant vindication of Darwin's surmise, but it is now clear that there was not just one hominid species, but several, all but one of which became extinct. The complexities of hominid evolution raise many questions about precisely when any mental attributes that might be uniquely human might have emerged. In the search for clues to the special nature of the human mind, therefore, we must not only look to the great apes, but we must also try to unravel the several stages and multiple species that characterize the transition from ape to human.

As background to the chapters that follow, this chapter reviews the stages of evolution from monkeys to apes, apes to hominids, and hominids to humans. Every branch point in this evolutionary progression is a potential point of mental discontinuity. In describing the different species, my emphasis here will be primarily on physical characteristics, as background to the discussion of psychological characteristics in the chapters that follow.

From monkeys to apes

The *primates* are an order of species that includes prosimians, monkeys, apes, and of course ourselves, and we all share a common primate ancestor dating from perhaps 80 million years ago (Martin 1990). Within the suborder known as *anthropoids*, the New World monkeys were cut adrift from the Old World monkeys in the Americas some 40 million years ago, and then about 35 million years ago the apes separated from Old World monkeys. Campbell (1996) suggests that the transition from monkey to ape can be understood as an adaptation to insect predation, but rather little is known about the earliest apes. Two early fossil specimens, discovered in Northern Egypt, are *Propliopithecus*, dated at about 33 to 35 million years ago, and *Aegyptopithecus*, dated at about 33 million years ago. Both are tentatively classified as apes mainly on the basis of their dental features, and although there is some suggestion that *Aegyptopithecus* might have been ancestral to monkeys (Kay *et al.* 1981), there are also indications that it was ancestral to the later Miocene ape known as *Proconsul* (Campbell 1996). This species, whose fossil remains were discovered in Kenya and date from 20 to 18 million years ago, so closely resembles the chimpanzee and gorilla that it has been generally assumed to be ancestral to living apes and humans. It has, however, recently been claimed that a newly-named species called *Morotopithecus*, whose remains have been discovered in Uganda, has more characteristics in common with modern apes than does *Proconsul*. *Morotopithecus* dates from at least 20.6

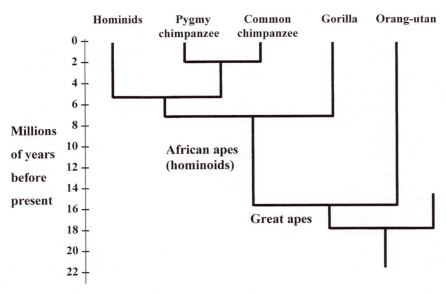

Fig. 3.1. Evolutionary tree for the great apes.

million years ago, and provides the earliest fossil evidence for an ape-like body (Gebo *et al.* 1997)

The various divisions among the apes are shown in Fig. 3.1. The first split occurred about 18 million years ago (Waddell and Penny 1996), when the ancestors of the modern gibbons and siamangs split from the line leading to the great apes, which comprise orang-utans, gorillas, two species of chimpanzee, and humans. The several species of gibbon (*Hylobatids*) are known as lesser apes. About 16 million years ago, there was a further split within the great apes (Waddell and Penny 1996), when the ancestors of the modern orang-utan split off to form a separate line. Orang-utans are now found in the wild only in the rainforests of Sumatra and Borneo. Examination of a fossil skull from a species known as *Sivapithecus*, dating from about 12 million years ago, clearly shows that it belongs to the orang-utan line (Pilbeam and Smith 1981). Within the remaining African apes, the gorillas are thought to have split off about 7.6 million years ago, and the chimpanzees to have split from the hominids about 5.6 million years ago. There was a further split between the two species of chimpanzee, the common chimpanzee and the pygmy chimpanzee (or bonobo), about three million years ago (Waddell and Penny 1996).

Locomotion

The differences between the different species of ape can be understood partly in terms of the way they move around. *Morotopithecus*, the earliest ape-like primate dating from 20.6 million years ago, was an arboreal animal, adapted to quadrupedalism, with the distinctive adaptation of the arm and shoulder for brachiation (swinging from branches). It is described as having a 'slow to moderate speed of brachiation'

(Gebo *et al.* 1997, p. 402). There might have been further refinements by the time the ancestor of the gibbon split off about 18 million years ago, with the shoulder adapted to allow the arms to swing directly above the head. Although this adaptation allows apes to hang easily from branches, it is something of a hindrance to quadrupedal walking, which monkeys do with ease (Byrne 1995). Gibbons are the most efficient brachiators, but the adaptation persists in the modern great apes, including humans, and is exploited by bowlers in cricket, trapeze artists, and tall people who play basketball. In the great apes, however, the hands and arms underwent further modifications to permit more efficient quadrupedal movement over open terrain. Orang-utans are less efficient brachiators than are gibbons, but they can clamber more efficiently on all fours and, like chimpanzees and gorillas, are also capable of limited bipedal walking.

Gorillas and chimpanzees are distinguished from orang-utans by a form of quadrupedal locomotion known as knuckle-walking, in which the back of the hand is in line with the lower arm and the supporting weight is taken on the middle phalanges of the fingers (Marzke 1996). Both species travel extensively in this fashion, and are less efficient brachiators than is the orang-utan. Since gorillas and chimpanzees probably separated independently from the line leading to the hominids, parsimony suggests that the common ancestor of gorillas, chimpanzees, and humans was also a knuckle-walker. Nevertheless Savage-Rumbaugh (1994) has proposed that bipedalism, which is the main feature distinguishing the early hominids from the other great apes, evolved more or less directly from brachiation, without an intervening phase of knuckle-walking. While this implies that chimpanzees and gorillas must have evolved knuckle-walking independently, which is unparsimonious from a cladistic point of view, there are a number of arguments in its favour.

First, detailed study of the ways in which monkeys, gibbons, chimpanzees, and humans walk suggests that 'the bipedal walking of the gibbon is closest to man' (Yamazaki 1985, p. 129). Moreover, the fossil remains of a relatively large-brained (400 cm^3) primate known as *Oreopithecus*, dating from eight to nine million years ago, reveal many of the characteristics of a common ancestor of the African ape and the hominids, including skeletal adaptations for bipedalism (Pilbeam 1972). Analysis of the human hand reveals no obvious trace of a knuckle-walking phase, although any such trace might have been masked by the more obvious changes that were probably related to tool use (Marzke 1996). Further, evidence from DNA sequences suggests that although the gorilla and chimpanzee lines split independently from the line leading to the hominids, the time-gap between the two splits was quite small, and it remains conceivable that the gorilla and chimpanzee lines separated from the ho-minid line before later diverging from each other (e.g. Campbell 1996). This raises the possibility that they might have become knuckle-walkers after the split from the hominid line, but before diverging into separate species.

The different styles of locomotion might also be related to different habitats. Up to about eight million years ago both East and West Africa consisted mainly of forests and woodlands, and the primates were adapted primarily to brachiation. Then the continent of Africa collided with Eurasia, creating an upward pressure that formed the highlands of Kenya and Ethiopia. This eventually caused the earth's crust to crack, creating the Great Rift Valley, and much of the forest and woodland to the east gave way to savanna, or open terrain. It has generally been assumed that the early hominids were restricted to the eastern habitat, which favoured bipedal walking over brachiation or quadrupedal walking, but the recent discovery of hominid fossils in Chad, which is considerably west of the Great Rift Valley, has raised doubts about this theory (M. Leakey and Walker 1997). Be that as it may, the habitats of modern great apes suggest that their ancestors were probably confined largely, if not completely, to the more forested area west of the Great Rift Valley. Modern gorillas live in two main areas, a lowland area north of the Zaire River, and a mountain area west of Lake Victoria (Schaller 1963). Pygmy chimpanzees inhabit the humid rainforests of Zaire, and have been described as 'the most forest-adapted of the African apes' (Susman 1987, p. 78), while common chimpanzees inhabit a wide area from near the Atlantic Coast in Western Zaire to the eastern side of the western Rift Valley, an area that is mostly heavily forested but includes some savanna with widely scattered trees (Goodall 1986).

Although these species live in largely forested areas, they make little use of brachiation. Gorillas spend most of their time on the ground, and their movement through trees has been described as 'quadrupedal climbing' (Schaller 1963, pp. 82–3) rather than brachiation. Pygmy chimpanzee are more versatile and make greater use of brachiation than the common chimpanzee. Noble and Davidson (1996) suggest that the common ancestor might have been arboreal 80 percent of the time, but that all three species evolved terrestrial modes of locomotion. It is conceivable, then, that the more open areas east of the Great Rift Valley led directly from brachiation to bipedalism among the hominids, while the ancestors of the gorilla and chimpanzee retained the long arms adapted to brachiation. These long arms enable the animal to reach down easily for support while on the ground, especially if the arm is lengthened slightly by holding the wrist firm and carrying the weight on the middle phalanges of the fingers, as in knuckle-walking. Since this device involves little anatomical adaptation, and was adequate for the largely forested terrain inhabited by these animals, it might well have been adopted independently in the two species.

This issue cannot at present be resolved from fossil evidence because there are no known fossil remains of the common ancestor, nor are there any fossil remains of creatures immediately ancestral to gorillas or chimpanzees (Szalay and Delson 1979). This is unfortunate, because the question of whether the ancestors of the hominids were knuckle-walkers or not might have an important bearing on the evolution of the hominid mind. Savage-Rumbaugh (1994) suggests that knuckle-walking and bipedalism were independent solutions, not just to the problem of locomotion across open terrain, but also to the problem of transporting infants. With knuckle-walking, the infant clings to the mother's body, and the placement of knuckles on the ground provides extra support for the infant's weight. Little parental monitoring is required, since the infant simply clings and can be largely ignored by the mother. But with bipedal walking, the infant must be actively carried in the parent's arms. This places more onus on parents to monitor their infants and ensure their well-being, and to remember to pick them up after putting them down. Savage-Rumbaugh suggests that these extra demands might have set the stage for the later evolution of the ability to take the mental perspective of others, leading perhaps to language. If she is correct in supposing that the hominid line did not pass through a phase of knuckle-walking, these adaptations might have taken place gradually since well before the gorilla and chimpanzee lines split off.

Evolution of the brain

There can be little doubt that it is the brain that holds the key to the mind. The simplest assumption is that mental capacity is a function of the *size* of the brain, as in the folk-psychology notion that some people are 'brainier' than others. Table 5.1 in Chapter 5 by Beran *et al.* (this volume) shows the cranial volumes of the apes, and it is clear that there is a general increase from monkeys through the lesser apes (Hylobates) to the great apes (orang-utans, gorillas, and chimpanzee), and a massive increase to humans. This might seem to support the idea that any discontinuity of mental function does indeed lie between humans and the other great apes.

Although humans are comfortably at the top, it may nevertheless be misleading to suppose that brain size is directly proportional to brain power. For example, the chimpanzee is generally reckoned the smartest of the great apes (humans excluded), but in terms of brain size lies a distant third behind the gorilla and orang-utan. Moreover, male brains tend to be larger than female, especially in orang-utans, gorillas, and humans. These anomalies occur, at least in part, because size depends to some extent on body size. One way to compensate for variations in body size is to compute the empirical relationship between brain size and body size across different species, and then express the actual brain size of a given species as a ratio of the predicted brain size. This is the so-called *encephalization quotient*, suggested by Jerison (1973). With this approach, Passingham (1982) was still able to conclude that the human brain is about three times the size one would expect for a primate of our build, which he regards as "perhaps the single most important fact about mankind" (p. 78). Yet even this is not conclusive, because the encephalization quotient depends on the species included in the computation of the relationship between brain and body sizes. Holloway (1996) notes that however quotient is computed, the relatively small-bodied chimpanzee is restored to its rightful place next to humans, and the gap between humans and chimpanzees is considerably larger than that between chimpanzees and gorillas, in defiance of the molecular evidence discussed earlier.

Even so, the encephalization quotient is still a crude measure of mental capacity since it does not differentiate one part of the brain from another. For example, the neocortex is presumably especially important in intellectual function, and Dunbar (1993) has suggested that what he calls the *neocortex ratio*, which is the ratio of the volume of neocortex to the volume of the rest of the brain, might be more indicative of mental capacity. He has shown that there is a positive relationship among monkeys and primates between the neocortex ratio and the size of the social group that the animals form, suggesting that cognitive capacity establishes an upper limit to the number of individuals with which the animal can maintain personal relationships. Byrne (1995) has further shown a linear relationship in primates between the neocortex ratio and the estimated prevalence of tactical deception. In humans, the ratio is 4.1:1, which is about 30 percent larger than that of any other primate. While this still places humans at the top of the intellectual tree, it is more suggestive of continuity than are measures based on total brain size.

But even within the non-human primates, there are reasons to doubt that the neocortex ratio is an altogether adequate measure of mental capacity. For example, as Byrne (1995) points out, the neocortex ratio is as large in the baboon as it is in the gorilla, yet the gorilla shows much more evidence of insightful behaviour. It is also clear that group size is not the only determinant of the neocortex ratio, since the great apes do not live in larger groups than monkeys do, and indeed the orang-utan is notably solitary—although this might have been a recent adaptation. Byrne therefore suggests that while an enlarged neocortex ratio might have been selected for by social pressures, it might also reflect intelligent behaviour in non-social contexts, such as the insightful solving of mechanical problems (Kohler 1925). Indeed, one might expect actual computational power to be dependent to some extent on actual brain size, uncorrected for body size. As Table 5.1 in Chapter 5 by Beran *et al.* (this volume) shows, it is this measure that clearly distinguishes the great apes from the other apes and monkeys, despite failing to do justice to the chimpanzee. The reader is referred to the chapters by Beran *et al.* and Byrne for further discussion.

Humans as hominids

Virtually nothing was known of the transition from ape to human until 1924, when Raymond Dart came into possession of a skull with both human-like and ape-like features that had been found in a cave in Taung, South Africa. He called it *Australopithecus africanus*, and hailed it as the 'missing link' between human and chimpanzee (Dart 1925, 1959). Although Dart was initially ridiculed for his claims, there has since been an avalanche of discoveries of hominid remains from Africa, and the missing link has become, not merely a chain, but a tangle of chains. Figs 3.2 and 3.3 show the hominid species thought to have occupied the time gap from the common ancestor of ourselves and the chimpanzee, some five or six million years ago, to the present-day survivor, *Homo sapiens*. This classification is based on the recent work by Groves (1989) and Wood (1992). There is some controversy over both the number and names of species involved, but we can be sure of at least one thing—the picture will become more not less complicated as further discoveries are made.

Bipedalism

The main characteristic distinguishing the hominids from the apes is habitual bipedalism, involving a reshaping of the pelvis to enable efficient upright walking. The earliest species to be tentatively classified as a hominid is the newly-discovered *Ardipithecus ramidus*, dating from some 4.4 million years ago. The evidence is not yet decisive as to whether or not it was bipedal, although the anterior placement of the foramen magnum (where the spine enters the skull) suggests that it might have been (White *et al.* 1994, 1995). Another recent discovery, named *Australopithecus anamensis*, dates from 3.9 to 4.2 million years ago, and a partial tibia suggests that it was not a knuckle walker, and was probably bipedal (M. G. Leakey *et al.* 1995). These two species lie very close to the common ancestor of the hominids and the chimpanzee,

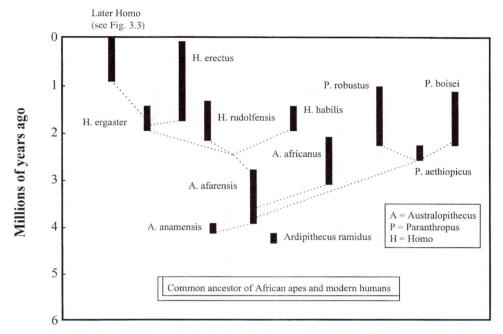

Fig. 3.2. Speculative evolutionary tree for the hominids, excluding later *Homo*.

and Wood (1994) suggests that if any species deserves to be called the 'missing link' it is *Ardipithecus ramidus*.

Australopithecus afarensis, dating from about 3.8 to 3.0 million years ago, was clearly bipedal (M. D. Leakey 1979). There is some evidence that the foot and ankle remained partially adapted to arboreal life (Susman *et al.* 1984), although this has been disputed (Latimer and Lovejoy 1990). The hands also retained ape-like charac- teristics, such as the potential to sustain a hook-like grasp on the branches of trees, but there is no evidence suggestive of knuckle-walking (Marzke 1996). The strong evidence for bipedalism in hominid species dating from quite near the chimpanzee- hominid split, together with some remnants of adaptations to arboreal life but no indications of knuckle-walking, lend further support to Savage-Rumbaugh's (1994) contention that the hominids might have progressed from brachiation to bipedalism without passing through a knuckle-walking stage.

Groves (1989) notes that the evolution of bipedalism should not be thought of as a gradual progression toward some goal, as though the model were being incrementally perfected—as Dawkins (1997, p. 83) remarks, "No animal ever made a living purely by being on the evolutionary path toward something better." The locomotory pattern of each hominid species was an adaptation to that species' habitat and behaviour pattern. He suggests that there were four different locomotory morphologies, each with some unique characteristics but all including a form of bipedalism. The first was the australopithecine morphology, in which bipedalism was only part of a pattern that included a sophisticated climbing ability. The habiline morphology included some

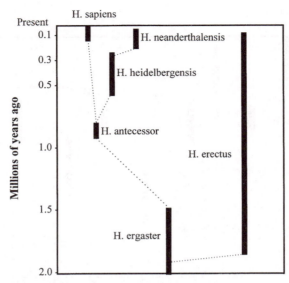

Fig. 3.3. Speculative evolutionary tree for later *Homo*.

climbing ability, but the overall pattern was more terrestrial, although without the striding bipedal walk characteristic of modern humans. The erectus morphology might have been similar, but with different body parts involved. Finally the sapient morphology involves a more linear body build and full-striding gait.

Although there are many other bipedal animals, there has been much speculation as to why bipedalism evolved in the hominids. Until recently, it has been generally supposed that it followed the formation of the Great Rift Valley, when the hominids were confined to the savanna-like habitat to the east. This forced the early hominids into a scavenging lifestyle, and bipedalism was not only more efficient for covering long distances, but would also have freed the arms and hands for carrying meat and other foodstuffs back to the home base (Lovejoy 1981). The question here, though, is why the hominids would have used the hands for transportation, since other bipedal animals have adopted different devices, such as cheek pouches or the abdominal pouch of the kangaroo.

Another problem for the savanna theory is the recent discovery of a 3.5-million-year-old fossil, identified as an australopthecine, in Chad (Brunet *et al.* 1995). This is some 2500 km to the west of the Great Rift Valley, and is a wooded area, suggesting that at least some australopithecines spent at least some of the time in woodlands rather than on the savanna (M. Leakey and Walker 1997). This creature appears to have been anatomically closer to *A. afarensis* than to other known hominids, suggesting that it migrated from eastern Africa, although it was sufficiently distinctive to be named a separate subspecies, now known as *Australopithecus bahrelghazali* (M. Leakey and Walker 1997).

If bipedalism was not an adaptation to locomotion on the savannah, how else are we to explain it? One possibility, suggested by Darwin (1871), is that it had to do with the freeing of the hands and arms for the more efficient manufacture and use of tools.

Tools

Until recently, the earliest known tools were the stone artefacts that M. D. Leakey (1971) discovered at Olduvai Gorge in Tanzania. These tools, comprising what is known as the Oldowan industry, were primitive sharp-edged flakes that were probably used for cutting and scraping meat from large carcasses (Butynski 1982). Leakey attributed them to *Homo habilis* ('handy man'), with the suggestion that this was a critical step toward the emergence of human culture. According to this scenario, then, the stone tool industry emerged relatively late in hominid evolution, and was there-fore not decisive in selecting for bipedalism in the australopithecines.

There is now evidence that the Oldowan industry precedes *H. habilis*, since stone tools of the same type found in Ethiopia have been securely dated to between 2.6 and 2.5 million years ago (Semaw *et al.* 1997). As shown in Fig. 3.2, the only species of *Homo* known to date from this period is *H. rudolfensis*. However, Wood (1997) observes that the Oldowan industry persisted long after *H. rudolfensis* disappeared from the fossil record, and that the one hominid species that spans the Oldowan was not a member of the *Homo* clade at all—it was *Paranthropus aethiopicus/boisei*. The idea that stone tools might have originated with *Paranthropus* rather than *Homo* is not new; Susman (1988) had earlier inferred from the anatomy of the hand that *P. robustus* might have been the first maker of stone tools, although his reasoning has been questioned (e.g. by Schick and Toth 1993). It is not inconceivable however that tools, even stone tools, go back even further. Marzke's (1996) analysis of the comparative anatomy of the hand shows that, while the hands of *A. afarensis* were more ape-like than human-like, there were a few distinctively human features that would have allowed firmer and more controlled grips of objects than are achievable by any of the great apes. These grips would have been especially effective in using stones for pounding or digging, or butchering small game, or for throwing stones with speed and accuracy. The tangible evidence for early tool use in the hominids was the discovery of *stone* tools dating from around the time of early *Homo*, but it is likely that earlier hominids used primitive tools made from perishable material, such as wood, just as present-day chimpanzees use sticks for activities such as extracting termites from their holes.

Indeed there is evidence that making simple Oldowan tools is within the compe-tence of modern chimpanzees (Wynn and McGrew 1989; Toth *et al.* 1993), and even an orang-utan (Wright 1972), and it has been claimed that the tool culture of Tai chimpanzees, although not including the manufacture of stone tools, represents a comparable stage of development (Boesch and Boesch 1984). It is not altogether unreasonable to suppose, therefore, that the precursors of the hominids already possessed manufacturing skills, and that the elaboration of those skills contributed to the selection for bipedalism and concomitant changes in the anatomy of the hand.

The association of tools with bipedalism may not have been simply a matter of the freeing of the hands. Marzke (1996) points out that many actions involving tools are more effectively accomplished from an upright stance. Activities like wielding an axe, using a club, or digging with a stick benefit from the extra leverage of the trunk obtained from an upright posture. Another activity to benefit from a bipedal posture is the throwing of rocks or spears, and a further advantage can be obtained by running and then throwing, as demonstrated by a skilled javelin-thrower. A number of authors have suggested that accurate throwing might have played a decisive role among the early hominids in self-protection and in the killing of small animals for food (e.g. Parker and Gibson 1979; O'Brien 1981; Calvin 1993; Noble and Davidson 1996). More specifically, Marzke (1986) suggested that even as far back as *A. afarensis*, the hand-grip, steady bipedal posture, and control of the trunk were adapted for accurate and potentially lethal throwing. It has also been suggested that the precision timing needed for accurate throwing might have pre-adapted neural circuitry for the subsequent evolution of speech. These specialized circuits are presumably in the left hemisphere in most people, which might explain why most of us are both right-handed and left-cerebrally dominant for speech (Calvin 1983, 1993).

Gesturing

There is also a growing consensus that language might have evolved from manual gestures (e.g. Hewes 1973; Corballis 1991, 1992; Kendon 1991; Armstrong *et al.* 1995; Givon 1995; Goldin-Meadow *et al.* 1996; Goldin-Meadow and McNeill, this volume), and the advantages of sophisticated communication might have created a further selective pressure toward bipedalism. Monkeys and apes are already partly bipedal, and the hands and arms are well adapted for activities requiring considerable flexibility, such as picking fruit, manipulating objects, making tools, throwing, and even gesturing. It is not surprising, then, that attempts to teach great apes to speak have failed almost completely (Hayes 1952), whereas attempts to teach them to use manual gestures have been at least moderately successful (Gardner and Gardner 1969; Patterson 1978; Savage-Rumbaugh and Lewin 1994). Communicative gesturing would of course be facilitated further by full bipedalism. Whiten (this volume) makes the additional point that silent manual gesturing would be advantageous among groups hunting prey. Unlike the 'professional' hunters, such as sabre-toothed cats and hyenas, the hominids were not equipped with sharp claws, great strength, or speed, and had to rely instead on cooperation, shared knowledge, and stealth. Had they communicated vocally, their prey might well have been alerted to the danger and fled to safety.

One reason for the growing popularity of the gestural theory is the recognition that ASL, and other indigenous sign languages, are natural human languages, with syntax as sophisticated as that of spoken language (Klima and Bellugi 1979; Poizner *et al.* 1987). ASL is acquired by children in the deaf community in very much the same way that hearing children acquire speech (e.g. Pettito and Marentette 1991), and, like speech, depends primarily on the left cerebral hemisphere (Poizner *et al.* 1987; Neville 1991). In some respects, though, gestural language is more straightforward than vocal language, since signs can represent objects and actions in iconic fashion much more readily than spoken words can represent onomatopoeically. It therefore seems entirely plausible that communication among visually sophisticated, bipedal, manually dexterous, but vocally challenged hominids would have begun as a manual system, and later switched to a predominantly vocal mode only when the vocal system became more refined and amenable to voluntary control.

The gestural theory is discussed further by Goldin-Meadow and McNeill (this volume). It remains controversial, however. Donald (this volume) argues that there was a bodily precursor to language that was *mimetic* rather than linguistic, closer to present-day dance and mime than to sign language. Another theory, developed by MacNeilage (this volume), is that speech was exapted from mandibular movements that emerged first as ingestive processes such as chewing, licking and sucking, then as visuofacial communicative movements such as lipsmacks, tongue-smacks, and teeth chattering, and only later became associated with vocalization. This theory need not wholly contradict the gestural theory because visuofacial communicative acts must certainly be considered gestural. In any event, both the gestural theory and Mac-Neilage's theory are consistent with the idea that language evolved gradually during hominid evolution, as Pinker (1994) has argued, and indeed has roots that might go far back in primate evolution. Others, such as Bickerton (1995), have argued that true language emerged as a 'big bang' with the emergence of *H. sapiens*, or even later (see Lock, this volume). Debates over the evolutionary origins of language depend to some extent on precisely when one can call a communication system 'language'.

Humans as *Homo*

It has generally been assumed that the emergence of *Homo* something over 2 million years ago was a decisive step in hominid evolution, separating the australopithecines from the line that was subsequently to evolve into humans. *Homo* is generally associated with an enlargement of the brain, the beginnings of human-like culture, a more advanced bipedal gait, and less emphasis on mastication in the preparation and consumption of food. The australopithecines, by contrast, are thought to have depended on large postcanine teeth for processing food, to have mixed climbing with bipedalism, and not to have advanced beyond the apes in relative brain size (Wood 1992)—although Kappelman (1996) observes that the australopithecine brain is clearly larger than that of the chimpanzee when body size is taken into account.

The main evidence for the emergence of human-like culture in *Homo* is the association with stone tools, but as we saw in the previous section there is now some doubt as to whether stone tools, or manufactured tools in general, were in fact restricted to *Homo*—although I shall argue below that they probably were. Even so, the possibility that the later australopithecines might have made the stone tools discovered by Semaw *et al.* (1997) raises the question of whether early so-called *Homo* (*H. rudolfensis* and *H. habilis*) should really be classified as *Homo* at all. Nevertheless, Wood (1992) has defended the classification on the basis of a cladistic analysis of 90 cranial, mandibular, and dental features, without reference to tool use. This analysis suggests that the *Homo* clade split from *A. africanus* around three million years ago, and that there was a later split between *H. rudolfensis* and *H. habilis*. The common characters possessed by these two species, and presumably by their common ancestor, are listed in Table 3.1. Also listed are the characters shared by all species of *Homo*, including *H. rudolfensis*, *H. habilis*, *H. erectus*, *H. ergaster*, and *H. sapiens*. These characters are not present in the australopithecines, and therefore serve to define the *Homo* clade as a whole.

Table 3.1 Defining characters of *Homo*

Characters unique to all species of Homo, as distinct from other hominids:

1. *Increased cranial vault thickness*
2. *Reduced postorbital constriction*
3. *Increased contribution of occipital bone to cranial sagittal arc length*
4. *Increased cranial vault height*
5. *More anterior foramen magnum*
6. *Reduced lower facial prognathism*
7. *Narrower tooth crowns, especially mandibular premolars*
8. *Reduction in length of the molar tooth row*

Characters shared by H. habilis and H. rudolfensis, and unique to these species:

1. *Elongated anterior basicranium*
2. *Higher cranial vault*
3. *Mesiodistally elongated first and second molars*
4. *Narrow mandibular fossa*

Source: Wood (1992).

The characters unique to *H. habilis* and *H. rudolfensis* also imply that the common ancestor of these two species split off from the common ancestor of the other hominids, as shown in Fig. 3.2. This supports the growing consensus that *H. habilis* (or *H. rudolfensis*) did not simply evolve into the larger-brained, technologically more sophisticated *H. erectus*, as has been commonly assumed, but was a separate species (Groves 1989; Wood 1992; Larick and Ciochon 1996). The two species might have coexisted for 500 000 years, because fossils of *H. erectus* discovered in Java have been dated at 1.8 million years ago (Swisher *et al.* 1994), whereas there is evidence for *H. habilis* dating from as recently as 1.3 million years ago. There is also evidence from Java suggesting that *H. erectus* may have persisted there until as recently as 27 000 years ago (Swisher *et al.* 1996). If these controversial dates for *H. erectus* in Java prove to be correct, then this species would have not only coexisted in the early stages with *H. habilis*, but would also have overlapped in the latter stages both with the Neanderthals and with anatomically modern humans (*H. sapiens*).

To complicate matters, however, there are recent suggestions that the fossils once grouped together as *H. erectus* might have belonged to two different species, one associated with fossil discoveries in Kenya, and the other, which includes the specimens from Java, associated with an early migration to east Asia. The Kenyan fossils are now categorized as *H. ergaster*, with the label *H. erectus* restricted to the species that migrated to Asia (Larick and Ciochon 1996). Besides the 1.8-million-year-old fossil discovered in Java (Swisher *et al.* 1994), there is other evidence of an early migration eastward from Africa; these include a fossil found in the former Soviet republic of Georgia and controversially dated at 1.8 million years ago (Gabunia and Vakua 1995), another fossil dated at 1.9 million years ago found in south-eastern Sichuan Province in China (Huang *et al.* 1995), and crude stone tools in Northern Pakistan thought to date from about two million years ago (Dennell *et al.* 1988*a*, *b*). This migration evidently occurred before the development of the relatively sophisticated Acheulian tool industry by the species now known as *H. ergaster* (Tattersall 1997). Larick and Ciochon (1996) suggest that it was a species of *Homo* ancestral to both *H. erectus* and *H. ergaster*, but parallel to *H. habilis*, that left Africa more than two million years ago, perhaps as a consequence of a cooling during the Middle Pliocene (3.0–2.4 million years ago) that also led to extinctions and dispersals among large African bovines.

It was *H. ergaster*, rather than *H. erectus*, who was probably ancestral to modern humans (Tattersall 1997). The earliest African evidence dates from about 1.9 million years ago, but the most complete specimen is the so-called Turkana Boy, whose skeletal remains were discovered in northern Kenya in 1984 (Brown *et al.* 1985; Walker and Leakey 1993). This skeleton dates from 1.6 million years ago, and gives a remarkably detailed impression of what *H. ergaster* was like. Had he lived beyond adolescence, the Turkana Boy would have grown to about six feet tall, with long slender limbs. The brain was about double the size of the ape brain, but still markedly smaller than the modern human brain. The Acheulian tool industry associated with this species, and discussed below, was clearly more sophisticated than the Oldowan industry.

Migrations

The early migration of *H. erectus* to east Asia perhaps over two million years ago might have been but the first of several migrations of the genus *Homo* out of Africa. Tattersall (1997) suggests that there might have been no fewer than five identifiable waves. As we have seen, the first migration seems to have left its traces in Georgia, Pakistan, and China, as well as in Java, but it evidently by-passed Europe. Migration to Europe was probably much more recent, within the last million years. Carbonell *et al.* (1995) have described primitive stone tools and some human fossil fragments found in northern Spain, and have attributed these to a species now known as *Homo heidelbergensis*. The primitive stone technology of this species shows no traces of the Acheulian technology now associated with *H. ergaster*, suggesting a separate lineage. It has been suggested that *H. heidelbergensis* might have been the starting point of an indigenous lineage that evolved into the Neanderthals, a species known only from Europe and Western Asia and dating from 200 000 to about 30 000 years ago. Recent evidence from the analysis of mitochondrial DNA extracted from a Neanderthal specimen supports the view that the line leading to the Neanderthals diverged from that leading to modern humans some 500 000 years ago (Ward and Stringer 1997). Another site in northern Spain has yielded fossils dating from about 300 000 years ago (Arsuaga *et al.* 1993), and these are said to anticipate the Neanderthals in some but not all respects.

An even older species, dating from about 800 000 years ago and named *Homo antecessor*, has recently been discovered in Spain, and seems to be ancestral to both the Neanderthals and *H. sapiens*, and probably to *H. heidelbergensis* also (Bermudez de Castro *et al.* 1997). One revealing specimen, comprising part of a boy's face, shows a fully modern mid-face set between a primitive jaw and brow. This specimen, along with others from the same site in Northern Spain, comprise the earliest well-dated fossils from Europe. According to the Spanish team, it might have been the African members of the species *H. antecessor* that gave rise to modern humans. A 600 000-year old skull found in Ethiopia, currently attributed to *H. heidelbergensis* (Tattersall

1997), might in fact represent a transitional species between *H. antecessor* and *H. sapiens*. Figure 3.3 summarizes the hypothesized lineages originating from *H. ergaster* in Africa.

Tools

Despite Wood's (1997) suggestion that the Oldowan stone industry might have been associated with *P. aethiopicus/boisei* rather than with *Homo*, cladistic analysis suggests otherwise. The evidence for association of stone tools with *H. habilis* is after all quite strong, and *H. ergaster* is associated with the more sophisticated Acheulian stone industry. Given that *H. habilis* and *H. ergaster/erectus* were separate species that overlapped in time, it seems likely that their common ancestor also made stone tools. If that common ancestor dates from some three million years ago, as Wood (1992) suggests, then it is not altogether surprising that stone tools dating from 2.5 million years ago have been discovered (Semaw *et al.* 1997)—and we might even expect to find still earlier ones.

The Acheulian stone industry traditionally associated with *H. erectus* emerges from about 1.4 million years ago in Africa (Asfaw *et al.* 1992), and has not been seen at Asian sites, supporting the idea that it was developed by the separate species known as *H. ergaster*. The Acheulian industry overlaps the Oldowan industry in time (Clark *et al.* 1994), but was clearly more sophisticated. It includes the manufacture of picks, cleavers, and bifacial hand-axes by striking several flakes from faces of a core, instead of just one as in the Oldowan industry. Their symmetry and often standardized form are often regarded as evidence of deliberate planning and even an aesthetic sense.

The Acheulian industry is generally reckoned to have been superseded by the more sophisticated Mousterian industry during the period from about 200 000 to 100 000 years ago (Schick and Toth 1993). With the Mousterian, the tools characteristic of the Acheulian gave way to smaller flake tools, made from a prepared stone core using a method known as the Levallois technique. The hafting of hand-axes was also introduced. There has actually been some dispute as to the transition point, with Bischoff *et al.* (1992) suggesting that the end of the Acheulian was not likely to have been much earlier than 100 000 years ago, but the recent discovery of sophisticated wooden spears at Schoningen in Germany dating from 380 000 to 400 000 years ago (Thieme 1997) suggests that the early colonisers of northern Europe had developed a much more sophisticated culture than has been previously thought. These spears, which can presumably be attributed to *H. heidelbergensis,* seem in marked contrast to the relatively primitive stone tools associated with that species in the artefacts found in Spain by Carbonell *et al.* (1995), and dating from about 780 000 years ago.

These 400 000-year-old spears confirm that these early humans were hunters—an idea that was once popular, but fell into disrepute from the early 1980s (Dennell 1997). They also reinforce the idea, introduced earlier, that throwing emerged quite early in hominid evolution. As Dennell (1997) points out, they reflect "a depth of planning, sophistication of design, and patience in carving the wood, all of which have been attributed only to modern humans" (p. 768).

Evolution of the brain

The brain sizes of the various hominid species, along with those of extant primates, are shown in Table 5.1 of Chapter 5 by Beran *et al.* (this volume). The absolute size of the australopithecine brain was about the same as that of the chimpanzee, although it was somewhat larger relative to body size (Kappelman 1996). The significant increase in brain size, however, was associated with the genus *Homo*, beginning some 2.5 million years ago. Again, interpretation of these data is complicated by differences in body size. For example, although absolute brain size increased dramatically over the successive stages from early *Homo* through to *H. sapiens*, it has been estimated that when body size is taken into account there was virtually no increase in brain size over nearly two million years of evolution in *Homo*, but then a dramatic increase from about 600 000 to 150 000 years ago. Although the Neanderthals seem to have had bigger brains than modern humans, they also had larger bodies, perhaps by as much as 24 per cent, so that modern humans have a slightly larger *relative* brain size than the Neanderthals (see also Beran *et al.*, this volume). There has also been a reduction in both brain and body size over the past 50 000 years (Kappelman 1997; Ruff *et al.* 1997).

As with the apes, however, brain size is probably not a very sensitive indicator of the evolution of intelligence, or cognitive capacity (call it what you will), even when corrected for body size. Holloway (1996) argues that we should also look at how the brain is organized. In particular, it seems reasonable to associate cognitive capacity with the so-called association areas of the brain, and not with sensory or motor areas (e.g. Wilkins and Wakefield 1995). One such area is contained within the parietal lobe, which is concerned with spatial relations among objects. In humans, the left parietal cortex also includes part of Wernicke's area, which is critically involved in the perception and comprehension of language. In humans, moreover, the parietal cortex is relatively enlarged, such that the lunate sulcus, separating the parietal and occipital lobes, is pushed back. According to Holloway (1996), the human brain has less than half the volume of primary visual striate cortex (part of the occipital lobe) than would be expected from a primate of the same overall brain size. Holloway also claims that endocasts made from the skulls of the original specimen of *A. africanus* from Taung, and of a specimen of *A. afarensis*, show a rearward shift of the lunate sulcus, implying that associative cortex had already begun to increase in the australopithecines. This has been challenged by Falk (1985, 1986), who suggests that Holloway has mistaken another sulcus for the lunate sulcus. This long-standing dispute has not been satisfactorily resolved, as Holloway (1996) himself acknowledges. Unfortunately, there are no data that bear on the location of the lunate sulcus, or the size of the parietal lobe, in the hominid species spanning the gap between the australopithecines and modern humans.

Another critical association area is contained within the frontal lobe, which is greatly enlarged in the human brain relative to that in apes. Again, though, Holloway and Falk are in dispute as to its evolution—Falk (1980, 1983) has claimed that the fronto-orbital sulcus in the specimen of *A. africanus* from Taung is located as it is in apes, but Holloway (1996) claims that none of the australopithecine endocasts shows sufficient evidence of brain convolutions to provide satisfactory evidence. Holloway

(1976) does suggest that an endocast of the skull of the species now known as *H. rudolfensis* has a human-like rather than an ape-like third frontal convolution, which is the area containing Broca's area in modern humans, and for once Falk (1983) seems to agree. On the basis of this evidence, Tobias (1987) argued that *H. rudolfensis* (then called *H. habilis*) had invented at least rudimentary language. This further suggests that the increase in brain size and the relative growth of association areas were driven at least in part by pressure for more effective communication, and began with the split of *Homo* from the australopithecines perhaps 3 million years ago (cf. Greenfield 1991; Wilkins and Wakefield 1995).

But it might have been the development of the prefrontal cortex, rather than Broca's area alone, that was critical in the evolution of the hominid mind. Deacon (1997) estimates that the human prefrontal cortex is about twice the size that would be predicted in an ape with a brain as large as a human's, and is probably the most divergently enlarged of any brain region. Deacon argues that the development of the prefrontal cortex underlay the emergence of symbolic thinking that is unique to our species.

Cerebral asymmetry

Another aspect of brain evolution is cerebral asymmetry. Most humans are right-handed and left-cerebrally dominant for language, and until quite recently it was thought that these asymmetries were uniquely human, and indeed constituted strong evidence of a discontinuity between humans and apes (e.g. Corballis 1989). That view has been eroded over the past decade. Hopkins (1996) has recently documented evidence of a population bias toward right-handedness in chimpanzees (and to a lesser extent in other great apes), and there is growing evidence, reviewed by Bradshaw and Rogers (1993), for cerebral asymmetries in other primates. Although this has led Bradshaw and Rogers to argue for continuity between animals and humans, it is still possible to argue that the pattern and strength of lateral asymmetries sets humans apart. Summarizing work on anatomical asymmetries of the brain, for example, Holloway (1996) remarks that "while asymmetries certainly exist in pongids, neither the pattern nor direction is anywhere near as strong as in *Homo*" (p. 94).

The data on chimpanzee handedness summarized by Hopkins (1996) suggest that, on the limited tasks in which handedness is evident in the chimpanzee, the ratio of right- to left-handers is only about 2:1, and there are several anatomical and postural asymmetries in humans that also approximate this ratio (Previc 1991). Previc suggests that it might have been cultural pressures that increased the ratio of right- to left-handers to about 8:1. The 8:1 bias, however, seems to be more or less constant across diverse human cultures (Corballis 1983). More tellingly, the bias in favour of the left hemisphere for the representation of speech is, if anything, even higher (Milner 1975), and this bias is difficult to explain in terms of cultural pressure. An alternative possibility is that the more pronounced bias underlying handedness and cerebral dominance for language depends on some additional genetic influence that emerged at some point in hominid evolution, to be superimposed on the already existing 2:1 bias. Annett (1985, 1995) and McManus (1985, this volume) have proposed genetic models in which some uniquely human allele might be responsible for the predominance of right handedness and left-cerebral dominance for language. I have proposed that this 'dextral' allele operates, not against a background of neutrality with respect to laterality, but against the background of the weak 2:1 asymmetry (Corballis 1997).

Precisely when this allele might have emerged is not clear, but it might have been relatively late in the evolution of the genus *Homo*. Toth (1985) has found that the shapes of flakes struck from stones by early hominids were characteristically asymmetrical. Those suggestive of right-handed operation outnumbered left-handed flakes by 57:43 among the earliest samples of up to 1.9 million years ago, and by 61:39 in the artefacts of 300000 years ago. The more extreme 8:1 ratio might therefore have emerged within the last 300000 years, possibly with the appearance of *H. sapiens*. However, Toth's figures on the ratio of right- to left-handed flakes need not reflect the ratio of right- to left-handed *individuals*; indeed Toth himself showed that similar ratios are produced when modern right-handers are given the task of producing flakes. On these grounds, McManus (this volume) makes the alternative suggestion that the dextral allele initially conferred right-handedness and left-cerebral dominance for language on *all* members of the genus, but later mutated to produce an alternative, 'null' allele that operates to cancel the dextral bias. According to this theory, left-handedness evolved more recently than right-handedness.

Why did laterality evolve? It is perhaps best understood in the context of bilateral *symmetry*, which is presumably an adaptation to the fact that the physical world, as it impinges on freely-moving animals such as ourselves, is largely indifferent with respect to left and right (Corballis and Beale 1976). Given that the shortest distance between two points is a straight line, locomotory systems are almost (but not quite) universally symmetrical, and since predator and prey might lurk on either side our sensory systems have followed suit. But the advantages of symmetry do not apply with equal force to actions that are internally generated, rather than being reactions to external events, and scarcely apply at all to purely cognitive activity. It might simply be more efficient in terms of neural space to have such highly computational skills as language represented asymmetrically. Deacon (1997) suggests, for example, that hemispheric specialization allows for more efficient parallel processing in the two cerebral hemispheres, which was especially critical to the evolution of language. Wilkins and Wakefield (1995) suggest that lateralization might have facilitated internally generated manual activities, such as manipulation and throwing, by shortening the feedback from somatosensory to motor areas. Lateralization would also eliminate the possibility of interhemispheric conflict, especially in praxic functions (Corballis 1991).

Another possibility can be derived from the theory, outlined above, that language originated in manual gesture, but was increasingly accompanied by vocalization. Kimura (1973*a*, *b*) observed that right handers make many more gestures with the right hand than with the left hand speaking, while left handers make more bilateral movements and show a more mixed pattern. This is consistent with the idea that the dextral allele underlies the left-hemispheric control of both speaking and gesturing, while in the absence of dextral allele the two activities might sometimes be controlled by opposite hemispheres. The importance of cerebral dominance might therefore have been to ensure that manual and vocal control were located in the *same* cerebral hemisphere. This might have been most critical at a time when spoken language began to emerge as an alternative to manual language, and this in turn might have been restricted to *H. sapiens*.

Heterochrony

Many of the differences among hominid species, and indeed among the primates generally, can be related to *heterochrony*, or differences between rates of development. Indeed, Groves (1989) was moved to remark that "The vast potential for evolutionary change opened up by heterochrony has perhaps not been appreciated by most biologists; in the last analysis it seems possible to ascribe a major proportion of evolutionary change to changes in rates of development" (p. 57). One aspect of heterochrony that seems to have characterized primate and hominid evolution is *neoteny*, in which the adult of a new species has characteristics of the juvenile of the parent species. For example, pygmy chimpanzees branched off from the chimpanzee line about three million years ago (Waddell and Penny 1996), and adult pygmy chimpanzees have the skull shape and body proportions of the juveniles of common chimpanzees. But neoteny is complex, involving dissociations between different aspects of growth; for example, despite the neotenous appearance of the adult pygmy chimpanzee, it is about the same size as the common chimpanzee and reaches sexual maturity at the same age.

According to Groves (1989) heterochronic events dominate the later stages of hominid evolution involving the various species of *Homo*. Many of the physical characteristics of adult *H. habilis* are neotenous, resembling juvenile characteristics of the australopithecines, including many aspects of the shape of the cranium. Indeed *H. habilis* was more neotenous than the sister species of *Homo* from which it split. But after the split of *H. ergaster*, neoteny seems to have emerged again: Groves states that "neotenous events arise with increasing frequency at each quasi-speciation event along the lineage from *H. ergaster* to modern humans" (p. 313).

An aspect of heterochrony that is often confused with neoteny is *hypermorphosis*, or prolongation of growth (McKinney and McNamara 1991). For example, adult humans somewhat resemble infant chimpanzees in that both have bulbous foreheads, but in humans the enlargement of the brain, and of the frontal lobes in particular, is a result of prolonged growth rather than the preservation of infant features. Further, compared with the new-borns of other apes, the human infant is born about nine months prematurely (Krogman 1972)—as Gould (1980) put it, the child is effectively an embryo for the first nine months of its life. The brain of the new-born chimpanzee is about 60 percent of its ultimate weight, compared with about 24 percent for the new-born human. This prolongation of infancy was probably critical to the evolution of the human mind, because the brain is most receptive to environmental influences during growth. It was probably especially important in the emergence of recursive, hierarchical skills like language, manufacture, and perhaps even music and dance (Corballis 1991; Greenfield 1991).

One index of hypermorphosis comes from dental development: In apes, the three molar teeth appear at ages 3.3, 6.6, and 10.5 years, whereas in human children the corresponding ages are 6, 12, and 18 years. Fossil evidence suggests that the dental patterns of *A. africanus* and *H. habilis* were more ape-like than human-like, implying that the prolonged childhood characteristic of our own species were not present in these species (Smith 1986). There is evidence, however, that it was present in *H. ergaster*. Judging from the skeleton of a fossil of a boy who died at around twelve years of age and from other data on sex differences in morphology, the birth canal in *H. ergaster* was significantly smaller in this species than in *H. sapiens*, yet *H. ergaster* grew to a size at least approaching that of modern humans. Brown *et al.* (1985), who describe this skeleton, conclude that "by 1.6 [million years] ago, the secondary altricial condition (which leads to increased fetal dependency) must have been present" (p. 792). That is, the premature birth that characterizes our species might have been present in *H. ergaster*, and might have been driven in part by restrictions on the size of the pelvic canal and the increase in brain size, perhaps forcing an early birth.

Language and speech

There has been much debate as to when generative language might have evolved. Pinker and Bloom (1989) argue that it evolved gradually in the course of hominid evolution, while Bickerton (1995) and Noble and Davidson (1996) maintain that true language is unique to *H. sapiens* (see also Lock, this volume). Given that an enlarged brain, cerebral asymmetry, and heterochrony might all be markers of language evolution, it is not unreasonable to suppose that language evolved from a relatively primitive system, which Bickerton (1994) has described as *proto-language*, to a fully-fledged, generative system during the course of the evolution of *Homo*. Proto-language might involve the ability to form internal representations of external objects and events, and might be already in place in the great apes (see Byrne, this volume). There seems fairly general agreement that it is syntax that makes human language unique, and that gives it its generative structure (Chomsky 1980; Pinker and Bloom 1989; Bickerton 1995).

But if language emerged gradually in the course of the evolution of the genus *Homo*, it is likely that speech itself was more recent. Lieberman (1984, 1991) has claimed that the production of speech was not possible until the larynx descended in the neck, and that this adaptation, as well as concomitant changes in the brain mechanisms involved in producing speech, occurred only recently in human evolution, and perhaps only with the emergence of *H. sapiens*. According to Lieberman (1992), even the Neanderthals of 30 000 years ago would have suffered gross speech deficits that not only kept them apart from anatomically modern humans, but led to their eventual extinction. Lieberman's claims have been disputed. For example Falk (1975), ever the critic, argued that if the reconstruction of the Neanderthal vocal tract proposed by Lieberman *et al.* (1972) were accurate, the creature would have been unable to swallow—although Lieberman (1982) has retorted in turn that if Falk were right the chimpanzee would be unable to swallow either! Duchin (1990) has argued that the evolution of the tongue was more critical than that of the larynx, and her analyses suggest that the tongue would have been capable of producing articulate speech sounds in *H. ergaster/erectus*. The slow and gradual evolution of language can be reconciled with the relatively sudden and recent evolution of speech if it is supposed that language emerged first as a primarily gestural system, as suggested above, and switched to a predominantly vocal system relatively late in the evolution of *Homo*.

Conclusions

In many respects, the evolution of distinctively human characteristics might be said to have begun with the emergence of the genus *Homo*. Brain size began its spectacular increase, stone tools were developed, and from about two million years ago various species of *Homo*, beginning with *H. erectus*, started to migrate from Africa, at first to east Asia and later to Europe. By about half a million years ago, the hominids had become large-bodied, large-brained creatures, with perhaps a more sophisticated manufacturing technology than is suggested by stone artefacts. In particular, they appear to have become hunters, at least in Europe, using sophisticated spears to kill or maim their prey. It is also likely that they had fairly sophisticated language, although it might still have been primarily manual. But the hunters of northern Europe were probably not the species that survives today. There is one more stage to consider.

Homo sapiens

There have been two different scenarios as to the emergence of anatomically modern humans, now known exclusively as *H. sapiens*. According to the 'regional continuity' model, championed by Wolpoff (1989), the species of *Homo* that radiated from Africa, beginning about two million years ago, evolved into modern humans more or less independently, although with some genetic exchange. The main evidence for this is the supposed continuity of the morphology of East Asian skulls over a period of more than a million years. The weight of evidence, however, appears to lie with the 'Out of Africa' model, which holds that *H. sapiens* emerged in Africa some 100–150 000 years ago, and migrated from there to the Old and New Worlds, beginning somewhere between 100 000 and 60 000 years ago (Cavalli-Sforza *et al.* 1993). This species replaced (to put it politely) the descendants of the earlier migrants, from *H. erectus* in Java to the Neanderthals in Europe and western Asia. The 'Out of Africa' model was developed from analysis of mitochondrial DNA, which implied that all modern humans were descended from Africa (Cann *et al.* 1987), although it had been suggested earlier on the basis of an analysis of the diversity of nuclear allele frequencies (Nei and Roychoudhury 1982). It has continued to receive support, not only from more recent analysis of mitochondrial DNA (Waddell and Penny 1996), but also from chromosomal analyses (Dorit *et al.* 1995; Hammer 1995; Tishkoff *et al.* 1996), and from independent analysis of fossil and subfossil remains (Stringer and Andrews 1988). Assuming an African origin for all modern humans, Cavalli-Sforza *et al.* (1993) have summarized the likely expansions that have taken place over the past 100 000 years.

But there are already signs that the dichotomy between the 'Out of Africa' and 'regional continuity' might be too simple. On the basis of the diversity of a region of the beta-globin gene among present day populations, Harding *et al.* (1997) have argued that populations ancestral to modern humans were located in Asia, as well as in Africa, over 200 000 years ago. Hammer *et al.* (1997) have examined the diversity of haplotypes on the Y chromosome, and their data appear to show that one of the haplotypes has an Asian rather than an African origin. They suggest that the distribution of haplotypes in the modern population might reflect several dispersions from Africa, but also one from Asia. The Asian challenge receives further support from a recent analysis of the similarities among various fossil crania—although the data were better fit by a 'single-origin' model than by a 'regional-continuity' one, the best-fitting single-origin model was one in which the origin of modern humans was assumed to lie in south-west Asia, not in Africa (Sokal *et al.* 1997).

It is too early to tell whether these developments will result in a serious challenge to the 'Out of Africa' scenario. Whatever the case, comparative linguistics is adding to the case for a recent and geographically localized origin of modern humans. Shevoroshkin (1990) and Ruhlen (1994), among others, have argued on the basis of the similarities among the spoken languages of the world that all of them must have evolved from a single 'mother tongue,' also known as 'Proto-World' (Shevoroshkin 1990, p. 20). For example, the word pronounced with relatively minor variations as 'akwa' occurs in a great many language families, and was probably a root word meaning 'water'. Just as genetic diversity is greater in Africa than in any other region, so linguistic diversity is greatest there. While this supports an African origin, it should be appreciated that diversity is as much a consequence of population size as of time-depth (Harding *et al.* 1997). Ruhlen (1994) notes that linguistic analysis is largely uninformative as to the dates of early linguistic evolution, but nevertheless "supports a recent, as opposed to a very ancient, date for the origin of modern languages" (p. 163).

Ruhlen was of course referring to *spoken* language. It would be equally consistent with his analysis to suppose that language emerged much earlier as a system of manual gestures, but switched to a predominantly vocal mode in *H. sapiens*. This is not to say that the switch was sudden; early gestural language would no doubt have been punctuated by vocalizations, just as present-day vocal language is embellished by gesture, as Goldin-Meadow and McNeill (this volume) make clear. What *H. sapiens* might have invented was a vocal language that was fully syntactic and fully autonomous. Indeed, it might even have been this invention that led to the ultimate triumph of *H. sapiens* over all other hominid species. The switch from a manual to a vocal language might also have been facilitated by the emergence of dextral gene, discussed earlier, that ensured that manual and vocal control were represented in the same (left) cerebral hemisphere (Corballis 1997).

There are several advantages to a spoken language over a gestural one. One is that it allows communication at night, or over distances at which manual signs would be visually indiscriminable, or when obstacles prevent the communicating parties from seeing each other. Goldin-Meadow and McNeill (this volume) make the more subtle point that communication is more effective if the voice carries the grammatical, combinatorial aspect of language, while the hands provide the more global, imagistic aspect. Reversing these roles would be less effective, since the hands and arms lend themselves more readily to holistic expression. Another important advantage of a largely autonomous vocal language is that it frees the hands for other activities, including tool making (Corballis 1991, 1992; Givon 1995); although we have seen that *H. heidelbergensis* and their probable successors, the Neanderthals, possessed spears for hunting, it might have been the invention of weapons that allowed our somewhat aggressive species to prevail over the other hominids. With predominantly vocal speech, moreover, an individual could demonstrate tool-making techniques while at the same time verbally explaining them. This could be why the manufacture of tools, having been relatively static for some two million years (Foley 1987), was suddenly launched on an upward curve *after* the emergence of *H. sapiens*.

Archaeologists have documented what has been called an 'evolutionary explosion' in artefacts dating from about 35 000 years ago in Europe and the Near East (Pfeiffer 1985), and it is sometimes said that the modern mind truly dates from this period (Lock this volume). It is characterized by cave drawings, the crafting of ornaments and objects that display visual metaphor (White 1989), and more sophisticated manufacture than was evident at earlier Eurasian sites. We should also include the remarkable development of water craft that took people from the Asian mainland to New Guinea and Australia (then joined) at least 40 000 years ago, and perhaps earlier (Allen and Holdaway 1995; Diamond 1997). It might be argued that the evolutionary explosion was too late to be attributable to a switch to vocal language that took place in Africa before the migration of *H. sapiens*. There is, however, good reason to suppose that the evolutionary explosion actually began earlier in Africa, and eventually expanded into Eurasia. Mellars (1989) writes that;

It is possible to point to at least certain features of the archeological record of the Middle Stone Age (roughly between 100 000 and 40 000 years ago) in Southern Africa which suggest a significantly more 'complex' (and perhaps more 'advanced') pattern of behavior than that reflected in the parallel records of the Middle Paleolithic in northern Eurasia over the same time range (p. 367).

Evidence of a sophisticated bone industry, including the possible manufacture of harpoons to catch fish, has been recently discovered in the Republic of Congo, and dates from some 90 000 years ago (Yellen *et al.* 1995).

Whatever the reason for their advantage, the migrating *H. sapiens* replaced the descendants of the hominids who had earlier migrated from Africa, including the descendants of *H. erectus* in east Asia and the Neanderthals in western Asia and Europe. Although the status of the Neanderthals remains controversial, the evidence largely supports the theory that they were a subspecies distinct from *H. sapiens* (Hublin *et al.* 1996), probably descended from *H. heidelbergensis* (Tattersall 1997). Neanderthal fossils have been dated in Europe and Asia from about 150 000 to about 34 000 years ago, and their disappearance coincides at least roughly with the appearance of the invading Cro-Magnons (Mellars 1996). Lest we be carried away with our own mental superiority over the hapless Neanderthals, it is as likely that they succumbed to invading diseases brought the Cro-Magnons as to any superiority of intellect or weaponry (Deacon 1997). There was nevertheless a period of coexistence, lasting from perhaps 40 000 to 34 000 years ago in France, during which the Cro-Magnons might have even traded technology to the Neanderthals (Hublin *et al.* 1996).

Despite the evolutionary explosion of 35 000 years ago, humans everywhere were probably hunter–gatherers until about 13 000 years ago. Indeed, by comparison with the apes, humans are probably biologically adapted primarily to a life of hunting and gathering. The sophistication of the 400 000-year-old wooden spears discovered in Germany (Thieme 1997) implies that hunting was already well established by that date, and had probably been a prominent aspect of life since well before that. Indeed the emergence of stone tools some 2.5 million years ago might have marked something of a transition from a scavenging of carcasses killed by other predators to active hunting. There are of course still bands of people, in remote parts of New Guinea and Amazonia, whose way of life is predominantly one of hunting and gathering (Diamond 1997). A major assumption of so-called 'evolutionary psychology' is that many, if not most, of the distinctive aspects of the human mind owe their origins to the lengthy period of adaptation to a hunter–gatherer way of life (Tooby and Cosmides 1989, 1992).

Hunting and gathering probably remained the dominant way of life in all humans until about 13 000 years ago, with the domestication of wild plants and animals, first in the Fertile Crescent of western Asia (comprising modern Syria, Jordan, Iraq, and part of Turkey), and perhaps slightly later in China. The emergence of agriculture led to surpluses of food, so that people were freed for other activities, such as the development of new technologies and social organizations, leading ultimately to what we are pleased to called civilizations. These historical and geographic forces have resulted in the remarkable difference in culture that we see in the modern world. While some authors have continued to argue that these differences reflect, at least in part, biological differences between groupings of people (e.g. Herrnstein and Murray 1994; Rushton 1995), the period of differential cultural evolution is surely too short to have produced significant biological adaptation, except in relatively superficial features such as hair, eye, or skin colour. As a counter to such notions, Diamond (1997) has argued compellingly and in considerable detail that cultural differences can be attributed entirely to features of geography and climate, along with some elements of chance.

For all that, the hunter–gatherer mind of *H. sapiens* must have possessed the flexibility to respond to the extraordinary and varied influences of culture that have emerged and accumulated in the last 13 000 years. One of the distinctive characteristics of the human biological condition is that we possess a cognitive capacity that extends well beyond our immediate needs (Suddendorf and Corballis 1997). It might have been the release of the hands from primary language duty that allowed us to indulge in art, music, and manufacture, and later in writing, which in turn made possible philosophy, science, mathematics, and yet more sophisticated technology. These activities all have a representational, generative character that evolved in the more restricted context of manual communication, which in turn evolved from the increasing complexities of hominid interactions (Corballis 1991, 1992).

Conclusions

As we have seen, the evolution of modern humans from African apes has been complex. There are several critical periods during which characteristics that we see as distinctively human might have emerged. To some, the step into apehood was the decisive one, providing at least the underpinnings for theory of mind and language (Byrne, this volume), although Suddendorf (this volume) suggests that what he calls *metamind* is the true mark of humanity and is not present in the apes. The next transition into the world of the hominids brought bipedalism, and perhaps it was the freeing of the hands that was decisive, leading to tool-making, throwing, and possibly gestural language. Whiten (this volume) argues that the decisive trigger to evolutionary change was life on the savannah, where the early hominids had to compete and contend with species, such as sabre-toothed cats and hyenas, that were physically much more obviously adapted to hunting and killing than the puny australopithecines. This forced them to resort to cognitive solutions—cunning, subterfuge, social cooperation. But there is a gap of some two million years before we see evidence of the dramatic increase in brain size that was to distinguish the genus *Homo* from the other hominids, and it might have been this period that saw the critical development of communicative, social, and perhaps hunting skills that set us apart. The emergence of *H. sapiens* a mere 150 000 to 100 000 years ago was clearly another critical event, because this species has succeeded in removing all other hominid species, and many others species as well, from the planet. I have suggested above that what might have been decisive here was the switch to a fully autonomous vocal language, freeing the hands for the varieties of mischief that we humans have wrought upon the earth.

The final transition began 13 000 years ago, with the switch from hunting and gathering to the systematic domestication of wild plants and animals, leading to more complex societies and even more rapid advances in technology. To some, this final phase, leading to the extraordinary advance of knowledge and understanding in the modern world, might seem to display most of what is truly characteristic of the human mind. In 1955, the astronomer Fred Hoyle wrote as follows:

Man's [sic] claim to have progressed beyond his fellow animals must be supported not by his search for food, warmth, and shelter (however ingenious), but by his very penetration into the very fabric of the Universe. It is in the world of ideas and in the relation of his brain to the Universe itself, that the superiority of Man lies. The rise of Man may justly be described as an adventure in ideas (p. 1).

Lest this claim seem hopelessly Eurocentric, not to say sexist, we should recall that the quality of mind that led to our remarkable understanding of the universe, and indeed of our own evolution within that universe, was probably biologically formed in our African (or Asian?) relatives of over 100 000 years ago. As Bloom (this volume) argues, however, the extraordinary accomplishments of modern science and technology depend not only on our biological endowment, but on the cultural accumulation of knowledge, sustained first through word of mouth, and then through books, the ever-growing complexity of machines themselves, and now through computers and the Internet. Go well.

References

Allen, J. and Holdaway, S. (1995). The contamination of Pleistocene radiocarbon determination in Australia. *Antiquity*, **69**, 101–12.

Andrews, P. (1995). Ecological apes and ancestors. *Nature*, **376**, 555–6.

Annett, M. (1985). Left, right, hand and brain: the right shift theory. Erlbaum, London.

Annett, M. (1995). The right shift theory of a genetic balanced polymorphism for cerebral dominance and cognitive processing. *Current Psychology of Cognition*, **14**, 427–80.

Armstrong, D. F., Stokoe, W. C., and Wilcox, S. E. (1995). *Gesture and the nature of language*. Cambridge University Press.

Arsuaga, J.-L., Martinez, I., Gracia, A., Carretero, J.-M., and Carbonell, E. (1993). Three new human skulls from the Sima de los Huesos Middle Pleistocene site Sierra de Atapuerca, Spain. *Nature*, **362**, 534–7.

Asfaw, B., Beyene, Y., Suwa, G., Walter, R. C., White, T. D., Wolde-Gabriel, G., *et al*. (1992). The earliest Acheulian from Konso-Gardula. *Nature*, **360**, 732–5.

Bermudez de Castro, J. M., Arsuaga, J. L., Carbonell, E., Rosas, A., Martinez, I., and Mosquera, M. (1997). A hominid from the Lower Pleistocene of Atapuerca, Spain: possible ancestor to Neanderthals and modern humans. *Science*, **276**, 1392–5.

Bickerton, D. (1995). *Language and human behavior*. University of Washington Press, Seattle.

Bischoff, J. L., Garcia, J. F., and Straus, L. G. (1992). Uranium-series isochron dating at El Castillo cave (Cantabria, Spain). *Journal of Archeological Science*, **19**, 49–62.

Boesch, C. and Boesch, H. (1984). Mental map in wild chimpanzees: an analysis of hammer transports for nut cracking. *Primates*, **25**, 160–70.

Bradshaw, J. L. and Rogers, L. J. (1993). *The evolution of lateral asymmetries, language, tool use, and intellect*. Academic Press, Sydney, Australia.

Brown, F., Harris, J., Leakey, R., and Walker, A. (1985). Early *Homo erectus* skeleton from west Lake Turkana, Kenya. *Nature*, **316**, 788–92.

Brunet, M., Beauvilain, A., Coppens, Y., Heintz, E., Moutaye, A. H. E., and Pilbeam, D. (1995). The first australopithecine 2500 kilometres west of the Rigt Valley (Chad). *Nature*, **378**, 273–5.

Butynski, T. M. (1982). Vertebrate predation by primates. *Journal of Human Evolution*, **11**, 421–30.

Byrne, R. W. (1995). *The thinking ape: evolutionary origins of intelligence*. Oxford University Press.

Calvin, W. H. (1983). *The throwing madonna*. McGraw–Hill, New York.

Calvin, W. H. (1993). The unitary hypothesis: a common neural circuitry for novel manipulations, language, plan-ahead, and throwing? In *Tools, language and cognition in human evolution*, (ed. K. R. Gibson and T. Ingold), pp. 230–50. Cambridge University Press.

Campbell, B. G. (1996). An outline of human phylogeny. In *Handbook of human symbolic evolution*, (ed. A. Lock and C. R. Peters), pp. 31–52. Oxford University Press.

Cann, R. L., Stoneking, M., and Wilson, A. C. (1987). Mitochondrial DNA and human evolution. *Nature*, **325**, 31–6.

Carbonell, E., Bermudez de Castro, J. M., Arsuaga, J.-L., Diez, J. C., Rosas, A., Cuenca-Bescos, G., *et al*. (1995). Lower Pleistocene hominids and artifacts from Atapuerca-TD6 (Spain). *Science*, **269**, 826–30.

Cavalli-Sforza, L. L., Menozzi, P., and Piazza, A. (1993). Demic expansions and human evolution. *Science*, **259**, 639–46.

Chomsky, N. (1980). *Rules and representation*. Columbia University Press, New York.

Clark, J. D., de Heinzelin, J., Schick, K. D., Hart, W. K., White, T. D., WoldeGabriel, G., *et al*. (1994). African *Homo erectus*: old radiometric ages and young Oldowan assemblages in the Middle Awash Valley, Ethiopia. *Science*, **264**, 1907–10.

Corballis, M. C. (1983). *Human laterality*. Academic Press, New York.

Corballis, M. C. (1989). Laterality and human evolution. *Psychological Review*, **96**, 492–505.

Corballis, M. C. (1991). *The lopsided ape: evolution of the generative mind*. Oxford University Press, New York.

Corballis, M. C. (1992). On the evolution of language and generativity. *Cognition*, **44**, 197–226.

Corballis, M. C. (1997). The genetics and evolution of handedness. *Psychological Review*, **104**, 714–27.

Corballis, M. C. and Beale, I. L. (1976). *The psychology of left and right*. Erlbaum, Hillsdale, NJ.

Dart, R. A. (1925). *Australopithecus africanus*: The man–ape of South Africa. *Nature*, **115**, 195–9.

Dart, R. A. (with Craig, D.) (1959). *Adventures with the missing link*. Hamish Hamilton, London.

Darwin, C. (1871). *The descent of man, and selection in relation to sex*. J. Murray, London.

Dawkins, R. (1997). *Climbing mount improbable*. Penguin Books, Harmondsworth.

Deacon, T. (1997). *The symbolic species*. Allen Lane, The Penguin Press, Harmondsworth.

Dennell, R. (1997). The world's oldest spears. *Nature*, **385**, 767–8.

Dennell, R. W., Rendell, H., and Hailwood, E. (1988*a*). Late Pliocene artefacts from Northern Pakistan. *Current Anthropology*, **29**, 495–8.

Dennell, R. W., Rendell, H., and Hailwood, E. (1988*b*). Early tool making in Asia: two million year old artefacts in Pakistan. *Antiquity*, **62**, 98–106.

Diamond, J. (1997). *Guns, germs, and steel: the fates of modern human societies*. Norton, New York.

Donald, M. (1991). *Origins of the modern human mind*. Harvard University Press.

Dorit, R. L., Akashi, H., and Gilbert, W. (1995). Absence of polymorphism at the ZFY locus on the human Y chromosome. *Science*, **268**, 1183–5.

Duchin, L. E. (1990). The evolution of articulate speech: comparative anatomy of the oral cavity in *Pan* and *Homo*. *Journal of Human Evolution*, **19**, 687–97.

Dunbar, R. I. M. (1993). Coevolution of neocortical size, group size and language in humans. *Behavioral and Brain Sciences*, **16**, 681–736.

Falk, D. (1975). Comparative anatomy of the larynx in man and chimpanzee: implications for language in Neanderthal. *American Journal of Physical Anthropology*, **43**, 123–32.

Falk, D. (1980). A re-analysis of the South African australopithecine natural endocasts. *American Journal of Physical Anthropology*, **53**, 525–39.

Falk, D. (1983). Cerebral cortices of East African early hominids. *Science*, **222**, 1072–4.

Falk, D. (1985). Apples, oranges, and the lunate sulcus. *American Journal of Physical Anthropology*, **67**, 313–5.

Falk, D. (1986). Reply to Holloway and Kimbel. *Nature*, **321**, 536–7.

Foley, R. (1987). Hominid species and stone tool assemblages. *Antiquity*, **61**, 380–92.

Gabunia, L. and Vakua, A. (1995). A Plio–Pleistocene hominid from Dmanisi, East Georgia, Caucasus. *Nature*, **373**, 509–12.

Gardner, R. A. and Gardner, B. T. (1969). Teaching sign language to a chimpanzee. *Science*, **165**, 664–72.

Gebo, D. L., MacLatchy, L., Kityo, R., Deino, A., Kingston, J., and Pilbeam, D. (1997). A hominoid genus from the early Miocene of Uganda. *Science*, **276**, 401–4.

Givon, T. (1995). *Functionalism and grammar*. Benjamins, Philadelphia.

Goldin-Meadow, S., McNeill, D., and Singleton, J. (1996). Silence is liberating: removing the handcuffs on grammatical expression in the manual modality. *Psychological Review*, **103**, 34–55.

Goodall, J. (1986). *The chimpanzees of Gombe*. The Belknap Press of Harvard University Press.

Goodman, M. (1992). Reconstructing human evolution from proteins. In *The Cambridge encyclopaedia of human evolution*, (ed. S. Jones, R. Martin, and D. Pilbeam), pp. 307–12. Cambridge University Press.

Gould, S. J. (1980). Human babies as embryos. In *Ever since Darwin*, (ed. S. J. Gould). Penguin Books, Harmondsworth, UK.

Greenfield, P. M. (1991). Language, tools, and the brain: the ontogeny and phylogeny of hierarchically organized sequential behavior. *Behavioral and Brain Sciences*, **14**, 531–95.

Groves, C. P. (1989). *A theory of human and primate evolution*. Clarendon, Oxford.

Hammer, M. F. (1995). A recent common ancestry for human Y chromosomes. *Nature*, **378**, 376–8.

Hammer, M. F., Spurdle, A. B., Karafet, T., Bonner, M. R., Wood, E. T., Novoletto, A., *et al.* (1997). The geographic distribution of human Y chromosome variation. *Genetics*, **145**, 787–805.

Harding, R. M., Fullerton, S. M., Griffiths, R. C., Bond, J., Cox, M. J., Schneider, J. A., *et al.* (1997). Archaic African *and* Asian lineages in the genetic ancestry of modern humans. *American Journal of Human Genetics*, **60**, 772–89.

Hayes, C. (1952). *The ape in our house*. Gollancz, London.

Herrnstein, R. and Murray, C. (1994). *The bell curve: intelligence and class structure in American life*. Free Press, New York.

Hewes, G. W. (1973). Primate communication and the gestural origins of language. *Current Anthropology*, **14**, 5–24.

Heyes, C. M. (1993). Imitation, culture and cognition. *Animal Behaviour*, **46**, 999–1010.

Heyes, C. M. (1998). Theory of mind in non-human primates. *Behavioral and Brain Sciences*, **21**, 101–48.

Holloway, R. L. (1976). Paleoneurological evidence for language origins. *Annals of the New York Academy of Sciences*, **280**, 330–48.

Holloway, R. L. (1996). Evolution of the human brain. In *Handbook of symbolic evolution* (ed. A. Lock and C. R. Peters), pp. 74–125. Oxford University Press.

Hopkins, W. D. (1996). Chimpanzee handedness revisited: 55 years since Finch (1941). *Psychonomic Bulletin and Review*, **3**, 449–57.

Hoyle, F. (1955). *Frontiers of astronomy*. Heinemann, London.

Huang, W., Ciochon, R., Yumin, G., Larick, R., Qiren, F., Schwarcz, H. *et al.* (1995). Early *Homo* and assorted artefacts from Asia. *Nature*, **358**, 275–8.

Hublin, J., Spoor, F., Braun, M., Zonnefeld, F. W., and Condemi, S. (1996). Late Neanderthal associated with Upper Palaeolithic artefacts. *Nature*, **381**, 224–6.

Jerison, H. J. (1973). *Evolution of the brain and intelligence*. Academic Press, New York.

Kappelman, J. (1996). The evolution of body mass and relative brain size in fossil hominids. *Journal of Human Evolution*, **30**, 243–76.

Kappelman, J. (1997). They might be giants. *Nature*, **387**, 126–7.

Kay, R. F., Fleagle, J. G., and Simons, E. L. (1981). A revision of the Oligene apes from the Fayum province, Egypt. *American Journal of Physical Anthropology*, **55**, 293–322.

Kendon, A. (1991). Some considerations for a theory of language origins. *Man*, **26**, 199–221.

Kimura, D. (1973a). Manual activity during speaking—I. Right-handers. *Neuropsychologia*, **11**, 45–50.

Kimura, D. (1973b). Manual activity during speaking—I. Left-handers. *Neuropsychologia*, **11**, 51–6.

Klima, E. and Bellugi, U. (1979). *The signs of language*. Harvard University Press.

Kohler, W. (1925). *The mentality of apes*. Routledge and Kegan Paul, New York.

Krogman, W. M. (1972). *Child growth*. University of Michigan Press.

Larick, R. and Ciochon, R. L. (1996). The African emergence and early Asian dispersal of the genus *Homo*. *American Scientist*, **84**, 539–51.

Latimer, B. and Lovejoy, C. O. (1990). Metatarsophalangeal joints of *Australopithecus afarensis*. *American Journal of Physical Anthropology*, **83**, 13–23.

Leakey, M. and Walker, A. (1997). Early hominid fossils from Africa. *Scientific American*, June, pp. 60–5.

Leakey, M. D. (1971). *Olduvai Gorge*, Vol. 3. Cambridge University Press.

Leakey, M. D. (1979). Footprints in the ashes of time. *National Geographic*, **155**, 446–57.

Leakey, M. G., Feibel, C. S., McDougall, I., and Walker, A. (1995). New four-million-year-old hominid species from Kanapoi and Allia Bay, Kenya. *Nature*, **376**, 565–71.

Lieberman, P. (1982). Can chimpanzees swallow or talk? A reply to Falk. *American Anthropologist*, **84**, 148–152.

Lieberman, P. (1984). *The biology and evolution of language*. Harvard University Press.

Lieberman, P. (1991). *Uniquely human: the evolution of speech, thought, and selfless behavior*. Harvard University Press.

Lieberman, P. (1992). On Neanderthal speech and Neanderthal extinction. *Current Anthropology*, **33**, 409–10.

Lieberman, P., Crelin, E. S., and Klatt, D. H. (1972). Phonetic ability and related anatomy of the new-born, adult human, Neanderthal man, and the chimpanzee. *American Anthropologist*, **74**, 287–307.

Lovejoy, O. C. (1981). The origin of man. *Science*, **221**, 341–50.

Martin, R. (1992). Classification and evolutionary relationships. In *The Cambridge encyclopaedia of human evolution*, (ed. S. Jones, R. Martin, and D. Pilbeam), pp. 17–23. Cambridge University Press.

Martin, R. D. (1990). *Primate origins and evolution*. Chapman and Hall, London.

Marzke, M. W. (1986). Tool use and the evolution of hominid hands and bipedality. In *Proceedings of the Tenth Congress of the International Primatology Society*, Vol. 1, (ed. J. G. Else and P. C. Lee), pp. 203–9. Cambridge University Press.

Marzke, M. W. (1996). Evolution of the hand and bipedality. In *Handbook of human symbolic evolution*, (ed. A. Lock and C. R. Peters), pp. 126–54. Oxford University Press.

McKinney, M. L. and McNamara, K. J. (1991). *Heterochrony: the evolution of ontogeny*. Plenum Press, New York.

McManus, I. C. (1985). Handedness, language dominance and aphasia: a genetic model. *Psychological Medicine* (Suppl. 8), 1–40.

Mellars, D. (1989). Major issues in the emergence of modern humans. *Current Anthropology*, **30**, 349–85.

Mellars, D. (1996). *The Neanderthal legacy: an archaeological perspective from Western Europe*. Princeton University Press.

Milner, B. (1975). Psychological aspects of focal epilepsy and its neurosurgical management. In *Advances in neurology*, Vol. 8, (ed. D. P. Purpura, J. K. Penry, and R. D. Walters), pp. 299–321. Raven, New York.

Nei, M. and Roychoudhury, A. K. (1982). Genetic relationship and evolution of human races. *Evolutionary Biology*, **14**, 927–43.

Neville, H. J. (1991). Whence the specialization of the language hemispherc? In *Modularity and the motor theory of speech perception*, (ed. I. S. Mattingley and M. Studdest-Kennedy), pp. 269–94. Erlbaum, Hillsdale, NJ.

Noble, W. and Davidson, I. (1996). *Human evolution, language and mind*. Cambridge University Press.

O'Brien, K. P. (1984). What was the Acheulian hand-axe? *Natural History*, **93**, 20–3.

Parker, S. T. and Gibson, K. R. (1979). A developmental model for the evolution of language and intelligence in early hominids. *Behavioral and Brain Sciences*, **2**, 367–408.

Passingham, R. E. (1982). *The human primate*. Freeman, San Francisco.

Patterson, F. (1978). Conversations with a gorilla. *National Geographic*, **154**, 438–65.

Pettito, L. A. and Marentette, P. F. (1991). Babbling in the manual mode: evidence for the ontogeny of language. *Science*, **251**, 1493–6.

Pfeiffer, J. E. (1985). *The emergence of humankind*. Harper and Row, New York.

Pilbeam, D. (1972). *The ascent of man: an introduction to human evolution*. Macmillan, New York.

Pilbeam, D. and Smith, R. (1981). New skull remains of *Sivapithecus* from Pakistan. *Memoirs of the Geological Survey of Pakistan*, **11**, 1–13.

Pinker, S. (1994). *The language instinct*. Morrow, New York.

Pinker, S. and Bloom, P. (1990). Natural language and natural selection. *Behavioral and Brain Sciences*, **13**, 707–84.

Poizner, H., Klima, E. S., and Bellugi, U. (1987). *What the hands reveal about the brain*. MIT Press/Bradford, Cambridge, MA.

Premack, D. (1988). 'Does the chimpanzee have a theory of mind?' revisited. In *Machiavellian intelligence: social expertise and the evolution of intellect in monkeys, apes and humans*, (ed. R. W. Byrne and A. Whiten), pp. 160–79. Clarendon Press, Oxford.

Premack, D. and Woodruff, G. (1978). Does the chimpanzee have a theory of mind? *Behavioral and Brain Sciences*, **4**, 515–26.

Previc, F. (1991). A general theory concerning the prenatal origins of cerebral lateralization in humans. *Psychological Review*, **98**, 299–334.

Ruhlen, M. (1994). *The origin of language: tracing the evolution of the mother tongue*. Wiley, New York.

Ruff, C. B., Trinkhaus, E., and Holliday, T. W. (1997). Body mass and encephalization in Pleistocene *Homo*. *Nature*, **387**, 173–6.

Rushton, J. P. (1995). *Race, evolution, and behavior: a life history perspective*. Transaction, London.

Sarich, V. and Wilson, A. C. (1967). Immunological time-scale for hominid evolution. *Science*, **158**, 1200–1203.

Savage-Rumbaugh, E .S. (1994). Hominid evolution: Looking to modern apes for clues. In *Hominid culture in primate perspective*, (ed. D. Quiatt and J. Itani), pp. 7–49. University of Colorado Press.

Savage-Rumbaugh, S. and Lewin, R. (1994). *Kanzi: an ape at the brink of the human mind*. Wiley, New York.

Schaller, G. B. (1963). *The mountain gorilla*. University of Chicago Press.

Schick, K. D. and Toth, N. (1993). *Making silent stones speak*. Weidenfeld and Nicolson, London.

Semaw, S., Renne, P., Harris, J. W. K., Feibel, C. S., Bernor, R. L., Fesseha, N., *et al.* (1997). 2.5-million-year-old stone tools from Gona, Ethiopia. *Nature*, **385**, 333–6.

Shevoroshkin, V. (1990). The mother tongue. *The Sciences*, **30**, 20–7.

Smith, B. H. (1986). Dental developments in *Australopithecus* and early *Homo Nature*, **323**, 327–30.

Sokal, R., Oden, N. L., Walker, J., and Waddle, D. M.. (1997). Using distance matrices to choose between competing theories and an application to the origin of modern humans. *Journal of Human Evolution*, **32**, 501–22.

Stringer, C. B. and Andrews, P. (1988). Genetic and fossil evidence for the origin of modern humans. *Science*, **239**, 1263–8.

Suddendorf, T. and Corballis, M. C. (1997). Mental time travel and the evolution of the human mind. *Genetic, Social, and General Psychology Monographs*, **123**, 133–67.

Susman, R. L. (1987). Pygmy chimpanzees and common chimpanzees. In *The evolution of human behavior*, (ed. W. G. Kinzey), pp. 72–86. State University of New York Press, Albany, New York.

Susman, R. L. (1988). Hand of *Paranthropus robustus* from Member 1, Swartkrans: fossil evidence for tool behavior. *Science*, **240**, 781–4.

Swisher, C. C., III, Curtis, G. H., Jacob, A. C., Getty, A. G., Suprojo, A., and Widiasmoro. (1994). Age of the earliest known hominids in Java, Indonesia. *Science*, **263**, 1118–21.

Swisher, C. C., III, Rink, W. J., Anton, H. P., Schwarcz, H. P., Curtis, G. H., Suprijo, A., *et al.* (1996). Latest *Homo erectus* of Java: potential contemporaneity with *Homo sapiens* in Southeast Asia. *Science*, **274**, 1870–4.

Szalay, F. S. and Delson, E. (1979). *Evolutionary history of the primates*. Academic Press, New York.

Tattersall, I. (1997). Out of Africa again ... and again? *Scientific American*, April, pp. 60–7.

Thieme, H. (1997). Lower Palaeolithic hunting spears from Germany. *Nature*, **385**, 807–10.

Tishkoff, S. A., Dietzsche, E., Speed, W., Pakstis, A. J., Kidd, J. R., Cheung, K., *et al.* (1996). Global patterns of linkage disequilibrium at the CD4 locus and modern human origins. *Science*, **271**, 1380–7.

Tobias, P. V. (1987). The brain of *Homo habilis*: a new level of organization in cerebral evolution. *Journal of Human Evolution*, **16**, 741–61.

Tooby, J. and Cosmides, L. (1989). Evolutionary psychology and the generation of culture, part 1. Theoretical considerations. *Ethology and Sociobiology*, **10**, 29–49.

Tooby, J. and Cosmides, L. (1992). The psychological foundations of culture. In *The adapted mind*, (ed. J. H. Barkow, L. Cosmides, and J. Tooby), pp. 19–136. Oxford University Press, New York.

Toth, N. (1985). Archeological evidence for preferential right-handedness in the lower and middle Pleistocene, and its possible implications. *Journal of Human Evolution*, **14**, 607–14.

Toth, N., Schick, K. D., Savage-Rumbaugh, S., Sevcik, R. A., and Rumbaugh, D. M. (1993). Pan the toolmaker: investigations into stone tool-making and tool-using capabilities of a bonobo (*Pan paniscus*). *Journal of Archeological Science*, **20**, 81–91.

Waddell, P. J. and Penny, D. (1996). Evolutionary trees of apes and humans from DNA sequences. In *Handbook of human symbolic evolution*, (ed. A. Lock and C. R. Peters), pp. 53–73. Oxford University Press.

Walker, A. and Leakey, R. E. (eds.) (1993). *The Nariokotome Homo erectus skeleton*. Harvard University Press, Cambridge, MA.

Ward, R. and Stringer, C. (1997). A molecular handle on the Neanderthals. *Nature*, **388**, 225–6.

White, R. (1989). Visual thinking in the ice age. *Scientific American*, January, pp. 74–81.

White, T. D., Suwa, G., and Asfaw, B. (1994). *Australopithecus ramidus*, a new species of early hominid from Aramis, Ethiopia. *Nature*, **371**, 306–12.

White, T. D., Suwa, G., and Asfaw, B. (1995). Corrigendum to '*Australopithecus ramidus*, a new species of hominid from Aramis, Ethiopia.' *Nature*, **375**, 88.

Wilkins, W. K., and Wakefield, J. (1995). Brain evolution and neurolinguistic preconditions. *Behavioral and Brain Sciences*, **18**, 161–226.

Wolpoff, M. H. (1989). Multiregional evolution: the fossil alternative to Eden. In *The human revolution: behavioural and biological perspectives on the origins of modern humans* (ed. P. Mellars and C. Stringer), pp. 62–108. University of Edinburgh Press.

Wood, B. (1992). Origin and evolution of the genus *Homo*. *Nature*, **355**, 783–90.

Wood, B. (1994). The oldest hominid yet. *Nature*, **371**, 280–1.

Wood, B. (1997). The oldest whodunit in the world. *Nature*, **385**, 292–3.

Wright, R. V. S. (1972). Imitative learning of a flaked-tool technology: the case of an orang-utan. *Mankind*, **8**, 296–306.

Wynn, T. and McGrew, W. C. (1989). An ape's view of the Oldowan. *Man*, **24**, 383–98.

Yamazaki, N. (1985). Primate bipedal walking: computer simulation. In *Primate morphophysiology, locomotor analyses, and human bipedalism*, (ed. S. Kondo), pp. 105–130. University of Tokyo Press.

Yellen, J. E., Brooks, A. S., Cornelissen, E., Mehlman, M. J., and Stewart, K. (1995). A Middle Stone Age worked bone industry from Katanda, Upper Semliki Valley, Zaire. *Science*, **268**, 553–6.

4

Human cognitive evolution

Richard W. Byrne

Introduction

Until recently most attempts to imagine the minds of our remote ancestors have begun with the archaeological and geological record of hominids—extinct creatures which are more closely related to modern humans than to any other living animal. Certain problems are inevitable with this approach. As with most groups of land animal, the fossil record of hominids is extremely limited. This difficulty is sometimes presented as if it were a special, and therefore perhaps temporary, setback for hominid reconstruction; in reality, the fossil record of hominids is probably as good as can be expected for any taxon of species close to the top of the food-chain and thus having low population density. As a result, new fossils often cause not just minor revisions but radical re-thinking, and it would be naive to hope for any sudden and final enlightenment. In addition, behaviour leaves few traces, compared with the many teeth and skulls that can be found in rock deposits. An exception is tools, objects for which the function is related to the form, but of the various materials that can be used for tools, only stone is highly durable. The consequent abundance of stone tools—even compared to teeth and skulls—has channelled theories of mental evolution firmly towards tool manufacture. It comes as no surprise, then, that the origin of human mentality was long thought to lie chiefly in the challenge of tool making: "when the immediate forerunners of man acquired the ability to walk upright habitually, their hands became free to make and manipulate tools—activities that were in the first place dependent on adequate powers of mental and bodily coordination, but which in turn perhaps increased these powers" (Oakley 1949, p. 1). This would lead to a prediction that tool sophistication and brain enlargement should go hand in hand, but testing this is impeded by the problems of dating tools and skulls relative to each other. Worse, often stone tools cannot be attributed to any particular hominid—either because no tools were preserved in the same deposits as fossils, or because more than one candidate tool-maker is evident in fossils. The classic assumption that 'the biggest brained must be the tool-maker' is obviously suspect.

Nevertheless, in the absence of positive evidence against the tool-maker hypothesis, and with the prominence of technology in modern human cultures, it was customary to accept something like Oakley's proposal—giving a special role to bipedalism (a defining characteristic of hominids) and to tool-use. Other animals, even primates, being on the whole neither bipedal nor tool-users, were not thought relevant to theories of human mental evolution. (It is true that some species show bipedalism, such as penguins and kangaroos, and some use tools, such as sea otters, Galapagos woodpecker finches, and chimpanzees, but evolution can readily account for a scatter of convergences as a result of parallel selection pressures in unrelated groups.) If anything, debate focused more on whether stone tools, which go back over 1.5 million years, were closely relevant to the evolution of the modern mind, or whether instead the more recent development of language was responsible for all interesting cognitive skills. In any case, it was assumed that cognition was a recent and uniquely human (hominid) development. Two discoveries have challenged this belief.

Firstly, the advent of molecular taxonomy has shown that humans are much more closely related to African great apes (Sarich and Wilson 1967), and in particular the two species of chimpanzee (Waddell and Penny 1996), than to other primates. Hominids were formerly considered to have separated from the great apes (then called *Pongidae*) before the apes diverged into orang-utan, gorilla and chimpanzee lines perhaps 30 million years ago. Now, we realize that 'Pongids' are simply the hairier part of a single taxon of great apes that includes humans; put at its most striking, for a chimpanzee a man is a closer relative than a gorilla. This evidently leaves less time for hominid ancestry, and indeed 5 million years is considered a better estimate for our last shared ancestor with the chimpanzee. If all the mental 'distance' which separates modern human cognition from the animal mind must be compressed into 5 million years of evolution, then a very rapid transformation must have occurred.

On the other hand, such a rapid transformation might not be needed. Recent studies of non-human primates and other species have questioned the dogma that mental faculties are similar in different species—a dogma that is partly a legacy of behaviourism and partly due to a failure to differentiate 'species intelligence' under laboratory conditions (Warren 1973). The new data mainly come from animals living under social conditions, often in the field. Before the surge of field studies in the 1950s and 1960s, there was little appreciation among researchers of the degree of sociality and scope for social complexity within the primates. There were anecdotal accounts of manipulative behaviour by pets, especially monkeys and apes, but in general it was assumed that humans were alone in using their mind and intelligence extensively for the business of social competition. Once observational studies in the wild and in naturalistic colonies began, however, it was found that non-human primates often rely on the support of other individuals in gaining rank (Kawai 1958; Sade 1967), and sometimes use decidedly subtle social tactics—such as 'protected threat' (Kummer 1967), reciprocation of help in contests (Packer 1977), reconciliation after disputes (de Waal and van Roosmalen 1979), and even deception (Goodall 1971). Also, the non-social skills of monkeys and apes began to be better understood. Following Goodall's pioneering work (Goodall 1963), it was not safe to use Franklin's phrase 'Man the Tool-maker' without a mention that chimpanzees *make* tools, also. In captivity, in fact, all species of great ape prove able to make tools to solve problems (McGrew 1989); note the contrast with tool use in the rest of the animal kingdom, which does not involve manufacture, and whose distribution is not clustered in a group of close relatives descended from a single common ancestor (Beck 1980). Researchers observing monkeys and apes in the moist tropical forests they mostly inhabit also pointed to another cognitive challenge that their subjects seemed well able to deal with—complexity of cognitive map. Tropical forest trees often fruit on non-annual cycles, out of synchrony with each other, and are distributed sparsely and patchily; remembering where trees of each important species grow is a major feat of memory (Mackinnon 1978; Milton 1981). Unless primates have 'specialized' neural structures for spatial memory (as do various bird species), their general cognitive ability must be great to cope with this challenge. In various ways, then, it would seem that apes and even monkeys (separated from humans by over 30 million years of independent evolution) show signs of what is called 'intelligence' in common usage. These signs include a good memory, both for the foibles and histories of social companions and for the confusing and time-varying distribution of fruit sources, and the ability to gain ends by employing subtle social tactics or by constructing novel objects to some pattern. Perhaps the mental substrate that underlies intelligence is a primate specialization, in the same way that speed is a specialization of cheetahs and antelopes, or insulation from cold a specialization of whales.

In this chapter I will examine the current evidence of intellectual skills in non-human primates for what their distribution across species shows about the evolutionary history of cognition. At the same time I will consider the theories of how this historical trajectory came about. In the environment of human ancestors, which selection pressures is intelligence an adaptation to? I shall argue that the evidence indicates that several different selection pressures were crucial at different points in early human ancestry, so that the modern mind passed through successive stages, with later changes building upon past adaptations.

Deducing ancestral species

The basic procedure I shall employ is called the comparative method. It begins with (and is therefore crucially dependent on) an evolutionary, or phylogenetic, taxonomy —one which reflects the path of evolution. In such a system, each group of species shared a single common ancestor that is unique to them. Groups of this kind are called *clades*, and discovering a clade is tantamount to predicting the existence of a particular extinct species. In the classification systems traditionally used in zoology, not all groups are clades. For instance, 'great-apes-but-not-humans' do not form a clade, because any ancestor of chimpanzee, orang-utan and gorilla is also an ancestor of humans; nevertheless this group was treated as a unit, named the *Pongidae* (and for some purposes, such as zoo housing, these species do indeed form a useful grouping). But the many similarities among the non-human great apes are *primitive* features, characteristics retained from pre-hominoid ancestry, such as body hair, flat noses, and small brains. Only *derived* features (i.e., ones novel to each clade) are properly used to construct a phylogenetic taxonomy. Nowadays, clade construction (cladistics) is usually done using patterns of molecular similarity, but the principles are the same—a set of shared, derived characters must be identified to define a clade. Once a firm cladistic taxonomy is available, then the property of 'predicting extinct species' comes into its own. Each clade 'predicts' a particular ancestor, and with molecular dating, the approximate time at which each predicted species lived can also be gauged. If all the clade members share a characteristic (whether derived or primitive), then it is a fairly safe bet that the ancestor did also. Thus the distribution patterns of modern characteristics—even behavioural ones—can be used to deduce the attributes of extinct forms, *even if the fossils of these species are never found*.

It cannot be stressed enough that this approach is *not* a matter of attempting to identify extant 'models' of ancestral stages. In certain cases, the set of features worked out to apply to a (deduced) human ancestor might enable identification of descendants which—as it happens—seem to have changed little, but such 'living fossils' cannot often be expected. More usually, the search for models leads to error—modern species, which have themselves changed greatly since they shared a common ancestor with us, are confusingly—libellously—hailed as 'ancestors.' This risks falsely attributing derived characters of modern primate species to our own ancestry. Instead, the logic of the comparative method is not unlike using a family tree to trace the origin of some distinctive characteristic, not shared with most people, like inherited haemophilia. Even without direct knowledge of the trait's distribution among the deceased, its current dispersion among living relatives can be used to trace back to the unique ancestor of all of them, from whom the trait must first have entered the family.

But the comparative method is limited by the range of modern species available for comparison. Little can be discovered of the ancestry of highly singular species with few close relatives, like the aardvark, whereas for antelopes many species diverge from each other in quite a short period of evolution, and descendants of most of these lines still survive. For humans, the situation is intermediate—we have relatives that branched from our lineage at about six million years (two species of chimpanzee), eight million years (two species of gorilla), 16 million years (the orang-utan), 30 million years (numerous Old World monkeys), 40 million years (New World monkeys), and 60 million years (the strepsirhine primates, like lemurs). The most frustrating 'gap' is of course the absence of other surviving hominids (aside from reports of orang pendek and yeti). At present we have quite good evidence for two phases of intellectual advance, at around 40 million years (with evidence from all monkeys and apes), and around 16 million years (with evidence from all great apes). Finer differentiation, in the period between 16 million years ago and the divergence of the hominid line, awaits more precise comparison among the living apes.

Machiavellian intelligence and the enlarged brain

There is now considerable evidence of sophisticated social skills among monkeys and apes, but this does not extend to the strepsirhine primates (lemurs and lorises), which appear similar in social sophistication to most other mammals. By contrast, monkeys and apes:

(1) use alliances and cooperation extensively, when directly competing for resources (Harcourt 1988);
(2) acquire dominance ranks on the basis of support given by others, particularly kin (Chapais 1992);

(3) show long lasting 'friendships' which predict the distribution of mutual help (Smuts 1983, 1985; Cheney *et al*. 1986);
(4) devote considerable time and effort to others, in Old World species principally via social grooming (Dunbar 1988), using this as a way of building up friendships with potentially useful individuals (Seyfarth and Cheney 1984);
(5) when friendships are perturbed by conflict, some species repair these relationships by targeted reconciliation after conflict (de Waal and van Roosmalen 1979; Cords 1997);
(6) show knowledge of the personal characteristics and affiliations of other members of the social group (Cheney and Seyfarth 1990); and
(7) use techniques of social manipulation, to gain personal ends while minimizing social disruption, including deception (Byrne and Whiten 1985, 1992; Whiten and Byrne 1988).

Although all these traits were first identified among Old World monkeys and apes, a steadily increasing number have subsequently been recorded in certain non-primate mammals. Zebras show decisive interventions by third-parties into dyadic conflicts (Schilder 1990); long-lasting alliances are seen in lions, cheetahs, mongooses, and coatis (Bygott *et al*. 1979; Russell 1983; Caro and Collins 1987; Waser *et al*. 1994)—occasionally these alliances certainly involve non-kin; wolves and hyaenas form more transient coalitions (Mech 1970; Zabel *et al*. 1992); dolphins and whales show both long-term friendships and temporary coalitions (Connor *et al*. 1992; Whitehead 1997). Reciprocal altruism, first identified among baboons (Noe 1992; Packer 1977), is now better documented among vampire bats than for any primate (Wilkinson 1984). Although deception has been little reported among wild mammals, under captive conditions pet dogs and cats readily learn tactics, usually for manipulating their owners (Byrne 1997). Some aspects still remain 'primate specialities,' such as informed choice of potential allies on the basis of individual characteristics (Harcourt 1992), and targeted reconciliation after conflict with certain long-term allies (de Waal 1992), but future research may challenge even these claims. Note that all these species are rather social ones, compared with a typical, solitary mammal.

In parallel with the growing realization of complexity in the social lives of monkeys, apes, and some other social groups of mammals, came suggestions that the social group might originally have stimulated the evolution of cognition (Chance and Mead 1953; Jolly 1966; Humphrey 1976; Byrne and Whiten 1988). In Humphrey's (strong) version, this would suggest that primate (and human) intelligence is an adaptation to social problem-solving, well suited to forward-planning in social interaction, but less suited to non-social domains. Other versions claim much less, but all are conveniently grouped under the title 'Machiavellian Intelligence,' a label inspired by de Waal's (1982) explicit comparison between chimpanzee social strategies and some of the advice offered four centuries earlier by Niccolo Machiavelli. Giving somewhat cynical recommendations to an aspiring prince, Machiavelli was prescient in his realization that an individual's success is often most effectively promoted by seemingly altruistic, honest, and pro-social behaviour: "(It) is useful, for example, to appear merciful, trustworthy, humane, blameless, religious—*and to be so*—yet to be in such measure prepared in mind that if you need to be not so, you can and do change to the contrary" (Machiavelli 1532/1979; my italics). 'Machiavellian Intelligence' seems an appropriate metaphor, when so many features of primate behaviour appear coopera-tive and helpful, yet evidently result from natural selection maximizing the inclusive fitness of certain individuals relative to others (Hamilton 1964). Compared with many of the challenges posed by the external environment, social complexity has the attractive feature of inherent positive feedback—since the competitors are con-specifics, any increase in intelligence will automatically spread in the population, thus raising the level of social sophistication needed to excel in future. Predator–prey interaction has a similarly dynamic character, and had already been invoked by Jerison (1973) to explain the steady increase, visible in the fossil record, of the brain size of carnivores and their ungulate prey.

Subsequently, much interest has centred on whether—as Humphrey supposed—the result of such a selection pressure would be *qualitatively* different from normal animal abilities, involving 'theory of mind' (Premack and Woodruff 1978), or simply a dramatic quantitative increase in memory and learning abilities. Evidence now favours the latter view. There is no systemic difference in group size or composition between monkeys and apes, so the Machiavellian Intelligence theory should apply equally to both taxa (indeed, several species of ape are less social than many monkeys). The evidence of theory of mind in non-human primates is largely observational, and as such it is disputed by some (Tomasello and Call 1994; Heyes 1998), but it is extensive for great apes (Byrne 1995; Russon *et al.* 1996). In contrast, there is at present no good evidence at all for theory of mind in monkeys. Something other than theory of mind underlies the shared social complexity of monkeys, apes, and the various other species mentioned above: The question is, what?

Complexity is not an automatic consequence of the number of individuals in a social group (a large but anonymous aggregation might be socially simple), but is rather a function of the range and subtlety of behaviour expressed by its members. The behavioural tendencies that give rise to complexity—grooming kin and powerful non-kin, supporting close associates, returning favours given, and so forth—appear likely to be strongly channelled genetically. Thus, each individual would not have to work out the tactics for itself. In species which show *one* of these tactics, although individuals differ in how much they use it, in most groups that have been studied the same general patterns have been observed. There appears no good reason why such behavioural traits should not evolve in any species that already has or can develop the cognitive capacity to execute them. No such trait could evolve, however, in any species in which individuals could not:

(1) distinguish conspecific group members as individuals and as kin;
(2) remember their relative ranks and past affiliations; and
(3) in some cases, remember even the personal histories of help given and received from various others.

Successful use of the tactics essentially demands good perception, discrimination, categorization, and memory, as well as attention to social attributes. Even for tactics of social manipulation which are idiosyncratic and evidently *learnt* by individuals, the main demand is for a good memory. Effective deception within a semi-permanent group of individuals, for instance, is bound to be frequency-dependent, and likely to be infrequent, accounting for the patchiness of its detection by primatologists; and precisely what tactics an individual learns will depend on its idiosyncratic experience. Yet the great majority of records of tactical deception, contributed by many experienced primatologists and spanning every taxon of monkeys and apes, could be explained solely as a result of learning from natural coincidences (Byrne and Whiten 1990, 1992; Byrne 1997). The only provisos were that individuals must first have a rich data-base of social knowledge and then be able to learn tactics over only a very few trials. This conclusion has been supported by the only study designed to elicit tactical deception under close observation, which found that a mangabey could learn to deceive a conspecific in only three trials (Coussi-Korbel 1994). Thus the key cognitive variable for tactical deception is simply an efficient memory for social characteristics, as is the case for more species-typical aspects of social complexity.

Social complexity is therefore likely to select for memory efficiency, including rapid learning of socially relevant information. In this selection process, the costs of increased memory efficiency trade off against the benefits of increased social sophistication: These costs are borne in brain development. Considerable brain capacity, in particular neocortical enlargement, seems to be necessary for the efficient memory needed to handle social complexity. This verdict has come from the use of brain size as a cognitive index. Attempts with laboratory tests to measure 'intelligence' of species directly were notably unsuccessful (Warren 1973; Macphail 1982). In contrast, brain weight (or for fossils, cranial capacity) is straightforward to measure and so is available for many species. These facts have led to its widespread use as an indication of cognitive capacity; unfortunately, none of the various indices derived from brain size is 'perfect' (Byrne 1996). *Absolute brain size* evidently tends to increase with body size (consider the impossibility of a mouse having a brain the size of a horse's), but not linearly (consider how large-brained a horse-sized mouse would appear). Brain size scales allometrically with body size, a power relationship with a slope of approximately 0.75. Because it seemed implausible that large animals should in general be more intelligent than small ones, theorists looked to brain enlargement in proportion to body size as an index of cognitive capacity. Various measures of *relative brain size* have been devised; these include the 'encephalization quotient', EQ (Jerison 1973), a species' actual brain size divided by that predicted by allometry for a mammal of its body size, and the 'comparative brain size', CBS (Clutton-Brock and Harvey 1980), which focuses on deviations from the allometric scaling line for a particular subgroup of mammals. However, this whole approach leads to odd implications. Two species, each with brains 50% greater than that predicted by allometric scaling, would be treated as cognitively equal (EQ = 1.5), even if one had a body weight of 5 g and the other a body weight of 500 g. Yet vastly different amounts of neural tissue are involved.

Also, deviations from the allometric scaling line may reflect selection on body size rather than brain size, yet using relative brain size as a measure implicitly treats body size as fixed. For instance, it is reliably found that frugivorous primates have relatively larger brains than folivorous ones (Clutton-Brock and Harvey 1980). This has been interpreted to support the theory that large brains are a consequence of selection for cognitive mapping skill, needed more by frugivores for remembering the seasonal location of fruit in a large range (Mackinnon 1978). The fruit-based diet of most monkeys and apes is patchy and ephemeral, so demanding of memory, but able to supply the energy needed to support energetically costly brain tissue (Milton 1981, 1988). But an alternative interpretation is that large *bodies* (and thus 'relatively small brains') may be a direct consequence of folivory, which requires a large gut and a proportionately large body to support it (Byrne 1994), and there is some evidence to favour the latter interpretation (Shea 1983; Deacon 1990). Rather than measuring computational power, relative brain size indexes the costs of brain tissue borne by a species. Brain tissue is metabolically expensive, using a significant part the energy supply of the whole body. Deviations from the allometric scaling line therefore give some estimate of the metabolic penalty borne by species with large brains, and the benefits accruing to species with relatively small brains. Depending on diet adaptations, these costs or benefits might be significant for species' brain evolution.

Clearly, to the extent that the brain is an 'on-board computer', body size is irrelevant to its power. However, to some extent the brain is more like a 'switchboard', dealing with the mundane neural traffic of input and output, traffic which inevitably increases with body size. Unfortunately, the two functions can only be separated in the imagination; in real brains they are intimately related. Various statistical methods of teasing out a brain's computational power have been proposed over the years, but none is entirely satisfactory; the most recent is *neocortex ratio*, the ratio between the size of the neocortex and the size the rest of the brain. At the simplest level, this takes the 'intellectual' part of the brain to be localized in the neocortex, which is naive. However, there is additional justification for the use of neocortex ratio in primates. Among primate species, variation in volume is much greater in the neocortex than in other brain areas; it thus appears that these other structures are more 'conservative', and neocortex ratio will measure recent selection for increases in brain size. It should be noted that neocortex ratio, like absolute brain size, is *not* independent of body size. In general, larger-bodied mammals have brains that are both larger, and more devoted to neocortex. Could it be, after all, that larger animals are simply more intelligent? While this might be so for a limited grouping, such as the primates, it is unlikely to apply to all brains; for example, the tiny brains of parrots appear capable of underwriting behaviour that is in many respects similar to that of apes (Pepperberg 1990).

Analyses with neocortex ratio have shown that, not only do socially complex mammals like monkeys, wolves, and dolphins have relatively large brains compared with solitary species of similar body size, but the precise degree of neocortical enlargement correlates with typical group size in both primates and chiropteran bats (Dunbar 1992; Barton and Dunbar 1997). No such relationship is found when neocortical enlargement is compared with simple correlates of environmental complexity, such as the size of the home range compared with that expected for a primate of given body weight. Group size is only an indirect estimate of the potential social complexity encountered by an individual, but in fact the frequency of deception observed in a primate taxon is also well predicted by neocortex size, after taking into account the time devoted to the study of each taxon (Byrne 1996), supporting the interpretation that brain enlargement is required for the efficient memory needed to manage complex social interactions. Additionally, this tight intercorrelation between social skill, group complexity and brain size gives strong support to the Machiavellian Intelligence hypothesis. The brain of a monkey or ape is strikingly larger than that of most similarly-sized mammals, including the prosimian primates, and several other taxa of highly social mammals also show relatively large brains; these facts are most likely to be a consequence of the intellectual challenges arising from permanent social living (Byrne 1995), including the consequent opportunities for enhanced learning (Caro and Hauser 1992; Russon 1997).

For human evolution, this takes the first step in the evolution of modern intelligence back to about 40 million years ago, when the highly social simian primates first arose. To judge from their modern descendants, these early primate/human ancestors showed a massive quantitative increase in memory efficiency and learning speed over their immediate ancestors—visible in pronounced brain enlargement, and put to use in subtle social tactics. This was most likely an evolutionary response to a need to deal with the sort of complexity that social circumstances create; the fact that other highly social mammals have large brains supports this conclusion. However, brain tissue is highly costly in metabolic terms. Only species with an energy-rich diet, or those able to show dietary flexibility to increase energy supply, are able to 'afford' large brains. This constraint is likely to limit the extent to which a species responds to a selection pressure that favours increased social complexity. It is not coincidental that the large-brained chiropteran bats, carnivores, pinnipeds and cetaceans have a high-energy diet, and the large-brained simian primates eat much more fruit than (small-brained) prosimian primates.

Representational intelligence

Assertions of representational, computational processes in primates have been made repeatedly in recent years. Although all such conclusions remain controversial, it is striking that they concern only one primate taxon, the great apes. In an eclectic range of studies, great apes have been found to engage in behaviour more subtle or more complex than that of any monkey, or to perform behaviour similar to that of monkeys but to acquire it in more powerful ways. Whereas monkeys routinely take account of third parties, chimpanzees have been described as using 'political' manoeuvres in playing one competitor off against another (de Waal 1982; Nishida 1983). Whereas monkeys of all taxa can learn subtle tactics of deception, only apes—of all four species—sometimes seem to understand the false beliefs involved (Byrne and Whiten 1991, 1992). Whereas monkeys learn rapidly in social circumstances, various apes have been considered to learn novel behaviour by imitation of others (for chimpanzees, see Tomasello *et al.* 1993; Custance *et al.* 1995; for orang-utans, see Russon and Galdikas 1993; Russon 1996; for gorillas, see Patterson and Linden 1981; Byrne and Byrne 1993). More striking still, occasional observations have been made suggesting deliberate instructional teaching by mother chimpanzees (Fouts *et al.* 1989; Boesch 1991). Interpopulation differences in chimpanzee behaviour are consistent with these signs of special mechanisms of social learning in great apes (Nishida 1986). Although many species of animal show persisting local traditions in their behaviour, chimpanzee tool usage goes well beyond this, and has been analysed as 'material culture' (McGrew

1992). The controversial nature of these claims is unsurprising, since they are used to argue that great apes possess a 'uniquely human' ability: to hold information in mind, in the absence of prompting by observable stimuli, about unobservable mental states —such as what other individuals think or know. Rightly, strong evidence is required of any such claim, and some would still dispute that any special explanation is needed for ape behaviour (Heyes *in press*; Tomasello and Call *in press*). Attempts with experiments to test directly for this ability in apes have been equivocal (Premack 1988; Povinelli and Eddy 1996). Caution is also urged by the fact that tactical deception in monkeys, although often superficially matching the forms of intentional deception in humans, can be convincingly explained as a consequence of rapid learning and a good social memory. Nevertheless, researchers are increasingly concluding that great apes possess an intellectual ability qualitatively different from that of monkeys (Parker *et al.* 1994; Byrne 1995; Russon *et al.* 1996).

In social circumstances this ability is described as mental state attribution, or theory of mind (Whiten and Perner 1991). However, the unusual capabilities of great apes do not appear particularly limited to social domains. This is clearest in the domain of tool-use. While monkeys under certain restricted circumstances can readily learn to use an object *as* a tool, they seem to have no concept of the essential properties an effective tool must possess; when their tool is removed, they do not select replacements on the basis of functional properties, nor do they seem to understand simple physical causality (Visalberghi and Trinca 1987; Visalberghi and Limongelli 1994; but see Hauser, 1997, for a contrary view). In contrast, tool-using chimpanzees select objects according to an appropriate pattern for the job in hand, even when this is done far from the site of need (Boesch and Boesch 1984), and where the tool is made by modification of natural materials this is sometimes done well in advance of use (Goodall 1986); chimpanzees also do show rudimentary understanding of physical causality (Limongelli *et al.* 1995). Some skills may be seen either as social or non-social. A young gorilla's developing ability to use a human as a 'social tool,' as a thing that can voluntarily provide help if properly requested, has been analysed as showing that gorillas can understand cause-and-effect and the nature of agency, rather than theory of mind (Gomez 1991). Even great apes' considerable achievements in social learning are not necessarily based on *social* comprehension. What is needed for imitation of novel behavioural routines is an ability to construct programmes of motor action by observation of a skilled model, and this might not need mental state attribution (Byrne 1993; Heyes 1993). However, it certainly does need an ability to comprehend (represent) the structured actions of others, in order to translate them into new motor programmes that the self can employ (Byrne and Russon 1998). The monkey/ape difference should therefore be described in terms of *mental representation*, rather than theory of mind. Great apes can apparently compute with mental representations of information, about physical or mental states, which are not physically present at the time, not yet in existence, or unobservable in principle (Byrne 1995).

This interpretation points to a second cognitive development in the ancestry of human mentality, crucial to the later establishment of language and other modern human abilities, occurring around 16 million years ago in the common ancestor of great apes and humans. Individuals of this species gained an ability to represent properties of the world, and to use these representations to compute future behaviour. Clearly, this is an essential precursor to the later development of language in the hominid line. The adaptations that enable mental representation and planning—'thinking,' in everyday terms—have perhaps arisen in no other animal group, although a case can be made for some parallel evolution in toothed whales (Byrne 1995).

The physical underpinning of this change is less clear. All the great apes possess brains absolutely larger than in any monkey, so mental representation might be an emergent property of sheer size (Gibson 1990); the possible cetacean convergence would support this interpretation. Or, an organizational change in information storage in the brain might have occurred—a 'software' adaptation—allowing the flexibility given by mental representation, instead of more rudimentary storage of unstructured associations (Byrne 1996); the lack of any systematic monkey/ape difference in neocortex ratio (Dunbar 1992) tends to point in this direction. What is certain is that the demands of living permanently in a large social group cannot explain such a difference. Great apes simply do not form systematically larger groups than monkeys: The Machiavellian Intelligence hypothesis is no explanation for the evolution in great apes alone of representational understanding.

Attention has therefore recently turned to challenges in the physical environment that might have applied with particular severity to ancestral great apes rather than monkeys. Several theories have been proposed, all centring on the large body size of apes relative to monkeys. Perhaps arboreal clambering, by large animals for whom a fall would be lethal, is best accomplished by advance planning, an engineering problem in which an ability to perceive the self as an object moving in space would be advantageous (Povinelli and Cant 1995). Thus locomotion could directly have selected for representational ability. This theory derived from studies of orang-utan's unusual mode of locomotion, rather deliberate 'four-handed' clambering through trees and vine tangles. Orang-utans' bulk causes the various supports to deform as they move, continually changing the problem that confronts them. Large size also indirectly puts a premium on efficient feeding, especially in direct competition with Old World monkeys, species able to digest a wider range of plant foods than great apes. Perhaps, then, the ability to process plant foods that are nutritious but difficult to separate from matrix or physical defences was selected in ancestral great apes (Byrne 1997). In extant mountain gorillas that confront this sort of problem, novel programmes of manual actions for handling hard-to-eat foods are acquired rapidly during development, and show complexity in structure and hierarchical organization (Byrne and Byrne 1991, 1993). A representational understanding of action would be of benefit here, both for remembering organized programmes of manual actions, and for understanding the actions of others and so learning from them. More narrowly, perhaps tool-use was advantageous to the ancestral ape population, for efficient extraction of certain embedded foods (Parker and Gibson 1977; Parker 1996). Only common chimpanzees and one orang-utan population show tool use now, but in captivity all great apes demonstrate the potential to be tool-users (McGrew 1989); possibly, more recent changes of diet in pygmy chimpanzees, gorillas and most orang-utans might have caused secondary loss of the trait. Finally, perhaps efficient food monopolization was enabled by a change to sleeping near food, involving the construction of arboreal platforms to give safety from predators (Fruth and Hohmann 1996; Byrne 1997). The 'nests' or 'beds' constructed by all extant great apes for sleeping and resting are often elaborate structures, and considering that they show skilful constructional behaviour and are made by all great apes their possible significance has been overlooked. At present, all these theories are speculative, and can be evaluated only by their relative plausibility, self-consistency, and partial match to the behaviour of modern great apes. It would be premature to attempt to decide among them, but it seems likely that physical challenges of some sort resulted in the evolution of mental representation capability among the great apes and ourselves.

Conclusions

On the interpretation developed here, the cognitive 'distance' between the abilities of modern humans and those of the last common ancestor shared with a living ape is considerably smaller than in other recent formulations (e.g. Corballis 1991; Donald 1991). In their accounts, the last common ancestor we share with a living ape—the ancestral pre-human stock—was a large-brained species, able to learn rapidly, with highly social tendencies and an ability to manage complex social relationships. These capacities are not, however, much different from those of many monkey species, and probably evolved much earlier, around 30–40 million years ago.

Between then and five million years ago, when human and chimpanzee lines diverged, great apes had evolved to be very different animals to monkeys, and this most likely extended to their cognition. The selective pressures to which our hominid ancestors were exposed would have very different effects on the cognition of monkeys and apes. Consider as an analogy, the parallel changes that occurred in locomotion. Monkeys are smallish, quadrupedal primates, at home in the larger branches of trees; great apes are heavy primates, adapted to hang beneath branches. Given this variation in body configuration, a move to savannah living creates a very different adaptive response in a monkey and an ape, as is shown in the fossil record of various (mostly *Therapithecus*) baboons and *Australopithecus* apes: The former simply became larger, more plantigrade quadrupeds, whereas the latter, from brachiating ancestral stock, developed striding bipedalism. Following the analysis of this chapter, the cognition of the last common ancestor stock *already* allowed mental representation of the cause-and-effect structure of the observable world, and of the mental states of other individuals. Given the dependence of human language on mutual representation of communicative intent (Grice 1957), I would suggest that only in species with ape-like cognition could language have possibly have evolved.

While we may never know precisely what combination of selection pressures was responsible for this dramatic human adaptation, exactly when it happened, or through what intermediate stages it passed, this interpretation would suggest that the cognitive underpinnings were already in place five million years ago. An appropriate 'test' of this hypothesis might be an attempt to instantiate language in a living great ape; and of course, this has repeatedly been tried already, for other reasons. The recent successes of at least one of these projects (Savage-Rumbaugh *et al.* 1993) are encouraging for the interpretation advanced here.

References

Barton, R. and Dunbar, R. I. M. (1997). Evolution of the social brain. In *Machiavellian intelligence II: Extensions and evaluations* (ed. A. Whiten and R. W. Byrne), pp. 240–63. Cambridge University Press.

Beck, B. B. (1980). *Animal tool behaviour*. Garland Press, New York.

Boesch, C. (1991). Teaching among wild chimpanzees. *Animal Behaviour*, **41**, 530–2.

Boesch, C. and Boesch, H. (1984). Mental maps in wild chimpanzees: an analysis of hammer transports for nut cracking. *Primates*, **25**, 160–70.

Bygott, J. D., Bertram, B. C. R., and Hanby, J. P. (1979). Male lions in large coalitions gain reproductive advantages. *Nature*, 282, 839–41.

Byrne, R. W. (1993). Hierarchical levels of imitation. *Behavioural and Brain Sciences*, **16**, 516–7.

Byrne, R. W. (1994). The evolution of intelligence. In *Behaviour and evolution*, (ed. P. J. B. Slater and T. R. Halliday), pp. 223–65. Cambridge University Press.

Byrne, R. W. (1995). The thinking ape: evolutionary origins of intelligence. Oxford University Press.

Byrne, R. W. (1996). Relating brain size to intelligence in primates. In *Modelling the early human mind* (ed. P. A. Mellars and K. R. Gibson), pp. 49–56. Macdonald Institute for Archaeological Research, Cambridge.

Byrne, R. W. (1997). What's the use of anecdotes? Attempts to distinguish psychological mechanisms in primate tactical deception. In *Anthropomorphism, anecdotes, and animals: the emperor's new clothes?* (ed. R. W. Mitchell, N. S. Thompson, and L. Miles), pp. 134–50. SUNY Press, New York.

Byrne, R. W. (1997). The technical intelligence hypothesis: an additional evolutionary stimulus to intelligence? In *Machiavellian intelligence II: Evaluations and extensions* (ed. A. Whiten and R. W. Byrne), pp. 289–311. Cambridge University Press, Cambridge.

Byrne, R. W. and Byrne, J. M. E. (1991). Hand preferences in the skilled gathering tasks of mountain gorillas (*Gorilla g. beringei*). *Cortex*, **27**, 521–46.

Byrne, R. W. and Byrne, J. M. E. (1993). Complex leaf-gathering skills of mountain gorillas (*Gorilla g. beringei*): variability and standardization. *American Journal of Primatology*, **31**, 241–61.

Byrne, R. W. and Russon, A. (1998). Learning by imitation: a hierarchical approach. *Behavioral and Brain Sciences* **21**, in press.

Byrne, R. W. and Whiten, A. (1985). Tactical deception of familiar individuals in baboons (*Papio ursinus*). *Animal Behaviour*, **33**, 669–73.

Byrne, R. W. and Whiten, A. (1988). *Machiavellian intelligence: social expertise and the evolution of intellect in monkeys, apes and humans*. Clarendon Press, Oxford.

Byrne, R. W. and Whiten, A. (1990). Tactical deception in primates: the 1990 data-base. *Primate Report*, **27**, 1–101.

Byrne, R. W. and Whiten, A. (1991). Computation and mind-reading in primate tactical deception. In *Natural theories of mind* (ed. A. Whiten), pp. 127–41. Blackwell, Oxford.

Byrne, R. W. and Whiten, A. W. (1992). Cognitive evolution in primates: evidence from tactical deception. *Man*, **27**, 609–27.

Caro, T. M. and Collins, D. A. (1987). Male cheetah social organization and territoriality. *Ethology*, **74**, 52–64.

Caro, T. M. and Hauser, M. D. (1992). Is there teaching in non-human animals? *Quarterly Review of Biology*, **67**, 151–74.

Chance, M. R. A. and Mead, A. P. (1953). Social behaviour and primate evolution. *Symposia of the Society of Experimental Biology*, **7**, 395–439.

Chapais, B. (1992). The role of alliances in social inheritance of rank among female primates. In *Coalitions and alliances in humans and other primates* (ed. A. H. Harcourt and F. B. M. de Waal), pp. 29–59. Oxford University Press.

Cheney, D. L. and Seyfarth, R. M. (1990). *How monkeys see the world: inside the mind of another species*. University of Chicago Press.

Cheney, D. L., Seyfarth, R. M., and Smuts, B. B. (1986). Social relationships and social cognition in nonhuman primates. *Science*, **234**, 1361–6.

Clutton-Brock, T. H. and Harvey, P. H. (1980). Primates, brains and ecology. *Journal of Zoology, London*, **190**, 309–23.

Connor, R. C., Smolker, R. A., and Richards, A. F. (1992). Dolphin alliances and coalitions. In *Coalitions and alliances in humans and other animals* (ed. A. H. Harcourt and F. B. M. de Waal), pp. 415–443. Oxford University Press.

Corballis, M. C. (1991). *The lopsided ape*. Oxford University Press, New York.

Cords, M. (1997). Friendships, alliances, reciprocity and repair. In *Machiavellian intelligence II: Extensions and evaluations* (ed. A. Whiten and R. W. Byrne), pp. 24–49. Cambridge University Press.

Coussi-Korbel, S. (1994). Learning to outwit a competitor in mangabeys *(Cercocebus t. torquatus)*. *Journal of Comparative Psychology*, **108**, 164–71.

Custance, D. M., Whiten, A., and Bard, K. A. (1995). Can young chimpanzees (*Pan troglodytes*) imitate arbitrary actions? Hayes and Hayes (1952) revisited. *Behaviour*, **132**, 11–12.

de Waal, F. B. M. (1982). *Chimpanzee politics*. Jonathan Cape, London.

de Waal, F. B. M. (1992). Coalitions as part of reciprocal relations in the Arnhem chimpanzee colony. In *Coalitions and alliances in humans and other animals* (ed. A. H. Harcourt and F. B. M. de Waal), pp. 233–257. Oxford University Press.

de Waal, F. B. M. and van Roosmalen, A. (1979). Reconciliation and consolation among chimpanzees. *Behavioral Ecology and Sociobiology*, **5**, 55–6.

Deacon, T. W. (1990). Fallacies of progression in theories of brain-size evolution. *International Journal of Primatology*, **11**, 193–236.

Donald, M. (1991). Origins of the human mind: three stages in the evolution of culture and cognition. Harvard University Press.

Dunbar, R. I. M. (1988). *Primate social systems*. Croom Helm, London.

Dunbar, R. I. M. (1992). Neocortex size as a constraint on group size in primates. *Journal of Human Evolution*, **20**, 469–93.

Fouts, R. S., Fouts, D. H., and Van Cantford, T. E. (1989). The infant Loulis learns signs from cross-fostered chimpanzees. In *Teaching sign language to chimpanzees* (ed. R. A. Gardner, B. T. Gardner, and T. E. Van Cantford), pp. 280–292. State University of New York Press, New York.

Fruth, B. and Hohmann, G. (1996). Nest building behavior in the great apes. In *Great ape societies* (ed. W. C. McGrew, L. F. Marchant, and T. Nishida), pp. 225–40. Cambridge University Press.

Gibson, K. R. (1990). New perspectives on instincts and intelligence: brain size and the emergence of hierarchical mental construction skills. In *'Language' and intelligence in monkeys and apes* (ed. S. T. Parker and K. R. Gibson), pp. 97–128. Cambridge University Press.

Gomez, J. C. (1991). Visual behaviour as a window for reading the mind of others in primates. In *Natural theories of mind* (ed. A. Whiten), pp.195–207. Blackwell, Oxford.

Goodall, J. (1963). Feeding behaviour of wild chimpanzees: a preliminary report. *Symposia of the Zoological Society of London*, **10**, 39–48.

Goodall, J. (1971). *In the shadow of man*. Collins, London.

Goodall, J. (1986). *The chimpanzees of Gombe: patterns of behavior*. Harvard University Press.

Grice, H. P. (1957). Meaning. *Philosophical Review*, **66**, 377–88.

Hamilton, W. D. (1964). The genetical theory of social behaviour. I & II. *Journal of Theoretical Biology*, **7**, 1–52.

Harcourt, A. (1988). Alliances in contests and social intelligence. In *Machiavellian intelligence: social expertise and the evolution of intellect in monkeys, apes and humans* (ed. R. W. Byrne and A. Whiten), pp. 132–52. Clarendon Press, Oxford.

Harcourt, A. (1992). Coalitions and alliances: are primates more complex than non-primates? In *Coalitions and alliances in humans and other animals* (ed. A. H. Harcourt and F. B. M. de Waal), pp. 445–71. Oxford University Press.

Hauser, M. D. (1997). Artifactual kinds and functional design features: what a primate understands without language. *Cognition*, **64**, 285–308.

Heyes, C. M. (1993). Imitation, culture and cognition. *Animal Behaviour*, **46**, 999–1010.

Heyes, C. M. (1998). Theory of mind in non-human primates. *Behavioral and Brain Sciences* **21**, 101–48.

Humphrey, N. K. (1976). The social function of intellect. In *Growing points in ethology* (ed. P. P. G. Bateson and R. A. Hinde), pp. 303–17. Cambridge University Press.

Jerison, H. J. (1973). *Evolution of the brain and intelligence*. Academic Press, New York.

Jolly, A. (1966). Lemur social behaviour and primate intelligence. *Science*, **153**, 501–6.

Kawai, M. (1958). On the system of social ranks in a natural group of Japanese monkeys. *Primates*, **1**, 11–48.

Kummer, H. (1967). Tripartite relations in hamadryas baboons. In *Social communication among primates* (ed. S. A. Altmann), pp. 63–71. University of Chicago Press.

Limongelli, L., Boysen, S. T., and Visalberghi, E. (1995). Comprehension of cause-effect relations in a tool-using task by chimpanzees (*Pan troglodytes*). *Journal of Comparative Psychology*, **109**, 18–26.

Machiavelli, N. (1532/1979). *The Prince*. Penguin Books, Harmondsworth, Middlesex.

Mackinnon, J. (1978). *The ape within us*. Collins, London.

Macphail, E. (1982). *Brain and intelligence in vertebrates*. Clarendon Press, Oxford.

McGrew, W. C. (1989). Why is ape tool use so confusing? In *Comparative socioecology: the behavioural ecology of humans and other mammals* (ed. V. Standen and R. A. Foley), pp. 457–72. Blackwell Scientific Publications, Oxford.

McGrew, W. C. (1992). *Chimpanzee material culture: implications for human evolution*. Cambridge University Press.

Mech, L. D. (1970). *The wolf*. Natural History Press, New York.

Milton, K. (1981). Distribution patterns of tropical plant foods as a stimulus to primate mental development. *American Anthropologist*, **83**, 534–48.

Milton, K. (1988). Foraging behaviour and the evolution of intellect in monkeys, apes and humans. In *Machiavellian intelligence: social expertise and the evolution of intellect in monkeys, apes and humans* (ed. R. W. Byrne and A. Whiten), pp. 285–305. Clarendon Press, Oxford.

Nishida, T. (1983). Alpha status and agonistic alliance in wild chimpanzees (*Pan troglodytes schweinfurthii*). *Primates*, **24**, 318–36.

Nishida, T. (1986). Local traditions and cultural transmission. In *Primate societies* (ed. B. B. Smuts, D. L. Cheney, R. M. Seyfarth, R. W. Wrangham, and T. T. Struhsaker), pp. 462–74. University of Chicago Press.

Noe, R. (1992). Alliance formation among male baboons: shopping for profitable partners. In *Coalitions and alliances in humans and other animals* (ed. A. H. Harcourt and F. B. de Waal), pp. 285–381. Oxford University Press.

Oakley, K. P. (1949). *Man the tool maker*. Trustees of the British Museum, London.

Packer, C. (1977). Reciprocal altruism in olive baboons. *Nature*, **265**, 441–3.

Parker, S. T. (1996). Apprenticeship in tool-mediated extractive foraging: the origins of imitation, teaching and self-awareness in great apes. In *Reaching into thought* (ed. A. Russon, K. Bard, and S. T. Parker) pp. 348–70. Cambridge University Press.

Parker, S. T. and Gibson, K. R. (1977). Object manipulation, tool use, and sensorimotor intelligence as feeding adaptations in early hominids. *Journal of Human Evolution*, **6**, 623–41.

Parker, S. T., Mitchell, R. W., and Boccia, M. L. (1994). Self-awareness in animals and humans: developmental perspectives. Cambridge University Press.

Patterson, F. and Linden, E. (1981). *The education of Koko*. Holt, Rinehart, and Linden, New York.

Pepperberg, I. (1990). Conceptual abilities of some non-primate species, with an emphasis on an African grey parrot. In *Language and intelligence in monkeys and apes* (ed. S. T. Parker and K. R. Gibson), pp. 469–507. Cambridge University Press.

Povinelli, D. J. and Cant, J. G. H. (1995). Arboreal clambering and the evolution of self-conception. *Quarterly Journal of Biology*, **70**, 393–421.

Povinelli, D. J. and Eddy, T. J. (1996). What young chimpanzees know about seeing. *Monographs of the Society for Research in Child Development*, **61**, (3), 1–189.

Premack, D. (1988). 'Does the chimpanzee have a theory of mind?' revisited. In *Machiavellian intelligence: social expertise and the evolution of intellect in monkeys, apes, and humans* (ed. R. W. Byrne and A. Whiten), pp. 160–79. Clarendon Press, Oxford.

Premack, D. and Woodruff, G. (1978). Does the chimpanzee have a theory of mind? *Behavioral and Brain Sciences*, **4**, 515–26.

Russell, J. K. (1983). Altruism in coati bands: nepotism or reciprocity? In *Social behaviour of female vertebrates* (ed. S. K. Wasser), pp. 263–90. Academic Press, New York.

Russon, A. E. (1996). Imitation in everyday use: matching and rehearsal in the spontaneous imitation of rehabilitant orang-utans (*Pongo pygmaeus*). In *Reaching into thought: the minds of the great apes* (ed. A. E. Russon, K. A. Bard, and S. T. Parker), pp. 152–76. Cambridge University Press.

Russon, A. E. (1997). Exploiting the expertise of others. In *Machiavellian intelligence II: Extensions and evaluations* (ed. A. Whiten and R. W. Byrne). Cambridge University Press.

Russon, A. E., Bard, K. A., and Parker, S. T. (Ed.). (1996). *Reaching into thought. The minds of the great apes*, pp. 174–206. Cambridge University Press, Cambridge.

Russon, A. E. and Galdikas, B. M. F. (1993). Imitation in free-ranging rehabilitant orang-utans. *Journal of Comparative Psychology*, **107**, 147–61.

Sade, D. S. (1967). Determinants of dominance in a group of free-ranging rhesus monkeys. In *Social communication among primates* (ed. S. Altmann), pp. 99–114. University of Chicago Press.

Sarich, V. and Wilson, A. (1967). Immunological time scale for hominid evolution. *Science*, **158**, 1200–3.

Savage-Rumbaugh, E. S., Murphy, J., Sevcik, R. A., Brakke, K. E., Williams, S. L., and Rumbaugh, D. M. (1993). Language comprehension in ape and child. *Monographs of the Society for Research in Child Development*, **58**, 1–252.

Schilder, M. B. H. (1990). Interventions in a herd of semi-captive plains zebra. *Behaviour*, **112**, 53–83.

Seyfarth, R. and Cheney, D. (1984). Grooming alliances and reciprocal altruism in vervet monkeys. *Nature*, **308**, 541–2.

Shea, B. T. (1983). Phyletic size change and brain/body allometry: a consideration based on the African pongids and other primates. *International Journal of Primatology*, **4**, 33–61.

Smuts, B. B. (1983). Special relationships between adult male and female olive baboons: selective advantages. In *Primate social relationships* (ed. R. A. Hinde), pp. 262–6. Blackwell, Oxford.

Smuts, B. B. (1985). *Sex and friendship in baboons*. Aldine Hawthorn, New York.

Tomasello, M. and Call, J. (1994). Social cognition of monkeys and apes. *Yearbook of Physical Anthropology*, **37**, 273–305.

Tomasello, M. and Call, J. (1997). *Primate cognition*. Oxford University Press, New York.

Tomasello, M., Savage-Rumbaugh, E. S., and Kruger, A. C. (1993). Imitative learning of actions on objects by children, chimpanzees, and enculturated chimpanzees. *Child Development*, **64**, 1688–705.

Visalberghi, E. and Limongelli, L. (1994). Lack of comprehension of cause-effect relationships in tool-using capuchin monkeys (*Cebus apella*). *Journal of Comparative Psychology*, **103**, 15–20.

Visalberghi, E. and Trinca, L. (1987). Tool use in capuchin monkeys: distinguishing between performing and understanding. *Primates*, **30**, 511–21.

Waddell, P. J. and Penny, D. (1996). Evolutionary trees of apes and humans from DNA sequences. In *Handbook of symbolic evolution* (ed. A. J. Lock and C. R. Peters), pp. 53–73. Clarendon Press, Oxford.

Warren, J. M. (1973). Learning in vertebrates. In *Comparative psychology: a modern survey* (ed. D. A. Dewsbury and D. A. Rethlingshafer), pp. 471–509. McGraw–Hill, New York.

Waser, P. M., Keane, B., Creel, S. R., Elliott, L. F., and Minchella, D. J. (1994). Possible male coalitions in a solitary mongoose. *Animal Behaviour*, **47**, 289–94.

Whitehead, N. (1997). Analysing animal social structure. *Animal Behaviour*, **53**, 1053–67.

Whiten, A. and Byrne, R. W. (1988). Tactical deception in primates. *Behavioral and Brain Sciences*, **11**, 233–73.

Whiten, A. and Perner, J. (1991). Fundamental issues in the multidisciplinary study of mind-reading. In *Natural theories of mind* (ed. A. Whiten), pp. 1–17. Blackwell, Oxford.

Wilkinson, G. S. (1984). Reciprocal food sharing in the vampire bat. *Nature*, **308**, 181–4.

Zabel, C. J., Glickman, S., Frank, L. G., Woodmansee, K. B., and Keppel, G. (1992). Coalition formation in a colony of prepubertal spotted hyaenas. In *Coalitions and alliances in humans and other animals* (ed. A. H. Harcourt and F. B. M. de Waal), pp. 113–35. Oxford University Press.

5

Predicting hominid intelligence from brain size

Michael J. Beran, Kathleen R. Gibson, and Duane M. Rumbaugh

Introduction

The cognitive capabilities of the extinct hominids have been debated since their fossil remains were first discovered. Research from the later part of this century, pointing to psychological as well as biological continuities between apes and humans, has increasingly challenged the idea of a discontinuity between humans and other species. In particular, the study of language (Rumbaugh 1977; Savage-Rumbaugh 1986; Savage-Rumbaugh et al. 1990), numerical competence (Rumbaugh et al. 1989; Boysen and Capaldi 1993; Beran et al. 1998), culture (McGrew 1992), hunting (Boesch and Boesch 1989), politics (de Waal 1982), tool use (McGrew 1993), mirror self-recognition (Povinelli et al. 1993), and theory of mind (Premack and Woodruff 1978) have provided evidence that the Great Apes share much more in common with humans than mere morphological similarity. The question remains whether the australopithecines (who first appeared more than 4 million years ago) and other extinct hominids were more intelligent than the great apes. Wynn (1981) has argued that the intelligence of Oldowan hominids was on a par with that of the modern pongids when intelligence is defined in terms of organizational ability. Specifically, he suggested that the crudity of Oldowan artefacts reflects an inability to organize space in the same way that modern humans can. He also argued that an increase in intelligence was not significant in hominid evolution until 1.6 million years ago, by which time hominids were capable of Piagetian functions characteristic of human children from approximately 7 to 12 years of age (Wynn 1979, 1981).

Intelligence has been associated with brain size and organization (Rumbaugh and Washburn 1994; Rumbaugh et al. 1996). Holloway and De LaCoste-Lareymondie (1982) stated that australopithecine fossils show human rather than pongid patterns of hemispheric asymmetry, suggesting a human pattern of cerebral organization early in human evolution. Observations of petalial asymmetry (greater protrusion of a cerebral lobe on one side relative to that on the other) in hominid and modern human endocasts show an identical pattern of left-occipital, right-frontal petalia, not present in the pongids. From this, Holloway and De LaCoste-Lareymondie speculated that human-like cognitive patterns evolved early in hominid evolution and were related to selection pressures for symbolic and visuospatial integration. They suggested that brain restructuring was an important early component in hominid evolution, despite the fact that the early hominids had brains that were clearly smaller than those of modern humans. Holloway (1996) has also argued that the site of the lunate sulcus was more posterior in australopithecines than in the great apes indicating enlargement of the parietal lobes in australopithecine brains. Blumenberg (1983) has also proposed that the brains of the australopithecines were organized in a more complex fashion than those of pongids. On the other hand, Falk (1985) has disputed Holloway's conclusions about the position of the australopithecine lunate sulcus. Falk considers that the sulcus is in the same position in the australopithecines as in the great apes. Falk (1980, 1983) and Tobias (1987) noted further that there were numerous changes in brain organization from the earlier hominids to *Homo habilis*. How these changes in brain morphology throughout hominid evolution affected intelligence has been a matter of speculation.

There has also been debate as to the intelligence of more recent hominids, such as the Neanderthal. Although Neanderthals had brains that were larger, on average, than those of modern humans, their brains were nevertheless smaller relative to body size than are modern human brains (Ruff *et al.* 1997). From this, Kappelman (1997) inferred that Neanderthals were less intelligent than modern humans, and supported his view by noting the simplicity of Neanderthal tools. Gibson (1996), however, suggested that Neanderthals were more intelligent than generally thought. Gibson *et al.* (1998, in preparation) extend this argument. They note that although Neanderthal tools were primitive by the standards of many later human cultures, they were nearly identical to tools made by early Homo sapiens and not demonstrably more crude than those made by some technologically unsophisticated modern populations. A major point of their argument is that measures of brain size in relation to body size have been found not to correlate with measures of ability to learn (and thus behave intelligently). They argue that previous work has shown that within the order Primates *absolute* brain size and body size correlate more highly with laboratory tests of learning and intelligence than does brain size relative to body size. Therefore, the large absolute brain size of Neanderthals implies greater intelligence than inferred by Kappelman (1997). Such findings on brain size, encephalization, body size, and intelligence provide an opportunity to consider how hominids would have performed on tests of complex learning given their brain and body sizes, and given the data now available on several taxa of non-human primates.

Investigations of the learning capabilities of non-human primates has pointed to the orderly progression of the evolution of brain size within the order Primates as being vitally important to cognitive capability (Rumbaugh *et al.* 1996; Rumbaugh 1997). There is a striking increase in the size of the brain as a whole and many of its regions, including the neocortex, basal ganglia, hippocampus, and cerebellum, as one moves from the most primitive primate forms, the Prosimians, to the New and Old World monkeys and the lesser apes, and finally to the great apes. It is also important to note that there are marked differences in brain size between the larger and smaller Old and New World monkeys. Along with these increases in size of the brain and many of its component parts come increases in the ability to organize information hierarchically (Gibson 1990; Byrne 1995), and increased performance on Piagetian tests of intelligence (Parker and Gibson 1979). There is also both a quantitative shift in the efficiency of cognitive functioning and a qualitative shift in learning (Rumbaugh and Pate 1984). The qualitative shift reflects an increased probability that the learning process will be relational and comprehensive, rather than simply the association of specific responses to specific stimuli (as in stimulus–response conditioning). Whereas the small-bodied, small-brained primates' learning is for the most part consistent with a stimulus–response model of learning, that of the larger-bodied, larger-brained primates becomes increasingly relational or mediational, suggestive of thought processes, albeit at a primitive level (Rumbaugh 1997).

The application of transfer index methodology and associated protocols (Rumbaugh 1970; Rumbaugh and Pate 1984) has objectively demonstrated this qualitative shift in learning. In transfer tests subjects have to achieve specific criteria of learning (e.g., a certain percentage of correct responses) as a prerequisite to the administration of test trials, from which the most important measures are obtained. On the transfer trials, the cue valences of the stimulus objects are reversed, so that the choice that previously netted food reward is now unrewarded. Operationally defined criteria of learning are established so that potentially confounding differences among species in complex learning and differential levels of readiness to attend to and learn a series of two-choice discrimination problems are minimized. Transfer skills are assessed in terms of transfer-of-learning proficiency relative to the amount of learning before transfer, rather than in terms of absolute levels of learning. This approach might be contrasted with earlier tests of transfer of learning that have used overtraining, in which animals were given additional trials beyond a criterion before being faced with a reversed discrimination (Bitterman 1979). Some researchers found this overtraining to result in greater transfer than in control animals not given overtraining, an effect known as the overtraining reversal effect, or ORE (Reid 1953; Siegel 1967; Mandler 1968). However, others have found the ORE to be elusive (Mackintosh 1962; Lukaszewska 1968). In general, over a wide range of studies, the ORE has failed to occur more often than not (Bitterman 1979).

Transfer index methodology, rather than overtraining a subject, aims to produce only low to moderate levels of learning before transfer tests. Two training levels are used, based on performance criteria of 67% and 84%, where the chance level of performance is 50%. Direction of transfer for a given species is assessed by examining the change in percentages of correct responses between two transfer tests. The first test is given after the 67% training criterion has been achieved on one discrimination, and the second after the 84% training criterion has been achieved on a different discrimination. An increase in the percentage of correct responses on transfer after the 84% criterion, over the percentage of correct responses on transfer following the 67% criterion, is referred to as positive transfer. A decrement in the percentage of correct responses after the 84% criterion, over the percentage of correct responses on transfer after the 67% criterion, is taken to indicate negative transfer (see Rumbaugh 1997 for more details on transfer index methodology). Positive transfer—that is the transfer of learning to advantage in new situations—is viewed as an indication of intelligence whereas negative transfer—the inability to use learning to other than a disadvantage—is taken to show a lack of intelligence. In a study with rhesus macaques using a battery of 18 psychological tasks Rumbaugh and Washburn (1994) reported that transfer of learning skills showed the highest item–total correlation, that is, no other learning measurement correlated more highly with overall achievement levels.

When testing was conducted on the transfer index with 12 primate species (a total of 116 subjects), a qualitative difference emerged between species. As the level of performance before transfer was increased, the Prosimians and smaller monkeys tended to perform more poorly (negative transfer), whereas additional learning in the great apes and the larger monkeys generally led to increased (positive) transfer abilities (Rumbaugh *et al.* 1996). This shift from negative to positive transfer implies a qualitative rather than a quantitative change in the nature of learning. Fig. 5.1 shows the transfer of learning for each of those species as reported by Rumbaugh *et al.* There were high rank–order correlations between brain size and transfer ability. The rank order of brain size was also found to correlate highly with 'extra brain volume' and 'extra neurons'. However, Jerison's (1985) 'encephalization coefficient' did not correlate significantly with transfer skills.

Humans show an even more profound shift in transfer ability than that seen in the apes and large monkeys (e.g. macaques). Humans perform very well on tests of

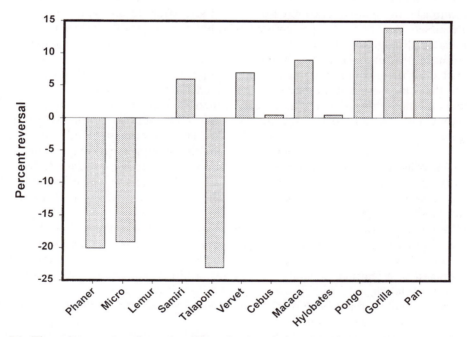

Fig. 5.1. The enhancement of transfer of learning in relation to brain complexity, based on 116 primates representing 12 taxa. The vertical axis defines change in percentage of responses correct on transfer-of-training test trials as a function of the pre-test criterion level of learning being increased from 67% to 84% choices correct. The higher the values, the more facile the transfer of learning. Species are rank-ordered according to brain complexity which is essentially a dimension of 'extra' brain and neurons. (See text and Rumbaugh 1997 for details.)

transfer. We will now consider how earlier hominids would have compared with the non-human primates on which comparative data, as defined above, are available.

We assume that with the evolution of large brains and large bodies in both the genus *Australopithecus* and the genus *Homo* the selective pressure toward increasing the ability to learn in a complex manner, to transfer whatever had been learned to a 'leveraged advantage', and to organize information hierarchically all became increasingly great. How did both bodies and brains become so large in the anthropoids and hominids?

We propose the following two-step model. The allometric relationship between brain and body sizes in the order Primates is very strong and positive—selection for a large body also leads to selection for a large brain. Large size is generally recognized as enhancing access to food and mates and as enhancing the probability of winning in fights. Thus, we propose (1) that *the basic selection was for body size*, and with that came a larger-brained primate. But selection for body size has its costs. Large bodies require more food, more of everything for sustenance. Large bodies can become advantageous only to a certain point, beyond which it can become difficult for the animal to move swiftly and in the highly coordinated patterns required for capturing prey, and so on. We therefore propose that there was a trend for primate taxa, including hominids, to be selected for large size only to that critical point. (2) Fortuitously, the consequent increase in brain size afforded an increased amount of brain tissue that could be pre-empted by whatever areas of the brain were most stimulated through experience. To the extent that the ability to learn complexly and to transfer learning served the interests of adaptation, the areas of the brain that provided for them could (and might) have incorporated and organized this extra brain tissue that otherwise had no specific role (Riesen 1982). At this point in evolution, let us assume that body size could no longer be increased to adaptive advantage because of attendant demands for agility, etc. With the constraint on further selection for largeness of body, the only way for this new-found brain-mass-based potential for intelligence (e.g. hierarchical organizational abilities, complex learning, and enhanced transfer skills) to develop further was by *enlargement of the brain relative to body size*. And enlargement of the brain might well have been both servant to and served by the emergence of an erect posture, which would provide for the balancing of a relatively heavy head on its top.

Observing that the various extinct hominid species differed markedly in both body size and brain size, let us now pursue an understanding of how cranial capacity and body size allow for estimates of extinct hominids' performance on the transfer index as a measure of learning capability. From this, a direct measure of their intelligence can be postulated.

Hominid evolution has been marked throughout by a significant increase in relative brain size, but a major expansion of absolute brain size is associated with the genus *Homo* (Foley and Lee 1991). Therefore, it is predicted that, although transfer skills will continue to increase in a linear fashion throughout the Hominidae, the most marked changes will occur with the appearance of *Homo*.

Table 5.1 presents the variables of interest for this analysis. Cranial capacities and body weights for 13 extant primate species are reported along with the variables for *Australopithecus afarensis*, *A. africanus*, *Paranthropus aethiopicus*, *P. boisei*, *P. robus-*

Table 5.1. *Cranial capacities and body weights for extant primates and for hominids*

Genus or species	Cranial capacity (cm³)	Body weight (g)
Microebus	2	60
Phaner	7	440
Lemur	23	1669
Samiri	24	914
Talapoin	39	1250
Vervet	63	3605
Cebus	76	2437
Macaca	83	4600
Hylobates (gibbon)	100	5442
Pan (chimpanzee)	393	45290
Pongo (orang-utan)	418	55000
Gorilla	465	114450
A. afarensis	433	44600
A. africanus	445	40800
A. aethiopicus	410	Unknown
P. boisei	487	48600
P. robustus	530	40200
H. rudolfensis	781	60000
H. habilis	612	51600
H. erectus/ergaster	988	63000
H. neanderthalensis	1520	71000
H. sapiens	1409	65000

Note: All values for extant primates (including humans) are from Martin (1990). Cranial capacities for the hominids and the body weight for *H. rudolfensis* are from Campbell and Loy (1996). Body weights for the hominids are from McHenry (1994), except the Neanderthal body weight, which is from Kappelman (1996).

tus, Homo habilis, H. rudolfensis, H. erectus, and H. neanderthalensis. The African equivalents of *H. erectus* are now generally referred to as *H. ergaster*, but for the purposes of this paper *H. erectus* and *H. ergaster* have been combined into the single designation *H. erectus*. The Spearman rank–order correlation between cranial capacity and transfer index score for the 12 extant (non-human) primates here represented is 0.83. The rank order correlation for body weight and transfer index score is 0.87, and cranial capacity and body weight measures are also highly correlated (0.97). Because cranial capacity correlated rather highly with the transfer index score for these primates, it was possible to determine a best-fit linear equation and then estimate hominid performance on the transfer index based on the cranial capacities for those hominids. The equation of the best-fit line is as follows:

$$\text{Transfer index score} = (0.05 \times \text{cranial capacity}) - 7.2 \qquad (5.1)$$

The regression equation was based on the numerical values of transfer index and cranial capacity, not on their ranks.

Figure 5.2 plots the estimated enhanced transfer of learning values for each extinct hominid species and for modern humans. The cranial capacities predict a continual, but not uniform, increase in transfer skills throughout hominid evolution. Predicted values for those species of the genus Australopithecus and the genus *Paranthropus* all

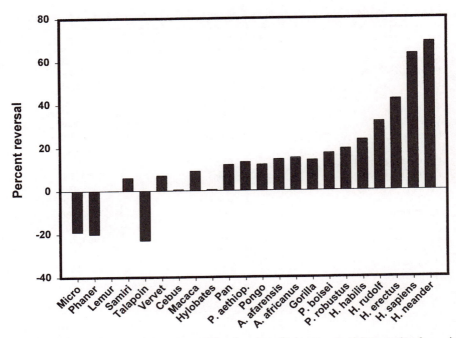

Fig. 5.2. The enhancement of transfer of learning in relation to cranial capacity for primate groups, presented in Fig. 5.1, and estimates of enhanced transfer of learning for nine extinct hominid species and *Homo sapiens*. The estimates are based on Equation 1 (see text). The estimated values for *Homo sapiens* and *H. neanderthalensis*, based on Equation 1, exceed a probable ceiling of about 40–50 percent change that can be obtained with the testing employed for extant primates here represented. Thus, the predicted values are relative, rather than absolute, estimates of the hominid and human species' transfer of learning abilities.

exceed those for the extant primates but are relatively close to the values for the great apes. The robust australopithecines do exhibit a slightly increased level of estimated transfer skill compared with the gracile forms of the genus, but the first relatively large change is for *Homo rudolfensis*. Although *Homo habilis* exhibits a greater estimated increase in transfer skills over the earlier hominids, the estimated performance is still well below that of *Homo rudolfensis*. There is a great increase in estimated transfer skill with the appearance of *Homo rudolfensis* and again with the appearance of *Homo erectus*. A third large increase occurs with the appearance of the Neanderthals and modern humans. In accordance with their large brain size, Neanderthals are estimated to perform as well as (if not better than) modern humans on tests of transfer.

What do these predicted enhanced transfer of learning values of the hominids tell us about the probable cognitive capacity of these species? These scores suggest that there was a progressive increase in the flexibility of learning. In the extant primates, the predicted enhanced transfer of learning values show that, with increases in cranial capacity learning becomes more relational, over-arching and rule-based. There is no reason to suppose that the same relationship did not hold during hominid evolution.

Hence, during that period, attention was becoming more controlled and focused. Small amounts of additional learning proved to be more valuable with the increases in cranial capacity, leading to advantages in exploiting the environment and controlling it. Therefore, it appears that hominids were continuing to exhibit a quantitative increase in cognitive capacity above and beyond that of the great apes. In particular, a clear increase in intelligence emerges with early *Homo*, and later species (*H. erectus* and *H. neanderthalensis*) probably come relatively close to the level of performance of current *Homo sapiens*—at least if we can judge from the fact that their cranial capacities began to approximate that of modern humans. Why, then, did *H. sapiens* proliferate while Neanderthals disappeared, despite their predicted ability to perform equally well on tests of transfer? Whatever the reason, we believe it wasn't a deficit of intelligence relative to that of early modern humans.

Acknowledgements

This research was supported by National Institutes of Health grant NICHD-06016 to the Language Research Center of Georgia State University. The authors would like to thank David A. Washburn, John Gulledge and Charles R. Menzel for their assistance with transfer index scores for the extant primates and cranial measures for extant primates and extinct hominids, and Andrew Whiten for his comments on an earlier draft of this chapter.

References

Beran, M. J., Rumbaugh, D. M., and Savage-Rumbaugh, E. S. (1998). Chimpanzee (*Pan troglodytes*) counting in a computerized testing paradigm. *The Psychological Record* **48**, 3–19.

Bitterman, M. E. (1976). Attention. In *Animal learning: survey and analysis* (ed. M. E. Bitterman, V. M. LoLordo, J. B. Overmier, and M. E. Rashotte), pp. 445–71. Plenum, New York.

Blumenberg, B. (1983). The evolution of the advanced hominid brain. *Current Anthropology*, **24**, 589–623.

Boesch, C. and Boesch, H. (1989). Hunting behavior of wild chimpanzees in the Tai National Park. *American Journal of Physical Anthropology*, **78**, 547–73.

Boysen, S. T. and Capaldi, E. J. (1993). *The development of numerical competence*. Erlbaum, Hillsdale, NJ.

Byrne, R. (1995). *The thinking ape*. Oxford University Press.

Campbell, B. G. and Loy, J. D. (1996). *Humankind emerging*. Harper–Collins, New York.

de Waal, F. B. M. (1982). *Chimpanzee politics*. Jonathan Cape, London.

Falk, D. (1980). Hominid brain evolution: the approach from Paleoneurology. *Yearbook of Physical Anthropology*, 23, 93–107.

Falk, D. (1983). Cerebral cortices of East African early hominids. *Science*, **221**, 1072–4.

Falk, D. (1985). Apples, oranges, and the lunate sulcus. *American Journal of Physical Anthropology*, **67**, 313–5.

Foley, R. A. and Lee, P. C. (1991). Ecology and energetics of encephalization in hominid evolution. *Philosophical Transactions of the Royal Society of London*, **334**, 223–32.

Gibson, K. R. (1990). New perspectives on instincts and intelligence: brain size and the emergence of hierarchical mental constructional skills. In *'Language' and intelligence in monkeys and apes: comparative developmental perspectives* (ed. S. T. Parker and K. R. Gibson), pp. 97–128. Cambridge University Press.

Gibson, K. R. (1996). The biocultural human brain, seasonal migrations, and the emergence of the upper Paleolithic. In *Modeling the early human mind* (ed. P. Mellars and K. R. Gibson), pp. 33–46. The McDonald Archaeological Institute, Cambridge.

Gibson, K. R., Rumbaugh, D. M., and Byrne, R. (1998). Brains: bigger is better. *American Journal of Physical Anthropology*, **29** (supplement), 9.

Gibson, K., Rumbaugh, D. M., and Byrne, R. (in preparation). Brains: bigger is better. To be published in *Modern human findings on human brain evolution* (ed. D. Falk and K. R. Gibson).

Holloway, R. (1996). Evolution of the human brain. In *Handbook of symbolic evolution* (ed. A. Lock and C. R. Peters), pp. 74–115. Oxford University Press.

Holloway, R. L. and De LaCoste-Lareymondie, M. C. (1982). Brain endocast asymmetry in pongids and hominids: some preliminary findings on the paleontology of cerebral dominance. *American Journal of Physical Anthropology*, **58**, 101–10.

Jerison, H. J. (1985). On the evolution of mind. In *Brain and mind* (ed. D. A. Oakley), pp.1–31. Methuen, London.

Kappelman, J. (1996). The evolution of body mass and relative body size in fossil hominids. *Journal of Human Evolution*, **30**, 243–76.

Kappelman, J. (1997). They might be giants. *Nature*, **387**, 126–27.

Lukaszewska, I. (1968). Some further failures to find the visual overlearning effect in rats. *Journal of Comparative and Physiological Psychology*, **65**, 359–61.

Mackintosh, N. J. (1962). The effects of overtraining on a reversal and a non-reversal shift. *Journal of Comparative and Physiological Psychology*, **55**, 555–9.

Mandler, J. M. (1968). Overtraining and the use of positive and negative stimuli in reversal and transfer. *Journal of Comparative and Physiological Psychology*, **66**, 110–5.

Martin, R. D. (1990). *Primate origins and evolution: a phylogenetic reconstruction*. Princeton University Press.

McGrew, W. C. (1992). *Chimpanzee material culture*. Cambridge University Press.

McGrew, W. C. (1993). The intelligent use of tools: twenty propositions. In *Tools, language, and cognition in human evolution* (ed. K. R. Gibson and T. Ingold), pp. 151–70. Cambridge University Press.

McHenry, H. M. (1994). Behavioral ecological implications of early hominid body size. *Journal of Human Evolution*, 27, 77–87.

Parker, S. T. and Gibson, K. R. (1979). A model of the evolution of language and intelligence in early hominids. *Behavioral and Brain Sciences*, **2**, 367–407.

Povinelli, D. J., Rulf, A. B., Landau, K., and Bierschwale, D. (1993). Self-recognition in chimpanzees (*Pan troglodytes*): distribution, ontogeny, and patterns of emergence. *Journal of Comparative Psychology*, **107**, 347–72.

Reid, L. S. (1953). The development of non-continuity behavior through continuity learning. *Journal of Experimental Psychology*, **2**, 107–12.

Riesen, A. H. (1982). Effects of environments on development in sensory systems. In *Contributions to sensory physiology* (ed. W. D. Neff) pp. 45–77. Academic Press, New York.

Ruff, C. B., Trinkaus, E., and Holliday, T. W. (1997). Body mass and encephalization in Pleistocene Homo. *Nature*, **387**, 173–6.

Rumbaugh, D. M. (1970). Learning skills of anthropoids. In *Primate behavior: developments in field and laboratory research* (ed. L. Rosenblum) pp. 1–70. Academic Press, New York.

Rumbaugh, D. M. (1977). *Language learning by a chimpanzee*. Academic Press, New York.

Rumbaugh, D. M. (1997). Competence, cortex, and primate models: a comparative primate perspective. In *Development of the prefrontal cortex: Evolution, neurobiology, and behavior* (ed. N. A. Krasnegor, G. R. Lyon, and P. S. Goldman-Rakic), pp. 117–39. Paul H. Brookes, Baltimore, MD.

Rumbaugh, D. M. and Pate, J. L. (1984). The evolution of cognition in primates: a comparative perspective. In *Animal Cognition* (ed. H. L. Roitblat, T. G. Bever, and H. S. Terrace), pp. 569–87). Erlbaum, Hillsdale, NJ.

Rumbaugh, D. M. and Washburn, D. A. (1994). Animal intelligence: primate. In *Encyclopedia of human intelligence* (ed. R. J. Sternberg), pp. 96–102. Macmillan, New York.

Rumbaugh, D. M., Hopkins, W. D., Washburn, D. A., and Savage-Rumbaugh, E. S. (1989). Lana chimpanzee learns to count to 'Numath': a summary of a videotaped experimental report. *The Psychological Record*, **39**, 459–70.

Rumbaugh, D. M., Savage-Rumbaugh, E. S., and Washburn, D. A. (1996). Toward a new outlook on primate learning and behavior: complex learning and emergent processes in comparative perspective. *Japanese Psychological Research*, **38**, 113–25.

Savage-Rumbaugh, E. S. (1986). *Ape language: from conditioned response to symbols*. Columbia University Press, New York.

Savage-Rumbaugh, E. S., Sevcik, R. A., Brakke, K. A., Rumbaugh, D. M., and Greenfield, P. M. (1990). Symbols: their communicative use, combination, and comprehension by bonobos (*Pan paniscus*). In *Advances in infancy research*, Vol. 6 (ed. C. Rovee-Collier and L. P. Lipsett), pp. 221–78. Ablex, Norwood, NJ.

Siegel, S. (1967). Overtraining and transfer processes. *Journal of Comparative and Physiological Psychology*, **64**, 471–7.

Tobias, P. V. (1987). The brain of *Homo habilis*: a new level of organization in cerebral evolution. *Journal of Human Evolution*, **16**, 741–61.

Wynn, T. (1979). The intelligence of later Acheulean hominids. *Man*, **14**, 371–91.

Wynn, T. (1981). The intelligence of Oldowan hominids. *Journal of Human Evolution*, **10**, 529–41.

6

Perception of personality traits and semantic learning in evolving hominids

James E. King, Duane M. Rumbaugh, and E. Sue Savage-Rumbaugh

Introduction

Anyone suffering from aspirations to indulge in evolutionarily-based speculations about faculties of the mind incurs large risks. Those risks would be greatly lessened if speculation were more expediently confined to overt behaviours, such as tool making, hunting, and cannibalism that often leave clear physical residue behind. The fundamental problem was expressed by George Gaylord Simpson (1964) in a scathing review of the then new science of exobiology, the study of presumed extraterrestrial life: "a curious development in view of the fact that this 'science' has yet to demonstrate that its subject matter exists" (p. 769).

The embarrassment of having no subject matter relating to mental evolution can be partly circumvented by performing detailed evolutionarily-oriented analyses of relevant mental faculties in humans, with particular emphasis on their possible fitness-enhancing properties and on how those properties related to and may have co-evolved with other adaptive capabilities. This strategy can be strengthened if similar mental faculties can be demonstrated in non-human primates. Of course, the warning that what is adaptive now might not have been adaptive in earlier evolutionary times, and vice versa, must be constantly borne in mind.

There are three main arguments that we will pursue in this chapter. First, human personality dimensions predict behaviour and other humans can accurately assess those dimensions based on that behaviour. Second, non-human primates also display personality dimensions that predict their behaviour. Human and probably non-human primates can also assess those personality dimensions based on behaviour. Finally we will tentatively suggest that the combined generalization and discrimination required to classify individual personality dimensions accurately within a complex, socially interacting group is similar to that in which the semantic meaning of a word or other linguistic symbol is inferred from experiencing that symbol in a variety of contexts, and indeed may have thereby contributed to the earliest emergence of the semantic dimension of language.

Personality in psychological science

The study of personality has traditionally been focused on humans, not animals, for reasons easy to understand from the history of personality research from the late 19th century through much of the 20th century. Conceptions of personality in the late 19th century were based on individual character (moral or otherwise) (Bain 1861), on self concepts (James 1890), and even on aspects of the soul (Myers 1903). The literature on personality was often a collection of case histories of people whose personalities were sagaciously interpreted by the author (Murphy 1949). A Freudian flavour relating personality traits to behaviour was increasingly evident in which, for example, it was assumed that projection predisposed people to paranoia and that repression in unwholesome quantities could lead to conversion hysteria (Sears 1948). The other main focus in early personality research was a social learning model (Miller and Dollard 1941) emphasizing the roles of society and culture in shaping personality that presumably led to distinctive personality expression in cultures such as those in Samoa (Mead 1928) and Japan (Benedict 1946). Thus, personality was viewed as either reflecting unconscious and Freudian dynamic processes or as a product of culture-specific learning. Either view would have placed personality well beyond the modest domain of the animal mind.

In addition, anyone considering the study of animal personality might have been charged with that old bugbear, anthropomorphism. The sin of anthropomorphism is usually committed by invoking human motives including intentional states to explain episodes of animal behaviour, particularly those displaying an endearing, human-like quality and seeming to show advanced cognition and possibly a theory of mind (see Premack 1988). However, attribution of long-lasting behavioural dispositions or personality traits from human psychology to non-humans would also probably qualify as anthropomorphism, something that many psychologists (e.g. Kennedy 1992) would view as more appropriate to Uncle Remus than to serious science. Therefore, it is not surprising that, until recently, personality had no role in animal behaviour research. We believe that part of the reluctance of animal behaviour researchers to incorporate personality constructs into their research might be because they were unaware of developments in the psychometric literature for rigorously testing the reliability and validity of latent variables, including personality factors (e.g. Wiggins 1973; Nunnally 1978). To apply these psychometric techniques to human personality while a priori proscribing their application to animals implies an assumption of a qualitative gap between human and non-human minds that has no biological justification.

An extensive literature does exist on animal temperament and personality based, not on subjective evaluation of personality traits, but on behaviour assumed to be related to temperament and personality. For example, Scott and Fuller (1965) described highly heritable differences among different breeds of dog. A similar set of temperament-related behaviours was observed in mice (Royce *et al.* 1973). Even octopus behaviour has been interpreted in terms of differences in temperament (Mather and Anderson 1993).

The lexical approach to personality

The study of personality, in common with most scientific disciplines, would benefit from a taxonomy or organized description of its subject matter. A useful basis for a personality taxonomy applicable to human and animal personality alike has been the natural language of personality description. Allport and Odbert (1936) identified a remarkable total of over 4000 words in the unabridged *Webster's New International Dictionary* referring to an individual's distinctive, consistent, long-lasting behavioural disposition. These words were the basis for the lexical approach to personality that soon emerged. Two obvious conclusions from the Allport and Odbert study having evolutionary implications were that humans have enormously differentiated personalities and that many of the vast number of possible nuances and subtleties of those personalities were important enough to warrant separate words. If the number of personality trait descriptors in human natural language is an indicator of human ability to make finely tuned personality discriminations, then we are all indeed acutely perceptive personality psychologists.

A large portion of human personality research in the 40 years after publication of the Allport and Odbert personality descriptor list was focused on simplifying the descriptors into a few dimensions or factors. After an inevitable period of confusion and disagreement (see John 1990; Digman 1996 for reviews) about the number and description of the factors, a consensus emerged that, as a first general approximation, most personality descriptors could be subsumed into five factors, usually described as the Big Five (Goldberg 1990). The ordering of the factors from I to V reflects, approximately, their importance in terms of the amount of variance in personality attribution that they explain.

The two most important factors, Surgency or Extroversion (Factor I) and Agreeableness (Factor II) are largely defined by interpersonal interactions. Therefore, overt behavioural expression related to the strength of these two factors should be more evident than that related to other factors that have less effect on social relationships and that are expressed more by personal subjective experience. Factor III, which has been labelled as Dependability or Conscientiousness, relates to behavioural self-control and persistence in pursuing goals. Emotional lability is incorporated in Factor IV which is usually designated Emotionality or Neuroticism. Finally Factor V, the least important of the Big Five, is centred on an individual's intellect, curiosity, and general openness to new experiences. It is now usually identified as Openness.

Biological foundations of personality factors

The validity of conclusions about the possible roles of these five factors in hominid evolution is dependent upon evidence that they are not just simple epiphenomena specific to our particular culture and language or on a particular behavioural context, but instead have a genetic and biological reality indicated by biological trait markers (Costa and McCrae 1992a; Zuckerman 1992). Phenotypic traits that contribute to evolutionary adaptation and are evolving in variable and uncertain social and physical environments typically have high heritabilities (Burger *et al.* 1989; Wilson 1994). Twin studies conducted mainly in the United States general population indicate that all five factors have heritabilities approaching 0.50 (Bouchard 1994), a fact consistent with the adaptive importance of personality traits during recent hominid evolution. However, these high heritabilities by themselves are necessary but not sufficient evidence for the biological reality for the specific five factors. They might simply reflect the more general fact that many personality descriptors have at least moderately high heritabilities, and therefore factor scores, which are simply linear combinations of intercorrelated descriptors, will also share the same moderately high heritabilities.

A further test of the biological reality of the Big Five is that they should show moderate but not necessarily perfect generality across both Western and non-Western cultures and languages. This prediction has been largely confirmed (see John 1990; Costa and McCrae 1992*a* for reviews) although a few minor discrepancies have been noted (Church and Katigbak 1989; Yang and Bond 1990; Narayanan *et al.* 1995).

The biological reality of personality factors would also be supported by evidence that precursors of those factors exist during infancy or early childhood in the form of temperament traits. Although the distinction between personality and temperament has always been somewhat blurred, temperament traits have traditionally been regarded as expressions of basic emotions, moods, social reactivity, and response speed that are highly heritable and present early in life. More differentiated personality traits presumably emerge from the fundamental temperament traits as an individual matures. Buss and Plomin's theory (1984) incorporates three temperament dimensions—emotionality, sociability, and activity. McCrae and Costa (1985), using a factor analysis of temperament and personality scales, showed that Buss and Plomin's activity and sociability temperament scales were related to Extroversion (Factor I) and their emotionality scale was related to Emotionality (Factor II).

If personality factors are adaptive strategies with long evolutionary histories we would expect to see evidence of their expressions in neurological and physiological functioning. There is some recent but limited support for this, at least with respect to Factors I and III (Extroversion and Dependability).

Behaviour at its most fundamental level is simply approach or avoidance elicited by some salient stimulus. The Extroversion factor with its facets of sociability, susceptibility to boredom, and attraction to sensation-seeking activity reflects a predisposition to approach new stimuli (MacDonald 1995). A possible mediator for Extroversion is the dopaminergic reward system (Newman 1987). Specifically, the affective state associated with dopaminergic rewards might contribute to the dominance–assertion behaviours and risk-taking associated with high levels of Extroversion, while the anhedonia and depression characterizing extremely low levels of Extroversion would reflect low operating levels of the dopaminergic reward system (MacDonald 1995). Furthermore, novelty seeking, a personality trait related to Extroversion and characterized by impulsivity, exploration, and extravagance, has recently been shown to be associated with polymorphism in the locus for the D4 dopamine receptor gene (Ebstein *et al.* 1996).

Dependability or Conscientiousness (Factor III) is related to the ability to delay gratification and to behave in a consistent, dependable way while paying attention and responding to important details. Expression of this factor might be mediated by sensitivity to anxiety, and predominance of behavioural inhibition that at extreme levels leads to obsessive–compulsive disorders (Gray 1987). A possible mediator of this effect is the prefrontal cortex (Mesulam 1986; Tucker and Derryberry 1992). The observations by Zametkin *et al.* (1993) of reduced metabolic rates in the left frontal lobes of hyperactive children are consistent with the interrelationship of Factor III with inhibition and frontal-lobe function.

Human behaviour and personality

The relationship between overt behaviour and personality factors is critical to the argument that personality and the perception of personality had a role in hominid evolution since it is unlikely that natural selection could greatly affect psychological processes with no reliable link to behaviour. Early attempts dating from the 1920s to predict behaviour from personality traits were largely unsuccessful (see Ross and Nisbett 1991 for a review). Scepticism about the association between behaviour and personality traits culminated in a widely-cited paper by Mischel (1968) strongly discounting the importance of personality traits for predicting behaviour. In the following decades, a vigorous argument, the person–situation debate, raged over the relative importance of constitutional personality traits versus situational or context-specific variables in directing behavioural expression. Accumulated evidence now indicates that long-lasting personality traits do exert significant behavioural influences, but against a background of sometimes strong situational effects (see Kendrick and Funder 1988 for a review of the person–situation debate). Personality traits are not mere artifacts of word meaning or sentence structure, nor are they the result of shared stereotypes or by-products of situational consistencies (Kendrick and Funder 1988). Personality factors are also not artifacts of our shared implicit personality theories about which traits should occur together in the same person (Borkenau 1992).

If personality expression and perception played a significant role in hominid evolutionary development, four fundamental properties should be demonstrable from human personality research. These are:

(1) Individual personality traits should have a permanence and stability across different contexts and should remain stable across time (see Costa and McCrae 1992b).
(2) The personality traits should be reliably related to a set of verbal and non-verbal behaviours, including postures and facial expressions.
(3) Other human observers should be able to use the observable behavioural expressions of personality traits to make accurate judgements about the type and magnitude of traits in target humans.
(4) Behaviourally signalled traits in target subjects that are accurately perceived by external observers should not be abstract concepts with little contribution to inclusive fitness, but should have direct relevance to social interactions in groups where problems involving competition, interdependence, coalitions, trust, and sexual selection are complex and subtle.

Recent evidence has provided some support for all four of the above properties. For practical reasons most human personality research has either been conducted in constrained, unnaturalistic laboratory settings on a single occasion with only a restricted range of behaviours measured, often on videotape, or else has been based on subjects' questionnaire responses. Despite these limitations, many studies have shown evidence of the consistency and durability of personality traits. However, they probably underestimate the size of effects that would be evident in long-term observations in naturalistic settings.

Small *et al.* (1983) showed that if a broad range of behavioural indices are taken in a naturalistic habitat, the relationship between rater-based personality traits and overt behaviours can be quite high. These investigators observed four groups of adolescents in wilderness-training programmes lasting from 23 to 30 days. Four categories of prosocial behaviour and eight categories of dominance behaviour involving a variety of acts were scored. The behaviours were highly consistent across situations for the duration of the programmes. Furthermore, across the four subject groups the mean correlation between peer ratings of the prosocial trait and overt prosocial behaviours was 0.73, while the corresponding correlation for dominance-related behaviours was 0.85. These correlations are strikingly higher than the corresponding values from more circumscribed laboratory-based studies where correlations rarely exceed 0.30 (see Ross and Nisbett 1991). Furthermore, they show that under naturalistic conditions, our first and second criteria for the evolutionary relevance of personality traits are supportable.

A fruitful way of conceptualizing the second and third criteria for the evolutionary relevance of personality traits is by means of the Brunswick Lens Model (Brunswick 1955, 1956). This model was originally proposed by Egon Brunswick as an ecologically-based model separating environmental perception into two components: One component defined the correspondence between stimuli and some actual characteristics of an animal's environment, and the other component defined a perceiver's use or interpretation of those stimuli or cues to make inferences about the environmental entity. Inaccurate perception could therefore result from an unreliable correspondence between the environmental entity and its associated cues as well as from an animal's invalid use of those cues. There has been recent interest in applying the model to personality perception (e.g. Borkenau and Lieber 1992, 1995; Gangestad *et al.* 1992; Funder and Sneed 1993) in which personality becomes the environmental entity.

Figure 6.1 shows the basic idea of the Lens Model adapted to personality perception. Two personality traits or latent variables, T1 and T2, are correlated with several behaviours, B1, B2, and B3 with T1 and B4, B5, and B6 with T2. The personality perceiver judges behaviours B2, B3, and B4 to be indicators of T1 by means of judgement J1, and behaviours B5 and B6 to be indicators of T2 by means of judgement J2. Two types of errors can occur. The first type occurs when a behaviour (e.g. B1) is correlated with a trait (viz. T1) but the perceiver fails to detect the association. The second type of error occurs when a perceiver assumes that a behaviour is associated with a trait (e.g. B4 with T1) but the behaviour is actually more strongly associated with another trait (B4 with T2). These two error categories are conceptually similar to misses and false alarms in signal-detection theory, which underscores the similarity between personality perception and detecting a signal in a noisy environment.

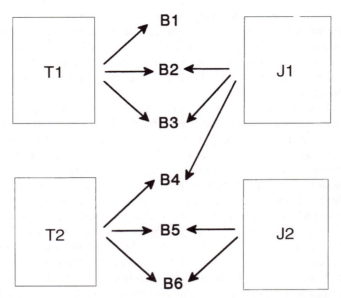

Fig. 6.1. Brunswickian Lens Model depiction of the relationship between latent variable personality traits (T), behaviours (B), and judgements (J) of the relationships between behaviors and traits. Adapted from Funder and Sneed (1993).

Overt behaviours are thus the lens through which personality traits are viewed with varying amounts of accuracy by the perceiver. Trait or T values for target subjects are estimated directly by self ratings or by ratings of well-informed acquaintances. Behaviours or B values are scored by independent subjects while viewing samples of the behaviour of target subjects. Finally the perceived diagnosticity of the behaviours (the links between J and B values) for the personality traits are estimated by a third group of subjects who judge how well each behaviour would predict different traits.

Experiments incorporating all or part of the Lens Model have, for practical reasons, used brief behaviour samples under laboratory conditions that were often video-taped. Considering the brief, restricted behaviour samples and the inevitable errors in successive stages of the Lens model, it is significant that impressive validities have sometimes been obtained.

A study by Funder and Sneed (1993) is a good example of how the Lens Model can be adapted to the components of personality perception. Measures of 62 overt behaviours and the Big Five were assessed by separate Q-sort procedures. After target subjects were video-taped in two-person interactions, the following information was obtained. First, target subjects were rated on each of the Big-Five personality dimensions by acquaintances and by strangers who viewed the subjects' video tapes. Both measures provided estimates of the personality scores (T_1 and T_2 in Fig. 6.1). Second, scores on 62 overt behaviours by the target subjects were scored by a separate group of behavioural coders who viewed the video tapes. These scores constituted the B values in Fig. 6.1 or the lens through which the independently assessed personality values could be assessed. Funder and Sneed assumed that these were the behavioural cues used by the strangers to assess the personalities of the target subjects. Finally, a third group of subjects rated each of the 62 behaviours on how well they were perceived as predicting each of the Big Five.

For each of the Big Five, two correlation vectors were calculated, one based on strangers' ratings and the other based on acquaintances' ratings, both showing correlations of the personality ratings with each of the 62 behaviours. Correlations for both types of vector were highest for the Extroversion dimension, moderately high for Agreeableness, Dependability, and Emotionality, but low and largely insignificant for Openness. The most important results were obtained by calculating the cross-correlations between each of the two correlation vectors and the independently calculated diagnosticity assessments of each behaviour for the personality traits (the third measure described in the preceding paragraph). The mean cross-correlations for the four personality factors excluding openness ranged from 0.54 to 0.93. Thus, the behavioural cues that people believe they use to rate a personality trait (the diagnosticity ratings) are in fact the cues that are used in judging personality from a behaviour sample. In other words, the perceived relevance of 62 behaviours for personality attribution actually predicted how strangers used these cues to make personality judgements that in turn were highly correlated with independent assessments of the subjects' personalities. Thus lay perceivers of personality were linking the J, B, and T values in Fig. 6.1 with surprisingly accuracy.

Borkenau and Lieber (1992) reported a similar study, also based on subjects' perceptions of the Big Five. The study was based on a sample of behaviour that was even more restricted than that in the Funder and Sneed study. Subjects were video-taped while entering a room, sitting down, and reading from a text. Behavioural measures were mainly physical attributes, facial expressions, and voices of the subjects. Borkenau and Lieber calculated three measures:

(1) the correlations between each of the behavioural attributes and subjects' self rating of their own personality traits;
(2) the correlation between each of the 45 behavioural measures and independent raters' inferences about how well the measures predicted different personality traits; and
(3) the cross correlations between the pairs of correlations vectors obtained from the preceding two measures.

The cross-correlations were highest for Extroversion (0.89), moderately high for Agreeableness (0.57), Dependability (0.76), and Emotionality (0.43) but non-significant for Openness.

We have described the two preceding experiments in some detail to make the argument that at least four of the Big Five personality dimensions are associated with a consistent set of behavioural expressions, and that lay perceivers not only can evaluate which of those behaviours are associated with each dimension but are also capable of discriminating among the different validities of the behavioural cues for predicting values on the dimension. In the aftermath of the person–situation debate some psychologists persist in the belief that personality traits are largely context-specific, linguistic phenomena, that they are not reliable predictors of behaviour, and that lay observers are poor judges of personality (e.g. Ross and Nisbett 1991). If this pessimistic view about personality were true, it is unlikely that personality could be a direct product of natural selection and speculation about the evolution of personality would share with exobiology the notoriety of being placed in George Gaylord Simpson's category of being a science without a subject matter. We believe that the above evidence shows this pessimism to be untenable. Specifically, the evidence indicates that personality traits are related to behaviours and that observers can use these behaviours to make accurate inferences about those traits. These are the second and third properties of personality, noted earlier, that are necessary to establish its evolutionary relevance.

The fourth property of human personality that was deemed necessary to show its evolutionary significance was its role in improving inclusive fitness, especially within a society of intelligent hominids with long-term, highly interactive relationships involving both cooperation and competition. Within the discipline of evolutionary psychology there has been considerable discussion about the evolutionary role of the Big Five (Hogan 1983; Buss 1996).

For example, Extroversion or Surgency has been linked to the ability to find and hold resources, and to the status or dominance that is important in regulating interactions within social groups. In addition to the obviously direct advantages of Surgency for resource accumulation, it also probably affects sexual selection. Buss (1989) showed that perceived aptitude for resource acquisition was valued more highly by females than by males across 37 different human cultures. The Agreeableness factor is predictive of an individual's suitability as a coalition partner and more generally predictive of whether an individual should be trusted or avoided. The persistence, conscientiousness, and self-discipline of individuals located high on the Dependability factor would predict the pay-off from an extended cooperative venture. The Emotionality factor predicts the adaptiveness of an individual's response to stressful, dangerous situations and might lead to preferences for stable individuals over those with more labile dispositions. Even the weakest of the Big Five, Openness, might have contributed to fitness through its effects on creative, novel, and intelligent solutions to problems. Finally, Buss (1992, 1996) has shown that manipulation tactics used by students in close human relationships (spouses, parents, close friends) could be related to independent assessments of all Big Five factors.

The striking fact about all of the Big Five is that their expression and detection have fitness consequences across the entire range of complex human interdependence. Interactions affected by the Big Five include such diverse social phenomena as coalitions, alliances, deception, sympathy, trust, justice, and even revenge.

Personality in non-human primates

In recent years lexical measurement of personality has been applied to non-human primate species (see Figueredo *et al.* 1995 for a review). In most of these studies human observers familiar with their primate subjects rated them on a five- or seven-point scale using adjectival personality descriptors. Usually between 20 and 30 adjectives were used. Typical findings were that inter-rater reliabilities were acceptably high and that the personality scores of individual animals remained stable over periods up to four years even when different human raters were employed over that interval (Stevenson-Hinde and Zunz 1978; Stevenson-Hinde *et al.* 1980; Figueredo *et al.* 1995).

Several animal studies have incorporated factor analysis of the personality ratings (e.g. Stevenson-Hinde and Zunz 1978; Bolig *et al.* 1992; Gold and Maple 1994). The most common outcome of the factor analysis has been the extraction of three factors, one of which is related to dominance, assertiveness, and sociability, all characteristics of the human Surgency factor. However, the factors emerging from a factor analysis are, of course, constrained by the items going into the factor analysis. Since personality descriptors representing both poles of the human Big Five were not included in the adjective lists used in these studies, it was not possible to make any conclusions about the generality of the Big Five to non-human primates.

King and Figueredo (1997) directly tested the applicability of the human five-factor model to a sample of 100 zoo chimpanzees. The chimpanzees were housed at 12 zoological parks participating in the ChimpanZoo program of the Jane Goodall Institute. The chimpanzees were rated by a mean of 4.05 raters who were either zoo employees who regularly worked in the chimpanzee enclosures or by ChimpanZoo volunteers who had extensive experience observing the chimpanzees as part of a separate behavioural project.

Raters at zoos scored the chimpanzees on 43 personality descriptive adjectives using a seven-point scale. Goldberg's (1990) taxonomy of adjective membership in the human Big Five was used to select the 43 adjectives. The adjectives were selected to insure approximately equal representation from both poles of each factor and to sample as many facets or subfactors within each of the five main factors as possible.

A principal-factor analysis with varimax rotation showed the presence of six factors accounting for 72.4% of the inter-item variance. Five of the six factors were clearly identifiable as being remarkably similar to the human Big Five. However, the factor explaining the most variance was obviously related to dominance but contained adjectives from each of the human Big Five. In contrast, human taxonomies of the Big Five place dominance as part of the Surgency dimension.

A sense of the content of the six chimpanzee factors can be seen by describing the individual traits of chimpanzees that would have high scores on particular factors. Thus, high-Dominance chimpanzees were dominant but not submissive, dependent, or fearful. High-Surgency chimpanzees were active, playful, and sociable, but not solitary or lazy. High-Agreeableness chimpanzees were helpful, sensitive, protective, and gentle. High-Dependability chimpanzees were predictable but not impulsive, reckless, or erratic. High-emotionality chimpanzees were excitable but not stable or unemotional. Finally, high-Openness chimpanzees were inventive and inquisitive.

Application of a general linear-model analysis to the chimpanzee personality data showed that neither the profile of scores across the 43 personality descriptors nor the profile across the six personality factors interacted significantly with zoos. In other words, the pattern of individual differences across personality descriptors and across factor scores were independent of zoo habitats despite the considerable differences in physical habitat and social groupings among the 12 zoos. This was important evidence that individual differences in personality expression of chimpanzees are at most only minimally affected by their social and physical surroundings. Instead, personality expression might be more an inherent characteristic of individual chimpanzees. This is indirect evidence that personality expression in hominids is relatively independent of context and might, therefore, have been subject to the forces of natural selection.

An additional oblique-rotation analysis did not affect the composition of the factors and showed that the mean absolute value of the 15 intercorrelations among the six factors was only 0.13 thereby showing good evidence of discriminant validity of the factors (Campbell and Fiske 1959). The correlation between Surgency and Dominance was only 0.04, thus confirming separate and independent status of the Dominance factor in chimpanzees.

Personality and behaviour in chimpanzees

A fundamental question about rated personality of non-human primates is whether the ratings predict specific overt behaviours consistent with the Lens Model. Evidence on this point for non-human primates is clearly far more limited than for humans. However Gaspar and King (1996), using a sample of only seven chimpanzees from the Lisbon Zoo, showed that the King and Figueredo personality traits could be used to predict overt behaviours. The study had four components. First, all chimpanzees were rated on a Portuguese version of the King and Figueredo scale and factor scores calculated. Second, after an interval of more than one year, behaviours from the ChimpanZoo ethogram (1991) were scored from video tapes. Each behaviour in this ethogram had two components, a social context and a specific behaviour. The main social contexts were *affinitive*, in which there was a general awareness and friendly responsiveness to other chimpanzees; *agonistic*, in which there was an aggressive response to other chimpanzees; *submissive*, in which there was a frightened withdrawal or appeasing gesture to another chimpanzee; *solitary*, in which the animal was psychologically isolated from other chimpanzees and the viewing public; and *public orientation*, in which the chimpanzee attended to or interacted directly with the general public. A total of 48 combinations of social contact and specific behaviour was scored.

The third component entailed construction of a behaviour-weighting matrix. Using adjectival personality descriptors with high loadings in the Dominance, Surgency, Agreeableness, and Emotionality factors as guides, the authors assigned each possible combination of behaviour and factor a weight of +1, −1, or zero depending upon whether occurrence of the behaviour was evidence consistent with the positive pole of the factor, the negative pole, or largely unrelated to the factor. Thus, for example, affinitive approach had a +1 weight for Surgency and Agreeableness and 0 weights for Emotionality and Dominance. Head-bobbing had a −1 weight for Dominance, a +1 weight for Emotionality, and 0 weights for Surgency and Agreeableness.

The fourth component involved cross-multiplication of the behaviour weights with the corresponding behaviour totals to produce a weighted behavioural score for each of the four factors. The correlation of these scores with the independently obtained questionnaire ratings of the personality traits was then a test of the chimpanzee personality Lens Model. The weighting matrix was the link between the J and B values while the behaviour scores were the link between the T and B values. Despite the small sample size afforded by only seven chimpanzees, the correlation for Surgency was significant; however, the others were not. Furthermore, individual behaviours that were most strongly correlated with personality scores showed a pattern consistent with the personality traits. For example, behaviours most strongly associated with Dominance were aggressive hunch and affiliative grab/pull; behaviours most strongly associated with Surgency were affiliative social play and embrace; behaviours most strongly associated with Agreeableness were affiliative embrace and touch; and behaviours most strongly associated with Emotionality were submissive avoidance, approach and head-bob.

In a more recent study (King, unpublished) multiple regressions were used to identify personality dimensions that significantly predicted the ChimpanZoo social contexts for 60 zoo chimpanzees. Dominance and Emotional Stability were positively related to aggressive context behaviours while Surgency and Openness were positively related to affinitive context behaviours.

Finally, in a wild habitat, Buirski and Plutchik (1991) reported a remarkable example of personality measurement predicting a spectacularly deviant behaviour by a Gombe chimpanzee in Tanzania after an interval of over two years. In 1973 these investigators scored a sample of Gombe chimpanzees on a version of Plutchik and Kellerman's (1974) emotions profile index adapted for chimpanzees. One chimpanzee, known as Passion, was scored as more aggressive, depressed, and distrustful but less timid, controlled and gregarious than other female chimpanzees. The authors' impression of Passion was that she was disturbed, isolated, and aggressive, with a profile of traits consistent with a human paranoid. About two years after these evaluations, warfare broke out between two communities within the Gombe chimpanzee population. During this time Passion was observed stealing three infants from their mothers and then killing and eating the infants. She might have been responsible for the deaths of up to seven infants during the two-year period of social upheaval.

Can non-human primates be personality psychologists?

We believe that the evidence described above gives reason for optimism about the scientific validity of personality and its correlation with behaviours that are relevant to inclusive fitness within a highly structured social group. However, in these studies it was the chimpanzees who had the personality traits and displayed the behaviours, but humans who judged the traits and scored the behaviours. For the Lens Model to give us fully convincing evidence of the evolutionary importance of personality factors, we should be able to show evidence that chimpanzees or other non-human primates can evaluate the behaviours and have the intelligence to attribute accurate personality traits to conspecifics. In other words, we should be able to demonstrate in non-human primates at least rudimentary abilities to form long-term personality-relevant social concepts about other conspecifics based on particular behaviours.

There are two necessary characteristics for personality perception in non-human primates. The first and conceptually simpler mechanism might be described as personality account-keeping, in which animal A uses its past encounters with animal B to guide future strategies involving B. This account-keeping is both simple and egocentric because all relevant experience directly involves behavioural interactions between the animal keeping the account and the animals whose personalities are being learned. The second mechanism occurs when animal A uses a history of past observed interactions between animals B and C to modify future responses toward B or C or possibly both B and C. In a more sophisticated version of this mechanism, A's responses toward D might be affected because A perceives a behavioural overlap between D and either B or C.

A few examples of social concepts in non-human primates having similarity to personality concept formation illustrate that the above mechanisms are widespread. De Waal and Luttrell (1988), in a methodologically sophisticated experiment, measured reciprocity of friendly and unfriendly behaviours in chimpanzees and two species of macaque monkeys. Reciprocal behaviours between two animals can only occur when both are present. If, hypothetically, all animals have a certain baseline level of friendly behaviour production independent of past experiences with other animals, then pairs of animals will show a positive correlation of friendly behaviours. However, the correlation does not imply reciprocity; rather, it might simply reflect that some animal pairs spend more time together than others. Those pairs spending much time together will have high reciprocity scores and those spending little time together will have low reciprocity scores. De Waal and Luttrell (1988), after controlling for the time pairs spent together and for matriline and sex combination, showed statistically significant positive or supportive reciprocity for the macaque monkeys and for the chimpanzees. However, only the chimpanzees showed reciprocity of negative interactions. One might speculate that the more intelligent chimpanzees displayed their superior psychological prowess by detecting Agreeableness and Dependability traits as well as Disagreeableness and Undependability traits in their conspecifics, while the macaques were capable of learning only about prosocial personality traits in their social companions.

Other reports of social learning consistent with the account-keeping model of personality include Seyfarth and Cheney's (1984) observation that vervet monkeys are particularly responsive to playbacks of vocalizations from previous grooming partners, an effect that might be viewed as a primitive expression of the generosity component of the Agreeableness factor. Cheney and Seyfarth (1988) also played alarm calls with no actual referent present, recorded from one vervet monkey of a troop. The other monkeys then ignored further alarm calls from that monkey with the same referent, e.g. an eagle, but they did respond to eagle calls from other monkeys. The other monkeys also responded when the previously unreliable monkey gave an alarm call indicating a new type of predator, such as a leopard. Thus, vervet monkeys would appear unable to conceptualize a fully developed Undependability personality factor, at least in the context of alarm calls.

A few examples of primate social constructs involving similarities between individuals might also be cited. Dasser (1988) trained two crab-eating macaque monkeys from a group of 40 monkeys to discriminate colour-slide pictures of mother–infant pairs from other monkey pairs. One monkey, after simultaneous discrimination training on one set of slides, correctly identified 14 out of 14 novel mother–infant pairs. Another monkey trained with a matching from sample technique correctly identified 20 out of 22 novel pairs. A variety of controls in the experimental design strengthened the author's conclusion that the mother–infant concepts were based on a history of affiliation. Although a mother–infant concept is not a personality concept, the cognitive demands of detecting a signal of highly affiliative mother–infant pairings within highly noisy, intensely interactive environments of 40 monkeys are at least as formidable as those of forming a simple personality construct based on behavioural overlap between monkeys. A complex mother–infant concept is also consistent with Cheney and Seyfarth's (1982) observation that infant distress calls will cause female vervet monkeys to look toward the mother of the calling infant.

There is considerable evidence that monkeys can use perceived dominance relationships between two or more other monkeys to form alliances (Bercovitch 1988; Datta 1992; Nok 1992). Furthermore Harcourt (1992), in a review of alliances in primates and non-primates, suggests that only primates form alliances based on future, not just immediate, support by alliance partners and that only primates form alliances within the context of a much larger cohesive group. Perceived competitive abilities, dominance status, and likelihood of reciprocity might well play a role in choosing alliance partners, perhaps based on primitive concepts that later evolved into Dominance, Surgency, and Agreeableness in early human societies.

Some final words about the earliest words

It has not escaped our notice that if symbols were attached to complex personality concepts they would have a striking similarity to linguistic concepts. The history of ape language research has clearly shown that learning to associate an arbitrary symbol with a single exemplar in one context is not sufficient for any meaningful language learning (see Savage-Rumbaugh *et al.* 1993; Rumbaugh and Savage-Rumbaugh 1994 for reviews). Instead, at the beginning level of individual symbol learning the meaning of the referent must be decontextualized. If, for example, a symbol is paired with a particular apple on a table, the meaning of the symbol is equivocal because the symbol could mean anything red, or round, or edible, or suitable for a paperweight. At the very least, the apple and its symbol must first be experienced in a variety of settings before a refined concept of apple is learned, by separating apple-like signal from apple-irrelevant noise. This has similarities to the process depicted in Fig. 6.1 for the Lens Model of personality. The process of linguistic decontextualization would be further enhanced by comprehending the symbol in a variety of sentence types.

The process of learning a refined version of a personality concept is similar to, and at least as complex as, that of learning the meaning of a symbol at the simplest single-word stage. Personality concepts such as dominance, trustworthiness, and reliability seem simple and obvious to us. But, in fact, within in a highly interactive group of intelligent primates they must be discerned out of a welter of hundreds or thousands of behaviour types, not the mere seven shown in our Fig. 6.1 Lens Model. Furthermore, instead of just the one context implied by Fig. 6.1, the number of possible social contexts in which personality concepts would be evident is immense. We believe that early hominids who had evolved aptitudes for personality trait discernment would have been well poised to begin rudimentary attempts at language.

We also believe that when those first words were spoken, a large portion of them were related to personality.

Robin Dunbar (1993, 1996) has proposed a theory about language origins emphasizing the socially cohesive effects of language, especially gossip about others. According to this theory, during early hominid evolution, group conversation, especially about others, replaced grooming as the main socially cohesive force in large-brained hominids who lived in large groups. The universal human fascination with gossip and the large portion of human conversation devoted to it was cited by Dunbar as evidence of its evolutionary underpinnings. If the early hominids spent large amounts of time around the metaphorical campfire listening to accounts of each other's exploits, treacheries, and kindnesses, those accounts would mainly concern past events. What possible fitness advantages could accrue to aficionados of gossip in these circumstances? After all, past misbehaviours cannot be changed. The answer, of course, is that it would provide many advantages, but only if personality traits were long lasting and could be inferred from gossip by viewing accounts of past behaviour through an early hominid Brunswickian personality lens. Those inferred traits could then be advantageously used in deciding upon alliance partners and sexual consorts as well in directing social tactics toward others. The earliest hominid psychologists would have learned whom to seek in times of crises and whom to avoid wherever possible, all without having to learn these lessons the hard way—by experience. We suspect that the resultant increase in inclusive fitness was not insubstantial.

References

Allport, G. W. and Odbert, H. S. (1936). Trait names: a psycho-lexical study. *Psychological Monographs*, **47** (No. 212).

Bain, A. (1861). *On the study of character, including an estimate of phrenology*. Parkeson and Bourne, London.

Benedict, R. (1946). *The chrysanthemum and the sword: patterns of a Japanese culture*. Houghton–Mifflin, Boston.

Bercovitch, F. (1988). Coalitions, cooperation, and reproductive tactics among adult male baboons. *Animal Behaviour*, **36**, 1198–209.

Bolig, R., Price, C. S., O'Neil, P. L., and Suomi, S. J. (1992). Subjective assessment of activity level and personality traits of rhesus monkeys. *International Journal of Primatology*, **13**, 287–306.

Borkenau, P. (1992). Implicit personality theory and the five factor model. *Journal of Personality*, **60**, 295–327.

Borkenau, P. and Lieber, A. (1992). Trait inferences: sources of validity at zero acquaintance. *Journal of Personality and Social Psychology*, **62**, 645–57.

Borkenau, P. and Lieber, A. (1995). Observable attributes as manifestations and cues of personality and intelligence. *Journal of Personality*, **63**, 1–25.

Bouchard, T. J. (1994). Genes, environment and personality. *Science*, **264**, 1700–1.

Brunswik, E. (1955). Representative design and probabilistic theory in a functional psychology. *Psychological Review*, **62**, 193–217.

Brunswik, E. (1956). *Perception and the representative design of psychological experiments* (2nd ed.). University of California Press, Berkeley, CA.

Buirski, P. and Plutchik, R. (1991). Measurement of deviant behaviour in a Gombe chimpanzee: relation to later behavior. *Primates*, **32**, 207–11.

Burger, R., Wagner, G. P., and Stettinger, F. (1989). How much heritable variation can be maintained in a finite population by mutation–selection? *Evolution*, **43**, 1748–66.

Buss, D. M. (1989). Sex differences in mate preferences: evolutionary hypotheses tested in 37 cultures. *Behavioral and Brain Sciences*, 12, 1–49.

Buss, D. M. (1992). Manipulation in close relationships: five personality factors in interactional context. *Journal of Personality*, **60**, 477–99.

Buss, D. M. (1996). Social adaptation and five major factors of personality. In *The five factor theory of personality: theoretical perspectives* (ed. J. S. Wiggins), pp. 180–207. Guilford Press, New York.

Buss, A. H. and Plomin, R. (1984). *Temperament: early developing personality traits*. Erlbaum, Hillsdale, NJ.

Campbell, D. T. and Fiske, D. W. (1959). Convergent and discriminant validation by the multitrait–multimethod matrix. *Psychological Bulletin*, **56**, 81–105.

Cheney, D. L. and Seyfarth, R. M. (1982). Recognition of individuals within and between groups of free-ranging vervet monkeys. *American Zoologist*, **22**, 519–29.

Cheney, D. L. and Seyfarth, R. M. (1988). Assessment of meaning and the detection of unreliable signals by vervet monkeys. *Animal Behaviour*, **36**, 477–86.

ChimpanZoo observer's guide (1991). Jane Goodall Institute, Ridgefield, CN.

Church, T. A. and Katigbak, M. S. (1989). Internal, external, and self-report structure of personality in a non-Western culture. An investigation of cross-language and cross cultural generalizability. *Journal of Personality and Social Psychology*, **57**, 857–72.

Costa, P. T. Jr. and McCrae, R. R. (1992a). Four ways the five factors are basic. *Personality and Individual Differences*, **13**, 653–65.

Costa, P. T. Jr. and McCrae, R. R. (1992b). Trait psychology comes of age. In *Nebraska symposium on motivation: psychology and aging* (ed. T. B. Sonderegger), pp. 169–204. University of Nebraska Press, Lincoln, NB.

Dasser, V. (1988). A social concept in Java monkeys. *Animal Behaviour*, **36**, 225–30.

Datta, S. B. (1992). Effects of availability of allies on female dominance structure. In *Coalitions and alliances in humans and other animals* (ed. A. H. Harcourt and F. B. M. de Waal), pp. 61–82. Oxford University Press.

de Waal, F. B. M. and Luttrell, L. M. (1988). Mechanisms of social reciprocity in three primate species: symmetrical relationship characteristics or cognition? *Ethology and Sociobiology*, **5**, 55–66.

Digman, J. M. (1996). The curious history of the five-factor model. In *The five-factor model of personality: theoretical perspectives* (ed. J. S. Wiggins), pp. 1–20. Guilford Press, New York.

Dunbar, R. I. M. (1993). Coevolution of neocortical size, group size, and language in humans. *Behavioral and Brain Sciences*, 16, 681–735.

Dunbar, R. I. M. (1996). *Grooming, gossip, and the evolution of language*. Harvard University Press, Cambridge, MA.

Ebstein, R. P., Novick, O., Umansky, R., Priel, B., Osher, Y., Blaine D., *et al.* (1996). Dopamine D4 receptor (D4DR) exon III polymorphism associated with the human personality trait of novelty seeking. *Nature Genetics*, **12**, 78–80.

Figueredo, A. J., Cox, R. L., and Rhine, R. J. (1995). A generalizability analysis of subjective personality assessments in the stumptail macaque and the zebra finch. *Multivariate Behavioral Research*, **30**, 167–97.

Funder, D. C. and Sneed, C. D. (1993). Behavioral manifestations of personality: an ecological approach to judgmental accuracy. *Journal of Personality and Social Psychology*, **64**, 479–90.

Gangestad, S. W., Simpson, J. A., DiGeronimo, K., and Biek, M. (1992). Differential accuracy in persona perception across traits: examination of a functional hypothesis. *Journal of Personality and Social Psychology*, **62**, 688–98.

Gaspar, A. D. and King, J. E. (1996). *Prediction of chimpanzee behavior by personality scores*.

Paper presented at the joint meeting of the International Primatological Society and the American Primatological Association, Madison, WI.

Gold, K. C. and Maple, T. L. (1994). Personality assessment in the gorilla and its utility as a measurement tool. *Zoo Biology*, **13**, 509–22.

Goldberg, L. R. (1990). An alternative 'description of personality': the Big-Five structure. *Journal of Personality and Social Psychology*, **59**, 1216–29.

Gray, J. A. (1987). *The psychology of fear and stress*. Cambridge University Press.

Harcourt, A. H. (1992). Coalitions and alliances: are primates more complex than non-primates? In *Coalitions and alliances in humans and other animals* (ed. A. H. Harcourt and F. B. M. de Waal), pp. 445–71. Oxford University Press.

Hogan, R. (1983). A socioanalytic theory of personality. In *Personality: current theory and research* (ed. M. M. Page), pp. 55–89. University of Nebraska Press, Lincoln, NB.

James W. (1890). *Principles of psychology*. Holt, New York.

John, O. P. (1990). The 'Big Five' factor taxonomy: dimensions of personality in the natural language and in questionnaires. In *Handbook of personality: theory and research* (ed. L. A. Pervin), pp. 66–100. Guilford Press, New York.

Kendrick, D. T. and Funder, D. C. (1988). Profiting from controversy: lessons from the person–situation debate. *American Psychologist*, **43**, 23–34.

Kennedy, J. S. (1992). *The new anthropomorphism*. Cambridge University Press.

King, J. E. and Figueredo, A. J. (1997). The five-factor model plus dominance in chimpanzee personality. *Journal of Research in Personality*, **31**, 257–71.

MacDonald, K. (1995). Evolution, the five factor model, and levels of personality. *Journal of Personality*, **63**, 525–67.

Mather, J. A. and Anderson, R. C. (1993). Personalities of octopuses (*Octopus rubescens*). *Journal of Comparative Psychology*, **107**, 336–40.

McCrae, R. R. and Costa, P. T. Jr. (1990). *Personality in adulthood*. Guilford Press, New York.

Mead, M. (1928). *Coming of age in Samoa*: *a psychological study of primitive youth for Western civilization*. W. Morrow, New York.

Mesulam, M. M. (1986). Frontal cortex and behavior. *Annals of Neurology*, **19**, 320–5.

Miller, N. F. and Dollard, S. (1941). *Social learning and imitation*. Yale University Press, New Haven, CT.

Mischel, W. (1968). *Personality and assessment*. Wiley, New York.

Murphy, G. (1949). *Historical introduction to modern psychology*. Harcourt Brace, New York.

Myers, F. W. H. (1903). *Human personality and its survival after bodily death* (Vol. 1–2). Longmans, Green, London.

Nanayanan, K., Menon, S., and Levine, E. L. (1995). Personality structure: a culture-specific examination of the five-factor model. *Journal of Personality Assessment*, **64**, 51–62.

Newman, J. P. (1987). Reaction to punishment in extraverts and psychopaths: implications for the impulsive behavior of disinhibited individuals. *Journal of Personality Research*, **21**, 464–80.

Nok, R. (1992). Alliance formation among male baboons: shopping for profitable partners. In *Coalitions and alliances in humans and other animals* (ed. A. H. Harcourt and F. B. M. de Waal), pp. 285–321. Oxford University Press.

Nunnally, J. C. (1978). *Psychometric theory*. McGraw–Hill, New York.

Plutchik, R. and Kellerman, H. (1974). *Manual for the emotions profile index*. Western Psychological Services, Los Angeles, CA.

Premack, D. (1988). 'Does the chimpanzee have a theory of mind?' revisited. In *Machiavellian intelligence: social expertise and the evolution of intellect in monkeys, apes, and humans* (ed. R. W. Bryne and A. Whiten), pp. 94–110. Clarendon Press, Oxford.

Ross, L. and Nisbett, R. E. (1991). *The person and the situation*. McGraw–Hill, New York.

Royce, J. R., Foley, W., and Yeudall, Y. T. (1973). Behavior genetic analysis of mouse emotionality: I. factor analysis. *Journal of Comparative and Physiological Psychology*, **83**, 36–47.

Rumbaugh, D. M. and Savage-Rumbaugh, E. S. (1994). Language in comparative perspective. In *Animal learning and cognition* (ed. N. J. Mackintosh), pp. 307–33. Academic Press, San Diego, CA.

Savage-Rumbaugh, E. S., Murphy, J., Sevcik, R. A., Brakke, K. E., Williams, S. L., and Rumbaugh, D. M. (1993). Language comprehension in ape and child. *Monographs of the Society for Research in Child Development*, **58**, Nos. 3 & 4, 1–221.

Scott, J. P. and Fuller, J. L. (1965). *Genetics of the social behavior of the dog*. University of Chicago Press.

Sears, R. R. (1948). Personality development in contemporary culture. *Proceedings of the American Philosophical Society*, **92**, 363–70.

Seyfarth, R. M. and Cheney, D. L. (1984). Grooming alliances and reciprocal altruism in vervet monkeys. *Nature*, **308**, 541–3.

Simpson, G. G. (1964). The non-prevalence of humanoids. *Science*, **143**, 769–75.

Small, S. A., Zelding, R. S., and Savin-Williams, R. C. (1983). In search of personality traits: a multimethod analysis of naturally occurring prosocial and dominance behavior. *Journal of Personality*, **51**, 1–16.

Stevenson-Hinde, J. and Zunz, M. (1978). Subjective assessment of individual rhesus monkeys. *Primates*, **19**, 473–82.

Stevenson-Hinde, J., Stillwell-Barnes, R., and Zunz, M. (1980). Subjective assessment of rhesus monkeys over fou successive years. *Primates*, **21**, 66–82.

Tucker, D. M. and Derryberry, D. (1992). Motivated attention: anxiety and the frontal lobe functions. *Neuropsychiatry, Neuropsychology, and Behavioral Neurology*, **5**, 233–52.

Wiggins, J. S. (1973). *Personality and prediction: principles of personality assessment*. Addison–Wesley, Reading, MA.

Wilson, D. S. (1994). Adaptive genetic variation and human evolutionary psychology. *Ethology and Sociobiology*, **6**, 59–73.

Yang, K. and Bond, H. M. (1990). Exploring implicit theories with indigenous or imported constructs: the Chinese case. *Journal of Personality and Social Psychology*, **58**, 1087–97.

Zametkin, A. J., Liebenauer, L. L., Fitzgerald, G. A., Minkunas, D. V., Hercovitch, P., Yamada, E. M., *et al.* (1993). Brain metabolism in teenagers with attention–deficit hyperactivity disorder. *Archives of General Psychiatry*, **50**, 333–40.

Zuckerman, M. (1992). What is a basic factor and which factors are basic? Turtles all the way down. *Personality and Individual Differences*, **13**, 675–81.

7

Whatever happened to articulate speech?

Peter F. MacNeilage

Introduction

Broca's deduction, in 1861 (anticipated by Dax in 1836—see Dax, 1865), that there is a relatively separable faculty of 'articulate speech' in the left frontal lobe of humans was a landmark in the history of human understanding (Broca 1861; Schiller 1992). According to Changeux (1985), "Broca gave the first demonstration of the discrete cortical localization of well-defined faculties..." (p. 19). He thought it involved memory for word production. This was also the first evidence that any capacity could be localized to one hemisphere of the brain. From our present perspective, Broca's evidence, and his deduction from it, marked the beginning of the field of cognitive neuroscience (Gazzaniga 1995). Although subject to a long history of debate, the claim that there is a region of inferior frontal cortex of the left hemisphere that is concerned with algorithms for speech production in most humans remains a valid one (Brown 1979; Galaburda 1982).

The question I wish to raise in this paper is: why has so little been made of this finding in the subsequent century and a half? Humans definitely do have a relatively separable capacity to produce speech, and it is the main observable action capacity that sets us apart from all other species. And in attempting to understand this capacity, we have the advantage that descriptive information about the *structure* of speech clearly exceeds that for any other complex output function. But while we have been happy to point to this capacity and its lateralization in the brain as evidence of human uniqueness, we have given relatively little attention to the question of what all this might mean for the understanding of humans. Some attention has been given to the question of why speech is in the left hemisphere, but virtually no attention has been given to the question of why speech is the way that it is. Certainly there has been no sustained effort to put speech in the context within which all 'why' questions regarding living forms must be asked—the context of the neo-Darwinian theory of evolution by natural selection. To take a single example of this neglect, in the recent 1400-page *Handbook of Cognitive Neuroscience* edited by Gazzaniga (1995) only five pages were devoted to speech production (Blumstein 1995), with no consideration of how it might have evolved.

A number of reasons for this neglect can be found in the history of science. The discipline of psychology has mirrored the history of Western thought in being more concerned with how humans assimilate the world, and perform mental operations on the products of this assimilation, than in the *actions* that humans perform, vocal or otherwise (e.g. MacKay 1987). Even in the behaviourist era, the response was only of interest for what it could reveal about learning, not for evidence regarding the nature of action control. Motor learning was a negligible component of behaviourism. A continued lack of interest in action in general is clearly revealed in modern cognitive science. Less than 10% of Gazzaniga's handbook of cognitive neuroscience was devoted to motor control. In an influential monograph on cognitive science (Posner 1991), the authors of one of the two chapters on motor control (68 pages out of 900 with no coverage of speech production) nicely illustrate the continued preoccupation with input and its mental manipulation (Jordan and Rosenbaum 1991). These authors thought it necessary to introduce their chapter apologetically, saying: "Thus cognitive science, insofar as it regards perception as one of its core problems, cannot afford to ignore action". And: "For cognitions to be communicated, they must be physically enacted" (p. 727).

This neglect of action is equally obvious in the area of the cognitive science of language most related to traditional psychology, namely, psycholinguistics. For every contribution on language production, there are a couple of dozen on comprehension: "Language production is the stepchild of psycholinguistics" (Levelt 1989, p. xiv). But if language production is a stepchild, speech production is positively feral. Even with a home field advantage, in the recent 1200-page *Handbook of Psycholinguistics* (Gernsbacher 1994) there was no chapter on speech production at all! Speech perception, yes (four chapters); eye movements in reading, yes (one chapter); speech production (or writing), no. Apart from psycholinguistics, the only area that has been concerned with speech production is the area of motor programming (e.g. Shaffer 1982, 1984).

In addition to suffering from a general neglect of action, speech has the additional problem that it is part of the discipline of linguistics that has been characterized in this century by a *principled* neglect of the *actual actions* involved in speaking. Early in the century, de Saussure (1916) formulated his distinction between *'la Langue'* (language form) and *'la Parole'* (language substance, or speech) and declared that the discipline should be concerned only with the former. Later in the century, Chomsky (1965), declaring that "the logical priority of the study of langue seems quite inescapable" (p. 52), formulated a similar distinction between *competence* and *performance*, according to which actual speech, like other performance phenomena such as memory lapses or speech errors, were deemed to be of no real interest. All this is in the classical Western philosophical tradition of essentialism (Mayr 1982) bequeathed to us by Plato, and reinforced by Descartes (e.g. see Chomsky's 1966 *Cartesian Linguistics*). In this tradition basic forms have a priori status, and substance—in Plato's terms, appearances—is trivial. Ironically, one cannot go to the major discipline most concerned with speech itself to find out much about how it is actually produced, let alone why it takes the form that it does. What little there is to be found on this topic is in the minor subdiscipline of phonetics (e.g. MacNeilage 1983; Hardcastle and Marchal 1997).

Another more general factor that has led to the neglect of articulate speech is that, while Darwin's theory of evolution has now been widely accepted, its implications are only beginning to be systematically explored for humans—as, for example, in the emerging field of evolutionary psychology. In Darwin's view, the engine of evolution is natural selection of adaptive actions. According to Mayr (1982):

Many if not most acquisitions of new structures in the course of evolution can be ascribed to selection forces exerted by newly acquired behaviors. Behavior, thus, plays an important role as the pacemaker of evolutionary change. Most adaptive radiations were apparently caused by behavioral shifts (p. 612).

From this standpoint it is what animals *do*, not how they perceive the world or how they think about it, that most determines the nature of all living forms. This way of looking at things puts the ability to *do* speech at centre stage. It should be conceded that there has been some interest in the actions underlying tool construction and use in the attempt to understand humans, but as with speech, the main tendency has been to (wrongly, it turns out) emphasize hominid tools as a badge of hominid uniqueness, not as a milestone in the relation of movement to mind.

Only an occasional voice has called for a focus on the study of action. In a little-known paper, Roger Sperry (1952) made the claim, requiring only minor qualification, that "The entire output of our thinking machine consists of nothing but patterns of motor coordination" (pp. 297–98). It was his belief that:

The unknown cerebral patterns in psychic experience must necessarily involve excitation patterns so designed that they intermesh in intimate fashion with motor and premotor patterns. ...It follows that the more we learn about the motor and premotor mechanisms, the more restrictions we add to the working picture of the unknown mental patterns and hence the closer our speculation will have to converge towards and accurate description of their true nature (p. 300).

This year (1998) is the 50th anniversary of the delivery of a much better known paper in which Lashley (1951) drew attention to what he considered to be "both the most important and the most neglected problem of cerebral physiology" (p. 114)—the problem of serial order in behaviour. This is basically the problem of how *any* output sequence is organized, including the formulation of any mental underpinnings. It was Lashley's opinion that "language presents in most striking form the integrative functions that are characteristic of the cerebral cortex and reach their highest development in human thought processes" (p. 113). Accordingly, he made considerable use of spoken language, including errors in speech, in his attempt to formulate the problem of serial order in a manner that would enable its comprehensive investigation.

The implications of Darwin's theory for articulate speech have not been pursued, and the exhortations of Sperry and Lashley have, for the most part, fallen on deaf ears. The best known idea about how speech might have evolved, the two-tubed vocal-tract hypothesis of Lieberman (e.g. 1984), does not transcend anatomy to include consideration of how hominids might have evolved the ability to produce sequences of these shapes in syllabic packages at rates as high as 15 tract shapes per second. A recent survey of the influence of Lashley's paper on modern cognitive science (Bruce 1994) finds it to be relatively modest.

My task in this paper is to use the neo-Darwinian perspective and some of Lashley's insights to give an account of the nature of articulate speech which might help us further understand its significance. Articulate speech actually presents *two* major explanatory problems, not just one. The first is why it is usually represented in the left hemisphere, and the second is why it takes the particular form that it does. I have recently considered the first question elsewhere (MacNeilage 1998a), arguing that there might be a left-hemispheric specialization for motor control of routine actions in vertebrates in general. It may underlie the widespread occurrence of left-hemi-spheric specializations for vocal communication in animals as diverse as humans, monkeys, mice, gerbils, birds, and frogs. Counter to the common assumption of a *causal* link between a tool-related manual specialization and a vocal specialization in hominids is the repeated finding that language laterality is more closely related to foot preference than to hand preference (e.g. Day and MacNeilage 1996). In my opinion, foot preference is indicative of a contralateral specialization for whole-body postural organization. The foot-mouth link is therefore considered to reflect an underlying generalized motor control specialization of the hemisphere. When devel-oped in detail (MacNeilage 1998a), this point of view is not necessarily antithetical to claims that the left hemisphere can be characterized as having a generalized special-ization for various metafunctional capabilities, such as analyticity (Bradshaw and Nettleton 1983), sequencing (Kimura 1979), or generativity (Corballis 1991). But these conceptions are far too non-specific to give us much help in saying exactly why speech is the way that it is. It is to that problem that I now turn.

While the location of speech specialization might have a deep-seated origin, there is no question that the detailed form of speech is unique to hominids. There is no close functional analogue with the composition of speech in other mammalian vocalization (MacNeilage 1998b). The syllable, a universal unit of speech, is produced by an open–close alternation of the mouth—open for the vowel, closed for the consonant(s). Individual consonants and vowels, called segments, or phonemes, can be described in terms of a limited number of subsegmental attributes called 'features'. Consonants are described in terms of the amount of vocal fold vibration (voicing) that accompanies them, the place in the mouth at which the accompanying constriction is made, and the amount of constriction. Vowels are described in terms of the height and front–back location of the tongue, and whether the lips are rounded. It is a felicitous fact that the most appropriate English translation of Broca's phrase 'lan-gage articulé' seems to be 'articulate speech' (Schiller 1992). Speech differs from other mammalian vocalization primarily in terms of the diversity of *articulatory* function—the articulators being the tongue, lips, jaw, and soft palate. The role of the other two components of the speech apparatus, the respiratory component, which supplies the outgoing air, and the phonatory component that modulates it in the form of vocal fold vibration, are relatively similar in all mammals. It is the evolution of the versatility with which modern hominids use the articulators to reconfigure the vocal tract at the rate of 15 consonants and vowels per second that constitutes the main explanatory problem for the understanding of speech production.

Lashley's views on serial order

Before we come to grips with this problem, let us review the contributions Lashley made to our task. The most important contribution resulted from a review of properties of language, a decade before the birth of psycholinguistics as a discipline (Miller 1962). Lashley concluded that in producing language and other skilled behaviours "The order must therefore be imposed upon the motor elements by some organization other than direct associative connections between them" (p. 115). To understand how profound this conclusion was—and it was made before a similar conclusion in linguistics (Chomsky 1957)—one needs to note that the prevailing view of serially ordered behaviour since the inception of behaviourism (J. Watson 1913) was that it was produced by a stimulus–response (S–R) arrangement of "chains of reflexes in which the performance of each element of the series provides the excitation of the next" (Lashley 1951, p. 114). J. Watson (1920) hypothesized that thought was simply talking to oneself, using just this kind of arrangement.

Part of Lashley's argument against the reflex-chaining view was that there was not time in fast serially-ordered behaviours such as piano playing, which could reach rates of 16 strokes per second, for feedback from the previous response to influence the next. Bruce (1994) has pointed out that more recent work has shown that sensorimotor linkages can in fact work fast enough for a response to *influence* the next one at these rates. But a more important criticism of the reflex-chaining view was that the *choice* of a subsequent response cannot be determined by the previous response because a particular response is followed by different responses on different occasions. Lashley illustrates this fact by the sentence: "The millwright on my right thinks it right that some conventional rite should symbolize the right of every man to write as he pleases." (p. 116). In such a sentence, as Lashley points out, "word arrangement is obviously not due to any direct associations of the word 'right' itself with other words, but to meanings that are determined separately" (p 116). He made a point about the organization of individual words—it is true to at least some extent that the production of words such as 'right' and 'tire' involve making the same motor elements in reverse order, the order being determined from above, so to speak. "No single letter invariably follows *g*, and whether *gh*, *ga* or *gu* is written depends upon a set for a larger unit of action, the word" (p. 116).

When Bruce asked Chomsky what influence Lashley's paper had on his linguistic theories, as expressed in the book *Syntactic Structures*, Chomsky responded "I don't think there was any" (Bruce 1994, p. 99). He pointed out that he did not know about the paper, and even if he had, it would not have been any help to him. Unfortunately, this is true—presumably Lashley had nothing to tell Chomsky about language structure. But Lashley was attempting to address the whole problem of how a speaker gets from an idea to a serially ordered set of actual movements, which are essential for transmission of the idea to a listener. Chomsky has only been concerned with an aspect of the middle part of this sequence of events—how do you characterize, in an idealized way, the grammatical structure of a language independent of the user? Chomsky's approach is in some ways reminiscent of Tolman, who attempted to get cognition into S–R behaviourism by arguing that maze learning was based on formation of cognitive maps, and involved the formation of concepts such as 'sign gestalt expectations' (Tolman 1948). However as Guthrie (1935) pointed out, "Signs, in Tolman's theory occasion in the rat *realization*, or *cognition*, or *judgement*, or *hypothesis*, or *abstraction*, but they *do not occasion action*...So far as the theory is concerned, the rat is left buried in thought" (p. 172). For Lashley, as for Guthrie, an acceptable theory must contain a link from cognition to action. Whatever the defects of orthodox behaviourism, the stimulus–response paradigm always had consequences for action. By analogy with Guthrie's point about Tolman, Chomsky's human stands there with a marvellous genetically determined universal grammar, but he/she can neither hook it up backwards, so to speak, to ideas, or forwards to actual movements. Lashley was trying to solve the problem that S–R behaviourism had with the existence of complex mental processes independent of stimuli, while retaining its capacity to give an account of action. (See Levelt 1989 for an attempt to conceptualize the *entire* sequence of events from idea to action, though without a single reference to Lashley, in 566 pages!).

Lashley then asked: "What determines the order?" His conclusion was that "the mechanism which determines the serial activation of the motor units is relatively independent of the motor units and of the thought structure" (p. 118). Evidence for independence from thought structure included the ability of bilinguals to express the same thought with two different sentence structures in the two languages. Evidence for independence of the serial order from the units at the phonological level of speech came from errors in typing and speaking. For example it was pointed out that in typing t-h-s-e-s for *these*, l-o-k-k for *look* and i-i-l for *ill* one can see the separation of the aspects of the programme controlling the letter repetition from the letters which need to be repeated. Examples are also given from speech errors, but discussion of this topic will be postponed until other aspects of Lashley's approach to the serial-ordering problem are outlined.

Lashley anticipated what has become the important concept of working memory (Baddeley 1986) with his concept of 'priming'. "There are indications that, prior to the internal or overt enunciation of the sentence, an aggregate of word units is partially activated or readied" (p. 119). Evidence for this claim came from speech or typing errors in which forthcoming material is erroneously inserted into the ongoing sequence. "Thus I wrote *wrapid* writing, carrying the *w* over from the second word to the first" (p. 119).

He also made an explicit distinction between overt and internal speech, thus addressing another issue that would never come up in formal linguistics. The recognition of a role of internal speech anticipated the English translation of Vygotsky's (1962) work and the advent of the *articulatory loop*, which involves subvocal rehearsal, as an important component of verbal working memory (Baddeley 1986). He also anticipated the *motor theory of speech perception* (Liberman *et al.* 1967; Liberman and Mattingly 1985) which, like the articulatory loop, requires a perceptual–motor linkage, by remarking that "The processes of comprehension and production of speech have too much in common to depend on wholly different mechanisms" (p. 120).

At the level of actual movement control, Lashley suggested that timing mechanisms might play an important role in serially-ordered behaviours because of their capacity to integrate widely separated strands of central neural activity. He cited early work by Graham Brown and von Holst showing that biphasic rhythms associated with relatively simple serially-ordered activities such as respiration and locomotion have some independence from peripheral control. He pointed out that rhythmic patterns similar to those observed in basic life-preserving activities are to be found in higher-order actions such as musical performance and speech. At the time Lashley made this suggestion, the possibility of totally autonomous central rhythms (now commonly attributed to *central pattern generators* (CPGs) was quite controversial, as many physiologists as well as S–R behaviourists thought that sensory stimulation was essential to rhythmic control, which therefore could simply be regarded as another instance of S–R chaining. It should be acknowledged that under ordinary ecological conditions rhythmic activities are modulated by sensory input. The question was whether sensory input was essential to their operation. Lashley's position was that these rhythms had properties beyond any postulated by S–R associationists. Here he has been richly vindicated. By 1980, Delcomyn was able to assert that "evidence from isolation, deafferentation and paralysis experiments provides overwhelming support for the idea that all nervous systems are capable of generating properly timed rhythmic output in the absence of peripheral feedback" (p. 497).

A pervasive feature of Lashley's discussion is his extreme conservatism regarding the mechanisms underlying serially ordered behaviour, and their phylogeny. He concludes that "Analysis of the nervous mechanisms underlying order in the more primitive acts may contribute ultimately to the solution even of the physiology of logic" (pp. 121–2). He also states that:

I am coming more and more to the conviction that the rudiments of every human behavioural mechanism will be found far down in the evolutionary scale and also represented even in the primitive activities of the nervous system. If there exist, in human cerebral action, processes which seem fundamentally different or inexplicable in terms of our present construct of the elementary physiology of integration, then it is probable that this construct is incomplete or mistaken, even for the levels of behaviour to which it is applied (p. 135).

Although Lashley does not mention Darwin, or evolutionary theory as such, this conservatism regarding the evolution of cerebral control mechanisms is consistent with Darwin's emphasis on 'descent with modification' (Darwin 1859, p. 420) as the basic event in evolution, and on the 'lowly origins' of humans (Darwin 1871, p. 597). An appropriate metaphor for this conservative view of evolution has been suggested by Jacob—evolution as tinkering (Jacob 1977). The implication is that nature does not build new structures or functions from scratch, but tinkers them into place by modifications of previously existing structures or functions. If Lashley's view on this matter had received a sympathetic reception, we would have a much less anthropocentric picture of the human mind than we have. It is interesting to note that this aspect of Lashley's thinking has had so little impact on cognitive science that it was not even mentioned in Bruce's 1994 survey.

Another thing to note about Lashley's evolutionary views, not only about serial order but in general, is that they have a distinctly old-fashioned non-modular ring about them. He asserts, for example that "not only speech, but all skilled acts seem to involve the same problems or serial ordering, even down to the temporal coordination of muscular contractions in such a movement as reaching and grasping" (pp. 121–2). This of course flies in the face of the relatively popular claim, arising from the essentialist mode of thought, that language results from a genetically programmed module only containing language-specific structure (e.g. Fodor 1983). In Chomsky's view:

We should, so it appears, think of knowledge of language as a certain state of the mind/brain, a relatively stable element in transitory mental states, once it is attained; furthermore, as a state of some distinguishable faculty of the mind—the language faculty—with its specific properties, structure and organization, one 'module' of the mind (Chomsky 1986, pp. 12–13).

Specifically in the domain of speech, Liberman and Mattingly, the proponents of the motor theory of speech perception, incorporate speech perception in Chomsky's module, declaring that it "is part of the natural human grammatical capacity that, together with syntax, distinguishes speech from all other forms of communication" (Liberman and Mattingly 1989, p. 491). With respect to neurolinguistics, Caplan (1994) has asserted that "language processing is carried out only in perisylvian association cortex" (p. 1043) because it contains a genetically determined system allowing "the activation of abstract linguistic codes and of computational processes applying to the representations specified in these codes" (p. 1045). He points out that:

The theory presented here contrasts sharply with the classical connectionist theory and many other localizationist models that maintain that language functions are localized in particular areas of perisylvian cortex because of the relationship of these areas to cortical structures supporting aspects of sensory and motor functions (p. 1046).

There is certainly a clear choice to be made here in attempting to answer the question of why speech is the way that it is.

Vindicating Lashley: the frame / content theory of evolution of speech production

We now come to the central question in this paper: How do we place the serial ordering of articulate speech in an evolutionary perspective? Elsewhere, I have presented in detail a *'frame/content'* theory of evolution of speech production which shows a debt to Lashley in a number of respects (MacNeilage 1998b, c). The specific task here is to present an outline of this theory, and to make clear the nature and extent of its debt to Lashley. The four aspects of Lashley's views discussed earlier are integral to this theory:

(1) the order/elements dichotomy;
(2) working memory;
(3) timing mechanisms; and
(4) the conservatism of evolution.

I will deal with each of these four themes as the occasion arises.

The basic proposition regarding the *order/elements dichotomy* is that the order of the motor elements in speech must be imposed by some organization other than the direct associative connections between them. What are the elements for speech production, and how is the order imposed on them? Lashley's suspicion that speech errors could be an important source of information on this problem has been richly born out. One speech element is by far the most frequent participant in serial ordering errors in speech (Shattuck-Hufnagel 1980): it is the segment or phoneme—the individual consonant or vowel. This is true of all five of the main types of error—segments can be omitted, added, shifted in location, or erroneously substituted for a correct one. In addition, in spoonerisms, two segments can exchange locations. The most important generalization to be made about these errors is that there is a syllable structure constraint on where a misplaced segment can go. Consonants can be moved into consonantal positions in syllables and vowels can be moved into vowel positions, creating spoonerisms, such as, for vowels 'odd hack' for 'ad hoc', and for consonants 'mel wade' for 'well made' (examples from Fromkin 1973). Vowels and consonants virtually never occupy each other's positions in syllable structure (Dell *et al.* 1993). These results lead us to what Levelt (1992) has called "Probably the most important insight from modern speech error research...". It is that "the word's skeleton or frame and its segmental content are independently generated" (p. 10). This conclusion provides the beginnings of an answer to Lashley' question about the relationship between serial order and motor elements, in regard to speech. The ordering device is *some kind of abstract representation of syllable structure*. Most simply put, it is something like this—the vowel is at the core, and a capacity for handling zero or more consonants is on the margins.

Although Lashley himself did not specifically note the syllable structure constraint on speech errors (though he gave an example of it in 'queer old dean' for 'dear old queen') he would no doubt find vindication in these latest developments. There has been a large number of attempts to model serially-ordered speech in terms of the learning of associations between elements, involving various activation regimes, but with no separate structural principle for ordering. But in a recent review Dell *et al.* (1997) conclude that "we are persuaded that structural frames are needed for serial order in language" (p. 132). They believe that "there is a fairly glaring empirical difficulty with the models without frames as theories of phonological encoding" (p. 132). In the other models "the predicted pattern of misorderings of phonemes involves rearrangement of the phonemes within a word. So /kaet/ would be predicted to slip to /tkae/, /aekt/ or /ktae/. Unfortunately, these kinds of error never happen. Most commonly, phonological errors on a word like /kaet/ involve the substitution of sounds from nearby syllables, where the substituting sound emerges in the same syllabic position, and where the resulting string of sounds is phonologically acceptable. For example 'the cat is chasing...' results in 'the chat...' or 'the cass...'. Categorically specified frames derived from the phonological patterns in the language, together with a mechanism that inserts sounds from particular categories into frame slots, provide for exactly the right kind of phonological errors' (p. 131). This is an interesting statement coming from Dell, because he has made use of more different models in his attempts to accommodate speech error patterns than has anyone else (see also Dell *et al.* 1993; Dell 1996). Dell *et al.* (1997) also claim that frames are necessary to account for our ability to order novel sets of elements (e.g. to produce /ae/, /m/ and /ng/ only as 'mang'). The frame might be here to stay as the prime candidate for the ordering mechanism underlying speech production.

I have argued that this frame/content view is the best general characterization of the end point of the evolution of speech production (e.g. MacNeilage *et al.* 1985), and I have given an account of how it might have evolved (MacNeilage 1998b) as well as an account of how it might have developed (MacNeilage and Davis 1990). However, in the field of psycholinguistics, researchers have been for the most part exclusively concerned with only one of the questions that Tinbergen (1952) poses for those seeking a complete explanation of communication in any animal. This might be paraphrased as the question of mechanism—how does it work? The other questions —'What does it do for the organism?' and 'How did it get that way, in both phylogeny and ontogeny?' have not been addressed.

The question of the origin of the syllabic frame takes us into a consideration of the role of timing mechanisms in speech evolution. The most important issue here is how did the most salient property of the frame evolve. This property is the vowel–consonant dichotomy and the mutual exclusiveness of these two parts of the frame, as evidenced by the lack of interaction of vowels and consonants in errors. My suggestion is that this dichotomy had a motor origin in the basic mouth open–close alternation that accompanies syllable production—open for vowels, closed for consonants (MacNeilage 1998b). Thus, what is now mutual exclusiveness of consonants and vowels at a *premotor* programming stage might have originated in the fact that from the moment the syllable came into being as a communicative entity the opening and closing phases of the mandibular cycle had a mutual exclusiveness at the *motor* level, and the evolving mechanism has never superseded this constraint. In short, from motor frames there evolved premotor frames and separate content specification. When speaking a single word, modern hominids retrieve a set of basic instructions for producing it which are stored in a mental dictionary. Studies of the 'tip of the tongue' state in which subjects can only retrieve part of the information about the word they want show that syllabic (frame) information—about how many syllables there are and where the stresses are (e.g. 'it's got two syllables and the first one is stressed')—is stored separately from segmental (content) information (e.g. 'it begins with *b*') (Levelt 1989). The independence of the frame and content components in modern hominid production begins in the mental dictionary.

In the open–close alternation of the mouth associated with the syllable we have a rhythmic biphasic cycle. Virtually all utterances in all languages are composed of syllables and virtually all syllables have an open phase—the vowel, often termed the syllable nucleus—and a closing phase. It is not so obvious to English speakers that this biphasic cycle underlies speech production. It is masked by the fact that there can be several consonants between vowels, and by the fact that the main contributor to the impression of rhythmicity in English is the fact that *stressed* syllables tend to sound equally spaced. But the fact that it is syllables that are stressed is evidence for a role of this unit in rhythmic control. In other languages (often called syllable-timed) such as Spanish, syllables make a more equal contribution to the impression of rhythm. The basic role of the open–close alternation in adult language is most readily seen in Polynesian languages such as Hawaiian, where the consonant–vowel (CV) syllable is the only syllable type with consonants in it, the other type being the vowel alone.

The basic role of the rhythmic mouth open–close alternation in speech is most evident in *early* speech, which has virtually the same structure as pre-speech babbling (MacNeilage 1997d) consisting primarily of CV syllables, alone or reiterated (e.g., 'bababa'). It is interesting to note that both babbling and early speech can be characterized by the phrase 'frame dominance' in that articulators other than the mandible (tongue, lips, soft palate) make only minor relatively undifferentiated

contributions to the sound patterns (Davis and MacNeilage 1995; MacNeilage *et al.*
1997). This is what early hominid speech would have been like according to the
frame/content theory, and the implications of this possible relationship are explored
elsewhere (MacNeilage 1994, 1998b). Thus, the biphasic cycle appears in modern
hominids at the onset of babbling, and only appears to go away in some languages.
However even in languages with complex syllable structure, it has been noted that
there are shorter segment durations in syllables which have more segments, reflecting
an adjustment of the segmental component (the content) to the rhythmic motor frame
of the syllable (Kozhevnikov and Chistovich 1965).

To try to address the most basic of Tinbergen's questions—How did this basic
rhythmic property of speech get that way?—I have argued that the use of the
mandibular cycle for speech was the third major stage in the evolution of this rhythm
(MacNeilage 1998b). The first stage, occurring in early mammals, was the use of the
mandibular cycles for ingestive processes such as chewing, sucking, and licking. A
possible second stage—an exaptation in Gould's (1991) terms—is seen in the use of
the cycle for various relatively widespread visuofacial communicative events in many
primates—lipsmacks, tongue-smacks, and teeth chatters (Redican 1975). The third
stage was the systematic pairing of phonation with mandibular oscillation, a pairing
only occasionally found in other primates (e.g., S. Green 1975; Andrew 1976). Dunbar
(1997) has suggested that talk, as a successor to grooming in contributing to social
solidarity in hominids, might have helped speech and therefore language to get off the
ground (see also Locke 1997). Rhythmic syllable reiteration is a simple device for
extending talk in the time domain.

Lest this suggestion of an early mammalian origin of the syllable frame seem too
extreme, I would point out that Cohen (1988) has argued that there has been an
evolutionary continuity in use of the basic biphasic vertebrate locomotory cycle of
flexion and extension over a period of half a billion years, beginning perhaps in
lampreys, and presumably still in use, in modified form, in humans.

If these conjectures are correct, then Lashley was correct in his surmise that
rhythm generators might play a key role in the realization of serial ordering at the
action level, even in such complex behaviours as speech. My specific suggestion is that
in this case use has been made of a hard-wired rhythm generator (CPG) presumably
located in the brain stem (Hiraba *et al.* 1988). Such hard-wired generators presumably
need to be distinguished from the generalized ability of humans to programme
rhythms of various kinds, as Lashley noted for musical performance. The present line
of argument also provides support for Lashley's extreme evolutionary conservatism.
The basic claim is that the abstract mental structure we now use for serial ordering of
human speech—the frame—evolved from a movement routine which may be one-fifth
of a billion years old. We lack the kind of evidence on the evolution of mandibular
oscillation that we have for the evolution of locomotion. But with respect to the
locomotory progression from lampreys to mammals, Cohen has concluded that "the
basic locomotor CPG need change very little to accommodate the increasing demands
natural selection placed on it" (p. 161).

It was Lashley's emphasis on rhythm generators that enables us to make direct
contact between his thinking and Broca's discovery. It is in lateral frontal cortex, the
region that contains Broca's area, that cortical control over ingestive processes,

including ingestive cyclicities, is exerted in mammals (Woolsey 1958). The part of lateral frontal cortex that has been most consistently considered to be part of Broca's area, is the *pars opercularis* of the inferior frontal gyrus—area 44 of Brodmann (Brown 1979; see Fig. 7.1, bottom). Lund and Enomoto (1988) conclude that the area of masticatory cortex is homologous in humans, monkeys, and cats. "When defined by electrical stimulation, the masticatory area...is found at the lateral end of area 6 in monkeys [see Fig. 7.1, bottom, for human area 6], and probably extends into area 44" (p. 57). In addition, Luschei and Goldberg (1981) have reported that a monkey with bilateral lesions in the homologues of area 6 and 44 "never produced repetitive phasic biting seen in other animals" (p. 1262). Foerster (1936; see summary in *Lancet*, 1931, **221**, pp. 309–12) first reported that effects of electrical stimulation of area 6 in humans included chewing and licking movements.

Area 6 has never been functionally distinguished from area 44 in attempts to establish the role of Broca's area in speech. Recent positron emission tomography (PET) studies of speech production show co-activation of area 6 and posterior area 44 (Peterson *et al.* 1988; LeBlanc 1992; Fox 1995) (see MacNeilage 1998b for a figure showing the area of activation in Talairach coordinates.) The research summarized here allows me to suggest an answer to another version of Tinbergen's phylogenetic question that has (surprisingly) rarely been asked: why is Broca's area in particular so important for articulate speech? Part of the answer might be: because the evolution of the syllable was achieved by modification of cortical ingestive control capabilities long resident in this vicinity. An additional part of the answer becomes more plausible when one again stresses the literal meaning of the term 'articulate' in the phrase articulate speech. It is in the articulatory component of vocal production (the articulators are the lips, the tongue, the mandible, and the soft palate), not in the phonatory or respiratory components, that the main advances over non-human primate vocal communication have been made (MacNeilage 1998b). I have suggested two main roles for the region containing Broca's area in speech evolution:

(1) modification of the mandibular cycle at the cortical level was responsible for the evolution of the syllable;
(2) because the mandibular cycle was already integrated with actions of the other articulators for ingestive purposes, its modification for communicative purposes provided a basis for subsequent modification of the functional role of the other articulators to provide the motor algorithms for the content component of speech.

As there is a tendency for more anterior sites in the inferior frontal cortex to be involved in higher-order functions (Deacon 1992) one might speculate that area 6 might be more involved in frame generation, and area 44 more involved in content generation.

The differentiation, in evolution, of separate content elements from the original frame state might have been a matter of self organization. Studdert-Kennedy (1987) has suggested that in speech acquisition, after a stage of more wholistic organization (frame dominance?) there is a stage during which "Under pressure from an increasing vocabulary, recurrent patterns of sound and gesture crystallize into encapsulated

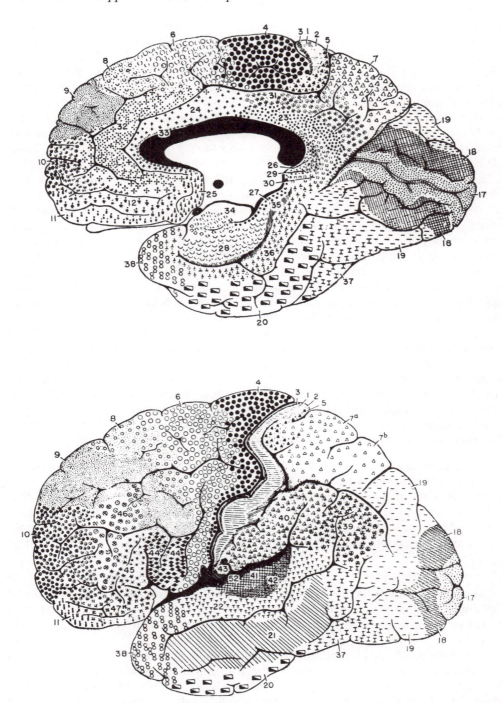

Fig. 7.1. Brodmann's (1909) cytoarchitechtonic classification of the medial (top) and lateral (bottom) regions of the cerebral cortex of humans.

phonemic control units" (p. 67)—see also Studdert-Kennedy (1998). This might have been what happened in evolution as vocabulary size increased in successive genera-tions. According to this view, once vocabulary reached a size sufficient to force this development, it would occur *during speech acquisition* in each generation. In this view there would be no need for genetic specification of the particulate structure of the content component, contrary to what Smathary and Maynard Smith (1995) believe is necessary for this major step in evolution.

At this point we need to deal with an apparent problem for a neo-Darwinian approach to speech evolution. It is that another area of the brain, the anterior cingulate cortex (ACC: Area 24 in Fig. 7.1, top), is generally acknowledged to be the cortical region controlling vocalization in non-human primates (Jurgens 1987). Elec-trical stimulation of this region evokes vocalization in monkeys, and damage to the region impairs the ability to produce conditioned vocalization. In contrast, bilateral damage to the monkey homologue of Broca's area and the surrounding cortex has no obvious effect on vocalization (Jurgens *et al.* 1982). This together with other findings has led many to believe that the neural basis of speech is entirely new (e.g. Lancaster 1973; Myers 1976; Robinson 1976). If so, this constitutes an exception to Darwin's principle of descent with modification. Parenthetically, while Broca was sympathetic to the concept of evolution (Schiller 1991), to my knowledge he never contemplated the question of how the faculty of articulate speech evolved from ancestral primate vocal capacities.

The problem here is only apparent. Contrary to Caplan's (1994) view, cited earlier, that language is restricted to the perisylvian cortex, the ACC is crucially involved in speech. For example, consistent with the fact that respiratory and phonatory aspects of vocalization have not changed much with the evolution of speech, Jurgens and von Cramon (1982) reported that a patient with a bilateral ACC lesion had not recovered normal phonation five years after the damage. In addition, Paus *et al.* (1993) concluded from a PET study of ACC activation during speech and non-speech tasks that the "ACC participates in motor control by facilitating the execution of the appropriate responses and/or suppression the execution of the inappropriate ones" (p. 453). This is certainly an activity integral to normal speech.

In addition to the ACC, there is another area of the medial cortex, immediately superior to the ACC (Brodmann's medial area 6—see Fig. 7.1, top) which, while unimportant in monkey vocalization, is intimately involved in speech. It is the supplementary motor area (SMA) which is closely related to the ACC. It is always active in speech-production tasks (Roland 1993), and two other aspects of its activity provide a clue as to its role in the evolution of speech. First, electrical stimulation of this area often makes patients involuntarily produce rhythmic syllable strings such as 'dadadada' (Brickner 1940; Erikson and Woolsey 1951; Penfield and Welch 1951; Penfield and Jasper 1954; Chauvel 1976; Woolsey *et al.* 1979; Dinner and Luders 1995). Second, Jonas (1981) has summarized eight studies of irritative lesions of the SMA which have reported involuntary production of similar sequences in 20 patients.

The SMA seems to be the part of the cortex most likely to be responsible for the production of speech frames in modern hominids. I have suggested that when visuofacial cyclicities became an important component of primate communication, the medial cortex, the SMA in particular, in its role as part of the medial communication region, took over the control of these cyclicities from lateral frontal cortex, to which it is intimately connected (MacNeilage 1998b). Therefore, in ordinary modern speech, when a lexical item is targeted for motor encoding, the requisite frame information (e.g., for 'landmark', two syllables, stress the first) is sent to the SMA, and information regarding the individual consonants and vowels is sent to Broca's area. There, the two are eventually put together, correctly or not, guided by the syllable-structure constraint, and the result is sent to the primary motor cortex (Brodmann's area 4—see Fig. 7.1, bottom).

If this view is correct, then Lashley's two necessary components of serially-ordered speech—the elements and the ordering mechanism—can be, at least in part, localized to two cortical premotor subsystems. The existence of these two motor subsystems, not only for speech but for action-control in general, is widely accepted in modern neurophysiology (e.g. Eccles 1982; Rizzolatti *et al*. 1983; Goldberg 1985, 1992; Passingham 1987). In terms of subcortical connectivities, the medial system is most closely related to the basal ganglia while the lateral system is most closely linked with the cerebellum. Both of these subcortical structures have been recently implicated in language production (for the basal ganglia, see Damasio and Damasio 1992; for the cerebellum, see Leiner *et al*. 1989), which I take to be another vindication of Lashley's evolutionary conservatism, and his non-modular emphasis.

Converging evidence from studies of monkeys and humans suggests that the medial subsystem is an 'intrinsic' one, most involved in spontaneous action generation *of all kinds*, whereas the lateral subsystem is 'extrinsic', that is, more responsive to external input *in any* modality (Goldberg 1992). Again I take this to be a vindication of Lashley's conservative non-modular view of neural mechanisms, and in stark contrast to the 'Speech is special' view (e.g. Liberman and Mattingly 1985). Relative to speech, medial cortex lesions tend to result in impaired ability to generate speech, but with preserved ability to repeat it (e.g. Rubens 1975), while one type of lateral patient, at least—the conduction aphasic—tends to have the opposite symptom pattern (e.g. Green and Howes 1977). Non-speech effects of medial lesions include an initial akinesia, followed by a difficulty in pantomiming acts—a situation in which direct external cueing is absent—relative to the ability to imitate them (R. Watson *et al*. 1986).

The ability of the extrinsic system to act on the basis of external input is supported by a number of lateral circuits from visual, auditory, and somatic sensory cortex to lateral frontal cortex (Pandya 1987; Deacon 1992). Some of the circuits presumably support our speech-repetition capacity. The well-known articulatory loop of working memory (Baddeley 1986) is one specific manifestation of the perceptuomotor capabilities supporting adult speech, localized, at least partially, in the lateral frontal cortex (e.g. Paulesu *et al*. 1993). From an evolutionary perspective, the ability to repeat what is said to us is not an important function in adults. Its importance lies perhaps mainly in the message it gives to us that we possess a capacity that makes speech learnable. Baddeley (1995) recently concluded that the articulatory loop of working memory evolved in order to make language learning possible. Our capacity to say the words we hear, either aloud or subvocally, is the basis for the building of the capacity to say words when we have not just heard them. While Lashley did not specifically consider either the evolution or the ontogeny of speech, he recognized the need for a capacity for short-term storage to support the assembly of on-line speech.

In my opinion, the evolution of learnability of speech played an important role in the evolution of the lateral cortex—the perisylvian cortex in general—as the most important region for control of communication in humans. But this capacity to learn —most basically to learn to make the *movements* of others—was presumably not specific to speech. Donald (1991) has argued persuasively that a major step in hominid evolution was the evolution of a general-purpose mimetic capability, seen in families of actions such as those supporting tribal rituals, dance, games, singing, and music in general. The human ability, noted by Lashley, to superimpose rhythms on various complex performances, even on an *ad hoc* basis, is presumably most related to the evolution of a general-purpose mimetic ability in hominids (Donald 1991). I take these considerations as supporting Lashley's evolutionary conservatism and his non-modular view of cerebral mechanisms. Just as the control of speech production by the two motor systems apparently evolved in the context of the general-purpose functions of these systems, so did speech learnability probably evolve in the context of the learnability of perceived movements in general.

Coda

I have argued, in accordance with Lashley's beliefs, that brain organization underlying many aspects of speech production is amenable to explanation in terms not specific to speech. But I don't want to give the impression that what is unique about speech production is relatively trivial. In what way then, is speech production unique? It is unique in the way in which its basic hard-wired syllabic rhythm generator is modu-lated. As pointed out earlier, in the most typical mode of operation of a rhythm generator, it is modulated by external stimuli. For example respiration is modulated by availability of oxygen, terrestrial locomotion by the structure of the terrain being traversed. Speech is unique among actions using hard-wired generators in that its basic rhythm is modulated *internally*, both in terms of syllable level inputs such as those related to stress, but more importantly, by the segmental sequence called for in any particular utterance. It is this internal programming of the rhythm generator with discrete sound units, arranged in combinations linked to specific meanings—both the units and the meanings being socially agreed upon—which in my opinion makes the greatest contribution to the uniqueness of speech production. No other mammalian vocal communication has these properties. This is a far from a minor matter. I believe that this development must have been a prerequisite for the development which was the crowning glory of hominid evolution. Before we evolved the ability to put words together in a rule-governed way, giving language its infinite capacity, we must have had a lot of words. Otherwise, where would the selection pressures have come from to force words into the superordinate categories necessary for the evolution of word-ordering rules? The frame/content mode gave us the capability of forming a lot of words.

It will perhaps not surprise the reader when I say that I think Lashley's serial order paper is one of the most important papers in the history of cognitive neuroscience. In my opinion, the paper set the stage, and still does, for the understanding of the relationship between cognition and action in higher organisms. If one accepts the views of Darwin and Sperry regarding the importance of action in the understanding of living forms, one might share my regard for Lashley's paper, and even the present paper, which is highly derivative of Lashley's paper.

Summary

Broca's localization of 'articulate speech' in the left lateral frontal lobe was a landmark in the history of human understanding, but one that has not yet been fully capitalized on. Action, and the Darwinian perspective on it, has generally been neglected in our attempts to understand ourselves. However, Lashley has provided us with a set of guidelines for the understanding of the cerebral organization underlying any serially ordered behaviour, and in this paper a 'frame/content' theory of the evolution of articulate speech is outlined which makes heavy use of four of these guidelines. They are:

(1) the necessity for an ordering process independent of the elements to be ordered;
(2) the importance of rhythm generators in achieving time-extended output;
(3) the necessity of a temporary priming stage (working memory) for the assembly of complex output sequences; and
(4) the extreme conservatism of evolution.

The preservation of the vowel–consonant distinction in the serial positioning of erroneously placed consonants and vowels ('content') in ordinary speech suggests that a syllable-structure ('frame') constraint, at the premotor level, provides the necessary ordering principle for modern adult hominid speech. The rhythmic open–close oscillation of the mandible for each syllable (the motor frame)—open for vowels, closed for consonants—was probably the phylogenetic motor base for the premotor frame. In a subsequent move which made speech truly unique, separable content elements probably originated by self-organization as languages evolved increasingly large message-differentiating capabilities. (They probably emerged then, as now, in development, though not in genetic structure.) The perceptual-motor relationships encoded in working memory serve on-line speech organization but also probably evolved so that language could be learned. A deep evolutionary base for the motor frame, and its origin as an exaptation, is suggested by the fact that the brain region containing Broca's area is the main cortical region for the control of ingestive processes, including ingestive cyclicities, in mammals. The conservatism of evolution is further reflected in the fact that the dichotomy between medial and lateral motor systems underlying speech production, and the motor-based learnability underlying speech evolution, are both aspects of more general-purpose hominid capabilities. In conclusion, using a neo-Darwinian perspective, and some of Lashley's guidelines for understanding serially ordered behaviours, the frame/content theory of speech evolution might give us a better understanding of what the human possession of articulate speech entails; this, in turn, might give us further insight into its significance.

References

Andrew, R. J. (1976). Use of formants in the grunts of baboons and other non-human primates. *Annals of the New York Academy of Sciences*, **280**, 673–93.

Baddeley, A. D. (1986). *Working memory*. Clarendon Press, London.

Baddeley, A. D. (1995). Working memory. In *The cognitive neurosciences* (ed. M. Gazzaniga), pp. 755–64. MIT Press, Cambridge, MA.

Blumstein, S. E. (1995). The neurobiology of the sound structure of language. In *The cognitive neurosciences* (ed. M Gazzaniga), pp. 915–30. MIT Press, Cambridge, MA.

Bradshaw, J. L. and Nettleton, N. C. (1983). *Human cerebral asymmetry*. Prentice Hall, Englewood Cliffs, NJ.

Brickner, R. M. (1940). A human cortical area producing repetitive phenomena when stimulated. *Journal of Neurophysiology*, **3**, 128–30.

Broca, P. (1861). Remarques sur la siège de la faculté du langage articulé, suivies d'une observation d'aphémie. *Bulletin de la Société Anatomique de Paris*, **2**, 330–57.

Brodmann, K. (1909). *Vergleichende Localizationslehre der Grosshirnrinde in ihren Prinzipien dargestelt auf Grund des Zellenbaues*. J. A. Barth, Leipzig.

Brown, J. W. (1979). Language representation in the brain. In *Neurobiology of social communication in primates* (ed. H. D. Steklis and M. J. Raleigh), pp. 133–95. Academic Press, New York.

Bruce, D. (1994). Lashley and the problem of serial order. *American Psychologist*, **49**, 93–105.

Caplan, D. (1994). Language and the brain. In *Handbook of psycholinguistics* (ed. M. A. Gernsbacher), pp. 1023–54. Academic Press, New York.

Changeux, J.-P. (1985). *Neuronal man*. Pantheon, New York.

Chauvel, P. C. (1976). Les stimulations de l'aire motrice supplementaire chez l'homme. Thesis, Université de Rennes.

Chomsky, N. (1957). *Syntactic structures*. Mouton, The Hague.

Chomsky, N. (1965). Current issues in linguistic theory. In *The structure of language* (eds J. A. Fodor and J. J. Katz), pp. 50–118. Prentice–Hall, Englewood Cliffs, NJ.

Chomsky, N. (1966). *Cartesian linguistics*. Harper and Row, New York.

Chomsky, N. (1986). *Knowledge of language: its nature, origin, and use*. Praeger, New York.

Cohen, A. H. (1988). Evolution of the vertebrate central pattern generator for locomotion. In *Neural control of rhythmic movements* (ed. A. Cohen, S. Rossignol, and S. Grillner), pp. 129–66. Wiley, New York.

Corballis, M. C. (1991). *The lopsided ape*. Oxford University Press.

Damasio, A. R. and Damasio, H. (1992). Brain and language. *Scientific American*, **267**, September, 63–71.

Darwin, C. (1859). *The origin of species*. John Murray, London.

Darwin, C. (1871). *The descent of man*. Great Books, Encyclopedia Britannica, Chicago, IL.

Davis, B. L. and MacNeilage, P. F. (1995). The articulatory basis of babbling. *Journal of Speech and Hearing Research*, **38**, 1199–211.

Dax, M. (1865). Lésion de la moitié gauche de l'encéphale coïncident avec l'oubli des signes de la pensée. *Gazette Hebdomadaire de Médecine et de Chirurgie* (*Paris*), **2**, 259–60. (Read at Montpelier, France, in 1836).

Day, E. and MacNeilage, P. F. (1996). Postural asymmetries and language lateralization in humans (*Homo sapiens*). *Journal of Comparative Psychology*, **110**, 88–96.

Deacon, T. W. (1992). Cortical connections of the inferior arcuate sulcus in the macaque brain. *Brain Research*, **573**, 8–26.

Delcomyn, F. (1980). Neural basis of rhythmic behavior in animals. *Science*, **210**, 492–98.

Dell, G. S. (1986). A spreading-activation theory of retrieval in sentence production. *Psychological Review*, **93**, 283–321.

Dell, G. S., Juliana, C., and Govindjee, A. (1993). Structure and content in language production: a theory of frame constraints in phonological speech errors. *Cognitive Science*, **17**, 149–95.

Dell, G. S., Burger, L. K., and Svec, W. R. (1997). Language production and serial order: a functional analysis and a model. *Psychological Review*, **93**, 123–147.

de Saussure, F. (1916). *Cours de linguistique générale*. Payot, Paris.

Dinner, D. S. and Luders, H. O. (1995). Human supplementary sensorimotor area: electrical stimulation and movement-related potential studies. In *Epilepsy and the functional anatomy of the frontal lobe* (ed. H. H. Jasper, S. Riggio, and P. S. Goldman-Rakic), pp. 261–72. Raven Press, New York.

Donald, M. (1991). *Evolution of the modern mind*. Harvard University Press, Cambridge, MA.

Dunbar, R. (1997). *Grooming, gossip, and the evolution of language*. Harvard University Press, Cambridge, MA.

Eccles, J. C. (1982). The initiation of voluntary movements by the supplementary motor area. *Archiv Psychiatrie Nervenkrankheiten*, **231**, 423–41.

Erickson, T. C. and Woolsey, C. N. (1951). Observations on the supplementary motor area of man. *Transactions of the American Neurological Association*, **76**, 50–2.

Fodor, J. A. (1983). *The modularity of mind*. MIT Press, Cambridge, MA.

Foerster, O. (1936). The motor cortex in man in the light of Hughlings Jackson's doctrines. *Brain*, **59**, 135–59.

Fox, P. T. (1995). Broca's area: motor encoding in somatic space. *Behavioral and Brain Sciences*, **18**, 344–5.

Fromkin, V. A. (ed.) (1973). *Speech errors as linguistic evidence*. Mouton, The Hague.

Galaburda, A. M. (1982). Histology, architechtonics and asymmetry of language areas. In *Neural models of language processes* (ed. M. A. Arbib, D. Caplan, and J. Marshall), pp. 435–44. Academic Press, New York.

Gazzaniga, M. (ed.) (1995). *The cognitive neurosciences*. MIT Press, Cambridge, MA.

Gernsbacher, M. A. (ed.) (1994). *Handbook of psycholinguistics*. Academic Press, New York.

Goldberg, G. (1985). Supplementary motor area structure and function: review and hypothesis. *Behavioral and Brain Sciences*, **8**, 567–616.

Goldberg, G. (1992). Premotor systems, attention to action and behavioral choice. In *Neurobiology of motor program selection* (ed. J. Kein, C. R. McCroha, and W. Winlow), pp. 225–49. Pergamon Press, London.

Gould, S. J. (1991). Exaptation: a crucial tool for an evolutionary psychology. *Journal of Social Issues*, **47**, 43–65.

Green, E. and Howes, D. H. (1977). The nature of conduction aphasia: a study of anatomic and clinical features and of underlying mechanisms. In *Studies in neurolinguistics Vol. 3* (ed. H. Whitaker and H. A. Whitaker), pp. 123–56. Academic Press, New York.

Green, S. (1975). Variations of vocal pattern with social situation in the Japanese monkey (*Macaca fuscata*): a field study. In *Primate behavior: Vol. 4. Developments in field and laboratory research* (ed. L. A. Rosenblum), pp. 1–102. Academic Press, New York.

Guthrie, E. (1935). *The psychology of learning*. Harper, New York.

Hardcastle, W. J. and Marchal, A. (ed.) (1997). *Handbook of phonetic sciences*. Blackwell, Oxford.

Hiraba, K., Taira, M., Yoshinori, S., and Nakamura, Y. (1988). Single unit activity in the bulbar reticular formation during food ingestions in chronic cats. *Journal of Neurophysiology*, **60**, 1333–49.

Jacob, F. (1977). Evolution and tinkering. *Science*, **196**, 1161–6.

Jonas, S. (1981). The supplementary motor region and speech emission. *Journal of Communication Disorders*, **14**, 349–73.

Jordan, M. and Rosenbaum, D. A. (1991). Action. In *Foundations of cognitive science* (ed. M. Posner), pp. 727–68. MIT Press, Cambridge, MA.

Jurgens, U. (1987). Primate communication: signalling, vocalization. In *Encyclopedia of Neuroscience* (ed. G. Adelman), pp. 976–9. Birkhauser, Boston, MA.

Jurgens, U. and Cramon, D. von (1982). On the role of the anterior cingulate cortex in phonation: a case report. *Brain and Language*, **15**, 234–48.

Jurgens, U., Kirzinger, A., and Cramon D. von. (1982). The effect of deep-reaching lesions in the cortical face area on phonation: a combined case report and experimental monkey study. *Cortex*, **18**, 125–40.

Kimura, D. (1979). Neuromotor mechanisms in the evolution of human communication. In *Neurobiology of social communication in primates* (ed. H. D. Steklis and M. J. Raleigh), pp. 197–220. Academic Press, New York.

Kozhevnikov, V. A. and Chistovich, L. (ed.) (1965). *Speech: articulation and perception*. Washington, Clearing House for Federal, Scientific and Technical Information, JPRS, **30**, 543.

Lancaster, J. (1973). *Primate behavior and the emergence of human culture*. Holt, Rinehart Winston, New York.

Lashley, K. S. (1951). The problem of serial order in behavior. In *Cerebral mechanisms in behavior: the Hixon symposium* (ed. L. A. Jeffress), pp. 112–36. Wiley, New York.

LeBlanc, P. (1992). Language localization with activation PET scanning. *Journal of Neurosurgery*, **31**, 369–73.

Leiner, H. C., Leiner, A. L., and Dow, R. S. (1989). Reappraising the cerebellum: what does the hindbrain contribute to the forebrain? *Behavioral Neuroscience*, **103**, 998–1008.

Levelt, W. J. M. (1989). *Speaking: from intention to articulation*. MIT Press, Cambridge, MA.

Levelt, W. J. M. (1992). Accessing words in speech production: stages, processes, and representations. *Cognition*, **42**, 1–22.

Liberman, A. M. and Mattingly, I. G. (1985). The motor theory of speech perception revised. *Cognition*, **21**, 1–36.

Liberman, A. M. and Mattingly, I. G. (1989). A specialization for speech perception. *Science*, **24**, 489–94.

Liberman, A. M., Cooper, F. S., Harris, K. S., MacNeilage, P .F., and Studdert-Kennedy, M. G. (1967). Some observations on a model for speech perception. In *Models for the perception of speech and visual form* (ed. W. Wathen-Dunn), pp. 68–87. MIT Press, Cambridge, MA.

Lieberman, P. (1984). *The biology and evolution of language*. Harvard University Press.

Locke, J. L (1997). *Social calls*. Simon and Shuster, New York.

Lund, J. P. and Enomoto, S. (1988). The generation of mastication by the central nervous system. In *Neural control of rhythmic movements* (ed. A. Cohen, S. Rossignol, and S. Grillner), pp. 41–72. Wiley, New York.

Luschei, E. S. and Goldberg, L. J. (1981). Neural mechanisms of mandibular control: mastication and voluntary biting. In *Handbook of physiology. Section 1: The nervous system, Vol. II, Part 2: Motor control* (ed. V. B. Brooks), pp. 1237–74. American Physiological Society, Washington, DC.

MacKay, D. G. (1987). The organization of perception and action: a theory for language and other cognitive sciences. Springer, New York.

MacNeilage, P. F. (ed.) (1983). *The production of speech*. Springer, New York.

MacNeilage, P. F. (1994). Prolegomena to a theory of the sound pattern of the first language. *Phonetica*, **51**, 184–94.

MacNeilage, P. F. (1997). Acquisition of speech. In *Handbook of phonetic sciences* (ed. W. J. Hardcastle and A. Marchal), pp. 301–32, Blackwell, Oxford.

MacNeilage, P. F. (1998a). Towards a unified view of cerebral hemispheric specializations in vertebrates. *Comparative neuropsychology* (ed. A. D. Milner). Oxford University Press (in press).

MacNeilage, P. F. (1998b). The frame/content theory of evolution of speech production. *Behavioral and Brain Sciences* **21**, 499–546.

MacNeilage, P. F. (1998c). Evolution of the mechanism of speech production: comparative neurobiology of vocal and manual communication. In *The evolution of phonology and syntax: social and cognitive bases for the evolution of language* (ed. J. Hurford, C. Knight, and M. G. Studdert-Kennedy), pp. 222–41, Cambridge University Press.

MacNeilage, P. F. and Davis, B. L. (1990). Acquisition of speech production: frames, then content. In *Attention and Performance XIII: motor representation and control* (ed. M. Jean-nerod), pp. 453–76. Erlbaum, Hillsdale, NJ.

MacNeilage, P. F., Studdert-Kennedy, M. G., and Lindblom, B. (1985). Planning and production of 'speech: an overview. *Planning and production of speech in normally hearing and deaf people* (ed. J. Lauter), pp. 15–22. ASHA Reports. American Speech and Hearing Association, Washington DC.

MacNeilage, P. F., Davis, B. L., and Matyear, C. L. (1997). Babbling and first words: phonetic similarities and differences. *Speech Communication*, **22**, 269–277.

Mayr, E. (1982). *The growth of biological thought*. Bellknap, Cambridge, MA.

Miller, G. A. (1962). Some psychological studies of grammar. *American Psychologist*, **17**, 748–62.

Myers, R. E. (1976). Comparative neurology of vocalization and speech: proof of a dichotomy. *Annals of the New York Academy of Sciences*, **280**, 745–57.

Pandya, D. (1987). Association cortex. In *The encyclopedia of neuroscience* (ed. G. Adelman), pp. 80–3. Birkhauser, Boston.

Passingham, R. E. (1987). Two cortical systems for directing movement. *Ciba Foundation Symposium No. 132*, (ed. G. Bock, M. O'Connor, and J. Marsh), pp. 151–64. Wiley, London.

Paulesu, E., Frith, C. D., and Frackowiak, R. S. J. (1993). The neural correlates of the component of working memory. *Nature*, **362**, 342–44.

Paus, T., Petrides, M., Evans, A. C., and Meyer, E. (1993). The role of the human anterior cingulate cortex in the control of oculomotor, manual and speech responses: a positron emission tomography study. *Journal of Neurophysiology*, **70**, 453–69.

Penfield, W. and Jasper, H. H. (1954). *Epilepsy and the functional anatomy of the human brain*. Little Brown, New York.

Penfield, W. and Welch, K. (1951). The supplementary motor area of the cerebral cortex: a clinical and experimental study. *A. M. A. Archives of Neurology and Psychiatry*, **66**, 289–317.

Petersen, S. E., Fox, P. T., Posner, M. I., Mintun, M., and Raichle, M. E. (1988). Positron emission tomographic studies of the cortical anatomy of single-word processing. *Nature*, **331**, 585–9.

Posner, M. (ed.) (1991). *Foundations of cognitive science*. MIT Press, Cambridge, MA.

Redican, W. K. (1975). Facial expressions in non-human primates. *Primate behavior: developments in field and laboratory research*, Vol. 4, (ed. L. A. Rosenblum), pp. 103–94. Academic Press, New York.

Rizzolatti, G., Matelli, M., and Pavesi, G. (1983). Deficits in attention and movement following the removal of postarcuate (area 6) and prearcuate (area 8) cortex in macaque monkeys. *Brain*, **106**, 655–73.

Robinson, B. W. (1976). Limbic influences on human speech. *Annals of the New York Academy of Sciences*, **280**, 761–71.

Roland, P. (1993). *Brain activation*. Wiley–Liss, New York.

Rubens, A. B. (1975). Aphasia with infarction in the territory of the anterior cerebral artery. *Cortex*, **11**, 239–50.

Schiller, F. (1992). *Paul Broca: explorer of the brain*. Oxford University Press.

Shaffer, L. H. (1982). Intention and performance. *Psychological Review*, **83**, 375–93.

Shaffer, L. H. (1984). Motor programming in language production—a tutorial review. In *Attention and performance X: control of language processes* (ed., H. Bouma and D. G. Bouwhuis), pp. 17–41. Erlbaum, Hillsdale, NJ.

Shattuck-Hufnagel, S. (1980). Speech units smaller than the syllable. *Journal of the Acoustical Society of America*, **72** (Suppl. 1), 548.

Sperry, R. W. (1952). Neurology and the mind/brain problem. *American Scientist*, **40**, 291–312.

Studdert-Kennedy, M. G. (1987). The phoneme as a perceptuomotor unit. In *Language perception and production* (ed. A. Allport, D. G. MacKay, W. Prinz, and E. Scheerer), pp. 67–84. Academic Press, London.

Studdert-Kennedy, M. G. (1998). The origins of generativity. In *The evolution of phonology and syntax: social and cognitive bases for the evolution of language* (ed. J. Hurford, C. Knight, and M. G. Studdert-Kennedy), pp. 202–221, Cambridge University Press.

Szathmary, E. and Maynard Smith, J. (1995). The major evolutionary transitions. *Nature*, **374**, 227–32.

Tinbergen, N. (1952). Derived activities: their causation, biological significance, origin and emancipation during evolution. *Quarterly Review of Biology*, **27**, 1–32.

Tolman, E. C. (1948). Cognitive maps in rats and men. *Psychological Review*, **55**, 189–208.

Vygotsky, L. S. (1962). *Thought and language*. MIT Press, Cambridge, MA.

Watson, J. B. (1913). Psychology as the behaviorist views it. *Psychological Review*, **20**, 158–77.

Watson, J. B. (1920). Is thinking merely the action of the language mechanisms? *British Journal of Psychology*, **11**, 86–104.

Watson, R. T., Fleet, W. S., Gonzales-Rothi, L., and Heilman, K. M. (1986). Apraxia and the supplementary motor area. *Archives of Neurology*, **43**, 787–92.

Woolsey, C. N. (1958). Organization of somatic sensory and motor areas of the cerebral cortex. In *Biological and biochemical bases of behavior* (ed. H. F. Harlow and C. N. Woolsey), pp. 63–82. University of Wisconsin Press, Madison, WI.

Woolsey, C. N., Erickson, T. C., and Gilson, W. E. (1979). Localization in somatic sensory and motor areas of human cerebral cortex as determined by direct recording of evoked potentials and electrical stimulation. *Journal of Neurosurgery*, **51**, 476–506.

8

Preconditions for the evolution of protolanguages

Merlin Donald

Introduction

Most theorists in the field of language evolution concede that the earliest forms of language must have emerged from adaptive elaborations on ape gesticulation and vocalization, and that these skills were gradually transformed by evolutionary pressures into the more flexible, and ultimately much more powerful, means of communication that we know as human language. There is such widespread agreement on this basic idea, from Darwin (1871) to Lieberman (1984), Bickerton (1990), Pinker and Bloom (1990), Corballis (1991), Greenfield (1991), Pinker (1994), and many others, including myself (Donald 1991), that one must conclude that, within the bounds of a neo-Darwinian theoretical framework, no viable alternative to this position has yet been proposed. The only exception of any influence is an extreme anti-Darwinian position once expressed by Chomsky (1965), that human language is based on a principle entirely different from that of animal communication. In essence, Chomsky's position holds that there are no precedents for language, and that language must have emerged by means of some discontinuous process that cannot be encompassed within the current neo-Darwinian framework. Unfortunately, this position does not generate dialogue, and is more an *ex cathedra* proclamation than a theory.

I will assume for the purposes of this article that the evolution of language, like all other aspects of life, must have been subject to the laws of natural selection, and that its emergence must therefore have been a continuous process. Given this assumption, there is still considerable room for disagreement on the details of the evolutionary transition from ape to human, and on the form that a credible theory of language evolution should take. There are early-versus-late language models; 'punctuated' models, with discrete stages of evolution, versus gradualistic models; vocalization-first versus language-first models; 'ontogeny-recapitulates-phylogeny' versus glottogenetic models; and encephalization versus lateralization models, to list just a few. The diversity of language-origin proposals reflects the fact that we have virtually no direct evidence on precisely what the cognitive skills of early hominids might have been. However, this diversity might be narrowed down if we consider the cognitive constraints that must be imposed on theories of language evolution.

The term 'protolanguage' has been used as a label for the earliest form that 'true' language must have taken. A protolanguage is thus a prototype, an approximation of the finished product that contains some of the essential features of language, and that could later have evolved into full-fledged language. Based upon his work on pidgins and creoles, Bickerton (1990) has proposed a specific definition of this phenomenon. He argues that protolanguage must resemble pidgins, which are very much like the language of two-year-old children, consisting of one- and two-word utterances combined with pointing, gesturing, and prosodic voice modulation. Pidgins are also grammarless. Bickerton proposes that protolanguage must have had all these characteristics. He locates protolanguage far back in hominid evolution, with the earliest members of species *Homo*, who lived in Africa over two million years ago. In line with his theory, he argues that grammars came later in hominid evolution, with *Homo sapiens*. He builds a credible case for this scenario, pointing out how a rudimentary vocabulary would have had immediate adaptive advantages for pre-sapient *Homo* (i.e. *Homo* before *Homo sapiens*), in tool-making, hunting, and social coordination.

Bickerton's approach thus places language early; it has an element of gradualism in it, although it acknowledges a period of accelerated change associated with the speciation of sapient humans; and it falls into the class of 'ontogeny-recapitulates-phylogeny' theories alongside those of Parker and Gibson (1979), Greenfield (1991), and others. But underneath these surface features there lies an assumption, one might say an axiom, that drives his particular theory, as well as a number of similar ideas about language origins.

The crucial axiom supporting Bickerton's argument is that *language is fundamental to all distinctly human thought and consciousness*. The root syllogism leading to his theory can be reconstructed thus:

(1) archaeological evidence shows that the culture of pre-sapient *Homo* was a major advance over what preceded it, manifesting the germ of human inventiveness, craft, and social coordination;
(2) this, combined with a large increase in the encephalization ratio of pre-sapient *Homo* implies a significant cognitive advance in the direction of symbolic thought;
(3) and symbolic thought is inherently dependent upon language capacity (Bickerton 1993).

Therefore, some primitive form of language skill must have been present in *Homo* before the emergence of *H. sapiens*.

A constraint acknowledged by Bickerton is that we must withhold some aspect of cognitive evolution from pre-sapient *Homo* to explain the tremendously accelerated recent cognitive advance of *H. sapiens*. For Bickerton, the extra advantage that sapient humans enjoy is the capstone of the Chomskyan conception of the linguistic world—grammar. Thus, Bickerton not only explains the achievements of pre-sapient *Homo*; he also preserves the most important component of Chomsky's treasured 'language acquisition device' for sapient humans.

Bickerton's approach is compatible with Daniel Dennett's belief that thought and consciousness are a direct product of language capacity. Dennett (1992) addressed this specific point, arguing that some form of language would have been necessary for pre-sapient hominid skills like fire-tending and complex tool-manufacture. In general, one might say that something like Bickerton's version of evolution is favoured by those who believe that human intellectual advantage is exclusively tied to language ability. This would probably include most classical A/I (Artificial Intelligence) theorists, many philosophers, and most linguists, who, not surprisingly, tend to be very language-centred in their bias. In this world-view, to explain the great cognitive leap that was obviously taken by pre-sapient *Homo*, one must push language back into that era.

I disagree with this world-view. The roots of my disagreement run very deep, and can be traced to the axiomatic level. Returning to the implicit syllogism I attributed to Bickerton, I would agree with its first two propositions, but not with the third, adding a supplementary caveat. The new (altered) argument would take the following form:

(1) archaeological evidence shows that the culture of pre-sapient *Homo* was a major advance over what preceded it;
(2) this, combined with a large increase in the encephalization ratio of pre-sapient *Homo*, implies a significant cognitive advance;
(3) such an advance would not have been possible without a more powerful form of representation; and then the caveat:
(4) *we must not assume that this early advance was in itself linguistic*, or that it conformed to conventional definitions of symbolic thought.

We should favour a theory that pays attention to the cognitive fundamentals, and does not make the leap to language until it is absolutely necessary. It also follows that we should explore statements (3) and (4) in some detail before trying to draw any conclusions.

The primacy of motor evolution

Could protolanguage have sprung 'fully-armed' from the cognitive armamentarium of primates? My answer to this question is a resounding 'no.' There are important fundamentals missing from the primate mind, without which protolanguages could not emerge; I shall call these the 'cognitive preconditions' of protolanguage. The nature of these preconditions becomes clear when we consider the collective, social nature of language. There are published reports of intentional gesticulation in individual chimpanzees and isolated 'pedagogical' interactions between chimpanzees (see, for example, Boesch and Boesch-Ackerman 1991), but the acid test for a species-wide representational capacity is its *general and spontaneous adoption in culture*, as shown by the presence of significant expressive variability across generations and between different social groups of the same species. This does not happen in modern apes, or in any other documented mammalian species (the variability found in bird-song forms an interesting parallel, but has no direct bearing on primate evolution). An adequate theory of language origin must therefore confront the problem of symbolic invention in groups. To cross the gap between symbolic and non-symbolic representation, hominids needed a capacity to invent expressive conventions—gestures and symbols —'in the wild.'

This focuses the question somewhat—what type of cognitive change would enable a group of primates to invent highly variable and culturally idiosyncratic forms of gesture and sound, and gradually develop distinctive cultures? Again, we must not assume that language was essential to achieve this end. A more fundamental requirement would appear to be a generalized capacity for deliberately refining action. All gestures and intentional vocalizations are ultimately actions of the musculature, and to generate greater varieties of gestures and sounds, primate motor behaviour must somehow have become much more plastic, less stereotyped, and subject to deliberate rehearsal. In other words, a breakthrough in hominid motor evolution must have preceded language evolution.

This revolution in the cognitive control of action required a break with the traditional scenario that evolutionary biology has developed to explain the evolution of animal behaviour. Throughout most of mammalian evolution the range of behaviours available to a species has been largely fixed in the genes, and closely attuned to its ecological niche; this is sometimes called a 'specialist' strategy (cf. Gamble 1993). While this mechanism enables tremendous diversity across species, and some specialization of roles within species, it forces virtual stereotypy on the behaviour of any single species. This is generally true of higher mammals; if you have seen one social group of lions or elephants, basically you have seen them all. The genetic concrete in which their behaviour is cast does not allow animal species to escape from the stereotyped shape of their own motor repertoire; their motor options are confined within a narrow 'morphological envelope'.

It is clear that human languages have broken out of this morphological straitjacket, and are constructed upon the virtually infinite variability of range and arbitrariness of human communicative behaviour. Where would such flexibility have begun? This question leads us logically back to one of the fundamentals of human motor skills, or what is sometimes called procedural learning. To vary or refine an action—any action, not only speech—one must carry out a sequence of basic cognitive operations. These are, traditionally: rehearse the action, observe its consequences, remember these, and then alter the form of the original act, varying one or more of the parameters dictated by the memory for the consequences of the previous action, or by an idealized image of the outcome. We might call an extended cognitive sequence of this sort—whose inherent complexity should not be underestimated—a 'rehearsal loop'. This is the familiar process of conscious review, whereby humans redirect their attention away from the world, and toward their own actions. The focus of attention thus becomes, not the reward or punishment that follows an act, or its social consequences, but the form of the act itself.

Apes seem to lack this option. They might repeat actions as a function of fairly obvious reinforcement contingencies, or socially-facilitated imitation, but they do not initiate and rehearse actions entirely on their own, for the sole purpose of refining their own movement-patterns. An important case in human prehistory is the skill-sequence known as throwing. Various species of primates throw projectiles, but they do not practise throwing projectiles, thus refining their accuracy and power, and creating variants on the execution of this skill. In contrast, even young children routinely practise and refine skills for endless hours, for example experimenting with various styles of throwing. This is a complex process; it demands that the skilled learner should be able to effortlessly change parameters such as starting position, grip, angle of arm and shoulder, release, velocity, acceleration, and so on, while evaluating the outcome of the modified action-pattern. Calvin (1983) has emphasized that humans need improved ballistic motor skills to become good at throwing, but surely the most critical element is a capacity for deliberately reviewing self-actions, so as to experiment with them. Systematic and repetitive experimentation with action is evident fairly early in human development, especially in infant babbling, including manual sign-babbling. It would be no exaggeration to say that this capacity is uniquely human, and forms the background for the whole of human culture, including language.

Those who believe in the primacy of language and symbols seem to think precisely the opposite, that this remarkable human control over motor behaviour came only after the evolution of language. Bickerton (1993), in a comment on my theory, proposed that, as humans developed better thinking skills (due presumably to protolanguage), they also developed better motor skills in general. In his 'language-first' version of evolution a child that is bouncing a ball off a wall and catching it would be able to do this only because everything in the set piece—the ball, the wall, the acts of throwing and catching—can be captured by language. Because the human child can think about the act linguistically, it is therefore able to experiment with it, and refine it through practice. Following the same logic, as Daniel Dennett (1992) has suggested, early hominids could have fashioned a complex tool only if they could 'talk' to themselves, in some primitive (proto)language, about the actions involved. Hence their conclusion—language in some form comes first, skill second.

But language-first theories run into many difficulties. Apes, and many other species, have thinking and symbol-using skills that are quite complex, without the use of language. For instance, the bonobo Kanzi recently learned how to make and use a primitive version of Oldowan tools (Toth *et al.* 1993). Such demonstrations contradict the notion that all higher cognitive skills depend on language. Second, a large experimental literature has shown that non-verbal representations and procedural learning are orthogonal to the presence of language. This widely-replicated finding has led to the dual-coding hypothesis, the notion that humans have two broadly different intellectual strategies available for representation and thinking (see Paivio 1991 for a review). Moreover, in evolutionary terms, language-first theories ask for a virtual saltation from ape cognition to language—which in the worst scenario becomes a kind of Creationism. Quite simply, it puts the cart before the horse. Where would the ability to think in primitive languages have come from in the first place? As every schoolchild knows, languages are made up of lexicons and grammars, and the sounds and grammars of specific language families are very different from one another. How could archaic hominids have broken out of the stereotypy imposed by the standard primate motor repertoire, and evolved the rich variability of action-patterning that would set the stage for the emergence of language, and even of protolanguage? The answer to this question is clear—*the ability to self-programme motor skills had to come first*. Lexicons could not have come into existence—that is, they could never have evolved 'in the wild'—unless a great advance in motor skill had already taken place. A capacity for the purposive rehearsal and refinement of skill had to come into existence first, and thus it had to come without the pre-existence of language, with its own evolutionary *raison d'etre*, and as I have argued (Donald 1991, 1993*a*, *b*, *c*, 1995, 1996, 1997, 1998) its own representational principle.

The preconditions of protolanguage were even more demanding than that. The key to purposive rehearsal and morphological variability is voluntary recall: Hominids had to gain *access to the contents of their own memories*. You cannot rehearse what you cannot recall. If an animal depends entirely upon environmental triggers to remember when and what to rehearse, skill-development becomes extremely difficult, since the animal cannot self-trigger the memories supporting the skill, and effectively hangs in suspended animation until the environment provides the cues needed for retrieval of a given response-pattern. Trainers of apes have to cope with precisely this limitation; for instance, it often takes thousands of trials to establish a reliable signing response in a chimpanzee (Greenfield and Savage-Rumbaugh 1990). In general, primates and other mammals have great difficulty in voluntarily self-triggering the contents of their own memory banks, and seem dependent upon conditioning by the environment. Even the enculturated apes of Savage-Rumbaugh *et al.* (1993) rely heavily on the human cultural environment provided by their caretakers for memory cues. Humans, in contrast, are able to 'think about' or 'imagine' things that are totally unrelated to the immediate environment, seeking out specific memory items, preferably without retrieving unwanted elements, and without relying on the environment to come up with the relevant cues to help find the target item.

To be able to do this—to focus selectively on one's own action-patterns, there has to be an *implementable* representation of action in the brain. Agents of actions must be able to trigger action sequences out of their own imaginations. In modern humans we recognize this highly-developed capacity for kinematic imagination; coaches of professional athletes and teachers of musicians and actors rely heavily on this skill. Another key to self-programmed action is that *imagery generated in kinematic imagination may be edited before being implemented in action* (Fig. 8.1). Without this capacity, there could be no refinement of human movement, no increase in its variation within the species. Without self-cued retrieval from memory, under the control of kinematic imagination, humans would remain locked into a reactive strategy, driven by the vicissitudes of the environment, like most mammals. The latter point is important—non-verbal representation is rooted in the human creative imagination, and operates by *analogue* principles. Mimetic meaning is driven by perceptual, rather than linguistic rules. Nevertheless, it is representational, even though, in the simplest case, that of skilled rehearsal, mimetic representations might serve only to represent themselves. In more complex social situations, however, mimetic communications can become highly intricate and complex, as they are in modern human society, without ever invoking a linguistic mode of representation.

Domain-general models of models—mimesis

These advances in the refinement of voluntary action—kinematic imagination, and a consciously-controlled rehearsal loop—might have taken the form of highly special-ized adaptations in humans. For instance, it is conceivable that humans might have evolved a greater degree of specialized manual or vocal control, with the latter

PLAN   EXECUTE   REVIEW

Fig. 8.1. The conscious review process. Actors can consciously review their own kinematic imagery before, during, and after execution of an act. This 'rehearsal loop' enables an actor to modify future acts until match is achieved to an idealized template of the act. The latter may be modified either in action or in imagination. This capacity suggests the existence of a consciously-accessible modelling process in the human brain, in which the actor's own movements can be integrated with an event-perceptual model of the external world.

following the same evolutionary route as bird song. But this would have led nowhere in terms of general intellectual progress. Judging from the capacities of modern humans, the advancement of motor skill in hominids was a more domain-general adaptation; that is, it applied to the whole primate voluntary motor repertoire.

There is an opposite viewpoint on this issue, epitomized by the work of Tooby and Cosmides (1989), and recently applied to hominid prehistory by Mithen (1996). These thinkers tend to treat language, and indeed all primate cognition, as if it were divided into cleanly-dissociable modules that evolved along independent trajectories. Thus we are supposed to have distinct social, spatial, and communicative modules, within which there may be even more specific modules, for a variety of specialized functions. It is significant that these theorists rarely cite cognitive or neuroscience research, yet do not hesitate to speculate at length about the organization of both the brain and cognition. Perhaps this is understandable, because the experimental literature contradicts their views. It contains many demonstrations that domain-general capabilities are, and always have been, an essential feature of the vertebrate brain. Tooby and Cosmides seem to have confused the term 'domain-general' with what they conceive as 'general-purpose' capabilities. While it is true that evolution could not, even in theory, generate general-purpose capabilities, the term 'domain-general' applies to cognitive architecture, not to the process of adaptation. Just as modular ones, domain-general capacities can be adaptations of a specialized nature. Human intentional communication cuts across all major sensory and motor modalities, and by definition must be considered domain-general.

Neurophysiologists sometimes refer to a domain-general control system as a supra-modal system. A supra-modal system is, literally, 'above modality;' that is, it can take its inputs from various sources, and implement its output in any set of voluntary muscles. Humans have excellent supra-modal capacities; thus, I might read the letter 'a' with my eyes, or my fingers, or for that matter, my nose; and I can write the letter 'a' with my finger, my wrist, my elbow, my lips, my head, or even my legs or trunk. This means that my abstract perceptual template for the latter 'a' can be mapped on to virtually any subset of my voluntary musculature. To a degree, supra-modal motor control exists in other mammals, but only for certain fixed classes of action, such as running, eating, or mating. Other mammals do not seem able to build a second-order 'model of models,' in which their own acts become part of the model, and thus subject to systematic rehearsal and refinement. Thus, baboons throw projectiles in a fight, but there is no evidence that they can improve their skill at this by deliberate rehearsal. To achieve this, they would have to shift their attention away from the external world, and redirect it towards their own bodies and actions, and they seem incapable of this. In contrast, even very young human children can spontaneously rehearse such actions, including apparently non-utilitarian actions such as standing on one's foot, making faces, or skipping stones.

The most compelling manifestation of this uniquely human domain-general motor skill is found in motor rhythms. Motor rhythms are transferable to any skeletomuscular system in the body, singly or in combination, and this illustrates the abstractness of the schemata that drive them. A rhythmic source—usually auditory, proprioceptive, or visual—might be tracked vocally, or with the fingers, the feet, or the whole body (Fig. 8.2). The controlling construct is an abstract temporal model that can be translated into various concrete kinematic images: For instance, in a jazz drummer's improvisations; in dance or marching; in coordinated group song; in many children's games; or in gymnastics.

The process that generates these action-patterns relies on a principle of perceptual resemblance; accordingly I have labelled this skill 'mimesis' or 'mimetic skill'. Mimesis is essentially metaphoric, or holistic. A mimetic action—for instance, a rhythm—can be grasped effortlessly in many variations and approximations, and the pattern cannot easily be reduced to a computational principle; that is, it cannot always be reduced to discrete or digital elements that are combined according to rules. Rather, it is more like the visual recognition of faces—the 'Gestalt,' or overall pattern, is primary.

This holistic feature distinguishes my notion of mimetic skill from Corballis's (1989, 1991) idea of 'generative praxis,' which operates according to computational, rather than holistic principles. Corballis's praxic adaptation was supposed to segment or parse action; that is, break it into irreducible fundamental components, and recombine these components at will. Thus, a tool-making sequence might be reduced to a few basic action-elements that are essentially symbolic in nature, and can be combined and recombined in various ways. These elements in turn can be parsed into

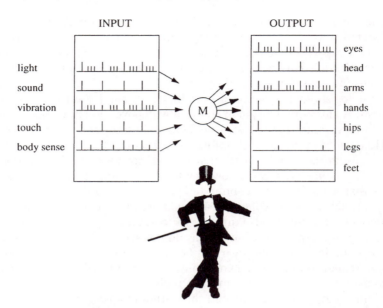

Fig. 8.2. The integration of mimetic expression with external stimuli. In rhythmic actions such as dance the actor maps from any or all of several input modalities to any or all of several output, or motor, modalities. Thus the whole body becomes an expressive device. This is, by definition, a domain-general capacity. These motor-mappings can be switched, altered, or recombined by the actor at very short notice. The acquisition or modification of such mappings is usually achieved during conscious rehearsal, using active kinematic imagery.

recombinable components. Mimetic action does not operate in this way. It is extremely difficult to reduce vocomimetic expressions, body-language, metaphoric gesture, or a complex re-enactive sequence, to discrete elements. Undoubtedly, the inspiration for Corballis's idea, and for Kosslyn's (1988) closely-related conceptualization of visual scene-analysis, is the modern computational habit of parsing and labelling events using explicit symbols. But just because programmers can find no alternative to using language-like symbols to parse perceptual events, it does not follow that the mammalian brain does the same. The denotative uses of language that support programming are extremely recent innovations, and a very unlikely source of their own invention.

Human mimetic capacity can model complex events that extend over fairly long time-scales, to include the sequencing of more complex patterns of action in context. Thus, if hominids could comprehend and remember a complex event, such as the killing of an animal or the manufacture of a tool, they should have been capable of re-enacting such events, individually or in groups, once mimetic capacity was established. Such re-enactments would have served the elementary pedagogical function of transmitting the sequence: Thus hunting and tool-making techniques could be extended and transmitted throughout the group. To some extent, this sort of imitative behaviour is present in apes, and they obviously understand many complex sequences when they are demonstrated by humans; but evidently they lack the critical capacities needed to ignite the spontaneous cultural innovations that mark human culture. Representationally-driven cultures are impossible without a public arena of modifiable action. This emphasizes once again the primacy of output—that is, production systems and ultimately motor control—in human evolution.

The cultural impact of mimetic skill distributed in social groups

An improvement in primate motor skill of this magnitude would inevitably have resulted in changes to hominid patterns of social expression, but it would not necessarily have led to anything that could qualify as protolanguage. The entire existing repertoire of primate expressive behaviour would have become raw material for this new motor-modelling mechanism. By 'parachuting' a domain-general device of this power on top of the primate motor hierarchy, previously stereotyped emotional expressions would have become rehearsable, refinable, and employable in intentional communication. This would have allowed a dramatic increase in the variability of facial, vocal, and whole-body expressions, as well as in the range of potential interactive scenarios between pairs of individuals, or within larger groups of hominids. This is precisely what we can see in modern humans. Importantly, because a supra-modal mimetic capacity would have extended to the existing vocal repertoire, it would have increased selection pressure for the early improvement of mimetic vocalization, a skill whose modern residue in speech is known as prosody.

Given a mechanism for intentional rehearsal and refinement, instrumental skills would also have moved to another plane of complexity through sharing and cultural diffusion. Sophisticated tool-making is in many ways the most solidly-established achievement of archaic *Homo*, but it is important to realize that the manufacture of a new kind of tool implies a perceived need for that tool, and corresponding advances in both tool use and pedagogy. Mimetic skill would have enabled widespread diffusion of new applications, and supported the underlying praxic innovations that led to new applications.

In addition to tool-making and emotional expression, motor mimesis would inevitably have allowed some degree of quasi-symbolic communication, in the form of a very simple shared semantic environment. The 'meaning' of mimed versions of perceptual events is transparent to anyone possessing the same event-perception capabilities as the actor; thus mimetic representations can be shared, and constitute a cognitive mechanism for creating unique sets of socially distributed representations. The expressive and social ramifications of mimetic capacity thus follow with the same inevitability as improved constructive skill. As the whole body becomes a potential tool for expression, a variety of new possibilities enter the social arena: complex games, extended competition, pedagogy through directed imitation (with a concomitant differentiation of social roles), and public action-metaphor, such as intentional group displays of aggression, solidarity, joy, fear, and sorrow. These would have perhaps constituted the first social 'customs,' and the basis of the first truly distinctive hominid cultures. This kind of mimetically-transmitted custom still forms the background social 'theatre' that supports and structures group behaviour in modern humans.

The emergence of mimetic skill would also have amplified the existing range of differences between individuals (and groups) in realms such as social manipulation, fighting and physical dominance in general, tool-making, tool use, group bonding and loyalty, pedagogical skill, mating behaviour and emotional control, and even in sexual behaviour, which would have become much more complex. This would have complicated social life, placing increased memory demands on individuals; but these communication tools would also have created a much-increased capacity for social coordination, which was probably necessary for a culture capable of moving a seasonal base camp or pursuing a long hunt.

It is important to consider the question of the durability of a hominid society equipped with mimetic skill—adaptations would not endure if they did not result in a stable long-term survival strategy for a species. Mimesis would have provided obvious benefits, allowing hominids to expand their territory, extend their potential sources of food, and respond more effectively as a group to dangers and threats. But it might also have introduced some destabilizing elements, especially by amplifying both the opportunities for competition, and the potential social rewards of competitive success.

Mimesis as a pre-adaptation for protolanguage

All these changes could have occurred without any form of what might properly be called 'linguistic' modelling of reality. In my version of events, the metaphorical, holistic pattern of thought that marks mimetic imagination would not have had the capacity to parse the visual display and label its component parts; it would have had no need for lexicons. Nevertheless, mimetic skill provided an essential pre-adaptation for speech and language, for at least one very obvious reason: the *primacy of mimetic skill in lexical morphophonology.*

Mimetic skill was necessary for the later evolution of language, because the evolution of mimetic skill made it possible to tamper with the morphology of action. But this development was only one of the two major preconditions for lexical invention, and thus for protolanguage. We should perhaps reflect on the nature of the lexicon for a moment. I will use Levelt's (1989) schematization of the lexicon as a basis for discussion. A lexical entry has to have two major components: the 'lemma', which contains the semantic and grammatical aspects of each word, and its morphophonology. In principle, the morphophonological components of a lexicon could have been constructed along purely mimetic lines. But the lemma would not have been provided by a mimetic motor adaptation, and without this side of the lexical entry, there can be no lexicon in the normal meaning of the word. There might be elements of 'speech acts' that could be supported mimetically; and there might be gesture, including vocal gesticulation; but this does not constitute a basis for constructing a true lexicon.

Mimesis was therefore necessary, but not sufficient; however, this does not diminish its importance in the later evolution of language. To invent a primitive lexicon, even in the halting, grammarless manner of a two-year-old, one must be capable of a considerable degree of mimetic invention and refinement. To be more precise, one must be able to produce *retrievable action-schemata*. Before any form of true oral language could appear, hominids had to be able to create large numbers of retrievable (or what I call 'autocuable') motor schemata. These would have provided the potential for developing a repertoire of lexical entries, the *sine qua non* of any protolanguage system.

To reiterate my major point, the fundamental principle of self-triggered voluntary retrieval of motor representations had to be established in the brain before the highly complex motor acts of speech would have been possible. Phonetic skill has been called 'articulatory gesture' by various investigators (Brownman and Goldstein 1989); the whole higher apparatus of speech depends on the basically mimetic ability of individuals to create rehearsable and retrievable vocal acts, usually in close connection with other mimetic acts. The same principle applies to sign language. Indeed, the iconic grammars of sign language have an even closer link to mimesis than the grammars of speech. This linkage has led Armstrong *et al.* (1995) to propose a gestural origin for language. Unfortunately, there is no evidence that sign languages are universal in human society, as speech grammars are. Moreover, there are no vestiges of a once-dominant universal sign language, as there should be if it was the original form of language. In my view, the fact that sign languages are possible does not suggest a gestural Ur-tongue for humans; rather it suggests that mimesis came first, as a whole-body skill, and that many linguistic constructions are mapped directly on to mimetic ones.

The universal form of language is undoubtedly speech. Language is thus normally layered on top of a mimetically-skilled phonological system during its development. Phonology has the special virtue of being able to generate a virtually infinite number of easily retrievable sound-patterns for symbolic use, to form the articulatory gestures that make up the phonological components of language. It provides the ideal vehicle for morphological experimentation. Human retrieval capacity for oral words is extraordinary—we carry around tens of thousands, and in the case of some multilinguals, hundreds of thousands, of words; in the wild, most other species, from bees to the great apes, seem to be limited to at most a few dozen expressions; and this limitation even applies to Cheney and Seyfarth's (1990) vervet monkeys. The only relatively close parallel to human phonological skill might be the vocal skill of certain birds, such as parrots and mynah birds. However, their adaptations were specialized at all levels—confined to sound, and to a very limited arena of communication.

In contrast, the human vocal adaptation came as part of a domain-general cognitive adaptation. This is evident in the fact that language is not confined to the vocal modality. Human mimesis is inherently supra-modal, cutting across all voluntary motor systems. Thus when phonology malfunctions in development, other mimetic subsystems may be harnessed by the language system, as they are in the deaf. This was shown most clearly in Petitto and Marentette's (1991) study of deaf infants' hand-babbling in sign-language environments, which occurs at exactly the same time as phonological babbling, and has the same properties. Deaf infants, growing up in deaf-signing households, are very good at miming the motor *principle* behind signing, if not the specific signs themselves. In this case, the motor principle is the same, whether vocal or manual; to produce actions repetitively at a certain rate, that most resemble those that they see others producing. Thus their manual 'babbling' reflects their expressive environments accurately, on a purely mimetic level. This is exactly what babbling infants do in hearing households—they create models, in their actions, of one of the most salient dimensions of motor behaviour observed in their families—repetitive phonological acts.

Babbling, whether oral or manual, is reference-free in the linguistic sense—that is, it has no linguistic meaning—but it is truly representational, in that babbling patterns are (eventually) excellent motor-models of the expressive patterns infants observe around them. These models are *morphological*, but not yet linguistic, because they are reference-free and grammar-free. They reproduce not only the elementary mor-phemes of language, but also the larger mimetic envelope of expression—for instance prosody, and the habit of alternation, or 'waiting one's turn' in expressive exchanges. Since babbling is free of a linguistic frame of reference, the brain mechanism that supports it does not have to be linked to language per se; rather, these eight- to ten-month old infants look like pretty good mime artists. The supra-modal nature of their babbling is very revealing—the fact that babbling is not confined to phonology is consistent with the idea that a domain-general mimetic adaptation evolved first, serving as the initial morphological foundation for language evolution. High-speed phonology seems to have developed later, as a specialized mimetic subsystem specifi-cally driven by selection pressures that favoured the use of sound as the major modality for language. This is not to say that ontogeny recapitulates phylogeny; the language of infants would not necessarily resemble the forms that early hominid communication took. But ontogeny can reveal something about the functional hierar-chies underlying language (see Nelson 1996, and my comment, Donald 1994, on Karmiloff-Smith's 1992 book *Beyond Modularity*). Skills are nested in contingent hierarchies and, in language, a capacity for morphological modelling precedes the emergence of lexical skill.

The other side of the lexical entry—lemmas

Language-first evolutionary theorists might try to hold the line at this point by conceding that, yes, basic motor skill advances might have been necessary for protolanguage, but were probably driven by the same selection pressures that pro-duced protolanguage, and indeed, were an integral component of it. Again, I disagree.

In protolanguage, as in fully-developed language, the construction of a lexical entry requires more than morphophonology; it also requires the other side of the lexical entry, the 'lemma' (Levelt 1989). This necessitates a second level of mental modelling, one that harnesses the mind's underlying morphological skills to construct linguistic statements and propositions. This second level—lexical semantics and grammar—is absent in mimesis. The integration of morphophonological addresses into a larger descriptive system is an inherently social activity, and one is tempted to predict that this process could not be confined within the isolated brain; that is, one should not expect to find the 'language acquisition device' that Chomsky (1965, 1988) predicted entirely inside the individual brain. Rather, the emergence of language depends on a community of brains in interaction. There is not yet any viable computational model of this process, and neural network models have not yet reached the point where anything so complex could be simulated. The process of mapping the 'lemma' or meaning-based side of the lexicon on to the form of the symbol—whether it is phonological or manual—involves much more than the association of a discrete form with a discrete meaning. Phonology, like any mimetic system, works according to a metaphorical principle, but the lemma involves incredibly subtle forms of meaning that cannot simply be reduced to other symbols, if Wittgenstein (1922) or Johnson-Laird (1983) are to be believed. Word-forms and meanings both tend to be fuzzy, and neither side of the lexical entry is clearly defined or discrete. The tension between word-form and meaning is a creative one that greatly increases the range of things that can be represented.

The shift here is very fundamental—mimetic models generally work on an *analogue* principle, whereas linguistic models work on the principle of segmentation, labelling and thus the *consensual definition* of reality. Where mimetic models are driven by perceptual similarity and metaphor, linguistic ones are driven by definable, specifi-able, and arbitrary relationships. Mimesis is truly representational on its own level; it underlies gesture, mime, body-language, dance, ritual, some music, and most non-verbal communication. But language captures reality in a different way; and linguistic knowledge emerges as an independent level of representation. The underlying enve-lope of speech-acts (see Fetzer 1993, and my reply at the end of the same article) is thus mimetic, not linguistic; and linguistic principles do not need to be introduced until some subset of mimetic inventions—call it the proto-lexicon—acquires a differ-ent cognitive role from mimesis.

The shift from mimesis towards protolanguage, which we can see in two-year-old children, is therefore a shift from motor homology and perceptual metaphor towards analysis and differentiation. Instead of being directly driven by perceptual metaphor, as mime is, words differentiate and specify the components of perceived relationships. Parsing the environment, that is, assigning labels to various 'views' of perceived events, is central to language. A linguistically-able mind must be able even to parse its own representations, and those of others.

The impact of this second level of skill on manifest group behaviour again changes the cultural picture of humanity. Able to perform such 'parsing,' the species produced a new, and very different, pattern of collective representations. It is still an open question whether grammar, and metalinguistic skills at the level of discourse, require a separate adaptation in addition to phonology and lexical invention. If one were to try to meet all of Fodor's (1983) requirements for a true linguistic 'module', a separate grammar module would surely fail, inasmuch as it seems to be completely interpene-trable with the rest of language, and closely tied to semantics. The neuropsychological case for a separate grammar module is further weakened by cross-linguistic studies of aphasia, which show that no specific brain lesion, nor specific pattern of grammatical deficit, is found in agrammatics of all languages (Bates *et al.* 1987). The whole perisylvian region of the left hemisphere seems to be dedicated to language, with function words and grammatical rules being stored in the same tissue as other aspects of the lexicon. Grammars are thus better regarded as a natural by-product of the process of parsing and definition; I see no compelling need to place grammatical invention in a separate category.

The invention of a symbol is a reciprocal process—form is mapped on to meaning, while meaning is *defined* by that same process, in a reciprocal tension that is revealed by the fact that language is never static. This tension is still evident, after at least 45 000 years of lexical invention. Languages are constantly changing their particular mappings of form on to meaning; for instance the entire Indo-European group of languages, including languages as diverse as Sanskrit, Gaelic, Latin, and Greek, seems to have evolved from a common ancestor within the past 7000 years (Renfrew 1987). This pattern of incessant innovation suggests that the cognitive process driving lexical invention—the need to define and redefine our maps of meaning on to form—is more fundamental and considerably less rigid than the specific forms and rules of language at any given moment.

In conclusion, hominids could not have evolved a capacity for 'protolanguage' without meeting at least two preconditions. The first was the prior evolution of a more powerful central motor capacity that gave hominids a degree of voluntary movement control that does not exist in any other species. This new motor-modelling skill, or 'mimesis', allowed them to vary and elaborate upon the entire voluntary motor repertoire of the primate line. This provided a capacity for considerable morphological invention, and thus, in theory, some of the morphophonetic capacities underlying language must have been in place first. However, their communicative use at this preliminary stage was probably restricted to action-metaphor, mime, and rudimentary gesture. On the present evidence, general mimetic skill would seem to have sufficed for the achievements of archaic *Homo* and could have served as the basis for shared expressive custom, leaving the human line with a legacy of non-verbal culture both in infancy, where language is acquired in a mimetic context; and in adults, where forms like dance, pantomime, and a public 'theatre' of expression still play a very major role, and remain largely independent of language in both their social function and guiding principles. This non-verbal background of custom and expression eventually set the cultural stage for protolanguage, by establishing a public arena for non-verbal representation, in which a disambiguating device would have been found useful.

The second precondition was the evolution of a more abstract capacity for expressive modelling, one that did not rely entirely on perceptual metaphor as the carrier of conventional meaning. This capacity, apparently unique to sapient humans, 'defines' and parses reality by employing specific classes of morphological invention as explicit memory labels; note that the evolution of this second capacity therefore depends upon the pre-existence of the first. In evolution, this second step provided the cognitive mechanism needed to construct the other side of the lexical entry, or lemma, and elevated the morphological inventiveness of hominids to a truly linguistic level. This innovation, probably first found in nascent form in early sapients, would have triggered the structural basis for evolving a capacity for lexical invention and the first protolanguages.

A corollary of this hypothesis is that the evolutionary origins of the elaborate mimetically-driven systems of expression common to all human cultures are distinct from the roots of language per se. Protolanguage, even in modern human infants, floats on the surface of such a system (Nelson 1996), and the latter must be at least partly in place before the child can begin to invent linguistic descriptions. Similarly, in its first appearance in evolution, protolanguage must have emerged slowly from a cultural environment ruled by mimetic principles—that is, by action-metaphor.

References

Armstrong, D., Stokoe, W., and Wilcox, S. E. (1995). *Gesture and the nature of language*, Cambridge University Press, Cambridge, MA.

Bates, E., Friederici, A., and Wulfeck, B. (1987). Grammatical morphology in aphasia: evidence from three languages. *Cortex*, **23**, 545–74.

Bickerton, D. (1990). *Language and species*. University of Chicago Press.

Bickerton, D. (1993). Putting cognitive carts before linguistic horses. *Behavioral and Brain Sciences*, **16**, 749–50.

Boesch, C. and Boesch-Ackermann, H. (1991). Dim forest, bright chimps. *Natural History*, **9**, 50–7

Brownman, C. P. and Goldstein, L. (1989). Articulatory gestures as phonological units. *Phonology*, **6**, 201–51.

Calvin, W. (1983). A stone's throw and its launch window: timing precision and its implications for language and the hominid brain. *Journal of Theoretical Biology*, **104**, 121–35.

Cheney, D. and Seyfarth, R. (1990). *How monkeys see the world*. University of Chicago Press.

Chomsky, N. (1965). *Aspects of a theory of syntax*. MIT Press, Cambridge, MA.

Chomsky, N. (1988). *Problems of knowledge*. MIT Press, Cambridge, MA.

Corballis, M. C. (1989). Laterality and human evolution. *Psychological Review*, **96**, 492–505.

Corballis, M. C. (1991). *The lopsided ape: evolution of the generative mind*. Oxford University Press, New York.

Darwin, C. (1871). *The descent of man*. John Murray, London.

Dennett, D. (1992). The role of language in intelligence. *Darwin Lecture*, Cambridge University, March 6, 1992. Publication CCS-92-3, Center for Cognitive Studies, Tufts University, Boston, MA.

Donald, M. (1991). *Origins of the modern mind: three stages in the evolution of culture and cognition*. Harvard University Press, Cambridge, MA.

Donald, M. (1993a). Précis of 'Origins of the modern mind', with multiple reviews and author's response. *Behavioral and Brain Sciences*, **16**, 737–91.

Donald, M. (1993b). Human cognitive evolution: what we were, what we are becoming. *Social Research*, **60**, 143–70.

Donald, M. (1993c). Hominid enculturation and cognitive evolution. *Archaeological Review from Cambridge*, **12**, 5–24.

Donald, M. (1994). Representation: ontogenesis and phylogenesis. *Behavioral and Brain Sciences*, **17**, 714–715.

Donald, M. (1995). The neurobiology of human consciousness: an evolutionary approach. *Neuropsychologia*, **33**, 1087–102.

Donald, M. (1996). The role of vocalization, memory retrieval, and external symbols in cognitive evolution. *Behavioral and Brain Sciences*, **19**, 159–64.

Donald, M. (1997). The mind from a historical perspective: human cognitive phylogenesis and the possibility of continuing cognitive evolution. In *The future of the cognitive revolution* (ed. D. Johnson and C. Ermeling), pp. 478–92. Oxford University Press.

Donald, M. (1998). Mimesis and the executive suite: missing links in language evolution. In *Approaches to the evolution of language: social and cognitive bases* (ed. J. Hurford, M. Studdert-Kennedy, and C. Knight), pp. 44–67. Cambridge University Press.

Fetzer, J. (1993). Evolution needs a modern theory of the mind. *Behavioral and Brain Sciences*. **16**, 759–60.

Fodor, J. A. (1983). *The modularity of mind*. MIT Press, Cambridge, MA.

Gamble, C. (1993). *Timewalkers: the prehistory of global colonization*. Harvard University Press, Cambridge, MA.

Greenfield, P. M. (1991). Language, tools and the brain: the ontogeny and phylogeny of hierarchically organized sequential behaviour. *Behavioral and Brain Sciences*, **14**, 531–95.

Greenfield, P. M. and Savage-Rumbaugh, E. S. (1990). Grammatical combination in *Pan paniscus*: processes of learning and invention in the evolution and development of language. In *Language and intelligence in monkeys and apes* (ed. S. T. Parker and K. R. Gibson), pp. 540–78. Cambridge University Press.

Johnson-Laird, P. N. (1983). *Mental models*. Harvard University Press, Cambridge, MA.

Karmiloff-Smith, A. (1992). *Beyond modularity: a developmental perspective on cognitive science*. MIT Press, Cambridge, MA.

Kosslyn, S. (1988). Aspects of a cognitive neuroscience of imagery. *Science*, **240**, 1621–6.

Levelt, W. J. M. (1989). *Speaking: from intention to articulation*. MIT Press, Cambridge, MA.

Lieberman, P. (1984). *The biology and evolution of language*. Harvard University Press, Cambridge, MA.

Mithen, S. (1996). *The prehistory of the mind*. Thames and Hudson, London.

Nelson, K. (1996). *Language in cognitive development: emergence of the mediated mind*. Cambridge University Press.

Paivio, A. (1991). *Images in mind: evolution of a theory*. Harvester Wheatsheaf, Toronto.

Parker, S. T. and Gibson, K. R. (1979). A developmental model for the evolution of language and intelligence in early hominids. *Behavioral and Brain Sciences*, **2**, 367–408.

Petitto, L. and Marentette, P. F. (1991). Babbling in the manual mode: evidence for the ontogeny of language. *Science*, **125**, 1493–6.

Pinker, S. (1994). *The language instinct: how the mind creates language*. Morrow, New York.

Pinker, S. and Bloom, P. (1990). Natural language and natural selection. *Behavioral and Brain Sciences*, **13**, 707–84.

Renfrew, C. (1987). *Archaeology and language: the puzzle of Indo-European origins*. Jonathan Cape, London.

Savage-Rumbaugh, E. S., Murphy, J., Sevcik, R. A., Braake, K. E., Williams, S. L., and Rumbaugh, D. (1993). Language comprehension in ape and child. *Monographs of the Society for Research in Child Development*.

Tooby, J. and Cosmides, L. (1989). Evolutionary psychology and the generation of culture. Part I. *Ethology and Sociobiology*. **10**, 29–49.

Toth, N., Schick, K. D., Savage-Rumbaugh, E. S., Sevcik, R. A., and Rumbaugh, D. A. (1993). Pan the tool-maker: investigations into the stone tool-making and tool-using capabilities of a bonobo (*Pan paniscus*). *Journal of Archaeological Science*, **20**, 81–91.

Wittgenstein, L. (1922). *Tractatus logico-philosophicus* (trans. D. F. Pears and B. V. McGuiness, 1961). Routledge and Kegan Paul, London.

9

The role of gesture and mimetic representation in making language the province of speech

Susan Goldin-Meadow and David McNeill

Introduction

Why, in all cultures in which hearing is possible, has language become the province of speech (the oral modality) and not of gesture (the manual modality)? This question is particularly baffling given that humans possess *equipotentiality* with respect to the two modalities—if exposed to language in the manual modality, that is, to a signed language, children will learn that language as quickly and effortlessly as they learn a spoken language (Newport and Meier 1985; Petitto 1992). Thus, on the ontogenetic time scale, humans can, without retooling, acquire language in either the manual or the oral modality. Why then, on an evolutionary time scale, has the oral modality become the channel of choice for languages across the globe?

Intuitively, one might suppose that the oral modality triumphed over the manual modality simply because it is so good at encoding messages in the segmented and combinatorial form that human languages have come to assume. We suggest, however, that this is not the case. In fact, the manual modality is just as good as the oral modality at segmented and combinatorial encoding. As a result, there would be little to choose between on these grounds.

Rather, we suggest that the oral modality assumed the segmented and combinatorial code not because of its strengths but to compensate for its weaknesses. The oral modality is *not* well suited to conveying messages mimetically, even though that function is also important to human language. This function is, however, very well served by the manual modality. The manual modality consequently assumes the role of mimetic encoding, in the form of spontaneous gestures found to accompany speech in all cultures (Feyereisen and de Lannoy 1991; McNeill 1992), leaving segmented and combinatorial encoding by default to speech.

This argument rests on several assumptions. The first is that the manual modality is as adept as the oral modality at segmented and combinatorial encoding. We describe data that support this assumption in our review of the structural properties of signed languages, both conventional and idiosyncratic. The second assumption is that mimetic encoding is an important aspect of human communication, well served by the manual modality. We describe data supporting this assumption in our review of the gestures that are spontaneously produced along with speech. We end with a discussion of the advantages of having a language system that contains both a mimetic and a seg-mented/combinatorial code (see also Donald, this volume), and of the role that gesture might have played in linguistic evolution.

Segmented and combinatorial encoding in the manual modality

We begin by describing the properties of communication systems in the manual modality that are codified and that are used, and learned, as native languages by deaf people—conventional sign languages that have been transmitted from one generation to the next over *historical time*. We then turn to idiosyncratic gesture systems invented over two different time spans. The first are the gesture systems invented by deaf children who have not been exposed to conventional sign language to communicate with the hearing individuals around them, that is, idiosyncratic gesture systems developed over *ontogenetic time*. The second are the gestures that hearing individuals create in an experimental situation when asked to communicate using their hands and not their mouths, that is, idiosyncratic gesture systems developed over *experimental time*.

Segmentation and combination in a manual system developed over historical time

Sign languages of the deaf are autonomous languages, independent of the spoken languages of hearing cultures (Klima and Bellugi 1979; Bellugi and Studdert-Kennedy 1980; Lane and Grosjean 1980). Despite the fact that they are processed by the hand and the eye and not the mouth and the ear, sign languages have the essential properties of segmentation and combination that characterize all spoken language systems. For example, American Sign Language (ASL) is structured at the level of the sentence (i.e. syntactic structure: Liddell 1980; Padden 1983; Lillo-Martin 1986), at the level of the sign (i.e. morphological structure: Klima and Bellugi 1979; Newport 1981; Supalla 1982; Schick 1990), and at the level of sub-sign, and meaningless, elements akin to phonemes (i.e. 'phonological' structure: Stokoe 1960; Lane *et al.* 1976; Liddell and Johnson 1986; Sandler 1986; Wilbur 1986; Padden and Perlmutter 1987; Coulter 1990).

As in all spoken languages, the signs of ASL combine to create larger wholes, that is, sign sentences. ASL sentences have a basic or canonical sign order (subject–verb–object), with other orders possible when one of the constituents is fronted and marked for topic (Friedman 1976; Fisher and Gough 1978; Liddell 1980; Padden 1983). Moreover, the signs that comprise the sentences of ASL are themselves composed of meaningful components, morphemes. Like spoken languages, ASL has grammatical markers that serve as inflectional and derivational morphemes, that is, systematic changes in form internal to the sign associated with changes in meaning (Supalla and Newport 1978; Klima and Bellugi 1979).

Unlike spoken languages, however, the form–meaning pairs that comprise the morphology of ASL are not produced in a linear string but are instead produced simultaneously. For example, the ASL verb 'ask both' is composed of two parts simultaneously produced—'ask' which involves moving the index finger away from the chest area and bending it as it moves, and 'both' which involves reduplicating the motion. The sign 'ask both' is therefore produced by superimposing the grammatical morpheme 'both' on the uninflected form of 'ask,' resulting in reduplication of the basic outward bending movement, once directed to the left and once to the right (Klima and Bellugi 1979).

The morphemes of ASL are produced simultaneously. Nevertheless, they appear to have psychological integrity as isolable parts. For example, children acquiring ASL produce the meaningful parts of signs (the morphemes) in isolation and before combining them into composite wholes (Newport 1981; Supalla 1982) despite the fact that the parts do not appear in isolation in their input. Thus, sign language, when developed within a community and passed down from generation to generation, is characterized by a system of segmented units that combine in rule-governed fashion.

Segmentation and combination in a manual system developed over ontogenetic time

Not only is segmentation and combination characteristic of communication in the manual modality when that communication has been conventionalized within a community, but it is also a salient feature of manual communication systems invented within a single generation by a deaf child of hearing parents. Deaf children exposed from birth to a conventional sign language such as ASL acquire that language by following stages comparable with those of hearing children acquiring a spoken language (Hoffmeister and Wilbur 1980; Kantor 1982; Caselli 1983; Newport and Meier 1985). However, 90 per cent of deaf children are not born to deaf parents who can provide early exposure to conventional sign language. Rather, they are born to hearing parents who, not surprisingly, speak to their children. Unfortunately, it is extremely uncommon for deaf children with severe to profound hearing losses to acquire spontaneously the spoken language of their hearing parents and, even with intensive instruction, their speech is very likely to be markedly delayed (Meadow 1968; Conrad 1979; Mayberry 1992). In addition, unless hearing parents send their deaf children to a school in which sign language is used, the children are not likely to be exposed to a conventional sign system.

Despite their lack of a usable model of conventional language, deaf children of hearing parents do manage to communicate and do so by means of a self-created system of gestures called 'homesign' (Tervoort 1961; Lenneberg 1964; Fant 1972; Moores 1974). Most interesting to our concerns is the fact that the homesign systems invented by individual deaf children are characterized by a variety of language-like properties, including segmentation and combination. Rather than mimetically display a scene, the child conveys the message using segmented gestures combined into a rule-governed string. For example, rather than going over to the cookie jar and pretending to remove the cookie and eat it, the child will point at the cookie and then jab her hand several times toward her mouth, effectively conveying 'cookie–eat'. Moreover, the gesture strings generated by each of the deaf children can be described in terms of very simple 'rules.' The rules predict which semantic elements are likely to be gestured and where in the gesture string those elements are likely to be produced

(Goldin-Meadow and Feldman 1977; Feldman *et al*. 1978; Goldin-Meadow and Mylander 1984, 1990). Thus, the gesture systems have sentence-like structure.

In addition to structure at the sentence level, each deaf child's homesign system also has structure at the word level. Each gesture is composed of a hand-shape and a motion component, and the meaning of the gesture as a whole is determined by the meanings of each of these parts (Goldin-Meadow *et al*. 1995). For example, a child moves his hand shaped like an O in a short motion arcing downward to request the experimenter to lay a penny down flat. The O-hand-shape represents 'roundness' (of the penny) in this gesture and in the child's entire corpus of gestures, and the short-arc motion represents 'putting down,' again across the entire gesture corpus. When produced together within a single gesture, the component parts combine to create the meaning of the whole, 'putting down roundness.' In addition to combining components to create the stem of a gesture, one deaf child also altered the internal parts of a gesture (the number of times a motion is performed, and the placement of the gesture) to mark the grammatical function of that gesture, in particular, to distinguish between a noun role and a verb role (Goldin-Meadow *et al*. 1994). For example, when using a 'twist' gesture as a noun, the child tended to produce the twisting motion only once and in neutral space (near the chest area); in contrast, when using the 'twist' gesture as a verb, the child produced the twisting motion several times and extended it toward (but not on) the object to be twisted. Thus, the parts of a gesture vary as a function of its role in discourse.

Interestingly, the structure found at the sentence and word levels in each of the deaf children's gesture systems could *not* be traced back to the spontaneous gestures that their hearing parents produced when talking to them (Goldin-Meadow and Mylander 1983, 1984; Goldin-Meadow *et al*. 1994, 1995). The systems thus appeared to be generated in large part by the children themselves. It is consequently of great interest that these self-created gesture systems contained the properties of segmentation and combination, properties that characterize all naturally evolving language systems, be they spoken or signed.

As a caveat, we note that the creation of language by deaf children cannot be taken as a simulation of first creation of language in hominid evolution. Deaf children are developing their gesture systems in a world in which language and its consequences are pervasive. The human cultural world may therefore be necessary for an individual child to create a communication system characterized by segmentation and combination, although it does not appear to be necessary for a child to be exposed to a model of a conventional language to do so. In any case, the findings from deaf children make it clear that segmentation and combination can blossom in the manual modality over a relatively short period of time (the deaf children were all under 5 years of age when observed). In the next section, we demonstrate that these properties can arise in the manual modality even within a single experimental session.

Segmentation and combination in a manual system developed over experimental time

In an effort to determine whether gesture, if divorced from speech, would assume the properties of speech, Goldin-Meadow *et al*. (1996) asked adults who had no previous experience with sign language to describe a series of videotaped scenes using their hands and not their mouths. They then compared the resulting gestures (the gesture condition) to the gestures these same adults produced when asked to describe the scenes using speech (the gesture + speech condition).The results showed that, in the gesture condition, the adults frequently combined their gestures into strings and those strings were reliably ordered, with gestures for certain semantic elements occurring in particular positions in the string; that is, there was structure across the gestures at the sentence level. In addition, the verb-like action gestures that the adults produced in the gesture condition could be divided into hand-shape and motion parts, with the hand-shape of the action frequently conveying information about the objects in its semantic frame—that is, there was structure within the gesture at the word level. Thus, the adults produced gestures characterized by segmentation and combination and did so with essentially no time for reflection on what might be fundamental to language-like communication.

Interestingly, however, the adults in the gesture condition did not develop all of the properties of a natural language, or even all of the properties found in the gesture systems of the deaf children studied by Goldin-Meadow and colleagues. In particular, they failed to develop a system of internal contrasts in their gestures. When incorporating hand-shape information into their action gestures, they rarely used the same hand-shape to represent an object, unlike the deaf child whose hand-shapes for the same objects were consistent in form and in meaning (Singleton *et al*. 1993). Thus, a system of contrasts in which the form of a symbol is constrained by its relationship to other symbols in the system (as well as by its relationship to its intended referent) is *not* an immediate consequence of symbolically communicating information to another. The continued experience that the deaf children had with a stable set of gestures (cf. Goldin-Meadow *et al*. 1994) might be required for a system of contrasts to emerge in those gestures.

Thus when gesture is called upon to fulfil the communicative functions of speech, it immediately takes on the properties of segmentation and combination that are characteristic of speech. The appearance of these properties in the adults' gestures is particularly striking given that these properties were *not* found in the gestures that these same adults produced when asked to describe the scenes in speech. In contrast to the gesture condition, when the adults produced gestures in the gesture + speech condition, they rarely combined those gestures into strings, and rarely used the shape of the hand to convey object information within a gesture (Goldin-Meadow *et al*. 1996). In other words, they did not use their gestures as building blocks for larger units, either sentence or word units. Rather, they used their gestures to holistically and mimetically depict the scenes in the videotapes, as speakers typically do when they spontaneously gesture along with their talk, a topic to which we now turn.

Mimetic encoding in the manual modality

We have shown that segmentation and combination are properties that appear in manual communication whether it was developed over a long or a short period of time. Thus, the manual modality can serve as a medium for language, suggesting that the capacity for creating and learning a linguistic system is modality independent. However, communication in the manual modality does not always assume language-like properties. When speakers use their hands to gesture as they talk, those gestures do not take on the analytic properties characteristic of speech (McNeill 1992).

Gesture conveys meaning differently from speech

In contrast to verbal behaviour which is assumed to be closely tied to a speaker's thoughts, non-verbal behaviour, including gesture, has traditionally been assumed to reflect the speaker's feelings or emotions (Wundt 1900/1973; see Feyereisen and de Lannoy 1991 for a review of studies focusing on gesture as a reflection of emotion and attitude). Recently, however, researchers who have focused on the hand gestures speakers produce while talking (e.g. Kendon 1980; McNeill 1985, 1987, 1992) have argued that gesture can convey substantive information and, as a result, can provide insight into a speaker's mental representations. Children too produce gestures (Jancovic *et al.* 1975; Evans and Rubin 1979; Church and Goldin-Meadow 1986; Perry *et al.* 1988; Crowder and Newman 1993) and those gestures convey substantive thoughts that even observers not trained in gesture-coding can interpret accurately (Goldin-Meadow *et al.* 1992; Alibali *et al.* 1997; Goldin-Meadow and Sandhofer 1998; Kelly and Church 1997; but see Krauss *et al.* 1991, who argue that gesture does not convey to listeners information above and beyond the information conveyed in speech).

Thus, gesture conveys meaning. However, it conveys meaning differently from speech. Speech conveys meaning by rule-governed combinations of discrete units, codified according to the norms of that language. In contrast, gesture conveys meaning mimetically and idiosyncratically through continuously varying forms. Mc-Neill (1992, p. 41) lists the fundamental properties of the gestures that accompany speech as follows:

(1) Gestures are global in meaning. The meanings of the parts of a gesture are determined by the whole (and not vice versa, as is the case in speech). Indeed, the parts of a gesture cannot really be considered isolable units, as they are dependent for their meaning on the whole. In contrast to the bottom-up structure of sentences, there is consequently a top-down structure *within a gesture*.

(2) Gestures are non-combinatoric. Gestures do not combine to form larger, hierarchically structured gestures. Most gestures are one to a clause and, even when there are successive gestures within a clause, each corresponds to an idea unit in and of itself. There is, as a result, no hierarchical structure *across* gestures (though there may be other kinds of non-hierarchical structure, as in 'catchments' described below).

(3) Gestures are context-sensitive. They are free to incorporate only the salient and relevant aspects of the context. Each gesture is created at the moment of speaking and highlights what is relevant. Because of gestures' sensitivity to the context of the moment, there is variability in the forms gesture takes *within a speaker*.

(4) Gestures do not have standards of form. Different speakers display the same meanings in idiosyncratic ways. There is consequently variability in the forms

gesture takes *across speakers*. Even when there is cross-speaker similarity, this is not because of standards but because of similarity of meaning—similar meanings engender similar gestures.

It is often easy to analyse a given gesture into parts, but these parts have a different status from the parts of sentences—they are individually constructed with meanings that are determined by the context and that percolate from the top down. For example, in describing an individual running, a speaker moved his hand forward while wiggling his index and middle fingers (McNeill 1992). The parts of this gesture gain meaning because of the meaning of the whole; the wiggling fingers mean 'running' only because we know that the gesture, as a whole, depicts someone running and not because this speaker uses wiggling fingers to mean running in any other context. Indeed, in other gestures produced by this same speaker, wiggling fingers may well have a very different meaning (e.g. indecision between two alternatives). To argue that the wiggling-fingers gesture is composed of separately meaningful parts, one would have to show that each of the three components that comprise the gesture—the V hand-shape, the wiggling motion, and the forward motion—is used for a stable meaning across the speaker's gestural repertoire. The data suggest that there is no such stability in the gestures that accompany speech (McNeill 1992).

Thus, the gestures that accompany speech are not composed of parts but instead have parts that derive from wholes. Moreover, they are wholes that represent by way of mimetic depiction. Because the gesture as a whole must be a good (i.e. relatively transparent) representation of its referent, the addition of semantic information to a spontaneous gesture never reduces its iconicity. Although the simultaneous occurrence of morphemes within a sign in a conventional sign language such as ASL can give that sign an iconic quality, mimetic depiction is *not* the principle underlying ASL. Thus, ASL will sacrifice iconicity if the rules of combination require it, while gesture never does. For example, the sign for 'slow' in ASL is made by moving one hand across the back of the other hand. When the sign is modified to be 'very slow,' it is made *more rapidly* because this is the particular modification of movement that denotes intensification (Klima and Bellugi 1979). As a result, modifying the meaning of the sign reduces its iconicity because the meaning of the sign as a whole is, in rule-governed fashion, made up of the meanings of the components that comprise it. In contrast, if a gesture is generated along with speech to depict something that is very slow, that gesture will be articulated particularly slowly—it would not work to increase the speed of the gesture if the goal is to convey extreme slowness (McNeill 1992).

Given that gesture and speech convey meaning differently, it is possible for the meanings expressed in each of the two modalities to complement one another, creating a richer picture than the view offered by either modality alone. For example, when describing Granny's chase after Sylvester in a cartoon narrative, a speaker said 'she chases him out again' while moving her hand as though swinging an umbrella (McNeill 1992). Speech conveys the ideas of pursuit and recurrence while gesture conveys the weapon used during the chase. Both speech and gesture refer to the same event, but each presents a different aspect of it. As a second example, a speaker who might not be able to convey a particular meaning in speech might well still be able to express that meaning in gesture. At a certain stage in the acquisition of mathematical equivalence, a child might explain that she solved a problem such as $4 + 3 + 5 = \_ + 5$ by adding all of the numbers on both sides of the equation (e.g. she says, 'I added the 4, the 3, the 5, and the 5 and got 17'), never commenting on the fact that the equal sign divides the equation into two parts. However, in her gestures, the same child manages to convey just this notion (e.g. she produces a sweeping gesture under the 4, the 3, and the 5 on the left side of the equation, and the same sweeping gesture under the blank and the 5 on the right side of the equation; Perry *et al.* 1988). Thus, gesture conveys aspects of equivalence that are not found anywhere in the child's speech (Alibali and Goldin-Meadow 1993a; Goldin-Meadow *et al.* 1993). In this way, gesture expands on the representational possibilities offered by the codified spoken system.

Gesture and speech form an integrated system

Despite the fact that gesture and speech represent meaning in different ways, the two modalities form a single, integrated system. Gesture and speech are integrated both semantically and temporally. For example, a speaker produced the following iconic gesture when describing a scene from a comic book in which a character bends a tree back to the ground (McNeill 1992): He grasped his hand as though gripping something and pulled the hand back. He produced this gesture as he uttered the words 'and he bends it way back'. The gesture was a concrete description of precisely the same event described in speech, and thus contributed to a semantically coherent picture of a single scene. In addition, the speaker produced the 'stroke' of the pulling-back gesture just as he said 'bends it way back'. The gesture was consequently synchronized with speech (see also Kendon 1980).

Even when gesture and speech convey different information, the two modalities adhere to the principles of gesture–speech integration described by McNeill (1992). Consider, for example, a child asked to explain why she thinks an amount of water has changed after it has been poured. The child says the amount is different because 'the glass is tall' while indicating the width of the glass in her gestures (Church and Goldin-Meadow 1986). Although this child is indeed expressing two different pieces of information in gesture and speech, she is nevertheless describing the same object in the two modalities. Moreover, the timing of the gesture–speech 'mismatch' also reflects an integrated system. The child produces the width gesture as she says 'tall', thus synchronously expressing her two perspectives on the glass.

Further evidence that gesture–speech 'mismatches' reflect an integrated system comes from two sources. First, children begin to convey different information in speech and its accompanying gesture for the first time *after* gesture and speech have become temporally synchronized; that is, mismatch appears for the first time after gesture and speech have been integrated into a single system (Butcher and Goldin-Meadow, in press). Second, children who produce many gesture–speech mismatches when explaining their solutions to a given task have been found to be in a transitional state with respect to that task; that is, they are particularly ready to learn the task (Church and Goldin-Meadow 1986; Perry *et al.* 1988). If gesture and speech were independent of one another, their 'mismatch' would be a random event and, as a result, should have no cognitive consequence whatsoever. The fact that mismatch is a reliable index of a child's transitional status suggests that the two modalities are, in fact, *not* independent of one another (see Alibali and Goldin-Meadow 1993*b*; Goldin-Meadow *et al.* 1993).

In addition, speech sometimes takes the form that it does precisely because of a prior gesture, thus making it clear that gesture and speech are part of the same communication system. For example, in his initial utterance, a speaker produced a gesture to the right for Sylvester and a second gesture to the left for Tweety. In a subsequent utterance, the speaker then used only pronouns in his speech, relying on gesture to disambiguate the utterance. The speaker said "so he knows that he's gonna come and get him," producing a gesture to the left, the space associated with Tweety, just as he uttered the first 'he.' The first 'he' is therefore understood as a reference to Tweety, and the two other pronouns are understood in relation to this starting point —a starting point that depends crucially on gesture and its synchronization with speech.

Gesture and speech therefore form an integrated system, with gesture providing a representational format that complements the format found in speech. The fact that gesture is used in combination with speech in all of the spoken languages that have been examined thus far (cf. McNeill 1992) suggests that the mimetic representation that gesture offers language might be essential to human communication. Humans can, of course, speak without gesturing (we can talk with our hands folded or even bound). Nevertheless, gesture is pervasive in human talk. We often produce gestures in situations where no observer is present to appreciate the output of the act. For example, speakers gesture when talking on the telephone or when they have their backs turned to their listeners (e.g. Rimi 1982). Even more compellingly, children who have been blind from birth and have never experienced the communicative value of gesture produce gestures along with their speech (Iverson and Goldin-Meadow 1997). Thus, gesture is a robust component of human communication, supplementing the analytic code that speech offers with a code that is analogue and mimetic. We turn next to a discussion of the advantages that a language system with both a segmented/combinatorial and a mimetic code can bring to human communication.

Some advantages of having a mimetic code along with a segmented / combinatorial code

Corballis (1989, p. 500) describes the benefits of a generative system based on categorical elements for human language and thought: "Generativity is a powerful heuristic, for it allows us to describe, represent, or construct an enormous variety of composites, given only a relatively small number of building blocks and rules of construction." At the same time, however, Corballis (1989) notes the limitations of generativity. A generative system becomes unworkable if the number of units in the system is too large; moreover, the relatively small number of units required to make the system manageable also makes it difficult to capture subtle distinctions. These distinctions might be more easily expressed via an analogue representational format. For example, a verbal description of the shape of the east coast of the United States is likely, not only to be very cumbersome, but also to leave out important information about the coastline (Huttenlocher 1973, 1976). It is just this information that can easily be captured in a mimetic gesture tracing the outline of the coast.

Categorization, which is at the heart of a segmented and combinatorial code, is the grouping of elements as alike and, as such, necessarily creates its complement—uncategorized elements. In general, there are two kinds of uncategorized elements—those that are distinguishable but are categorized in the same way (i.e. elements that fall within a codified category), and those that are not categorized at all (i.e. elements that fall outside of the codified categories for that language). A mimetic code is able, at least in principle, to capture both types of uncategorized elements. In fact, we find that the mimetic characteristics of gesture not only enable it to capture both, but enable it to do so alongside the segmented and combinatorial code provided by speech.

Capturing information within a codified category

As an example of how gesture can convey distinctions not captured by a linguistic category, a child participating in a conservation task (Church and Goldin-Meadow 1986) explained his belief that an amount of water had changed after it had been poured from a tall, thin glass into a short, wide dish as follows: He said 'it's different because this one's fatter than this one' while varying the distance between his thumb and fingers to indicate, first, the exact width of the dish and, next, the exact width of the glass. The child's speech arbitrarily categorized the two containers into more fat and less fat, while his gestures indicated not only the relative widths of the containers but also the precise value of each container on the width dimension. Although it would have been possible to explicitly describe the width of each container in English (e.g. "it's different because this one's 5 inches and fatter than this one which is 3 inches"), such a statement detracts from the focus of the sentence (which is the relative widths of the objects, not their exact values). Moreover, the child is not likely to be able to describe the widths of the containers in inches, although he clearly knows, at some level, precisely how much the containers vary in width.

Conveying information not found in any codified category

Mimetic encoding fills in where categorization reaches its limit. Exactly where this limit is and thus where the filling in occurs varies across languages. The way manner is conveyed in Spanish and English is a good example. Manner is *how* a motion is performed. Contrasts in manner are illustrated by English verbs of locomotion: 'walk', 'run', 'stroll', 'limp', 'hop', 'sidle', etc., all involve motion with the feet but differ in how the motion is done. Slobin (1996) notes that while manner can be encoded in Spanish, Spanish speakers rarely include manner in their motion descriptions. Indeed, McNeill and Duncan (in press) have confirmed that, when asked to describe a cartoon, Spanish speakers infrequently convey manner information in their speech. However, they do express manner in their gestures. For example, one Spanish speaker described Sylvester's ascent up a drainpipe without mentioning in speech how the cat accomplished the feat; at the same time, the speaker's hands continuously displayed Sylvester's clambering style of ascent throughout the spoken description. Thus, Spanish speakers can use gesture to expand the resources of their codified system.

Downplaying unwanted information within a codified category

Gesture can also be used to focus attention away from an element that is obligatorily encoded in speech. In contrast to Spanish, the codified categories English offers a speaker come equipped with manner as an obligatory semantic component (cf. the locomotion verbs cited above). The spoken code therefore does not easily allow a speaker to omit manner information. Gesture, however, can be used to focus attention away from the manner of motion—it can be used to trim manner when it is not part of the speaker's communicative focus. For example, an English speaker describing Sylvester's descent down the drainpipe said "and he rolls down the drain spout" while plunging his hand straight down. The speaker's words convey manner information (rolling), but his gesture downplays that semantic component by focusing exclusively on the path of motion. English speakers can, of course, use gesture to highlight manner, as in the following example. Once again to describe Sylvester's trajectory, the speaker said "but it rolls him out" while arcing his two hands to the left with his fingers wiggling. The speaker thus reinforced the rolling manner conveyed in speech with a gesture mimetically displaying the motion that propelled Sylvester along the path. In these ways, the mimetic properties of gesture allow it to modulate the verb semantics of the spoken code to fit the speaker's immediate communicative needs.

Creating impromptu coherence across sentences

A mimetic code is, by definition, transparently related to its referents and, as a result, can be fashioned on the spur of the moment and still be understood. Links that might otherwise be difficult to make within the bounds of a codified system can therefore be made via the mimetic properties of gesture. For example, discourse context is not richly categorized by the spoken language system. Gesture, however, offers resources to fill the gap. A 'catchment' displays the cohesive relations that bind a gesture to the larger discourse. Catchments are conveyed mimetically by gesture features (e.g. hand-shape, locus in space, hand choice) that recur across successive gestures (Kendon 1972). Such recurrence links a given gesture to earlier (anaphoric) and later (cataphoric) gestures that share the same feature(s). As a consequence of this recurrence, gesture has the ability to create larger discourse units.

For example, in a series of four gestures, a speaker consistently used her left hand to represent Sylvester who was climbing up a pipe, and her right hand to represent a bowling ball that was rolling down the pipe. In addition, across the same four gestures, the speaker consistently placed the hand that represented Sylvester below the hand representing the bowling ball. Finally, and again across the four gestures, the speaker made her hands play symmetrical roles when describing events before the bowling ball was dropped, and asymmetrical roles when describing events after the drop. Thus, hand choice (left versus right), spatial configuration (up versus down), and the relationship between the hands (symmetrical versus asymmetrical) functioned together to unify these four gestures and the utterances they accompanied into a cohesive discourse unit—a unit that was not displayed in the accompanying speech.

In sum, a mimetic code offers its own advantages. Having a mimetic code provides a way for speakers to combine into one representation the specific advantages of both the categorical and the mimetic modes of representation. Equipped with a mimetic code, speakers can express information that is indistinguishable within a codified category (without diluting the category itself), they can express information that is not captured in any codified category, they can downplay unwanted information that comes along obligatorily within a codified category, and they can create larger units, particularly discourse units, that are not easily captured within the codified system. Mimetic encoding thus offers speakers a way of enhancing their categorical spoken system, a system which has the advantages of generativity but the disadvantages of stodginess. Mimetic encoding offers speakers flexibility so that their communicative needs of the moment can be met—and gesture provides an ideal medium with which to accomplish mimetic encoding.

Gesture and linguistic evolution

Given that there are advantages to having a mimetic code as well as a segmented and combinatorial code, we can now understand why speech has taken over language across the globe. While both the manual modality and the oral modality are able to assume a segmented and combinatorial representational format, only the manual modality is well suited to a mimetic representational format. Mimetic representation thus falls to the manual modality, leaving segmented and combinatorial representation to the oral modality. Having segmented structure in the oral modality as we currently do leaves the manual modality free to co-occur with speech and to capture the mimetic aspects of communication along with speech. Thus, our current arrangement allows us to retain, along with a segmented representation and *in a single stream of communication*, the imagistic aspects of the mimetic that are so vital to human communication. The alternative arrangement—in which the manual modality would assume the segmented code and the oral modality would serve the mimetic functions —has the disadvantage of forcing the oral modality to be unnaturally imagistic in form (although see Haiman 1985 for evidence that the oral modality does exhibit some iconic properties). If our hypothesis is correct, speech became the predominant medium of human language not because it is so well suited to the segmented and combinatorial requirements of symbolic communication (the manual modality is equally suited to the job), but rather because it is not particularly good at capturing the mimetic components of human communication (a task at which the manual modality excels).

This speculation about the importance of maintaining a vehicle for mimetic representation along with speech raises an interesting question about sign language. In sign, it is the manual modality that assumes the segmented and combinatorial form essential to human language. Can the manual modality at the same time also be used for holistic and mimetic expression? In other words, do signers gesture along with their signs and, if not, how is the mimetic function filled? One possibility is that the mouth movements associated with particular sounds might assume the mimetic function for signers. Although such movements have frequently been observed in fluent signers (cf. Padden 1990), as far as we know, no work has been conducted to investigate whether these behaviours (or any others, for that matter) serve for sign the mimetic function that gesture serves for speech.

Mimetic encoding as we have used the term is reminiscent of, but narrower than, Merlin Donald's notion of mimesis. Donald (1991, p. 16; see also Donald, this volume) defines mimetic representation as the ability to use the body to mime, or re-enact, events. This function is part of a wider mimetic culture, underlying ritual, play, acting, and sport. Donald reconstructs the emergence of human cognitive and cultural systems as an evolution in which mimesis is a key stepping-stone through a series of four stages: the *episodic* (shared by all apes), the *mimetic* (the system of *Homo erectus*, the creator of sophisticated stone tool industries), the *mythic* (the evolution of language and of narrative modes of thinking of our own *Homo sapiens* culture), and the now-dawning *theoretic* (moving toward effortless propositional representations). Each stage is characterized by its own memory stores (including external memories), representation modes, technical potential, and limits. Donald speculates, as did Condillac in the eighteenth century, that a mimetic stage was a pre-speech style of cognitive representation. It supported a language of some kind in which the main principle of expression was mimesis. The form of such a language, both Condillac and Donald argue, would naturally have been gestural (see also Hewes 1973; Kendon 1974; Wescott 1974; Corballis 1992; and Armstrong *et al.* 1995, who express similar views). Gradually, the mimetic stage and its language of gestures gave way to the mythic stage, and its language of sounds. Out of this evolutionary process came narrative discourse and oral language as we know it. Donald emphasizes that the new stage absorbed the old, the representational forms of the mimetic system being reformatted into mythic ones based on spoken linguistic models. The outcome is the old mimetic system encapsulated within the new mythic system. The crucial point in Donald's model is that gesture and speech evolved separately and successively.

We agree that mimesis is an important mode of representation, one that could well have been a way-station along the route to language as we know it. However, we disagree that the mythic system embodied in speech replaced the mimetic system found in gesture, or that the two representational systems continued to develop independently of one another. Rather, we suggest that the spoken system we have today evolved hand-in-hand, as it were, with gesture. Indeed, there is no evidence in modern-day gesture to suggest that speech and gesture evolved separately. Donald himself finds evidence for the independence of gesture and speech in emblems (Ekman and Friesen 1969), gestures that have conventional paraphrases or names and that can be used, often without speech, as if they were spoken words (e.g. the 'okay' sign can be used without speech in American culture to mean 'things are fine'). While emblems might well be independent of speech (but see Kendon 1995 for arguments against this claim), they are a very small part of a speaker's repertoire of gestures. Iconic and metaphoric gestures of the sort we have focused on here constitute the bulk of the gestures speakers spontaneously produce—and these gestures are not at all independent of speech. Donald (1991, p. 223) notes that 'in some situations gestures may actually override a linguistic message' and suggests that the ability of gesture and speech to, at times, go their separate ways is evidence that the two constitute separate systems (see also Donald 1993, p. 744). However, as described earlier, even when gesture and speech convey different messages, the two modalities adhere to the principles of gesture–speech integration described by McNeill (1992)—that is, they form a single unified system, with gesture assuming the mimetic functions and speech the mythic.

In summary, we have provided evidence suggesting that the manual modality is as good as the oral modality at segmented and combinatorial encoding—the manual modality assumes such a format whenever it is required to take on the full burden of communication. Why then do all hearing cultures place language in the oral modality? We have suggested that it is because the segmented and combinatorial format is not sufficient to capture all the essential components of human communication—a mimetic and imagistic format is needed to integrate discourse and get beyond the limits of categorical thinking that underlie the segmented code. Having a mimetic code alongside a segmented and combinatorial code creates a composite communication system that not only is generative but also is responsive to the context-specific communicative needs of human speakers. Such an integrated system retains the virtues of categorical generativity, while avoiding the unworkability of an over-refined linguistic code. A mimetic code is therefore needed to realize the advantages of the categorical code.

It is, moreover, the manual modality—and not the oral modality—that is particularly well suited to mimetic representation. As a result, the manual modality takes over the mimetic aspects of human communication, leaving the analytic aspects by default to speech. Under this scenario, the mimetic and linguistic sides of language evolved together, producing a single system. Our current-day arrangement therefore allows the simultaneous production of both formats, making possible the flexibility and scope of human language.

Acknowledgements

This work was supported by Grant No. RO1 DC00491 from the National Institute on Deafness and other Communication Disorders and Grant No. R01 HD31185 from the National Institute of Child Health and Human Development to S. Goldin-Meadow; and Grant No. RO1 DC10561 from the National Institute on Deafness and other Communication Disorders and grants from the Spencer Foundation to D. McNeill.

References

Alibali, M. W. and Goldin-Meadow, S. (1993a). Gesture–speech mismatch and mechanisms of learning: what the hands reveal about a child's state of mind. *Cognitive Psychology*, **25**, 468–523.

Alibali, M. W. and Goldin-Meadow, S. (1993b). Modelling learning using evidence from speech and gesture. *Proceedings of the 15th Annual Conference of the Cognitive Science Society*, **15**, 203–8.

Alibali, M. W., Flevares, L., and Goldin-Meadow, S. (1997). Assessing knowledge conveyed in gesture: do teachers have the upper hand? *Journal of Educational Psychology* (in press).

Armstrong, D. F., Stokoe, W. C., and Wilcox, S. E. (1995). *Gesture and the nature of language*. Cambridge University Press, New York.

Bellugi, U. and Studdert-Kennedy, M. (ed.) (1980). *Signed and spoken language: biological constraints on linguistic form*. Verlag Chemie, Deerfield Beach, FL.

Butcher, C. and Goldin-Meadow, S. (in press). Gesture and the transition from one- to two-word speech: when hand and mouth come together. In *Language and gesture: window into thought and action* (ed. D. McNeill). Cambridge University Press.

Caselli, M. C. (1983). Communication to language: deaf children's and hearing children's development compared. *Sign Language Studies*, **39**, 113–44.

Church, R. B. and Goldin-Meadow, S. (1986). The mismatch between gesture and speech as an index of transitional knowledge. *Cognition*, **23**, 43–71.

Conrad, R. (1979). *The deaf child*. Harper and Row, New York.

Corballis, M. C. (1989). Laterality and human evolution. *Psychological Review*, **96**, 492–505.

Corballis, M. C. (1992). On the evolution of language and generativity. *Cognition*, **44**, 197–226.

Coulter, G. R. (1990). Emphatic stress in ASL. In *Theoretical issues in sign language research, Vol. 1. Linguistics* (ed. S. D. Fisher and P. Siple), pp. 109–25. University of Chicago Press.

Crowder, E. M. and Newman, D. (1993). Telling what they know: the role of gesture and language in children's science explanations. *Pragmatics and Cognition*, **1**, 341–76.

Donald, M. (1991). *Origins of the modern mind: three stages in the evolution of culture and cognition*. Harvard University Press, Cambridge, MA.

Donald, M. (1993). Précis of 'Origins of the modern mind: three stages in the evolution of culture and cognition'. *Behavioural and Brain Sciences*, **16**, 737–91.

Ekman, P. and Friesen, W. (1969). The repertoire of non-verbal behavioural categories. *Semiotica*, **1**, 49–98.

Evans, M. A. and Rubin, K. H. (1979). Hand gestures as a communicative mode in school-aged children. *The Journal of Genetic Psychology*, **135**, 189–96.

Fant, L. J. (1972). *Ameslan: an introduction to American Sign Language*. National Association of the Deaf, Silver Springs, MD.

Feldman, H., Goldin-Meadow, S., and Gleitman, L. (1978). Beyond Herodotus: the creation of language by linguistically deprived deaf children. In *Action, symbol, and gesture: the emergence of language* (ed. A. Lock), pp. 351–414. Academic Press, New York.

Feyereisen, P. and de Lannoy, J.-D. (1991). *Gestures and speech: psychological investigations*. Cambridge University Press.

Fischer, S. and Gough, B. (1978). Verbs in American Sign Language. *Sign Language Studies*, **18**, 17–48.

Friedman, L. A. (1976). The manifestation of subject, object, and topic in American Sign Language. In *Subject and topic* (ed. C. Li), pp. 125–48. Academic Press, New York.

Goldin-Meadow, S. and Feldman, H. (1977). The development of language-like communication without a language model. *Science*, **197**, 401–3.

Goldin-Meadow, S. and Mylander, C. (1983). Gestural communication in deaf children: the non-effects of parental input on language development. *Science*, **221**, 372–4.

Goldin-Meadow, S. and Mylander, C. (1984). Gestural communication in deaf children: the effects and non-effects of parental input on early language development. *Monographs of the Society for Research in Child Development*, **49**, 1–121.

Goldin-Meadow, S. and Mylander, C. (1990). Beyond the input given: the child's role in the acquisition of language. *Language*, **66**, 323–55.

Goldin-Meadow, S. and Sandhofer, C. (1998). The role of gesture in communicating a child's thoughts to an adult onlooker. (Under review.)

Goldin-Meadow, S., Wein, D., and Chang, C. (1992). Assessing knowledge through gesture: using children's hands to read their minds. *Cognition and Instruction*, **9**, 201–19.

Goldin-Meadow, S., Alibali, M. W., and Church, R. B. (1993). Transitions in concept acquisition: using the hand to read the mind. *Psychological Review*, **100**, 279–97.

Goldin-Meadow, S., Butcher, C., Mylander, C., and Dodge, M. (1994). Nouns and verbs in a self-styled gesture system: what's in a name? *Cognitive Psychology*, **27**, 259–319.

Goldin-Meadow, S., Mylander, C., and Butcher, C. (1995). The resilience of combinatorial structure at the word level: morphology in self-styled gesture systems. *Cognition*, **56**, 195–262.

Goldin-Meadow, S., McNeill, D., and Singleton, J. (1996). Silence is liberating: removing the handcuffs on grammatical expression in the manual modality. *Psychological Review*, **103**, 34–55.

Haiman, J. (1985). *Iconicity in syntax*. John Benjamins, Amsterdam.

Hewes, G. W. (1973). Primate communication and the gestural origin of language. *Current Anthropology*, **14**, 5–24.

Hoffmeister, R. and Wilbur, R. (1980). Developmental: the acquisition of sign language. In *Recent perspectives on American Sign Language* (ed. H. Lane and F. Grosjean). Erlbaum, Hillsdale, NJ.

Huttenlocher, J. (1973). Language and thought. In *Communication, language and meaning: psychological perspectives* (ed. G. A. Miller), pp. 172–84. Basic Books, New York.

Huttenlocher, J. (1976). Language and intelligence. In *The nature of intelligence* (ed. L. B. Resnick), pp. 261–81. Erlbaum, Hillsdale, NJ.

Iverson, J. and Goldin-Meadow, S. (1997). What's communication got to do with it: gesture in blind children. *Developmental Psychology*, **33**, 453–67.

Jancovic, M. A., Devoe, S., and Wiener, M. (1975). Age-related changes in hand and arm movements as non-verbal communication: some conceptualizations and an empirical exploration. *Child Development*, **46**, 922–8.

Kantor, R. (1982). Communicative interaction: mother modification and child acquisition of American Sign Language. *Sign Language Studies*, **36**, 233–82.

Kelly, S. and Church, R. B. (1997). Can children detect conceptual information conveyed through other children's non-verbal behaviours? *Cognition and Instruction*, **15**, 107–34.

Kendon, A. (1972). Some relationships between body motion and speech. In *Studies in dyadic communication* (ed. A. Siegman and B. Pope), pp. 177–210. Pergamon Press, New York.

Kendon, A. (1974). Kinesics, speech, and language. In *Language origins* (ed. R. W. Wescott), pp. 181–4. Linstok Press, Silver Spring, MD.

Kendon, A. (1980). Gesticulation and speech: two aspects of the process of utterance. In *Relationship of the verbal and non-verbal communication* (ed. M. R. Key), pp. 207–28. Mouton, The Hague.

Kendon, A. (1995). Gestures as illocutionary and discourse structure markers in southern Italian conversation. *Journal of Pragmatics*, **23**, 247–79.

Klima, E. and Bellugi, U. (1979). *The signs of language*. Harvard University Press.

Krauss, R. M., Morrell-Samuels, P., and Colasante, C. (1991). Do conversational hand gestures communicate? *Journal of Personality and Social Psychology*, **61**, 743–54.

Lane, H. and Grosjean, F. (1980). *Recent perspectives on American Sign Language*. Erlbaum, Hillsdale, NJ.

Lane, H., Boyes-Braem, P., and Bellugi, U. (1976). Preliminaries to a distinctive feature analysis of hand-shapes in American Sign Language. *Cognitive Psychology*, **8**, 263–89.

Lenneberg, E. H. (1964). Capacity for language acquisition. In *The structure of language: readings in the philosophy of language* (ed. J. A. Fodor and J. J. Katz), pp. 579–603. Prentice–Hall, New Jersey.

Liddell, S. (1980). *American Sign Language syntax*. Mouton, The Hague.

Liddell, S. and Johnson, R. (1986). American Sign Language compound formation processes, lexicalization, and phonological remnants. *Natural Language and Linguistic Theory*, **4**, 445–513.

Lillo-Martin, D. (1986). Two kinds of null arguments in American Sign Language. *Natural Language and Linguistic Theory*, **4**, 415–44.

Mayberry, R. I. (1992). The cognitive development of deaf children: recent insights. In *Child Neuropsychology, Vol. 7. Handbook of Neuropsychology* (ed. S. Segalowitz and I. Rapin), pp. 51–68. Elsevier, Amsterdam.

McNeill, D. (1985). So you think gestures are non-verbal? *Psychological Review*, **92**, 350–71.

McNeill, D. (1987). *Psycholinguistics*. Harper and Row, New York.

McNeill, D. (1992). *Hand and mind: what gestures reveal about thought*. University of Chicago Press.

McNeill, D. and Duncan, S. D. (in press). Growth points in thinking-for-speaking. In *Language and gesture: window into thought and action* (ed. D. McNeill). Cambridge University Press.

Meadow, K. (1968). Early manual communication in relation to the deaf child's intellectual, social, and communicative functioning. *American Annals of the Deaf*, **113**, 29–41.

Moores, D. F. (1974). Non-vocal systems of verbal behaviour. In *Language perspectives: acquisition, retardation, and intervention* (ed. R. L. Schiefelbusch and L. L. Lloyd), pp. 377–417. University Park Press, Baltimore, MD.

Newport, E. L. (1981). Constraints on structure: evidence from American Sign Language and language learning. In *Minnesota Symposium on Child Psychology, Vol. 1* (ed. W. A. Collins), pp. 93–124. Erlbaum, Hillsdale, NJ.

Newport, E. L. and Meier, R. P. (1985). The acquisition of American Sign Language. In *The cross-linguistic study of language acquisition, Vol. 1. The data* (ed. D. J. Slobin), pp. 881–938. Erlbaum, Hillsdale, NJ.

Padden, C. (1983). *Interaction of morphology and syntax in American Sign Language*. Unpublished doctoral dissertation, University of California at San Diego.

Padden, C. (1990). Rethinking fingerspelling. *Signpost*, October 2–4. International Linguistics Association, University of Durham.

Padden, C. and Perlmutter, D. (1987). American Sign Language and the architecture of phonological theory. *Natural Language and Linguistic Theory*, **5**, 335–75.

Perry, M., Church, R. B., and Goldin-Meadow, S. (1988). Transitional knowledge in the acquisition of concepts. *Cognitive Development*, **3**, 359–400.

Petitto, L. A. (1992). Modularity and constraints in early lexical acquisition: evidence from children's early language and gesture. In *Minnesota Symposium on Child Psychology*, Vol. 25 (ed. M. Gunnar), pp. 25–58. Erlbaum, Hillsdale, NJ.

Rimi, B. (1982). The elimination of visible behaviour from social interactions: effects on verbal, non-verbal and interpersonal variables. *European Journal of Social Psychology*, **12**, 113–29.

Sandler, W. (1986). The spreading hand autosegment of American Sign Language. *Sign Language Studies*, **50**, 1–28.

Schick, B. S. (1990). The effects of morphological complexity on phonological simplification in ASL. *Sign Language Studies*, **66**, 25–41.

Singleton, J. L., Morford, J. P., and Goldin-Meadow, S. (1993). Once is not enough: standards of well-formedness in manual communication created over three different timespans. *Language*, **69**, 683–715.

Slobin, D. I. (1996). Two ways to travel: verbs of motion in English and Spanish. In *Grammatical constructions: their form and meaning* (ed. M. Shibatani and S. A. Thompson), pp. 195–219. Oxford University Press.

Stokoe, W. C. (1960). Sign language structure: an outline of the visual communications systems. *Studies in linguistics*, Occasional papers No. 8.

Supalla, T. (1982). *Structure and acquisition of verbs of motion and location in American Sign Language*. Unpublished doctoral dissertation, University of California at San Diego.

Supalla, T. and Newport, E. (1978). How many seats in a chair? the derivation of nouns and verbs in American Sign Language. In *Understanding language through sign language research* (ed. P. Siple), pp. 91–132. Academic Press, New York.

Tervoort, B. T. (1961). Esoteric symbolism in the communication behaviour of young deaf children. *American Annals of the Deaf*, **106**, 436–80.

Wescott, R. W. (1974). The origin of speech. In *Language origins* (ed. R. W. Wescott), pp. 103–23. Linstok Press, Silver Spring, MD.

Wilbur, R. (1986). Interaction of linguistic theory and sign language research. In *The real world linguist: linguistic applications for the 1980s* (ed. P. C. Bjarkman and V. Raskin), pp. 166–82. Ablex, Norwood, NJ.

Wundt, W. (1900/1973). *The language of gestures*. Mouton, The Hague.

---------------------------- **10** ----------------------------

The evolution of deep social mind in humans

Andrew Whiten

Introduction: the puzzle of the hominid niche

An influential postulate of evolutionary psychology is that the latter part of hominid evolution—a part which saw the final phases of encephalization and the shaping of mind related to these phases—was one in which our ancestors exploited a particular ecological niche, described as hunting-and-gathering (Isaac 1978; Tooby and Cosmides 1989). This inference is based on integration of two quite different kinds of data: archaeological evidence that our distant ancestors were hunters, and the finding that amongst present-day tropical hunting peoples, hunting is but a part (typically the minor part) in a system of foraging which also depends heavily on gathering vegetable foods[1]. If the inference that our ancestors were gatherer–hunters over an evolutionarily significant timescale is correct, it follows that it is adaptation to this particular niche that will explain much about the nature of the human psychological system (Tooby and DeVore 1987).

So are we dealing with an 'evolutionarily significant timescale'? There is some evidence of identifiable hominid specialization along this pathway in stone tool cut-marks on bones that date from as much as 1.8 million years ago (Potts 1988, 1992). These are signs of a new hominid adaptation to carnivory, not observed in the carnivorous repertoire of other apes (Boesch and Boesch 1989). Strictly, such cut-marks do not in themselves demonstrate an *increase in reliance* on meat—they are too few in number to permit such inferences. However, the qualitative innovation which they represent does define the differentiation of a new meat-exploiting niche at this time—and this is really the second major hominid niche differentiation we know of after the earlier emergence of bipedalism.

---

[1] In this chapter I shall focus more on hunting than gathering as a potential explanatory factor in the evolution of the hominid mind. This should not be misinterpreted as a reincarnation of the kind of 'hunting hypothesis' favoured by some earlier authors (e.g. Ardrey 1976; Washburn and Lancaster 1968) as the core explanation for human evolutionary change, to the exclusion of the gathering process (and therefore women, who typically perform most of the gathering and little or none of the hunting). This omission was well recognized some time ago, for example by Hrdy (1981) and Dahlberg (1981), although, as I remark elsewhere in this chapter, the empirical gaps in our knowledge about the nature of gathering behaviour and the psychological phenomena involved remain disappointingly under-studied. This is one reason for my focus on hunting. The other is that I am able to cite hard archaeological evidence charting the prehistory of hunting, but not of gathering.

It is possible that stone tools, dated at approximately 2.5 million years ago (Semaw *et al.* 1997), represent an even earlier component of this change, but we do not know their function and they might have been used to process vegetable foods, with no necessary implication of either gathering (in the sense of accumulating foodstuffs for later consumption) or hunting.

Just how access to animal carcasses for butchery was achieved by early hominids is also unclear and the subject of extensive controversies amongst archaeologists. Cut marks in themselves demonstrate only butchery, which is consistent with either scavenging or hunting. Because chimpanzees (with whom we share our most recent pre-hominid ancestor) and baboons (who share adaptation to savannah niches) both hunt small mammal prey, it would be surprising if early hominids did not themselves catch at least some of the animals that they butchered with stone tools 1.8 million years ago. The alternative, that they scavenged their meat, seems to be assumed as the 'simpler' hypothesis by some archaeologists, but this would in fact have been a more radical departure insofar as it seems rare even in non-human primates with a predilection for meat (Blumenschine 1992, p. 60). Ingenious attempts by archaeologists to supplement the cut-mark evidence with analyses testing whether body-part remains of prey conform to those predicted by hunting or by scavenging have yielded suggestive data (e.g. Blumenschine 1992), yet they do not seem to have resolved these controversies in the eyes of commenting archaeologists themselves (see, for example, Mithen 1996, p. 103).

Evidence that more clearly demonstrates hunting, rather than butchery only, has until recently come only with records of stone implements of a design suitable for hafting to shafts, for spears or arrows. Evidence of this sort becomes stronger only in much more recent periods, from 200 000 to 100 000 years ago (Gowlett 1996). However Thieme (1997) has now described wooden spears well dated at approximately 400 000 years ago. These spears have been fashioned with a balance similar to that of modern javelins, the centre of gravity being one third back from the sharpened tip. Found alongside numerous horse skeletons, they not only present the earliest clear evidence for hunting, but were equally clearly not first attempts—hunting must have been active for a long time before this.

These two items of evidence—early butchery cuts and later projectiles—offer the clearest dated points in charting this hominid niche differentiation. Assemblages of stone tools and bones from often quite large prey found throughout this two-million-year period, whilst difficult to interpret by themselves, are consistent with, and indeed reinforce, the picture of a new way of life that evolved during this period, its distinctive feature being the exploitation of large mammal prey.

The main point I want to emphasize about this picture is that in many ways it represents an extraordinary evolutionary pathway for hominid evolution to have taken. It is surely one of the big puzzles about why hominids evolved as they did. The reason this pathway was extraordinary lies in the conditions under which it developed. Hominid evolution occurred in the context of a loss of forest cover creating seasonal savannah habitats in a wide belt which included much of South and East Africa where the hominid fossil record is preserved (R. Foley 1987). Chimpanzees, gorillas, and presumably their ancestors have remained closely associated with the habitats to which they were already well adapted, in the dwindling forests and woodlands of the west. Early hominids, by contrast, opted for the new and relatively hostile, more open, savannah-like habitats, which clearly presented challenges for an animal shaped by arboreal adaptations.

One major factor that made these habitats so hostile was that a high biomass of large mammals, supported by the growing seasonal nutrients offered by grasslands, came to be preyed upon by a large community of formidable predators, in a landscape more sparsely provided with the predator-avoidance resource to which primates are adapted—stands of large trees. This community of large carnivores peaked in the early Pleistocene, when it included at least twelve species of sabre-tooth cats, eight species of other felines and nine hyena species (Maglio 1978; R. Foley 1984). What is extraordinary about the hominids' successful utilization of this habitat is not so much coping with the dangers of being caught by any of these many predators, but going beyond such dangers to compete directly with them at their own carnivorous game.

Scavenging prey already killed by carnivores such as lions, an evolutionary scenario supported by many, would surely have courted direct dangers from the primary predators themselves. But there is a more fundamental way in which increased hominid carnivory seems remarkable. The luxuriant large-carnivore component of the complex early Pleistocene community reconstructed by R. Foley (1987) included numerous formidable 'professional predators'—obligatory carnivores reliant on daily kills for which they were thoroughly adapted in terrestrial speed of running, hunting behaviour patterns, and morphology such as sharp teeth and claws. Enter puny *Australopithecine* apes with little in the way of such adaptations—how could it be that some of these kinds of creature would carve a new ecological niche involving greater carnivory in the context of a community ecology so dominated by these 'professionals'? One answer is that the hominid niche became differentiated in a new way: as a 'cognitive niche'.

The cognitive niche

The concept of a cognitive niche was outlined by Tooby and DeVore (1987). A capacity for "conceptually abstracting from a situation a model of what manipulations are necessary to achieve proximate goals that correlate with fitness" is "the core of our zoological distinctiveness" (p. 209). This has allowed humans rapidly to escalate the arms race between predator and prey, effectively mounting 'surprise attacks' on such prey—attacks perfected over short time-scales relative to the ability of prey to counteract them through the effects of natural selection. Such prey should be thought of as including both animal and plant species—use of a digging stick is one example of an evolutionary surprise attack on a tuber!

Tooby and DeVore discussed their conception of the cognitive niche in general terms and did not cite specific manifestations. It might help, therefore, to see how the idea of a distinctive cognitive niche is demonstrated graphically when the repertoires of hunter–gatherers documented in recent decades is compared with that of other large mammalian carnivores. This, of course, represents an 'end-state' in hominid evolution rather than a concerted reconstruction of early hominid capacities, but it serves to underscore the nature of the niche differentiation that has occurred.

Take the case of hunting with projectiles by !Kung San (Lee 1979). What is remarkable is the extent to which so much of the process is 'abstracted' from the kind of direct contact with the prey which constitutes hunting done by other species. Even at the point of maximum contact with the live prey, when a poison arrows finds its mark, the hunters do not even try to pursue large prey they hit, but instead converge on the site of the hit to recover parts of the multi-component arrow and read the signs, such as how much poison will have been taken and how much blood will have been lost. The prey might be tracked for many kilometres, but then the hunters return to camp. It will usually be the next day before a party sets out to track the prey to the point where it died and butcher it.

These core hunting actions of carcass acquisition are embedded in wider activities that further extend the cognitive nature of the process. For example, each hunt is preceded on at least the previous evening by the preparation of some hunting plan informed through communication with other band members who have travelled recently and witnessed a variety of signs of good locations to search. Also, after the hunt, campfire debriefings dissect the hunt and encode lessons for the future. In addition, hunting by tracking and stalking is supplemented by the laying of traps, which again involves a characteristic cognitive abstraction in dealings with a predatory niche.

This is all very different from the approaches of other species of predator, which operate throughout by maintaining sensory contact with the prey. Their actions are, of course, subject to the operations of cognitive mechanisms—memory, decision-making, and so on. Distinguishing the hominid niche as 'cognitive' is to this extent a misnomer and it must be read instead as signalling ways in which the hominid approach is in certain respects 'more intelligent'. In the case of the San hunting described above, the human approach 'replaces' direct sensory contact with prey with such sophisticated cognitive operations as planning (not to chase, to return later, etc.), representation and mental manipulation of objects in their absence, understanding of technology and reasoning about signs such as animal tracks. To be sure, these are cognitive refinements more advanced than those likely to have *begun* cognitive niche differentiation in early hominids, but delineating them is important because they demonstrate vividly the nature of the differentiation that natural selection has driven hominids to, in the face of such competition as occurs in African community ecology. That the selection pressures to differentiate in this way have been so strong in pushing humans so far down this cognitive track implies, I suggest, that the pressures in this direction would have been great in the early phases of the differentiation.

The social-cognitive niche

According to what has been said above, to describe the hominid hunting–gathering niche as 'cognitive' picks out a real and probably crucial aspect of the way in which that niche became differentiated from those exploited by other species that were specialized for carnivory. However, this should not allow us to miss another, no less fundamental aspect of the human approach—its *social interdependence*.

To return to our !Kung example, hunting is indeed differentiated from that of other large predators by its cognitive sophistication, but the intellectual operations of the individual hunter are only part of the story, for they are in turn reliant on a new level of social differentiation from competitor species. That new level involves processes of cooperation and communication.

The hunting patterns of several species of felid and canid are importantly social and cooperative also, of course. What differentiates the human approach is the level of cognitive sophistication at which the social integration operates. This is at least one aspect that I mean to convey by the expression 'deep social mind', which is explained more fully below. I am suggesting that the differentiation of the hominid niche must be characterized in its fundamentals not only by being 'cognitive' (at a uniquely high level) but also 'deeply social' (where the 'social' operates at a uniquely, cognitively, interdependent level). This means that components of social cognition have been moulded both to provide social support for exploiting the 'non-social' components of the niche (e.g. procuring large prey) and also to handle complexities of the social structures themselves.

In this chapter I shall treat three aspects of deep social mind. First there is cooperation. Hominid cooperation became unusually deep in several respects, including *coordination* in such enterprises as hunting, and the maintenance of an egalitarian society. Second there is culture. Increasingly, hominids came to be what they were through a social process of cultural transmission, and in this further sense have deeply social—that is, extremely socially shaped minds. Third is what I shall call mind-reading, the capacity to recognize and discriminate the states of mind of others (and oneself—but that will concern us less here). Reading others' minds makes minds deeply social in that those minds *interpenetrate* each other. Cognitive social interdependence is what binds all these three components to constitute deep social mind.

There is an obvious fourth candidate for this list—language. Language clearly facilitates deep cognitive social interdependence. I put it to one side in this chapter in favour of treating the other three aspects for at least two main reasons. One is that it is dealt with elsewhere in this volume (see also Corballis 1991; W. Foley 1997; Goody 1997). The other is that it is possible to say more about the evolution of the other three components from pre-hominid primate origins, on the basis of my own empirical research and that of others.

Methodological approach

I shall use several very different sources of evidence to reconstruct aspects of hominid social and cognitive evolution. One is the literature on hunter–gatherer societies which have been studied earlier this century. By examining the hunting–gathering way of life across many different geographical locations and local conditions, one can search for those cognitive and social features they share, which are thus revealed as the core adaptations involved when humans live by gathering and hunting. Such common features offer our best, and in several cases our only, sources of inference about the recent evolutionary ancestry of hominid society[2]. The validity of such inferences obviously attenuate the further back in time they are cast and to some extent the archaeological record can be used to judge this—reconstructions of hunting patterns, for example, clearly become tenuous if projected back to periods for which the direct archaeological evidence of hunting does not exist.

For earlier periods of our evolutionary history, an analogous process of comparison across the different taxa of great apes can be used to reconstruct the social patterns from which those of hominids evolved. Between these inferences to several million years ago and those based on contemporary hunter–gatherers, valid for the most recent period of perhaps only tens or most optimistically hundreds of thousands of years, there exists a large gap which has to be filled by a process of extrapolation, tempered by archaeological evidence. In domains such as tool-making the latter can be rich, but has obvious limits with respect to inferences about social matters.

The evolution of hominid cooperation

Under the broad heading of cooperation I include several patterns of behaviour in which individuals coordinate their actions to their mutual benefit, or the benefit of a part or whole of the group. Lee (1979) has described cooperation as the social core of the hunter–gatherer way of life. It takes several different forms, which are inter-related in various ways.

Egalitarianism

In an attempt to delineate those patterns of cooperation commonly associated with hunter–gatherer life, my colleague David Erdal has combed detailed ethnographies from two dozen such societies from different continents. One of the principal results of this survey was to agree with previous commentators that hunter–gatherer society can generally be described as markedly egalitarian (Erdal and Whiten 1994, 1996; see also Woodburn 1982; Knauft 1991). Egalitarianism means social equality and hunter–gatherers cooperate to achieve this. Such equality is manifested in a number of different ways, in each of which we see social actions very different to those which can be assumed in pre-hominid ancestors.

Sharing

The sharing of food, particularly meat (which more often comes in large, shareable packages than does vegetable food), was found to be effectively universal (Erdal and

---

[2] The pitfalls of using modern-day hunter–gatherers as models of ancestral behaviour have been well debated in the literature (e.g. Solway and Lee 1990). This is a complex issue, but my principal responses are to note that: (1) the rich information about behaviour and mental processes obtainable from hunter–gatherers is too valuable to ignore and indeed that richness is matched by no other source of data; and (2) the most serious pitfalls of naive interpretation are to be avoided (a) by the analysis of common patterns amongst large numbers of different hunter–gatherer societies, as pursued by Erdal and by me; and (b) by 'triangulating' inferences to past populations by treating these data not in isolation, but together with other sources, particularly archaeology (Mithen 1996).

Whiten 1996; Table 1). Social equality is seen in a levelled distribution of food resources. Both quantitative (weighed food) and qualitative data (observations, interviews) converge to show that meat is not only shared with kin and with reciprocators, but according to who needs it, approximating to a 'generalized altruism', coupled with an ideology of generous sharing.

When we come to compare these findings with what obtains in other primates, and in particular to describe the evolutionary change implied, we find that, interestingly, food sharing has been described in both of the two main groups of primates of most relevance. These are, first, chimpanzees (as the taxon with whom we share our most recent common pre-hominid ancestor) and baboons (with whom our ancestors shared the open country habitat of seasonal savannah). In both groups it is meat eating which, where it achieves levels not seen in other non-human African primates, provides the context for sharing between adults (Strum 1981; Boesch and Boesch 1989). However, such food sharing is rarely unsolicited or even active in the way it is among humans, nor does it approximate distribution by need. Hunter–gatherer food sharing appears a quite distinctive evolutionary innovation in the thorough egalitarianism it embodies[3].

Status and leadership

A second aspect of equality concerns status and power. Hunter–gatherers typically do not claim formal leadership or rank. Such informal leadership as occurs tends to emerge in particular contexts such as tracking prey, where particular individuals might earn respect for their competence, but this does not translate to rank in any generalized sense.

Again, this contrasts markedly with both chimpanzees and baboons, where differential ranks are manifested in the ability of individuals to displace others with respect to such resources as food, reproductive opportunities and safe refuges—gross inequalities in acquisition of such resources follow.

Reproduction

Although a majority of human societies have been classed as polygamous, monogamy appears typical for hunter–gatherers and this suggests that it is humans' ancestral pattern. Compared with the sexual patterns of either baboons or chimpanzees, in which several males will compete to fertilize each fertile female (some with disproportionate success), monogamy generates a greater amount of equality of reproductive success, an effect most significant amongst males, where the intrinsic potential for inequality is greater than for females.

---

[3] I am not the first to suggest that sharing was a key factor in hominid evolution. However, what I have to say is not dependent on the quite complex models for sharing, including the use of home bases, inferred most notably by Isaac (1978) from early Pleistocene excavations (see Schick 1987 and Potts 1992 for recent appraisals of that evidence).

A U-shaped evolutionary curve?

If these egalitarian patterns are extrapolated back to an ancestral phase of hunting and gathering, a U-shaped historical curve is suggested, albeit an asymmetric one (Fig. 10.1) (Knauft 1991; Erdal and Whiten 1996). The saddle of the U would be the meat-sharing, egalitarian phase, assumed to have become increasingly evident between the markers of butchery and hunting outlined earlier, and the rise of settlement, herding and agriculture in the last 10000 years. Because this latter period was so short on an evolutionary timescale, the right-hand limb of the U looks almost vertical. Because it lasted just a few hundred generations, it is unlikely to have seen much genetic change, so that it is principally the genetic legacy of the saddle of the U that we inherit, with its attendant psychological elements. The left-hand arm of the curve, representing the transition from hierarchical ape societies to the egalitarian pattern, is likely to have spread over a much longer period, but its timing and precise shape are uncertain, as we have noted.

   If the U-curve is at least approximately correct as a picture of our past, it raises many questions. For example, what were the reasons for the two transitions implied by the U-shape? Although anthropologists have tended to assume the first transition to egalitarianism represents a cultural imposition, Erdal and Whiten (1994) suggested that the period over which gatherer–hunter egalitarianism operated was long enough for biologically based psychological changes to have been selected for. Certainly an analysis of the details of both hunter–gatherer and non-human primate societies suggests potential behavioural and psychological continua through which the first transition could have occurred.

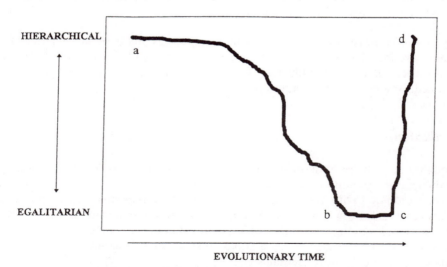

Fig. 10.1. The U-curve hypothesis of hominid evolution. The 'saddle' of the U (b–c) represents a period of hunter–gatherer egalitarianism, which evolved from more hierarchically structured ancestral ape societies in the period a–b: c–d represents a swing back to social inequality as reliance on wild foods came to be replaced by agriculture, herding and/or settlement in the majority of human populations (after Erdal and Whiten 1996).

First amongst these are details of the hunter–gatherer ethnographies which show that the egalitarian ethos is undermined intermittently by non-egalitarian, 'Machiavellian' behaviour. Erdal and Whiten (1996) note that sharing is often 'vigilant sharing', where the sharing operation is watched intently by spectators who might intervene to ensure that fairness is accomplished; in addition, cases of cheating and stealing occur, as, for example, when small pieces of meat are siphoned off to an individual's own family. Likewise, social equality is punctuated from time to time by individuals trying to rise in status: Then, however, we see another common pattern which we called 'counter-dominance', in which all other members of the group cooperate to put down the upstart by such tactics as ignoring, ridiculing, or ostracizing them. Thus, the remarkable egalitarianism of hunter–gatherers is probed from time to time by selfish undercurrents and Machiavellian skirmishes (see Boehm 1997 for a more thorough review).

Complementing this picture, in both of the two important primate groups noted above, baboons and chimpanzees, we see simple forms of social behaviour which in an ancestral state could have provided more of a platform for the emergence of egalitarianism than is often appreciated. Thus, whereas much meat-sharing is indeed merely tolerated scrounging, in a population of chimpanzees found to rely particularly heavily on meat as much as 38% of sharing was 'active' in the sense that the owner was prepared to facilitate the transfer of meat to an individual requesting it (Boesch and Boesch 1989).

Turning to counter-dominance, the occurrence of coalitions and alliances in baboons and chimpanzees can mean that an individual who would otherwise hold the alpha rank is deposed by others acting in concert (de Waal 1982; Nishida 1983). Erdal and Whiten (1994, 1996) proposed that an important phase in the evolution of egalitarianism might have arisen when the social skills of would-be-alphas and counter-dominants escalated to a ceiling where it became uneconomic for any individual to try to dominate the rest. Thus, although at first sight there seems to be a yawning gap between Machiavellian primates and egalitarian humans, according to this scenario the latter would actually have been the product of an arms race of Machiavellian expertise. This is consistent with the picture of hunter–gatherer society as showing a state of egalitarianism which is effectively a stable state for their niche, but probed intermittently by Machiavellian explorations.

Coordination

Egalitarianism represents one sense in which hunter–gatherers cooperate—they cooperate in the *levelling* of differentials of status and resource-holding. But they also cooperate in the sense of *coordinating* their actions. This coordination is also achieved through high-level cognitive operations which set it apart from that found in other species in both its nature and its extent. These two aspects of cooperation—egalitarianism and coordination—are probably linked to each other as well as to other aspects of deep social mind in various ways, an issue we shall return to later.

Cooperative coordination is seen in many aspects of hunter–gatherer life, but the evidence reviewed above for a niche differentiation founded on this subsistence pattern of gathering and hunting leads me to focus here particularly on coordination in the foraging quest.

We have not systematically catalogued the frequency with which hunting is done by groups in the sample surveyed by Erdal and Whiten, but it is common and is the dominant mode in the African groups for which there are good descriptions, such as the San (e.g. Lee 1979) and the Hadza (Hawkes *et al.* 1992). Hunting parties might be small, however—in small bands of San, for example, the modal size is only two (a fact which might be telling us something important, insofar as the logically minimum size for the cognitively advanced phenomenon of an ambush is two).

Despite the small size of such hunting groups, the nature of the coordination they rely on is deep in several respects, evident in the detailed descriptions given by Lee (1979). If we begin with the activities of a San hunting party itself, we find that analysis of the meaning of animal tracks is a social affair, involving much discussion and consensual decision-making. If tracks fade, the group might fan out to gather information as a group, sometimes using bird calls to coordinate their movements with each other without warning potential prey. Once prey is approached, communication switches to sign-language, another way of avoiding disturbance to the prey. These non-verbal signs can be used to signal type of prey, age, health, speed, and direction, and thus coordinate the intelligent approach of a spread of strategically placed hunters. Once a kill has been attempted and if prey bolt, hunters will coordinate their movements so as to drive prey towards each other to get further shots in. As we noted earlier, the abstract, socio-cognitive nature of hunting often then involves a further analysis of signs from wounded prey, which again involves much discussion and social decision-making.

The coordination on which this 'core' part of the hunt rests is further extended by other cooperative actions in the larger frame of effort in which it is embedded, the sophisticated cognitive nature of which was noted earlier. Thus even before the hunt begins there is much sharing of relevant information by hunters and gatherers who have witnessed prey, or other relevant information like grazing and water sources or fresh burrows. At this level the group functions like a coordinated net of information-processing which spans very large areas around the camp. After a hunt, the return of hunters to the camp, followed by the organization of a party to recover the prey, makes yet more elaborate the manner in which human hunting works as a coordinated group activity. Such coordination is no doubt enhanced over the long term by the recounting of the day's events that occurs amongst the group in the aftermath, typically around the evening camp-fire.

Such deep coordination is clearly the product of minds that are deeply social: They exploit the cognitive hunting niche through processes of planning and decision-making in which such an enormous part of the information processed is about, or derived from, other group members (as opposed to the prey itself), that the group operates as one big, unique kind of predator. But this latter epithet is appropriate for all animals who hunt in packs or prides—what differentiates the human approach seems to be, first, the way in which the 'group-level predator' description applies across large spaces and times (coordination spans the activities of hunters and gatherers even when they are exploiting quite different parts of their range or working at the camp, and even over long periods); and second, the degree of differentiation of the roles combined in the group effect.

These features contrast with the hunting behaviour of those non-human primates that eat significant amounts of meat, such as certain populations of chimpanzees and baboons. At the same time, chimpanzees and baboons do reveal levels of coordination that suggest the kinds of precursors from which the special hominid approach is likely to have evolved. Strum (1981) was fortunate to observe significant increases in hunting frequency in one group of baboons, apparently through an interplay between the carnivorous propensities of one individual baboon and the availability of prey. Accompanying the greater prevalence of hunting came more meat-sharing, a tendency for some individuals to become sensitive to others' intention to hunt, and more coordinated group hunting in which individuals chased prey in 'relays'. However, even at its most advanced point, this hunting appeared to be opportunistic in that each hunter became skilled at reacting to the particular social and predatory configuration of the moment. In chimpanzees, the most frequent hunters are in the populations of the Tai forest (Boesch 1994) and again this focus on hunting seems to be associated with greater levels of coordination than reported for other populations such as that at Gombe. Boesch and Boesch distinguish four levels of cooperation, the most complex being 'collaboration', in which "hunters perform different complementary actions...examples are driving, blocking escape ways, and encirclement" (p. 550). At Tai, they assigned 68% of hunts to this category. Just how such cases are discriminated from opportunism remains to be described in any detail, but clearly Boesch and Boesch perceive a high level of coordination, of a kind which could have formed an evolutionary platform for the sophistication we now observe in human hunters.

I have purposely concentrated much of the foregoing analysis on hunting rather than gathering, even though gathering also seems to evidence high levels of coordination and typically contributes the greater part of calorific income to the group, at least in the tropics. This is principally because of the nature of the data to hand. We have little information on which to judge the prehistory of gathering, in contrast to hunting. Nor do we appear to have very full accounts of the nature of gathering, of a kind which would enable inferences about the cognitive processes involved. However gathering, like hunting, is typically a social activity, coordinated by group discussion and decision-making which extends beyond the confines of any one gathering trip (Lee 1979). Moreover, because of the information flow between gatherers and hunters, there is a coordination between hunting and gathering activities which means that the concept of a band as a 'group-level predator' should encompass all edible components of the environment.

Finally, we should note that this analysis which has focused on coordination in the service of foraging omits reference to others spheres of social life in which cooperative coordination is elaborate amongst hunter–gatherers. Arranging marriages between members of different bands and care of the sick are but two further examples from San society (Lee 1979).

Culture

Extensive components of hunter–gatherer behavioural repertoires seem to be acquired by cultural rather than genetic transmission between individuals. My use of 'seem' here might seem over-cautious, but I want to start this section by noting that, by the standards of evidence debated in the recent literature on the question of animal culture (e.g. Galef 1992; Heyes and Galef 1996), we seem to have remarkably little systematic evidence on just how much of the behaviour of humans in any society is socially transmitted.

Perhaps the clearest exception to this remark—the best model for what is otherwise so lacking—is demonstrated by the literature on first-language acquisition. On this subject, systematic, scientifically rigorous observations (e.g. McShane 1980), coupled with experimental studies which intervene to test hypothesized transmission processes (e.g. Tomasello and Kruger 1992), have much refined our knowledge about how social learning operates in language acquisition, at least in certain non-hunter–gatherer societies. By contrast, if we turn to ask what we know at a similar level of rigour about cultural transmission of the behavioural repertoire of hunter–gatherers, the answer is: very little indeed. Despite the vast size and scope of the Kalahari San project, for example, we cannot be sure how much of either hunting or gathering skill is derived respectively from all the individual practice and learning that takes place before adolescence, from intentional teaching, or from observation of skilled foragers. Lee (1979), for example, although providing some of our best detail on hunting behaviour, remarks only that San boys "receive little formal instruction from men until they are about 12 years old" (p. 236). From this age, boys begin to accompany their elders on hunts and presumably learn much of their very sophisticated hunting repertoire from them—it will usually be another three to six years before they have the competence to kill good-sized prey, such as an adult antelope. Coupled with the contrast between intergenerational consistency in hunting techniques within societies, and variation in such techniques across societies, such observations suggest that social transmission plays a major part in the construction of each individual hunter's repertoire. This is likely to be true also for gathering, although once again we have to lament that we do not have any systematic data by which to make any kind of thorough comparison with hunting.

Despite the surprising lack of empirical documentation of hunter–gatherer cultural transmission, there will probably be little dissent from the observation that the human mind is typically much more a product of the culture within which it grows than is that of any great ape. This aspect of deep social mind facilitates a wide range of acquisitions, including the local language, subsistence and social customs. Why did this process become so marked only in hominids?

Social transmission and the cognitive niche

It was argued above that the exploitation of a novel cognitive niche has been crucial in hominid evolution, and this might provide the explanation for the evolution of the cultural component of deep social mind. Learning from others enables faster, deeper penetration of the cognitive niche than an individual can manage by their own efforts in their lifetime. This is because with succeeding generations, the most profitable cognitive advances of the past can be accumulated—any one hominid does not merely exploit the cognitive niche by their own mental powers, but does so on the back of a string of progressive niche penetrations by their ancestors, as techniques such as those for hunting are progressively improved, refined and differentiated from those of competitor species. In this way, the 'surprise attacks' highlighted by Tooby and DeVore (1987) can become bigger and bigger surprises for prey.

To compound our metaphors, we can see that through what Tomasello *et al.* (1993) described as the 'ratchet effect' of cultural transmission, the cognitive niche can become a progressively deepening furrow. Cognitive achievements such as the acquisition of difficult-to-obtain knowledge and the solving of specific problems do not need to be repeated in each generation because they can be acquired socially, and each advance builds on the shoulders of the last. An example of such rarefied knowledge is expressed in the ability of San hunters to travel several kilometres from camp to places where they recognize particular surface signs, on the basis of which they dig down very deep to obtain grubs, from which in turn they extract arrow poison through a complex series of operations. It is unimaginable that the fund of knowledge which is used here could be built up by any single isolated individual, however excellent an example of a cognitive-niche-exploiter they might be. A parallel example to illustrate this point with respect to problem solving is the use of a special snare by which San efficiently hook spring-hares from the burrow in which the hares typically hide from other, less cognitively-resourceful, predators.

As a result of such cultural acquisitions, hunter–gatherers (and in this case, humans generally) have minds which are deeply social in senses different from, but I suggest importantly related to, the cooperating/egalitarian/sharing senses already described in the previous sections—such minds are deeply social, first, with respect to the source of their *content* (they contain extensive behavioural repertoires got from others) and second, in their learning *mechanisms* (the highly structured processes which are used to build those repertoires by absorption from others). The first of these, the content, is typically extensive, including, for example, a whole range of often intricate hunting and gathering techniques, and social customs ranging from the local language to marriage practices. The second, social learning processes, include observation and imitation, which might be supported by active teaching.

Hominid culture

If the above analysis is essentially correct, cultural learning is one important strand in the process through which deep social mind permits hunter–gatherers to extend their crucial penetration of the cognitive niche. As in the case of other observed correlates of modern-day hunting and gathering, like egalitarianism, the hypothesis is that the scope of cultural acquisition came to fulfil this important function during the rise of the hunting–gathering way of life as it emerged in the Pleistocene.

However, unlike egalitarianism, we do have archaeological remains—stone tools in particular—which help us to assess how realistic this hypothesis is. In fact, assemblages of stone tools are typically referred to as cultures, traditions or industries—first, the 'Oldowan culture' from about 2.5 million years ago, then the 'Acheulian culture' from about 1.5 million years ago (Gowlett 1992a). Although we do not have any direct evidence, it is assumed that the techniques which generated these tools were typically socially acquired, rather than generated each time by individual inventiveness. This is probably a reasonable assumption, but it is worth dwelling briefly on the comparison between this state of affairs and recent debates about animal culture, alluded to earlier.

Galef (1992) noted that psychologists have drawn distinctions between several different processes of social learning which operate in the animal kingdom. These include simple processes such as stimulus enhancement, in which an individual's attention is merely drawn to relevant objects or parts of the environment by the actions of a companion, the remainder of the matching of the observer's behaviour to that of the original performer then being produced by learning at the individual level. Imitation, by contrast, would involve actually copying something about the actions of the model. Galef noted that in humans social transmission occurs through processes which include both imitation and teaching, and he went on to argue that where an animal acquires a behaviour pattern only through the simpler methods like stimulus enhancement, it is important to acknowledge that the mental process is *not homologous* with the human ones. He proposed that we should not refer to 'culture' in such a case, but use the term 'tradition' instead.

In Galef's terms, then, did the first stone toolmakers have a culture, or only traditions? In the case of the earliest Oldowan tools, its seems difficult if not impossible to say. It is conceivable that an onlooker, having had their attention drawn to a tool being used on its target (animal matter? plant matter? we don't know) could learn how to use it by experimenting themselves, rather than learning about the techniques as such. This is the kind of scenario that, according to some authorities, is not ruled out in the case of wild chimpanzees' tool use, including the smashing of hard shelled fruit with stone (Tomasello 1990, 1996; Galef 1992; Heyes 1993). In principle, the same argument could apply to early hominids' manufacture of stone tools also. However, it seems likely that stone tool-making was acquired through *some* form of social learning: The alternative is that the many thousands of Oldowan choppers and flakes recovered are the result of repeated reinventions.

When Acheulian tools appear, however, we seem driven to different levels of inference. As Gowlett (1992*b*) describes it, "the working of a stone to a set form was plainly established by 1.5 [million years] ago, when early humans made large, bifacial cutting tools, or Acheulian handaxes" (p. 342). He goes on to remark that "this tells us a great deal: that an 'arbitrary', preconceived form was held in the mind, and could be impressed on stone". This new degree of clearly intended symmetry is what distinguished the Acheulian, although it remains possible that "in even earlier, Oldowan stone industries similar ideas may underlie the careful flaking of discoid cores or core tools" (Gowlett 1992b, p. 342).

That such tools were carefully worked to a 'pattern' is the feature most commonly commented on as evidence of an important cognitive leap forward, when compared with Oldowan or chimpanzee tools. However this considers mental implications only at the individual level and it is likely that what these tools tell us about cultural learning is no less profound. However functional the symmetrical patterns were (and presumably they conferred significant benefits since they were reproduced for over a million years), it is unlikely they could have been products of the simpler social learning processes, like stimulus enhancement, distinguished above. Instead, we surely have to accord their makers quite refined abilities for imitative copying, both of the final tool-pattern to be achieved, and how to set about achieving it. These in turn represent advances over the Oldowan products, so by then hominids ploughed the cognitive furrow deeper by exploiting the progressive achievements of a long chain of tool-making ancestors.

Pre-hominid foundations of culture

Like each of the aspects of deep social mind I am picking out, this new level of culture was attainable in hominid evolution because it could be shaped from the capacities of the ancestral ape mind. It is true that in recent years, several critiques have appeared which together cast strong doubt on whether the available observational and experimental evidence showed the imitative capacities which for so long had been assumed in apes (Galef 1990, 1992; Tomasello 1990, 1996; Visalberghi and Fragaszy 1990; Whiten and Ham 1992). But apparently as a result of this onslaught, a new wave of more rigorous studies has been embarked upon, such that we have a properly documented 'reinstatement' (Russon 1997) of the notion that apes have a well elaborated capacity for imitation, and thus for 'culture' in Galef's (1992) stringent terms. Experimental studies have mainly involved chimpanzees and have revealed a number of respects in which imitative capacities they share with humans, and therefore, we assume, our common ancestor, are of a kind from which the advances of Acheulian culture could have taken off. These capacities include the imitation of functional actions on objects (opening novel, 'artificial' fruits—Whiten *et al.* 1996); imitation of arbitrary or non-functional acts (relevant to the extent that the fine symmetry of Acheulian patterns is often assumed to have conventional rather than any obvious functional significance—Tomasello *et al.* 1994; Custance *et al.* 1995); and delayed imitation (relevant to cases where cultural transmission depended on recall of techniques on occasions when the original model is absent—Tomasello *et al.* 1994). New and more fine-grained observational studies complement these results by offering stronger evidence for cultural transmission in wild chimpanzees (Boesch 1996), whilst close observational analysis of orang-utan behaviour has suggested that these capacities might be shared by all great apes and thus by the common ancestor which lived as long ago as 16 million years ago (Russon and Galdikas 1993).

All this suggests that early hominids would have had a highly structured imitative capacity of this type. With the Acheulian period we see this capacity extended to replication of tools to a specific pattern, indicating a deepening of this component of social mind. This in turn would have enabled the deepening of the cognitive niche that differentiated the beginnings of hunting–gathering from the competing foraging strategies of other species. This analysis agrees with a major examination of such evolutionary transitions by Donald (1991), in identifying a significant advance beyond the capacity of the ancestral ape mind in the Acheulian stage, although there is disagreement on the correct characterization of the ape–*Homo* psychological contrasts involved (Donald 1991; Whiten *et al.* 1996b).

Mind-reading

The third piece of the jigsaw of the deep social mind I am outlining here is the ability to read other minds, an ability known variously in the relevant literatures as mind-reading, natural psychology, or operating a theory of mind (Whiten 1994; see also Baron-Cohen, this volume). Strangely, the bulk of what has become a vast scientific literature on the subject over the last ten years has been almost exclusively devoted to the development of this capacity in young children (see Lewis and Mitchell 1994, for an overview). Apart from the efforts of philosophers of mind, there has been relatively little work done to chart everyday mind-reading in adults—how we do it and what we use it for, for example—and the same dearth of empirical investigation is apparent if we want to know about the nature of mind-reading in non-literate societies, including those of hunter–gatherers. One exception to the latter vacuum is a study by Avis and Harris (1991), rather grandly subtitled 'evidence for a universal conception of mind'. Avis and Harris showed that five-year-old Baka pygmy children have the same grasp as do European and American children of the mental state of *belief*—they recognize the circumstances in which false beliefs arise and can predict ensuing actions accordingly. This is sufficient for our present purposes, because although our system of mind-reading can become very much more sophisticated than that of a five-year-old, everyday psychology is already an elaborate system by this age, which recognizes numerous states of mind including desires, perceptions, intentions, knowledge, and ignorance, as well as belief, and predictively models people's actions using a mentalistic scheme. It seems we can safely assume *at least* this level of mind-reading for hunter–gatherer societies, and in doing so we recognize a further aspect of deep social mind—to an extent not apparent in other animals, such people mentally penetrate other minds and are in turn mentally penetrated by them. The minds in such a society are deeply *interwoven* in a manner unprecedented in evolution (we shall discuss how far apes get, below).

This phenomenon is distinct from the other aspects of deep social mind discussed earlier, but surely related to them—egalitarianism, coordination, and culture all operate in the way they do because the actors' minds are interwoven in this deep way.

Like cultural learning, mind-reading seems to enable a deepening of the cognitive niche. Given the lack of empirical investigation what we can say on this must remain quite speculative but if, for illustration, we stick again to the example of hunting as described for the San above, it is clearly plausible that the social coordination and communication involved rests on each hunter utilizing a model of his co-hunters' psychology, including states of mind like those listed earlier as within the five-year-old's grasp—visual perspectives, desires, intentions, ignorance, knowledge, and belief. This suggests that selection pressures were active with respect to mind-reading in the same way as for other aspects of deep social mind, as differentiation into this cognitive niche was favoured during hominid evolution. An additional possibility is that reading the mind of one's prey, and perhaps that of competitors (have the lions who made the kill lost interest sufficiently to make scavenging safe?) were bonuses in yet more successfully exploiting the cognitive niche.

The evolution of mind-reading

As far as the archaeological record goes, there is not much room for optimism that lessons can be learned about early hominids' capacity for mind-reading. However, like the other capacities we have considered, we can hope to reconstruct the relevant mentality of the common ancestor we share with chimpanzees by establishing what mind-reading abilities the chimpanzee has in common with ourselves. These abilities might help to explain how the extraordinary apparatus that is our present-day mind-reading system arose as part of the hunter–gatherer mentality.

This issue has been tackled empirically through two main routes. One involves descriptive analysis of naturally occurring primate behaviour, particularly deception (e.g. Whiten and Byrne 1988a). The other involves experimentation (e.g. Premack and Woodruff 1978; Povinelli and Eddy 1996a). There is not the space to review this corpus of work adequately here and to do so properly requires a quite extensive conceptual framework to accompany it (see Whiten 1994, 1996a; Heyes in press). Fortunately, recent reviews are to hand (Povinelli 1996; Whiten in press; Heyes 1998).

Perhaps the most general of the key points which should be drawn out of these efforts for present purposes is that the identification of non-verbal mind-reading is not an all-or-none affair—for one thing, there are many different states of mind and it is clear in the child research, at least, that some (e.g. *seeing, wanting*) are recognized more easily and earlier than others (e.g. *false belief, ironic intention*) (Whiten 1991; Baron-Cohen 1995); for another, mind-reading is not done by telepathy but by reading observables, so the distinction between sophisticated behaviour-reading and mind-reading is more like a continuum than a dichotomy (Whiten 1994, 1996a). This means that whether the limited capacities of either human infants or chimpanzees along this continuum are best classed as the first signs of mind-reading, or as precursors to mind-reading, is not a productive debate—as Baron-Cohen (this volume) and Byrne (this volume) note, *elements* of mind-reading might be older than six million years. A major candidate for such a transitional ability is that for reading *visual attention*.

Reading visual attention deserves special interest for several reasons. One is that it seems to be foundational in the development of normal human mind-reading, because deficits in autistic individual's theory of mind are predicted by earlier deficits in shared attention (Baron-Cohen 1995, this volume). Another is that the monitoring and manipulation of attention accounts for the major part of Byrne and Whiten's (1990) corpus of episodes of tactical deception in primates, indicating that tuning into visual attention is a major component of primate's social expertise (Whiten and Byrne 1988b).

Accordingly, several recent experimental studies have focused on just what chimpanzees are capable of in this domain. Although in some studies subjects have shown a remarkable lack of sensitivity to relevant aspects of others' visual attention, such as whether the eyes of the other are open or closed, or otherwise covered (Povinelli and Eddy 1996a), other studies have shown sensitivity to such factors (Gomez 1996), as well as an appreciation of visual occlusion by barriers and the likelihood that the focus of another's gaze will have an object or referent, which might be the subject of further communication (Povinelli and Eddy 1996b; Whiten in press). Such abilities are a far cry from the mind-reading of humans, but they nevertheless express a capacity to compute something of the other's view of the world. The likelihood that such an ability was present in our common ancestor of six million years ago would mean that a significant platform existed from which the advanced mind-reading of humans could evolve. Although it is a little difficult to tell from the kinds of description given, the most sophisticated primate hunting, done by chimpanzees of the Tai forest, seems already to depend on skilled reading of the intentions and attention of those others engaged in the hunt (Boesch and Boesch 1989).

Conclusion—the integration of components of deep social mind

A final word should be added about the ways in which the various aspects of deep social mind distinguished here might interact. The ways in which they might do so suggests they act together as an adaptive complex, reinforcing the effects each has on the depth of penetration of the cognitive niche:

1. *Mind-reading* can support *cultural transmission*, both in terms of acquiring mental contents from others and teaching others (e.g. one's offspring).
2. *Culture* supports *mind-reading*, through the transfer of the underlying social skills. This is likely to be particularly powerful once a linguistically coded folk psychology is a cultural phenomenon to be transmitted.
3. *Mind-reading* supports *egalitarianism*, at least near the 'ceiling' outlined earlier, because it exposes minds to the public appraisal which makes counter-dominance powerful, and exposes cheating.
4. *Egalitarianism* encourages a certain kind of cooperative *mind-reading* such as operates in teaching and sharing of information. This cooperative pole of mind-reading seems to be the first to be expressed in human infancy (Whiten 1997).
5. *Culture* can also support *egalitarianism*, for example through the acquisition of counter-dominant tactics.
6. *Egalitarianism* can support *culture* through the generalized sharing of information.

In such suggestions I have limited cooperation to 'egalitarianism' rather than distinguishing sharing, status-levelling, and coordination, in order to prevent a combinatorial explosion in the interactions I could list. However, this in itself highlights the possibility that just such a combinatorial explosion might have occurred in our past, producing an adaptive socio-cognitive complex that might explain the rapid encephalization and extraordinary niche differentiation of hominids.

References

Ardrey, R. (1976). *The hunting hypothesis*. Collins, London.

Avis, J. and Harris, P. L. (1991). Belief–desire reasoning among Baka children: evidence for a universal conception of mind. *Child Development*, **62**, 460–7.

Baron-Cohen, S. (1995). *Mindblindness: an essay on autism and theory of mind*. Bradford/MIT Press, Cambridge, MA.

Blumenschine, R. J. (1992). Hominid carnivory and foraging strategies, and the socio-economic function of early archaeological sites. In *Foraging strategies and natural diet of monkeys, apes and humans* (ed. A. Whiten and E. M. Widdowson), pp. 51–61. Oxford University Press.

Boehm, C. (1997). Egalitarian behaviour and the evolution of political intelligence. In *Machiavellian intelligence II: evaluations and extensions* (ed. A. Whiten and R. W. Byrne), pp. 341–64. Cambridge University Press.

Boesch, C. (1994). Cooperative hunting in wild chimpanzees. *Animal Behaviour*, **48**, 653–67.

Boesch, C. (1996). The emergence of cultures among wild chimpanzees. In *Evolution of social behaviour patterns in primates and man* (ed. W. G. Runciman, J. Maynard Smith, and R. I. M. Dunbar), pp. 251–68. Oxford University Press.

Boesch, C. and Boesch, H. (1989). The hunting behaviour of wild chimpanzees in the Tai National Park. *American Journal of Physical Anthropology*, **78**, 547–73.

Byrne, R. W. and Whiten, A. (1990). Tactical deception in primates: the 1990 database. *Primate Report*, **27**, 1–101.

Corballis, M. C. (1991). *The lopsided ape: evolution of the generative mind*. Oxford University Press, New York.

Custance, D. M., Whiten, A., and Bard, K. A. (1995). Can young chimpanzees imitate arbitrary actions? Hayes and Hayes (1952) revisited. *Behaviour*, **132**, 839–58.

Dahlberg, F. (1981). *Woman the gatherer*. Yale University Press, New Haven, CT.

de Waal, F. B. M. (1982). *Chimpanzee politics*. Jonathan Cape, London.

Donald, M. (1991). *Origins of the human mind: three stages in the evolution of culture and cognition*. Harvard University Press.

Erdal, D. and Whiten, A. (1994). On human egalitarianism: an evolutionary product of Machiavellian status escalation? *Current Anthropology*, 35, 175–83.

Erdal, D. and Whiten, A. (1996). Egalitarianism and Machiavellian intelligence in human evolution. In *Modelling the early human mind* (ed. P. Mellars and K. Gibson), pp. 139–50. McDonald Institute Monographs, Cambridge, UK.

Foley, R. (1984). Early man and the Red Queen: tropical African community evolution and hominid adaptation. In *Hominid evolution and community ecology: prehistoric human adaptation in biological perspective* (ed. R. Foley), pp. 85–110. Academic Press, London.

Foley, R. (1987). *Another unique species: patterns in human evolutionary ecology*. Longman Scientific and Technical, Harlow.

Foley, W. A. (1997). *Anthropological linguistics*. Blackwell, Oxford.

Galef, B. G. (1990). Tradition in animals: field observations and laboratory analyses. In *Interpretations and explanations in the study of behaviour: comparative perspectives* (ed. M. Bekoff and D. Jamieson), pp. 74–95. Westview Press, Boulder, Colorado.

Galef, B. G. (1992). The question of animal culture. *Human Nature*, **3**, 157–78.

Gomez, J.-C. (1996). Non-human primate theories of (non-human primate) minds: some issues concerning the origins of mind-reading. In *Theories of theories of mind* (ed. P. Carruthers and P. K. Smith), 330–43. Cambridge University Press.

Goody, E. (1997). Social intelligence and language: another Rubicon. In *Machiavellian intelligence II: evaluations and extensions* (ed. A. Whiten and R. W. Byrne), pp. 365–96. Cambridge University Press.

Gowlett, J. A. J. (1992a). Early human mental abilities. In *The Cambridge encyclopaedia of human evolution* (ed. S. Jones, R. Martin, and D. Pilbeam), pp. 341–5. Cambridge University Press.

Gowlett, J. A. J. (1992b). Tools—the Palaeolithic record. In *The Cambridge encyclopaedia of human evolution* (ed. S. Jones, R. Martin, and D. Pilbeam), pp. 350–60. Cambridge University Press.

Gowlett, J. A. J. (1996). Mental abilities of early *Homo*: elements of constraint and choice in rule systems. In *Modelling the early human mind* (ed. P. Mellars and K. Gibson), pp. 191–215. McDonald Institute Monographs, Cambridge.

Hawkes, K., O'Connell, J. F, and Blurton-Jones, N. G. (1992). Hunting income patterns among the Hadza: big game, common goods, foraging goals and the evolution of the human diet. In

Foraging strategies and natural diet of monkeys, apes and humans (ed. A. Whiten and E. M. Widdowson), pp. 83–91. Oxford University Press.

Heyes, C. M. (1993). Imitation, culture, and cognition. *Animal Behaviour*, **46**, 999–1010.

Heyes, C. M. (1998). Theory of mind in non-human primates. *Behavioral and Brain Sciences*, **21**, 101–48.

Heyes, C. M. and Galef, B. G. Jr. (ed.) (1996). *Social learning in animals: the roots of culture*. Academic Press, London.

Hrdy, S. B. *The woman that never evolved*. Harvard University Press.

Isaac, G. (1978). The food-sharing behaviour of protohuman hominids. *Scientific American*, **238**, 90–108.

Knauft, B. M. (1991). Violence and sociality in human evolution. *Current Anthropology*, **32**, 391–428.

Lee, R. B. (1979). The !Kung san: men, women and work in a foraging society. Cambridge University Press.

Lewis, C. and Mitchell, P. (ed.) (1994). *Children's early understanding of mind: origins and development*. Lawrence Erlbanm, Hove, UK.

McShane, J. (1980). *Learning to talk*. Cambridge University Press.

Mithen, S. (1996). *The prehistory of the mind*: a search for the origins of art, religion, and science. Thames and Hudson, London.

Maglio, V. J. (1978). Patterns of faunal evolution. In *evolution of African mammals* (ed. Maglio, V. J. and Cooke, H. B. S.), pp. 603–20. Harvard University Press.

Nishida, T. (1983). Alpha status and agonistic alliance in wild chimpanzees. *Primates*, **24**, 318–36.

Potts, R. (1988). *Early hominid activities at Olduvai*. Aldine, Hawthorne, NY.

Potts, R. (1992). The hominid way of life. In *The Cambridge encyclopaedia of human evolution* (ed. S. Jones, R. Martin, and D. Pilbeam), pp. 325–34. Cambridge University Press.

Povinelli, D. J. (1996). Chimpanzee theory of mind: the long road to strong inference. In *Theories of theories of mind* (ed. P. Carruthers and P. K. Smith), pp. 293–329. Cambridge University Press.

Povinelli, D. J. and Eddy, T. J. (1996a). Chimpanzees: joint visual attention. *Psychological Science*, **7**, 129–35.

Povinelli, D. J. and Eddy, T. J. (1996b). What young chimpanzees know about seeing. *Monographs of the Society for Research in Child Development*, **61**, (2), Ser. No. 247.

Premack, D. and Woodruff, G. (1978). Does the chimpanzee have a theory of mind? *Behavioral and Brain Sciences*, **1**, 515–26.

Russon, A. E. (1997). Exploiting the expertise of others. In *Machiavellian intelligence II: evaluations and extensions* (ed. A. Whiten and R. W. Byrne), pp. 174–206. Cambridge University Press.

Russon, A. E. and Galdikas, F. B. M. (1993). Imitation in ex-captive orang-utans. (Pongo pygmaeus). *Journal of Comparative Psychology*, **107**, 147–61.

Schick, K. D. (1987). Modelling the formation of stone artifact concentrations. *Journal of Human Evolution*, **16**, 789–807.

Semaw, S., Renn, P., Harris, J. W. K., Feibel, C. S., Bernor, R. L., Fesseha, N., *et al.* (1997). 2.5-million-year-old stone tools from Gona, Ethiopia. *Nature*, **385**, 333–6.

Solway, J. S. and Lee, R. B. (1990). Foragers, genuine or spurious? Situating the Kalahari san in history. *Current Anthropology*, **31**, 109–46.

Strum, S. C. (1981). Processes and products of change: baboon predatory behavior at Gilgil, Kenya. In *Omnivorous primates: gathering and hunting in human evolution* (ed. R. S. O. Harding and G. Teleki), pp. 255–302. Columbia University Press, New York.

Thieme, H. (1997). Lower Palaeolithic hunting spears from Germany. *Nature*, **385**, 807–10.

Tomasello, M. (1990). Cultural transmission in the tool use and communicatory signalling of chimpanzees? In *'Language' and intelligence in monkeys and apes: comparative developmental perspectives* (ed. S. Parker and K. Gibson), pp. 274–311. Cambridge University Press.

Tomasello, M., Savage-Rumbaugh, E. S. and Kruger, A. C. (1993). Imitative learning of actions on objects by children, chimpanzees and encutturated chimpanzees. *Child Development*, **64**, 1688–705.

Tomasello, M. (1996). Do apes ape? In *Social learning in animals: the roots of culture* (ed. C. M. Heyes and B. G. Galef, Jr), 319–46. Academic Press, London.

Tomasello, M. and Kruger, A. (1992). Joint attention on actions: acquiring verbs in ostensive and non-ostensive contexts. *Journal of Child Language*, **19**, 311–34.

Tomasello, M., Kruger, A. C., and Ratner, H. H. (1993). Cultural learning. *Behavioral and Brain Sciences*, **16**, 495–552.

Tooby, J. and Cosmides, L. (1989). Evolutionary psychology and the generation of culture, Part 1. Theoretical considerations. *Ethology and Sociobiology*, **10**, 29–49.

Tooby, J. and DeVore, I. (1987). The reconstruction of hominid behavioral evolution through strategic modelling. In *The evolution of human behavior: primate models* (ed. W. G. Kinzey), 183–237. SUNY Press, New York.

Visalberghi, E. and Fragaszy, D. (1990). Do monkeys ape? In *Language and intelligence in monkeys and apes: comparative developmental perspectives* (ed. S. Parker and K. Gibson), pp. 247–73. Cambridge University Press.

Washburn, S. L. and Lancaster, C. S. (1968). The evolution of hunting. *In Man the hunter* (ed. R. B. Lee and I. DeVore), pp 293–303. Aldine, Chicago.

Whiten, A. (1991). The emergence of mindreading. In *Natural theories of mind*. (ed. A. Whiten) Basil Blackwell, Oxford.

Whiten, A. (1994). Grades of mind-reading. In *Origins of an understanding of mind* (ed. C. Lewis and P. Mitchell), pp. 47–70. Erlbaum, Hove, UK.

Whiten, A. (1996*a*). When does smart behaviour reading become mind-reading? In *Theories of theories of mind* (ed. P. Carruthers and P. K. Smith), pp. 277–92. Cambridge University Press.

Whiten, A. (1996*b*). Imitation, pretence and mind-reading: secondary representation in comparative primatology and developmental psychology? In *Reaching into thought: the minds of the great apes* (ed. A. E. Russon, K. A. Bard, and S. T. Parker), pp. 300–24. Cambridge University Press.

Whiten, A. (1997). The Machiavellian mind-reader. In *Machiavellian intelligence II: evaluations and extensions* (ed. A. Whiten and R. W. Byrne), pp. 144–73. Cambridge University Press.

Whiten, A. (1998). Evolutionary and developmental origins of the mind-reading system. In *Piaget, evolution and development* (ed. J. Langer and M. Killen), pp. 73–99. Erlbaum, Hove, UK.

Whiten, A. (*in press*). Chimpanzee cognition and the question of mental re-representation. In *Metarepresentation* (ed. D. Sperber). Oxford University Press.

Whiten, A. and Byrne, R. W. (1988*a*). Tactical deception in primates. *Behavioral and Brain Sciences*, **11**, 233–73.

Whiten, A., and Byrne, R. W. (1988*b*). The manipulation of attention in primate tactical deception. In *Machiavellian intelligence: social expertise and the evolution of intellect in monkeys, apes and humans* (ed. R. W. Byrne and A. Whiten), pp. 211–23. Oxford University Press.

Whiten, A. and Ham, R. (1992). On the nature and evolution of imitation in the animal kingdom: reappraisal of a century of research. In *Advances in the study of behavior* (ed. P. J. B. Slater, J. S. Rosenblatt, C. Beer, and M. Milinski), pp. 239–83. Academic Press, San Diego.

Whiten, A., Custance, D., Gomez, J.-C., Teixidor, P. and Bard, K. (1996). Imitative learning of artificial fruit-processing in children (*Homo sapiens*) and chimpanzees (*Pan troglodytes*). *Journal of Comparative Psychology*, **110**, 3–14.

Woodburn, J. (1982). Egalitarian societies. *Man*, **17**, 431–51.

11

Handedness, cerebral lateralization, and the evolution of language

I. C. McManus

Introduction

To those proverbial and seemingly almost ubiquitous biologists and anthropologists from Mars, visiting planet Earth and trying to make sense of the vast and diverse animal kingdom, one of the most difficult phenomena to explain would be language. In a fully developed, practical and useful form it would seem to be restricted to just the one species, *Homo sapiens*, where it is apparently correlated with such overwhelming technical advantages that without it civilization and technology would seem impossible, and indeed its organizational advantages would seem to threaten the very existence of many other species on the planet. Perhaps most problematic in explaining why only one species exhibits language would be that the brain, which embodies the central nervous system whence all complex behaviours stem, would seem to be not substantially different in any qualitative morphology from that of many other vertebrates, particularly from that of other primates. Our Martians might observe that the human brain, and especially the frontal lobes, is somewhat larger relative to body size than in other species, but the differences are not immense. Neither are there in human brains any obvious 'language organs', any sets of nuclei or particular gyri which are conspicuously absent in apes or primates.

Eventually one of the Martians, perhaps one of a more experimental turn of mind, would cease observing and instead begin a little vivisection on the single peculiar species with language. And from that would come what is really the strangest of all the truths about language—that in most of the humans studied, the faculty of language would be destroyed by removing the *left* half of the brain, but almost unaffected by removing the right half. And to mystify the Martian yet further, the two halves of the brain when viewed anatomically would be barely distinguishable. The shock would be all the more surprising because the Martian would know that the function of the left lung is similar to that of the right lung—to exchange gases—and that the function of the left kidney is the same as that of the right kidney—to excrete waste products—and so on; so why on earth (or indeed, for that matter, why on Mars) should language be functionally asymmetric in an anatomically symmetric brain? And just to clinch it, why is functional asymmetry of similar extent found in almost none of the other myriad different brains found on earth—with the exception of the asymmetrical control of song in birds (Nottebohm 1977) and possibly of 'speech' in parrots (Snyder and Harris 1997)? There can be little doubt that our inquisitive Martian would feel sure that lurking in the asymmetry of language, in the phenomenon of cerebral dominance, was an answer to the question of what had happened in the evolutionary past that resulted in just this single species having that most crucial and sophisticated of faculties, language.

Broca, the lateralization of language, and its relationship to handedness

The above account makes a few small exaggerations—'always' should sometimes be 'almost always', and so on—but the key observation is correct, and it dates back to the findings of Paul Broca in the 1860s (Broca 1865; Hécaen and Dubois 1969; Schiller 1979) who observed that in a series of patients with aphasia, a loss of language, there was a concomitant paralysis of the right side of the body. Since the central nervous system shows decussation, the left cerebral hemisphere controlling the right half of the body, and *vice versa*, the implication was that in most people language was present in the *left* half of the brain. The general principle was rapidly confirmed by other researchers, although it did become apparent that a small proportion of individuals, perhaps 10% or so, had their language disrupted by damage to the right rather than the left side. At first it was often assumed that these individuals were left-handed (Eling 1984; Harris 1991, 1993)—in effect restoring some form of conceptual symmetry to an otherwise asymmetric brain. But it soon became clear from observations of patients with brain damage, then later from studies of language function during intra-carotid sodium amytal testing (Woods *et al.* 1988; Milner 1994), unilateral electroconvulsive therapy (Kopelman 1982), and also from dichotic-listening tests (Bryden 1988) and visual tachistoscopic studies (Beaumont 1982; Strauss *et al.* 1985) that the true relationship between handedness and language dominance was more subtle and more complex. A consensus view of this relationship is that between 2 and 10% of *right*-handers have language in the *right* hemisphere, and between 20 and 30% of *left*-handers have their language in the *right* hemisphere.

Notice that a majority of right-handers *and a majority of left-handers* have language in their left hemispheres, and that although right-hemisphere language is proportionately more common in right-handers, the majority of individuals with right-hemisphere language are actually right-handed, because right handers are about ten times more common than left handers. In practice the situation is made yet more complex by the fact that a moderate number of left-handers seem to show some form of bilateral language, whereas that pattern is rare in right-handers (Snyder *et al.* 1990).

The nature of hemispheric specialization

The precise nature of hemispheric specialization is still far from clear, and is complicated by a number of observations. After Broca's discoveries in the nineteenth century, it was felt that the left hemisphere was the 'dominant' or 'major' hemisphere, and that the right hemisphere, often referred to as the 'minor' or 'non-dominant' hemisphere, had no specific function. However, it soon became apparent that there was also a specific class of syndromes, typically the agnosias, but also including the constructional apraxias and other disorders of spatial organization, that were associated with right-hemisphere lesions. This led to the concept of *complementarity* between the hemispheres, with the left hemisphere principally processing verbal, sequential, analytic tasks, and the right hemisphere instead being spatial, parallel, or holistic in its approach. Analysis of the dissociations between different neuropsychological syndromes after right- and left-hemisphere lesions showed, however, that in a number of patients there could be verbal functions and spatial functions seemingly in the same hemisphere (Bryden *et al.* 1983). More recent work has used dichotic listening to measure ear advantages for verbal distinctions (typically with a right-ear advantage) and for emotional judgements (typically showing a left-ear advantage) in the same normal subjects at the same time, and shown that there was no correlation between the strength of the two forms of lateralization (Bulman-Fleming and Bryden 1994). The implication is that the lateralization of functions in the two hemispheres is independent, and seems to be complementary only because a majority of the population is left-hemisphere dominant for verbal tasks and right-hemisphere dominant for other tasks. The modal pattern in the population therefore misleadingly suggests causal complementarity rather than the true situation of mere statistical complementarity (Bryden 1990).

The differences between the two hemispheres have stimulated many investigators to look for a deeper, more primitive asymmetry. Perhaps the most interesting asymmetries are those reviewed by Nicholls (1994, 1996) which suggest that there are differences in temporal processing between the two hemispheres, the left hemisphere being able to distinguish small time intervals more accurately, be they in the auditory, visual, or tactile modes. The potential for explaining language dominance is that the perception of subtle phonemic distinctions often requires judgements of voicing and other features that differ in onset by perhaps only 20 ms or so. Although this is an attractive idea, it must be remembered that language and speech are not the same thing. Recent work on deficits in sign language after brain damage suggests that although sign language is essentially spatial rather than temporal, with very different timing characteristics, it is still based in the left hemisphere (Hickok *et al.* 1996). The possibility therefore arises that it is some high-level feature of language *per se* that is lateralized, rather than a low-level process to do with perception of speech sounds. One obvious possibility is grammar. It is possible that this also is connected with superior temporal processing, because the active, dynamic parsing of sentences requires fast timing of sequentially ordered words, perhaps also benefiting from a left-hemisphere temporal processing advantage; although it could be argued that grammar in sign language is spatial, it does include a temporal dimension, and it also seems to be quintessentially left rather than right hemispheric (Hickok *et al.* 1996). That possibility might also fit in with the proposal of Corballis (1991) that the principal advantage of the left hemisphere is as a 'generative assembling device' (GAD), which enables not just grammar, but also praxis in the form of complex motor actions, together with the decomposition of complex visual images into their components in the form of a 'visual grammar' (a position much influenced by Biederman's 1987 theory of 'geons').

A complete and adequate theory of cerebral lateralization must not only explain how and why language is typically located in the left hemisphere and visuo-spatial processing of complex images is typically located in the right hemisphere. It must also explain how these processes can be independently located so that in some individuals they are seemingly in the same hemisphere, so they can be either ipsilateral or contralateral to the writing hand. Finally, it must also be accepted that there are probably many lateralized processes in the brain which have not yet been discovered, or are only just being discovered. Perhaps one of the most surprising to psychologists must be the highly lateralized processes of encoding and retrieval of memory. Memory research has dominated psychology ever since the pioneering experiments of Ebbinghaus in the late nineteenth century, and particularly since the advent of the cognitive psychology revolution in the 1960s. Memory was felt to be reasonably well understood and unlikely to show any major surprises in its neural organization. However with the advent of positron emission tomography in the late 1980s there were many studies of subjects encoding and retrieving information, and to the amazement of some of the leading researchers in the field it was found that there were baffling asymmetries. In particular, for episodic memory, the left prefrontal cortex appears to be involved in encoding whereas the right prefrontal cortex is involved in retrieval. Just to confuse matters even further, for semantic memory it is the left prefrontal cortex that is involved in retrieval (Nyberg *et al.* 1996). (There is no information on whether the encoding of semantic information is lateralized, because it is virtually impossible to perform the necessary experiments.) The so-called HERA model (hemispheric encoding/retrieval asymmetry) poses many problems for neuropsychology and, given the importance of semantic memory in language usage, those questions are likely also to be important for understanding the evolution of language.

The nature of handedness

Handedness is a deceptively simple phenomenon. Most people use just one hand for writing, usually the right, and if asked their handedness will refer to that hand. In a few cases they might preface their answer by saying that at school they had tried to write with the left hand but had been persuaded or forced to use the right, and are therefore 'naturally left-handed'. And in other cases people will explain that they seem to do some tasks with their right hand and some with their left, making them ambidextrous; in practice, true ambidexterity, if defined as the ability to write equally well with either hand, seems to be almost unknown. The details of handedness, however, are more complex. Firstly, one must distinguish between *direction* and *degree* of handedness. Direction refers to whether it is the right or left hand that is dominant, and degree refers to the extent of that dominance. These two phenomena are logically separate although many studies have confounded them by calculating a single 'laterality index' and then carrying out conventional statistics (McManus 1983). Direction of handedness undoubtedly runs in families, but whether degree does so is not at all clear, some studies finding it that does and others that it does not (McManus and Bryden 1992).

A further complication in defining handedness concerns the difference between *preference* and *skill*. For example, I am right-handed in two distinct senses—when asked to perform a task I *prefer* to use my right hand, and when I carry out a task with each hand I am more *skilled* with my right hand. In principle either skill or preference could be prior to the other: Thus I might have an innate preference for the right hand, which makes me use it more often, and hence it becomes more skilled, or I may be innately more skilled with my right hand, making me prefer it for more complex actions. Teasing the two apart is not easy, but one intriguing piece of evidence has been found in children with childhood autism (McManus *et al.* 1992), and has recently also been replicated in children with fragile-X syndrome (Cornish *et al.* 1997). In these individuals there is a clear overall *preference* for the right hand but half the individuals are more *skilled* with the right hand and half are more *skilled* with the left hand. The implication is that preference may be developmentally prior to skill, with preference normally causing subsequent skill asymmetry. That is, preference is the fundamental asymmetry.

Yet another problem for handedness concerns its dimensionality—is it a single entity or are there several independent components to it? Traditional handedness inventories and questionnaires have implicitly assumed that all items are equivalent and that there is a single underlying component. That assumption has been challenged in recent years by factor analytical studies of questionnaires suggesting that there might be between two and four underlying dimensions (Healey *et al.* 1986; Liederman and Healey 1986; Steenhuis and Bryden 1989). These studies are almost certainly flawed, not least in that they take no notice of the highly skewed distributions of scores on the individual items, which are effectively binary, and which almost certainly result in the artefactual factor structures known in psychometrics as 'difficulty factors' (Corballis 1968; Maxwell 1977; Gorsuch 1983; Bernstein and Teng 1989). Far more substantial is recent work by Peters and coworkers suggesting that there is a subgroup of left-handers who write with their left hand but are better at throwing, among other things, with their right hand (Peters and Servos 1989; Peters 1990; Peters and Pang 1992). Recent questionnaire analyses have suggested that about one third of left-handers are inconsistently left-handed in this sense, and in addition about 1 or 2% of the population are inconsistent right-handers, writing with the right hand but preferring to throw with the left (Gilbert and Wysocki 1992; McManus *et al.* in press). This separation of handedness into two components, one intimately linked with written language and the other with throwing, has clear evolutionary implications, particularly given the work of Calvin (1982, 1983*a*, *b*) on the possible importance of throwing in hominid evolution (and in particular of the crucial importance of precise *timing* in throwing).

The ontogeny and phylogeny of handedness

Handedness in some form or other is found in most mammalian species. Thus a cat, for instance, when given food at the bottom of a can, will automatically use one paw to scrape out the food, and in most cases individual cats will consistently use the same paw. That is, individual animals show handedness, footedness, pawedness, or whatever. Where humans differ from most other animals is that they show a population-level asymmetry, with about 90% of individuals choosing to use their right hand, whereas in cats, mice, and other species about 50% of individuals use the right paw and 50% the left paw for skilled activities (Collins 1968; Fabre-Thorpe *et al.* 1993). Although there is some evidence that in mice there are minor differences between strains in the frequency of right paw usage (Signore *et al.* 1991), the proportions never differ dramatically from 50% or begin to approach the 90% found in humans. One exception is the toad, in which there is a population-level functional asymmetry approximating that in humans (Bisazza *et al.* 1996), but it would seem that this is secondary to anatomical asymmetries that are probably related in turn to the asymmetry of the cardiovascular and gastrointestinal systems (Naitoh and Wassersug 1996). There is also the intriguing problem of handedness (or more accurately 'footedness') in parrots, where there does indeed seem to be a population level asymmetry, but only, it seems, for Australasian parrots, perhaps representing an evolutionary cul-de-sac (Harris 1989; Snyder *et al.* 1996). Recent controversy has surrounded the question of whether there is a population-level handedness in primates (MacNeilage *et al.* 1987). Some of the evidence for this is statistically inadequate (McManus 1987; Marchant and McGrew 1991), and in other cases there is clear evidence of a lack of population-level asymmetry, notably in gorillas (Annett and Annett 1991; Byrne and Byrne 1991). However, recent evidence does suggest that right-handedness in great apes might be above 50% (Hopkins 1995, 1996), but still well below the 90% incidence found in humans, and perhaps restricted to bimanual rather than unimanual actions (Hopkins and Rabinowitz 1997). A conservative conclusion might be that there are weak population-level asymmetries for handedness in primates, in particular in chimpanzees, but that none of these shows the extreme 90:10 ratio evident in humans.

In the hominid evolutionary record there is only a little adequate evidence for the evolution of handedness, most of which has been excellently reviewed by Steele (1997). The literature is complex but two important conclusions seem to be possible, although there is still much controversy (Noble and Davidson 1996). The first is that right-handedness seems to have been present between about 1.5–1.6 million years ago, based on asymmetries of the post-cranial skeleton (Walker and Leakey 1993) and in the production of asymmetric artefacts in the form of stone tools (Toth 1985). From these data the only sensible estimate we can make of the incidence of left-handedness in the population is that *none* of the population was left-handed—the relative proportions of left- and right-handed tools are the same as those produced by a fully right-handed sample of modern humans, although the statistics are not totally compelling. Certainly, the conclusion that there was an excess of right-handers seems robust, particularly when coupled with evidence suggesting that cerebral asymmetries were also present at about the same time and are different in form from those in non-hominid primates (Holloway and de Lacoste-Lareymondie 1982). More problematic is evidence concerning the existence of left-handedness, and its proportion in the population. Recent only partially reported findings at Boxgrove suggest clear evidence of at least one left-handed flint knapper (Pitts and Roberts 1997, p.175) dating from about 500 000 years ago, but statistics have not yet been reported on the other 150-plus stone tools found (and additional evidence based on teeth (p. 265) or butchery marks (p. 198) suggests right-handedness). The analysis of handedness as depicted in works of art by Coren and Porac (1977) suggest strongly that left-handedness has been present in proportions similar to those of modern populations for at least 5 000 years (i.e. from about 3 000 BC), and that figure is compatible with the data of Spennemann (1984) on a large sample of Neolithic stone tools with right-handed and left-handed wear patterns. A very specific early example of left-handedness is associated with 'Ötzi', the Neolithic hunter found in a glacier in the Italian Alps (Spindler 1994), dated to about 5 300 years ago; he was found to be carrying two arrows, one of which had clearly been fletched by a right-hander and the other by a left-hander (BBC television, *Horizon: A Life in Ice*, 6 February 1997). These data suggest that left-handedness in its modern proportions could have arisen at any time between about 1.6 million and 10 000 years ago.

Little need be said about the ontogeny of human handedness except to emphasize that its direction seems to be set up quite early, typically between 18 months and two years of age, although degree of handedness continues to develop throughout childhood (McManus *et al.* 1988) and possibly even throughout the adult life-span (Porac *et al.* 1990). It is also possible that handedness is set up in utero, and the elegant data of Hepper *et al.* (1991), using dynamic ultrasound imaging of human fetuses, suggest that 90% or more of human infants are preferentially sucking their right rather than their left thumb by 15–20 weeks of gestation (although as yet there has been no reported follow-up into childhood to demonstrate that fetal thumb-sucking does indeed predict child and adult hand-preference). Data such as these, together with the lack of evidence for intra-familial learning of handedness (Leiber and Axelrod 1981) and the suggestion that in adopted children handedness correlates more strongly with biological parents' handedness than with adoptive parents' handedness (Carter-Saltzmann 1981), support the idea that handedness is probably under genetic control, and is little influenced by social learning—at least in the absence of coercion.

Genetic models of handedness

The central tenet of this chapter will be that handedness is under genetic control, that the peculiar aspects of its transmission in families can readily be explained by a simple genetic model, and that genetic model can also explain the association of handedness with language dominance. The problem will then be to explain how those genes evolved. Any such explanation, however, will necessarily be a partial theory of the evolution of language itself.

The important thing in understanding genetic theories of laterality is to realize that they are heavily constrained by biology. All other things being equal, there is a strong tendency for organisms to be approximately symmetrical, not least because symmetric organisms can cope better with a physical world in which it is necessary to swim, stand, walk, run, etc., and in which information is as likely to come from one point as another (Dawkins 1997). Building a symmetric body does, however, pose certain problems, mainly because parts of the body that are physically distant from one another cannot readily influence one another. Thus if one considers the embryological mechanisms that result in the eventual growth of a limb, complete with upper arm, forearm, hand, and fingers, then the development of the left arm is independent of that of the right arm. In effect each limb is like a ballistic missile, each being launched into space with its own in-built program, coded in the genes, which should result in a similar limb being built on each side. Of course, just as two precisely identical ballistic missiles would not land at exactly the same spot, so the limbs on each side will not be exactly the same size or shape, each being buffeted by a myriad of tiny forces and disturbances, broadly described as 'biological noise', which result in the limb being deviated randomly from its target. The result is that the two limbs will not be quite identical; one will be slightly larger than the other, for instance, and in half of individuals it will be the left limb that is larger, and in half the right that is larger. This is the situation known as *fluctuating asymmetry* and it represents the biological baseline from which all lateralities develop. In the absence of any other form of control a population will show fluctuating asymmetry, and in the presence of noise or other randomness, fluctuating asymmetry will tend to override *directional asymmetries*, returning the symmetry towards 50:50. An example in which the asymmetry is actually reversed is the phenomenon of pathological left-handedness (Satz 1972).

Producing directional asymmetry in a biological system is not easy, and it is perhaps therefore not surprising that very few systems under genetic control have been described. Quite the best understood is that of control of *situs*, the side of the body on which the heart is placed, from which also flows all other asymmetries of the viscera, normally resulting not only in a left-sided heart but also asymmetric lungs, a liver and an appendix on the right, a spleen and a stomach on the left, and so on, including a mass of smaller asymmetries, such as those of the testes and ovaries (McManus 1976; Mittwoch 1988). In about 1 in 20 000 humans the normal situation of *situs solitus* is reversed to give *situs inversus*, with the heart on the right, and all other organs also reversed, resulting in an individual who is anatomically a mirror-image of the normal. A similar situation occurs in mice, produced by the *iv* mutation, which has been extensively studied; the gene has been located (Brueckner *et al.* 1989, 1991), and recently has been sequenced in its entirety and been shown to be a mutant form of dynein (Supp *et al.* 1997). Individual mice with the normal 'wild type', $+/+$, or with a single copy of the *iv* gene, $+/iv$, all have the heart on the left side, but homozygotes for the iv gene, with genotype *iv/iv*, show precisely 50% with their heart on the left side and 50% with their heart on the right side—that is, pure fluctuating asymmetry. A similar mechanism almost certainly underlies many cases of human *situs inversus*, which also runs in families (Afzelius 1979; Arnold *et al.* 1983), and in at least one case is based on the X chromosome (Casey *et al.* 1993), where there seems to be mutations in a specific zinc finger gene (Gebbia *et al.* 1997). The biological basis of *situs* is very similar to that proposed for the genetic control of handedness and language dominance in humans.

The problem for any genetic model of handedness is to explain several well understood observations:

(1) although left-handedness tends to run in families, it does so only weakly, almost half of all left-handers having no known left-handed relatives (McManus 1995*a*);

(2) two right-handed parents can have left-handed children in about 5–10% of cases;
(3) two left-handed parents have left-handed children in only about 25–30% of cases (McManus and Bryden 1992); and
(4) monozygotic (identical) twins often differ in their handedness, although the proportion of discordant pairs is slightly lower in monozygotic pairs than in dizygotic pairs (McManus and Bryden 1992).

I have proposed a simple model (McManus 1985a) which explains this pattern of inheritance. According to this model, there are two alleles, D (Dextral) and C (Chance). Individuals with two copies of the D allele, D/D, are all right-handed. Individuals with two copies of the C allele, C/C, show pure fluctuating asymmetry, with 50% being right-handed and 50% being left-handed. Heterozygotes, the individuals with one of each allele, D/C, are midway between the homozygotes in their expression, 25% being left-handed and 75% being right-handed. This model is successful at explaining why handedness runs only weakly in families, and why neither right-handers nor left-handers 'breed true'—right-handers can be of any of the three genotypes, D/D, D/C or C/C, and hence can transmit C alleles to their offspring, who might well then be left-handed; likewise left-handers will be either of genotype D/C or C/C, and because the D allele is necessarily much more common than the C allele (since right-handedness is much more common than left) many of the children of left-handers will have D alleles, making them more likely to be right-handed. Even those rare individuals who are of the C/C genotype will still only have a 50% chance of being left-handed. The discordance of monozygotic twins is also readily explained, because in individuals who are C/C (or D/C) handedness will partly be determined by chance factors and those chance effects will be statistically independent in the two developing fetuses, resulting in discordant pairs. The model has also been developed somewhat to account for known sex differences in handedness (McManus and Bryden 1992).

Annett has produced a slightly different genetic model of handedness, the right-shift theory, the central feature of which is also fluctuating asymmetry. This model can also produce a good account of family data (Annett 1985). Detailed comparison of the two models suggests to me that the McManus model is somewhat superior, both in accounting for the family data (McManus 1985a) and also in accounting for the phenotypic distributions (McManus 1985b); perhaps unsurprisingly, Annett claims the converse (Annett 1996).

The relationship between handedness and language dominance

Earlier, I described the relationship between handedness and language lateralization. It is one of the successes of the modern genetic models of handedness that they naturally and elegantly produce the proportions illustrated by a simple extension of the models for handedness alone. In the model detailed above, all that is required is to postulate that the D and C alleles influence language lateralization in exactly the same way as they determine handedness. Thus D/D individuals are all right handed and are expected all to be left-language dominant. In contrast, C/C individuals show fluctuating asymmetry for handedness and are expected also to show fluctuating asymmetry for language dominance, with half being left-dominant and half being right-dominant, and with handedness and language dominance again statistically independent, so that a quarter are right-handed and right-language dominant, a quarter are right-handed and left-language dominant, and so on for the four possible combinations. The D/C heterozygotes follow the pattern for handedness, so one quarter are right-language dominant and three quarters are left-language dominant, handedness and language-dominance again being statistically independent. Such a model not only produces almost exactly the proportions reported earlier, but can also be extended to consider the situation of there being two language centres, each being determined independently both of each other and of handedness. This extended model predicts very well the differences between aphasia occurring acutely after brain damage (if either centre is damaged), and chronically (when both centres have to be damaged), and also explains the fact that left-handers are somewhat more likely to recover from aphasia after brain damage than are right handers (McManus 1985*a*). A conceptually almost identical approach using the right-shift theory has also been put forward recently (Annett and Alexander 1996).

It can now be seen that this pleiotropy of the handedness gene, with independent effects on different cerebral lateralities resulting in what might be better called 'cerebral heterotaxy', can not only explain the association of handedness and language dominance but can also be invoked to explain many other problems of cerebral organization. Thus if the same gene determines some form of visuo-spatial functioning, which typically would be in the right hemisphere of D/D individuals, then one can see that in individuals with other genotypes it could instead be in the left hemisphere. And likewise, it might also be possible to explain the seemingly correlated but nevertheless independent location of writing hand and throwing hand to the right and left hemispheres. The genetic model therefore by means of a single, simple genetic mechanism—fluctuating asymmetry—can potentially explain much of the rich diversity of lateralized cortical organization for higher functions, and yet can also explain why many of the population—about 70% or so—will show the conventional textbook patterns of right-handedness, with language on the left, visuo-spatial function on the right, because they have the D/D genotype. The importance of diverse patterns of cortical lateralization is clear in conditions such as aphasia, and is now also becoming apparent in conditions such as stuttering, where positron emission tomography shows the presence of atypical speech-related centres in the right hemisphere (Fox *et al.* 1996).

The evolution of right handedness and language dominance

Thus far this chapter has argued that handedness and language dominance are under genetic control, with most individuals being right-handed and left-language dominant as a result of the effects of the D allele. Two things now need to explained: firstly, why do most individuals have the D allele, and secondly, why do some individuals have the C allele and hence are left-handed and right-language dominant. I wish to argue that what I will call the D^* allele is a specifically human innovation, that it occurred some time before approximately 2.5 million years ago, when humans were becoming tool-users (Semaw *et al*. 1997) and properly bipedal, with locomotor bipedalism rather than postural bipedalism (Wood 1993), and that it was responsible for the right handedness found in *Homo ergaster*. Additionally, it was also responsible not only for right handedness but also for some form of early cerebral dominance, either for language or, more likely, for some form of proto-language. Before the evolution of the *D** allele I shall assume that handedness in hominids was 'determined' by what I shall call the *C** allele, which results entirely in fluctuating asymmetry in just the same way as does the *C* allele. For reasons that will become apparent later I will not however call it *C*, and neither will I wish to equate *D** and *D*. Either way, *C** is a null gene with no effect upon the development of handedness, so that handedness is 50% to the right and 50% to the left (as I presume is probably the case for most modern primates and particularly in their shared ancestors with the hominid line, although it is possible this proportion is 66:33, as has been suggested by Corballis 1997). The *D** allele must have had significant benefits for the early hominids and I presume that in some sense it was responsible for the shared characteristics of proto-language, throwing ability, manual dexterity, and the other characteristics which all seem to have co-evolved, and which might be intimately related neurologically and functionally (Calvin 1993). One possibility is that this gene directly affected the timing of processing in the left hemisphere, making it faster (perhaps even simply increasing what in a computer would be called the 'clock speed') and thereby making possible tasks such as accurate throwing, fine motor tasks, sophisticated locomotor bipedalism, and complex vocal gestures, all of which would benefit from greater processing power. Because these characteristics would be of enormous survival benefit to those carrying the *D** allele, it seems reasonable to assume that the *D** allele rapidly went to fixation, the *C** allele being eliminated from the gene-pool, and the entire early hominid population becoming right-handed (see Fig. 11.1).

Where did this *D** allele come from? As a general rule, new genes can only come from old genes, by mutation or, more likely, copying of an existing gene to a new location, followed by mutation. It has already been suggested that genes affecting laterality are surprisingly rare in biological evolution, a fact that tends to be forgotten principally because we are all so aware of the asymmetry in our own bodies and those of other vertebrates in the form of the heart. The genes and the control mechanisms which determine *situs* in vertebrates, including frogs, chicks, and mice, seem to be very similar (Ryan *et al*. 1998). They result in the otherwise morphologically symmetric early embryo showing a greater rate of growth in the cells on one side of the heart rudiment, causing it to kink to one side and eventually end up as a left-sided heart, with all other organs following the direction laid down by the initial cardiac asymmetry. A simple scenario for the evolution of the *D** allele is that a mutation occurred in a copy of one of the genes which normally causes the cardiac rudiment to grow slightly more on the left side. Instead, therefore, of causing the *heart* to grow slightly more on the left side, it caused early *neural* tissue to start to develop differently on the left side. That would have resulted in a directional asymmetry of precisely the kind required. Recent discoveries in the molecular biology of the control of *situs* make this situation quite feasible. Before the developing chick, frog, toad, or mouse

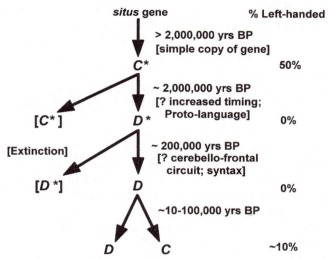

Fig. 11.1. A summary of the proposed evolution of the various genes underlying handedness and cerebral dominance for language. The *situs* gene is that found in all vertebrates which makes the heart be on the left side, and firstly a copy of that is made to produce the 'null' *C** gene. About two million years ago the *C** gene mutated to the *D** gene, which perhaps affected the timing of the left hemisphere and thereby enabled protolanguage, throwing, and tool-making, with the result that *C** gene rapidly became extinct, and almost all of the population were right-handed. About 200 000 years ago, the *D** gene mutated to the modern *D* gene, perhaps allowing a fronto-cerebellar circuit which resulted in proper syntax, and resulting in the *D** gene becoming extinct. Finally somewhere between 10 000 and 100 000 years ago the modern *C* allele mutated out of the *D* allele and the *D* and *C* alleles formed a balanced polymorphism, with about 10% of the population being left-handed.

shows any anatomical asymmetries, there are clear asymmetries in growth factors such as *sonic hedgehog, activin receptor IIa, cNR-1* (Levin *et al.* 1995), *lefty* (Meno *et al.* 1996), *nodal* (Colignon *et al.* 1996; Lowe *et al.* 1996) and *Vg1* (Hyatt *et al.* 1996); interestingly, the action of these growth factors has been shown to be downstream from the *iv* gene and also from the *inv* gene, which reverses lateralization completely (Yokoyama *et al.* 1993). Integrating all of these findings into a single ontogenetic model which includes both the *iv* gene and the X-linked situs mutations is not straightforward, but seems possible (Srivastava 1997).

If I am correct that the gene for handedness can only have mutated from some pre-existing gene, then the most probable scenario, following the finding of Supp *et al.* (1997), is that the *iv* mutation results from a mutation to axonemal dynein. This provides a direct test: The genes for handedness should be largely homologous with the sequence of the wild-type *iv* gene. Finding the gene ought therefore to be relatively straightforward. Take a core sequence from the DNA of the left–right dynein (*lrd*) specified by the *iv* gene, carry out a moderately low stringency screen of the entire human genome and look for DNA sequences which are close homologues of the *lrd* sequence, exclude any which are also present in the mouse genome because they are not specifically human, and then look for linkage to handedness, or for the presence of mutations or polymorphisms in left-handers not present in right-handers.

The model described also provides an answer, albeit a prosaic one, to the question of why most people are right-handed rather than left-handed—it is ultimately because our heart happened to be on the left, that there were genes that made the left side grow more, and these could then make the left brain grow more. In other words, historical contingency plays a large part, as in so many evolutionary situations (Gould 1989). The answer to why the heart should itself be on the left side is complex and interesting, and seems to depend on events occurring about 550 million years ago (Jefferies 1986, 1991; Gee 1996), but that is another story.

If the above scenario is to be acceptable as an explanation, it is necessary to show that alteration of the normal route for producing cardiac asymmetry can result in alterations of neural development. At present not all the links in that causal chain are present, not least because it will probably be necessary to study morphogens in early human embryos, who have and express the modern *D* (or *C*) alleles, rather than in non-human embryos, who necessarily only have the ancient *C** allele. Nevertheless there are several suggestions that the mechanisms might be present. Firstly, it is now becoming apparent that the asymmetries of growth factors being found in early embryos are not restricted to the region that will form the future heart, but are also present asymmetrically in the floor-plate of the developing mid- and hind-brain (Meno *et al.* 1996), where one might speculate that they could be responsible for the otherwise bizarre asymmetry of cerebral decussation in the motor and sensory tracts, and adjacent to the developing notochord (Colignon *et al.* 1996). Additional evidence for the feasibility of the mechanism comes from the seemingly unlikely source of a mouse gene called *legless*, which causes the back legs to fail to develop (McNeish *et al.* 1988; Singh *et al.* 1991). When this insertional mutation was mapped it was shown to be at precisely the same location as the *iv* gene, and subsequently it was shown to be co-allelic with it, so that *legless/iv* heterozygotes are also more likely to show *situs inversus*. Of particular interest for the present story is that individuals of a *legless/legless* genotype also showed wide-ranging abnormal development of the brain (McNeish *et al.* 1988), in particular showing a failure of the normal differentiation of the two cerebral hemispheres. The *legless* mutation therefore confirms that abnormalities of a gene which normally determine *situs* can result in failure of normal neural development. If a further link is needed between laterality and limb development then it should also be remembered that *sonic hedgehog* is now deeply implicated in both (Tickle and Eichele 1994; Levin *et al.* 1995), although to complicate matters a knockout mouse lacking the *sonic hedgehog* gene does not seem to show abnormal visceral lateralization (Chiang *et al.* 1996).

A final important point is that the modern *D* allele cannot be the same as the human genes controlling *situs solitus*. Although there is no doubt that cardiac asymmetry is the primary asymmetry which determines as a secondary consequence many of the asymmetries of the human body, handedness is not so caused. The evidence for this comes primarily from two large-scale studies (Cockayne 1938; Torgersen 1950) in which it was found that the incidence of left-handedness is almost exactly the same in individuals with *situs inversus* as in the rest of the population with *situs solitus*. The clear implication is that two entirely separate genetic systems are involved. Almost nothing is known at present about cerebral organization in *situs inversus*, too few cases having been described (Woods 1986). It should be emphasized that although no phenotypic correlation is proposed between handedness and *situs*, there is of course a strong evolutionary correlation in the sense that the gene sequences responsible are probably very similar indeed.

Language and proto-language

Jean-Jacques Rousseau speculated in his *Essay on the origin of languages* that what must have come first was a language of the passions or of primitive instinct, and that only later would come the complex grammatical structures necessary for articulating abstract thoughts (Norris 1987). There is now a growing consensus (Donald 1991; Leakey 1995; Maynard Smith and Szathmáry 1995; Bickerton 1996; Noble and Davidson 1996) that during human evolution there are at least two broad stages. The first stage, some 2 million or so years ago, when humans first started tool-making and using some form of proto-language, was followed by a remarkable period of techno-logical stasis—as Schick and Toth (1993, p. 284) remark: "considering that we see the Acheulean spread across thousands of miles, lasting almost one and a half million years, and continuing through considerable biological change among hominids, this conservatism is absolutely astounding". The Acheulean was followed suddenly by an "evolutionary explosion" (Corballis 1992) perhaps 30–40 000 years ago, when lan-guage might have started to be present in a form which would be recognizably modern, and when it might also have been associated with an anatomically modern larynx which would support a complex vocal language (Lieberman 1991); after this there was the diversification of languages presently found (Cavalli-Sforza *et al.* 1988). The implication must surely be that if the evolution of proto-language and its associated right-handedness and cerebral lateralization was the result of the mutation of a key developmental gene that made the left half of the brain grow differently, then the most likely explanation of the equally sudden onset of modern language was that a further mutation of the D^* gene had occurred, and that it produced the modern D allele. This allele provided the neurobiological substrate for a rich, grammatically complex language that was modern in form, and had the generativity which would also enable complex analyses of visual objects and manual skills (Corballis 1991). Just as the D^* allele rapidly took over the gene pool with the extinction of the C^* allele, so we must presume that the D allele would have soon also gone to fixation, eliminating the D^* allele.

Thus far no consideration has been given to the question of *how* in neurobiological terms it is possible for single mutations to change cognitive functioning qualitatively. For the evolution of the D^* allele no obvious mechanism is available at present, although some relatively low-level change in the migration patterns of developing central neurones or their proliferation kinetics (Rakic 1995; Caviness *et al.* 1997) could well change their interconnectivity or other properties, with dramatic effects perhaps on timing or the nature of the neural calculations for which they are optimized. The shift from the D^* to the D allele is of greater interest, not least because Bickerton (1996) has proposed that this specifically involves a novel connection between the cerebellum and the fronto-lateral cortex, via the thalamus (Leiner *et al.* 1991; Fiez *et al.* 1989, 1997), and that this connection is responsible for syntax. The evidence in favour of the hypothesis is broad, covering not only the fact that agrammatism can occur after thalamic and cerebellar lesions, but also that the cerebellum has been shown to have been implicated in other high-level cognitive functions (Leiner *et al.* 1989, 1991; Barinaga 1996), including defects of timing (Nicolson *et al.* 1995). The relationship to handedness is made all the more interesting by the fact that in autism, fragile-X, and Rett's syndrome there not only seem to be unusual abnormalities of handedness, but neural imaging suggests that there are anatomical anomalies in the cerebellum (McManus and Cornish 1997). This is therefore a prime site for the *D* allele to work. Certainly, current work on cortical embryology is entirely compatible with the idea that a single mutation could radically alter the way that neurons in different parts of the brain interconnect, and result in a profoundly different form of functional organization (Molnar and Blakemore 1995); as Humphrey (1992) has pointed out, a tiny change such as allowing 'sensory' inputs to monitor internal neural states rather than external events can transform the life of the mind.

The evolution of left-handedness

If the scenario of the previous paragraphs is correct, there remains the mystery of why left-handedness should occur at all. Primitive, pre-hominid left-handedness was the 'result' (if the non-action of a null gene can be so-called) of the *C** allele. But modern left-handedness cannot possibly result from some atavistic reversion to the primitive *C** allele, because if the above story is correct then right-handedness and proto-language, and then language proper, have been intimately linked in cerebral terms. If left-handers were merely carriers of the *C** genes then they should be expected not even to have proto-language, to have difficulties in throwing, to have poor manual coordination, etc., none of which, of course, is true, despite a few occasional attempts to stereotype sinistrals in such a fashion. The only conclusion must be that the modern *C* allele is a further mutation of the *D* allele, presumably relatively recent in time, which enables the allele to have most of its beneficial effects on neurobiological development but does not require the locus of the effects to be in the left hemisphere. Far from the *C* allele being a reversion, it must be more recent in origin than the *D* allele, with new advantages of its own. We can do little at present to date this mutation except to state that it was almost certainly present in its modern form by 5000 years ago, since when there seems to have been a stable proportion of left-handers in the population (Coren and Porac 1977).

The origins of left-handedness are more complex still because left-handedness represents what in genetics is called a *balanced polymorphism*, with two separate phenotypic forms each being present in the population at quite high frequencies. Genetic theory (Cavalli-Sforza and Bodmer 1971) is entirely clear that balanced polymorphisms which result from the actions of two separate alleles in the gene-pool cannot maintain themselves spontaneously. If the two alleles have even slightly different fitnesses then the less fit will inevitably be removed from the population; and indeed even if the two alleles have precisely identical fitnesses then by random genetic drift resulting from populations being of finite size then, just as surely, one or other of the alleles will be eliminated. Balanced polymorphisms therefore cannot just passively happen, but must be actively maintained by equally balancing forces. It is like a pencil being balanced on its point—by chance one may just happen to get it poised there for a fraction of a second but the apparent stability is ephemeral, and is in reality only metastability, and the slightest unequal push from an air molecule or one side or other will provide a turning moment which will rapidly grow by positive feedback and push the pencil off balance so that it falls over. The pencil can only be maintained on its point for any length of time by equally balanced forces such as two fingers holding it in position. Likewise with a balanced polymorphism, there must be forces maintaining the instability, or the polymorphism will disappear by genetic drift in a few instants of geological time. Occasionally, polymorphisms are maintained by frequent new mutations, but that seems an unlikely explanation for handedness.

The most common explanation for balanced polymorphisms is in terms of heterozygote advantage, which in the case of handedness would mean that D/C individuals are fitter than both D/D and C/C individuals. This would not mean that left-handers are fitter than right-handers (because the inheritance is additive, with heterozygotes midway in proportion of left-handedness between the homozygotes, the fitness of left-handers will be precisely the same as the fitness of right-handers), but rather that *some* left-handers and right-handers (the D/C genotypes) are fitter than the other right- and left-handers. At present there is no clear idea what the advantage might be. Annett and coworkers have proposed that homozygotes might have intellectual problems, with lower IQ, as well as specific problems with reading (Annett and Manning 1989; Annett 1995; Annett *et al.* 1996); detailed calculations suggest, however, that there are severe problems with that model which as yet have not been adequately circumvented (McManus *et al.* 1993; McManus 1995*b*). Additionally, a series of empirical studies has failed to find the postulated increased intelligence of individuals with moderate degrees of handedness (Klicpera and Gasteiger-Klicpera 1994; Corballis and Palmer 1996; Natsopoulos *et al.* 1997; Resch *et al.* 1997). Perhaps the problem is that, although it is tempting to assume that any advantage associated with genes to do with handedness must be neurological or psychological in its effect, that is not in fact the case. The proposed fitness advantage ultimately only has to mean that the heterozygotes have more children and grandchildren, and that might be because they can run faster, digest food more efficiently, have better thermo-regulation, or a myriad of other effects all of which could result in biological advantages. Balanced polymorphisms can also be affected by sexual selection, and Crow (1989, 1993) has argued that cerebral specialization for language might be explained in terms of sexual selection. Specifically he argues that the genes for cerebral dominance and handedness (and also the genes for psychosis, which he suggests are mutations of the normal cerebral dominance gene (Crow 1990*b*)), might be located in the homologous regions of the X and Y chromosomes. That theory produces some highly counter-intuitive patterns of inheritance of handedness in families in relation to the sex of offspring, and, to what I confess is my surprise, the predictions have been found correct in a very large sample of families (Corballis *et al.* 1996). The data do not, however, yet give totally compelling support for the handedness/cerebral dominance gene being on the sex chromosomes; Bryden and I have previously argued that the gene itself could be autosomal and it is merely a modifier gene that is on the X-chromosome (McManus and Bryden 1992).

Testing the model and its predictions

Evolutionary models are very easy to produce—there are usually far more explanatory variables than there are data points, and as a result the models always seem convincing. Or to put it more crudely, they are often merely 'Just So' stories (Gould and Lewontin 1979; Pinker and Bloom 1990; Barkow *et al.* 1992)—nice stories or fairy tales but hardly science in any serious sense of the word. Steve Jones is even blunter about the problems of evolutionary theories:

Evolution is to allegory as statues are to birdshit. It is a convenient platform upon which to deposit badly digested ideas (*New York Review of Books*, July 17th, 1997, p.39).

So is the above model testable? I think so, mainly because molecular genetics is progressing at an enormous rate. The first step of course must be to find the genes responsible for handedness, and if the above scenario is correct they should show strong homologies of sequence with the genes controlling *situs*. More interestingly, they should also produce gene-products which control growth asymmetrically in the early nervous system, and that should certainly be the case in humans. Intriguingly, this might also be the case in a transgenic mouse with the human gene inserted; if so, then we will also have an excellent model system for studying brain lateralization experimentally. A further possibility is that a wide range of human pathologies will show abnormalities of sequence in the *D* or *C* alleles, which will be responsible for atypical nervous system development. It is also possible that, as Crow (1990*b*) has suggested, schizophrenia is due to a mutation of the cerebral dominance gene—and the analogy presumably extends to the hundreds of diseases and conditions produced by minor sequence changes in the haemoglobin gene, such as sickle-cell anaemia. Supporting Crow's suggestion is the important finding that schizophrenia does indeed seem to involve an abnormality of cerebral dominance (Crow 1990*a*). There is also a group of other conditions which are characterized by atypical lateralization, problems of communication, and interestingly also tend to occur more frequently in males, namely, autism (McManus *et al.* 1992), dyslexia (McManus 1991; Eglinton and Annett 1994), and stuttering (Bishop 1990), and these are also good candidates for explanation in terms of abnormalities of the cerebral dominance gene. Finally there is a growing group of defects (Gopnik 1991; Van der Lely and Stollwerck 1996) that seems to be specific to grammar itself; these seem to run in families, suggesting that they also might be explained in terms of abnormalities of the cerebral dominance gene. Of course none of these findings would explicitly prove the relationship of the evolution of the gene to the evolution of language, but it is more than possible that detailed study of the sequences of the genes and analogous genes in modern humans and modern apes and primates would provide crucial insights into the evolution of language.

References

Afzelius, B. A. (1979). The immotile-cilia syndrome and other ciliary diseases. *International Review of Experimental Pathology*, **19**, 1–43.

Annett, M. (1985). *Left, right, hand and brain: the right shift theory*. Lawrence Erlbaum, New Jersey.

Annett, M. (1995). The right shift theory of a genetic balanced polymorphism for cerebral dominance and cognitive processing. *Cahiers de Psychologie Cognitive*, **14**, 427–80.

Annett, M. (1996). In defence of the right shift theory. *Perceptual and motor skills*, 82, 115–37.

Annett, M. and Alexander, M. P. (1996). Atypical cerebral dominance: predictions and test of the right shift theory. *Neuropsychologia*, **34**, 1215–27.

Annett, M. and Annett, J. (1991). Handedness for eating in gorillas. *Cortex*, **27**, 269–75.

Annett, M. and Manning, M. (1989). The disadvantages of dextrality for intelligence. *British Journal of Psychology*, **80**, 213–26.

Annett, M., Eglinton, E., and Smythe, P. (1996). Types of dyslexia and the shift to dextrality. *Journal of Child Psychology and Psychiatry*, **37**, 167–80.

Arnold, G. L., Bixler, D., and Girod, D. (1983). Probable autosomal recessive inheritance of polysplenia, situs inversus and cardiac defects in an Amish family. *American Journal of Medical Genetics*, **16**, 35–42.

Barinaga, M. (1996). The cerebellum: movement coordinator or much more? *Science*, **272**, 482–3.

Barkow, J. H., Cosmides, L., and Tooby, J. (eds) (1992). *The adapted mind: evolutionary psychology and the generation of culture*. Oxford University Press, New York.

Beaumont, J. G. (1982). *Divided visual field studies of cerebral organization*. Academic Press, London.

Bernstein, I. H. and Teng, G. (1989). Factoring items and factoring scales are different: spurious evidence for multidimensionality due to item categorization. *Psychological Bulletin*, **105**, 467–77.

Bickerton, D. (in press). Catastrophic evolution: the case for a single step from protolanguage to full human language. In *Evolution of language: social and cognitive bases for the emergence of phonology and syntax* (ed. J. Hurford, M. Studdert-Kennedy, and C. Krugar). Cambridge University Press.

Bickerton, D. (1996). *Language and human behaviour*. UCL Press, London.

Biederman, I. (1987). Recognition-by-components: a theory of human image understanding. *Psychological Review*, **94**, 115–47.

Bisazza, A., Cantalupo, C., Robins, A., Rogers, L. J., and Vallortigara, G. (1996). Right-pawedness in toads. *Nature*, **379**, 408.

Bishop, D. (1990). *Handedness and developmental disorder*. Blackwell, Oxford.

Broca, P. (1865). Sur le siège de la faculté du langage articulé. *Bulletin de la Société d'Anthropologie*, **6**, 337–93.

Brueckner, M., D'Eustachio, P., and Horwich, A. L. (1989). Linkage mapping of a mouse gene, *iv*, that controls left–right asymmetry of the heart and viscera. *Proceedings of the National Academy of Sciences, USA*, **86**, 5035–8.

Brueckner, M., McGrath, J., D'Eustachio, P., and Horwich, A. L. (1991). Establishment of left–right asymmetry in vertebrates: genetically distinct steps are involved. In *Biological asymmetry and handedness* (Ciba Foundation symposium 162) (ed. G. R. Bock and J. Marsh), pp. 202–18. John Wiley, Chichester.

Bryden, M. P. (1988). An overview of the dichotic listening procedure and its relation to cerebral organization. In *Handbook of dichotic listening: theory, methods and research* (ed. K. Hugdahl), pp. 1–43. John Wiley, London.

Bryden, M. P. (1990). Choosing sides: the left and right of the normal brain. *Canadian Psychology*, **31**, 297–309.

Bryden, M. P., Hécaen, H., and De Agostini, M. (1983). Patterns of cerebral organization. *Brain and Language*, **20**, 249–62.

Bulman-Fleming, M. B. and Bryden, M. P. (1994). Simultaneous verbal and affective laterality effects. *Neuropsychologia*, **32**, 787–97.

Byrne, R. W. and Byrne, J. M. (1991). Hand preferences in the skilled gathering tasks of mountain gorillas (*Gorilla g. berengei*). *Cortex*, **27**, 521–46.

Calvin, W. H. (1982). Did throwing stones shape hominid brain evolution? *Ethology and Sociobiology*, **3**, 115–24.

Calvin, W. H. (1983a). *The throwing madonna: essays on the brain.* McGraw–Hill, New York.

Calvin, W. H. (1983b). A stone's throw and its launch window: timing, precision and its implications for language and the hominid brain. *Journal of Theoretical Biology*, **104**, 121–35.

Calvin, W. H. (1993). The unitary hypothesis: a common neural circuitry for novel manipulations, language, plan-ahead, and throwing? In *Tools, language and cognition in human evolution* (eds. K. R. Gibson and T. Ingold), pp. 230–50. Cambridge University Press.

Carter-Saltzmann, L. (1981). Biological and socio-cultural effects on handedness: comparison between biological and adoptive families. *Science*, **209**, 1263–5.

Casey, B., Devoto, M., Jones, K. L., and Ballabio, A. (1993). Mapping a gene for familial situs abnormalities to human chromosome Xq24-q27.1. *Nature Genetics*, **5**, 403–7.

Cavalli-Sforza, L. L. and Bodmer, W. F. (1971). *The genetics of human populations.* W. H. Freeman, San Francisco.

Cavalli-Sforza, L. L., Piazza, A., Menozzi, P., and Mountain, J. (1988). Reconstruction of human evolution: bringing together genetic, archaeological, and linguistic data. *Proceedings of the National Academy of Sciences USA*, **85**, 6002–6.

Caviness, V. S., Jr., Takahashi, T., and Nowakowski, R. S. (1997). Numbers, time and neocortical neurogenesis: a general developmental and evolutionary model. *Trends in Neurosciences*, **18**, 379–83.

Chiang, C., Litingtung, Y., Lee, E., Young, K. E., Corden, J. L., Westphal, H., *et al.* (1996). Cyclopia and defective axial patterning mice lacking *sonic hedgehog* gene function. *Nature*, **383**, 407–13.

Cockayne, E. A. (1938). The genetics of transposition of the viscera. *Quarterly Journal of Medicine*, **31**, 479–93.

Colignon, J., Varlet, I., and Robertson, E. J. (1996). Relationship between asymmetric nodal expression and the direction of embryonic turning. *Nature*, **381**, 155–8.

Collins, R. L. (1968). On the inheritance of handedness. I: Laterality in inbred mice. *Journal of Heredity*, **59**, 9–12.

Corballis, M. C. (1968). Some difficulties with difficulty. *Psychological Reports*, **22**, 15–22.

Corballis, M. C. (1991). *The lop-sided ape: evolution of the generative mind.* Oxford University Press, New York.

Corballis, M. C. (1992). On the evolution of language and generativity. *Cognition*, **44**, 197–226.

Corballis, M. C. (1997). The genetics and evolution of handedness. *Psychological Review*, **104**, 714–27.

Corballis, M. C. and Palmer, R. E. (1996). Predicting reading ability from handedness measures. *British Journal of Psychology*, **87**, 609–20.

Corballis, M. C., Lee, K., McManus, I. C., and Crow, T. J. (1996). Location of the handedness gene on the X and Y chromosomes. *American Journal of Medical Genetics (Neuropsychiatric Genetics)*, **67**, 50–2.

Coren, S. and Porac, C. (1977). Fifty centuries of right-handedness: the historical record. *Science*, **198**, 631–2.

Cornish, K. M., Pigram, J., and Shaw, K. (1997). Do anomalies of handedness exist in children with Fragile-X syndrome? *Laterality*, **2**, 91–101.

Crow, T. J. (1989). Pseudoautosomal locus for the cerebral dominance gene. *Lancet* ii, 339–40.

Crow, T. J. (1990a). Temporal lobe asymmetries as the key to the etiology of schizophrenia. *Schizophrenia Bulletin*, **16**, 433–43.

Crow, T. J. (1990b). Strategies for biological research: psychosis as an anomaly of the cerebral dominance gene. In *Search for the causes of schizophrenia, Vol. II* (ed. H. Hdfner and W. F. Gattaz), pp. 383–96. Springer, Heidelberg.

Crow, T. J. (1993). Sexual selection, Machiavellian intelligence, and the origins of psychosis. *Lancet*, **342**, 594–8.

Dawkins, R. (1997). *Climbing Mount Improbable*. Penguin Books, London.

Donald, M. (1991). *Origins of the modern mind: Three stages in the evolution of culture and cognition.* Harvard University Press, Cambridge, MA.

Eglinton, E. and Annett, M. (1994). Handedness and dyslexia: a meta-analysis. *Perceptual and Motor Skills*, **79**, 1611–6.

Eling, P. (1984). Broca on the relation between handedness and cerebral speech dominance. *Brain and Language*, **22**, 158–9.

Fabre-Thorpe, M., Fagot, J., Lorincz, E., Levesque, F., and Vauclair, J. (1993). Laterality in cats: paw preference and performance in a visuomotor activity. *Cortex*, **29**, 15–24.

Fiez, J. A., Petersen, S. E., Cheney, M. K., and Raichle, M. E. (1992). Impaired non-motor learning and error detection associated with cerebellar damage. A single case study. *Brain* **115** Pt 1, 155–78.

Fiez, J., Peterson, S. E., and Raichle, M. E. (1997). Impaired habit learning following cerebellar hemorrhage: a single case study. *Society for Neuroscience Abstracts*, **16**, 287.

Fox, P. T., Ingham, R. J., Ingham, J. C., Hirsch, T. B., Downs, J. H., Martin, C., *et al.* (1996). A PET study of the neural systems of stuttering. *Nature* **382**, 158–61.

Gebbia, M., Ferrero, G. B., Pilia, G., Bassi, M. T., Ayslworth, A. S., Penmann-Splitt, M., *et al.* (1997). X-linked situs abnormalities result from mutations in ZIC3. *Nature Genetics*, **17**, 305–8.

Gee, H. (1996). *Before the backbone: views on the origins of the vertebrates*. Chapman and Hall, London.

Gilbert, A. N. and Wysocki, C. J. (1992). Hand preference and age in the United States. *Neuropsychologia*, **30**, 601–8.

Gopnik, M. (1991). Familial aggregation of a developmental language disorder. *Cognition*, **39**, 1–50.

Gorsuch, R. L. (1983). *Factor analysis* (2nd edn). Lawrence Erlbaum, Hillsdale, NJ.

Gould, S. J. (1989). *Wonderful life: the Burgess shale and the nature of history.* W. W. Norton, New York.

Gould, S. J. and Lewontin, R. C. (1979). The spandrels of San Marco and the Panglossian program: a critique of the adaptationist programme. *Proceedings of the Royal Society of London, Series B*, **205**, 281–8.

Harris, L. J. (1989). Footedness in parrots: three centuries of research, theory, and mere surmise. *Canadian Journal of Psychology*, **43**, 369–76.

Harris, L. J. (1991). Cerebral control for speech in right-handers and left-handers: an analysis of the views of Paul Broca, his contemporaries, and his successors. *Brain and Language*, **40**, 1–50.

Harris, L. J. (1993). Broca on cerebral control for speech in right-handers and left-handers: a note on translation and some further comments. *Brain and Language*, **45**, 108–20.

Healey, J. M., Liederman, J., and Geschwind, N. (1986). Handedness is not a unidimensional trait. *Cortex*, **22**, 33–53.

Hécaen, H. and Dubois, J. (1969). *La naissance de la neuropsychologie du langage* (1825–1865). Flammarion, Paris.

Hepper, P. G., Shahidullah, S., and White, R. (1991). Handedness in the human fetus. *Neuropsychologia*, **29**, 1107–11.

Hickok, G., Bellugi, U., and Klima, E. S. (1996). The neurobiology of sign language and its implications for the neural basis of language. *Nature*, **381**, 699–702.

Holloway, R. and de Lacoste-Lareymondie, M. C. (1982). Brain endocast asymmetry in pongids and hominids: some preliminary findings on the paleontology of cerebral dominance. *American Journal of Physical Anthropology*, **58**, 101–10.

Hopkins, W. D. (1995). Hand preferences for a coordinated bimanual task in 110 chimpanzees (*Pan troglodytes*): cross-sectional analysis. *Journal of Comparative Psychology*, **109**, 291–7.

Hopkins, W. D. (1996).Chimpanzee handedness revisited: 55 years since Finch (1941). *Psychonomic Bulletin and Review*, **3**, 449–57.

Hopkins, W. D. and Rabinowitz, D. M. (1997). Manual specialization and tool use in captive chimpanzees (*Pan troglodytes*): the effect of unimanual and bimanual strategies on hand preference. *Laterality*, **2**, 267–77.

Humphrey, N. (1992). *A history of the mind*. Chatto and Windus, London.

Hyatt, B. A., Lohr, J. L., and Yost, H. J. (1996). Initiation of vertebrate left–right axis formation by maternal Vg1. *Nature*, **384**, 62–5.

Jefferies, R. P. S. (1986). *The ancestry of the vertebrates*. British Museum (Natural History), London.

Jefferies, R. P. S. (1991). Two types of bilateral asymmetry in the Metazoa: chordate and bilaterian. In *Biological asymmetry and handedness (Ciba Foundation symposium 162)* (ed. G. R. Bock and J. Marsh), pp. 94–127. John Wiley, Chichester.

Klicpera, C. and Gasteiger-Klicpera, B. (1994). Linkshaendigkeit und Legasthenie: Kein Beleg fuer dir Rechsverschienungstheorie bei Wiener Kindern, aber Hinweise auf Verzerrungen bei der Auswahl von Kindern fuer Foerdermassnahmen. *Paediatrie und Paedologie*, **29**, 11–15.

Kopelman, M. D. (1982). Speech-dominance, handedness and electro-convulsions. *Psychological Medicine*, **12**, 667–70.

Leakey, R. (1995). *The origin of humankind*. Phoenix, London.

Leiber, L. and Axelrod, S. (1981). Intra-familial learning is only a minor factor in manifest handedness. *Neuropsychologia*, **19**, 273–88.

Leiner, H. C., Leiner, A. L., and Dow, R. S. (1989). Reappraising the cerebellum: what does the hindbrain contribute to the forebrain? *Behavioral Neuroscience*, **103**, 998–1008.

Leiner, H. C., Leiner, A. L., and Dow, R. S. (1991). The human cerebro-cerebellar system: its computing, cognitive, and language skills. *Behavioral Brain Research*, **44**, 113–28.

Levin, M., Johnson, R. L., Stern, C. D., Kuehn, M., and Tabin, C. (1995). A molecular pathway determining left–right asymmetry in chick embryogenesis. *Cell*, **82**, 803–14.

Lieberman, P. (1991). *Uniquely human: the evolution of speech, thought, and selfless behavior*. Harvard University Press, Cambridge, MA.

Liederman, J. and Healey, J. M. (1986). Independent dimensions of hand preference: reliability of the factor structure and the handedness inventory. *Archives of Clinical Neuropsychology*, **1**, 371–86.

Lowe, L. A., Supp, D. M., Sampath, K., Yokoyama, T., Wright, C. V. E., Potter, S. S., *et al.* (1996). Conserved left right asymmetry of nodal expression and alterations in murine *situs inversus*. *Nature*, **381**, 158–61.

MacNeilage, P. F., Studdert-Kennedy, M. G., and Lindblom, B. (1987). Primate handedness reconsidered. *Behavioral and Brain Sciences*, **10**, 247–303.

Marchant, L. F. and McGrew, W. C. (1991). Laterality of function in apes: a meta-analysis of methods. *Journal of Human Evolution*, **21**, 425–38.

Maxwell, A. E. (1977). *Multivariate analysis in behavioural research*. Chapman and Hall, London.

Maynard Smith, J. and Szathmáry, E. (1995). *The major transitions in evolution*. W. H. Freeman, Oxford.

McManus, I. C. (1976). Scrotal asymmetry in man and in ancient sculpture. *Nature*, **259**, 426.

McManus, I. C. (1983). The interpretation of laterality. *Cortex*, **19**, 187–214.

McManus, I. C. (1985*a*). Handedness, language dominance and aphasia: a genetic model. *Psychological Medicine*, Monograph Supplement No.8.

McManus, I. C. (1985*b*). Right- and left-hand skill: failure of the right shift model. *British Journal of Psychology*, **76**, 1–16.

McManus, I. C. (1987). On the one hand, on the other hand: statistical fallacies in laterality. *Behavioral and Brain Sciences*, **10**, 282–3.

McManus, I. C. (1991). The genetics of dyslexia. In *Vision and Visual Dysfunction*: Vol. 13, Dyslexia (ed. J. F. Stein), pp. 94–112. Macmillan Press, London.

McManus, I. C. (1995*a*). Familial sinistrality: the utility of calculating exact genotype probabilities for individuals. *Cortex*, **31**, 3–24.

McManus, I. C. (1995*b*). Achilles' right heel: the vulnerabilities of the right-shift theory. *Cahiers de Psychologie Cognitive*, **14**, 565–74.

McManus, I. C. and Bryden, M. P. (1992). The genetics of handedness, cerebral dominance and lateralization. In *Handbook of Neuropsychology, Volume 6, Section 10: Child neuropsychology (Part 1)* (ed. I. Rapin and S. J. Segalowitz), pp. 115–44. Elsevier, Amsterdam.

McManus, I. C. and Cornish, K. M. (1997). Fractionating handedness in mental retardation: what is the role of the cerebellum? *Laterality*, **2**: 81–90.

McManus, I. C., Sik, G., Cole, D. R., Mellon, A. F., Wong, J., and Kloss, J. (1988). The development of handedness in children. *British Journal of Developmental Psychology*, **6**, 257–73.

McManus, I. C., Murray, B., Doyle, K., and Baron-Cohen, S. (1992). Handedness in childhood autism shows a dissociation of skill and preference. *Cortex*, **28**, 373–81.

McManus, I. C., Shergill, S., and Bryden, M. P. (1993). Annett's theory that individuals heterozygous for the right shift gene are intellectually advantaged: theoretical and empirical problems. *British Journal of Psychology*, **84**, 517–37.

McManus, I. C., Porac, C., Bryden, M. P., and Boucher, R. (in press). Eye dominance, writing hand, and throwing hand. *Laterality*.

McNeish, J. D., Scott, W. J., Jr., and Potter, S. (1988). Legless, a novel mutation found in PHT1–1 transgenic mice. *Science*, **241**, 837–9.

Meno, C., Saijoh, Y., Fujii, H., Ikeda, M., Yokoyama, T., Yoyoyama, M., *et al.* (1996). Left–right asymmetric expression of the TGF-β-family member *lefty* in mouse embryos. *Nature*, **381**, 151–5.

Milner, B. (1994). Carotid-amytal studies of speech representation and gesture control. *Discussions in Neuroscience*, **10**, 109–18.

Mittwoch, U. (1988). Y chromosome and sex determination. *Lancet* ii, 52–3.

Molnar, Z. and Blakemore, C. (1995). How do thalamic neurons find their way to the cortex? *Trends in Neurosciences*, **18**, 389–97.

Naitoh, T. and Wassersug, R. (1996). Why are toads right-handed? *Nature*, **380**, 30–1.

Natsopoulos, D., Kiosseoglou, G., Xeromeritou, A., and Alevriadou, A. (1997). Do the hands talk on mind's behalf? Differences in language ability between left- and right-handed children. *Brain and Language*, in press.

Nicholls, M. E. R. (1994). Hemispheric asymmetries for temporal resolution: a signal detection analysis of threshold and bias. *Quarterly Journal of Experimental Psychology*, **47A**, 291–310.

Nicholls, M. E. R. (1996). Temporal processing asymmetries between the cerebral hemispheres: evidence and implications. *Laterality*, **1**, 97–137.

Nicolson, R. I., Fawcett, A. J., and Dean, P. (1995). Time estimation deficits in developmental dyslexia: evidence of cerebellar involvement. *Proceedings of the Royal Society of London: Series B. Biological Sciences*, **259**, 43–7.

Noble, W. and Davidson, I. (1996). *Human evolution, language and mind: a psychological and archaeological enquiry.* Cambridge University Press.

Norris, C. (1987). *Derrida.* Fontana, London.

Nottebohm, F. (1977). Asymmetries in neural control of vocalization in the canary. In *Lateralization in the nervous system* (ed. S. Harnad, R. W. Doty, L. Goldstein, J. Jaynes, and G. Krauthamer), pp. 23–44. Academic Press, New York.

Nyberg, L., Cabeza, R., and Tulving, E. (1996). PET studies of encoding and retrieval: the HERA model. *Psychonomic Bulletin and Review*, 3, 135–48.

Peters, M. (1990). Subclassification of non-pathological left-handers poses problems for theories of handedness. *Neuropsychologia*, 28, 279–89.

Peters, M. and Pang, J. (1992). Do 'right-armed' left-handers have different lateralization of motor control for the proximal and distal musculature? *Cortex*, 28, 391–99.

Peters, M. and Servos, P. (1989). Performance of subgroups of left-handers and right-handers. *Canadian Journal of Psychology*, 43, 341–58.

Pinker, S. and Bloom, P. (1990). Natural language and natural selection. *Behavioral and Brain Sciences*, 13, 707–84.

Pitts, M. and Roberts, M. (1997). *Fairweather Eden: life in Britain half a million years ago as revealed by the excavations at Boxgrove*. Century, London.

Porac, C., Izaak, M., and Rees, L. (1990). *Age trends in handedness: an environmental approach*. Paper presented at the meeting of the Canadian Psychological Association, Ottawa, May 1990.

Rakic, P. (1995). A small step for the cell, a giant leap for mankind: a hypothesis of neocortical expansion during evolution. *Trends in Neurosciences*, 18, 383–8.

Resch, F., Haffner, J., Parzer, P., Pfueller, U., Strehlow, U,. and Zerarn-Hartung, C. (1997). Testing the hypothesis of the relationships between laterality and ability according to Annett's right shift theory: findings in an epidemiological sample of young adults. *British Journal of Psychology* 88, 621–35.

Ryan, A. K., Blumberg, B., Rodriguez-Esteban, C., Yonei-Tamura, S., Tamura, K., Tsukui, T., *et al.* (1998). Pitx2 determines left-right asymmetry of internal organs in vertebrates. *Nature*, 394, 545–51.

Satz, P. (1972). Pathological left-handedness: an explanatory model. *Cortex*, 8, 121–35.

Schick, K. D. and Toth, N. (1993). *Making silent stones speak: human evolution and the dawn of technology*. Weidenfeld and Nicholson, London.

Schiller, F. (1979). *Paul Broca: explorer of the brain*. Oxford University Press.

Semaw, S., Renne, P., Harris, J. W. K., Feibel, C. S., Bernor, R. L., Fesseha, N., *et al.* (1997). 2.5-million-year-old stone tools from Gona, Ethiopia. *Nature*, 385, 333–6.

Signore, P., Chaoui, M., Nosten-Bertrand, M., Perez-Diaz, F., and Marchaland, C. (1991). Handedness in mice: comparison across eleven inbred strains. *Behavior Genetics*, 21, 421–29.

Singh, G., Supp, M., Schreiner, C., McNeish, J., Merker, H., Copeland, N. G., *et al.* (1991). *legless* insertional mutation: morphological, molecular, and genetic characterization. *Genes and Development*, 5, 2245–55.

Snyder, P. J. and Harris, L. J. (1997). Lexicon size and its relation to foot preference in the African Grey parrot (*Psittacus erithacus*). *Neuropsychologia*, 35, 919–26.

Snyder, P. J., Novelly, R. A., and Harris, L. J. (1990). Mixed speech dominance in the intracarotid sodium amytal procedure: validity and criteria issues. *Journal of Clinical and Experimental Neuropsychology*, 12, 629–43.

Snyder, P. J., Harris, L. J., Ceravolo, N., and Bonner, J. A. (1996). Are psittacines an appropriate model of handedness in humans? *Brain and Cognition*, 32, 208–11.

Spenneman, D. R. (1984). Handedness data on the European Neolithic. *Neuropsychologia*, 22, 613–5.

Spindler, K. (1994). *The man in the ice*. Weidenfeld and Nicolson, London.

Srivastava, D. (1997). Left, right … which way to turn? *Nature Genetics*, 17, 252–4.

Steele, J. (1997). Evolution of laterality in hominids, including humans: archaeological perspectives. (Unpublished).

Steenhuis, R. E. and Bryden, M. P. (1989). Different dimensions of hand preference that relate to skilled and unskilled activities. *Cortex*, **25**, 289–304.

Strauss, E., Wada, J., and Kosaka, B. (1985). Visual laterality effects and cerebral speech dominance determined by the carotid amytal test. *Neuropsychologia*, **23**, 567–70.

Supp, D. M., Witte, D. P., Potter, S. S., and Brueckner, M. (1997). Mutation of an axonemal dynein affects left–right asymmetry in *inversus viscerum* mice. *Nature*, **389**, 963–6.

Tickle, C. and Eichele, G. (1994). Vertebrate limb development. *Annual Review of Cell Biology*, **10**, 121–52.

Torgersen, J. (1950). Situs inversus, asymmetry and twinning. *American Journal of Human Genetics*, **2**, 361–70.

Toth, N. (1985). Archaeological evidence for preferential right handedness in the lower and middle Pleistocene and its possible implications. *Journal of Human Evolution*, **14**, 607–14.

Van der Lely, H. K. J. and Stollwerck, L. (1996). A grammatical specific language impairment in children: an autosomal dominant inheritance. *Brain and Language*, **52**, 484–504.

Walker, A. and Leakey, R. (1993). The postcranial bones. In *The Nariokotome* Homo erectus *skeleton* (ed. A. Walker and R. Leakey), pp. 95–160. Springer, Berlin.

Wood, B. (1993). Four legs good, two legs better. *Nature*, **363**, 587–8.

Woods, R. P. (1986). Brain asymmetries in situs inversus: a case report and review of the literature. *Archives of Neurology*, **43**, 1083–4.

Woods, R. P., Dodrill, C. B., and Ojemann, G. A. (1988). Brain injury, handedness and speech lateralization in a series of amobarbital studies. *Annals of Neurology*, **23**, 510–8.

Yokoyama, T., Copeland, N. G., Jenkins, N. A., Montgomery, C. A., Elder, F. F. B., and Overbeek, P. A. (1993). Reversal of left–right asymmetry—a novel situs inversus mutation. *Science*, **260**, 679–82.

12

The rise of the metamind

Thomas Suddendorf

Cogito ergo sum—Descartes

Introduction

Every culture and epoch has had its ideas about the nature of mind and existence. We can reflect upon ourselves, upon others, and upon the world. Do animals do that too? Do they sit around and think that they are because they can think? Are they to be considered mindless if they do not reflect? How did our ability to think beyond the immediately present evolve?

The self-awareness implied by '*cogito ergo sum*', or 'I think, therefore I am', demands a reflective level of thinking that develops by about age four in children. Only then, recent research suggests, do children begin to reflect on their own mental states. It would be quite difficult, however, to convince people that younger children are mindless—mind can surely exist without being able to reflect upon its own existence. One can know, regardless of whether one knows that one knows. This means that the Cartesian assumption that the mind is necessarily transparent to the self is flawed (cf. Wimmer and Hartl 1991; Gopnik 1993). Instead, the reflective mind, or what I want to call the metamind, seems to depend on mental computations that gradually develop over the first four years of life and that have evolved over the last five million years of human evolution.

Rather than being given by God, as Descartes would have had it, metamind is the product of natural selection. It is not a basic starting block, but the product of a long process of cognitive evolution. The fundamental problem to be addressed is how, from a time when there was no consciousness on Earth, mind developed to the phenomenological experiences we have today. While physical features such as bipedal locomotion, the opposable thumb, increased cranial size, and stone-tool production mark important developments in human evolution, I maintain that it was the evolution of *mind* that takes prime responsibility for the extraordinary story of the human species.

In this chapter I will attempt to outline the natural history of the human mind, with special reference the emergence of representational skills. There are several evolutionary proposals that are in parts similar to the one that will be presented here (e.g. Lorenz 1973; Bischof 1985; Tulving 1985; Humphrey 1986, 1992; Whiten and Byrne

1991; Olson 1993; Dennett 1995). Perner (1991) proposed perhaps the most influential account of children's growing representational skills. I will extend and update Perner's developmental model and apply it to evolution. From this model one can derive various testable hypotheses about children's development and about other animals' capacities. I will show that there is a general fit to the data and that this model is very useful for understanding the basic progression in the evolution of the hominid mind.

Perner (1991) suggested that children's understanding of mind reflects their level of understanding representation in general. In brief, his theory suggests that children advance in conceptual capacity from the ability to form (1) primary representations of reality, to (2) entertaining secondary representations beyond current reality (e.g. representing past, future, or imaginary objects or events; or representing the representational content of other representational systems), to (3) understanding representational relations themselves—or in other words, metarepresenting representations *as* representations. This progression, which may seem confusing at first, can be illustrated with the example of understanding the representational nature of television. With primary representations one can merely perceive the reality of the TV image as a quickly colour-changing set of dots or as two-dimensional shapes that might be mistaken for the objects they resemble. Following these pictures in terms of the 3-D characters and events they represent means creating secondary representations (i.e., the content of the TV image is represented). With metarepresentation, one can further appreciate that this is just television (an American soap, say, with lots of bad acting). At this level, then, one can simultaneously follow the programme and evaluate whether the story is true or fictional, whether the editing is good or bad, and whether the actor always has this funny accent.

The mind can be regarded as a representational system (cf. Dretske 1995). Understanding mind might develop in the same fashion as understanding other representational systems such as televisions. For example, with primary representation one simply perceives other's actions. With secondary representations these actions can be interpreted in terms of what the person wants, intends, or pretends (i.e., in terms of not directly perceivable mental states). Only with metarepresentation, however, can one appreciate that these mental states are *just* representations. One can simultaneously entertain somebody else's beliefs and evaluate them as true or false, and wonder whether the other wants to deceive or how one could change his or her mind.

Children, animals, and human ancestors can, according to my model, be categorized in terms of their level of representational capacity (see Table 12.1). The representational level determines what an organism can mentally conceive of. With primary representations an animal can form only a *single updating model* of reality. With secondary representations the organism can entertain *multiple models*. That is to say, in addition to a model of current reality, such an organism can consider models representing past, future, or hypothetical situations. Furthermore, it can interpret the representational content of other representational systems (e.g. a picture or someone's pretend play). Because the different models can be compared I refer to this mentality as the *collating mind*. Finally, with metarepresentations an individual can form *metamodels*. The representational relations themselves can be represented (new ones can even be invented). With this capacity the individual can conceive concurrently of

Table 12.1. *A model of the natural history of the representational mind*

	Primary mind	*Collating mind*	*Metamind*
Model of reality	single updating model	multiple models	metamodels
Representational level	primary representation	secondary representation, representing representations	metarepresentation, representing representations *as* representations.
Evolution	>150 million years ago birds, mammals	~ 15 million years ago great apes	~ 1.5 million years ago *H. erectus / ergaster*, humans
Development	fetus (~ 30 weeks)	end of infancy (~ 1.5 years)	pre-schooler (~ 3.5 years)
Characteristics	sensation, perception, emotion, schemes, instincts, reflexes, conditioning...	plus secondary representation	plus metarepresentation, executive control
High expressions and applications	play, exploration, latent learning	pretence, planning, insight, self-awareness, other awareness, attribution of desire and intention	theory of mind, mental time travel, symbolic representation, generativity, creativity, teleology...
Resulting culture	no culture but nature	simple tool cultures, basic politics	mimesis, morality, religion, language, narrativity, history, science...

different ways the same object or event can be represented (e.g., by different people, by different media, by different plans, in different times, etc.). This capacity to form reflective metamodels is the cornerstone of *metamind*, which, I propose, further entails the ability to dissociate from primary perceptions and response tendencies to create a distinct level of mental executive control over actions. Metamind, I will argue, is uniquely human and at the root of humans' extraordinary position in the animal kingdom.

I acknowledge that any attempt at reconstructing the evolution of mind is inevitably an outrageous simplification. The story I will tell encompasses and connects recent findings from various research fields, to create a plausible and coherent—perhaps even true—account of the evolution of the representational mind. But a couple of hundred citations in the reference list merely scratch the surface of the complex debates in the disciplines. So even if I succeed at constructing a harmonious interdisciplinary picture, it is only one of several possible interpretations. Further-more, to answer the question as to how we got to where we are now, I will need to employ two controversial strategies—I shall argue from currently living organisms to ancestral organisms, and from ontogeny (development) to phylogeny (evolution). Both of these strategies require some justification.

The main problem with arguing from living to ancestral species is one of deciding what features are based on common ancestry. Functionally or structurally similar phenotypes can depend on either homology or analogy. The decision between them is sometimes difficult to make, especially when it comes to behaviour and underlying cognition. For example, I observed a sub-adult male orang-utan maintaining in a horizontal position between two trees until a juvenile climbed down the trunk and used him as a living bridge. Ants can also be observed to build such bridges. Does the bridging behaviour indicate some level of self-awareness in orangs (cf., Povinelli and Cant 1995) but not in ants? The decision should be based on what I want to call *evolutionary parsimony*. Parsimony usually refers to Lloyd Mogan's canon which proclaims that we should use no higher level explanation for behaviour than is strictly necessary. Unfortunately, it is not at all clear what constitutes a higher and what a lower level of explanation. Evolutionary parismony, however, can be defined more readily. We should favour the phylogenetic scenario that requires the least number of assumptions to explain the current phenotypes of species. For example, if all species of a particular family share a feature, it is more parsimonious to assume that they share that feature because a common ancestor had it, than to postulate that each species developed that feature independently. On the other hand, if two distantly related species (such as orangs and ants) share a feature that is not present in closer relatives, then it is more parsimonious to assume that the feature developed through convergent evolution, because otherwise one would have to assume that each of the closer related species had lost that feature during evolution. In this chapter, this reasoning will be applied chiefly in the context of similarities between humans and our closest relatives, the other great apes. Features shared between all these species are probably homologous and thus were present in our common ancestor some 12 to 15 million years ago. While analogous features can tell us something about selective pressures, only homologous features suggest that the same underlying mechanism is at work. Human characteristics not shared with our closest relatives, not even with the chimpanzees, most likely evolved after our ancestry split from the line that led to modern chimpanzees and have therefore emerged in the last five million years.

The second controversial strategy is to reason from development to evolution. Haeckel's notion that ontogeny recapitulates phylogeny has long been rejected. There appear to be as many cases violating this 'rule' as following it (e.g. Parker and Gibson 1978). However, this should not stop us from using developmental information to construct hypotheses about evolutionary history (see also Donald, this volume). From a state of no mind, a mind capable of reasoning *cogito ergo* sum evolved in phylogeny, and the same metamorphosis also occurs in the development of an individual human. For our discussion it is mainly the fact that one has to be able to form primary representations before one can form secondary representations, and secondary representations before one can form metarepresentations, that will be mapped from ontogeny onto phylogeny. My model predicts that various capacities and skills should co-emerge both in development or in evolution, because in both cases their emergence reflects the two representational transitions. Thus, recent empirical findings of developmental associations between markers of each representational level and other skills bear on the debate as to when these skills could have made their debut in evolutionary history.

Finally, the stage-like model I present does not imply strong claims about abrupt quantum leaps. The development and evolution of mental skills is a gradual process, but qualitative changes can emerge from gradual changes, just as water changes qualitatively from solid to liquid to gas as temperature gradually increases. Potentials and characteristics change in each qualitatively new level (cf. Lorenz 1973; Bischof 1985). I shall propose that, in children, the change from primary mind to the collating mind occurs at approximately age one and a half, and the change from collating mind to metamind occurs at approximately age three and a half. The corresponding changes in hominid evolution, I suggest, occurred approximately 15 million and approximately one and a half million years ago, respectively. However, the new skills might at first be crude; application and generalization might involve inconsistencies and might generally invoke a picture of gradual transition. Yet, if only to contribute to an easier understanding, I believe it to be useful to model this development as a simplified stage-like progression. Thus, I shall present the model in a three-stage manner—first discussing primary mind, then the collating mind, and finally the metamind.

I will place special emphasis on the emergence of metamind and its corollaries and present relevant findings from my own research. This change to metamind, I suggest, began in *Homo erectus/ergaster* about 1.5 million years ago. It marked the dawn of a new self-reflective force that challenged instincts and simple stimulus–response learning for the driver's seat of behaviour. Once it emerged, the metamind was to change the face of the Earth. It is so powerful (creative, self-aware, and communicative) that it might help life itself to spread beyond the boundaries of the planet; so powerful, on the other hand, that it might destroy the whole enterprise of life on Earth.

The primary mind

Evolution of mind

Before discussing the evolution of complex representational abilities, I must briefly outline the basic assumptions about the origin of mind. During evolution more complex levels arose out of, and are ultimately dependent upon, less complex levels of organization while at the same time being profoundly different from those levels. Physical evolution gave rise to biological evolution, which gave rise to mental evolution, which gave rise to cultural evolution.

Various regulating mechanisms preceded mind, or mental functions, in biological evolution. Living organisms, by their very definition, reproduce, have metabolism, and respond to environmental change. These characteristics can be achieved by varied processes including regulating cycles and hard-wired response patterns. The entire plant world seems to run on such processes. Behaviour in early animals might also have been largely based on innate processes like today's instincts, reflexes, and other "innate releasing mechanisms" (Lorenz 1973) that filter the environmental stimuli and select the appropriate response. Even modification of innate response patterns during an individual's life-span can be achieved through classical conditioning, habituation, sensitization etc., and these are usually not regarded as affording anything mental (but see Lea, this volume).

Mental experience might have first emerged with the evolution of reinforceable plasticity. Dennett (1995) calls organisms with this capacity 'Skinnerian Creatures'. The organism performs various actions and then selects the one 'that works' or that is 'reinforced'. This is natural selection extended to the individual behavioural level. The selection process, however, is *not* within the environment but within the individual. Which environmental stimuli are reinforcing is ultimately a function of what the organism evaluates as 'good' or 'bad'. The same stimulus may be good for one creature and bad for another; good today and bad tomorrow. But how does the individual 'know' what is good and what is bad, and why should it bother? These are surprisingly important questions that bear on the evolution of mind. Dennett (1995) suggests that some early candidates for this category 'were no better off than their hard-wired cousins, since they had no way of favouring (selecting for an encore) the behavioural options they were equipped to 'try out', but others, we might suppose, were fortunate enough to have wired-in 'reinforcers' that happened to favour Smart Moves, actions that were better for their agents' (p. 374).

But how are the 'wired-in reinforcers' of those lucky creatures supposed to work? In our experience something is positively reinforcing if it 'feels good'. Perhaps the mind or mental experience evolved for this very reason—to represent certain stimuli as *feel-goods*, or, if they happen to be negative reinforcers, *feel-bads*. According to Humphrey (1992), evolution favoured organisms with affect-laden sensitivity (this is good versus this is bad) to events at their boundaries. Organisms evolved *interests*. Leahy (1994) traces this argument back to William James (1890) who claimed that consciousness evolved to make survival an imperative rather than a chance rule. 'Minding' created the adaptive striving for survival that marks the vertebrate world.

The legacy of Descartes' philosophy is a popular idea of mind that is far too intellectualized. As Milan Kundera (1991) put it: "'I think therefore I am' is the statement of an intellectual who underrates toothache" (p. 200). Humphrey's (1992) alternative—'I feel therefore I am'—might come closer to the true essence of mind. That 'to feel' is the essence of consciousness is reflected in the everyday use of the word. Losing consciousness means more than being unable to think or reason, it means being unable to feel. Just as well, because being unconscious is supposed to mean that one cannot feel anything when one is cut open on an operating table.

Basic to Humphrey's (1992) analysis is the distinction between sensation (what is happening to me) and perception (what is happening out there), and the insight that sensations or feelings are the product of active neuronal processes separate from those producing perception. He cites phenomena such as blindsight and agnosia to make his case for a double dissociation between sensation and perception. The distinct activity of sensing, the logic goes, involves a reactivating loop with a particular duration in projection areas of the central nervous system, creating a subjective experience of sensation. The projection areas have a correspondence with the site of stimulation at the organism's boundary that determines the characteristic modality of the sensation. Sensation with an attached positive or negative evaluation is the fundamental non-intellectual assessment machinery which can be expected to be present in any organism with sufficiently developed sensory projection areas. Higher vertebrates such as birds and mammals are probably capable of this feat. They mind!

This assumption is substantiated by the resemblance of those animals' behaviour to the kinds of human behaviour that we ordinarily describe as based on feelings. Dogs, horses, and cats seem to *enjoy* being stroked and *dislike* being pinched, much as we do. This phenotypical correspondence is most likely of homologous rather than of analogous origin. That is, there is no apparent reason why convergent evolution, rather than ancestry, should have produced such strikingly similar phenotypes in all mammalian species. That in turn means that, just as we can assume that other people experience pain the way we do (e.g. when we see them scream while being hit), so too can we assume, with much the same certainty, that mammals (and birds and possibly some other species) experience pain when we see them 'scream' while being hit. These creatures are sentient beings.

Nonetheless, the evolution and nature of feeling remain controversial. We do not need to resolve that controversy here. For my model of the evolution of representational skills it is the second kind of organismic information-processing that is important.

Perception is how the organism uses sensory information to gain knowledge about the outside world. This, of course, is of immense adaptive value. An organism that can respond appropriately to stimuli that indicate the proximity of, say, food or a predator, *before* that external object comes in direct contact with the body surface has an adaptive advantage. Organisms with highly fallible indication systems are soon starved or eaten. So, evolution favoured those with increasingly sophisticated and fine-grained categories for indicating stimuli of significant external events. Sensory organs became the means of inferring the state of the outside world. Stimulation of these specialized areas of the body surface (e.g. the retina) was used decreasingly for sensation and increasingly for perception. Some surface areas, such as the skin on our hands, maintained a double function of sensation (when being stroked) and perception (when touching objects). At specialized perception areas like the retina, however, the stimulation is no longer evaluated simply as 'feels good' or 'feels bad'. It is the configuration of the stimuli and what they indicate that is evaluated emotionally. Furthermore, perception does not happen to a *tabula rasa*. Animals form concepts, and concepts guide perception. These processes require an integrating central processor.

The brain processes the constantly changing incoming information to create a relatively stable picture of the environment. Size, shape, and colour constancy are formidable computational achievements that ensure that an object is perceived as *one continuing* object. Cross-modal integration of sensory information is an even greater achievement. Auditory, olfactory, and visual inputs are all taken as indicators of one and the same object in the environment. The brain creates a *single integrating* model of the outside world. All major primate groups have been shown to have cross-modal abilities (Ettlinger and Wilson 1990).

We can call this mental model, created by perception, a *representation*, since the inner and outer worlds are matched according to definable rules. Because it is an integrating model, it is not entirely stimulus-bound, as is often suggested. Indeed, a mental model might not only integrate information across modalities but also across time. If a cat were to stop hunting as soon as its prey disappeared behind a bush, it would have a very inefficient mental model indeed. This, of course, does not happen. The mental model maintains a representation of the prey as being behind the bush until there is new information displacing it (e.g. the prey re-emerges on the other side). Bischof (1985) called this capacity *diachronic identity*, as the mental model bridges past, present, and future, albeit to a very limited extent. The main limitation is that we are talking about a single model of reality that is constantly updated (cf. Perner 1991).

The ancestors of today's vertebrates were already armed with these devices of sensation, perception, and representation, and so exploited the potential design space to evolve in their diverse ways. Thus, what I present here as one basic category of mind is a very heterogenous class with very diverse degrees of sophistication, all of which are equally successful adaptations. They all share the same fundamental characteristics of mind, but lumping them into one category does their diversity an injustice. This rough treatment is inevitable, though, given the scope of this chapter and its primary focus on mental evolution in hominids.

There are two further refinements I wish to highlight because they lead up to the next level of representational capacity. One is curiosity. Some species developed active ways of improving their internal conception of the environment, and thus improving the information contained in the model. Exploratory behaviour is used to gather information about the environment, but the animal only engages in it in the absence of any competing serious motivation. A rat, for example, explores a maze and, when a stimulus elicits a flight response, uses the information gained to directly choose the most appropriate escape route. Such *latent learning* does not involve any operant conditioning but is a pre-emptive measure. The single updating mental model is enlarged to cover a wider spectrum of the current situation, including routes through the maze, by the information gathered through exploration. This is specifically adaptive for unstable or diverse environments, because it provides the information necessary for flexible appropriate responses in novel situations. It is not surprising therefore to find this trait especially in what Lorenz (1973) called the "specialists in non-specialization, ... the rats from among the rodents, corvids from among the song birds, and man [sic] from among the primates" (p. 148).

Closely related to curiosity is play. Playing animals not only acquire information about the environment but also train their responses to it. Just as in exploratory behaviour, the organism usually stops the play activity when serious threats or motivations (e.g. hunger) emerge. This suggests that the action is implicitly tagged as a 'non-serious' drive only to be followed in the absence of 'serious' motives. Learning activities such as play or exploration are inherently future-oriented and lead up to the next level of representational thought. But first we need to consider human development.

Development of mind

How did we develop from a non-conscious cell to a minding, perceiving, playing, and exploring infant? From the moment of birth, human infants seem to feel and to perceive the world, albeit in limited ways. Indeed, there is reason to believe that the child 'minds' long before it is born. Prenatal voice recognition and other effects suggest such early developments (e.g. DeCasper and Spence 1986). While electrical activity above the brainstem starts to emerge from the 14th week after conception, it is not until the 30th week that cortical electrical activity is recorded. It is not clear when exactly the sensory projection areas of the fetal brain have matured enough to produce the reverberatory loops that, according to Humphrey (1992), produce sensation, and it will not become clear until we have identified the precise nature of these proposed neural loops in the mature brain. But it is clearly some time before birth, and in medical practice painkillers are now being used for the fetus in prenatal surgery, in apparent recognition that the sentient mind begins its development before birth (cf. Concar 1996).

There is early evidence for the existence of a single updating mental model (Perner 1991). From birth the infant seems capable of cross-modal integration, as is evident through imitation of facial expression (Meltzoff and Gopnik 1989). And by three months the time-bridging capacity becomes evident. Baillargeon has shown in several experiments that three- to four-month-old infants represent an object that is no longer perceptible (Baillargeon 1987; Baillargeon and DeVos 1991). The infants show significant signs of surprise when viewing a screen that appears to move through the space occupied by an obscured object without any signs of resistance. Apparently, the infants' model includes information about the no longer visible object, and expectations about its effect on other objects. The internal model therefore holds the information (e.g. there is this object) until it is erased through forgetting or until incompatible information updates the model (Perner 1991). The model's time-bridging capacity seems to be quite limited at first. Searching for an object hidden under one of two cloths deteriorates to chance level if the delay between witnessing the placement and starting the search is more than 8 s in ten-month-olds (Diamond 1985), and more than only 20 s in 16-month-olds (Daechler *et al.* 1976). This does not mean, however, that the infant does not store information and accumulate knowledge. Indeed, recent research has shown that young infants learn from single events and show deferred imitation (e.g. Bauer 1996; Rovee-Collier 1997).

The first two years witness an increasing sophistication in other areas of the infant's mental and physical capabilities. Piaget (e.g. 1954) aptly called this phase the sensorimotor period. Perceptions form mental concepts—or *schemas*, in Piagetian terminology. New experiences are incorporated or *assimilated* into existing schemas (applying an old schema to a new stimulus) and these schemas themselves are altered or *accommodated* to new experiential demands (adapting an old schema to a new stimulus). Piaget (e.g. 1951, 1952, 1954) described in detail the invariant sequences of sensorimotor development in regard to imitation, causality, means–ends, and object concept. Exploration and play soon make the formation and extension of the inner mental model an active preoccupation for the infant.

The development of the object concept, and other aspects of human sensorimotor development, are now being systematically studied in other primates. Indeed, a whole new research programme is devoted to this study. Parker (1990) called it *comparative developmental evolutionary psychology*. Monkeys and apes follow the same developmental sequence as humans, although they have fewer schemas, achieve the various stages at different rates, and reach different levels as their highest achievement. The general pattern of cognitive development appears to be an invariant sequence across the primate species (see, for example, Parker and Gibson 1990). Because this quasi-universal development in primates points to homology, it seems to be most plausible and parsimonious to assume that subjective phenomenological (mental) correlates of this development are homologous, also. In other words, the quality of mental experience in young infants and young monkeys might be very similar, and might have existed already in infants of our common ancestor.

However, in the second year the human infant acquires a new capacity to go beyond a single updating model to form multiple models. This has far-reaching consequences, and among the primate species this development might be shared by the other great apes only.

The collating mind

The next transition of representational capacity sets the stage for mental detachment from the immediate present. The mind goes beyond the single updating model of reality to entertain other hypothetical models. The creation of multiple models or secondary representations allows for a whole new set of skills. Throughout the discussion I will adhere to Perner's (1991) analysis of the nature of representations. In brief, a representation comprises a representational medium which represents something as having certain properties. For example, the medium might be a picture, the thing represented a house, and it might be represented as being blue (even if it's actually red).

A single updating model is based on primary mental representations. Its main function is to represent significant features of the outer world accurately. Secondary representations, on the other hand, are decoupled from the causal link to the real world. They can represent imaginary, past, or future situations. In this sense, play and curiosity might be precursors of the ability to consider multiple models. The collating mind can bring primary and secondary representations into propositional relation. That is, one can *think* of x (secondary representation) while looking at y (primary representation) and collate x and y (cf. Olson 1993). The mind can now not only feel, perceive and represent the world, but it can also *think* about things or events while feeling, perceiving, and representing the same or other things or events. This also enables the individual to interpret the representational content of other representations (e.g. of pictures, or others' thoughts). The primary perception of the pixel configuration on a two-dimensional TV screen is set aside, in favour of a secondary representation of the three-dimensional objects and events that the pictures represent. Note that these TV events are not simply mistaken for reality, although they might provoke emotional reactions and so forth appropriate to the realities they depict.

In the following section I will discuss some of the most important new skills a mind with multiple models possesses. I shall present and compare developmental and comparative data for each of these skills. My model predicts that they should all make their debut from around the same time in human development (by about one and a half years), and that our closest phylogenetic relatives, the great apes, are in principle capable of all these skills. This would support the claim that the ability to form secondary representations is a domain-general skill, and that this skill evolved before the line that led to modern apes and humans began to split, some 12 to 15 million years ago.

Several developmental and evolutionary theorists have recognized the significance of the transition to multiple models. Many names have been used, depending on the authors' theoretical positions: these include *synchronous identities* (Bischof 1985), *imagining other possible worlds* (Byrne and Whiten 1992), *metarepresentation* (Leslie 1987), *representation* (Olson 1993), *secondary representation* (Perner 1991), and *symbolic function* (Piaget 1951). Dennett (1995) coined the term *Popperian Creature*, after Sir Karl Popper, who once observed that the new skill allows hypotheses to die instead of the individual. What he meant was that multiple models can be used as mental testing grounds for behaviour rather than having to try out the real world and suffer real consequences. This, of course, is what we call insight—the search for new means to goals by mental operations rather than physical trial and error.

Insight, planning, and object permanence

Insight involves the creation of a propositional relation between the reality model (primary) and the hypothetical model of a desired goal state (secondary). Simple planning, too, can be understood as requiring the perception of the current situation (primary) and keeping a goal state in mind (secondary). These primary and secondary models need to be collated in order to conceive how one can get from the current to the desired situation. Piaget's search tests for (stage 6) object permanence might also require secondary representation (Perner 1991), but here the secondary model represents a past, rather than a future, state of the world. A classic procedure is as follows: The child watches a desired object being put into a box. The box is then placed under a rug where the object is covertly hidden. Finally the empty box is revealed to the child. With a single updating model of the world the individual only has access to the current situation. An infant does not know where the object might be. With multiple models, the individual can consider, not only the primary representation (box is empty), but also a secondary representation (past—object inside box under the rug) to create a good guess as to where the object is (under the rug).

By one and a half years most children pass these hidden-displacement tests (Haake and Somerville 1985) and show signs of insight (Piaget 1952). Planning, too, becomes evident in that the children begin to show signs of monitoring, correcting, and controlling goal-directed actions, and showing positive affective responses to mastery (Kagan 1981; Bullock and Luetkenhaus 1988). The emotional pleasure appears to be the result of achievement; the primary representation of the present reality now matches the preconceived secondary representation of the goal state.

Great apes have been observed solving problems in a way that strongly suggests insight. Köhler's (1917/1927) classic experiments illustrate this. Faced with the problem of bananas hanging out of reach from the roof, the chimpanzee apparently contemplated the situation and suddenly enacted a solution (e.g. stacking boxes upon each other) without hesitation. The chimpanzee seemed to mentally manipulate components of the situation in its imagination until hitting upon a solution to the problem. In contrast with great apes, monkeys and other animals have not yet provided convincing evidence of insightful behaviour (cf. Visalberghi and Limongelli 1994).

The same applies to planning where, again in contrast with monkeys, great apes have shown considerable skill. Döhl (1970), for example, showed that the chimpanzee Julia was able to look up to five steps ahead in a sequential-planning task. The chimpanzee was confronted with a series of two keys in transparent boxes. She had to choose the right key at the first trial to get to the right key at the second, the right key at the second to get the right key at the third, and so on, in order to finally reach the food reward. Only by working mentally backwards from the goal could the initial right key be determined. In other words, in addition to the primary representation of the situation, Julia considered the goal state (secondary representation) and worked out the steps towards the goal state *before* acting (see Suddendorf and Corballis 1997 for further examples).

While the first stages in the developmental sequence towards object permanence are commonly passed by many species, hidden displacement has been proven in few, including the great apes (Chevalier-Skolnikoff 1983; Natale and Antinucci 1989; Miles 1990). There is also evidence that African grey parrots can pass such tests (Pepperberg and Kozak 1986), but it is debatable as to whether secondary representations are implied by the particular tests used in this work (Natale and Antinucci 1989). Although monkeys can extrapolate hidden movement (Filion *et al.* 1996), they fail object permanence tasks (deBlois and Novak 1994). Natale *et al.* (1986) showed by employing 'catch' trials that a macaque used simple search rules in hidden displacement tasks, in contrast to a gorilla who, like a one-and-a-half-year-old human, showed systematic search implying secondary representation of the past path of the object.

Great apes and children from about one and a half years therefore appear to possess secondary representational skill as evidenced through planning, insight, and object permanence.

The beginning of symbolism—pretence, pictures, and language

Pretending that one object is another entails secondary representation because the object of perception (primary representation) is treated as if it were a different object (secondary representation). This requires decoupling from the primary representation (Leslie 1987). Further, in representing what *someone else* is pretending, one is interpreting their actions in terms of secondary representation; Leslie refers to this as metarepresentation, but in this chapter I reserve that term for the ability to represent representations as representations (cf. Pylyshyn 1978; Perner 1991; Astington 1994). As already noted, metarepresentation in this original sense does not emerge until about the fourth year of life—even in the realm of pretend play (Lillard 1993; Jarrold *et al.* 1994; Suddendorf *et al.*, in press). But already in earlier pretence, the child has to create secondary representations (the *as if* situation) in addition to the primary representation (real situation). This behaviour begins by about one and a half years (e.g., Leslie 1987).

There is some controversial evidence suggesting that great apes can pretend. Sign-trained chimpanzees, orang-utans, and gorillas have been reported to engage in pretend play with dolls (Gardner and Gardner 1969; Patterson and Linden 1981; Miles 1990). Patterson and Linden claim, for instance, that the gorilla Koko frequently pretends that one of her plastic alligators has 'real' properties, and uses it to 'frighten' her human caregivers (Patterson and Linden 1981). There are also some anecdotes of imaginary toy play (e.g. Hayes 1951; Savage-Rumbaugh and McDonald 1988). Although these examples all involve zoo or home-reared animals, they are still evidence that apes can engage in such behaviours. Other species do not seem to pretend. A cat's prey-catching behaviour with a ball probably does not constitute pretence, because it is stimulus-elicited and inflexible (Whiten and Byrne 1991).

Pictures usually represent something, for example the characters and events in a story. Understanding what they represent, therefore, involves representing representational content. While infants in their first year treat pictures as just a piece of colourful paper, during the second year pictures develop a magical attraction. The child can now interpret pictures in the sense of forming a mental model of the depicted situation (Perner 1991). This requires multiple models, because the true current situation (e.g. mum holding the family photo album) and the one pictured (e.g., mum at a beach holiday) have to be differentiated. A mental model of a depicted situation (photo, drawing, or TV), like a model of a pretended situation, is a secondary representation. Great apes interpret pictorial information appropriately and show interest in videos and picture books (e.g. Premack and Woodruff 1978; Patterson 1991).

The interpretation of symbols such as words or signs also begins during the second year. This also might be based on the emerging ability to entertain secondary representations in addition to the primary representation of the sound or the sight. Attempts at teaching signs to animals have resulted in moderate successes in a few species. Chimpanzees, bonobos, gorillas, and orang-utans have been successfully taught production and comprehension of words (signs), often numbering in the hundreds (Gardner and Gardner 1969; Greenfield and Savage-Rumbaugh 1990; Miles 1990; Patterson 1991). Limited success has also been reported in dolphins (e.g. Herman *et al.* 1993), sea lions (e.g. Schusterman *et al.* 1993), and African grey parrots (e.g. Pepperberg 1990, 1993). The most linguistically competent animal so far appears to be the bonobo Kanzi, whose capacity for language has been assessed as approximating that of a two-year-old human (Savage-Rumbaugh *et al.* 1993). Other aspects of early symbolic understanding such as classification and negation (cf. Olson 1993) or the ability to deduce word reference from the speaker's focus of attention (cf. Baldwin 1993) might also be facilitated through secondary representational skills and great apes might be quite capable in these respects.

Self awareness: mirror self-recognition

Reflections are similar to pictures, and the development of an understanding of reflective surfaces might parallel that of understanding pictures. Reflective surfaces can be used to discover what one looks like. Researchers have developed a formal test to assess mirror self-recognition (e.g. Amsterdam 1972; Gallup 1970). Individuals pass the test by retrieving a mark, such as a sticker or rouge covertly placed by the experimenter, from their faces while viewing their mirror image. This test has become a standard tool for the non-verbal measurement of an early cognitive understanding of self.

An understanding of the properties of a mirror is implied by the realization of the identity between directly and indirectly (mirrored) perceived objects (object match) and between directly and indirectly observed actions (event match or contingency testing). Self-recognition is a special case of object and event matching. Parts of the visible body (e.g. hands) match their mirrored counterparts, and proprioceptive and visual information about action also correspond with their mirrored equivalents. Such identification, or what Bischof (1985) called *synchronous identity*, seems to require secondary representation because one event or object has to be held in mind (secondary representation) while the perceptual system engages with the other (primary representation), in order that the relation between the two can be recognized.

The mirror mark test provides stronger evidence for the presence of secondary representations than the mere use of mirrored information, because the latter can be based on associative learning. For mirror self-recognition the individual has to hold in mind a picture of what the reflection 'ought' to look like, based on past experience (secondary), in order to realize that the mirror image it currently perceives (primary) is different. The reflection might, for example, show an unexpected red dot on the forehead. Only if this discrepancy is noted does it make sense for the individual to investigate its own forehead in search of the dot. Thus, passing the test is evidence for secondary representation and the existence of some kind of mental image of self (as seen from the outside). In human development the mark test is passed at about one and a half years and co-emerges with self-recognition in photos (Amsterdam 1972; M. Lewis and Brooks-Gunn 1979). Some argue that it marks the onset of autobiographic memory (Howe and Courage 1993, 1997), but I argue against this in the metamind section below.

Over the last twenty years the mirror self-recognition test has been used to study a wide variety of animals ranging from birds to dolphins (Parker *et al.* 1994). Macaques (Anderson 1986), elephants (Povinelli 1989), and parrots (Pepperberg *et al.* 1995) have all been shown to use mirrors appropriately, but only great apes have been shown to pass the classic mark test. This includes at least some chimpanzees, bonobos, orang-utans, and gorillas (Gallup 1970; Suarez and Gallup 1981; Patterson 1991; Hyatt and Hopkins 1994). Event-matching is clearly present in these species. Menzel *et al.* (1985) produced additional evidence that chimpanzees, but not macaques, could relate indirect perception and proprioception, because they could use a video image to guide their hand movements. Interestingly, dolphins, while not testable in the classic way, might also engage in contingency testing (Marten and Psarakos 1994, 1995).

Other-awareness—synchronic imitation, empathic behaviour, and mental attribution

To be aware of the perspective of others, or other-awareness, might entail secondary representations. Another individual's perspective is not part of the perceptual field but is an inference, a propositional relationship between a secondary representation and a primary representation. Other-awareness and self-awareness emerge together, presumably because they both depend on the ability to form secondary representation (cf. Asendorpf *et al.* 1996).

During the second year other-awareness in children becomes evident in various ways, including self-consciousness while the centre of another's attention (M. Lewis *et al.* 1989), cooperation with peers (Brownell and Carriger 1990), prosocial behaviour towards victims of distress (Zahn-Waxler *et al.* 1979), and communication through synchronic imitation (Asendorpf and Baudonniere 1993). The last two have been found to be strongly associated with self-recognition (Bischof-Köhler 1989; Asendorpf and Baudonniere 1993; Asendorpf *et al.* 1996). At the same age, children also begin to attribute mental states to others (e.g. Dunn 1991). For example, they might re-enact what an adult (but not an inanimate object) seemed to *intend* to do rather than what the adult actually did (Meltzoff 1995). Early mental attribution is about desires and intentions (Wellman 1990). Because mental states are not observable, they cannot be derived from direct perception. Rather, they result from cognitive processes relating conception (secondary) and perception (primary) in the observing individual. Secondary representations are therefore critically important for the attribution of intentionality.

Of course, most animal species must have some awareness of the presence of others. But evidence for other-awareness based on secondary representation is again strongest for the great apes. An example in chimpanzees was reported by de Waal (1982)—a subordinate male who displayed sexual interest to a female immediately covered his erect penis with his hand when he noticed that a dominant male was approaching. Macaques, on the other hand, failed to show an understanding of another's perspective even after training (e.g. Kummer *et al.* 1996). A collection of anecdotes of primate tactical deception (Whiten and Byrne 1988; Byrne and Whiten 1990, 1992) contain many examples of self-conscious behaviour shown by great apes when they were the centre of others' attention.[1] The record for lesser apes and monkeys is much scantier and more controversial.

In deception, other-awareness is used to take advantage of another individual. It might also be used for mutual advantage. Cooperation is of course common throughout the animal (and even the plant) kingdom. In most cases, however, it takes the form of long-term symbiotic behaviour. It is short-term cooperation in innovative problem solving that is more likely to involve some kind of perspective taking. There are many records of such cooperative innovation in chimpanzees (e.g. Köhler 1917/1927; Menzel 1974; de Waal 1989), but without a clear behavioural definition of when cooperation entails taking the perspective of the other, such anecdotes cannot be cited with confidence as evidence of secondary representation skills. Experimental work by Povinelli and colleagues (Povinelli *et al.* 1992*a, b*) showed that chimpanzees, but not rhesus monkeys, were capable of role reversal in a cooperative task, and the authors argued that only the chimpanzees showed 'empathy', that is, understood their

---

[1] At face value, the anecdotes of tactical deception in great apes appear to suggest metarepresentational capacities (cf. Whiten and Byrne 1991). I argue, however, that the difference between monkey and ape deception can be explained on the basis of the difference between a primary and a collating mind. Since writing this chapter my attention has been drawn to a paper by Whiten (1996) in which he re-evaluates the deception data. Independently, considering imitation, pretence and mindreading, he comes to the same conclusion that great apes can entertain secondary representations, but not metarepresentations.

partner's role—although Heyes (1993) has provided an alternative account of these data, based on associative learning.

There are very few records of spontaneous empathic behaviour in animals. There are the classic tales of dolphins helping humans in distress. Some credible accounts relating to great apes have been published. Washoe, the Gardner's home-reared chimpanzee, saved a young chimp, who had fallen into a moat, from drowning (Fouts and Fouts 1993). Boesch (1992) has reported evidence for chimpanzee compassion and empathy from the field. Most recently a gorilla saved a three-year-old boy, who fell 15 feet into the gorilla enclosure at Chicago's Brookfield Zoo, by carrying him to a door and alerting zoo-keepers. Although controversy still surrounds the issue, O'Connell (1995) reviewed the evidence and concluded that chimpanzees do have empathy.

Opinions about imitation in animals have changed dramatically in the last decades. Behaviours that were formerly considered as clear examples of imitation have recently been explained in terms of social learning processes such as stimulus enhancement and social facilitation (Meador *et al*. 1987). The most frequently cited case is the learning of song by birds, but this behaviour seems to be based on an innate program enabling direct comparison of the individual's own sound production with the memory trace ('tape recording') of the model sound (e.g. Lorenz 1973; Byrne 1994). Imitation of visually perceived behaviour might be significantly more difficult, because motor tasks might look very different from different perspectives. Indeed, it might be necessary to take the perspective of the model if one is to compare one's own behaviour with that of the model, particularly if imitation is to occur *synchronously* with the model behaviour. Contrary to common belief, there is *no* convincing evidence for imitation in monkeys (Cheney and Seyfarth 1990; Whiten and Ham 1992). The evidence for 'aping' in great apes is also scant, but more convincing (Goodall 1986; Meador *et al*. 1987; Byrne 1994). Dolphins also seem to be capable of imitation (Herman *et al*. 1993).

Great apes have also provided evidence for mental attribution of intention and desire. Indeed, the whole enterprise of studying the development of 'theory of mind' stemmed from a seminal article presenting evidence for the attribution of intention in a chimpanzee (Premack and Woodruff 1978). The conclusions remain controversial (cf. Heyes, 1998, and commentaries), but experimental (e.g. Povinelli *et al*. 1998*a*) and observational (e.g. Whiten and Byrne 1988) data suggest at least limited understanding of mind in great apes—perhaps comparable with that of a two-year-old child.

Summary and conclusion

In accordance with my model, comparative and developmental data seem to converge across skills. Great apes show evidence for a collating mind through their apparent knowledge about self and others, and skills such as pretence, planning, insight, sign-language learning, and mental attribution. In human development the child begins to display these capacities during the second year. Thus, it was argued that children of this age and great apes have collating minds.

To many developmental and comparative psychologists, this kind of generalization is a challenge. They are eager to show that much younger children can pass this or that test, if it is appropriately simplified, or that some bird or insect can solve the problem, if the test uses species-relevant stimuli. Despite this tendency, and the accumulation of some evidence for gradual improvement, I maintain that these changes, in the second year of human life, and between the monkey and ape lines of descent, can best be described as a qualitative shift in representational capacity. The capacity for secondary representation shows itself in a range of domains, but these domains themselves might have their roots in earlier developments. Thus, precursors of the later skills might suggest more gradual development.

The proposal does not, of course, exclude the possibility that some other lines of descent have also evolved collating minds, and strong arguments might be made for secondary representation in large-brained birds, such as parrots, and in aquatic mammals, especially dolphins. Any ape-like abilities in these species, however, must be the result of convergent evolution. But among the primates, the fact that all our closest sister species, the great apes, show evidence for a secondary representation in all of the respects discussed above is strong support for Darwinian evolution of mind. Evolutionary parsimony suggests that our common ancestors had already evolved the basis of a collating mind some 15 million years ago.

Metamind

During the fourth year children seem to change quite dramatically in the way they see the world, others, and themselves. Parents observe that their children begin to make their own plans, have their own long-term goals (such as what they will do when they grow up), recall what one told them last week (especially when it contradicts today's explanation), consider other people's minds, deceive and lie, restrain themselves, start to read and to follow complex story lines, invent their own stories (generating entirely novel scenarios), their own symbols, and perhaps an imaginary friend, draw moral conclusions, and actively ask *why* and *what for* in their attempts to make sense of the world. While these pre-schoolers are clearly just children, prone to all sorts of mistakes and silliness, we adults notice, often with pride, their first precocious attempts at reason and reflection. A fascinating new realm has opened up to the child. Almost out of the blue, the young person's mind is completely and without a doubt far beyond the reaches of any animal's mind. What happened?

I propose that the child has developed a *metamind*. A key aspect of metamind is the ability to metarepresent. Metarepresentations, according to Pylyshyn (1978), are representations of representational relations. Representations themselves can now be represented *as* representations (Perner 1991). This has far-reaching implications. Perner emphasized that to understand (i.e. metarepresent) something (e.g. a picture) as a representation one has to master the distinction between what something represents (e.g. my house) and how it represents it as being (e.g. the house is blue in the picture although it has since been painted red).

Through making this distinction one can form higher-order predicates such as 'is true' or 'is false' about the representation (cf. Olson 1993). Many different representations (e.g. an old picture, my memory, your memory, or an 'artist's impression' from a real-estate advertisement) might refer to the same object or event (e.g. my house) and represent it in very different ways (e.g. as new, beautiful, and blue, while it is truly old, shabby, and red). With metarepresentation, then, representational relations can be tagged with predicates (e.g. your view; my memory), and the individual can now simultaneously entertain several distinct representations of the same object or event in reality without running into paradoxical conflicts. It is not clear, however, whether the relationship is not the other way round. It might be that the ability to entertain various conflicting representations simultaneously is what enables the individual to create representations of representational relations (i.e. metarepresentations). Here, I will treat both abilities as the two sides of the same coin. With metamind the child can appreciate representations as representations and can entertain various conflict-ing representations of the same object or event. It follows that the child can now understand that people's minds, as well as pictures, words, and other representational systems, might represent the same world in different (e.g., true, false, exaggerated, imprecise, outdated, wishful...) ways.

This is also important for reflections on one's own mind. One can be wrong. Things are not always what they seem. A distinction between appearance and reality requires one to represent the same object or event in two conflicting ways simultaneously (e.g. what it looks like and what it really is). With a metamind, children can grasp that their own primary representations might be false or distorted, whereas to the collating mind the primary representation defines reality, even though the secondary represen-tation might deviate from it.

Metamind enables the individual to entertain various ways of looking at the same thing—representing what it is, looks like, was, could be, should be, and so on. Consideration of these various perspectives allows for a greater, and more informed, choice of behavioural options. On a social level, they help the individual to under-stand that other views are taken as the truth by other representers. The child can now understand that people will search for a desired object where they think it is, not necessarily where the child knows it is. And, as will become evident in later discussion, these examples only scratch the surface of the vast number of skills that are dependent on the representational advance to metamind.

The term *metamind* comprises all those kinds of thought and reasoning that are based on metarepresentational understanding. At times, metamind can be somewhat disengaged from immediate primary representations. It can 'wander off', as it were, and entertain a variety of propositions. It is the stage for complex reasoning, considering 'what if?', theorizing, reconstructing the past, and planning the future. Metamind enables the cognitive apparatus to function off-line (cf. Bickerton 1995). I am referring to that part of our mind that is dreaming or reasoning while the on-line processes are, say, driving the car. We can be so far removed from the on-line processes that we sometimes wonder how we drove to where we are now, with no recollection of the journey.

The second key aspect of metamind is an increase in executive control. It is important to note that metamind is only adaptive because the results of this disen-gaged thinking *can* be related to current perceptions. The conclusions drawn from these mental exercises can positively affect survival and procreation. Instead of acting simply on the basis of the current situation (i.e., what seems to be true—according to primary representation), the individual can now cognitively base behavioural decisions on what was, what could be, what should be, and what might be true, as well as on what seems to be true for others. In order to benefit from these considerations the individual has to be able to (at times) suspend 'lower-level' impulsive response patterns.

Metamind requires an ability to disengage or dissociate from the immediate response to perception. Mental computation increasingly demands priority in determining behaviour. Thus, executive control is crucially important to any adaptive advantage of the metamind. Of course, even we adults are not entirely rational and are often guided by immediate impulse rather than reason. Metamind emerges as a new addition to a cognitive apparatus that is already sophisticated. Instincts or 'gut-feelings' might sometimes be better than our best reasoning processes at assessing what is good or bad for us. However, large parts of our lives and our culture are based on our capacity to override immediate behavioural predispositions and base our decision on our reflective metamind.

In sum, metamind comprises advances in representational and executive abilities. Metarepresentation enables the individual to form higher-order predicates such as 'is true' and 'is false' or 'your belief' and 'my belief'. Various conflicting representations of the same object or event can now be entertained concurrently. These representations can be brought into complex relations, and reasoning with and about things well beyond the immediately present becomes possible. For this ability to unfold fully, the individual must learn to disengage from the preoccupation with immediate perceptions. Metamind enables a more accurate and present-transcending modelling of reality. If it is to be of any adaptive advantage, metamind must be able to override impulsive response patterns and replace them with responses based on reflective reasoning. In other words, the mind increasingly exerts executive control.

While there is ample evidence that our closest relatives, the great apes, have also evolved a collating mind, there is a marked lack of evidence that they possess the key elements of metamind. Although they have the rudiments of many human capacities, it seems that they lack precisely those aspects that catapult these capacities to new heights, beginning in humans at about age four. However, it is of course impossible to prove that a species is *not* capable of X or Y. After all, it takes only one individual at any one point in time to disprove the claim. Nevertheless, in the light of current evidence it is most parsimonious to assume that none of the great ape species, or any other animal for that matter, has developed a metamind (cf. Heyes 1993, 1998). Indeed, naturalistic observations confirm that despite the great apes' remarkable skills, they did not invent morality, history, music, justice, art, religion, language, or any other human cultural universal that, as will be seen, implies metamind.

The achievements of the growing cognitive apparatus between ages three and four have been studied intensely over the last decade, but authors have emphasized different aspects. Some have referred to the 'inner eye' (Humphrey 1986), others talk of 'theory of mind' (Premack and Woodruff 1978; Wimmer and Perner 1983), 'mental time-travel' (Suddendorf and Corballis 1997), 'second-order intentionality' (Dennett 1978), or 'executive function' (Russell *et al.* 1994; Zelazo *et al.* 1996). The achievements in all these domains, I suggest, are based on metarepresentation and increased executive control. That is, the concept of 'metamind' embraces the reflective self-reference of 'inner eye' (an introspection organ), the social and abstract component of 'theory of mind' (a mind-reading organ), the temporally extended sense of reality implied in 'mental time-travel' (autobiographic memory and remote future plans), the active association of 'second-order intentionality' (action plans and strategies), as well as the regulatory aspect of 'executive function' (the mental government of behaviour). I shall provide logical and empirical grounds for bringing together all these changes that occur at the transition between three and four years of age under the single heading metamind.

It is the theory-of-mind aspect that has received most attention over the last decade. 'Theory of mind' refers to the explanation and prediction of behaviour based on the attribution of mental states such as intention, knowledge, or belief. There is a fast-paced on-going debate about such questions as whether the underlying mechanisms are innate or socially constructed (e.g. Carruthers and Smith 1996), whether imitation or pretence is the precursor (e.g. Moore 1996), or whether theory of mind develops through simulation or through theory construction, but the debates are really about the relative importance of these factors (Astington 1994). In respect of whether theory of mind is based on simulation or on theory construction, for example, it is clear that adults can use both strategies—they can reason abstractly about, say, the probable mental state of someone they have betrayed, but they can also gain further insight into what the other might feel by mentally putting themselves into his or her position. Thus, instead of entering these debates (see Carruthers and Smith 1996), I want to look at the overall interconnected change that occurs at age four. It is now time to put empirical 'flesh' to the theoretical bone structure I have presented so far.

'Theory-of-mind' tests of metamind

Ever since Wimmer and Perner's (1983) pioneering research on mental attribution, understanding false beliefs has been the crucial test for metarepresentation and 'theory of mind'. People act according to how they represent the world, rather than according to how the world actually is. In the case of true beliefs, representation and reality are identical, but in the case of false beliefs they differ. Only the attribution of false beliefs can therefore unequivocally reveal an understanding of the representational nature of mind (Dennett 1978; Wimmer and Perner 1983). False-belief attribution also implies the other metamind skills, namely, the ability to dissociate or disengage from the immediate perception (e.g. regardless of where a desired object truly is, the person will look where she thinks it is) and to simultaneously entertain two conflicting representations of the same object or event (e.g. I know the object is here but she thinks the object is there).

At about the same age that children become able to ascribe false beliefs to others (by about three and a half to four years) they become able to attribute false beliefs to themselves. Gopnik and Astington (1988) showed that younger children fail on tests of representational change—when their belief was changed, they reported having held the current belief all along. When asked what they thought was inside a candy box before they were shown that there were pencils (not candy) inside, they stated that they originally thought there were pencils inside. Again, in order to entertain the past false belief (that there was candy in the box), the child has to be able to metarepresent the beliefs as true and false (or current and past) and disengage from the current knowledge about the true state of affairs.

Flavell and colleagues (e.g. Flavell *et al*. 1986) showed that children begin to distinguish between appearance and reality at around the same time. Younger children have problems understanding the difference. Pouring milk into a blue glass does not change the milk's colour but only our perception of it. To differentiate between the two, the child has to establish a relationship between the propositional relation held in mind and the perceived situation (Olson 1993). The two representations (e.g. 'is blue' and 'is white') have to be metarepresented or tagged as 'looks like' and 'is truly' and the child has to disengage from the current perception (blue) to answer the question about the reality (white).

One might be concerned about whether young children simply fail these tasks because they do not know what the researchers mean or want (e.g. Siegal 1995). Flavell *et al*. (1987) showed in various ingenious ways that children's conceptual problems are genuine. For example, a white card was held under a blue filter and the experimenter detached a pre-cut piece from the card and presented the child with this white piece and a corresponding blue piece. Asked which piece was taken from the card three-year-olds tended to point to the blue piece, thereby failing to recognize the distinction between appearance and reality. Passing false-belief, representational change, and appearance–reality tasks have been found to be correlated (Gopnik and Astington 1988; Moore *et al*. 1990), substantiating the notion of a common underlying representational mechanism (e.g. Flavell 1993).

Another aspect of how the representational mind works is the basic relationship between informational access (i.e. perception) and knowledge. Children younger than three and a half do not fully comprehend that, for example, seeing leads to knowing (Wimmer *et al*. 1988; Perner and Ruffman 1995; but see Pratt and Bryant 1990). Again, children need to metarepresent the other's perception (or ensuing representation) and to disengage from their own perception in order to reason about what is and what is not available to the other's mind. Further, this seems to be true also for the reconstruction of how information entered one's own system. Asked how they know what they know (e.g. being told, having seen, or having inferred the location of an object) three-year-olds fail to respond above chance (Gopnik and Graf 1988; O'Neill and Gopnik 1991; Woolley and Bruell 1996). Indeed, even four-year-olds tend to claim that they have always known what in fact they have just learned today (Taylor *et al*. 1994). Source memory also requires that the current mental state is set aside and a different past state is entertained.

Like conflicting knowledge and belief, conflicting desires seem to be understood only by about age four (Moore *et al*. 1995). Younger children ascribe desires and intentions to others. But, when children younger than five hold a strong desire they seem unable to recognize that another person might desire something different. Their own desire might be too overwhelming to dissociate from. If there is no strong desire on the part of the ascriber, the attribution does not pose a problem. Older children, through metarepresentation, can tag the desires as 'mine' and 'yours' and the conflict is resolved since both desires can be simultaneously entertained.

Once again, a task that is similar except that it involves the self rather than others produces comparable results. Zelazo and colleagues (e.g. Frye *et al*. 1995; Zelazo *et al.* 1996) found that changing the rules in a card-sorting task poses a problem for three but not for five-year-olds. For example, children had to sort cards first according to shape and then according to colour. The younger children continued to sort according to the first rule. They needed to disengage from the first rule (or desire to order by shape) in order to sort according to the second rule. Understanding embedded rules (i.e. use rule 1 in game A and rule 2 in game B) might also require representing representational relations (cf. Zelazo and Jacques 1997). The younger children showed evidence of understanding both rules, but they could not use this knowledge to guide their action. Similarly, there is evidence that even three-year-olds can remember their earlier false beliefs (Freeman *et al.* 1995 used cued recall to elicit such memory), yet without support this knowledge is not accessible for action control.

Some recent research suggests that in particular circumstances children's performance on theory-of-mind tasks can be enhanced (e.g. Chandler and Hala 1994; Saltmarsh *et al.* 1995). Mitchell (1997) argues that younger children's problems with theory-of-mind tasks are due to of an attentional magnetism to a tangible reality. Thus, theory-of-mind tasks that involve the child and provide tangible objects corresponding to, say, false beliefs, can be passed even by three-year-olds. In effect, these easier theory-of-mind tasks impose less of a demand on the child's ability to disengage. Recent research by Clements and Perner (1997) suggests that children might have some implicit understanding of false beliefs before developing it explicitly. In any case, the point of the research was *not* to show that three-year-olds lack a theory of mind; rather, it was to find a way of *showing* that a child might have a representational theory of mind (Dennett 1978). When children reliably pass false-belief tasks we know that they understand that people act according to their representations of the world.

Evidence from animals has proven elusive, because few theory-of-mind tests have been successfully adapted for comparative research. Povinelli *et al.* (1990) argued that chimpanzees recognized the distinction between a 'guesser' and a 'knower', and this result seemed to have promising implications for chimpanzees' capacity to recognize the relationship between perception and knowledge. Further studies, however, proved that the design did not yield evidence for mental attribution performance even in humans (Gagliardi *et al.* 1995), and that young chimpanzees are ignorant of the fact that seeing leads to knowing (Povinelli and Eddy 1996). Premack (1988) provided the only attempt to test false-belief attribution in a chimpanzee, and the single subject in that study failed to provide evidence. Premack concluded that chimpanzees do not have a fully-fledged theory of mind (Premack and Dasser 1991; see also Heyes 1998). What they appear to lack is a metamind.

Metamind and social knowledge

Being able to understand that others have minds is, of course, of tremendous value for all kinds of social interaction. By age four, children have developed an impressive basic understanding of the workings of mind. Contrary to the impression gained from the literature, the particular theories of how mind and world interact vary profoundly between cultures. Lillard (1998) identifies four basic types of variation between different folk psychologies: "magic, unmandated conceptual distinctions, denial of the negative, and varying values" (p. 23). Vast differences can also be observed within western culture. Some groups, for example, believe in mental powers such as telekinesis or telepathy. Others believe in spirits and in 'god' having access to one's private thoughts. Children acquire their 'theory of mind' within these socio-cultural contexts. While there is great variation between these theories, the basic capacity for generating such concepts about the mental (i.e., having a metamind), I argue, is a human cultural universal.

In general, others' beliefs, intentions, and knowledge are great predictors of their behaviour, and cooperation as well as deception become far more effective if one knows what is on the other's mind. Indeed, changing others' behaviour is usually most effective when one changes their minds. Research (mainly in western cultures) has shown that when children pass theory-of-mind tasks, they improve in their social understanding. Lalonde and Chandler (1995), for example, found that teachers rated children who pass false-belief tasks to be higher in social-emotional maturity than those who fail. The new level of social understanding also shows in particular areas such as deception (Peskin 1992; Ruffman *et al.* 1993). With metamind children begin to appreciate the subtler and more sophisticated aspects of the social world. The vast majority of our stories, histories, and fairy tales, for example, revolve around mental states like intentions, knowledge, false beliefs, surprise, betrayal, selflessness, goals, deceits, and morals. Only with metamind can such narratives be truly understood and the lessons inherent in the stories be learned (cf. Peskin 1996). Indeed, cultural learning in the sense of instructed learning, verbal self-regulation, and collaboration depends on metamind skills (cf. Tomasello *et al.* 1993). It is not surprising then that many researchers emphasize the social effect of metamind skills (e.g. Wimmer and Perner 1983; Dunn 1991; Byrne and Whiten 1992; Astington and Jenkins 1995; Baron-Cohen 1995). For a thorough discussion of the development of social understanding, see Barresi and Moore (1996).

The hypothesis of Machiavellian intelligence, which postulates that human intelligence was born out of increasing social intelligence in primates (Jolly 1966; Humphrey 1976; Byrne and Whiten 1988, 1992), fits in nicely with these effects. However, even if its origin was social, metamind must have had significant non-social side effects. These have been largely overlooked. To balance the score I want to emphasis these non-social effects here.

Metamind and self knowledge

Understanding other minds is bound to go hand in hand with understanding one's own mind. If one assumes that other minds are understood through simulation or putting oneself into the other's shoes (e.g. Harris 1991), then understanding one's own mind must come first.

Self-awareness can be viewed from a functional or structural perspective (Gibson 1995). The origin of self might lie in functional developments (e.g. experience of agency). Perceived control is of paramount importance, and primates prefer tasks in which they experience control over tasks where rewards are received independently of own action, even if the actual reward is greater in the latter tasks (e.g. Rumbaugh *et al.* 1994). Interactions with the environment, especially the experience of agency, give rise to knowledge about the agent (the self), its features, and competencies. This amounts to what from a structural perspective is 'the' concept of self. This idea of self, me, I, or soul, is universally generated (cf. Brown 1991). I am not arguing that there is such a core entity, far from it, but it is important to explain why, how, and when children form the idea we might structurally call a personal identity. In the following I will present several ways in which metamind functionally influences aspects of self which add to the new structural conceptualization of self.

As we have seen already, the attribution of mental states to self appears to co-emerge with the attribution of mental states to others (Gopnik and Astington 1988). By age four children begin to know *that* and *what* they know, believe, want, etc. With this reflective thought we have the transparency necessary for Descartes' *cogito*. The child can now reflect on her own mental states and can potentially come to the conclusion: I think therefore I am. But who or what is the structure of this I?

The ultimate question of where we come from, what we are, and where we are going (Humphrey 1986) can now, at least in principle, be addressed by the child. I have argued elsewhere (Suddendorf 1994; Suddendorf and Corballis 1997) that episodic memory is an active reconstructive process that depends on metamind skills. To travel mentally into one's past and inspect one's history requires mental disengagement from the present, tagging of tense (i.e. 'pastness') to the representation, and active metarepresentational reconstruction of episodes. Past mental states need to be appreciated and the source of current knowledge needs consideration in this process. Perner and Ruffman (1995) found evidence for an association between free recall and understanding the relationship between knowing and perceiving. Following Tulving (1985), they reasoned that episodic memory is based on autocueing through episodic traces which is reflected in free recall but not cued recognition. They found a robust correlation between free recall and perception–knowing tasks that was independent of variations in age and verbal intelligence. This substantiates the notion that episodic memory emerges with metamind (cf. Suddendorf and Corballis 1997). Recent neuropsychological work links this with the prefrontal cortex (Wheeler *et al.* 1997).

This new function, episodic memory, has an impact on self conceptualization in that it is the origin of autobiographical memory: 'that episode is what happened to me' (but see Howe and Courage 1997). Personal identity depends on a personal history. The development of autobiographical memory is often described as a social interactive process (e.g. Nelson 1992) suggesting gradual improvements. Without denying that social effects are important (Welch-Ross 1995), the metamind model predicts a sharper transition. Events that occurred before metamind are not part of autobiography, whereas events after this transition can be. As there is an age-correlate, the model predicts that four but not three year-olds would create an episodic memory of a salient event that is retrievable years later. Pillemer *et al.* (1994) recently provided empirical support for this assertion. Two groups of pre-schoolers (mean age three and a half and four and a half) were interviewed two weeks after a school evacuation in response to a fire. All children had some memory of the event. Seven years later, only children of the older group produced an accurate narrative memory of the event. Only 18 percent of the younger children were able to produce even a fragmentary memory while 57 percent of the older children did. With the rise of metamind around age four, childhood amnesia ceases and one's personal history (i.e. autobiographical memory) begins (Suddendorf 1994; Perner and Ruffman 1995; Suddendorf and Corballis 1997).

But the platform of metamind is not only used to reflect on what is and what *was*, but also on what *will* or *could be*. That is, the same mechanism is used to extrapolate from the past so as to conjure up scenarios of the future (Suddendorf 1994; Suddendorf and Corballis 1997).[2] Indeed, the mechanism's selective advantage must lie in its benefits for future survival, not in reminiscence per se. Secondary representation makes limited planning possible, but the individual is tied to the present, as primary representations alone represent reality. This might be especially limiting with respect to one's own drives and needs. Without anticipation of future needs and drives there is no point in imagining a future more remote than the satisfaction of current needs. With such anticipations, on the other hand, it seems imperative to secure not only the fulfilment of present but also of future needs. The idea that only humans have developed the capacity to anticipate future needs and drives is called the Bischof-Köhler hypothesis, and might be illustrated by the, admittedly over-simplified, claim that "while a full-bellied lion is no threat to nearby zebras, a full-bellied human may well be" (Suddendorf 1994, p. 45). Humans, presumably from about age four onwards, can consider possible or likely future states of need and alter their current behaviour in accordance with these anticipations.

The agent (the self) travels mentally in time (Suddendorf and Corballis 1997). A personal identity through time is the natural consequence by which the past, present, and future can be united under one umbrella. This is necessary to make the mental representations of past and future relevant to the present acting self. While we are changing dramatically in physical and mental make-up over time, all these stages are considered aspects of the same *me*. An extraordinary new structure appears to emerge: a sense of self that is not bound to time and body.[3]

With understanding and reflecting upon own mental states also comes the ability to form attitudes about oneself. Self-esteem is an important aspect of the new personhood, and early developments might have long-lasting effects on a person's life. More specifically, the child can now form attitudes about particular mental states such as: 'I don't like myself bossing others around' or 'I don't want to know'. Metamind includes self-assessment and self-control. Metavolition (e.g. 'my desire to play will not interfere with my concentration on work') makes the child capable of governing its own motives (cf. Frankfurt 1988). Perner (1991) submitted that the observation that children around age four become 'reasonable' might not so much be a result of them becoming 'logical' (in concrete operational thinking) but of them becoming rational about their own desires.

---

[2] Since writing this chapter I have been made aware of a manuscript by Bischof-Köhler (in press) in which she makes a similar argument and reports having found supporting correlations between the development of theory of mind and future-oriented behaviour (see also Moore *et al.* in press).

[3] Povinelli *et al.* (1996) have studied a variant of the mirror self-recognition test by showing children a three-minute-old video recording of themselves being unknowingly marked with a sticker on their foreheads. On being showed the video, most four-year-olds removed the mark, while only a minority of three-year-olds did, leading Povinelli (1995) to conclude that, although a present sense of self might exist by age two, a time-travelling sense of self does not emerge until about age four. However my own research, while confirming this result, showed that a similar paradigm involving the introduction of an unexpected object in the room, rather than an unexpected sticker in the child's hair, yielded the same pattern of results. This study raises doubts as to whether the video test has any bearing on the concept of self (Suddendorf, unpublished manuscript, 1997).

Mischel and colleagues (e.g. Mischel *et al.* 1989) demonstrated that by age four children can successfully delay gratification in order to receive a greater reward later. Choice between an immediate small and a delayed but greater reward clearly depends on the values of the rewards and the expected waiting time. However, other factors have been identified which are more relevant to the discussion of the impact of metamind. Exposure to the reward decreased average delay time for the children, and so did thinking about the reward versus thinking about something else. Disengaging from the primary representation of the reward and from one's desire for it increased self-control. Focusing on abstract qualities of the reward or exposure to the image of rather than the actual rewards also increased delay. In fact, merely imagining that the actually exposed reward was an image increased delay time. These findings support the idea that mental disengagement is crucial for executive control of the metamind and that abstractions (e.g., through symbolic representation) improve this ability.

Only the great apes have proven that they understand what they look like in the mirror self-recognition test. But whether they have evolved mental time-travel and a personal identity through time is highly questionable. Although apes have good memory (e.g. Fouts and Fouts 1993) and planning skills (e.g. Boesch and Boesch 1984), analysis of the existing evidence suggests that they do *not* have an autobiographic memory and are not capable of anticipating future drives (Suddendorf 1994; Suddendorf and Corballis 1997). Chimpanzees have shown considerable skill in delaying gratification (e.g. de Waal 1982) and Boysen and Berntson (1995) showed how symbols can help them to gain executive control to override impulsive responses: Chimpanzees who had great difficulty in choosing a smaller pile of sweets in order to obtain a larger one found the task much easier when the piles were replaced with numerical symbols. Language and metamind evolution seem to be linked on several planes. Nevertheless, the fact remains that great apes did not invent symbols by which to override impulses or to communicate with others, even if they can use symbols which we invent and teach to them.

Metamind and symbols: the connection between self and others

Zaitchik (1990) showed that three-year-olds have problems understanding not only mental misrepresentations but also physical misrepresentations. In an analogue of the classical false-belief task, Zaitchik asked children about a photograph of a previous situation that had now been altered. Three-year-olds expected the photo to represent the current situation while four-year-olds understood that the photo was of the past situation. A metamind explanation of this finding may be that three-year-olds cannot yet disengage from the current situation and fail to understand the photo as representing the situation as it was before the change. On the other hand, these tasks might not require metarepresentation because the pictures are true representations of the past, rather than false representations of the present, and indeed performance is not correlated with false-belief tasks (Perner 1995). However, Thomas *et al.* (1994) showed that young children have severe problems with the representational nature of pictures. Appearance–reality distinctions for pictures were found to be as difficult as classic appearance–reality tasks. Young pre-schoolers have difficulty simultaneously representing the distinct properties of picture and depicted (Robinson et al. 1994).

Similarly, 'false maps' and 'false drawings' are only understood by around age four

(Charman and Baron-Cohen 1992; Leslie and Thaiss 1992). Understanding these 'false' symbolic representations might imply metamind, because the symbol needs to be brought into relation with an internal memory representation of the previous situation, and might require disengagement from the current perception and metarepresentational tagging as 'past' or as 'false'. Symbolic representation, like mental representation, is understood only once the individual acquires metamind. Parkin (1994) found a robust correlation between false-belief task performance ('where does P think X is?') and a parallel false-symbol task involving a misleading direction sign ('where does this sign show X is?'). There is some evidence suggesting that physical misrepresentation is understood earlier than mental misrepresentation (e.g. Robinson *et al.* 1996), which is not really surprising when one considers that the former has a primary reality that can be examined (e.g. a photo), while the latter has no directly accessible medium.

The most significant symbols are of course those involved in language. It is not surprising, therefore, that strong correlations between metamind tasks and language abilities have been reported. Fletcher-Flinn and Snelson (1997), for example, found an association between metalinguistic skills (that is, syllable segmentation and rhyming tasks) and false-belief task performance. Doherty (unpublished, cited in Perner 1995) found a similar association between synonym monitoring and false-belief tasks. In another study, Suddendorf and Fletcher-Flinn (1996) found a strong correlation between verbal intelligence as measured by the British Picture Vocabulary Scale (BPVS; Dunn *et al.* 1982) and false-belief understanding. One might argue that a particular level of linguistic skill is necessary to comprehend the false-belief task and that the correlation merely reflects this. However, Jenkins and Astington (1996) found an association with performance on the Test of Early Language Development (TELD, Hresko *et al.* 1981) that appeared to go beyond this suggestion. While a certain level of language skill is required to pass false-belief tasks (98% of the children who passed at least one task scored 14 or higher, while only 33% of children who failed on all tasks reached this level), the authors found a significant correlation between the number of different tasks passed and the TELD scores even when analysed only for those who were above the threshold of 14. This suggests a more fundamental relationship than passing a threshold. Some have argued that the ability to comprehend the recursive nature of syntax is also involved in false-belief tasks (e.g. Feldman 1988), others point to semantic abilities involved in understanding metarepresentational terms such as remember, forget or surprise (Olson 1988; Lyon and Flavell 1994). Furthermore, pragmatic aspects of communication might be linked to false-belief task performance (Baron-Cohen 1988). Whatever the exact connection to language, the two abilities are apparently linked. Bickerton (1995) has even argued that they are fundamentally the same.

Plaut and Karmiloff-Smith (1993) have suggested a reason for this association that ties in closely with my interpretation of metamind. They appeal to the symbolic representation entailed by language as a mediating factor for false-belief task performance. They argue that symbolic representations need to be generated by the child that can effectively override the immediate reality bias of the present experience. In other words, disengagement from the immediate present is fostered by symbolic representation. This is supported by the above-mentioned results of Boysen and

Berntson's (1995) study on chimpanzees' increased executive control when confronted with numerals rather than treats.

Gestural communication might have preceded vocal language in evolution (Hewes 1973; Corballis 1992; Goldin-Meadow and McNeill, this volume) and this capacity might have already depended on metamind. In a recent study we investigated whether there is an association between metamind (as measured by false-belief understanding) and gestural representation in the absence of real objects (Suddendorf *et al.* in press). Earlier research has identified two successive levels in the development of gestural representation: body-part-as-object (BPO) and imaginary object (IO) pantomimes (Overton and Jackson 1973; Boyatzis and Watson 1993; O'Reilly 1995). We found that when asked to pretend to perform a common action such as brushing teeth with a toothbrush, most children without metamind substitute a body part (finger) for the object. Children with metamind, however, significantly more often act as if there were an object (toothbrush) to interact with. Modelling such 'imaginary object' pantomimes to pre-metamind children did not improve their performance; they continued to use body parts as objects. Metamind appears to be important for imaginary object pantomime and thus gestural communication.

But correlations do not tell us much about causal connections. We do not know whether language influenced the evolution of metamind or vice versa. Moreover, language is a prime example of how it can be misleading to reason from ontogeny to phylogeny. Children grow up in a verbal environment. Our forebears, on the other hand, must have invented language. To invent a symbolic representational system one has to have metarepresentation, because one has to understand symbols as representations. It is not surprising, then, that apes like the bonobo Kanzi, who grow up in a language environment, can learn language up to a level comparable to a two-year-old child (Savage-Rumbaugh *et al.* 1993), while chimpanzees in the wild have not invented such a linguistic system at all. Although their collating mind enables them to use symbols and interpret pictures or videos (e.g., Premack and Woodruff 1978), apes might not understand them as representations, and can therefore not invent a symbolic language or draw pictures that represent something. Premack and Premack (1983) went to elaborate lengths to teach their chimpanzees to utilize maps or scale models. All these efforts turned out to be fruitless, as not even identical rooms led the apes to look at the same baited place in the second room after discovering the treat in the first. The very idea that one thing represents the situation of another was beyond their grasp. However, there are at least two studies in which primates were quite successful at using video information about their enclosure (Menzel *et al.* 1978; Vauclair 1996), but it seems plausible that these animals mistook the video for reality (like a window), rather than understood the representational nature of the video.

With metamind the child becomes capable of understanding that something is represented by self, others, and symbols. The world becomes an entirely different place to the child. The way the child thinks is revolutionized.

Metamind and thought

The tasks presented earlier already exemplify the new mental experiences of the child. There are dramatic new developments such as the conceptualization of one's own and others' minds, personal history and future, self concept and control. There are further ways in which the metamind changes the way the child interprets and understands the world. With metamind matures what Dennett (1987) calls the intentional stance, which is a way of interpreting the events in the world by invoking mental states such as intentions and beliefs, rather than physical or design explanations. Heider and Simmel (1944) showed in now classic experiments how humans tend to interpret the world in mental terms. They showed subjects a silent film in which geometric figures moved about and the subjects were asked to describe what they saw. Descriptions generally were based on ascribing intentions and agency to the shapes. Adopting the intentional stance is a helpful heuristic in describing and understanding the world. Explanations often appear to have a wider appeal when proposed as narratives and when they anthropomorphize. Cultural mythologies are ample evidence for this inclination. This might well be due to the Machiavellian origin of human intelligence.

When this view is coupled with other aspects of metamind such as mental time-travel, it seems inevitable that teleology (cf. Kelemen, this volume) emerges. This is the idea that the things around us are here for some purpose. Adopting this view must have been of momentous adaptive value for our ancestors, as it encouraged the search for new uses of objects in the environment and thus must have fostered human control over events. Human cultures have experimented with many religious and natural technologies to influence significant events, sometimes successfully (e.g. making fire) and sometimes not (e.g. making rain). Predicting the future, one of the main features of metamind, is of course most reliable when one is shaping the future. The natural curiosity of our species had therefore been extended into a new era. In childhood, too, this teleological stance becomes increasingly (sometimes irritatingly) obvious when the child asks more and more questions about *why* or *what for*. Every detail of the world is investigated as to its function and purpose. Understanding the world on the explicit metalevel becomes one of our main preoccupations. You and I are devoting significant parts of our lives to this quest for knowledge—why else would I write and you read this chapter? And if you attempt to answer this question, you could be said—thanks to the virtue of recursive thought—to be on yet another teleological quest.

Complementary to generating questions through knowing 'that' and 'what' we *do not* know is generating answers through knowing 'that' and 'what' we *do* know. This metaknowledge can be very beneficial in the way knowledge is utilized. Metarepresentation and disengaging from present perception may be crucial for creative problem solving. Actively searching the knowledge base beyond currently activated areas of mental content appears to be at the very heart of divergent thinking. In our own research we have found that three- to four-year-old children who passed false-belief tasks were able to generate more items on creativity tests requiring them to generate ideas or items according to given criteria (Suddendorf and Fletcher-Flinn 1997). In a recent longitudinal study we then showed that children improve in divergent thinking once they pass theory of mind tasks (Suddendorf and Fletcher-Flinn, in press).

Divergent thinking, like language, requires informational access to varied domains of knowledge in the generative process of combining and recombining items into virtually infinite numbers of novel sequences. This generativity has been recognized as unique to the human condition (Corballis 1991). Metamind might have been crucial to the emergence of this important feat. Even apparently intelligent behaviour in animals is often characterized by a lack of transfer or flexibility. Non-human primates that act 'intelligently' in one domain fail to transfer their knowledge to another—they have a 'laser-beam intelligence' (Cheney and Seyfarth 1990). With metamind this domain specificity may be overcome. "Flexible transfer of knowledge between different domains is one of the hallmarks of humans' relentless creativity and invention" (Suddendorf and Fletcher-Flinn 1997, p. 67).

Is metamind domain general or modular? Evidence from autism

While some authors agree with the proposal of an across-the-board cognitive change (e.g. Perner 1991; Gopnik 1993), others have suggested the existence of domain-specific modules. In particular a theory-of-mind module, specific to understanding *mental* representation, has been proposed (Leslie and Thaiss 1992; Baron-Cohen 1995, this volume). The argument for a specific mind-reading module derived from the finding that autistic children fail theory-of-mind tasks while passing other tasks that are seemingly identical except that they require physical rather than mental representations (e.g., false photographs, drawings, and models—Leekam and Perner 1991; Charman and Baron-Cohen 1992, 1995).

But are autistic children deficient only in understanding mental representations? Perhaps the physical representations in these experiments were not really equivalent to mental representations. Physical representations are not only propositions about referents but also external real things themselves. So while they might misrepresent the current situation, they are themselves true existing objects in their own right. Perhaps it is easier to learn about their properties without invoking metarepresentation because they, in contrast to mental states, have a physical existence. In other words autistic children, even though lacking metamind, might learn to pass these non-mental tasks indirectly without metarepresentation. For example, the autistic children might have learned that photographs are stable and unchanging in nature, while the three-year-olds generalize, apply their immature representational understanding, and believe that what is happening in reality is also happening in the photograph (Leekam and Perner 1991; Robinson *et al.* 1994). Most studies match control and autistic sample according to mental age. This disguises the fact that the autistic sample is much older and thus has had much more opportunity to learn contingencies between observables. High functioning autistic people appear to solve many tasks through indirect computation of what 'comes naturally' to clinically normal people. For an autistic person, emotional states may not simply be perceived in somebody else's face, but need to be deduced on the basis of observed covariations between facial cues and behaviour. In other words, autistic children might learn via association and reward where normal children are applying pre-programmed short-cuts. Indeed, autistic children appear to tackle emotional and social problems in much the same dry way as they address mathematical problems (Sigman *et al.* 1995). In some respects autistic people seem to be behaviourists in a mentalists' society (cf. Baron-Cohen 1989).

While autistic children show evidence for a collating mind, through, for example, mirror self-recognition (Dawson and McKissick 1984) and pretend play (V. Lewis and Boucher 1988), there is a lack of evidence for metamind. Besides consistently failing classic theory-of-mind tasks (Baron-Cohen *et al.* 1985; Leslie and Frith 1988; Baron-Cohen 1989; Perner *et al.* 1989; Prior *et al.* 1990), autistic children do not seem to develop autobiographic memory (Boucher and Warrington 1976; Boucher and Lewis 1989; Powell and Jordan 1993), have severe problems with mental disengagement and executive control (Ozonoff *et al.* 1991; Hughes and Russell 1993; Hughes *et al.* 1994), lack generativity in pretend play (Jarrold *et al.* 1996), have problems imagining unreal things (Scott and Baron-Cohen 1996), have a gross language-acquisition deficit (Sigman and Ungerer 1984), are characteristically engaging in stereotyped and routinized actions rather than flexible planned behaviour (e.g. Prior and Hoffman 1990; Harris 1991), and are basically acultural (Loveland 1991). Autistic children seem to lack executive control and skills in regards to knowledge about self, about others, symbols and thought. In other words they appear to lack a metamind.

Even if mental attribution can be dissociated from other metamind skills in the autistic condition, metamind may still have evolved as a single capacity applied to varied modules. The theory-of-mind aspect might be a subsystem that can be disturbed while other parts remain intact. One reason to assume that metamind is a domain-general skill (or module) is the lack of evidence that any part of metamind exists in other species. The case would be further strengthened if it could be shown that the different components of metamind co-emerged in evolution.

Some words of caution

Although I have referred to 'pre-metamind' and used expressions like "once the child acquires metamind", this development is of course not as abrupt as these words suggest. Children who pass some metamind tasks continue to fail others (Jenkins and Astington 1996). Further, the test–retest reliability of false-belief tasks has been judged to be low to moderate (Mayes *et al.* 1996)—although it depends of course on the age range considered, because two-year-olds will always fail and five, six, seven, or eight-year-olds will reliably pass. Thus, there appears to be no clear transition point; rather, we should assume that there is a transition period. Indeed, abilities entailed by metamind continue to develop throughout childhood, and indeed we appear never to stop learning about people's minds. It is all the more surprising, then, that we do find robust associations between false-belief-task performance and various other skills such as imaginary object pantomime and creativity. The gradual change seems to produce a qualitative shift during this transition period.

The stark difference between monkeys and great apes might also be softened in future by more intensive studies of the lesser apes. Non-primate species (such as parrots and sea mammals) might also turn out to show sophisticated skills, reminding us that evolution is more like a tree branching in all directions than a ladder pointing to heaven.

While the sum of correlational evidence paints a picture of a domain-general metamind faculty emerging around age four, this is not certain. Even partialling out age and IQ does not entirely eliminate the worrisome fact that most things develop at this age period—and that correlations between skills are to be expected. Indeed, most of the experimental data reviewed, especially the comparative research, is mined with qualifications and reservations. Overall, however, the trends in the data can be assembled into an account that makes evolutionary sense, even if the model I am advancing is in some respects merely a 'just so' story. Ultimately, the findings from developmental and comparative research have to fit into a coherent evolutionary theory. The model I present is a first attempt.

When did metamind come on to the scene?

Since no other animal has developed metamind, we might reasonably assume that it evolved some time after the phylogenetic split from the line that led to modern chimpanzees some five million years ago. The prime candidates for introducing this new cognitive machinery are *Homo erectus* and *ergaster*. We do not have evidence suggesting any major changes in mental capacity among the australopithecines (5 to 2 million years ago), as there are no artefacts and their relative brain size did not exceed that of the apes (Wood 1992). At the other end of the time scale, the oldest representational art is about 35 000 years old and burials are up to 100 000 years old. The recent discovery of sophisticated 400 000 year-old spears in Germany (Thieme 1997) prove much earlier extensive planning skills (suggesting mental time-travel). The emergence of metamind thus appears to lie somewhere between two million and 400 000 years ago.

Around two million years ago (perhaps even two and a half million, according to Semaw *et al.* 1997) we have the beginning of the *Homo* clade with slightly increased brain size and the first stone tools (Corballis, this volume). These early tools, however, seem to be within the capacity of chimpanzees (Wynn and McGrew 1989; Toth *et al.* 1993) and there are no other hints of metamind. This changes with the emergence of *H. ergaster/erectus* some two million years ago.

Donald (1991, 1993, this volume) proposed the perhaps most plausible psychological account of the emergence of *H. erectus/ergaster*. At the centre of what he calls mimetic culture stands a new level of motor skill, which allows the whole body to be used as a communication and representation device. Crucial to such bodily or gestural communication would have been an ability to represent imaginary objects. Imaginary object pantomime, as argued above, is associated with metamind. Another aspect emphasized by Donald is the capacity for autocueing. The individual became able to consciously stop, replay, and edit bodily movement and thereby gain voluntary access to memory. Intentional rehearsal and refinement enabled *H. ergaster/erectus* to begin developing intentional symbolic communication and culture. Autocueing is crucial to free recall and episodic memory which are also implicated in metamind (Perner and Ruffman 1995).

But what is the 'hard' evidence for metamind in *H. ergaster/erectus*? The hardest evidence, literally, is that deriving from stone tools. While the Oldowan tools associated with *H. habilis* can be produced quickly, and were possibly used 'on the spot', *H. ergaster's* Acheulian tool kit implies some premeditation. The production of a symmetrical bifacial hand-axe requires time and precision. A tool like that would not be manufactured for one-time, on-the-spot use and it has thus been taken as evidence for mental time-travel (Suddendorf 1994; Suddendorf and Corballis 1997). Not only must the future need be anticipated, but the persistence and uniformity of this tool culture implies instructed cultural learning based on metamind.

Another line of evidence is the relatively sudden first wave of migration of *H. erectus* from Africa across the old world. This suggests that *H. erectus* were capable of altering the various environments to their distinct needs, although they had not developed the Acheulian tool kit of their African relatives *H. ergaster*. In practice this might have meant quick adaptation to different food resources, clothing for colder climates, and eventually fire for heat, light, cooking, and defence (the earliest evidence of the use of fire is about 500 000 years old). These things could not have been achieved without a metamind and without the evolving mimetic culture with generative thought and gestural communication. The origins of human cultural universals such as morality, justice, religion, language, narrative, mythology etc., might then go as far back as the emergence of the mental machinery I have called metamind.

The arrival of *H. sapiens* on the scene some 150 000 years ago probably brought with it a vocal apparatus capable of transforming the gestural communication systems of their forebears into speech. But it took yet another representational revolution to catapult humanity into a position from which the extraordinary development to world domination could begin. Only five thousand years ago did we begin to utilize our understanding of mental and vocal representational systems to create lasting symbolic representations. We invented writing. This external memory storage allowed cultures to share their knowledge across space and time (cf. Donald 1991). The consequential rapid accumulation of information was embraced and utilized for the erection of magnificent cultures such as that of the Egyptians where science, art, agriculture, astronomy, religion, and architecture flourished to new heights. Our current techno-logical leap is a continuation of this process of extended use of external memory storage into our computer age.

With the help of external memory storage we can still today reflect on the reflections of a long-dead Frenchman. Descartes' cogito implies a self-awareness firmly seated in the present. With an evolutionary approach that includes the human species, indeed the human mind, our self-awareness can go far beyond the immedi-ately present. We can realize that we are only a link in our species' evolution with a long past and, hopefully, a long future.

Acknowledgement

I would like to thank Michael C. Corballis, Russell M. Genet, Kennedy McLachlan, Josef Perner, and Kevin Waugh for their valuable comments on earlier versions of this paper. They are not responsible for my views, however.

References

Amsterdam, B. K. (1972). Mirror self-image reactions before age two. *Developmental Psychobi-ology*, **5**, 297–305.

Anderson, J. R. (1986). Mirror-mediated finding of hidden food by monkeys (*Macaca tonkeana* and *M. fascicularis*). *Journal of Comparative Psychology*, **100**, 237–42.

Asendorpf, J. B. and Baudonniere, P. M. (1993). Self-awareness and other-awareness: mirror self-recognition and synchronic imitation among unfamiliar peers. *Developmental Psychology*, **29**, 88–95.

Asendorpf, J. B., Warkentin, V., and Baudonniere, P. M. (1996). Self-awareness and other-awareness II: mirror self-recognition, social contingency awareness, and synchronic imitation. *Developmental Psychology*, **32**, 313–21.

Astington, J. W. (1994). *The child's discovery of the mind*. Fontana Press, London.

Astington, J. W. and Jenkins, J. M. (1995). Theory of mind development and social understanding. *Cognition and Emotion*, **9**, 151–65.

Baillargeon, R. (1987). Object permanence in 3.5- and 4.5-month old infants. *Developmental Psychology*, **23**, 655–64.

Baillargeon, R. and DeVos, J. (1991). Object permanence in young infants: further evidence. *Child Development*, **62**, 1227–46.

Baldwin, D. A. (1993). Infants' ability to consult the speaker for clues to word reference. *Journal of Child Language*, **20**, 395–418.

Baron-Cohen, S. (1988). Social and pragmatic deficits in autism: cognitive or affective? *Journal of Autism and Developmental Disorders*, **18**, 379–401.

Baron-Cohen, S. (1989). Are autistic children behaviorists? An examination of their mental–physical and appearance–reality distinctions. *Journal of Autism and Developmental Disorders*, **19**, 579–600.

Baron-Cohen, S. (1995). *Mindblindness*. MIT Press, Cambridge, MA.

Baron-Cohen, S., Leslie, A., and Frith, U. (1985). Does the autistic child have a 'theory of mind'? *Cognition*, **21**, 37–46.

Barresi, J. and Moore, C. (1996). Intentional relations and social understanding. *Behavioral and Brain Sciences*, **19**, 107–54.

Bauer, P. J. (1996). What do infants recall of their lives? Memory for specific events by one-to two-year-olds. *American Psychologist*, **51**, 29–41.

Bickerton, D. (1995). *Language and human behavior*. University of Washington Press, Seattle.

Bischof, N. (1985). *Das Rätzel Ödipus* [The Oedipus riddle]. Piper, Munich.

Bischof-Köhler, D. (1989). *Spiegelbild und Empathie* [Mirror image and empathy]. Hans Huber, Bern.

Bischof-Köhler, D. (in press). Zusammenhänge zwischen Kognitiver, motivationaler und emotionaler Entwicklung in der frühen Kindheit und im Vorschulalter [Relationships between cognitive, motivational and emotional development in early childhood and in preschoolers]. In *Lehrbuch Ebtwicklungs psychologie* (ed. H. Keller). Huber, Bern.

Boesch, C. (1992). New elements of a theory of mind in wild chimpanzees. *Behavioral and Brain Sciences*, **15**, 149–50.

Boesch, C. and Boesch, H. (1984). Mental map in wild chimpanzees: an analysis of hammer transports for nut cracking. *Primates*, **25**, 160–170.

Boucher, J. and Lewis, V. (1989). Memory impairments and communications in relatively able autistic children. *Journal of Child Psychology and Psychiatry*, **30**, 99–122.

Boucher, J. and Warrington, E. K. (1976). Memory deficits in early infantile autism: some similarities to the amnesic syndrome. *British Journal of Psychology*, **67**, 73–87.

Boyatzis, C. J. and Watson, M. W. (1993). Preschool children's symbolic representation of objects through gestures. *Child Development*, **64**, 729–35.

Boysen, S. T. and Berntson, G. G. (1995). Responses to quantity: perceptual versus cognitive mechanisms in chimpanzees (*Pan troglodytes*). *Journal of Experimental Psychology: Animal Behavior Processes*, **21**, 82–6.

Brown, D. E. (1991). *Human universals*. McGraw–Hill, New York.

Brownell, C. A. and Carriger, M. S. (1990). Changes in cooperation and self–other differentiation during the second year. *Child Development*, **61**, 1164–74.

Bullock, M. and Luetkenhaus, P. (1988). The development of volitional behavior in the toddler years. *Child Development*, **59**, 664–74.

Byrne, R. W. (1994). The evolution of intelligence. In *Behavior and evolution* (ed. P. J. B. Slater and T. R. Halliday), pp. 223–65. Cambridge University Press.

Byrne, R. W. and Whiten, A. (ed.) (1988). *Machiavellian intelligence*. Clarendon Press, Oxford.

Byrne, R. W. and Whiten, A. (1990). Tactical deception in primates: the 1990 database. *Primate Report*, **27**, 1–101.

Byrne, R. W. and Whiten, A. (1992). Cognitive evolution in primates. *Man*, **27**, 609–27.

Carruthers, P. and Smith, P. K. (1996). *Theories of theories of mind*. Cambridge University Press.

Chandler, M. and Hala, S. (1994). The role of personal involvement in the assessment of early false belief skills. In *Children's early understanding of mind* (ed. C. Lewis and P. Mitchell), pp. 403–25. Erlbaum, Hove.

Charman, T. and Baron-Cohen, S. (1992). Understanding drawings and beliefs: a further test of the metarepresentation theory of autism. *Journal of Child Psychology and Psychiatry*, **33**, 1105–12.

Charman, T. and Baron-Cohen, S. (1995). Understanding photos, models, and beliefs: a test of the modularity thesis of theory of mind. *Cognitive Development*, **10**, 287–98.

Cheney, D. L. and Seyfarth, R. M. (1990). *How monkeys see the world*. University of Chicago Press.

Clements, W. A. and Perner, J. (1997). When actions really speak louder than words—but only implicitly: young children's understanding of false belief in action. Unpublished manuscript.

Concar, D. (1996). Into the mind unborn. *New Scientist*, **152**, 40–5.

Corballis, M. C. (1991). *The lopsided ape*. Oxford University Press.

Corballis, M. C. (1992). On the evolution of language and generativity. *Cognition*, **44**, 197–226.

Daechler, M., Bukatko, D., Benson, K., and Myers, N. (1976). The effects of size and color cues on the delayed response of very young children. *Bulletin of the Psychonomic Society*, **7**, 65–8.

Dawson, G. and McKissick, F. C. (1984). Self-recognition in autistic children. *Journal of Autism and Developmental Disorders*, **14**, 383–94.

deBlois, S. T. and Novak, M. A. (1994). Object permanence in rhesus monkeys (Macaca mulatta). *Journal of Comparative Psychology*, **108**, 318–27.

Dennett, D. C. (1978). Beliefs about beliefs. *Behavioral and Brain Sciences*, **4**, 568–70.

Dennett, D. C. (1987). *The intentional stance*. MIT Press, Cambridge, MA.

Dennett, D. C. (1995). *Darwin's dangerous idea*. Simon & Schuster, New York.

de Waal, F. B. M. (1982). *Chimpanzee politics*. Jonathan Cape, London.

de Waal, F. B. M. (1989). *Peacemaking among primates*. Harvard University Press.

DeCasper, A. J. and Spence, M. J. (1986). Prenatal maternal speech influences newborns' perception of speech sounds. *Infant Behavior and Development*, **9**, 133–50.

Diamond, A. (1985). Development of the ability to use recall to guide action, as indicated by infants' performance on AB. *Child Development*, **56**, 868–83.

Döhl, F. (1970). Zielorientiertes Verhalten beim Schimpansen [Goal-directed behavior in chimpanzees]. *Naturwissenschaft und Medizin*, **34**, 43–57.

Donald, M. (1991). *Origins of the modern mind*. Harvard University Press.

Donald, M. (1993). Human cognitive evolution: what we were, what we are becoming. *Social Research*, **60**, 143–70.

Dretske, F. (1995). *Naturalizing the mind*. MIT Press, London.

Dunn, J. (1991). Young children's understanding of other people: evidence from observations within the family. In *Children's theories of mind* (ed. D. Frye and C. Moore), pp. 97–114. Lawrence Erlbaum, Hillsdale, NJ.

Dunn, L. M., Dunn, L., Whetton, C., and Pintillie, D. (1982). *British picture vocabulary scale*. Nfer–Nelson, London.

Ettlinger, G. and Wilson, W. A. (1990). Cross-modal performance: behavioral processes, phylogenetic considerations and neuronal mechanisms. *Behavioral Brain Research*, **40**, 169–92.

Feldman, C. F. (1988). Early forms of thought about thoughts: some simple linguistic correlates of mental state. In *Developing theories of mind* (ed. J. W. Astington, P. L. Harris, and D. R. Olson), pp. 126–137. Cambridge University Press.

Filion, C. M., Washburn, D. A., and Gulledge, J. P. (1996). Can monkeys (Macaca mulatta) represent invisible displacement? *Journal of Comparative Psychology*, **110**, 386–95.

Flavell, J. H. (1993). The development of children's understanding of false belief and the appearance–reality distinction. *International Journal of Psychology*, **28**, 595–604.

Flavell, J. H., Green, F. L., and Flavell, E. R. (1986). Development of knowledge about the appearance–reality distinction. *Monographs of the Society for Research in Child Development*, **51**, (1, Serial No. 212).

Flavell, J. H., Green, F. L., Wahl, K. E., and Flavell, E. R. (1987). The effects of question clarification and memory aids on young children's performance–reality tasks. *Cognitive Development*, **2**, 127–44.

Fletcher-Flinn, C. M. and Snelson, H. (1997). The relation between metaphonological abilities, metarepresentation and cognition. *New Zealand Journal of Psychology*, **26**, 20–8.

Fouts, R. S. and Fouts, D. H. (1993). Chimpanzees' use of sign language. In *The great ape project*, (ed. P. Cavalieri and P. Singer), pp. 28–41. Fourth Estate, London.

Frankfurt, H. G. (1988). *The importance of what we care about*. Cambridge University Press.

Freeman, N. H., Lacohee, H., and Coulton, S. (1995). Cued-recall approach to 3-year-olds' memory for an honest mistake. *Journal of Experimental Child Psychology*, **60**, 102–15.

Frye, D., Zelazo, P. D., and Palfai, T. (1995). Theory of mind and rule-based reasoning. *Cognitive Development*, **10**, 483–527.

Gagliardi, J. L., Kirkpatrick-Steger, K. K., Thomas, J., Allen, G. J., and Blumberg, M. S. (1995). Seeing and knowing: knowledge attribution versus stimulus control in adult humans (*homo sapiens*). *Journal of Comparative Psychology*, **109**, 107–14.

Gallup, G. G., Jr. (1970). Chimpanzees: self recognition. *Science*, **167**, 86–7.

Gardner R. and Gardner, B. (1969). Teaching sign language to a chimpanzee. *Science*, **165**, 664–72.

Gibson, E. J. (1995). Are we automata? In *The self in early infancy* (ed. P. Rochat), pp. 3–15. Elsevier, Amsterdam.

Goodall, J. (1986). *The chimpanzees of Gombe: patterns of behavior*. Harvard University Press.

Gopnik, A. (1993). How we know our own minds: the illusion of first-person knowledge of intentionality. *Behavioral and Brain Sciences*, **16**, 1–14.

Gopnik, A. and Astington, J. W. (1988). Children's understanding of representational change and its relation to the understanding of false belief and the appearance–reality distinction. *Child Development*, **59**, 26–37.

Gopnik, A. and Graf, P. (1988). Knowing how you know: young children's ability to identify and remember the source of their belief. *Child Development*, **59**, 1366–71.

Greenfield, P. M. and Savage-Rumbaugh, E. S. (1990). Grammatical combination in Pan paniscus: processes of learning and invention in the evolution and development of language. In *'Language' and intelligence in monkeys and apes* (ed. S. T. Parker and K. R. Gibson), pp. 540–78. Cambridge University Press.

Haake, R. J. and Somerville, S. C. (1985). Development of logical search skills in infancy. *Developmental Pschology*, **21**, 176–86.

Harris, P. L. (1991). The work of imagination. In *Natural theories of mind: evolution, development, and simulation of everyday mind-reading* (ed. A. Whiten), pp. 283–304. Basil Blackwell, Oxford.

Hayes, C. (1951). *The ape in our house*. Harper and Brothers, New York.

Heider, F. and Simmel, M. (1944). An experimental study of apparent behavior. *American Journal of Psychology*, **57**, 243–59.

Herman, L. M., Pack, A. A., and Morel-Samuels, P. (1993). Representational and conceptual skills of dolphins. In *Language and communication: comparative perspectives* (ed. H. L. Roitblat, L. M. Herman, and P. E. Nachtigall), pp. 403–42. Lawrence Erlbaum, Hillsdale, NJ.

Hewes, G. W. (1973). Primate communication and the gestural origin of language. *Current Anthropology*, **14**, 5–24.

Heyes, C. M. (1993). Anecdotes, training, trapping, and triangulation: do animals attribute mental states? *Animal Behaviour*, **46**, 177–88.

Heyes, C. M. (1998). Theory of mind in nonhuman primates. *Behavioral and Brain Sciences*, **21**, 101–48.

Howe, M. L. and Courage, M. L. (1993). On resolving the enigma of infantile amnesia. *Psychological Bulletin*, **113**, 305–26.

Howe, M. L. and Courage, M. L. (1997). The emergence and early development of autobiographical memory. *Psychological Review*, **104**, 499–523.

Hresko, W. P., Reid, D. K., and Hammill, D. D. (1981). *The Test of Early Language Development (TELD)*. Pro-Ed, Austin.

Hughes, C. and Russell, J. (1993). Autistic children's difficulty with mental disengagement from an object: its implications for theories of autism. *Developmental Psychology*, **3**, 498–510.

Hughes, C., Russell, J., and Robbins, T. W. (1994). Evidence for executive dysfunction in autism. *Neuropsychologia*, **32**, 477–92.

Humphrey, N. K. (1976). The social function of intellect. In *Growing points in ethology* (ed. P. P. G. Bateson and R. A. Hinde), pp. 303–17. Cambridge University Press.

Humphrey, N. K. (1986). *The inner eye*. Faber and Faber, London.

Humphrey, N. K. (1992). *A history of the mind*. Chatto and Windus, London.

Hyatt, C. W. and Hopkins, W. D. (1994). Self-awareness in bonobos and chimpanzees: a comparative perspective. In *Self-awareness in animals and humans* (ed. S. T. Parker, R. W. Mitchell, and M. L. Boccia), pp. 248–53. Cambridge University Press.

James, W. (1890). *Principles of psychology*, Vol. 1–2. Holt, New York.

Jarrold, C., Carruthers, P., Smith, P. K., and Boucher, J. (1994). Pretend play: is it metarepresentational? *Mind and Language*, **9**, 445–68.

Jarrold, C., Boucher, J., and Smith, P. K. (1996). Generativity deficits in pretend play in autism. *British Journal of Developmental Psychology*, **14**, 275–300.

Jenkins, J. M. and Astington, J. W. (1996). Cognitive factors and family structure associated with theory of mind development in young children. *Developmental Psychology*, **32**, 70–8.

Jolly, A. (1966). Lemur social behavior and primate intelligence. *Science*, **153**, 501–6.

Jolly, A. (1985). *The evolution of primate behavior*, (2nd edn). MacMillan, New York.

Kagan, J. (1981). *The second year*. Harvard University Press.

Köhler, W. (1927). *The mentality of apes* (trans. E. Winter). Routledge and Kegan Paul, London. (Original work published 1917).

Kummer, H., Anzensberger, G., and Hemelrijk, C. K. (1996). Hiding and perspective taking in long-tailed macaques (*Macaca fascicularis*). *Journal of Comparative Psychology*, **110**, 97–102.

Kundera, M. (1991). Immortality. Grone Weidenfeld, New York.

Lalonde, C. E. and Chandler, M .J. (1995). False belief understanding goes to school: on the social-emotional consequences of coming early or late to a first theory of mind. *Cognition and Emotion*, **9**, 167–85.

Leahy, T. H. (1994). Is this a dagger I see before me? Four theorists in search of consciousness. *Contemporary Psychology*, **39**, 575–81.

Leekam, S. R. and Perner, J. (1991). Does the autistic child have a metarepresentational deficit? *Cognition*, **40**, 203–18.

Leslie, A. (1987). Pretence and representation in infancy: the origin of 'theory of mind'. *Psychological Review*, **94**, 412–26.

Leslie, A. and Frith, U. (1988). Autistic children's understanding of seeing, knowing, and believing. *British Journal of Developmental Psychology*, **6**, 315–29.

Leslie, A. and Thaiss, L. (1992). Domain specificity in conceptual development: neuropsychological evidence from autism. *Cognition*, **43**, 225–51.

Lewis, M. and Brooks-Gunn, J. (1979). *Social cognition and the acquisition of self*. Plenum, New York.

Lewis, M., Sullivan, M. W., Stranger, C., and Weiss, M. (1989). Self development and self-conscious emotions. *Child Development*, **60**, 146–56.

Lewis, V. and Boucher, J. (1988). Spontaneous, instructed and elicited play in relatively able autistic children. *British Journal of Developmental Psychology*, **6**, 325–39.

Lillard, A. S. (1993). Pretend play skills and the child's theory of mind. *Child Development*, **64**, 348–71.

Lillard, A. S. (1998). Ethnopsychologies: cultural variations in theory of mind. *Psychological Bulletin*, **123**, 3–32.

Lorenz, K. (1973). *Die Rueckseite des Spiegels. Versuch einer Naturgeschichte menschlichen Erkennens* [Behind the mirror: A search for a natural history of human knowledge]. Piper, Munich.

Loveland, K. A. (1991). Social affordances and interaction: II autism and the affordances of the human environment. *Ecological Psychology*, **3**, 99–119.

Lyon, D. L. and Flavell, J. H. (1994). Young children's understanding of 'remember' and 'forget'. *Child Development*, **65**, 1357–71.

Marten, K. and Psarakos, S. (1994). Evidence of self-awareness in bottlenose dolphins (*Tursiops truncatus*). In *Self-awareness in animals and humans*, (ed. S. T. Parker, R. W. Mitchell, and M. L. Boccia), pp. 361–79. Cambridge University Press.

Marten, K. and Psarakos, S. (1995). Using self-view television to distinguish between self-examination and social behavior in the bottlenose dolphin (*Tursiops truncatus*). *Consciousness and Cognition*, **4**, 205–24.

Mayes, L. C., Klin, A., Tercyak, K. P., Cicchetti, D. V., and Cohn, D. J. (1996). Test–retest reliability for false-belief tasks. *Journal of Child Psychology and Psychiatry*, **37**, 313–19.

Meador, D. M., Rumbaugh, D. M., Pate, J. L., and Bard, K. A. (1987). Learning, problem solving, cognition, and intelligence. In *Comparative primate biology*, Vol. 2B (ed. J. Erwin), pp.17–83. Alan R. Liss, New York.

Meltzoff, A. N. (1995). Understanding the intentions of others: re-enactment of intended acts by 18-month-old children. *Developmental Psychology*, **31**, 838–50.

Meltzoff, A. N. and Gopnik, A. (1989). On linking nonverbal imitation, representation, and language learning in the first two years of life. In *The many faces of imitation in language learning* (ed. G. E. Speidel and K. E. Nelson), pp. 23–51. Springer, Berlin.

Menzel, E. W. (1974). A group of young chimpanzees in a one-acre field. In *Behavior of nonhuman primates*, Vol. 5, (ed. A. M. Schrier and F. Stollnitz), pp. 83–153. Academic Press, New York.

Menzel, E. W., Premack, D., and Woodruff, G. (1978). Map reading by chimpanzees. *Folia Primatologica*, **29**, 241–49.

Menzel, E. W., Savage-Rumbaugh, E. S., and Lawson, J. (1985). Chimpanzee (*Pan troglodytes*) problem solving with the use of mirrors and televised equivalents of mirrors. *Journal of Comparative Psychology*, **99**, 211–17.

Miles, L. (1990). The cognitive foundations for reference in a signing orang-utan. In *'Language' and intelligence in monkeys and apes* (ed. S. T. Parker and K. R. Gibson), pp. 511–39. Cambridge University Press.

Mischel, W., Shoda, Y., and Rodriguez, M. L. (1989). Delay of gratification in children. *Science*, **244**, 933–8.

Mitchell, P. (1997). *Introduction to theory of mind*. Arnold, London.

Moore, C. (1996). Theories of mind in infancy. *British Journal of Developmental Psychology*, **14**, 19–40.

Moore, C., Pure, K., and Furrow, D. (1990). Children's understanding of the modal expression of speaker certainty and uncertainty and its relation to the development of a representational theory of mind. *Child Development*, **61**, 722–30.

Moore, C., Jarrold, C., Russell, J., Lumb, A., Sapp, F., and MacCallum, F. (1995). Conflicting desires and the child's theory of mind. *Cognitive Development*, **10**, 467–82.

Moore, C., Barresi, J., and Thompson, C. (in press). The cognitive basis of future-oriented prosocial behavior. *Social Development*.

Natale, F. and Antinucci, F. (1989). Stage 6 object-concept and representation. In *Cognitive structure and development in nonhuman primates* (ed. F. Antinucci), pp. 97–112. Lawrence Erlbaum, Hillsdale, NJ.

Natale, F., Antinucci, F., Spinozzi, G., and Poti, P. (1986). Stage 6 object concept in non-human primate cognition: a comparison between gorilla (*Gorilla gorilla gorilla*) and Japanese macaque (*Macaca fuscata*). *Journal of Comparative Psychology*, **100**, 335–9.

Nelson, K. (1992). Emergence of autobiographical memory at age 4. *Human Development*, **35**, 172–7.

O'Connell, S. M. (1995). Empathy in chimpanzees: evidence for theory of mind? *Primates*, **36**, 397–410.

O'Neill, D. K. and Gopnik, A. (1991). Young children's ability to identify the sources of their beliefs. *Developmental Psychology*, **27**, 390–7.

O'Reilly, A. W. (1995). Using representations: Comprehension and production of actions with imagined objects. *Child Development*, **66**, 999–1010.

Olson, D. R. (1988). On the origin of beliefs and other intentional states in children. In *Developing theories of mind* (ed. J. W. Astington, P. L. Harris, and D. R. Olson), pp. 414–26. Cambridge University Press.

Olson, D. R. (1993). The development of representations: the origins of mental life. *Canadian Psychology*, **34**, 1–14.

Overton, W. F. and Jackson, J. P. (1973). The representation of imagined objects in action sequences: a developmental study. *Child Development*, **44**, 309–14.

Ozonoff, S., Pennington, B. F., and Rogers, S. (1991). Executive function deficits in high-functioning autistic children: relationship to theory of mind. *Journal of Child Psychology and Psychiatry*, **32**, 1081–105.

Parker, S. T. (1990). Origins of comparative developmental evolutionary studies of primate mental abilities. In *'Language' and intelligence in monkeys and apes* (ed. S. T. Parker and K. R. Gibson), pp. 3–64. Cambridge University Press.

Parker, S. T. and Gibson, K. R. (1979). A developmental model for the evolution of language and intelligence in early hominids. *Behavioral and Brain Sciences*, **2**, 367–408.

Parker, S. T. and Gibson, K. R. (1990). *'Language' and intelligence in monkeys and apes*. Cambridge University Press.

Parker, S. T., Mitchell, R. W., and Boccia, M. L. (eds.). (1994). *Self-awareness in animals and humans*. Cambridge University Press.

Parkin, L. (1994). *Normal and autistic children's theory of representation*. Unpublished doctoral thesis, University of Sussex.

Patterson, F. (1991). Self-awareness in the gorilla Koko. *Gorilla*, **14**, 2–5.

Patterson, F. and Linden, F. (1981). *The education of Koko*. Holt, Rinehart and Winston, New York.

Pepperberg, I. M. (1990). Conceptual abilities of nonprimate species, with an emphasis on an African grey parrot. In *'Language' and intelligence in monkeys and apes* (ed. S. T. Parker and K. R. Gibson), pp. 469–507. Cambridge University Press.

Pepperberg, I. M. (1993). Cognition and communication in an African grey parrot (*Psittacus erithacus*): studies on nonhuman, nonprimate, nonmammalian subject. In *Language and communication: comparative perspectives* (ed. H. L. Roitblat, L. M. Herman, and P. E. Nachtigall), pp. 221–48. Lawrence Erlbaum, Hillsdale, NJ.

Pepperberg, I. M. and Kozak, F. A. (1986). Object permanence in the African grey parrot *Psittacus erithacus*). *Animal Learning and Behavior*, **14**, 322–30.

Pepperberg, I. M., Garcia, S. E., Jackson, E. C., and Marconi, S. (1995). Mirror use by African grey parrots. *Journal of Comparative Psychology*, **109**, 182–95.

Perner, J. (1991). *Understanding the representational mind*. MIT Press, Cambridge, MA.

Perner, J. (1995). The many faces of belief: reflections on Fodor's and the child's theory of mind. *Cognition*, **57**, 241–69.

Perner, J. and Ruffman, T. (1995). Episodic memory and autogenetic consciousness: developmental evidence and a theory of childhood amnesia. *Journal of Experimental Child Psychology*, **59**, 516–48.

Perner, J., Frith, U., Leslie, A., and Leekam, S. (1989). Exploration of the autistic child's theory of mind. *Child Development*, **60**, 689–700.

Peskin, J. (1992). Ruse and representations: on children's ability to conceal information. *Developmental Psychology*, **28**, 84–9.

Peskin, J. (1996). Guise and guile: children's understanding of narratives in which the purpose of pretense is deception. *Child Development*, **67**, 1735–51.

Piaget, J. (1951). *Play, dreams and imitation in childhood*. Heinemann, Melbourne.

Piaget, J. (1952). *The origins of intelligence in children*. International University Press, New York.

Piaget, J. (1954). *The construction of reality in the child*. Basic Books, New York.

Pillemer, D. B., Picariello, M. L., and Pruett, J. C. (1994). Very long-term memories of a salient preschool event. *Applied Cognitive Psychology*, **8**, 95–106.

Plaut, D. C. and Karmiloff-Smith, A. (1993). Representational development and theory-of-mind computations. *Behavioral and Brain Sciences*, **16**, 70–1.

Povinelli, D. J. (1989). Failure to find self-recognition in Asian elephants (*Elephans maximus*) in contrast to their use of mirror cues to discover hidden food. *Journal of Comparative Psychology*, **103**, 122–31.

Povinelli, D. J. (1995). The unduplicated self. In *The self in early infancy* (ed. P. Rochat). North–Holland–Elsevier, Amsterdam.

Povinelli, D. J. and Cant, J. G. H. (1995). Arboreal clambering and the evolution of self-conception. *Quarterly Review of Biology*, **70**, 393–421.

Povinelli, D. J. and Eddy, T. J. (1996). What young chimpanzees know about seeing. *Monographs of the Society for Research in Child Development*, **61**, v–247.

Povinelli, D. J., Nelson, K. E., and Boysen, S. T. (1990). Inferences about guessing and knowing by chimpanzees (*Pan troglodytes*). *Journal of Comparative Psychology*, **104**, 203–10.

Povinelli, D. J., Nelson, K. E., and Boysen, S. T. (1992). Comprehension of social role reversal by chimpanzees: evidence for empathy? *Animal Behaviour*, **43**, 633–40.

Povinelli, D. J., Parks, K. A., and Novak, M. A. (1992). Role reversal by rhesus monkeys, but no evidence of empathy. *Animal Behaviour*, **44**, 269–81.

Povinelli, D. J., Landau, K. R., and Perilloux, H. K. (1996). Self-recognition in young children using delayed versus live feedback: evidence for a developmental asynchrony. *Child Development*, **67**, 1540–54.

Powell, S. D. and Jordan, R. R. (1993). Being subjective about autistic thinking and learning to learn. *Educational Psychology*, **13**, 359–70.

Pratt, C. and Bryant, P. (1990). Young children understand that looking leads to knowing (so long as they are looking into a single barrel). *Child Development*, **61**, 973–82.

Premack, D. (1988). 'Does the chimpanzee have a theory of mind?' revisited. In *Machiavellian intelligence* (ed. R. W. Byrne and A. Whiten), pp. 160–79. Clarendon Press, Oxford.

Premack, D. and Dasser, V. (1991). Perceptual origins and conceptual evidence for theory of mind in apes and children. In *Natural theories of mind: evolution, development and simulation of everyday mind-reading* (ed. A. Whiten), pp. 253–66. Basil Blackwell, Oxford.

Premack, D. and Premack, A. J. (1983). *The mind of an ape*. W. W. Norton, New York.

Premack, D. and Woodruff, G. (1978). Does the chimpanzee have a theory of mind? *Behavioral and Brain Sciences*, **4**, 515–26.

Prior, M. and Hoffman, W. (1990). Neuropsychological testing of autistic children through an exploration of frontal lobe tests. *Journal of Autism and developmental Disorders*, **20**, 581–90.

Prior, M., Dahlstrom, B., and Squires, T. L. (1990). Autistic children's knowledge of thinking and feeling states in other people. *Journal of Child Psychology and Psychiatry*, **51**, 587–601.

Pylyshyn, Z. W. (1978). When is attribution of beliefs justified? *Behavioral and Brain Sciences*, **1**, 592–3.

Robinson, E. J., Nye, R., and Thomas, G. V. (1994). Children's conceptions of the relationship between pictures and their referents. *Cognitive development*, **9**, 165–91.

Robinson, E. J., Riggs, K. J., and Samuel, J. (1996). Children's memory for drawings based on a false belief. *Developmental Psychology*, **32**, 1056–64.

Rovee-Collier, C. (1997). Dissociations in infant memory: rethinking the development of implicit and explicit memory. *Psychological Review*, **104**, 467–98.

Ruffman, T., Olson, D. R., Ash, T., and Keenan, T. (1993). The ABCs of deception: do young children understand deception in the same way as adults? *Developmental Psychology*, **29**, 74–87.

Rumbaugh, D. M., Savage-Rumbaugh, E. S., and Washburn, D. A. (1994). Learning, prediction, and control with an eye to the future. In *The development of future-oriented processes* (ed. M. M. Haith, J. B. Benson, R. J. Roberts, and B. Pennington), pp. 120–38. University of Chicago Press.

Russell, J., Jarrold, C., and Potel, D. (1994). Executive factors in preschoolers' strategic deception. *British Journal of Developmental Psychology*, **12**, 301–14.

Saltmarsh, R., Mitchell, P., and Robinson, E. (1995). Realism and children's early grasp of mental representation: belief-based judgements in the state change task. *Cognition*, **57**, 297–325.

Savage-Rumbaugh, E. S. and McDonald, K. (1988). Deception and social manipulation in symbol-using apes. In *Machiavellian Intelligence* (ed. R. W. Byrne and A. Whiten), pp. 224–37. Clarendon Press, Oxford.

Savage-Rumbaugh, E. S., Murphy, J., Sevick, R. A., Brakke, K .E., Williams, S. L., and Rumbaugh, D. M. (1993). Language comprehension in ape and child. *Monographs of the Society for Research in Child Development*, **58**, v–221.

Schusterman, R. J., Gisiner, R., Grimm, B. K., and Hanggi, E. B. (1993). Behavioral control by exclusion and attempts at establishing semanticity in marine mammals using match to sample paradigms. In *Language and communication: comparative perspectives* (ed. H. L. Roitblat, L. M. Herman, and P. E. Nachtigall), pp. 249–74. Lawrence Erlbaum, Hillsdale, NJ.

Scott, F. J., and Baron-Cohen, S. (1996). Imagining real and unreal things: evidence of a dissociation in autism. *Journal of Cognitive Neuroscience*, **8**, 371–82.

Semaw, S., Renne, P., Harris, J. W. K., Feibel, C. S., Bernor, R. L., Fesseha, N., et al. (1997). 2.5-million-year-old stone tools from Gona, Ethiopia. *Nature*, **385**, 333–336.

Siegal, M. (1995). Becoming mindful of food and conversation. *Current Directions in Psychological Science*, **4**, 177–81.

Sigman, M. and Ungerer, J. A. (1984). Cognitive and language skills in autistic, mentally retarded, and normal children. *Developmental Psychology*, **20**, 293–302.

Sigman, M., Arbelle, S., and Dissanayake, C. (1995). Current research findings on childhood autism. *Canadian Journal of Child Psychiatry*, **40**, 289–98.

Suarez, S. D. and Gallup, G. G., Jr. (1981). Self-recognition in chimpanzees and orangutans, but not gorillas. *Journal of Human Evolution*, **10**, 175–88.

Suddendorf, T. (1994). *Discovery of the fourth dimension: mental time travel and human evolution.* Master's thesis, University of Waikato, Hamilton, New Zealand. Internet: http://cogprints.soton.ac.uk

Suddendorf, T. (1997). *Children's understanding of the relation between delayed video representation and current reality: a test for self-awareness?* Unpublished manuscript, University of Auckland, New Zealand. Internet: http://cogprints.soton.ac.uk

Suddendorf, T. and Corballis, M. C. (1997). Mental time travel and the evolution of the human mind. *Genetic, Social, and General Psychology Monographs*, **123**, 133–67.

Suddendorf, T. and Fletcher-Flinn, C. M. (1996). Some correlates of the emerging theory of mind. *Australian Journal of Psychology*, **48**, (suppl.), 26–7.

Suddendorf, T. and Fletcher-Flinn, C. M. (1997). Theory of mind and the origins of divergent thinking. *Journal of Creative Behavior*, **31**, 59–69.

Suddendorf, T. and Fletcher-Flinn, C. M. (in press). Children's divergent thinking improves when they understand false beliefs. *Creativity Research Journal*, special issue.

Suddendorf, T., Fletcher-Flinn, C. M., and Johnston, L. (in press). *Pantomime and theory of mind. Journal of Genetic Psychology*.

Taylor, T., Esbensen, B. M., and Bennett, R. T. (1994). Children's understanding of knowledge acquisition: the tendency for children to report that they have always known what they have just learned. *Child Development*, **65**, 1581–604.

Thieme, H. (1997). Lower Palaeolithic hunting spears from Germany. *Nature*, **385**, 807–10.

Thomas, G. V., Nye, R., and Robinson, E. J. (1994). How children view pictures: children's responses to pictures as things in themselves and as representations of something else. *Cognitive Development*, **9**, 141–64.

Tomasello, M., Kruger, A. C., and Ratner, H. H. (1993). Cultural learning. *Behavioral and Brain Sciences*, **16**, 495–552.

Toth, N., Schick, K. D., Savage-Rumbaugh, S., Sevcik, R. A., and Rumbaugh, D. M. (1993). Pan the toolmaker: investigations into stone tool-making and tool-using capabilities of a bonobo (*Pan paniscus*). *Journal of Archeological Science*, **20**, 81–91.

Tulving, E. (1985). How many memory systems are there? *American Psychologist*, **40**, 385–398.

Vauclair, J. (1996). *Animal cognition*. Harvard University Press, London.

Visalberghi, E. and Limongelli, L. (1994). Lack of comprehension of cause–effect relationships in tool-using capuchin monkeys (*Cebus apella*). *Journal of Comparative Psychology*, **108**, 15–22.

Welch-Ross, M. K. (1995). An integrative model of the development of autobiographical memory. *Developmental Review*, **15**, 338–65.

Wellman, H. M. (1990). *The child's theory of mind*. MIT Press, Cambridge.

Wheeler, M. A., Stuss, D. T., and Tulving, E. (1997). Toward a theory of episodic memory: the frontal lobes and autonoetic consciousness. *Psychological Bulletin*, **121**, 331–54.

Whiten, A. (1996). Imitation, pretence and mindreading. In *Reaching into thought: the minds of the great apes* (ed. A. Russon, K. A. Bard and S. T. Parker), pp. 300–24. Cambridge University Press.

Whiten, A. and Byrne, R. W. (1988). Tactical deception in primates. *Behavioral and Brain Sciences*, **11**, 233–73.

Whiten, A. and Byrne, R. W. (1991). The emergence of metarepresentation in human ontogeny and primate phylogeny. In *Natural theories of mind: evolution, development, and simulation of everyday mind-reading* (ed. A. Whiten), pp. 267–81. Blackwell, Oxford.

Whiten, A. and Ham, R. (1992). On the nature and evolution of imitation in the animal kingdom: reappraisal of a century of research. In *Advances in the study of behavior*, Vol. 21, (ed. P. J. B. Slater, J. S. Rosenblatt, C. Beer, and M. Milinski). Academic Press, New York.

Wimmer, H. and Hartl, M. (1991). Against the Cartesian view of mind: young children's difficulty with own false beliefs. *British Journal of Developmental Psychology*, **9**, 125–38.

Wimmer, H. and Perner, J. (1983). Beliefs about beliefs: representation and constraining function of wrong beliefs in young children's understanding of deception. *Cognition*, **13**, 103–28.

Wimmer, H., Hogrefe, G. J., and Perner, J. (1988). Children's understanding of informational access as source of knowledge. *Child Development*, **59**, 386–96.

Wood, B. (1992). Origin and the evolution of the genus *Homo*. *Nature*, **355**, 783–90.

Woolley, J. D. and Bruell, M. J. (1996). Young children's awareness of the origins of their mental representations. *Developmental Psychology*, **32**, 335–46.

Wynn, T. and McGrew, W. C. (1989). An ape's view of the Oldowan. *Man*, **24**, 383–98.

Zahn-Waxler, C., Radke-Yarrow, M., and King, R. A. (1979). Child-rearing and children's prosocial imitations toward victims of distress. *Child Development*, **50**, 319–30.

Zaitchik, D. (1990). When representations conflict with reality: the preschooler's problem with false beliefs and 'false' photographs. *Cognition*, **35**, 41–68.

Zelazo, P. D., and Jacques, S. (1997). Children's rule use: representation, reflection and cognitive control. *Annals of Child Development*, **12**, 119–76.

Zelazo, P. D., Frye, D., and Rapus, T. (1996). An age-related dissociation between knowing rules and using them. *Cognitive Development*, **11**, 37–63.

The evolution of a theory of mind

Simon Baron-Cohen

Introduction

Homo sapiens is arguably the only species that possesses a developed 'theory of mind.' By this I mean the ability to attribute the full range of mental states (both goal states and epistemic states) to ourselves and to others, and to use such attributions to make sense of and predict behaviour. 'Theory of mind' is the phrase coined by Premack and Woodruff (1978), and there is a set of synonyms for this ability: mind-reading (Whiten 1991), mentalizing (Morton *et al.* 1991), folk psychology (Wellman 1990), and the intentional stance (Dennett 1987). In this chapter, I will use the term theory of mind, for convenience, whilst assuming that any of these alternative synonyms would be equally applicable.

There is considerable interest in tracing the evolution of a theory of mind, because of its central importance in modern human behaviour. Like language or bipedalism, a theory of mind can be taken as a major milestone in primate evolution. The importance of language and bipedalism is in some sense easier to see, or at least, the arguments are more familiar. Among other things, language enabled primates to manipulate the behaviour of conspecifics at a distance (a form of remote control), to obtain information about events that they had not directly witnessed, to inform others about events they had not directly witnessed, and to act cooperatively. Bipedalism enabled primates to use their forelimbs for activities other than just locomotion, such as carrying, throwing, and transforming objects. It also enabled foraging into new niches by reducing water loss. For at least these reasons, language and bipedalism have been justifiably the subject of considerable research. But why might a theory of mind be important? In what way might it have transformed primate evolution? Is it really justifiable to equate the importance of a theory of mind with that of language or bipedalism?

In this chapter I try to do two things. First, I want to persuade you that actually the evolution of a theory of mind is not only *as* important as these other developments, but it is in some respects *more* important. The main argument I will use here is that without a theory of mind, having the ability to speak or perceive speech would have been of little value. You can guess therefore that I will be arguing that a theory of mind must have *preceded* any ability to use language in the communicative way in which it is used today. Secondly, I want to question the claim by Mithen (1996) that a theory of mind evolved around six million years ago. This claim is made on the basis that existing species of ape have a full theory of mind, and our common ancestor with modern apes would have lived around that time. My reason for questioning this date is that recent experimental evidence throws doubt on the idea that modern apes have a full theory of mind. Instead, from available evidence, I will argue that all we can conclude is that a theory of mind proper was certainly evident 40 000 years ago, but before then there is no substantive evidence for its existence.

The importance of a theory of mind

To grasp the importance of a theory of mind, consider the following list of eight behaviours that depend on it: For each behaviour, I spell out the reason why each depends on a theory (or concept) of mind.

Intentionally communicating with others

We can define intentional communication as requiring a theory of mind, if we restrict it to those communicative acts that are produced in order to change the knowledge state of the listener. Thus, when a dog barks at a cat, this is not intentional communication because the dog is not intending to update the knowledge state of the cat. The effect of the bark might well be that the cat becomes aware (i.e. comes to know) that there is a dog nearby, but the dog's intention might have been far simpler: to make the cat run away. If there was an intention behind the bark, it was simply to change the cat's behaviour, without any necessary reference to changing the cat's knowledge state or mind.

In contrast, when I tell you that Liverpool won the football match, I am doing so in order to give you new information that I believe you do not have, and that you might be interested in or want. I am trying to change your knowledge state. Boring as it might be, this little utterance counts as intentional communication, and necessarily requires a theory of mind.

So, to intentionally inform others, one needs a concept that *others have minds* that can be informed or uninformed. Indeed, one needs a concept of information, which is itself intrinsically mentalistic—or at least this is true as long as one defines the goal of intentional informing as being to change the other animal's knowledge state. Two more examples should serve to clarify why this definition is needed. If a person shouts 'watch out!' to inform the listener of an impending danger, the intention is to change the other person's knowledge about the current state of the environment. Notice, though, that for this example to count, the utterance must be intended to change the listener's knowledge, not just their behaviour. Equally, if a person produces a bus timetable to inform another person about the times of future events, the intention is to change another person's knowledge about the future state of the environment.

Whereas intentionally informing others necessarily requires a theory of mind, unintentionally informing others does not. For example, if a trail of footprints in the sand was left unintentionally, the animal producing them was probably not thinking about how another animal's knowledge state might be changed by this information. Indeed, the animal producing the footprints was probably not thinking about the footprints as information at all. In contrast, if a trail of footprints in the sand was left intentionally, the animal producing the footprints was probably thinking about another animal's thoughts—for example, wanting to make it possible for the other animal to *know* how to find him or her, or wanting to make the other animal *believe* the footprints lead to where the prey is.

Repairing failed communication with others

Conversational repair is another good index of a speaker's theory of mind. If one animal is attempting to communicate with a listener, but is failing, the speaker can do one of two things: repeat the utterance in an identical fashion, or try to communicate the same message in a different way. The latter strategy is likely to indicate that the speaker believes the listener has not *understood* the intended message, and that the speaker is trying a different method to get the listener to understand.

Thus, if I say 'Have you seen it?' you are likely either to look at me quizzically, or ask me what on earth I'm talking about. If I simply repeat the utterance, you'll probably repeat your last response. If however I rephrase the utterance to 'Have you seen my wallet?', you'll probably answer usefully. My rephrasing of the utterance depended on me assuming that my first attempt at communication failed because it was ambiguous in some way, and that by using less ambiguous words, you (the listener) would then understand it—all very mentalistic.

Teaching others

Teaching others also necessarily requires a theory of mind. Again, this assumes we are restricting the definition of teaching to those behaviours produced by a more knowledgeable animal, with the intention of changing the knowledge state of a less knowledgeable listener. For example, a mother showing her juvenile daughter how to use a tool would count as an instance of teaching.[1]

Intentionally persuading others

Persuasion is an aspect of intentional communication, and as such it necessarily requires a theory of mind. But it is worth special mention here, because it is produced with the specific intention of changing someone else's belief about the value of something. I might try to persuade you to buy A rather than B, or to go down route x rather than route y, or to choose me rather than him. Admittedly all of these also are produced with the intention of changing your behaviour, but the means to doing this is by changing your beliefs about the value of the different options.

In contrast, if a deer grows a huge pair of antlers, this might make a doe choose him over the deer with the smaller antlers, but this does not count as an act of intentional persuasion, according to the above definition. The deer's body did not set

---

[1] Even teaching could at a simple level just involve attempting to change behaviour. This is true for all 8 behaviours listed here, any single instance of which *could* be purely behaviourally driven. One needs to check for the intention to change another's knowledge states (see Caro and Hauser 1992).

out to change the beliefs of the doe. Equally, a male gorilla beating his chest might have the effect of making another male gorilla turn and run away, but this again does not count as an act of intentional persuasion. It might be no more complex than the earlier example of the dog barking, causing the cat to run away. There is no evidence that the animal is considering the mental states of the audience.

Intentionally deceiving others

Intentional deception also requires a theory of mind. Indeed, we will define intentional deception as occurring when one animal attempts to place false information in the mind of another, or attempts to withhold true information from the mind of another. Thus, making a trail of footprints lead from locations A to B, and then swinging through the trees (thereby leaving no footprints) to hide in location C, would count as an instance of intentional deception. Rubbing out the trail of footprints from A to B would also count as intentional deception. In both cases, the first animal is attempting to influence the knowledge state of another animal.

In contrast, a stick insect, whose appearance saves it from being eaten by a predator, is not engaging in a deception that requires any theory of mind. Indeed, the stick insect might not be thinking about anything, let alone the mind of its predator. The same applies to an animal with camouflage. It is true that, by staying still, it might not be seen by its predator, but it was probably not aiming to make other animals *think* it was not there. It was not necessarily thinking about what other animals were thinking at all.

Building shared plans and goals

Sharing a plan or goal with another animal requires a 'meeting of minds.' Both animals must recognize the intention of the other animal, and subsequently work out how to mesh their actions with those of the other animal to achieve the shared goal. Take this example. A troop of chimpanzees are hunting a baby monkey, to eat it. The goal is to get the infant monkey away from its mother, scare off the adult monkeys, and kill the baby. They hunt as a team, and achieve the goal. This might not be evidence of building a shared plan in that each individual chimpanzee might simply be pursuing their own individual goals, which just happen to coincide. Thus, an infant monkey comes into sight, and adult male chimpanzees love the taste of baby monkeys, so all the adult male chimps in the troop recognize the reward and aim for it. The adult male chimps' goals all coincide because they all share the same taste or food preference. They mesh their actions with those of the other chimps, in the sense that as one chimp attempts to grab the infant monkey and gets beaten off, the next one jumps in and tries to do the same thing. Each chimp might even recognize the intentions of the others, representing for example that 'He is trying to get the infant monkey.' But this still falls short of being an example of building shared plans, in that a shared plan involves both animals recognizing that they are both holding the same goal.

In contrast, consider another example. Two chimps carry a log, then lean it up against a high wall. One holds it still whilst the other scrambles up it. When the climber reaches the top, he then turns and holds the log whilst the other chimp scrambles up it. This counts as a convincing example of building a shared plan in that the goal is not achievable without the help of the other animal, and both animals cannot help each other without realizing what both are aiming at. With this joint plan in mind, each can recognize why the other is taking the different role that they are (e.g. the holder of the log versus the climber up the log).

Intentionally sharing a focus or topic of attention

The same argument applies to the sharing of a focus of attention. Two animals can coincidentally look at the same target. This is not shared attention, if each animal is simply aware only of his or her own viewpoint. Shared attention is necessarily mentalistic in that both animals must be aware of the other animal being aware of looking at the same target as they are. Thus, I see you turn to look out of the window. If I then look out of the window, this is not necessarily shared attention. If I see you have looked back and have seen me looking out of the window, then this probably is. More convincing is when you point out the window, and keep pointing until I turn to look out the window. The chances are that if this is genuine shared attention, then I will acknowledge in some way that I have seen what you were trying to get me to see. I will turn back to look at you, and smile, or nod, etc.

Pretending

Last on this list is pretending. This is different from intentional deception in that the intention is not to mislead or plant a false belief in an audience, but simply to pretend. The intention is to temporarily treat one object as if it is another, or as if it had attributes that it clearly does not have. Pretending necessarily requires a theory of mind in that one has to be able to switch between thinking about one's *knowledge* of the real identity of the object, and its current *pretend* identity. Pretending only exists in the mind of the pretender. It is not an intrinsic part of the object.

The empirical contribution of studying autism

Let us take stock. We have surveyed eight behaviours which all usually require a theory of mind. The reason for this brief survey was to illustrate how important a theory of mind is. Without a theory of mind, none of these behaviours would be seen.

This is true by definition, if the analysis of the above eight behaviours is correct. But it is also true empirically: Children with autism are a natural test of this in that many of these children fail the standard test of understanding false beliefs, suggesting they have difficulties in the development of a theory of mind, and they fail to show the above behaviours in the normal way (see Baron-Cohen 1995 for a review of the evidence, which is:

(1) First-order mind-reading tests:
   (a) The *mental–physical* distinction (Wellman and Estes 1986; Baron-Cohen 1989a).

(b) The *functions of the mind* test (Wellman and Estes 1986; Baron-Cohen 1989a).

(c) The *appearance–reality distinction* (Flavell *et al.* 1986; Wellman and Estes 1986; Baron-Cohen 1989a).

(d) *First-order false belief* tasks (Wimmer and Perner 1983; Baron-Cohen *et al.* 1985, 1986; Perner *et al.* 1989; Reed and Peterson 1990; Leekam and Perner 1991; Swettenham *et al.* 1996).

(e) The *seeing leads to knowing* test (Leslie and Frith 1988; Pratt and Bryant 1990; Baron-Cohen and Goodhart 1994).

(f) *Recognizing mental state words* test (Baron-Cohen *et al.* 1994).

(g) Simple *causes of emotion* (such as situations and desire) versus complex causes of emotion (such as beliefs) (Harris *et al.* 1989; Baron-Cohen 1991; Baron-Cohen *et al.* 1993).

(h) *Recognizing the eye-region of the face* as indicating when a person is thinking and what a person might *want* (Baron-Cohen and Cross 1992; Baron-Cohen *et al.* 1995; Baron-Cohen, 1989b).

(i) The *accidental–intentional* distinction (Phillips 1993).

(j) *Deception*, premised on the understanding that people's beliefs can differ and can therefore be manipulated (Baron-Cohen 1992; Sodian and Frith 1992; Yirmiya *et al.* 1996).

(k) Tests of understanding *metaphor, sarcasm, and irony*—these all being *intentional, non-literal* statements (Happe 1993).

(l) *Pragmatics* (Baron-Cohen 1988b; see also Tager-Flusberg 1993), e.g. recognizing violations of pragmatic rules, such as the Gricean maxims of conversational cooperation (Surian *et al.* 1996). Since many pragmatic rules involve tailoring one's speech to what the listener needs to *know*, or might be *interested* in, this can be seen as intrinsically linked to a theory of mind.

(2) Second-order mind-reading tests:

(a) Second-order *false-belief* tests (Perner and Wimmer 1985; Baron-Cohen 1988b), that is, tests of understanding what one character thinks another character thinks. Such second-order reasoning is usually understood by children of 5–6 years of age (Sullivan *et al.* 1994).

(b) *Bluff and double-bluff* (Happe 1994).

(c) Decoding *complex mental states from the expression in the eye-region of the face* (Baron-Cohen *et al.* 1997a, b).

Indeed, autism is a clear illustration of what human life would be like if one lacked a theory of mind. The most devastating effect is on the ability to socialize, communicate, and use imagination. It is hard to think of aspects of our psychology that are more central or important than these. Certainly, I hope you agree, they are at least as important as language (syntax), or bipedalism.

Language without a theory of mind

Children with autism also show us how useless a language capacity is without a theory of mind. Strip out a theory of mind from language use and you have an individual who might have some syntax, the ability to build a vocabulary, and a semantic system.[2] Crucially, what would be missing from their language use and comprehension is 'pragmatics'—being able to decipher the speaker's communicative intentions, decipher non-literal language, read 'between the lines,' understand jokes, and tailor one's speech to fit the listener's background mental states (their knowledge, interest, expectations, etc.). This is the aspect of language that is missing from the language of most children with autism (Paul and Cohen 1985; Baron-Cohen 1988*a*, *b*; Tager-Flusberg 1992, 1993; Surian *et al.* 1996). The relationship between language and theory of mind is likely to be a very complex one, for several reasons. First, understanding that words refer presumes a concept of intention or goal. Second, mapping reference correctly, in language acquisition, is massively facilitated by joint attention (Baldwin 1991), itself an early form of mind-reading (Baron-Cohen 1995). These two points imply that normal 12- to 18-month-old language learners benefit from first having the mental-state concepts of intention and attention. Without these, the infant would be left with the puzzle of what people are doing while they are talking. Third, language serves as a virtual 'print-out' of a speaker's mind for the listener, giving the listener access to a description of the speaker's thoughts. Fourth, syntax can serve to disambiguate a speaker's intended meaning; that is, syntax can be used for the informing function (Cheney, personal communication). For example, shouting 'Leopard!' is quite ambiguous. Shouting 'Leopard in the tree above your head!' is not. Given this set of connections between language and theory of mind, it might be no surprise that children with autism, who are impaired in theory of mind, invariably show language delay.

When did a theory of mind evolve?

Let us turn to the question of most relevance to this book: the question of evolution. Here, things are necessarily speculative, as we attempt to peer into the mists of time, but there are two strategies available to us to answer this question. First, we can ask whether existing monkey and ape species have a full theory of mind. If so, we can assume that a theory of mind evolved as early as the common ancestor between us and the existing primate species. Second, we can ask what clues the palaeo-archaeological record gives us about the early hominids, and try to infer their behaviour and hence their cognitive abilities from fossil records, and from their tool use, cave paintings, ornamentation, etc.

The six-million-years hypothesis

The first strategy, that of looking at extant species of monkeys and apes, has led field observers to conclude that monkeys show little if any evidence of a theory of mind, but that modern apes do. That is, they show signs of deception in their natural behaviour, and this is one hallmark of a theory of mind (Byrne and Whiten 1991;

[2] Language without a theory of mind is not of course entirely useless. It allows literal communication, acquisition of information from others, requesting, ordering, etc.

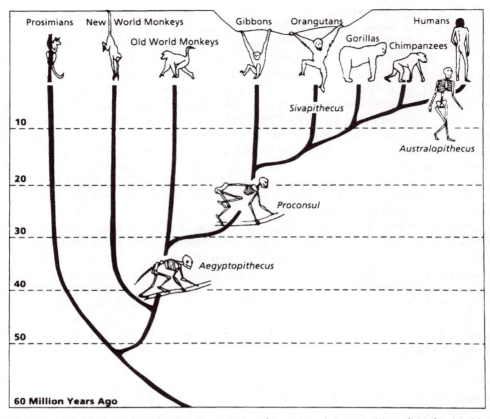

Fig. 13.1. Simplified model of primate evolution (reproduced from Mithen (1997) with kind permission).

Byrne this volume). This leads Byrne and Whiten to conclude that the common ancestor of modern humans and apes, had at least elements of a theory of mind. This is not so very old in evolutionary terms—for example, the common ancestor of modern humans and monkeys lived around 35 million years ago (see Fig. 13.1)—but it is still very old compared with the alternative hypothesis, reviewed next.

There is reason to doubt the six-million-years hypothesis. Experimental tests of a theory of mind in modern apes have found it hard to obtain convincing evidence of the ability to attribute beliefs to others. Even Premack, who was one of the first to ask the question of whether chimpanzees could attribute false beliefs (Premack and Woodruff 1978), finally concluded that they could not when their chimpanzees failed a better test of that ability (Premack 1988). In fact Povinelli and Eddy (1996) have found it hard to obtain evidence that chimpanzees even understand gaze as an indicator of the mental state of attention, in the way human children do.

There is a second reason to doubt the six-million-years hypothesis. If modern apes (chimpanzees, orang-utans, and gorillas) have a theory of mind, why don't we see signs of the eight behaviours listed above in their natural behaviour? Cheney and Seyfarth

(1990) put forward some interesting data suggesting that monkeys might have 'words,' but they conclude that monkeys only use these 'words' to change the behaviour of the listener, and not the listener's mental state. Equally, to take the last item on the earlier list, why don't we see evidence of pretend play in monkeys or apes—a behaviour which in human children emerges very early, around 18 months of age (Leslie 1987)?

Palaeo-archaeological evidence: The 40 000 years hypothesis

We can then turn to the alternative strategy for dating the evolution of a theory of mind, namely, that of addressing the palaeo-archaeological record. This tells us that *tool use* was evident from some two to three million years ago (see Corballis, this volume), and became more sophisticated over time. By itself, this is not sufficient evidence that these hominid ancestors had a theory of mind.

Around 30 000 years ago one sees the earliest examples of *cave paintings*, but again this is not evidence that the artists had a theory of mind. Some people might be drawn to conclude that any animal capable of art must have a theory of mind, but many children with autism, who fail tests of a theory of mind, and who show none of the eight behaviours listed earlier, are able and even gifted artists (Selfe 1977; Charman and Baron-Cohen 1992, 1993). Art clearly requires an ability to represent representations, but not necessarily an ability to represent mental states like beliefs. (For more on this distinction, see Leekam and Perner 1991; Leslie and Thaiss 1992; Charman and Baron-Cohen 1995).

The first fiction

Mithen (1996) has performed an invaluable service to cognitive neuroscience in reviewing some much more relevant evidence from palaeo-archaeology. Around the same time, 30 000 years ago, we see the first evidence of special forms of art: statues of *impossible entities*, such as the half-man-half lion ivory statuette from Hohlenstein-Stadel, southern Germany, dated around 30–33 000 years ago (see Fig. 13.2), and the painting of the half-man-half-reindeer, from Trois-Freres, Ariege, in France (see Fig. 13.3).

These are of interest because they are representations of *fictions*. They are necessarily representations of the artist's mind, of the artist thinking about his or her own thoughts. They are also, incidentally, direct evidence of the capacity for pretend play. Animals that are half-man-half-lion have never existed, except in the world of the imagination, of pretence (I am happy to be corrected on this point). So, we can say with some confidence that a full theory of mind must be at least as old as 30- to 40 000 years.[3]

Supporting evidence: adornment

There is further evidence that *H. sapiens* had a theory of mind by then. The

---

[3] Peter Carruthers (pers. comm.) argues that pretence and fiction may not necessarily require a theory of mind—merely the capacity to reason suppositionally. This is logically correct, but psychologically pretence may well involve representing the mental attitude of *pretending*.

Fig. 13.2. Statuette from Hohlenstein-Stadel, 30–33 000 years old (reproduced from Mithen (1996) with kind permission).

archaeological record shows the existence of burial at this time, which implies that our ancestors then were concerned about death. By itself, this does not tell us that they could think about the mind. But Mithen points out that burials around 28 000 years ago also include the dead person being *adorned with jewellery*. For example, at Sungir, in Russia, a 60-year-old man was buried with an adolescent male and female. All three individuals were decorated with thousands of ivory beads, necklaces, and bracelets (see Fig. 13.4).

Now why would someone adorn themselves, or adorn their dead relative? This behaviour can be taken as evidence that the decorator cared about how other people perceived the adorned person—they wanted an audience to *think* the person was beautiful, or of high status, or worthy of an after-life, or whatever. If this is not an excessively rich interpretation of jewellery-use, then it is an additional strand of evidence that around 30- to 40 000 years ago, our ancestors had a theory of mind.

Is early religion relevant?

If the archaeological evidence from these burials also indicates the existence of

Fig. 13.3. Painting from Trois-Freres, 30 000 years old (reproduced from Mithen (1996) with kind permission).

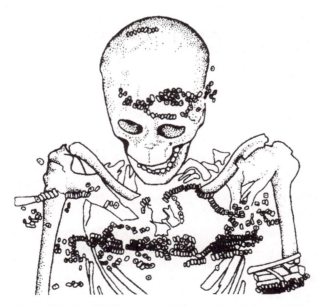

Fig. 13.4. Skeleton from Sringir, 30 000 years old (reproduced from Mithen (1996) with kind permission).

religion, then this might also be supportive evidence of the existence of a theory of mind 40 000 years ago. This is because anthropological evidence (Boyer 1990) suggests that the common feature of all current religions is that a supernatural agency—a god, a spirit—is postulated who can *communicate* with you, possibly judge (i.e. *think about*) you, and who can be appeased by ritual acts. The idea of a supernatural agency of this kind would be impossible without a theory of mind. Indeed, the idea that ritual actions might cause good outcomes or ward off bad ones is itself a belief in intentional causation rather than purely physical causation.

But let us leave religion out of it, since adorned skeletons in graves are not clear evidence of religion. Rather, let us stick to our two strong clues—art of a purely fictional kind (Figs 13.2 and 13.3) and adornment (Fig. 13.4). Here we can jump back to ask about these behaviours in autism, since children with autism who lack a theory of mind should also not produce art of a purely fictional kind, or bother with adornment. What does the evidence show?

Back to autism

Consistent with this idea, children with autism do draw, but tend to draw objects they have seen (buildings, cars, electricity pylons, train-stations, etc.). When challenged to draw purely fictional entities, like a 'man that could never exist,' normal 4-year-old children oblige by producing sketches of men with two heads or three arms or some such (Karmiloff-Smith 1990), whereas children with autism have difficulty doing so (Scott and Baron-Cohen 1996). Those children with autism who are more able, and who can pass first-order theory of mind tests, can draw such fictional entities (Craig *et al*. submitted). This is empirical evidence that the kind of art we think of as involving pretend play is a good indicator of whether the artist has a theory of mind. There is no systematic evidence about adornment in autism, but it is widely noted that children with autism pay little attention to how they appear to others, for example, showing little if any signs of embarrassment (Baron-Cohen *et al*. 1993) or interest in fashion (Baron-Cohen 1993).

Conclusions

Mithen (1996) clearly supports the six-million-years hypothesis:

A specialized domain of social intelligence first appeared in the course of human evolution after 55 million years ago. This gradually increased in complexity with the addition of further mental modules, such as that for a theory of mind between 35 and six million years ago (p. 94).

He bases this conclusion on the evident 'social intelligence' of monkeys and apes today. However, there is a danger of confounding social intelligence with theory of mind. It is clear that many monkey species and the apes show social intelligence in that they form alliances, keep track of social status, and behave tactically in grooming those allies they depend on (de Waal 1989; Whiten 1991). Whilst this is fascinating, and might be evidence of social intelligence evolving independently of general intelligence, it is not necessarily evidence of the possession of a theory of mind. For

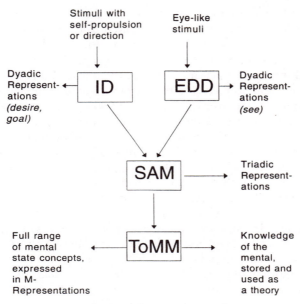

Stimuli with
self-propulsion
or direction

Eye-like
stimuli

Dyadic
Represent-
ations
*(desire,
goal)*

ID

EDD

Dyadic
Represent-
ations
(see)

SAM

Triadic
Represent-
ations

Full range
of mental
state concepts,
expressed
in M-
Representations

ToMM

Knowledge
of the
mental,
stored and
used as
a theory

Fig. 13.5. The mind-reading system (*from* Baron-Cohen 1995).

the latter, it would be more convincing if there were signs of one or more of the eight behaviours listed earlier. For that reason, in this chapter I remain more cautious, concluding simply that a theory of mind had in all likelihood evolved by 40 000 years ago, but that before this time there is as yet no clear evidence for it.

Mithen's conclusions are also based on his claim that "both monkeys and apes also engage in intentional communication" (p. 161). Here again one sees a potential confound. Clearly, monkeys and apes vocalize or gesture intentionally, but this is not the same as 'intending to communicate', as defined in the first section above. Monkeys and apes might be vocalizing or gesturing with the intention to alter the behaviour of the listener or audience, but there is no compelling evidence yet that they are vocalizing or gesturing with the intention to alter the mental states of their listener or audience (Cheney and Seyfarth 1990).

Using a model of the mind-reading system shown in Fig. 13.5, there is better evidence for the ability to attribute goal states (involving ID, or the Intentionality Detector) being as old as Mithen suggests, in that chimpanzees can clearly recognize *goal* states (Premack and Woodruff 1978). They are also acutely aware of gaze direction (EDD, or the Eye Direction Detector), suggesting they are monitoring when they might be the target of another's perception (Chance 1967). Less clear cut is whether they show shared attention (SAM, or the Shared Attention Mechanism) (Povinelli and Eddy 1996). This means that elements of mind-reading might be as old as 6–35 million years, and evolution might have 'tinkered with old parts' under selection pressure, to produce a theory of mind mechanism (ToMM) more recently.

Finally, we might consider that the presence of a Broca's area in the brain 200 000 years ago (as inferred from cranial evidence—Mithen 1996, and see Corballis, this volume) implies a theory of mind might be at least this old, in that language without a theory of mind would be functionally very limited. But this is only indirect evidence for the existence of a theory of mind. A more powerful logical argument is that 'theory of mind' must have been present in *H. sapiens* 100—150000 years ago, or at least before the dispersion from Africa. Otherwise, one would have to assume parallel evolution of theory of mind (see also Byrne, this volume; Suddendorf, this volume).[4]

A theory of mind is a powerful means of making sense of the social world. It enables explanations and prediction of the behaviour of agents, and communication (beyond animal signalling). Given its centrality to what makes the human mind essentially human, its evolution needs investigation. Palaeo-archaeological evidence shows that it was in place at least 40000 years ago, and comparative data from studies of existing primates shows that aspects of a theory of mind might be as old as six million years. Specifically, recognizing *volitional* states and a sensitivity to *eye-direction* might be a skill we share with the apes, and therefore with our common ancestor six million years ago. In contrast, *shared attention* and recognizing *epistemic* states might be unique to *H. sapiens* and may therefore have evolved more recently. In terms of the model of the 'mind-reading system' shown in Fig. 13.5, ID and EDD might be phylogenetically older (at least six million years) than the more recent SAM and ToMM. This leads to the idea that a theory of mind did not necessarily evolve all at once, but by degrees.

Acknowledgements

The author was supported by the Medical Research Council, the Wellcome Trust, and the Gatsby Foundation, during the period of this work. I am grateful to Steve Mithen, Peter Carruthers, Michael Corballis, and Andy Whiten for their comments on the first draft of this chapter.

References

Baldwin, D. (1991). Infants' contribution to the achievement of joint reference. *Child Development*, **62**, 875–90.

Baron-Cohen, S. (1988*a*). Without a theory of mind one cannot participate in a conversation. *Cognition*, **29**, 83–4.

Baron-Cohen, S. (1988*b*). Social and pragmatic deficits in autism: cognitive or affective? *Journal of Autism and Developmental Disorders*, **18**, 379–402.

Baron-Cohen, S. (1989*a*). The autistic child's theory of mind: a case of specific developmental delay. *Journal of Child Psychology and Psychiatry*, **30**, 285–98.

Baron-Cohen, S. (1989*b*). Perceptual role taking and protodeclarative pointing in autism. *British Journal of Developmental Psychology*, **7**, 113–27.

Baron-Cohen, S. (1991). Do people with autism understand what causes emotion? *Child Development*, **62**, 385–95.

Baron-Cohen, S. (1992). Out of sight or out of mind: another look at deception in autism. *Journal of Child Psychology and Psychiatry*, **33**, 1141–55.

---

[4] To clarify, I am arguing that there is quite persuasive evidence for a full theory of mind 30–40000 years ago, and some evidence for it as far back as 150000 years ago. Beyond this, we await better clues.

Baron-Cohen, S. (1993). Are children with autism acultural? Commentary on Tomasello *et al.* *Behavioral and Brain Sciences*, **16**, 512–3.

Baron-Cohen, S. (1995). *Mindblindness: an essay on autism and theory of mind*. MIT Press/Bradford Books.

Baron-Cohen, S. and Cross, P. (1992). Reading the eyes: evidence for the role of perception in the development of a theory of mind. *Mind and Language*, **6**, 173–86.

Baron-Cohen, S. and Goodhart, F. (1994). The 'seeing leads to knowing' deficit in autism: the Pratt and Bryant probe. *British Journal of Developmental Psychology*, **12**, 397–402.

Baron-Cohen, S., Leslie, A. M., and Frith, U. (1985). Does the autistic child have a 'theory of mind'? *Cognition*, **21**, 37–46.

Baron-Cohen, S., Leslie, A. M., and Frith, U. (1986). Mechanical, behavioural and intentional understanding of picture stories in autistic children. *British Journal of Developmental Psychology*, **4**, 113–25.

Baron-Cohen, S., Spitz, A., and Cross, P. (1993). Can children with autism recognize surprise? *Cognition and Emotion*, **7**, 507–16.

Baron-Cohen, S., Ring, H., Moriarty, J., Shmitz, P., Costa, D., and Ell, P. (1994). Recognition of mental state terms: a clinical study of autism, and a functional neuroimaging study of normal adults. *British Journal of Psychiatry*, **165**, 640–9.

Baron-Cohen, S., Campbell, R., Karmiloff Smith, A., Grant, J., and Walker, J. (1995). Are children with autism blind to the mentalistic significance of the eyes? *British Journal of Developmental Psychology*, **13**, 379–98.

Baron-Cohen, S., Jolliffe, T., Mortimore, C., and Robertson, M. (1997a). An even more advanced test of the theory of mind: evidence from very high functioning adults with autism or Asperger Syndrome. *Journal of Child Psychology and Psychiatry*, **38**, 813–22.

Baron-Cohen, S., Wheelwright, S., and Joliffe, T. (1997b). Is there a 'language of the eyes'? Evidence from normal adults and adults with autism/Asperger's Syndrome. *Visual Cognition*, **4**, 311–31.

Boyer, P. (1990). *Tradition as truth and communication: cognitive description of traditional discourse*. Cambridge University Press, New York.

Byrne, R. and Whiten, A. (1991). Computation and mindreading in primate tactical deception. In *Natural theories of mind*, (ed. A. Whiten), pp. 127–41. Blackwell, Oxford.

Caro, T. M. and Hauser, M. D. (1992). Is there teaching in nonhuman animals? *Quarterly Review of Biology*, **67**, 151–74.

Chance, M. (1967). The interpretation of some agonistic postures: the role of 'cut-off' acts and postures. *Symposium of the Zoological Society of London*, **8**, 71–89.

Charman, T. and Baron-Cohen, S. (1992). Understanding beliefs and drawings: a further test of the metarepresentation theory of autism. *Journal of Child Psychology and Psychiatry*, **33**, 1105–12.

Charman, T. and Baron-Cohen, S. (1993). Drawing development in autism: the intellectual to visual realism shift. *British Journal of Developmental Psychology*, **11**, 171–85.

Charman, T. and Baron-Cohen, S. (1995). Understanding models, photos, and beliefs: a test of the modularity thesis of metarepresentation. *Cognitive Development*, **10**, 287–98.

Cheney, D. and Seyfarth, R. (1990). *How monkeys see the world*. University of Chicago Press.

Craig, J., Baron-Cohen, S., and Scott, F. (submitted). An investigation of genuine creativity in autism.

De Waal, F. B. M. (1989). *Peace-making among primates*. Harvard University Press.

Dennett, D. (1987). *The intentional stance*. MIT Press/Bradford Books.

Flavell, J. H., Green, E. R., and Flavell, E. R. (1986). Development of knowledge about the appearance–reality distinction. *Monographs of the Society for Research in Child Development*, **51**.

Happé, F. (1993). Communicative competence and theory of mind in autism: a test of relevance theory. *Cognition*, **48**, 101–19.

Happé, F. (1994). An advanced test of theory of mind: understanding of story characters' thoughts and feelings by able autistic, mentally handicapped, and normal children and adults. *Journal of Autism and Developmental Disorders*, **24**, 129–54.

Harris, P., Johnson, C. N., Hutton, D., Andrews, G., and Cooke, T. (1989). Young children's theory of mind and emotion. *Cognition and Emotion*, **3**, 379–400.

Karmiloff-Smith, A. (1990). Constraints on representational change: evidence from children's drawings. *Cognition*, **34**, 57–83.

Leekam, S. and Perner, J. (1991). Does the autistic child have a metarepresentational deficit? *Cognition*, **40**, 203–18.

Leslie, A. M. (1987). Pretence and representation: the origins of a 'theory of mind.' *Psychological Review*, **94**, 412–26.

Leslie, A. M. and Frith, U. (1988). Autistic children's understanding of seeing, knowing, and believing. *British Journal of Developmental Psychology*, **6**, 315–24.

Leslie, A. M. and Thaiss, L. (1992). Domain specificity in conceptual development: evidence from autism. *Cognition*, **43**, 225–51.

Mithen, S. (1996). *The prehistory of the mind*. Penguin, London.

Morton, J., Frith, U., and Leslie, A. (1991). The cognitive basis of a biological disorder: autism. *Trends in Neuroscience*, **14**, 434–8.

Paul, R. and Cohen, D. J. (1985). Comprehension of indirect requests in adults with autistic disorders and mental retardation. *Journal of Speech and Hearing Research*, **28**, 475–9.

Perner, J. and Wimmer, H. (1985). 'John thinks that Mary thinks that …': attribution of second-order beliefs by 5–10 year old children. *Journal of Experimental Child Psychology*, **39**, 431–71.

Perner, J., Frith, U., Leslie, A. M., and Leekam, S. (1989). Exploration of the autistic child's theory of mind: knowledge, belief, and communication. *Child Development*, **60**, 689–700.

Phillips, W. (1993). *Understanding intentions and desire by children with autism*. University of London Press.

Povinelli, D. and Eddy, T. (1996). Chimpanzees: joint visual attention. *Psychological Science*, **7**, 129–35.

Pratt, C. and Bryant, P. (1990). Young children understand that looking leads to knowing (so long as they are looking into a single barrel). *Child Development*, **61**, 973–83.

Premack, D. (1988). 'Does the chimpanzee have a theory of mind?' revisited. In *Machiavellian intelligence: Social expertise and the evolution of intellect in monkeys, apes, and humans* (ed. R. W. Byrne and A. Whiten), pp. 160–79. Clarendon Press, Oxford.

Premack, D. and Woodruff, G. (1978). Does the chimpanzee have a 'theory of mind'? *Behavioral and Brain Sciences*, **4**, 515–26.

Reed, T. and Peterson, C. (1990). A comparative study of autistic subjects' performance at two levels of visual and cognitive perspective taking. *Journal of Autism and Developmental Disorders*, **20**, 555–68.

Scott, F. and Baron-Cohen, S. (1996). Imagining real and unreal objects: an investigation of imagination in autism. *Journal of Cognitive Neuroscience*, **8**, 400–11.

Selfe, L. (1977). Nadia: a case of extraordinary drawing ability in an autistic child. Academic Press, London.

Sodian, B. and Frith, U. (1992). Deception and sabotage in autistic, retarded, and normal children. *Journal of Child Psychology and Psychiatry*, **33**, 591–606.

Sullivan, K., Zaitchik, D., and Tager-Flusberg, H. (1994). Preschoolers can attribute second-order beliefs. *Developmental Psychology*, **30**, 395–402.

Surian, L., Baron-Cohen, S., and Van der Lely, H. (1996). Are children with autism deaf to Gricean maxims? *Cognitive Neuropsychiatry*, **1**, 78–88.

Swettenham, J., Baron-Cohen, S., Gomez, J.-C., and Walsh, S. (1996). What's inside a person's head? Conceiving of the mind as a camera helps children with autism develop an alternative theory of mind. *Cognitive Neuropsychiatry*, **1**, 73–88.

Tager-Flusberg, H. (1992). Autistic children's talk about psychological states: deficits in the early acquisition of a theory of mind. *Child Development*, **63**, 161–72.

Tager-Flusberg, H. (1993). What language reveals about the understanding of minds in children with autism. In *Understanding other minds: perspectives from autism*, (ed. S. Baron-Cohen, H. Tager-Flusberg, and D. J. Cohen), Oxford University Press.

Wellman, H. (1990). *Children's theories of mind*. Bradford/MIT Press.

Wellman, H. and Estes, D. (1986). Early understanding of mental entities: a re-examination of childhood realism. *Child Development*, **57**, 910–23.

Whiten, A. (1991). *Natural theories of mind*. Blackwell, Oxford.

Wimmer, H. and Perner, J. (1983). Beliefs about beliefs: representation and constraining function of wrong beliefs in young children's understanding of deception. *Cognition*, **13**, 103–28.

Yirmiya, N., Solomonica, D., and Shulman, C. (1996). The ability to manipulate behaviour and to understand manipulation of beliefs: a comparison of individuals with autism, mental retardation, and normal development. *Developmental Psychology*, **32**, 62–69.

14

Beliefs about purpose: on the origins of teleological thought

Deborah Kelemen

'We humans have purpose on the brain... Show us almost any object or process, and it is hard for us to resist the 'Why' question—the 'What is it for?' question' (Dawkins 1995, p. 95).

Introduction

For many decades, cognitive developmentalists generally assumed that children are fundamentally different kinds of thinkers from adults. It was believed that young children's reasoning, unlike that of adults, is concrete, pre-causal, and uniform across all domains of content. Thus, it was assumed that children reason no differently about the behaviour of people than they do about the properties of physical objects such as bricks. However, through the application of a set of general inferential mechanisms, it was argued that cognition becomes globally re-organized. Children pass through a series of hierarchically-ordered developmental stages and finally reach an adult state in which reasoning about different kinds of phenomena is differentiated into a variety of abstract causal–explanatory structures or 'domain-specific theories'.

Increasingly, this account of knowledge acquisition has come to be regarded as untenable by many contemporary researchers. The criticism is that, in real developmental time, children are so bombarded by input that they could never induce the kinds of causal theories adults possess, on the basis of unconstrained inferential mechanisms (see Carey 1988, 1991; Keil 1989; S. Gelman and Kremer 1991). An alternative theory has consequently emerged which argues for a greater continuity between children's and adults' thought. It suggests that, like adults, children's thinking is constrained by 'domain-specific' ways of viewing the world (see Hirschfeld and Gelman 1994). These modes of construal or 'stances' (Keil 1992; see Dennett 1987 for the origin of the term) embody adaptive causal notions that predispose children to interpret environmental regularities in certain ways, limiting the hypotheses they entertain and aiding the development of richer explanatory theories.

By adopting this perspective, many developmental researchers have found themselves in step with a body of evolutionary theorists who, in viewing the mind as a product of natural selection, have also rejected the domain–generalist position. Paralleling the developmentalist claim, evolutionists argue that the mind could not have been designed as a general-purpose processor because our hunter–gatherer ancestors could never have induced solutions to the adaptive problems they faced in time to secure their survival. The mind must therefore have developed with special-ized inferential devices adapted to deal with specific tasks and aspects of the environment (Cosmides and Tooby 1994; Pinker 1994; Hauser 1997).

This shared view of the mind has also led cognitive and evolutionary scientists to converge on a common research enterprise—identifying the modes of construal young children possess with an eye towards pinpointing the domain-specific theories that the human mind seems built to acquire. Note, however, the proposal is not that ontogenetic sequences in contemporary children reveal the way skills were progres-sively accumulated across successive generations of our ancestors. Rather the sugges-tion is that as human development is, in part, the unfolding of an adaptive, genetic blueprint, so children's early competences can provide unique insights into the mind's species-typical structure and constrain speculations on the ecological conditions that might have led to that structure. So far, developmental psychologists have uncovered several modes of construal—for example, from about 3 months of age infants adopt a 'physical stance' and can reason about physical causality and the properties of material objects—an understanding that underlies the later emergence of a naive theory of physics (e.g. Spelke 1990; Leslie 1994). Between 9 and 12 months, children are also able to adopt an 'intentional stance' (see Dennett 1987 for alternative use of this term), interpreting others as rational agents who act on the basis of goals and other internal states. This knowledge underlies the development of a more elaborate mind-reading 'naive psychology' or 'theory of mind' between ages 2 and 4 (e.g. Bartsch and Wellman 1989; Premack 1990; Leslie 1994; Gopnik and Meltzoff 1997). Finally, by the time they are in pre-school, children have also been found to adopt an 'essentialist stance' and show a bias to view natural objects as possessing core properties that determine their appearance, identity, and category membership. This tendency has been variously argued to underlie the later development of a naive theory of biology (e.g. Springer and Keil 1989; Atran 1994), a naive theory of race (Hirschfeld 1994), and a naive theory of personality (S. Gelman *et al.* 1994).

Recently a further candidate for early knowledge has been suggested. In addition to these other modes of construal, children might also possess a 'teleological stance', or a tendency to view objects as 'designed for a purpose' (Keil 1992; Atran 1994; Kelemen 1996, submitted; see also Dennett 1987). One reason for making this proposal is that this kind of reasoning is common in adults. On an everyday basis it helps constrain their reasoning about why something exists, what its future behaviour might be, why it has the properties that it does, and what role it plays in the larger scheme of things. As a consequence, when seeing a strange feature on an animal or an unfamiliar machine for the first time, the question an adult will usually ask is 'what's that for?—an assumption of purpose that, in addition to constraining naive reasoning, has also contributed a great deal to the development of academic fields such as palaeontology, archaeology, evolutionary psychology, and biology (Mayr 1982).

But what is the nature of the teleological stance and why are people driven to think about the purpose of objects? In this chapter I examine these questions and speculate on some possible answers. In the first part, I lay out some general assumptions and argue that adopting the teleological construal is not just something people find useful to do, but is something that we are *compelled* to do because of the way our minds are designed. In support of this I briefly overview some of the evidence demonstrating the pervasiveness of teleological ideas through human history and across cultures. In the second part of the paper, I examine various developmental theories about the origins of the teleological stance, beginning with the traditional explanation—Piaget's domain–generalist ideas about 'childhood artificialism'— and then turning to consider three more recent 'domain-specific' hypotheses. One theory by Frank Keil (1992, 1994a, b, 1995) suggests that the teleological stance is a basic aspect of cognition that is triggered by 'functional things' such as artefacts and biological parts and is the source of an innate sensitivity to biology. The second theory by Scott Atran (1994, 1995a) argues that the stance evolved as part of a specialized mental module for classifying and reasoning about biological kinds. Finally, my own hypothesis, 'Promiscuous Teleology' (Kelemen 1995, 1996, 1997, submitted), argues that the teleological construal of objects develops as part of children's understanding of goal-directed behaviour in intentional agents. As a result, humans are prone to systematic biases in their reasoning about the natural world and, before the elaboration of formal scientific ideas, children might have an overzealous tendency to view entities of all kinds as 'designed for a purpose'.

Teleology as a fundamental aspect of adult cognition

One of the best indicators that people are compelled to reason in teleological terms is provided by the ubiquitous phenomenon of religion. Adults' propensity to view objects and events as purposefully caused by intentional agents or gods is so prevalent that some have gone so far as to equate it to our susceptibility to disease (Dawkins 1993). Certainly, it seems likely that by the time hominids had the capacity to organize socially for hunting purposes and manufacture sophisticated tools, they had begun to engage in religious activities directed at forces thought to influence nature. Although archaeological evidence from earlier periods is equivocal, burial artefacts suggest that religious culture by the time of the Neanderthals was quite advanced. Our primate ancestors not only seem to have believed in life after death—burying individuals with diverse tools, flowers and jewellery—but might also have revered particular animals as possessing supernatural powers (Parrinder 1983; Wynn 1989; Shreeve 1995).

In contemporary times, the conceptualization of gods and supernatural causality varies greatly from culture to culture—some religions are monotheistic, others polytheistic, some deist, and others theist. For some cultures, supernatural agency influences humanity through its immanence in material objects, while in others it has no material or earthly form. But for all the profound differences between religions and their associated mythologies, a common moral tends to underlie most: objects and events have an intended purpose. Everything has a function to perform within a contrived natural order of which humanity is a significant part.

Teleological ideas such as these have of course extended far beyond the realms of religion. Throughout the history of Western philosophy, explanations of physical phenomena that make reference to notions of divine and other purposing forces have been central in science (see, for example, Aristotle's *Physics* (1930) for the influential teleological notion of 'final cause'). Probably because of its great intuitive appeal, one kind of teleological rationale that has been particularly prevalent is the Argument from Design. This can be traced at least to Cicero, who persuasively argued that the intricacy, order, and purpose in the universe could not possibly has arisen by chance —just as a clock or globe is obviously intentionally designed, so the world is clearly the handiwork of gods. Over the centuries, scholars such as Augustine, Aquinas, Boyle, Newton, and Malebranche echoed these sentiments with the nineteenth-century naturalist William Paley (1856) providing one of the most eloquent versions of the argument:

The works of nature want only to be contemplated... at one end we see an intelligent Power arranging planetary systems... and, at the other,... providing an appropriate mechanism, for the clasping... of the filaments of the feather of the humming bird. We have proof... One Being has been concerned in all (pp. 294–295).

Sir Isaac Newton himself, the father of mechanistic scientific explanation, was a vehement proponent of the Design Argument and argued that his accounts of the laws underlying natural events simply indicated that God was skilled in mathematics. As a result, Newton became a central figure in a seventeenth-century philosophical debate that ensured that science remained tied to the practice of religion well into the nineteenth century (Hurlbutt 1985; Shapin 1995).

Nowadays of course, the teleological explanations that characterize religions are regarded as a counterpoint to the mechanistic explanations that characterize most sciences. The great catalyst for this schism—the publication in 1859 of Darwin's *Origin of Species*—was a turning point for both science and theology. To date, natural selection is still the most plausible way of explaining the apparent design of biological entities without reference to a creator. Darwin's achievement was in describing how, without foresight or purpose, the brute mechanical forces of nature could generate the kinds of adaptive complexity found in the natural world. However, it is perhaps the clearest indicator of the depth of our teleological intuitions that even those individuals who subscribe to evolutionary rather than religious explanations still seem compelled to distort the theory into a teleological form. In general, natural selection is misconceived of as a goal-directed process akin to intentional design in which nature shapes organisms to function adaptively in their environment (see also Dennett 1983)—thus, hearts exist to pump blood because nature made them that way for the good of the species, and eyes were made for seeing so that animals could move around in the world. Add to this a general scientific tendency to over-generate functional–adaptationist explanations for cultural or physical phenomena and the teleological stance has all the appearances of a mode of reasoning run amok (see Pinker and Bloom 1990 on adaptationist explanations for why humans have two breasts; see also Gould and Lewontin 1979).

In sum, teleological intuitions are a central feature of adult thought. Consistently across societies and throughout history, people have expressed belief in a similar idea —that objects and events occur for a purpose. Contemporary teleological ideas, as expressed through sciences such as ecological theory, continue to impact palpably on our lives because they dictate the environmental policies that influence the current and future development of our species. But even aside from scientific and religious beliefs, it takes only a cursory reflection upon everyday 'naive' reasoning to see how fundamental teleological thought is. If encountering a person making small chirping noises at a bush, one's first assumption would be that they were doing it on purpose and wonder why. Similarly, when seeing a large and unfamiliar metal object standing in an enclosure, one's first reaction is to look at it and wonder what it is there for. Given that adults seem bound to engage in this kind of thought, several questions emerge—how does teleological thought originate and what light can developmental-ists shed on the issue?

The development of the teleological bias

Piaget (1929) was the first developmental psychologist to suggest that a bias to reason in teleological terms is inherent from childhood. On the basis of interviews in which children claimed, for example, that clouds exist to make rain and result from the steam off kettles, he argued that young children are 'artificialists' who believe that all things are caused by human activity. Piaget proposed that this belief occurs because children instinctively construe nature as goal-directed and consequently succumb to an 'animistic' tendency to attribute life to inanimate objects. This leads to artificialism because, drawing on their own experience, children assume that things only act in goal-directed ways because human agents such as parents tell them to. Children therefore conclude that people purposefully cause natural objects and events.

More generally, Piaget believed that misconceptions such as artificialism are the unavoidable result of undifferentiated and unsophisticated thinking. These false ideas arose, he argued, because before acquiring a particular stage of biological maturity, children cannot conceive of events occurring through pure mechanical causality. They therefore use knowledge of their own intentions as a basis for reasoning about all domains—a tendency that results in an inability to draw a true conceptual distinction between natural kinds and artefacts or even entertain that events can happen by chance. Similarly, Piaget argued, adults of non-technological cultures engage in animism and artificialism because their more 'primitive' evolutionary state engenders more cognitively 'primitive' conceptions.

Current developmental research indicates that Piaget substantially underestimated children's early abilities. As mentioned earlier, work on the intentional and physical stances demonstrates that, from infancy, children distinguish between mechanical and intentional cause. Other studies suggest that by pre-school, children do in fact draw conceptual distinctions between animate and inanimate objects in terms of these objects' capacity to experience feel, think, and eat (R. Gelman *et al.* 1983; Keil 1989) and on the basis of their underlying 'essential' properties (Wellman and Gelman 1992). Research also indicates that children's artificialism is not as extensive as Piaget suggested. Four-year-olds know that people make artefacts but not living things (S. Gelman 1988; Keil 1989; S. Gelman and Kremer 1991), although they often identify God as the cause of non-living natural objects (S. Gelman and Kremer 1991; see also Petrovich 1993).

Nevertheless, although Piaget might have underrated young children's capacities, two of his observations ring true. First, he proposed that young children are biased to believe that all events or environmental regularities have a cause and that they find it hard to think in terms of chance outcomes. In support of this, when young children are shown objects that behave randomly such as spinners, they tend to insist that they can predict where the pointer will land (Piaget and Inhelder 1975). Furthermore, infants show surprise when witnessing events with no obvious cause (Baillargeon 1993), and pre-schoolers will try to dismantle an apparatus that seems to produce events that violate physical causal laws (Chandler and Lalonde 1994; see also Brown 1990). S. Gelman *et al.* (1994) have proposed that this 'causal determinism' allows children to insert 'mental place-holders' as they develop explanations for events that are currently inexplicable. Later on, I will argue that people have difficulty resisting this tendency into adulthood, thus providing a consistent motivation for developing teleological explanations.

Second, Piaget also suggested that in the absence of certain kinds of knowledge, children over-rely on intentional thinking. Research by Carey (1985) and others (S. Gelman and Kremer 1991; Evans 1994; Evans *et al.* 1995) suggests that even with an understanding of physical causality, children do indeed compensate with intentional explanations when lacking knowledge about both biological and non-biological objects. Similarly, the predominance of religious kinds of explanations in earlier points in Western history suggests that this a default for adults as well— another point that I will be returning to later. In the next section, I am going to describe two more recent hypotheses as to the origins of the teleological stance.

Teleology and naive biology

Keil's autonomous teleological stance

A more recent account of teleological thinking is provided by Frank Keil (1992, 1994*a*, *b*, 1995). Keil suggests that the tendency to view objects as designed for purposes is probably innate. Indeed, he argues that the teleological stance is one of a handful of basic modes of construal that form the core of early cognition and which, in combination with each other, provide children with their earliest explanatory mechanisms. Principally, he proposes that the teleological stance is pre-school children's first truly biological mode of explanation and in combination with the essentialist stance, provides them with the developmentally invariant foundation of a rudimentary biological theory. This hypothesis stands in sharp contrast to arguments by Carey and others (Carey 1985; Solomon 1995) that children do not construct a biology that is autonomous from their naive psychology until the elementary school years.

Specifically, Keil's characterization of the teleological stance involves several claims. First, he argues that the teleological stance is, from the outset, an autonomous mode of construal. It does not derive from any other more basic biases or theories such as a physical stance or intentional stance. Instead, it is a primary building-block of cognition that is possibly elaborated from an instinctive sensitivity to functionality and first stimulated by children's perception of the functional parts of animate entities.

Second, Keil suggests that children and adults selectively apply the teleological stance. For, although it is not innately linked to any particular kinds of entity, the teleological stance is nevertheless triggered more by some real-world objects than others. Keil (1995) describes this class of objects as the set of 'functional things' which are, in effect, biological properties and artefacts. People directly perceive the relevance of functional thinking for artefacts and their parts because these objects are obviously designed to serve purposes for external agents. The functional construal is also compelling with respect to biological parts such as legs and arms because they exist to perform functions for the organisms possessing them. But Keil suggests that the tendency to adopt the teleological stance largely stops there. People do not find it appropriate to reason teleologically about non-living natural entities and their parts such as clouds or mountain peaks, because such entities do not seem designed for any obvious purpose. For similar reasons, the non-functional nature of most whole biological organisms (e.g. tigers and bears) also makes them bad candidates for teleological construal. In short, Keil states that although a child might spontaneously ask 'What's that for?' about a pointy part on an insect they would never ask the same question about a pointy part on a rock (or a whole rock or a whole tiger).

Keil and his collaborators have conducted several studies to explore the discriminating nature of children's teleological stance and its relationship to biological understanding. In one study, kindergarten and second-grade children were asked to consider why biological kinds such as plants or non-living natural kinds such as emeralds were green, and to indicate whether they preferred a physical explanation ('they are green because tiny parts mix together to give them a green color') or a teleological explanation ('they are green because it helps there be more of them'). The study found that second graders preferred functional explanations for plants and physical explanations for emeralds. While kindergartners had no significant preferences, this finding is interpreted as consistent with the idea that, from early on, teleological intuitions demarcate biological kinds from other natural kind domains (Keil 1992). A further study (Keil 1995) has shown that when children are presented with parallel parts in artefacts and living things (for example, barbs on barbed wire and thorns on a rose), even three-year-olds can identify that the biological part is self-serving ('good for itself') and the artefact part is other-serving ('good for others'). Additional research has focused on the way teleology applies to biological processes such as inheritance. Springer and Keil (1989) found that when asked to make inheritance judgements, pre-schoolers were more likely to judge an abnormal trait (e.g. stretched out eyes) as heritable if had 'biological' functional consequences for the offspring (e.g. helped it see its enemies) than if it did not. They also placed more weight on this information than on the more relevant issue of whether the defect was congenital or not. This finding has been taken as support for the idea that 'biological' functional beliefs underlie children's reasoning about inheritance.

Keil's theory has changed the face of the debate over children's biological knowledge. It also raises a number of interesting questions. By Keil's view, the teleological stance is, along with the physical and intentional stances, a basic aspect of human cognition—one that plays a central role in elucidating the biological domain. However, from an evolutionary perspective one feature of his account is puzzling. While Keil presents the relevance of teleology to biological reasoning as a primary motivation for positing the teleological stance's existence, he eschews the suggestion that there is any a priori link to living things. Instead, he argues that while it interacts with the essentialist stance, the teleological stance itself is free-standing and unspecialized to any local object domain. It is therefore not clear by this account what particular selection pressures led to the evolution of the teleological stance, or how it became linked with the essentialist stance to demarcate biology, since the suggestion is that the two stances have distinct origins (see Atran 1995*b* for full discussion). In this respect, Keil's theory falls prey to evolutionary plausibility problems in ways that a related account by Scott Atran does not.

Atran and the 'Living Thing' module

Atran's central thesis is that something like a teleological stance evolved as part of a mental module for reasoning about living things (Atran 1994, 1995, 1995*a*). Specifically he argues that children innately possess a 'teleo-essentialist' stance which leads them to automatically interpret the overt physical morphology that is characteristic of distinct biological species as resulting from an underlying essence. Although children initially have no explicit understanding of why biological kinds develop the functional parts that they use to distinguish them, their hard-wired teleological and essentialist intuitions are gradually elaborated. Over the course of development, children develop a more theoretical understanding of how non-obvious inherited properties cause superficial biological parts to grow and function as they do. As Atran (1995*a*) sees it:

Virtually all people, in all cultures cannot help but follow through this innately driven 'research program' which compels them to deepen and extend the domain of information relevant to living kinds into an all-embracing taxonomy (p. 220).

Thus, Atran argues that human's sensitivity to functionality and essence universally leads them to create similar systems for categorizing living things. His support for this hypothesis is based on two kinds of evidence—pre-school children's demonstrations of 'essentialism' and cross-cultural observations of the way disparate peoples categorize the biological world. With respect to the first kind of evidence, from early in development children treat natural kinds as having inviolable properties that determine their identity. Thus, they know that a porcupine is not transformed into a cactus by superficially changing its appearance because its underlying cactus 'essence'—the stuff that makes it what it is—remains unchanged (Keil 1989; S. Gelman *et al.* 1994). In relation to the second kind of evidence, Atran's own field-work suggests that Midwestern Americans and the Itza Maya of Guatemala divide up the living world in comparable ways. Both cultures make a primary division between plants and animals and then subdivide animals at various levels starting with major categories such as fish, birds, and mammals and concluding with primary taxa such as bear, wolf, deer. Classification at this last level, in particular, is thought to be guided by teleo-essentialist intuitions about the relationship between physical morphology and inherent essence.

According to Atran, then, teleological intuitions about function are a specific adaptation for categorizing the biological world and share a common origin with the essentialist stance. He proposes that the selection pressures leading to the evolution of the teleo-essentialist stance were those relating to the immediate necessity of categorizing toxic and non-toxic foods and identifying predators. Furthermore, he suggests that although people also have functional intuitions about artefacts, these might only occur through the process of drawing analogies to biological structures—the argument is that the obvious evolutionary advantage of spontaneously categorizing living species far outweighs any advantage from categorizing artefacts, and because children also demonstrate 'ontogenetic precocity' in biologically-based essentialist reasoning, there is substantial motivation for positing a teleo-essentalist 'living thing' module.

It should be noted, however, that the strength of Atran's evidence for cross-cultural equivalence in biological taxonomy is controversial (Carey 1995), and that, in addition, the hypothesis of a teleological component to the 'living thing' module could be discarded, without substantially damaging the theory. Nevertheless, one particular aspect of Atran and Keil's proposals seems certain—like adults, young children's reasoning about living things is, at least by kindergarten, influenced by intuitions about function. Our own studies (Kelemen *et al.* 1997a, b) have found that when kindergarten children are asked whether a behavioural property of one animal is likely to be true of another animal, they make inferences based on the presence of relevant functional structures rather than on the basis of either overall similarity or even shared category membership. Hence, kindergartners judge that an otter spends time in water because it has webbed feet like a water-living booby bird even though it looks like a land-living weasel. We have found similar intuitions guiding children's induction strategies in other tasks as well. However, these demonstrations of children's propensity to think about animal properties in teleological terms do not provide substantial support for the hypothesis that such intuitions result—as both Atran and Keil's theories suggest they should—from truly 'biological' notions about animals as 'living–growing–reproducing' organisms. Even the reasoning of ten-year-old American children in biological induction tasks often provides no obvious indication of a 'biological' basis to their answers (Kelemen *et al.* 1997b; see also Carey 1995). This suggests another possibility regarding the origins of children teleological responses: Rather than viewing animals as *biologically*-adapted organisms, young children may construe them in a slightly different way—as quasi-artefacts that have been purpose-fully constructed in some way. This possibility is explored in the next section.

Teleology and the intentional stance

The theory of an intention-based 'Promiscuous Teleology'

Two notions are central in teleological reasoning: goal and purpose. Although these concepts can be applied in many contexts, when adults talk about creatures possessing goals and purposes—"his goal was to build a house", "she hit him on purpose"—paradigmatically they are talking about intentional goal-directed behaviour mediated by mental states. Promiscuous Teleology argues that it is not accidental that phrases which are loaded with intentional meaning, such as 'design', 'made for', or 'purpose', are used when describing the functions of biological and non-biological entities. The relationship arises because, as social animals, humans are very good at thinking in intentional terms and because teleological thinking is an outgrowth of that expertise.

In short, Promiscuous Teleology (PT) makes two claims: First, it argues that the tendency to view objects as designed for purposes develops as part of our ability to view intentional agents as having purposes. Thus, it develops as part of the intentional stance and might never become autonomous from the intentional domain. Second, PT suggests that, because of the way our minds are designed, intention-based teleological explanations come easily to us. One consequence of this is that we might over-zealously apply teleological reasoning to inappropriate domains unless we have learned not to. Before acquiring alternative explanations then, children (and scientifically naive adults) might, by default, construe almost any sort of living and non-living entity —clocks, rivers, bears, and their parts—as intentionally caused for a purpose. In Western children this promiscuous teleological belief might only become appropriately restricted to artefacts and biological traits when they acquire formal scientific ideas both indirectly, through hearing the way adults talk about different kinds of phenomena, and directly, through schooling.

Turning to the first part of the claim, one reason for arguing that teleological thinking originates as part of the intentional domain is that there is a close association between intentional and teleological reasoning in adults. Artefacts provide the clearest instance of this because ideas about artefact function are bound to notions of intentional purpose. My refrigerator exists to keep things cool because it was created with the intent that it perform that function. Even if it works in such a way as to melt my dinner rather than chill it, it isn't *for* melting that is just something it *does*. The true function of my refrigerator is to chill things and when it does not, I will probably think it is broken and in need of repair (for discussion, see Wright 1973; Millikan 1989; Neander 1991; Bloom 1996; Kelemen 1996).

Interesting relationships between teleology and intentionality also exist in adults' conceptions of biological function. For some people, the connection is exactly the same as it is with artefact functions—ears are for hearing and eyes are for seeing because God made them that way. For other people—those well-versed in evolutionary biology—the teleological mode of construal has become almost entirely independent of the intentional stance and teleological phrases such as 'design' and 'purpose' are used in a purely metaphorical sense. However, the majority of Western adults probably fall somewhere between the creationist and the evolutionary biologist. Although they consider evolution to be the causal force underlying biological function, they understand it as a goal-directed process analogous to intentional design (see Brumby 1985). They know that natural selection does not *literally* have intentional states but for a non-biologist, understanding nature as a force that designs creatures to function in response to their needs makes intuitive sense. Such a belief obviates conceptually difficult ideas such as randomness and instead treats evolution just like an intentional agent with 'foresight', 'goals', 'purpose' and 'a design'—an agent who even 'knows about' and 'responds' to a species requirements.

Of course, intention-based teleological intuitions have not always been limited to biological traits and artefacts. Before mechanistic theories such as Newtonian physics and Darwinism became widespread, non-living natural objects were also considered in these terms (Paley 1856; Glacken 1967; Corey 1993; Livingstone 1993). The earth, its land-forms, water sources, climates, and elements were seen as intentionally designed to create a habitat for people, and to meet their needs. Thus, all varieties of natural objects were open to construal as quasi-artefacts, particularly if they played a significant role in people's lives or inspired awe through beauty or complexity of structure. This is not to imply that distinctions were not drawn between natural objects such as lakes and human-made objects such as houses; it is only to suggest that beliefs about purpose might not have been the basis of that distinction.

In relatively recent times, however, teleology has encountered tough competition as an explanatory mechanism. Aided by technology, people now have a greater understanding of the physical mechanisms that cause entities to form and behave as they do. Natural phenomena such as mountain ranges and meteor storms can now be explained by reference to natural processes alone—without invoking purpose. However, while suggesting that science has done much to ameliorate over-zealous intention-based teleological reasoning, some qualifications are in order. For all the scientific sophistication we acquire, people are built in a particular way—intentional explanations are a powerful way of making sense of the world and consequently an intention-based teleology remains a part of most of us throughout development. It does not take much for it to reassert itself into domains where it should not be applied when explanations seem inadequate or difficult to grasp. For example, it is revealing that a widespread response to first reports of the AIDS epidemic in both the US and Europe was that the disease was an intentionally contrived global punishment —such ideas are easy for people to latch onto. It would appear that even the most advanced scientific education can have a thin veneer.

This brings me back to the issue of the development of the teleological bias. Although imperfect, a useful analogy can be drawn between the cultural theory shifts that have occurred in the wake of historic scientific advances and those that occur in children as they acquire sophisticated scientific ideas over development (see Gopnik and Meltzoff 1997). At the outset, children's teleological ideas are embedded in a theory of intention and they might come to be applied quite broadly: In making sense of the world, and in the absence of other explanations, biological kinds, artefacts, and non-biological natural kinds may be construed, in some sense, as artefacts existing for a purpose.

Why would children overextend intentional explanations in this way? Why not overextend physical explanations, given that children have an understanding of physical causality also? Comparative and developmental research suggests that, to a degree as yet unmatched by other primates (Cheney and Seyfarth 1990; Tomasello and Call 1997), evolution has endowed humans with a propensity for intention-based reasoning. Naive physical reasoning is also central but because mechanical causes are constrained by time and space there are limitations on the range of phenomena they can explain. You can use the physical stance to manoeuvre around places and dodge arrows but because it is largely restricted to the 'here and now', it does not have the predictive power to tell you whether the animal by the trees is planning to jump on you (because it thinks that you have not noticed it) or be your friend (because it thinks you have). In contrast, the capacity to explain complex events and behaviour on the basis of non-physical causes such as goals and desires, liberates individuals from proximate causal explanations so that they can hypothesize about all kinds of possible *future* outcomes. It is therefore a potent and compelling way of making predictions about the world such that you continue to survive in it—a point sadly emphasized by people whose 'theory of mind' development has been impaired by autism (Leslie and Thaiss 1992; Tager-Flusberg 1994; Baron-Cohen 1995).

In essence, intention-based teleological notions are adaptive and work well for us. People rely heavily on them, and if as a consequence of that they sometimes apply them inappropriately, then that is a small price to pay for the net gain of having them available. There is nothing actively maladaptive to believing that 'clouds exist to rain' and 'bears exist to attack people' (see Humphrey 1979; Jolly 1983 for related arguments). Indeed, while these ideas might be mistaken, such intuitions help to bring order to our world by answering the 'why' questions for which we so frequently have no plausible answers.

Given then that the intentional stance provides a powerful and necessary way of reasoning, the intention-based teleological assumption that intentional agents act to achieve future goals is one of the first aspects of that capacity to emerge developmentally. Between 6 and 9 months babies construe animate objects as intentional goal-directed agents (Leslie 1994; see also Premack 1990) and by 12 months infants use this mode of construal to predict a novel object's future behaviour (Gergely *et al.* 1995). Shortly thereafter, babies show a growing awareness that intentional agents act upon objects and use them for purposes (Abravenel and Gingold 1985; see Leslie 1994) and begin to categorize objects according to functional properties (Madole and Cohen 1995; Madole *et al.* 1993). In other words, from early on, children's sensitivity to agents' object-centred activity might lead them to view objects of all kinds in functional terms because, from the infant's perspective, entities exist in their environment to be used for specific purposes. This early understanding of intentional causality might then become generalized as it interacts with the general 'determinist' bias or 'drive to explain' described earlier (Bullock *et al.* 1982; Brown 1989, 1990; S. Gelman *et al.* 1994; see also Gopnik and Meltzoff 1997). In search of explanations for their experience, and with a bias to think in intentional terms, children may draw on their knowledge of agency and object use to conclude that all kinds of entities are intentionally caused, by some kind of agent, for a purpose.

Further research is needed but evidence from several sources provides preliminary support for such a hypothesis. Irrespective of whether they come from Christian Fundamentalist or non-religious backgrounds, American six-year-olds strongly endorse the idea that animals and inanimate natural objects are made by God (Evans 1994; Evans *et al.* 1995; see S. Gelman and Kremer 1991 and Petrovich 1993 for evidence of similar intuitions in younger children and European samples). Furthermore, my own studies have found that, in addition to broadly attributing functions to non-living natural objects such as clouds, artefacts such as jeans, and biological organisms such as tigers, four- and five-year-olds strongly endorse the notion that entities of all types are 'made for something' (Kelemen 1996). Finally, a recent study has found, in contrast to Keil's (1992) result, that first and second graders prefer teleological explanations to physical explanations for both living or non-living natural object properties despite having physical explanations of non-living natural objects modelled for them in a pre-trial (Kelemen 1998, submitted).

Summary

Research indicates that both children and adults make the fundamental assumption that objects exist for a purpose. In this chapter, I have presented three recent developmental accounts for why these teleological intuitions occur. Two theories argue for a degree of selectivity in children's and adults' teleological intuitions. Keil suggests that the teleological stance is primary mode of thinking that, from early on, is selectively applied to biological traits and artefacts. Atran suggests that a 'teleo-essentialist stance' is a modularized way of reasoning about 'living things' which also happens to be applied to artefacts. In contrast to these hypotheses, my own theory, Promiscuous Teleology, argues that the teleological construal of objects derives from our domain-specific understanding of goal-directed agency and is not inherently restricted to any category of objects.

Further research is required to determine which of these accounts, if any, is most accurate. However, each raises a number of interesting issues. If the functional construal is essentially innate and human primates are predisposed to reason in teleological terms, at what evolutionary point did the stance emerge and what cognitive abilities were concomitant? Some speculations can be made in relation to each of the three theories presented in this chapter:

As noted earlier, the current account of Keil's autonomous teleological stance makes it difficult to assess what selection pressures would have led to this kind of adaptation. Keil has mentioned briefly that the evolutionary origin of the teleological stance might be tied in some way to the development of tool use. If this is the case, archaeological evidence suggests that such intuitions could have occurred by the point when early *Homo* was generating stone tools for use as meat-butchering implements (Wynn 1989). However, the blossoming of systematic tool manufacture only occurred relatively recently in the context of evolutionary time (perhaps even as recently as the last 50 000 years) and it seems likely that its emergence was associated with shifts in the complexity of hominid social arrangements and mind-reading capacities.

With respect to Atran's hypothesis of a 'Living Thing' module, a wide variety of animal species have the capacity to perceptually sort other living things into functional categories such as 'food versus non-food' or 'predators versus prey'. Atran's claim however, is that human taxonomic systems result from an intuitive recognition that perceptual similarities between organisms are caused by deeper 'teleo-essential' properties. No human culture, he argues, generates purely utilitarian classification systems of the 'predator versus prey' type. The insights provided by the literature on non-human primate classification strategies are equivocal because almost all of the work has involved the sorting of artefacts or abstract shapes. However, spontaneous classification of objects according to general morphology has been observed in a human-raised bonobo and primates do create non-utilitarian categories of natural objects that show some sensitivity to species-level differences (e.g. crow versus sparrow) (see Tomasello and Call 1997 for review). Whether these are simply perceptual categories is difficult to determine without further exploring primates' responses in something akin to the transformation tasks that have examined essentialism in human children. For example, would a monkey treat a familiar animal that has been made to *look* like something else as though it *were* something else? If, like pre-school children, they do not, then it might imply that something like the 'teleo-essentialist' module could have been in place from early on in primate evolution.

Finally, at what point in evolution might a promiscuous teleological construal have evolved? Promiscuous Teleology suggests that intuitions about object purpose derive from our expertise as intentional reasoners about goal-directed agents. Although there is no doubt that our primate relatives are able to construe other creatures as animate and goal-directed, their capacity to attribute intentions or mental states to others is still a source of great debate. Even Premack and Woodruff's (1978) classic study demonstrating Sarah the chimpanzee's somewhat sophisticated knowledge of another's intentions is controversial (Tomasello and Call 1997). Given this, the recent observation by Jane Goodall that chimpanzee 'display behaviour' at a waterfall has elements of human religious ritual is intriguing, but it is unlikely that the cause is anything akin to the intention-based teleological notions underlying most human religious belief. These kinds of intuitions probably developed quite late in hominid history in relation to increases in the socio-cultural complexity of *Homo sapiens*' lives and thus the growing need for successful inference of others' intentional states (see also Tomasello and Call 1997 for an interesting discussion of the emergence of 'theory of mind' capacities).

To conclude, human beings are compelled to think about aspects of the world in terms of their purpose. Indeed, what is fascinating about teleological reasoning is not just that we find it a convenient way to think, but that we sometimes behave as if it were the only way to think. It therefore provides fertile ground for future inter-disciplinary research examining both its nature in contemporary hominids and its emergence in evolutionary time.

Acknowledgements

I am grateful to Michael Corballis, Stephen Lea, Paul Bloom, Mark Holman and Deborah Widdowson for their very helpful comments on an earlier version of this manuscript.

References

Abravenel, E. and Gingold, H. (1985). Learning via observation during the second year of life. *Developmental Psychology*, **218**, 614–23.

Aristotle (1930). *Physics*. Clarendon Press, Oxford.

Atran, S. (1994). Core domains versus scientific theories: evidence from systematics and Itza-Maya folk biology. In *Mapping the mind: domain specificity in cognition and culture* (ed. L. A. Hirschfeld and S. A. Gelman), pp. 316–40. Cambridge University Press, New York.

Atran, S. (1995*a*). Causal constraints on categories. In *Causal cognition: a multi-disciplinary debate*. (ed. D. Sperber, D. Premack, and A. J. Premack), pp. 205–33. Clarendon Press, Oxford.

Atran, S. (1995*b*). Discussion. In *Causal cognition: a multi-disciplinary debate* (ed. D. Sperber, D. Premack, and A. J. Premack), pp. 263–5, Clarendon Press, Oxford.

Baillargeon, R. (1993). The object concept revisited. In *Visual perception and cognition in infancy* (ed. C. Granrud), pp. 265–315. Erlbaum, Hillsdale, NJ.

Baron-Cohen, S. (1995). *Mindblindness: an essay on autism and theory of mind*. MIT Press, Cambridge, MA.

Bartsch, K. and Wellman, H. C. (1989).Young children's attribution of action to beliefs and desires. *Child Development*, **60**, 946–64.

Bloom, P. (1996). Intention, history and artefact concepts. *Cognition*, **60**, 1–29.

Brown, A. (1989). Analogical transfer in young children: analogies as tools for communication and exposition. *Applied Cognitive Psychology*, **3**, 275–93.

Brown, A. (1990). Domain-specific principles affect learning and transfer in children. *Cognitive Science*, **14**, 107–33.

Brumby, M. (1985). Misconceptions about the concept of natural selection by medical biology students. *Science Education*, **68**, 493–503.

Bullock, M., Gelman, R., and Baillargeon, R. (1982). The development of causal reasoning. In *The developmental psychology of time* (ed. W. F. Friedman), pp. 209–54. Academic, New York.

Carey, S. (1985). *Conceptual change in childhood*. MIT Press, Cambridge, MA.

Carey, S. (1988). Conceptual differences between children and adults. *Mind and Language*, **3**, 167–81.

Carey, S. (1991). Knowledge acquisition: enrichment or conceptual change? In *The epigenesis of mind: essays on biology and cognition* (ed. S. Carey and R. Gelman). pp. 13–69. Erlbaum, Hillsdale, NJ.

Carey, S. (1995). The growth of causal understandings of natural kinds. In *Causal cognition: a multi-disciplinary debate* (ed. D. Sperber, D. Premack, and A. J. Premack), pp. 268–302. Clarendon Press. Oxford.

Chandler, M. J. and Lalonde, C. (1994). Surprising, magical and miraculous turns of events: children's reactions to violations of their theories of mind and matter. *British Journal of Developmental Psychology*, **12**, 83–95.

Cheney, D. and Seyfarth, R. L. (1990). *How monkeys see the world*. University of Chicago Press.

Corey, M. A. (1993). *God and the new cosmology: the anthropic design argument*. Rowan and Littlefield, Maryland.

Cosmides, L. and Tooby, J. (1994). Origins of domain-specificity. In *Mapping the mind: domain specificity in cognition and culture* (ed. L. A. Hirschfeld and S. A. Gelman), pp. 85–115. Cambridge University Press, New York.

Darwin, C. (1859). *The origin of species by means of natural selection*. John Murray, London.

Dawkins, R. (1993). Viruses of the mind. In *Dennett and his critics*, (ed. B. Dahlbom) pp. 13–27. Blackwell, Cambridge, MA.

Dawkins, R. (1995). *River out of Eden*. Basic Books, New York.

Dennett, D. (1983). Intentional systems in cognitive ethology: the 'Panglossian Paradigm' defended. *Behavioral and Brain Sciences*, **3**, 343–54.

Dennett, D. (1987). *The intentional stance*. MIT Press, Cambridge, MA.

Evans, E. M. (1994). *God or Darwin? The development of beliefs about the origin of species*. Unpublished Doctoral Dissertation, University of Michigan.

Evans, E. M., Andress, C. C., and Stewart, S. S. (1995). *God or nature? The role of essentialism in the development of beliefs about origins*. Paper presented at the Biennial Meeting of the Society for Research in Child Development, Indianapolis. March 30–April 2.

Gelman, R., Spelke, E. S., and Meck, E. (1983). What preschoolers know about animate and inanimate objects. In *The acquisition of symbolic skills* (ed. D. Rogers and J. A. Sloboda), pp. 297–324. Plenum, New York.

Gelman, S. A. (1988). Development of induction within natural kind and artefact categories. *Cognitive Psychology*, **20**, 65–95.

Gelman, S. A. and Kremer, K. E. (1991). Understanding natural cause: children's explanations of how objects and their properties originate. *Child Development*, **62**, 396–414.

Gelman, S. A., Colby, J. D., and Gottfried, G. (1994). Essentialist beliefs in children: the acquisition of concept and theories. In *Mapping the mind: domain specificity in cognition and culture* (ed. L. A. Hirschfeld and S. A. Gelman). pp. 341–65. Cambridge University Press, New York.

Gergely, G., Nadasdy, Z., Csibra, G., and Biro, S. (1995). Taking the intentional stance at 12 months of age. *Cognition*, **56**, 165–93.

Glacken, C. J. (1967). *Traces on the Rhodian shore. Nature and culture in Western thought from ancient times to the end of the eighteenth century*. University of California Press, Berkeley, CA.

Gopnik, A. and Meltzoff, A. (1997). *Words, thoughts, and theories*. MIT Press, Cambridge, MA.

Gould, S. J. and Lewontin, R. C. (1979). The spandrels of San Marco and the Panglossian paradigm: a critique of the adaptationist programme. *Proceedings of the Royal Society of London*, Vol. B, **205**, 581–98.

Hauser, M. D. (1997). The functional properties of artefacts: a nonhuman primate's point of view. *Cognition*, **64**, 285–308.

Hirschfeld, L. (1994). Anthropology, psychology and the meanings of social causality. In *Causal cognition: a multi-disciplinary debate* (ed. D. Sperber, D. Premack, and A. J. Premack), pp. 313–44. Clarendon Press, Oxford.

Hirschfeld, L. and Gelman, S. A. (1994). *Mapping the mind: domain specificity in cognition and culture*. Cambridge University Press, New York.

Humphrey, N. K. (1976). The social function of intellect. In *Growing points in ethology* (ed. P. P. G. Bateson and R. A. Hinde) pp. 303–17. Cambridge University Press.

Hurlbutt, R. H. (1985). *Hume, Newton, and the design argument*. University of Nebraska Press.

Jolly, A. (1983). Dennett's 'Panglossian Paradigm'. *The Behavioral and Brain Sciences*, **6**, 366–7.

Keil, F. C. (1989). *Concepts, kinds, and cognitive development*. MIT Press, Cambridge, MA.

Keil, F. C. (1992). The origins of an autonomous biology. In *Modularity and constraints in language and cognition. Minnesota Symposium on Child Psychology*. Vol. 25 (ed. M. R. Gunnar and M. Maratsos), pp. 103–38. Erlbaum, Hillsdale, NJ.

Keil, F. C. (1994*a*). Explanation, association, and the acquisition of word meaning. *Lingua*, **92**, 169–98.

Keil, F. C. (1994*b*). The birth and nurturance of concepts by domains: the origins of concepts of living things. In *Mapping the mind: domain specificity in cognition and culture* (ed. L. A. Hirschfeld and S. A. Gelman), pp. 234–54. Cambridge University Press, New York.

Keil, F. C. (1995). The growth of causal understandings of natural kinds. In *Causal cognition: a multi-disciplinary debate* (ed. D. Sperber, D. Premack, and A. J. Premack), pp. 234–62. Clarendon Press, Oxford.

Kelemen, D. (1995). *The nature and development of the teleological stance*. Paper presented at the Society for Research in Child Development, Indianapolis. March 30–April 2.

Kelemen, D. (1996). *The nature and development of the teleological stance*. Unpublished Doctoral Dissertation. University of Arizona.

Kelemen, D. (1997). *The development of teleological reasoning*. Symposium paper presented at the Biennial Meeting of the Society for Research in Child Development, Washington DC, April 3–6.

Kelemen, D. (1998). *Why are rocks pointy? Children's preference for functional explanations*. Paper presented at the Meeting of the Society for Philosophy and Psychology, Minneapolis, June 11–14.

Kelemen, D. (submitted). The scope of teleological thinking in preschool children. Available upon request from the author.

Kelemen, D. (submitted). Why are rocks pointy? Children's preference for teleological explanations of the natural world. Available upon request from the author.

Kelemen, D., Posner, T., Widdowson, D., and Brown, A. (1997*a*). *Teleological reasoning: structure–function relations in biology*. Poster presented at the American Educational Research Association, Chicago, March 25–28.

Kelemen, D., Widdowson, D., Posner, T., and Brown, A. (1997*b*). *Teleological reasoning in the biological domain*. Poster presented at the Biennial Meeting of the Society for Research in Child Development, Washington, DC, April 3–6.

Leslie, A. (1994). ToMM, ToBY, and agency: core architecture and domain specificity. In *Mapping the mind: domain specificity in cognition and culture*. (ed. L. A. Hirschfeld and S. A. Gelman), pp. 119–48. Cambridge University Press, New York.

Leslie, A. and Thaiss, L. (1992). Domain-specificity in conceptual development: neuropsychological evidence from autism. *Cognition*, **43**, 225–51.

Livingstone, D. N. (1993). *The geographical tradition*. Blackwell, Oxford.

Madole, K. and Cohen, L. B. (1995). The role of object parts in infants attention to form–function correlations. *Developmental Psychology*, **31**, 637–48.

Madole, K. L., Oakes, L. M., and Cohen, L. B. (1993). Developmental changes in infants' attention to function and form–function correlations. *Cognitive Development*, **8**, 189–209.

Mayr, E. (1982). *The growth of biological thought*. Belknap, Cambridge, MA.

Millikan, R. (1989). In defense of proper functions. *Philosophy of Science*, **56**, 288–303.

Neander, K. (1991). The teleological notion of function. *Australasian Journal of Philosophy*, **69**, 454–68.

Paley, W. (1856). *Natural theology*. Baldwyn and Co., London.

Parrinder, G. (1983). Man's religions: from ancient history to the present. Hamlyn, New York.

Petrovich, O. (1993). *Children's explanations of the origin of natural objects: understanding of non-natural causality*. Paper presented at the 60th Anniversary Meeting of the Society in Child Development, New Orleans, March 25–28.

Piaget, J. (1929). *The child's conception of the world* . Routledge and Kegan Paul, London.

Piaget, J. and Inhelder, B. (1975). *The origin of the idea of chance in children*. Norton, New York.

Pinker, S. (1994). *The language instinct*. William Morrow and Company, New York.

Pinker, S. and Bloom, P. (1990). Natural language and natural selection. *The Behavioral and Brain Sciences*, **13**, 707–84.

Premack, D. (1990). The infant's theory of self-propelled objects. *Cognition*, **36**, 1–16.

Premack, D. and Woodruff, G. (1978). Does the chimpanzee have a theory of mind? *The Behavioral and Brain Sciences* **1**, 515–26.

Shapin, S. (1995). *The scientific revolution*. University of Chicago Press.

Shreeve, J. (1995). The Neanderthal enigma: solving the mystery of modern humans. Morrow, New York.

Solomon, G. (1995). *Against the claim that preschoolers already have constructed an autonomous conceptual domain of biology*. Paper presented at the Biennial Meeting of the Society for Research in Child Development. Indianapolis, March 31–April 2.

Spelke, E. S. (1990). Principles of object perception. *Cognitive Science*, **14**, 29–56.

Springer, K. and Keil, F. C. (1989). On the development of biologically specific beliefs: the case of inheritance. *Child Development*, **60**, 637–48.

Tager-Flusberg, H. (1994). Predicting and explaining behaviour: a comparison of autistic, mentally retarded, and normal children. *Journal of Child Psychology and Psychiatry and Allied Disciplines*, **35**, 1059–75.

Tomasello, M. and Call, J. (1997). *Primate cognition*. Oxford University Press.

Wellman, H. M. and Gelman, S. A. (1992). Cognitive development: foundational theories of core domains. *Annual Review of Psychology*, **43**, 337–75.

Wright, L. (1973). Functions. *The Philosophical Review*, **82**, 139–68.

Wynn, T. (1989). *The evolution of spatial competence*. University of Illinois Press.

15

The evolution of certain novel human capacities

Paul Bloom

Introduction

The human mind is sometimes said to be a set of distinct modules, or mental organs, each of which has evolved to solve a particular task, such as communication, object perception, and mate selection. There is no single central processor; instead these diverse cognitive modules work together to underlie human thought and action. This theory goes under different names—modularity, multiple intelligences, the 'Swiss-army knife' model of the mind, and 'evolutionary psychology'—and it is a natural marriage of the modular perspective within cognitive science and the adaptationist perspective within evolutionary biology (Cosmides and Tooby 1987, 1994; Pinker 1997).

This is not a popular view within the social sciences. Most scholars prefer to look at human psychology from more of a Cartesian perspective. While specialized modules might exist, humans also possess some seat of consciousness, some 'self' that learns, makes decisions, comes up with the good ideas, and so on. Even Jerry Fodor, one of the most ardent defenders of modularity (e.g. 1983), argues that this view applies only to perceptual and motor systems—the rest of the mind is, he argues, profoundly *non*-modular.

There is also a widespread antipathy toward applying natural selection to human psychology. The minds of rats and birds might have been shaped by selection pressures and this might also be true for less central aspects of humans such as the senses and the appetites. But many would insist that evolutionary biology has little to say about the more interesting aspects of human thought. Derek Bickerton (1995), for instance, says of evolutionary psychology that "it is perhaps not unfair to say that this approach can tell us all we need to know about the least interesting aspects of human behavior. Surely what is most interesting about human behavior ... is precisely the part of it that we do *not* share with other creatures" (p. 5). And Alan Wolfe (1997) insists that "biology per se has little to tell us about those aspects of human behavior, such as how we make our way in the world, which are most interesting to social scientists (p. 5)".

There is something odd about these authoritative assertions of what is and is not interesting. Even if it were true that evolutionary psychology could tell us only about what we share with other creatures, this would still leave us with insights about perception, memory, communication, taste in food, love for our offspring, fear, play, rage, and lust. And, anyway, it isn't true that evolutionary theory cannot account for traits that are unique to a given species. Pinker (1994) notes that the elephant's trunk is just as singular as, say, human language, but nonetheless poses no special mystery for biologists.

The attack on modularity is logically independent of the attack on natural selection. There are those (such as Chomsky) who accept modularity but are sceptical about selectionist theories of how the modules evolve, and those (such as Skinner) who reject modularity but endorse natural selection as having a crucial role in the shaping of how the mind works. But these objections are related—if you believe that natural selection has played little role in shaping the mind (just as it played little direct role in shaping the human chin), then you are likely to sympathize with the view that the mind lacks internal complexity (just like the chin). And if you don't think that the mind is composed of complex and specialized modules, much of the motivation for appealing to natural selection to explain its origin goes away.

This chapter will address what I see as the most serious attack on evolutionary psychology, one that has been raised by many critics. This attack concerns the proper explanation of certain complex human capacities. I will suggest that, contrary to what is often claimed by these critics, theories that reject the tenets of evolutionary psychology fail to explain how these capacities evolved. Instead, the most likely explanation emerges from a modular adaptationist perspective on the mind, though one that must be elaborated in certain surprising ways.

Objections to evolutionary psychology

Humans have complex and unique abilities that are not biological adaptations. As Bickerton (1995) puts it: "humans are a species produced like all other species by the natural workings of biological evolution, yet the behavior of humans differs dramatically from that of all other species" (p. 5). Steven Mithen (1996) considers a group of scholars he once ate with at Trinity Hall, and asks rhetorically: "Could these surgeons, linguists, and theoretical physicists be expanding the boundaries of human knowledge in such diverse and complex fields by using minds which were adapted for no more than a hunter–gatherer existence?" (p. 47).

There are different ways to react to these concerns. One extreme is to reject the idea that the human mind is solely the result of biological evolution. This would be the route of scholars like Eccles (1989) and Penrose (1989), as well as that of Charles Darwin's contemporary, Alfred Russel Wallace, who had independently discovered natural selection. Wallace made the same sort of observations as Mithen, noting that humans have 'higher' intellectual capacities. He suggested that these capacities could not be the direct result of natural selection because they only exist in certain societies; some groups of humans ('savages') get along just fine without them. He then concluded that they must have a divine origin (see Cronin 1992).

Darwin's response to Wallace was harsh ("I hope you have not murdered too completely your own and my child"—see Cronin 1992), and many evolutionary psychologists today are just as dismissive about the worries expressed by their own contemporaries. After all, it is fully consistent with the process of natural selection that something can evolve for one purpose and then be co-opted for another. Darwin (1859) called this 'preadaptation' and more recently Gould and Vrba (1982) have redescribed it as 'exaptation', but the idea is the same. The nose, having evolved as a sense organ, can be used to support glasses; our feet, evolved for locomotion, can be used to kick a soccer ball; and so on. If the worry is simply that our minds can do things that are of no selective advantage, then we can quickly dismiss it—the existence of preadaptation poses no special problem for the study of human psychology.

I think this response fails to appreciate the real force of the problem posed by Bickerton, Mithen, and others, ignoring the fact that at least some of the unique capacities humans possess are complex—to put it the way some biologists would, they show signs of 'good design'. The problem is most obvious when one considers science and technology. Humans study physics and number theory, invent birth-control devices and portable computers, construct huge buildings and fly to the moon. Not only do none of these abilities have any selective advantage in the Darwinian sense, it is also far from clear how any of them can be accidental by-products of abilities that *do* have selective advantages.

There is no real mystery, in contrast, in explaining how senses that have evolved to savour the taste of fruit and flesh will crave a hot fudge sundae, how a motor system evolved for the manipulation of objects can learn to use a computer mouse, or even how a mind evolved to contemplate entities moving through space can come to appreciate a mathematical theorem. This isn't to say we *can* explain all this, but there are at least candidate theories as to how our evolved cognitive systems can be extended in these diverse ways (see, e.g. Pinker 1997). This also holds for aspects of mental life such as the appreciation of music, dance, and the visual arts (Lerdahl and Jackendoff 1983; Corballis 1992; Bloom 1996). But when it comes to the human ability to *create* ice cream sundaes, soccer games, and mathematical theorems, evolutionary psychology seems to offer us little insight.

The reason for this relates to one of the central issues in evolutionary biology—the proper application of selectionist explanation (Williams 1966; Gould and Lewontin 1979; Dawkins 1986). All sorts of traits *can* be the result of natural selection, from a moth's colour to the number of vertebrae in a monkey's spine to echolocation in bats. But which ones *have* to be adaptations, as opposed to being the products of mutation, genetic drift, and so on? When *must* we involve what Williams (1966) has called the 'quite onerous' notion of adaptation?

The answer is that natural selection is the only known explanation for adaptive complexity (Williams 1966; Dawkins 1986; Cronin 1992). Adaptively complex entities are ubiquitous in nature; they include such things as eyes and hands and camouflage and cats. Before Darwin, the only explanation for how these came to exist was an intelligent designer, God (e.g. Paley 1802). Darwin's fundamental accomplishment was to show how a non-intentional process can give rise to good design. The eye, for example, looks like something that has been cleverly constructed for the purpose of seeing. But it hasn't—it arose through the accumulation of random variations, each of which led to some improvement over the preceding form, and, over the course of time, led organisms along the path in the astronomically vast space of possible bodies leading from a body with no eye to a body with a functioning eye.

Some psychologists and linguists are sceptical about how important a role natural selection plays in the shaping of organisms (see, e.g. Chomsky 1988; Piattelli-Palmarini 1989), so it is important to realize that the above claim is not a matter of debate among biologists. Stephen Jay Gould is the most prominent critic of the purported excesses of adaptationism, but even he is adamant that this process is "the most important of all evolutionary mechanisms" (Gould and Lewontin 1979 p. 589). He made the point more recently, in a rather exasperated tone: "Yes, eyes are for seeing and feet are for moving. And, yes again, I know of no scientific mechanism other than natural selection with the proven power to build structures of such eminently workable design" (Gould 1997 p. 35). As he goes on to point out, the substantive debates about the scope of natural selection are over traits that do *not* show such clear-cut signs of design.

This brings us to psychology. There are many considerations that suggest that a certain aspect of the mind is a biological adaptation, but perhaps the strongest consideration is the one above—adaptive complexity. Abilities such as object recognition, syntactic processing, and spatial navigation arguably require cognitive mechanisms that are, on computational grounds, sufficiently complex so as to require an explanation in terms of natural selection. From this you get the argument at the core of evolutionary psychology—the complex design of the mind cries out for an adaptive explanation (e.g. Pinker and Bloom 1990; Cosmides and Tooby 1994; Pinker 1997). But here's the problem. The cognitive structures required to develop theories of quantum physics and create moon rockets *are intuitively at least as complicated as tasks such as object recognition.*

There are thus two sources of good design. The first is natural selection, and we have some understanding of how this works. The second is human creative powers, as exemplified in science and technology. Humans somehow have the ability to understand and manipulate aspects of the world in unique and novel ways. By any normal criteria, quantum physics and space flight reflect good design, but they are neither the direct result of natural selection nor, in any direct sense, the by-products of evolved abilities. How can we explain their origin?

General intelligence as a source of creative powers

The traditional answer is that we should start by rejecting the modular view of the mind. Like other animals, humans might possess at least some modules (or, more generally, specialized capacities). But we have also developed—or have developed to a much greater degree—some general ability that allows us to do complex and interesting things that evolution could not have prepared us to do.

Does such an ability exist? This proposal does have a strong introspective pull; we do not *feel* like a collection of special-purpose devices. Intuitively we are singular Cartesian egos, and it is in this way that we face new problems, make decisions, and so on. We often think of others in the same way. And we sometimes even judge that some people are just plain *smarter* than others, and make the same comparisons across species—dogs are smarter than cockroaches, and humans are smarter than dogs. In contrast, it is not very intuitive to claim that people differ from animals, and from other people, in terms of the number or type of modules that they possess.

Furthermore, learning processes that work across domains do exist, in both artificial intelligence and in the biological world. There are the principles of association, discussed by philosophers such as Hume and Locke, which link together arbitrary units that are spatially or temporally adjacent. If a person hears a bark every time she sees a dog, the sound and the image will be linked together and one will bring to mind the other. There is habituation, the adaptive mechanism through which an organism stops attending to familiar stimuli. When entering a room a person might notice the loud ticking of a clock, but if he waits long enough, this ticking retreats from consciousness. There are statistical algorithms, such as the back-propagation algorithm instantiated in many connectionist networks. Such procedures have had some success with tasks such as learning to recognize written words. And there are learning models that work on analogy with natural selection—randomly generating some set of hypotheses, weighing these hypotheses according to some criteria, and then repeating the process over again by generating variants of the hypothesis that has the most success. This is the logic behind 'genetic algorithms', which have been argued to underlie everything from the development of fine motor skills to scientific innovation.

These processes are quite general. One can habituate to the sound of an alarm clock or the smell of brownies; statistical learning algorithms can learn everything from how to play backgammon to how to identify different faces. Can they therefore explain the origin of human creative powers?

One immediate worry is that these processes are not uniquely human. In fact, for most of them, the best evidence for their existence comes from studies of animals, typically rats. This calls into question their utility in explaining abilities that only humans have. In response, one might argue that humans have evolved to be much smarter than other animals and that this increase in general intelligence has led to the unprecedented jump in our creative abilities. The problem here is that there is little evidence that animals such as chimpanzees really *are* deficient relative to humans in these ways, that they are less able to make associations, habituate, and so on.

A more general problem is that while such learning procedures might be used across different domains—for instance, some have argued that language processing and object perception employ the same statistical learning algorithm—the procedures are, by themselves, useless. There are countless theories of different facets of human learning, and many employ one or more of the mechanisms listed above. But each inevitably also has some special way of tailoring the mechanism for its particular domain. A connectionist system for learning to read, for instance, will have pre-set nodes corresponding to letters and sounds; a genetic algorithm for learning tic-tac-toe will have the configurations of the board already encoded; a classical conditioning mechanism for the acquisition of food aversion will have built-in expectations about the nature of the stimulus and how to respond to it. The notion that learning algorithms are sufficient to solve real-world problems has no empirical or theoretical support.

This might sound more tendentious than it actually is. There is of course much debate over the extent of task-specificity that the brain has evolved, and over the precise nature of this specificity. But even the most rabid empiricist would agree that innate learning principles (typically the principles of association) requires a pre-established set of representations, such as a 'sensorium' (Hume) or an 'animal similarity space' (Quine). And, in fact, the most ardent contemporary critics of modularity do not deny the need for *multiple* pre-existing cognitive systems, though they would argue that the way in which different parts of the brain are evolved to solve different problem is not in terms of specialized representational content, but through special modes of computation (e.g., Elman *et al*. 1996).

Maybe we have given up too soon on the search for an all-purpose mechanism that could explain how humans can adapt to new situations. The expectation that such a mechanism must exist is not limited to psychology. Before Darwin, Lamarck proposed that the adaptive fit between organisms and their environments is due to the inheritance of acquired characteristics. In response to heavy lifting, a labourer's arms get stronger and this strength is passed onto his offspring; to get food high in trees, a giraffe's neck grows and this increased neck length is passed onto its offspring; and so on. But Lamarck knew that such an account presupposes some mechanism that causes arms to get stronger in response to lifting, necks to stretch to reach food, and so on. To explain this, he proposed the principle: "New needs which establish a necessity for some part really bring about the existence of that part ..." (Mayr 1982, p. 355). The notion of intelligence that many scholars wish to appeal to is a cognitive version of Lamarck's principle—the human mind is such that it can adapt creatively to any novel situation or problem, just because it needs to do so.

Philosophers such as Goodman (1983) and Quine (1960), however, have offered certain reasons to believe that such a principle cannot exist. For any case of inductive learning, there are infinitely many logically possible—and from an a priori standpoint equally meritorious—generalizations that one can make. Thus, for learning to be successful, it must be constrained—some subset of the possible hypotheses must be privileged and the rest ignored. A learner that was so unbiased as to find everything equally interesting could learn nothing. To make matters worse, which generalizations are reasonable depends on contingent properties of the world, and differs from domain to domain. The properties that one should pay attention to when learning about the best foods to eat are different from those that are relevant when choosing a mate, or parsing a sentence, or figuring out how far away an object is. So while there is nothing logically incoherent about a learning procedure that is general in the sense that it treats everything the same, with no pre-existing knowledge of different domains, such a procedure would be useless from the standpoint of coping with the world.

Language as a source of creative powers

When it comes to finding the source of uniquely human creative powers, a sensible strategy is to look for some other capacity that only humans have. Capacities such as habituation and the principles of association do not meet this criterion, but language certainly does. An average adult knows tens of thousands of words; these refer to categories and to individuals, to entities as diverse as objects, actions, social institutions, distances, emotions, and numbers. And even young children unconsciously command a rich set of syntactic and morphological principles that enable them to combine these words to produce and understand a potential infinity of sentences that nobody has ever produced or understood before. There is nothing comparable in other primates, and attempts to teach non-humans the same sort of lexical and generative systems used by humans have been abysmal failures (see Pinker 1994).

Some relationship between the richness of human thought and the evolution of language clearly exists. This is true even if the most modular view of the origin of language (as a distinct neural system evolved for the purpose of communication) is correct. For one thing, it is likely that our language is richer than the communication systems of other creatures just because our thoughts are richer. We can say more because we have more to say. For another, language and non-linguistic cognition might well have co-evolved in the course of human evolution in a 'cognitive arms race', in which the increased communicative abilities of members of our species gave rise to selective pressure for enhanced cognitive skills (most notably, social cognition), which in turn made communication more important, and so on. Finally, there is the obvious fact that language is an excellent tool for the transmission and storage of information, and hence plays a central role in the development of culture.

But can the evolution of language entirely explain the unique human capacities that we are interested in? Darwin (1871) thought so: "If it could be proved that certain high mental powers, such as the formation of general concepts, self-consciousness, [etc.], were absolutely peculiar to man ... it is not improbable that these qualities are merely the incidental results of other highly-advanced intellectual faculties; and these again mainly the result of the continued use of a perfect language" [p. 126]. More recently, Daniel Dennett (1996) entertains an even more radical proposal: "Perhaps the kind of mind you get when you add language to it is so different from the kind of mind you can have without language that calling them both minds is a mistake" (p. 17).

There are many different versions of this view, including Bickerton's (1995) proposal that the evolution of language is tantamount to the evolution of intelligence—because human language just *is* an expanded mode of thought (see Pinker 1992 and Bloom 1998*a* for discussion). What I will focus on here is the somewhat different claim that the child's learning a natural language (such as English) gives rise to the creative powers we are concerned with, either because it enables the mind to appreciate new concepts or because it allows for richer patterns of deduction, planning, and inference. This is the proposal suggested by Darwin as well as by Carruthers (1996), Dennett (1996), Mithen (1996), and Jackendoff (in press).

We can start by dismissing the strongest version of this claim—that there is no mental life without language. Even putting aside research into the mental life of animals, there is by now abundant evidence that pre-linguistic infants are capable of imposing considerable structure on the world. They expect objects to continue to exist once they go out of sight, can determine the numerosities of small arrays of objects, and even compute the results of simple additions and subtractions performed over these arrays. They also show some ability to individuate sounds and actions, to recall spatial location, make simple causal inferences, and predict the actions of an agent based on its previous intentional behaviour (see, e.g. Spelke 1994; Gergely *et al*. 1995; Wynn 1996).

Furthermore, young children learn the meanings of many words easily, sometimes through only a single exposure. Their earliest words include not only names for middle-sized objects, such as 'dog' and 'truck', but also names for events, times, spatial relations, mental states, and all sorts of abstract entity. In fact, by the time a child is about two years of age, roughly half of her words refer to entities that are *not* middle-sized objects. The precocity and rapidity of this learning is consistent with the view that the concepts these words map on to exist before language development, and are not the product of language learning (see Bloom 1998*b*).

Of course, it is hardly surprising that some conceptual resources exist independently from language, and this does not preclude the proposal that the role of language is to instil into the human mind more concepts and enhanced sorts of conceptual abilities. But there is some concern about how coherent even this more moderate proposal is. There is something suspect, after all, in claiming that you cannot think of something until you learn a word for it. How could you have learned the word in the first place if you couldn't grasp the concept it corresponds to? This concern holds if concepts are, as Fodor (1975) suggests, symbols in a language of thought ("Nothing can be expressed in a natural language that can't be expressed in the language of thought. For if something could, we couldn't learn the natural language [word] that expresses it") but it applies with equal force under other theories. If a concept is, say, a vector in multi-dimensional space (Churchland 1989), a word corresponding to that concept can only be learned if the capacity to encode such a vector exists before exposure to the word.

But even in light of this, language could still play an important role in shaping our conceptual life, because possessing the conceptual resources to have the concept X is not the same as actually having the concept X. Fodor himself notes that while language cannot cause previously unthinkable concepts to emerge, it might affect the sorts of concepts one will consciously entertain. To take a somewhat fanciful example, continued use of a language in which verbs differ according to the shape of the object that is acted upon (as in Navajo, in which one verb is used for describing the giving of a long thin object like a stick while a different verb is used for describing the giving of a spherical object like a rock) might lead the language-user to consciously think about object shape more so than if she was using a language, such as English, that did not make such a distinction.

Does such an effect actually occur? Benjamin Lee Whorf (1956) made the argument in terms of cross-linguistic comparisons, arguing that speakers of distinct languages think in significantly different ways. His most famous claim was that Hopi speakers do not think about time in the same way as speakers of languages such as English, and that this is because Hopi expresses this notion differently than English. This claim has not weathered well; there is no real evidence for the cognitive difference that Whorf cited, and his linguistic statements about the Hopi language were inaccurate; upon careful scrutiny, Hopi is much more similar to languages such as English than Whorf had assumed (Malotki 1983). Further research, in domains as disparate as color memory and counterfactual reasoning, have either found that speakers of different language have identical non-linguistic capacities (e.g. Brown 1958; Au 1983), or that they differ only in tasks that are themselves language-dependent, such as explicit recall memory (e.g. Kay and Kempton 1984). As a result, many psychologists view the idea that differences in language can correspond to differences in mental life as having been decisively refuted.

Recently, however, Steven Levinson (1996) has presented some quite striking evidence in favour of the Whorfian view. When describing the relative locations of objects, the preferred frame of reference differs across languages. For objects in proximity, Dutch, like English, tends to use a *relative* system of reference which is based on spatial properties relative to the speaker or to the objects being described, as in 'in front of' or 'to the left of'. Other languages, such as Tzeltal, tend to use an *absolute* system, roughly akin to 'North', 'South', 'East/West'. In a series of experiments, Levinson found that Dutch speakers and Tzeltal speakers encode their spatial experience of the world differently, even in situations that do not involve language, such as visual recall and production of gesture. Dutch speakers tend to think about objects in close proximity in terms of relative notions like right and left while Tzeltal speakers tend to think about them in terms of absolute notions such as north and south—exactly in accord with how their languages work. Levinson concludes that: "The frame of reference dominant in the language, whether relative or absolute, comes to bias the choice of frame of reference in various kinds of non-linguistic conceptual representation" (p. 125).

One objection is that the convergence of language and spatial cognition might be due to some *third* factor, such as the different cultural and physical environments that the speakers of these languages live in. What one would need to do to dismiss this alternative would be to study the spatial cognition of speakers of different languages in cases where there is not such a radical difference in early experience, such as between speakers of English and Spanish who have both grown up in urban United States. Such research is in progress, by Levinson and others.

But even assuming that Levinson's interpretation is correct, it is critical to realize that it is not a case of language giving genuinely new capacities. Both relative and absolute systems are encoded in brain mechanisms that underlie the navigation of humans and of other animals, and hence exist independently of language (O'Keefe and Nadel 1978; Peterson *et al.* 1996). Furthermore, Dutch speakers *can* think in absolute terms, and Tzeltal speakers can think in relative terms—it is just that they tend not to. What Levinson's finding suggests is that the acquisition of a given language might *exercise* certain pre-existing ways of thinking about the world, affecting what Whorf (1956) called 'habitual thought and behaviour'.

More generally, this finding is consistent with the proposal that the acquisition of language allows for increased access to modular processes, making it possible for one to ruminate consciously on the workings of different modules, and allowing for different parts of the mind to 'talk to' each other. Many scholars believe that this can considerably expand the flexibility and adaptability of thought, though there is some disagreement as to whether such 'accessibility' requires language (see Rozin and Schull 1988; Clark and Karmiloff-Smith 1993; Dennett 1993).

This is an intriguing idea, and it might well be right. But it should be noted that there is little evidence to support it. This isn't to dismiss the many empirical demonstrations that children's behaviours grow more flexible through development, nor to deny that they gain increasingly more insight into mental processes such as language, memory, and emotion. But it is a huge jump from these data to the conclusion that children's knowledge and ability are due to increasing conscious access to the workings of their modules—'representational redescription' as Annette Karmiloff-Smith (1992) puts it. After all, it might be instead the result of children applying the same learning processes to their own thoughts and actions as they do to the external world. That is, children might come to know about the inner workings of their minds in exactly the same way they learn about the inner workings of their stomachs, or the inner workings of insects—through observation, theory construction, inference, pedagogy, and so on, not through any direct access. At this point, the claim that learning language gives one access to the inner workings of the mind is, at best, speculative.

The same thing holds for the view that it is only through language that we can construct a conscious workspace with which to carry out long chains of thought, and hence reason in sophisticated ways (Bickerton 1995; Jackendoff in press). This is intuitively plausible; many of us *feel* as if our long deductive chains, our internal soliloquies, are carried out in our native tongue. But there is again no evidence for it, and the fact that being deprived of language does not inevitably lead to severe cognitive impairments (see below) gives us reason to doubt it.

In any case, suppose it were true that language gives rise to capacities such as modular access and internal chains of reasoning. This would allow for some cognitive abilities to be used by other cognitive systems in novel ways, and could lead to some interesting exaptations. But it does not begin to explain the emergence of the creative powers we are concerned with here (Bloom and Wynn 1994). I think, incidentally, that the reason why the notion of 'access' is so tempting as an explanation for everything that is unique to humans is the implicit premise that humans start off with some smart central processor and language makes it possible for the modules to talk to it. But if one holds that there is no central processor and all these modules will have to talk to are *each other*, then this perspective becomes a lot less attractive.

A similar worry applies to the proposal that exposure to language can affect mental life by drawing people's attention to novel categories. Such an effect does occur. If you are a wine novice, all wines might taste the same. But because of the linguistic cues repeatedly provided in the context of a wine tasting class—this is a Merlot, this is a Beaujolais; this is dry, this is sweet—you can come to organize your unruly impressions into discrete categories and hence acquire the functional ability to distinguish the wines *and* come to have a different, richer, phenomenal experience of the taste of these wines. In general, labels are an excellent cue to the boundaries of categories; even two- and three-year-olds believe that if two entities are described with the same common noun they are likely to belong to the same category (Markman and Hutchinson 1984; Gelman 1996).

Again, however, this is not a creative process. The fact that labels can convey the boundaries of a category allows for a convenient way through which a person can *learn* a new concept from someone else, but it doesn't give any hint as to how new concepts can be *created* in the first place. Because of this, it does not bear on the question we are dealing with here.

Finally, consider the mental life of linguistic isolates, such as deaf adults who have grown up having never been exposed to sign language. As Sacks (1988) reviews, the cognitive abilities of such people have long been a matter of debate for scholars interested in the relationship between language and thought. One central case-study was Theophilus d'Estrella, who did not acquire sign language until the age of nine. After he had acquired language, he wrote an autobiographical account of his early experience in which he described his thoughts about religion and other abstract matters. William James (1893) concluded that this narrative "tends to discountenance the notion that no abstract thought is possible without words. Abstract thought of a decidedly subtle kind, both scientific and moral, went on here in advance of the means of expressing it to others."

There is good reason to be sceptical of autobiographical reports, and many of James' contemporaries rejected his conclusion on these grounds. But there is more recent evidence that bears on this issue. Susan Schaller (1991) studied contemporary deaf isolates in the United States and Mexico, people who have never acquired a natural language, either spoken or signed. She found that they have rich social skills and elaborate spatial knowledge and abilities, including the ability to repair complicated machinery, and they can handle money—in fact, some of them can do so well enough to live on their own. Furthermore, they can actively describe events from the past, using pantomimed narratives. This seems to refute the claim that learning a natural language is necessary for the emergence of mental powers such as reasoning about other people, spatial cognition, numerical cognition, complex reasoning, and even conscious reflection on the past. There seems to be no sense in which these linguistic isolates lack a normal mental life (see also Pinker 1994 for discussion).

It is sometimes the case that being deprived of language *does* have a terrible effect. Often such a person is severely deprived of personal contact, and, as Sacks discusses, there are many instances in which a languageless adult becomes cognitively lost. But the people described by James and Schaller suggest that this is not inevitable and hence should lead us to question the view that language is essential for human thought.

In the end, it might well be that there is a substantial amount of truth to the claim that language facilitates cognition—perhaps it *can* bring unconscious concepts to conscious light, lead to the shaping of new concepts, cause the unfolding of modular processes, and facilitate long chains of reasoning. This is nothing to sneer at. And there is no doubt that language is a great tool for the accumulation and dissemination of culture. But language does not, in itself, spark creative powers in individuals, and humans without language are, nonetheless, conscious and complete individuals.

Interaction and accumulation as the source of creative powers

So what is the solution to the question of the origin of genuinely new capacities? The proposal that I will endorse here is an old one, perhaps obvious to many, and it starts with the observation that there is a sense in which the claim that humans can do number theory and fly to the moon is false. After all, individual humans *cannot* do such things. Such creative powers exist only as the result of the accumulation of the efforts of many humans over many generations. Hence a psychological theory need not and cannot entirely explain the genesis of human creative powers, as such powers emerge under certain limited circumstances, over many generations and through the extended interactions of many people.

This leads to the following suggestion. There is no extra-modular capacity in humans, no general intelligence. Humans are nothing more than souped-up primates, chimpanzees with certain enhanced abilities, and a naked human, without history and without society, is no more capable of creating science or technology than is a naked chimp. But our special abilities allow for the accumulation and storage of information, and this makes it possible, over the course of many generations, for science and technology to emerge. This type of good design emerges not through natural selection, but out of the interaction of humans with other humans and with the external world.

To see the general idea, consider some examples. It is a fact about people that we can move thousands of pounds of objects from one place to another in a short period of time. But we would be wrong to look for the specific physiological adaptations that individual humans possess that gives rise to this ability. Individual humans have *not* evolved such an ability; instead the cumulative and coordinated behaviour of individuals leads to this emergent phenomena. In this case, the mechanism underlying this emergence is simple—the world works such that if many people each move a single object, many objects will be moved. Now consider the acquisition of knowledge. If a hundred people each move in a different direction, observe their environment, and then meet again and report to each other what they saw, each individual can rapidly gain information that would otherwise be impossible to have attained in so short a time.

The same kind of emergence might explain the emergence of science and technology. Each individual human has certain limited abilities to manipulate the world and learn from the environment. But humans can work in a coordinated fashion and can build on the accomplishments of other humans, across both time and space. We can build tools and then use them to make other tools; we can learn about different domains and then bootstrap from this knowledge to new knowledge (see also Whitehead 1926; Vygotsky 1978; Bruner 1990; Dennett 1995; Clark 1997).

This is admittedly not a solution to the puzzle of where human creative powers come from; at best it is an idea as to what a solution might look like. A solution would have two parts—one, a description of the cognitive prerequisites for accumulation, and, two, an explanation as to how this accumulation leads to the emergence of abilities that show signs of good design, or adaptive complexity. The prerequisites probably include adaptations such as language, which is essential to the dramatic sort of accumulation and transfer of cultural knowledge we find in our species (Tomasello *et al.* 1993). There is also a 'theory of mind'—an understanding of the thoughts, emotions, desires, and goals of others. While other primates possess some abilities in this domain, much of the innate human capacity appears to be special to our species (Povinelli and Preuss 1995). Other relevant proposals include the capacity to deal with meta-representation (Sperber 1994), and some ability to appreciate generativity and recursion (Corballis 1992).

It is the second part of the explanation that might be hardest. Exactly *how* is it that the limited abilities of humans can give rise to this unprecedented type of accumulation? To see why this is such a problem, imagine we found a species of fish that, by rubbing against undersea plants, shaped the plants into sculptures of dead American presidents. Plainly this could not be a biological adaptation on the part of the fish. Suppose someone said: "Here's the solution to this mystery. No individual fish has the ability to create such statues. But individual fish have evolved the tendency to swim close to the plants so as to evade predators. Well, it so happens that, over time, the continued motion of the fish brushing against the plants has a cumulative effect, and the plants come to take the form of dead American presidents." Suppose that close observation showed that this was actually *correct*—that plants only took their forms over the course of generations of fish (just as it is likely to be correct that science and technology only emerge over the course of generations of humans). This response would still be severely lacking as an explanation, as we would be left with the question as to why nature works this way.

There is, however, an interesting difference between the fish example and the human case. In the fish example, the relationship between the actions of the individual fish and the eventual outcome that these actions produced is arbitrary. There is no reason why continued brushing against plants should cause them to look like dead presidents. But the relationship between the abilities that humans have evolved and the products of our creative powers is not arbitrary. Humans have certain beliefs about the world, in part as the result of our perceptual mechanisms. We can then draw inferences on the basis of these beliefs, and communicate them to others. If it turns out that some of these beliefs are *true*, and some of these inferences are truth-preserving, then this might enable the creative process that we are concerned with.

Such an account of human creative accomplishments cannot fail to have metaphysical implications. The fact that science can give rise to successful manipulation of the external world is evidence that some of the beliefs held by scientists are true of the world (Weinberg 1992). This argument extends as well to the beliefs that make science possible in the first place. In general, the notion that natural selection guides organisms to true beliefs about the world is not tenable; evolution selects for adaptive beliefs and there are many cases in which these are not the right ones (see Stein 1996). But the fact that our beliefs can accumulate so as to lead to improved understanding and manipulation suggests that they have some external warrant, that they sometimes accurately reflect the external world. This is a surprising fact about humans.

Even once the prerequisites for this accumulation process were present in our species, the emergence of these creative powers probably still reflects, to a large extent, historical accident. It might be that good design is never inevitable. But we can hopefully gain some insight as to how it is even possible. I have suggested that the answer in the case of human creative powers will not involve rejecting a modular view of the mind, but instead will require a careful analysis of the interaction between evolved modules, human interaction, and the external world.

Acknowledgements

I am grateful to Gil Diesendruck, Bill Ittelson. Lori Markson, and Karen Wynn for helpful comments on an earlier draft of this manuscript.

References

Au, T. K.-F. (1983). Chinese and English counterfactuals: the Sapir–Whorf hypothesis revisited. *Cognition*, **15**, 155–87.
Bickerton, D. (1995). *Language and human behavior*. University of Washington Press, Seattle.
Bloom, P. (1996). Intention, history, and artifact concepts. *Cognition*, **60**, 1–29.
Bloom, P. (1998*a*). Some issues in the evolution of language and thought. In *The evolution of mind* (ed. D. D. Cummins and C. Allen) pp. 205–23. Oxford University Press.
Bloom, P. (1998*b*). Roots of word learning. In *Conceptual development and language acquisition* (ed. M. Bowerman and S. Levinson), in press. Cambridge University Press.
Bloom, P. and Wynn, K. (1994). The real problem with constructivism. *Behavioral and Brain Sciences*, **17**, 707–8.
Brown, R. (1958). *Words and things*. Free Press, New York.
Bruner, J. (1990). *Acts of meaning*. Cambridge University Press.
Carruthers, P. (1996). *Language, thought, and consciousness: an essay in philosophical psychology*. Cambridge University Press.
Chomsky, N. (1988). Language and problems of knowledge: the Managua lectures. MIT Press, Cambridge, MA.
Churchland, P. M. (1989). *A neurocomputational perspective: the nature of mind and the structure of science*. MIT Press, Cambridge, MA.
Clark, A. (1997). *Being there: putting brain, body, and world together again*. MIT Press, Cambridge, MA.
Clark, A. and Karmiloff-Smith, A. (1993). The cognizer's innards: a psychological and philosophical perspective on the development of thought. *Mind and Language*, **8**, 487–519.
Corballis, M. (1992). On the evolution of language and generativity. *Cognition*, **44**, 197–226.
Cosmides, L. and Tooby, J. (1987). From evolution to behavior: evolutionary psychology as the missing link. In *The latest on the best: essays on evolution and optimality* (ed. J. Dupre), p. 277–306. Cambridge University Press.
Cosmides, L. and Tooby, J. (1994). Origins of domain specificity: the evolution of functional organization. In *Mapping the mind: domain specificity in cognition and culture* (ed. L. A. Hirschfeld and S. A. Gelman), pp. 88–116. Cambridge University Press.
Cronin, H. (1992). *The ant and the peacock: altruism and sexual selection from Darwin to today*. Cambridge University Press.
Darwin, C. R. (1859/1964). *On the origin of species*. Harvard University Press, Cambridge, MA.
Darwin, C. R. (1871). *The descent of man and selection in relation in sex*. Hurst, New York.
Dawkins, R. (1986). *The blind watchmaker*. Norton, New York.
Dennett, D. C. (1993). Learning and labeling. *Mind and Language*, **8**, 540–8.
Dennett, D. C. (1995). *Darwin's dangerous idea*. Simon and Schuster, New York.
Dennett, D. C. (1996). *Kinds of minds*. Basic Books, New York.
Eccles, J. C. (1989). *Evolution of the brain: creation of the self*. Routledge, London.
Elman, J. L., Bates, E., and Johnson, M. (1996). *Rethinking innateness: a connectionist perspective on development*. MIT Press, Cambridge, MA.
Fodor, J. A. (1975). *The language of thought*. Crowell, New York.
Fodor, J. A. (1983). *The modularity of mind*. MIT Press, Cambridge, MA.

Gelman, S. (1996). Concepts and theories. In *Perceptual and cognitive development* (ed. R. Gelman and T. Au), pp. 117–50. Academic Press, San Diego, CA.

Gergely, G., Zoltan, N., Csibra, G., and Biro, S. (1995). Taking the intentional stance at 12 months of age. *Cognition*, **56**, 165–93.

Goodman, N. (1983). *Fact, fiction, and forecast*. Harvard University Press, Cambridge, MA.

Gould, S. (1997). Darwinian fundamentalism. *The New York Review of Books*, **44**, (10), 34–7.

Gould, S. J. and Lewontin, R. (1979). The spandrels of San Marco and the Panglossian paradigm: a critique of the adaptationist programme. *Proceedings of the Royal Society*, **205**, 581–98.

Gould, S. J. and Vrba, E. (1982). Exaptation: a missing term in the science of form. *Paleobiology*, **8**, 4–15.

Jackendoff, R. (1996). How language helps us think. *Pragmatics and Cognition*, **4**, 1–34.

James, W. (1893). Thought before language: a deaf–mute's recollections. *American Annals of the Deaf*, **38**, 135–45.

Karmiloff-Smith, A. (1992). Beyond modularity: a developmental perspective on cognitive science. MIT Press, Cambridge, MA.

Kay, P and Kempton, W. (1984). What is the Sapir–Whorf hypothesis? *American Anthropologist*, **86**, 65–79.

Lerdahl, F. and Jackendoff, R. (1983). *A generative theory of tonal music*. MIT Press, Cambridge, MA.

Levinson, S. C. (1996). Frames of reference and Molyneux's question: crosslinguistic evidence. In *Language and space* (ed. P. Bloom, M. Peterson, L. Nadel, and M. Garrett), pp. 109–69. MIT Press, Cambridge, MA.

Malotki, E. (1983). *Hopi time: a linguistic analysis of the temporal concepts in the Hopi language*. Mouton, New York.

Markman, E. M. and Hutchinson, J. E. (1984). Children's sensitivity to constraints in word meaning: taxonomic versus thematic relations. *Cognitive Psychology*, **16**, 1–27.

Mayr, E. (1982). *The growth of biological thought*. MIT Press, Cambridge, MA.

Mithen, S. (1996). *The prehistory of the mind*. Thames and Hudson, London.

O'Keefe, J. and Nadel, L. (1978). *The hippocampus as a cognitive map*. Clarendon Press, Oxford.

Paley, W. (1802/1851). *Natural theology: evidence of the existences and attributes of the deity, collected from the appearances of nature*. Gould and Lincoln, Boston.

Penrose, R. (1989). *The emperor's new mind*. Oxford University Press.

Peterson, M., Nadel, L., Bloom, P., and Garrett, M. (1996). Space and language. In *Language and space* (ed. P. Bloom, M. Peterson, L. Nadel, and M. Garrett), pp. 553–77. MIT Press, Cambridge, MA.

Piattelli-Palmarini, M. (1989). Evolution, selection, and cognition: from 'learning' to parameter-setting in biology and the study of language. *Cognition*, **31**, 1–44.

Pinker, S. (1992). Review of *Language and Species*. *Language*, **68**, 375–82.

Pinker, S. (1994). *The language instinct*. Morrow, New York.

Pinker, S. (1997). *How the mind works*. Norton, New York.

Pinker, S. and Bloom, P. (1990). Natural language and natural selection. *Behavioural and Brain Sciences*, **13**, 585–642.

Povinelli, D. and Preuss, T. (1995). Theory of mind: evolutionary history of a cognitive specialization. *Trends in Neurosciences*, **18**, 418–24.

Quine, W. V. O. (1960). *Word and object*. MIT Press, Cambridge, MA.

Rozin, P. and Schull, J. (1988). The adaptive–evolutionary point of view in experimental psychology. In *Stevens' handbook of experimental psychology, Vol. 1: Perception and motivation*, (2nd edn), (ed. R. Atkinson, R. J. Herrnstein, G. Lindzey, and R. D. Luce), pp. 503–46. Wiley, New York.

Sacks, O. (1988). *Seeing voices: a journey into the world of the deaf*. University of California Press, Berkeley, CA.

Schaller, S. (1991). *A man without words*. Summit Press, New York.

Spelke, E. S. (1994). Initial knowledge: six suggestions. *Cognition*, **50**, 431–45.

Sperber, D. (1994). The modularity of thought and the epidemiology of representations. In *Mapping the mind: domain specificity in cognition and culture* (ed. L. A. Hirschfeld and S. A. Gelman), pp. 39–67. Cambridge University Press.

Stein, E. (1996). *Without good reason: the rationality debate in philosophy and cognitive science*. Oxford University Press, New York.

Tomasello, M., Kruger, A. C., and Ratner, H. H. (1993). Cultural learning. *Behavioural and Brain Sciences*, **16**, 495–552.

Vygotsky, L. S. (1978). *Mind in society: the development of higher psychological processes*. Harvard University Press, Cambridge, MA.

Weinberg, S. (1992). *Dreams of a final theory*. Pantheon Books, New York.

Whitehead, A. N. (1926). *Science and the modern world*. Macmillan, New York.

Whorf, B. L. (1956). *Language, thought, and reality*. MIT Press, Cambridge, MA.

Williams, G. C. (1966). *Adaptation and natural selection*. Princeton University Press.

Wolfe, A. (1997). [Editorial correspondence]. *The New Republic*, **216**, correspondence starts on p. 5 and continues on p. 49 of issue 4 (February 17, 1997).

Wynn, K. (1996). Infants' individuation and enumeration of actions. *Psychological Science*, **7**, 164–9.

16

Social influences on human assortative mating

Del Thiessen

Introduction

Mating is never random within a species—presenting some of the most exciting and perplexing problems in the biological and social sciences. Various explanations for non-random mating are summarized in Table 16.1. The explanations are of two kinds, those that depend on individual mate selection and those that depend on social-demographic or ecological factors.

Sociobiologists and evolutionary psychologists emphasize that mate choice is based on Darwinian natural selection for individual fitness (column one of Table 16.1). I refer to this as the *individual imperative*. According to this view individuals choose each other for traits that potentially increase reproductive competence, including traits that underlie complex social behaviours. Advocates for alternative formulations (column two of Table 16.1), while acknowledging individual choice behaviour, stress the organizing nature of social-demographic and ecological processes. For them social systems are not merely the outgrowth of individual strivings for reproduction, but are the environmental surround for determining individual survival and reproduction. These multiple features of the environment that determine individual success or failure I refer to as the *collective imperative*. Ecologist Eric Pianka (1974) stressed the importance of the collective imperative by saying:

Every individual is simultaneously a member of a population, a species, and a community, and must therefore be adapted to cope with each, and must be considered in that context. An individual's fitness, or its ability to perpetuate itself as measured by its reproductive success, is determined not only by its status within its own population, but also by the various interspecific associations of its species, and especially by the particular community in which it finds itself. Similarly, every community is composed of many populations and numerous individuals, which determine many, but by no means all, of its properties (p. 5).

There is no doubt that the individual and collective imperatives of mate choice are two sides of a single coin, yet they are often seen as distinctive and in opposition. The ageless arguments, often highlighted as a struggle between nature and nurture, have resulted in a theoretical chasm between those who pursue a Darwinian fitness explanation of behaviour and those who believe that individual behaviours emerge

Table 16.1. *Explanation for non-random mating*

Individual mate choice	Social-demographic and ecological constraints
Natural selection for traits of fitness in monogamous or polygamous mating systems (Williams 1966)	Age, sex, and class distributions, restraining availability of mates (Krebs and Davies 1991)
Natural selection for trait similarity and compatibility of reproductive functions [assortative mating] (Rushton 1995; Thiessen and Gregg 1980)	Habitat selection which parses populations according to behavioural and other characteristics (Bouchard *et al.* 1990)
Sensory dispositions for unique traits that may have fitness value (Ryan and Kirkpatrick (1995)	Uneven distribution of resources, requiring unique foraging and mating strategies (Bronson 1989)

from a complex interaction between ecosystems and genomes (Cosmides and Tooby 1992). Eventually we can expect a resolution between these perspectives, perhaps when sociobiological notions about individual imperatives have been pushed to their limits. Already there are signs that natural selection theory can be merged with alternative models of evolutionary change, many of which are only indirectly associated with individual reproduction. Among the recent additions to natural selection theory are concepts of self-organization of individuals and communities (Kauffman 1993), phylogenetic and ecological constraints on behavioural variations (Eldredge 1995; Raff 1996), and principles of scaling that show inevitable relationships between structures and functions (Thiessen and Villarreal 1997). These and other efforts show that individual drives for self-perpetuation are linked with pervasive historical and environmental influences. As theoretical advances continue we can look forward to a more pluralistic and inclusive theory of complex behaviour.

In this discussion on assortative mating of couples I touch on the complex interactions between individual mate selection and human social ecology. There are compelling ties between individual goals of assortment and social influences on couples, even to the point that it is difficult to argue a separation between the two. Couples might gain reproductive advantages by selecting mates who share similar traits and genes, but the overall success of the assortment strategy hinges on social forces that support or undermine the strategy of individuals. I first present the genetic argument for human mate assortment, showing how Darwinian ideas of natural selection have influenced our view. I then refer to experimental data, suggesting that the social perceptions of couples by others influence the mate assortment process. This social-perceptual influence extends to incestual relations where mate assortment is extreme. Finally, I attempt to generalize these findings to a more formal theory of individual and social influences on human mate selection.

Genetic benefits of human assortative mating

Humans and other species tend to choose mates (as well as friends and possibly work associates) for phenotypic similarity. On the average married couples tend to correlate highly on age ($r \sim 0.85$; Susanne and Lepage 1988), demographic and socioeconomic parameters ($r \sim 0.40$–0.70; Lykken and Tellegen 1993; Herrnstein and Murray 1994), and intellectual measures ($r \sim 0.40$–0.60; Jensen 1978). Couples correlate to a lesser extent on personality variables ($r \sim 0.25$; Mascie-Taylor and Vandenberg 1988) and on physical attributes ($r \sim 0.30$; Spuhler 1968). This non-random distribution of mate selection is referred to as 'positive assortment', or just 'assortment' unless specified (Vandenberg 1972). The assumption is that choosing others on the basis of phenotypic similarity results in choosing for gene similarity. Indeed, heterosexual couples tend to select mates on traits that have high heritability (J. Rushton 1995). What this means is that couples who assort on phenotypic similarity, as with cognitive abilities, personality, and physical traits, are assorting on identical or similar genes for those traits. There is almost no support for the notion that couples converge in similarity over time (Griffiths and Kunz 1973; Thiessen and Gregg 1980; Epstein and Guttman 1984; Buss 1985; however, see Price and Vandenberg 1980; Zajonc *et al.* 1987). Couples are about as assorted on physical and psychological traits when they meet as they ever will be (Keller *et al.* 1996).

Several explanations have been advanced for positive assortment (Eckland 1968). These include mating for similarity because of the propinquity of individuals, because of economic benefits associated with mating, or because individuals who assort feel more comfortable together. While these proximate factors of everyday life might mediate mate choice, they do not address the underlying reasons for their existence—the ultimate causations. They do not suggest *why* propinquity of similar genotypes exists and *why* it leads to assortment, or *why* economic variables drive mate selection, or *why* one is more comfortable with others who are similar. The answers to such questions depend on deeper mechanisms, having to do with reproductive fitness.

There might be multiple biological reasons for positive assortment. Certainly, inclinations for assortment are strong. For one thing, assortment seems ubiquitous across species and cultures (Thiessen and Gregg 1980). It is even evident in cultures where marriages are arranged by parents or marriage brokers (unpublished observation, Muise and Thiessen 1997). The advantages seem to lie at the genetic level. As expected from notions of inclusive fitness (Hamilton 1964), couples who are genetically highly similar tend to have longer relationships and increased numbers of offspring (Thiessen and Gregg 1980; Bereczkei and Csanaky 1996). Apparently the tendency to assort can minimize the costs of mate cooperation, leading to increases in the probability of reproduction. The obvious limitation to this tendency involves high levels of inbreeding where the viability of offspring might be compromised (van den Berghe 1983) or where heterozygosity at the major histocompatibility complex is essential for optimal immune reactivity (Khlat and Khowry 1991; Ferstl *et al.* 1992).

The second apparent benefit of positive assortment is that offspring are related to each parent by the Mendelian expectation of 50% plus the extent to which partners assort on identical genes. For example, if two parents are highly assorted on some trait their offspring might be related to each parent by 52%, rather than the expected 50%. If natural selection tends to maximize gene reproduction then assortment for gene similarity would be a definite advantage—a reproductive bonus without an additional reproductive cost. Hypothetical differences between random mating (pan-

Table 16.2. *Number of offspring required to transmit all variable genes under different assumptions**

Percent of genes transmitted to each offspring each generation		*Number of offspring needed for total gene transmission*	
Degree of assortment	*% genes transmitted*	*20 000 genes*	*40 000 genes*
0 (panmixia)	50	15	16
10 (~first cousins)	55	13	14
50 (siblings)	75	8	8

* Each successive offspring carries 50% of those variable genes not expressed in other siblings. Some genes are obviously reproduced frequently, some only rarely. It is the rare statistical event that determines the high number of offspring necessary to include all genes. Thus, parents only rarely transmit *all* of their genes. I wish to thank David and Jason Cohen for the computer programme used to calculate number of offspring.

mixia) and assortment are shown in Table 16.2, based on the assumptions that we could possibly assort on 20 000–40 000 variable genes.

In practice it is difficult to measure the amount of increased gene similarity obtained between parent and offspring because of assortative mating. It is certainly much less than that obtained because of inbreeding for genes common by descent. Assortment is achieved through the selection of specific genes regardless of ancestry —a horizontal capture of limited gene similarity, rather than a wholesale increase in similarity because of vertical transmission of genes within a common lineage. If we assume that we possess 20 000 variable genes and that we tend to assort on 50 traits with high heritability, and that each trait is controlled by four genes, then increased similarity between parents and offspring due to assortment might be around one or two percent. Even though these increases of gene similarity seem rather insignificant in a single generation, a small difference extended over many generations can spell the difference between success and failure of alternative mating strategies.

Considering the genetic consequences of assortment one can begin to understand the reasons for the proximate mechanisms of mate choice. Propinquity, economic motivations, and feelings of comfort might be indirect ways to enhance gene similarity. Propinquity increases the likelihood of assortment because of the tendency of individuals with similar genes to select similar environments (Bouchard *et al.* 1990). Likewise, selection for economic benefits might be a stratification based on similarities of abilities among competing individuals (Herrnstein and Murray 1994). Finally, psychological comfort and compatibility might be the result of assortment rather than its cause, depending heavily on cost/benefit ratios of gene similarity (P. Rushton 1989).

The genetic argument, then, is that the proximate reasons for assortment might simply be the facets of natural selection that enhance individual gene replication (Table 16.1 column 1). The limitations of this explanation is that Darwinian views do not account for variations in assortment due to social, demographic, or ecological influences. These 'environmental' factors are generally considered by sociobiologists to be less directly involved in reproduction. We shall see, however, that they have the potential to modify how individuals optimize genetic fitness. In simplistic terms, the environment does not benignly *permit* natural selection to occur; the environment structures the constraints within which natural selection *can* occur.

The social world of mate assortment

Not only do males and females sense the amount of similarity they share, but others do as well. In one study of 59 dating couples we found that the couples typically report positive correlations for physical and psychological traits (Thiessen *et al.* 1997*a*). The range of correlations averaged between 0.34 and 0.66. When 50 strangers (upper-division undergraduate students) were presented with randomly displayed individual photographs of 12 of these couples (upper body photographs), strangers reassorted the dating couples at a statistical level far greater than chance ($\sim 23\%$ of the couples were correctly paired). This level of reassortment is astounding, considering that 'mispaired' couples might, in fact, also show similarities.

During the experiment we did not suggest to the subjects that they use cues of similarity to pair the couples, but only that they try to pair up the individuals of real dating couples. Similarity was in fact the critical cue. When subjects were later asked to rate the couples' similarity on a five-point scale, we found that the average correlation between the frequency with which the couples were paired and the rating of similarity was 0.50. Clearly, strangers detect similarity of couples, even for a limited number of traits for which assortment is generally low ($r \sim 0.30$).

Strangers not only assess similarity within couples but they make definite judgements about couples based on the degree of similarity they see. In this same experiment strangers were asked to estimate the extent to which the following questions applied (five-point scale):

1. Is this couple compatible?
2. Will this couple stay together?
3. Will this couple marry?
4. Will this couple reproduce?
5. Will others like this couple?
6. Will this couple cheat in this relationship?

The correlations between assessments of similarity and the extent to which strangers made attributions to the couples were all positive and highly significant except for the attribution about cheating, which in this study was slightly negative. These relations are seen in Fig. 16.1. Apparently strangers are using assessments of facial similarity to judge behavioural traits that might relate to reproductive fitness (Buss 1994). The value they place on couples depends upon the extent of perceived similarity.

Social intimacy and assortment

Attributions given couples by strangers could affect the reproductive process of couples through decisions about the degree and quality of social support provided by strangers. Strangers might, for example, show differing levels of intimacy toward couples depending on couple similarity. This could mean differential allocation of resources or social support to couples.

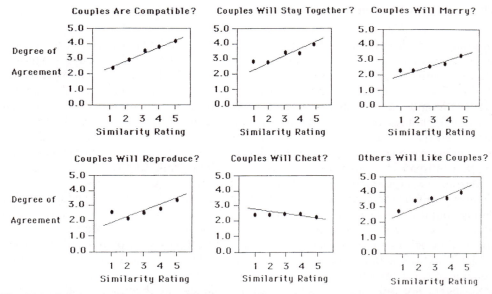

Fig. 16.1. Judgements by strangers of the relationships between ratings of couple similarity and strangers' agreement with attributions about those couples.

In a study of 60 upper-division undergraduate college students Thiessen *et al.* (unpublished observation 1997*c*) found that strangers' judgements of couple similarity were related to their willingness to be intimate with these couples. As in the earlier study we asked the strangers to rate the similarity and make attributions about couples displayed simultaneously on a projection screen. The pictures were of five couples selected randomly from those in an upper-division psychology course. Each couple was displayed with only the shoulders and heads visible; each individual wore the same black sweat shirt.

The amount of intimacy that strangers agreed to was based on a scale of intimacy developed on an independent sample of 61 upper-division undergraduate students, using a derivation of the Bogardus social distance scale (Bogardus 1933). Table 16.3 shows the correlations between assessments of couple similarity and the willingness of strangers to engage in various amounts of intimacy. Table 16.4 gives the correlations between assessments of couple similarity and attributions about these couples.

Table 16.3. *Correlations between ratings of couple similarity and level of desired intimacy*

	Couple designation				
Intimacy desired	*1*	*2*	*3*	*4*	*5*
Be friends with	0.17	0.18	0.41*	0.19	0.22
Dinner with	0.13	0.22	0.59**	0.30	0.15
Play with children	0.06	0.17	0.42**	0.51	0.23
Neighbour with	0.09	0.03	0.39*	0.38*	0.30
Vacation with	0.05	0.12	0.56**	0.19	0.22

*$P < 0.01$; **$P < 0.001$

Table 16.4. *Correlations between ratings of couple similarity and judgements of attributions*

Attributes	Couple designation				
	1	*2*	*3*	*4*	*5*
Compatibility of couple	0.29	0.46**	0.53**	0.58**	0.52**
Will relationship last?	0.21	0.48**	0.44**	0.51**	0.35*
Will couple marry?	0.41*	0.42**	0.35**	0.47**	0.38*
Will couple have children?	0.37*	0.41**	0.46**	0.61**	0.10
Will others like couple?	0.33*	0.28	0.60**	0.33**	0.40*
Will couple cheat?	−0.10	−0.11	−0.25	−0.48**	−0.11

$*P < 0.01$; $**P < 0.001$

For every level of intimacy, perceived similarity of couples seems to be important for the willingness of strangers to be intimate with couples. The relations are consistently positive but are statistically significant for only two of the five couples. This variation across couples suggests that attributes other than similarity might be of importance. There are several variables that went uncontrolled in this study, including (1) possible influences of correlations in similarity between strangers and couples, and (2) the influences of couple attractiveness. One should note that the correlations are higher between estimates of couple similarity and the amount of attributions, suggesting that judgements of reproductive attributes might be somewhat independent of the amount of intimacy that strangers prefer.

Social perception of couple similarity and incest

We predicted that positive evaluations of couples by strangers would decrease if the couples were relatives, or were depicted as relatives, and that the amount of positive regard would decrease as the degree of relatedness was thought to increase. We predicted this knowing that positive assortment goes down in communities where endogamy is practised (Thiessen and Gregg 1980) and that nuclear family incest is thought to be inappropriate by many individuals (van den Berghe 1983). Our second and related prediction was that the negative bias toward genetically related couples would be *less* for those couples who did not seem to be similar, and hence might seem not to share as many genes and would be at a lesser risk for inbreeding depression.

In a preliminary study with Russell Kingston to generate couples that differed in similarity we asked 70 upper-division undergraduate students to judge the similarity of pairs of heterosexual couples chosen and randomly paired from a university year book. Determinations of similarity of facial characteristics were made on a five-point scale for the 100 couples presented in a booklet form to each student. The students were not told what the relationship was between couples (zero), but many seemed to infer that they were dating couples.

From these determinations of couple similarity we constructed four sets of twenty pairs, four pairs from each of five levels of similarity. For each set, pairs were randomly labelled as Dating Couple, Brother/Sister Couple, Uncle/Niece Couple, or First Cousin Couple. Eighty three upper-division undergraduate students were asked

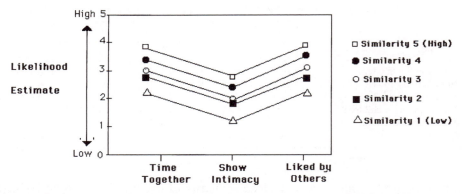

Fig. 16.2. Judgements by strangers of the likelihood that couples who differ in similarity will spend time together, be intimate, or be liked by others.

to judge these couples on a five-point scale for the likelihood of the couple (1) spending time together, (2) exhibiting signs of intimacy, (3) being likeable. All photographs of couples were counterbalanced for the labelling of the four amounts of genetic relatedness. Thus, the somewhat complicated analysis of variance design is four replications of a similarity (5) ×relatedness (4) ×questions (3). The experimental design enables us to test for interactions between assumed amounts of genetic relatedness, perceived facial similarity, and expectation of intimacy within couples.

Our predictions were variably supported. Regardless of our labels of genetic relatedness, couples who had previously been judged to be more similar were estimated to spend more time together, exhibit more signs of intimacy, and were seen to be liked more by others. As was expected for incestual relationships, there was a significant reduction in estimation of couple intimacy, but contrary to prediction, couples who were more similar were still judged to be more intimate. Apparently the bias for positive attributions associated with similarity extend to incestual relationships. These data are depicted in Fig. 16.2.

More in keeping with the negative attributions associated with incest, all amounts of relatedness reduce the subjects' estimate of the couple spending time together and especially the extent to which related couples were expected to show signs of intimacy. These findings are depicted in Fig. 16.3. What the data seem to indicate is that dating couples are expected to spend more time together and show more intimacy. Whether others are seen to like the couples depends on couple similarity and not family relatedness.

Thus, perceived similarity is still a determining factor in attributing positive traits to couples, but positive attributions are significantly attenuated for expressions of intimacy. Put another way, strangers believe that couples who are similar will spend more time together, display more intimacy, and be more likeable by others. Nevertheless, strangers are less likely to expect intimacy from couples at any level of familial relatedness from brother and sister, to uncle and niece, or to first cousins. Incest taboos are operative regardless of the amount of couple similarity.

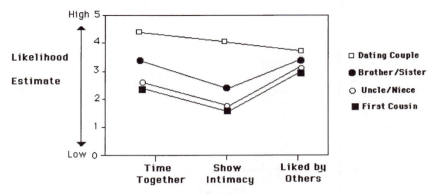

Fig. 16.3. Judgements by strangers of the likelihood that couples who differ in genetic relatedness will spend time together, be intimate, or be liked by others.

Can one talk another out of the incest taboo?

We still had not found that genetically related couples would be expected to be more intimate if they lacked phenotypic and hence genetic similarity. In the experiment just discussed estimates of intimacy were correlated with higher levels of phenotypic similarity, but all amounts of relatedness reduced the expectation of couple intimacy. In that study even first cousins were not considered to be kissing cousins no matter how dissimilar. We therefore wanted to extend judgements of strangers to second cousins, where inbreeding effects would be of lesser concern for observers (Thiessen *et al.* unpublished 1997*b*). We expected that dissimilar second cousins would be acceptable as reproductive partners.

In this experiment on attitudes toward incestual couples we asked upper-division undergraduate college students to look at pictures of two couples that we knew to differ widely in perceived similarity (1 or 5 on our scale of similarity). Four different sets of pictures were randomly presented to 85 students. Sometimes the pictures of the couple with low similarity was on the left of the page, sometimes on the right. Each of our subjects was asked to answer 'yes' or 'no' to the following three questions about each couple:

1. Do you think it is likely for this couple to date?
2. Do you think it is likely for this couple to marry?
3. Do you think it is likely for this couple to have children?

All couples, regardless of similarity, were described as second cousins. We emphasized the low genetic relatedness in several ways. We presented judges with a table of genetic relatedness for various degrees of relatedness including second cousin. In addition, we depicted a genetic pedigree leading to second-cousin marriage. Finally, we stressed that second cousins are only related to each other by 6.25% of their genes and that in most states it is legally permissible for second cousins to marry.

The data are summarized in Fig. 16.4. Students seem to condone second cousin relationships to the extent that the relationships are not associated with reproduction.

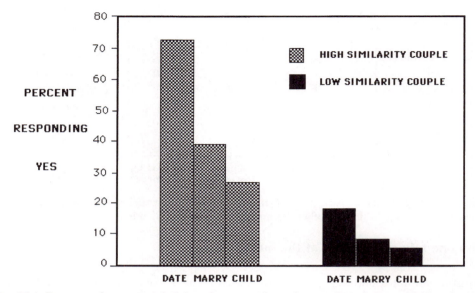

Fig. 16.4. Percent of strangers judging that second-cousin couples who are high or low in similarity would be expected to date, marry, or have children.

Dating is thought to be more likely than marriage, and marriage more likely than having offspring. Females more than males (81% versus 48%) believe that dating is likely between second cousins. Otherwise the sexes do not differ significantly in their judgements. Perhaps dating does not have the same sexual connotation for females as it does for males (Buss 1994). Second-cousin marriages, especially those leading to offspring, are not seen as likely by either sex.

Just as striking, all three behaviours are perceived as more likely among couples who are phenotypically similar. Once again we have negative conformation that low similarity in couples is associated with more positive attributions of dating, marrying, and reproduction. Similarity is a very robust regulator of reproductive expectations by strangers. However its influence is apparently overpowered by an incest taboo, even where the breeding effects on homozygosity is extremely low.

A theory of assortative mating

The evolutionary logic for positive assortative mating is consistent with Hamilton's (1964) concept of inclusive fitness. Assortment reduces the cost of social interactions for couples who share genes in common (Thiessen and Gregg 1980) and increases the likelihood of reproduction (Bereczkei and Csanaky 1996). Couples who assort on gene similarity seem to have more stable relations and ultimately transmit more genes to subsequent generations. Assortative mating does increase individual genetic fitness and is therefore likely to be enhanced through natural selection.

The expression of individual assortment for similarity is enriched by the social environment surrounding couples. Other individuals, including kin and non-kin often influence this process. It seems that couples might be adjusting their mate choices according to social influences. Individual decisions involving assortment take place in a sea of social approval or disapproval. Strangers as well as kin can potentially exert influences through their expressed attributions or through their decisions to help or not help the couple.

Merely knowing that others adjust their reactions to couples on the basis of similarity might be enough to influence choice behaviour. It is worth noting that the *individual imperative* for selecting mates with similar traits and genes is congruent with the social *collective imperative* that influences individuals in the same direction. The social influences compliment the individual tendencies to assort, suggesting that the individual and social benefits of assortment occur all around, perhaps as a part of people's reciprocal social exchange.

Physical similarity seems to direct a great deal of our attitudes toward couples. Couples who are highly similar are thought to possess positive traits, seem to be moving toward reproduction, and are those others are willing to interact with. We do not know how widely this halo effect spreads, as our focus was only on reproductive capabilities. It is possible that couples who are seen as similar are also believed to be more intelligent, more competent, and perhaps more attractive. Later research will enable us to make some estimate of the generality of the bias. Clearly people see the similarity within couples and adjust their attitudes accordingly.

In our experiments incest among relatives is not generally condoned, even for second cousins where genetic similarity is low. Nevertheless, beyond the general distaste for incest there is an influence of similarity on attributions. Strangers are more apt to attribute reproductive possibilities to genetic relatives to the degree that they are similar. The strongest negative biases are for genetic relatives possessing low similarity. In a sense, couples who are similar can do little wrong, even when they violate accepted incest taboos.

In these studies we have deliberately separated out the individual's evolutionary inclination to assort (the *individual imperative*) and the social milieu within which assortment takes place (the *collective imperative*). We did this mainly to emphasize that the genetic strategies of natural selection are part of a larger social, demographic, and ecological domain. We wish to point out their crucial interdependence. One cannot understand the individual expressions of strategies without knowing the larger environment. It is the complexity of the environment that facilitates or restrains the genetic code of reproduction, and it is the individual strategy that must adapt to the larger domain. The social sciences offer analyses of this wider domain within which natural selection acts and the individual prospers or fails.

Assortative mating is evident in many species (Thiessen and Gregg 1980), but only in humans is there a social pressure from peers to assort positively. The complexity of the central nervous system is no doubt responsible for this species-specific quality. It is not that humans have shifted away from the general animal pattern, but rather that humans have added a new influence to reinforce the genetic benefits of assortment. The evolutionary trajectory remains common to many species, but the proximate mechanisms are more cognitive in nature among humans.

The addition of social cognitive pressures for assortment suggests that assortment might be more important and more evident in humans than in other species. It is possible that our long life-span, the extended interval between births, and the associated increase in the necessity for parental investment in offspring increase the imperative for positive assortment. The paradox is that the increase in cognitive complexity might have reduced rather than increased the flexibility of mating choices. I have said little about the possible advantages for strangers. The mechanisms are not necessarily associated with kin relatedness, although related could enhance the pressure to assort. The question remains—why should strangers care whether or not couples assort? Their short-term benefits could be in the increased ability to understand couples who assort. What a stranger learns about one individual of a couple might facilitate the understanding of the other ('know one, know the other'). High similarity could thus enhance cooperation, or make deception by the stranger more advantageous. Deviations from high positive assortment, like any other deviation, might be treated with suspicion and avoidance. Whatever the reasons, it is clear that peers as well as relatives are motivated to reinforce phenotypic and genetic similarity between individuals within couples.

References

Bereczkei, T. and Csanaky, A. (1996). Mate choice, marital success, and reproduction in a modern society. *Ethology and Sociobiology*, **17**, 17–35.

Bogardus, E. S. (1933). A social distance scale. *Sociological and Social Research*, **17**, 265–71.

Bouchard, T. J., Jr., Lykken, D. T., McGue, M., Segal, N. L., and Tellegen, A. Sources of human psychological differences: the Minnesota study of twins reared apart. *Science*, **250**, 223–50.

Bronson, F. H. (1989). *Mammalian reproductive biology*. The University of Chicago Press.

Buss, D. M. (1985). Human mate selection. *American Scientist*, **73**, 47–51.

Buss, D. M. (1994). *The evolution of desire*: strategies of human mating. Basic Books, New York.

Cosmides, L. and Tooby, J. (1992). Cognitive adaptations for social exchange. In *The adapted mind*, (ed. J. H. Barkow, L. Cosmides, and J. Tooby), pp. 163–228. Oxford University Press, New York.

Eckland, B. K. (1968). Theories of mate selection. *Eugenics Quarterly*, **15**, 71–84.

Eldredge, N. (1995). *Reinventing Darwin*. Wiley, New York.

Epstein, E. and Guttman, R. (1984). Mate selection in man: evidence, theory, and outcome. *Social Biology*, **31**, 243–77.

Ferstl, R., Eggert, F., Westphal, E., Zavazova, N., and Müller-Ruchholtz, W. (1992). MHC-related odors in humans. In *Chemical signals in vertebrates 6*, (ed. R. L. Doty and D. Müller-Schwarze), pp. 205–12. Plenum, New York.

Griffith, R. W. and Kunz, P. O. (1973). Assortative mating. a study of physiognomic homogamy. *Social Biology*, **20**, 448–53.

Hamilton, W. D. (1964). The genetical evolution of social behaviour, I and II. *Journal of Theoretical Biology*, **7**, 1–52.

Herrnstein, R. J. and Murray, C. (1994). *The bell curve: intelligence and class structure in American life*. The Free Press, New York.

Jensen, A. R. (1978). How much can we boost IQ and scholastic achievement? *Harvard Educational Review*, **11**, 1–223.

Kauffman, S. A. (1993). *The origins of order: self-organization and selection in evolution*. Oxford University Press, New York.

Keller, M. C., Thiessen, D., and Young, R. K. (1996). Mate assortment in dating and married couples. *Personality and Individual Differences*, **2**, 217–21.

Khlat, M. and Khowry, M. (1991). Inbreeding and diseases: demographic, genetic, and epidemiologic perspectives. *Epidemiologic Reviews*, **13**, 28–41.

Krebs, J. R. and Davies, N. B. (ed.) (1991). *Behavioural ecology*. Blackwell, Oxford.

Lykken, D. T. and Tellegen, A. (1993). Is human mating adventitious or the result of lawful choice? A twin study of mate selection. *Journal of Personality and Social Psychology*, **65**, 56–68.

Mascie-Taylor, C. G. N. and Vandenberg, S. (1988). Assortative mating for IQ and personality due to propinquity and personal preference. *Behaviour Genetics*, **18**, 339–45.

Muise, J. and Thiessen, D. (1997). Evidence for assortative mating in cultures where marriages are arranged. In preparation.

Pianka, E. R. (1974). *Evolutionary ecology*. Harper and Row, New York.

Price, R. A., and Vandenberg, S. (1980). Spouse similarity in American and Swedish couples. *Behaviour Genetics*, **10**, 59–71.

Raff, R. A. (1996). *The shape of life: genes, development, and the evolution of animal form*. University of Chicago Press.

Rushton, J. P. (1995). *Race, evolution, and behaviour*. Transaction Publishers, New Brunswick.

Rushton, P. (1989). Genetic similarity, human altruism, and group selection. *Behavioral and Brain Sciences*, **12**, 503–59.

Ryan, M. J. and Kirkpatrick, M. A. (1995). Sexual selection. *Discovery*, **13**, 29–33.

Spuhler, J. N. (1968). Assortative mating with respect to physical characteristics. *Social Biology*, **15**, 128–40.

Susanne, C. and Lepage, Y. (1988). Assortative mating for anthropometric characters. In *Human mating patterns: society for the study of human biology symposium series No. 28*, (ed. C. G. N. Mascie-Taylor and A .J. Boyce), pp. 61–82. Cambridge University Press.

Thiessen, D. and Gregg, B. (1980). Human assortative mating and genetic equilibrium: an evolutionary perspective. *Ethology and Sociobiology*, **1**, 111–40.

Thiessen, D. and Villarreal, R. (1997). Allometry and comparative psychology: technique and theory. In *Encyclopedia of Comparative Psychology*, (ed. G. Greenberg and M. Haraway), pp. 1–30. Garland Press, New York.

Thiessen, D., Young, R. K., and Delgado, M. (1997*a*). Social pressures for assortative mating. *Personality and Individual Differences*, **22**, 157–64.

Thiessen, D., Young, R. K., and Kingston, R. (1997*b*). Modification of the incest taboo by variations in couple similarity. In preparation.

Thiessen, D., Young, R. K., and Rosenbaum, S. (1997*c*). Couple similarity affects willingness to be intimate. In preparation.

van den Berghe, P. L. (1983). Human inbreeding avoidance: culture in nature. *Behavioral and Brain Sciences*, **6**, 91–123.

Vandenberg. S. G. (1972). Assortative mating, or who marries whom? *Behaviour Genetics*, **2**, 127–58.

Williams, G. C. (1966). *Adaptation and natural selection: a critique of some current evolutionary thought*. Princeton University Press.

Zajonc, R. B., Adelmann, P. K., Murphy, S. T., and Niedenthal, P. M. (1987). Convergence in the physical appearance of spouses. *Motivation and Emotion*, **1**, 335–46.

17

On the recent origin of symbolically-mediated language and its implications for psychological science

Andrew Lock

Introduction

When might humans have begun to use language? The recent literature that deals with this question provides hypotheses of all shades. For example, Pinker (1994, pp. 352–3) claims that "the first traces of language could have appeared as early as *Australopithecus africanus*. ... It is easy to imagine some form of language contributing to [the success of *Homo erectus*]." Holloway (1969) and Tobias (1987, 1991) also argue for an early emergence of language, not with australopithecines, but perhaps with *Homo habilis*. Bickerton (1990) is more conservative. He draws a distinction between protolanguage and language, and argues that "protolanguage did not develop until *erectus* emerged. This would give protolanguage a time depth of around a million and a half years" (p. 141). In his view, real language, as distinct from protolanguage, arose more recently, with modern humans, giving it a time-depth of at least 100 000 years. Bickerton is thus in agreement with Lieberman (1991) who is confident that "we can date language as we know it back to at least ... 100 000 years ago at the edge of Africa and Asia" (p. 172). Noble and Davidson (1996) are more conservative still, concluding that it was "sometime between about 100 000 and 70 000 years before the present [that] the behaviour emerged which has become identified as linguistic" (p. 217).

Yet there is precious little evidence for language even at that late stage: As Halverson (1993) notes, "we do not know whether the Cro-Magnons [at 35 000 bp] even had a fully developed, *grammaticized language*" (p. 762). And if we were to appeal to direct data, then the earliest incontrovertible evidence that humans could speak is not much more than 100 years old (i.e. Edison's recordings). Beyond that, we must work by inference from less direct evidence. What do these sources tell us?

Setting the boundaries

The earliest dates for the appearance of the species to which we belong, *Homo sapiens*, are unclear. The earliest specimens which might be 'like us', such as those from Petralona and Heidelberg at around 300 000 years ago, are theoretically indistinguishable from the later members of *Homo erectus*. Current evidence points to anatomically modern *Homo sapiens* as being a very recent species, less than 200 000 years old. The earliest dates for anatomically-modern human fossil remains are around 100 000 years ago (e.g. those from Klasies River Mouth, South Africa, and from Skhül and Qafzeh, both Near East—see Campbell 1996; Waddell and Penny 1996). Mitochondrial and nuclear DNA studies are consistent with the conclusion that the human species had an African origin within the past 200 000 years, and began to move out of Africa from around 100 000 years ago or later (though not necessarily in one wave). What do we know about these early modern humans?

Human species characteristics

We are faced today with an organism that would appear to have possessed a human-like brain for at least 1.5 million years; that has an upper respiratory tract modification, dating back around 0.75 million years, that is most parsimoniously explained as an adaptation for human-like vocalization capabilities; and whose technological skills seem to have been based on modern intellectual capacities for around 0.3 million years. The evidence for these claims is reviewed below.

Brain organization

The first member of the human genus, *Homo habilis*, is dated to a little over 2 million years ago (Wood 1992). *Homo habilis*, or its conspecific *Homo rudolfensis*, provides the first evidence for a human-like specialization of the brain. There is a consensus that the endocast of the specimen KNM-ER 1470 shows a somewhat more complex and modern-human-like third inferior frontal convolution than is typical of modern apes, suggesting that by this point the brain was becoming organized into a more human rather than ape form (see Holloway 1996 for a review). Also evident from this skull is a reorganization of the posterior cortex, which Wilkins and Wakefield (1995, p.171) take as indicative of a shift in cognitive functioning from that of apes to a "uniquely human modality-free sensory representation". Thus, from very early in our genus, with respect to the inferior frontal and inferior parieto-temporal cortices, there is evidence of a more human-like structure than previously seen. However, no data are available from this time about the configuration of the basicranium[1], and thus there is no way of telling whether the evidence on the development of Broca's area provides a basis for enhanced right-hand motor control or the voluntary control of vocalization (see Peters 1996). Later endocasts through *Homo erectus* and archaic *sapiens* specimens are devoid of clear convolutional detail (Holloway 1996), thus making it impossible to be certain about any further possible re-organizational changes within our own genus. Evidence as to the appearance of modern brain organization is scarce. But, a reasonable assumption would be that the brain of modern humans is a species characteristic, and as such, the brains of early examples

---

[1] Laitman and Heimbuch (1982) have examined the contemporaneous specimen OH24, and this indicates, despite a somewhat distorted basicranial region, a configuration closer to extant apes than to modern humans. However the data are not conclusive.

of our species at around 100 000 years ago would be the same kinds of organ as those we find in individuals who have existed since then.

Vocal capabilities

It is not until *Homo erectus sensu stricto*, particularly specimen KNM-ER 3733 (*Homo ergaster sensu*; Wood 1992), that an incipient flexion of the basicranium is found. This partial flexion might well correspond to a partial descent of the larynx, which would have increased this specimen's ability to make more human-like sounds (Laitman and Heimbuch 1984; Laitman *et al.* 1992). The configuration of the basicranium of the skull of earlier hominid fossils, as well as later Neanderthal ones, indicates that their upper respiratory anatomy was not fully modern, but was more akin to the general primate configuration (which allows for simultaneous swallowing and breathing without the danger of choking that modern humans risk). Data are not available for later *H. erectus* specimens other than the Salé specimen—possibly early *sapiens* rather than late *erectus* (Hublin 1985)—which appears to show the modern configuration. Other specimens of middle to late Pleistocene hominids assigned as archaic *H. sapiens*, such as those found at Petralona and Broken Hill, have basicranial configurations that lie within the modern range. On the basis of these analyses it can be inferred that their upper respiratory tracts were also similar to our own (e.g. Laitman *et al.* 1992). This would suggest sound production (or speech) capability on a par with that of current humans (see Laitman and Reidenberg 1988; Arensburg *et al.* 1989), but this point has perhaps been over-emphasized in the literature. Thus it would appear that there have been changes in the structure of the hominid upper respiratory system over a period of at least 750 000 years which can only be explained as an adaptation to vocal communication[2]. The full adaptive anatomical suite is a species characteristic of anatomically modern *Homo sapiens*.

Intelligence

When might modern cognitive abilities have come into being? How far back in the record can we go before we fail to find evidence of capabilities that would fall within the range we can infer for modern humans? The only source of evidence is the material record.

H. habilis is regarded as having made those stone tools referred to as the Oldowan industry, consisting of simple core and flake tools of basalt, quartz, and quartzite.

---

[2] The change in the hominid basicranial configuration with its concomitant repositioning of the larynx could represent either an adaptation for vocal communication or a change brought about by other means that was subsequently co-opted for vocal communication. These other means could either be adaptive in themselves—that is, to meet some 'pressure' other than a communicative one—or 'accidental'—for example a structural response to the torsional stresses of reconfiguring the upper spinal and thoracic anatomy to deal with a bipedal posture. The former possibility seems unlikely on the weak grounds that no such 'pressure' has ever been proposed. The latter is also unlikely on two stronger grounds: that hominid bipedalism was well established before the reconfiguration of the basicranium becomes apparent, and the reconfiguration is not marked in Neanderthal specimens which were clearly bipedal. Similarly, had these changes occurred as mechanical responses to stresses generated by the enlargement of the brain, they should be apparent in Neanderthal specimens.

Wynn (1996) notes of these tools that:

There is considerable question as to the reality of the tool types in the Oldowan. If by type we mean a well-defined category of tool that existed in the minds of the tool-makers, then we would be unable to argue for their existence. ...It is doubtful whether there were any design criteria whatsoever, beyond perhaps big and little (p. 267).

Similarly, Toth and Schick (1993) note that the so-called 'core tools' are 'not necessarily tools, nor do they necessarily correspond to 'mental templates' held by their early makers' (p. 349). Toth and Schick (1993) and Fagan (1989) agree that this is an ad hoc technology, and Wynn (1996) concludes that "Oldowan tools did not require a particularly sophisticated intelligence" (p. 267). Nevertheless, these writers are of the view that the cognitive capabilities of these tool-makers might show some advance over that of modern apes in two ways: first in the planning of the sequences of motor actions needed to produce such tools; and second in judging the angles and overhangs of the 'blank' cores with respect to the angle and force of the blow required to effectively flake the stone.

The technology associated with early forms of *H. erectus*, by contrast, seems to be much more sophisticated, and the typical Acheulean hand-axe or biface is "the first type tool that is clearly outside the range of an ape technology" (Wynn 1996, p. 269). The symmetrical nature of the early bifaces could be produced without their makers having any mental concept of symmetry (Wynn 1996; see also Davidson and Noble 1993), and there is, in fact, no consensus that these bi-faces were actually tools, as distinct from the cores or debris left from making flake tools (e.g. Bradley and Sampson 1986; Potts 1989)[3]. But the later bifaces show such a high degree of three-dimensional symmetry that to regard them as being only core remains and not the intended finished artefact seems to be stretching it. For example, both of the cores in Fig. 17.1 appear to have been worked on in order to modify their final shape, and the flakes that have been removed appear to be waste rather than cutting flakes that were intended as such. With respect to the upper tool in Fig. 17.1, Wynn (1979) comments that "here the symmetry has been created by four short sections of retouch (A, B, C and D) which are not contiguous. In order to do this the maker had to have a competence in the relation of whole to parts" (p. 377): thus, the end result seems to have been anticipated before the observable retouching. And with respect to the lower tool in Fig. 17.1 he notes that:

Both faces of the original flake have been retouched to yield a remarkably straight edge. ...in order to have produced such artificial straightness the knapper had to have related each flake removal to all the others and also to a stable point of view (p. 378).

That stable point of view had to be "conserved in the knapper's imagination during the actual flaking process" (p. 380). On this basis, Wynn concludes that:

these artefacts required the organizational abilities of operational intelligence and...therefore, the hominid knappers were not significantly less intelligent than modern adults (p. 371).

---

[3] It is not even clear that Acheulian bi-faces deserve their traditional name of 'hand-axe'. Personal experience suggests that trying to use any of these forms as an axe is as likely to result in butchering one's own hand as it is in chopping the material it is aimed at.

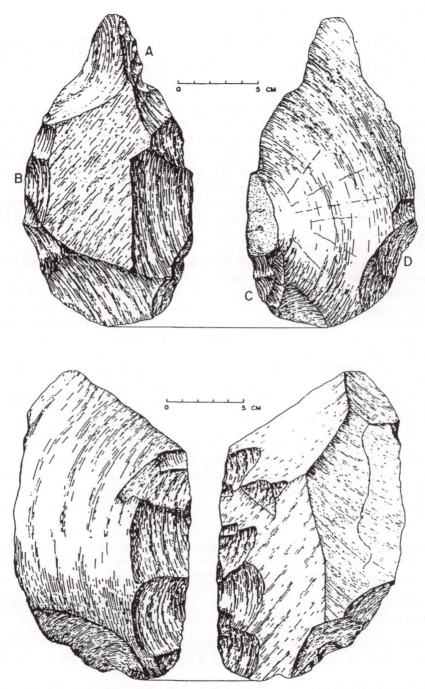

Fig. 17.1. a (above) and b (below). Acheulian cores that give evidence of part–whole relations being used to inform the planning of their making (from Wynn 1979, pp. 376 and 379).

His overall conclusion is that 'essentially modern intelligence was achieved 300 000 years ago' (p. 371).

It would seem, then, that early modern humans had an essentially modern intelligence, and on that basis also had the capacity to act in the ways that later modern humans do. What evidence is there that they used this capacity?

Indices of intelligent behaviour

The material artefacts associated with these early moderns actually lack many of the characteristics of the modern tool-kit, and overall, early anatomically-modern human remains are associated with industries of greater antiquity and non-modern characteristics, leading Stringer (1989), for example, to conclude that:

if the postulated dispersal of anatomically modern humans from Africa was associated with new forms of cultural or behavioural expression, this was not reflected in any simple or direct way in the character of the associated lithic industries (p. 7).

Thus, *modern human behaviour is not a species characteristic*. In fact, there is an emerging consensus in palaeoanthropology of a marked temporal disjunction between the appearance of anatomically-modern human forms—the species *Homo sapiens*—and modern species-typical behaviour (for a marshalling of the evidence, see Noble and Davidson 1996). For, quite remarkably, the period from the emergence of our species through to around 40 000 years ago shows little substantive change in the archaeological record associated with modern human forms as compared with more archaic ones. Throughout this period the artefacts of modern humans suggest remarkably un-modern activities. The complexity of the technology associated with both premodern and modern humans stays fairly constant with respect to technique, raw materials, number of components combined together, and the number of stages involved in the construction of tools (see Fig. 17.2, and Tables 17.1 and 17.2). And perhaps most tellingly, there is *no evidence of any symbolic practices* (e.g. Chase and Dibble 1987; Lindly and Clark 1990). As Lindly and Clark (1990) conclude from their review, "neither archaic *H. sapiens* nor morphologically modern humans demonstrate symbolic behaviour prior to the Upper Palaeolithic" (p. 233).

'Modern' behaviour

What characteristics must behaviour have to count as modern? Contemporary human activities rely on the social and cultural maintenance of symbolic resources. The means of both the maintenance and transmission of these symbols are conservative; the symbols themselves are volatile. The physical instantiations of contemporary human symbolic activities show temporal volatility, differential spatial distribution, and spatial relocation. *Temporal volatility* is not necessarily associated with functional utility. Clothing, for example, is functional, but fashion is volatile in entirely non-functional ways; hem lines on dresses go up and down for reasons unrelated to the non-symbolic function of wearing a dress, just as accepted male and female garb differs according to custom rather than function. *Differential spatial distribution* means that the pool of cultural products of human activities that would be found within five

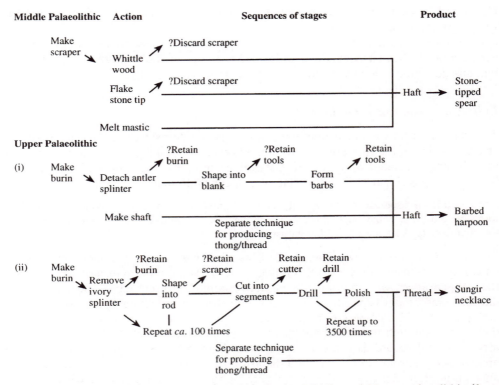

Fig. 17.2. Stages in tool (and ornament) making in the Middle and Upper palaeolithic (from Dennell 1983, p. 85).

kilometres of where you are reading this chapter will have a different constitution from those within five kilometres of another person in Tibet or New Guinea. If an inventory were available for your actual present location five years ago, then the temporal volatility of those products would again be apparent. *Spatial relocation* is demonstrable in the same way—the natural availability of the products that make up cultural materials within five kilometres of any particular point is vastly different from the proportions in which they have been assembled by that culture. The resources available to us move over large distances; even the food on one's plate can be a geography lesson.

Taking these properties as criteria for characterizing modern human cultural practices, we can ask when, in the archaeological record, is there evidence that humans acted in characteristically modern ways? That is, when did the material artefacts associated with humans show patterns of temporal volatility, differential spatial distribution, and spatial relocation?

1. The evidence is almost completely negative before 40 000 years ago. Before that time there is abundant evidence, in the form of artefacts, that cultural activities were a characteristic of human life, way back to non-modern *Homo* species approximately 2 million years ago—but there is very little unequivocal evidence of symbolic mediation, as indexed by the above characteristics.

Table 17.1. *Techniques for working raw materials in the Middle and Upper palaeolithic (from Dennell 1983, p. 82).*

Middle Palaeolithic		Upper Palaeolithic	
Technique	*Material*	*Technique*	*Material*
Percussion	Bone, stone		
Whittling	Wood		
Scraping	Wood, skin		
Cutting	Wood, skin, meat		
		Pressure flaking	Stone
		Drilling	Bone, ivory, antler
		Splintering	Bone, ivory, antler
		Twisting	Fibres
		Lashing	Skins, wood
		Carving	Stone
		Engraving	Stone
		Kneading	Clay
		Grinding/polishing	Stone, bone
		?Matting	Animal hair
		Compression:	
		straightening	Ivory
		bending	Wood
		?Tension:	
		stretching	?Bow string

2. The evidence is conclusively positive after 20 000 years ago (a point in time often referred to as the 'symbolic explosion'); the evidence of the intervening 20 000 years is less clear cut, but strongly supportive of human life being a symbolically-mediated activity, even if the spatial and temporal distribution of cultural artefacts were not fully modern in their characteristics.

Table 17.2. *Numbers of components in Middle and Upper Palaeolithic artefacts (from Dennell 1983, p. 83).*

	1	*2*	*3*	*More than 3*
Middle Palaeolithic	Wooden spears ?Clothing Scrapers, knives, etc. if unhafted	Stone-tipped spears Scrapers, knives, etc. if hafted		
Upper Palaeolithic	As above plus: needles ivory spears bone/antler polishers etc. if unhafted, grinding stones	Bone/antler polishers etc. if hafted		
			Arrows (shaft/ tip/flights)	Ladders Multi-piece clothing Necklaces Nets
		Bows (single or composite) Traps		

Thus, there is a temporal gap of around 60 000 years between the appearance of anatomically-modern humans, and their giving evidence of acting in characteristically modern ways (for reviews, see Lindly and Clark 1990; Gamble 1993; Conkey 1996; Noble and Davidson 1996; White 1996; Wynn 1996).

Note that here the distinction between modern and not-modern is being drawn on grounds of artefact *style* and its *volatility* rather than *inventory*. The transition point noted above at about 40 000 years ago has been referred to as the 'Mid/Upper Palaeolithic Transition'. Before that time, there is little in the archaeological inventory that is comparable with the typical subsequent inventory. It is generally accepted that certain lithic techniques (blades as opposed to flakes), tool forms (e.g. hafted spears), and materials (e.g. no bone or antler-based tools) distinguish the two periods. Such a distinction is probably a conceptual oversimplification, and if held rigidly both raises unnecessarily the issue of the continuity or discontinuity of 'traditions' and draws attention away from the interactive assemblage of mosaically-patterned developments that feed into each other to provide bases for new possibilities. In addition, the distinction is always open to empirical refutation, such as evidence of otherwise modern bone tool technologies reported by Yellen *et al.* (1995) at around 90 000 years ago in Zaire.

But it is not the *particularities* of individual artefacts that is the dividing line. Rather, the distinction being drawn here is based on the suite of recovered indices. Thus, Gamble (1993) has speculated that:

elements of the full Upper Palaeolithic package such as modern skulls, blade technologies, hearths, even, I would suggest, undecorated bone tools, will be found over wide areas and throughout periods from 200 000 BP to 40 000 BP (p. 170).

What is presently lacking is evidence for the assembled suite being in place before the Upper Palaeolithic. Before 40 000 years ago there was no art, and no spatial or temporal volatility of style in the tool-kit record. Foraging patterns were apparently based more on scavenging than hunter–gathering, and there was less geographical movement of tool materials. After the transition, a tool, even if still made of stone rather than 'new' materials such as ivory or bone, might be found 900 or more kilometres from the nearest known natural source of that stone. After the transition, too, the archaeological record contains evidence of typically modern human *practices* of a symbolic nature. (The one piece of present evidence that is problematic for this transitional date of 40 000 years ago is the date for the human colonization of Australia. Whenever this was—and it could have been around 60 000 years ago—it is unlikely it could have been accomplished accidentally, but required the deliberate building of a boat. Whether a boat could be built by a human group that lacked language is a moot point (see Davidson and Noble 1992).)

Social life

The above change in 'technological' assemblages is correlated with changes in the social organization of human groups. Social life before this transition might be inferred as still not fully modern. There is some early evidence for the use of fire, and perhaps cooking, as early as 700 000 years ago at Zhoukoudian (Stringer 1985), but there is no substantive evidence for hearths, storage pits, or architecture. Again, there is some early evidence for true hunting, if only of smaller mammals (Shipman and Rose 1983; Binford 1985; Thieme 1997), even if scavenging was still the major source of animal remains. Particular sites seem to have been used for particular activities (e.g. Keller 1973; de Lumley 1975; Freeman 1975), suggesting a spatial division of labour. But the overall picture here is complex and difficult to interpret, and the evidence is scanty. Gamble (1993) concludes his review of this technologically pre-modern period by noting that, with respect to social life:

It leaves an overwhelming impression of spontaneous, highly episodic behaviour where stone tools were made to do the job in hand before being dropped and their makers moving on. ... What is lacking ... is any indication for such modern practices as detailed planning, widespread contracts (sic), or elaborate social display. There is no physical evidence of storage, raw materials all come from within a radius of 50 km, and usually less than 5 km of the sites where they were used and any form of art, ornament, jewelry, or decoration is entirely absent. ... [But] the fifteen minute culture as revealed in the manufacture and use of stone tools is a poor guide to the length of time over which social information could be retained. The occupation of seasonal environments provides a clear indication that such memory was now substantial (pp. 138–9, 143).

After the transition to modernism, the evidence indicates changes in social organization in two directions. First, there is an increasing spatial and temporal extension that elaborates and sustains

extended kinship networks, communication beyond face-to-face encounters and exchange of information beyond the here-and-now, the organization of logistical economic strategies, and the extension of the time-depth of adaptation to environmental fluctuations (Whallon 1989, p. 451).

Second, there is an intensification in the organization of the immediate social environment. Built shelters and semi-permanent 'villages' are found after 40 000 years ago, but not before (see, for example, Gamble 1986). At first sight it might seem paradoxical, but these two changes can reinforce each other with respect to their effects in elaborating a linguistically-mediated awareness of the world. Both increasingly break the commonalities of shared knowledge between an individual and others —on the one hand in the meeting of strangers, and on the other in the creating of strangers through the implicit demarcation of the public and private within the domestic society (see, for example, Wilson 1988, for a fuller discussion). I will address this issue of the structuring social relations as providing a 'zone of proximal development' in a later section.

What might we make of all this? The conclusion to be drawn from all of the sources of evidence just reviewed is that modern human languages were established *after* the emergence of our biological species. The biology that supports these languages therefore evolved in the absence of such languages, and was subsequently co-opted to support present abilities as a result of quasi-historical changes in human social and technological practices through a long process of 'bootstrapping'. What follows is, then, a socially-driven account, similar to that recently put forward by Noble and Davidson (1996), who argue that:

'understanding' describes an interpersonal achievement, full stop. Brains are needed for this, but they are not where understanding occurs. ... Far from 'mind' as a personal possession, it is better characterized as *socially* distributed (p. 105).

This social distribution of mind is part-and-parcel of the communicative use of symbolic signs, which they regard as the defining feature of language. It is these symbolically-mediated social practices 'which happen to be unique to humans, [that] recruit the structures of the brain [to support them], rather than being determined by them. ... *Practices* interact with structures" (p. 18).

The central point to be made in what follows is that social structures put varying pressures on the communication systems that sustain them, through the different levels of presuppositionality a society's members share with each other. With low social differentiation and interchangeable roles, people communicate with each other against a background of a shared or common orientation, in a context of interpersonal relations founded on common perceptions, values, interpretive competence and so on. As social structure differentiates, presuppositionality decreases. Thus, the communicative practices within an increasingly elaborated society must develop ways of creating common contexts within the medium of communication itself. The contexts which make interpersonal communication possible have to be lifted out of the everyday milieu and created within the symbolic system of the lingua franca. Essentially, contexts will be 'pressured' into symbolic codes, and become conceptualized as objects of knowledge rather than remaining solely as implicit processes which sustain knowledge. In the process of this translation from context to code, grammar can be seen as emerging from the co-option of hierarchical ordering abilities that were already pregnant within the human mental apparatus. Grammar functions to 'freeze' the implications of otherwise immediate contexts into explicit forms. Grammar keeps track of these implications by structuring them into a symbolic tool kit that mediates our relation with the world we live in. The evidence broadly supports a view of communicative symbol systems as the providers of 'cognitive technologies' or 'tool-kits' that variously afford analytic, context-independent thought. This is not to claim that language determines thought, but rather that particular symbol systems can make some universal mental operations more or less difficult to carry out.

Culture, biology, and development

The internalization of cultural forms of behaviour involves the reconstruction of psychological activity on the basis of sign operations. ... The internalization of socially rooted and historically developed activities is the distinguishing feature of human psychology, the basis of the qualitative leap from animal to human psychology. As yet, the barest outline of this process is known (Vygotsky 1978, p. 57).

The evidence on human evolution reviewed above indicates that the 'biology' required to support modern behaviours was present well before those behaviours were put in place. Thus, when we ask questions about 'the evolution of language', which I include as a prime component of modern behaviours, we need to jettison the notion of language having an innate basis—that there is some 'module' in the human brain that is specifically given and evolved to support 'grammar'. We need to do this because there is no evidence that modern, grammatically-structured languages were in existence during the period when the biological substrate of the modern brain was being selected for. Thus, it would appear that whatever hardware we bring to support current-day tasks was put in place before the behaviours they now support were elaborated.

This is not as outlandish as it might at first sound. An example is suggested by the practices of reading and writing. The claim here is that all of the 'biological machinery' that evolution had to construct to enable people to write was in place 100 000 years ago, yet reading and writing were not accomplished until about 95 000 years later. In technical terms, writing systems are *extrasomatic* achievements. In the process of learning to read and write, it is quite likely that the structural and functional characteristics of our simultaneously developing and maturing brains are modified from the final patterns they might have ended with in the absence of this extrasomatic environment. However, these changes are not directly related to any changes in the phenotypic information that evolutionary processes are typically conceived to operate on. In this way, evolutionary questions with respect to modern behaviours, such as speaking a language, are shifted to the extrasomatic domain. The biology that enables them was there. The real questions are, firstly, *how were linguistic systems put together by the possessors of this biology*? And secondly, *how do these systems, once they are established, interact with the ontogenetic elaboration of the biology that supports them*? But before I can tackle these questions, there is some groundwork to be done.

My emphasis on the extrasomatic domain needs some clarification. I am not looking to present arguments that cultures 'evolve' in a fashion analogous to the way organisms evolve. Rather, it is quite clear that evolution is a far more complex process than proponents of the neo-Darwinian *Modern Synthesis* have made out. That view is exceptionally 'individualistic' in locating the site of evolution as the individual animal (or even the individual gene). It is characterized by a rigid separation of organisms from their environments. But evolution is not just based in the differential culling of variations between individuals by autonomous and natural selection forces emanating from a fixed environment. Environments evolve along with the organisms that inhabit them. And as environments evolve, they can be used by the evolutionary process itself, to enable biological structures to be put to new functions.

Such an expanded view both legitimizes and makes orthodox our approaching human evolution in terms of an extrasomatic emphasis, because there are good grounds for assuming that this is a viable way for an evolutionary process to do things. In the present context, if we eject the so-called information required to sustain language 'out of the brain', we do not need to account for how a language module evolved. This is a useful move, for two reasons. First, it is extremely difficult to elaborate an evolutionary account of a 'mental organ' which is by its nature discontinuous with anything that has gone before it (cf. Chomsky 1968, p. 60). Second, how else might we account for the temporal gap between the completion of the biology and the emergence of the behaviour? Brain mechanisms cannot have been selected to better adapt people to something that was not present in their environment.

Instead, we can look to processes of co-option or exaptation (Gould 1991). Hence, if we now, as modern adults, can be shown to have something that can be described as a 'language module', then this can be seen as developing as a result of the interaction between phenotypic information and extrasomatic information. Biological processes are co-opted by environmentally-conserved information to support new ends and outcomes. What I will be arguing is that, for the elaboration of human languages and linguistically-mediated behaviour, we are becoming aware of how these extrasomatic factors have their influence. They work by *changing the structuring of the attention of those who grow up within them*, and thereby enter into determining the phenotypic outcome of the developmental process.

There is evidence that different social structures facilitate the development of different mental ways of dealing with the world (see Lock and Symes 1996, for a review). How we attend to what we see is mediated in our developing years (a period when 60% of brain development occurs) by the actions of others. And part of our development is taking over these patterns of attending into our own conduct. As what we 'see' becomes increasingly symbolic, so our patterns of 'thinking' get differently founded. This point is implicit in the central concepts of Vygotsky's (1978) developmental account, that:

Every function in the child's cultural development appears twice: first, on the social level, and later on the individual level; first, *between* people (*interpsychological*), and then *inside* the child (*intrapsychological*). This applies equally to voluntary attention, to logical memory, and to the formation of concepts. All the higher functions originate as actual relations between individuals (p. 57).

The argument here is that structuring principles and information for developmental processes are conserved extrasomatically, both in durable artefacts and durable cultural practices. These provide new substrates for the developmental experiences of later generations. Hence, as patterns of social interaction change, they enable new ways for attention to be structured (because the individual is immersed in a perceptual world increasingly structured by social interaction and its products). We therefore need to look to the changing patterns of human social interaction for an explanation of our ability to have elaborated pre-existing communicative abilities into linguistic abilities that are symbolically mediated and constituted. Emerging brains of an already-modern sort handle these culturally-conserved sources of structuring information as best they can, by the use of pre-existing potentials rather than the deployment of already-given, task-specific modules. Those language-related modules, when (or if) they exist, are most likely the result of development under particular conditions of environmental input—they are not inevitable, in the way that modules for recognizing faces, say, are likely to be.

A central question in this exploration asks how what Vygotsky has called the 'zone of proximal development' can be generated *sui generis*, in the absence of more enculturated others. Many developmental processes have come to be seen as creative ones. For example, from a Piagetian perspective we conceive of the child as an active problem-solver; and from a Chomskyan perspective we see the child as creatively elaborating language. But in each case there is a model, something there to be mastered, an agreed end-point. The Vygotskyan perspective has been read as one of 'apprenticeship' or 'implicit tutoring'—through the actions of someone who has already mastered the end point, the child is assisted in getting there. Development is scaffolded by its embeddedness within social interactions that point to a known outcome. But when we turn to evolution, we have the problem of the outcomes not being there already. The development of the ability to count, for example, can be seen to be scaffolded by those who can already count, but what enables counting to be constructed when no-one can count? Fortunately, we have some clues as to how to refine and pursue this question.

Clues

Implicit properties

Popper (1972) has pointed out very clearly how particular symbol systems contain the seeds of their future elaboration. He points to the number system as one example. Many four-year-olds can count from 1 to 10, at least after a fashion. But they do so in complete ignorance of the properties of the numbers they are using. Among those properties are the distinction between odd and even numbers, the nature of prime numbers, and the nature of perfect numbers, for example. Hence, there is built into the system a whole new order of distinctions that could be made explicit. Making these things explicit is not necessarily easy. First, the way in which numbers come to be represented or symbolized can affect the likelihood of these implicit properties being discovered. Basic mathematical operations such as addition, subtraction, division, and multiplication are made more or less easy depending on how the number system is notated—the Arabic system is better suited to this than the Roman one; an abacus is better still.

Second, similar views have been put forward for alphabetic literacy. One such view (e.g. Goody 1968) is that writing functions to abstract the events it deals with from their ongoing context, and so helps foster abstract thinking. But the empirical evidence suggests that coming to exploit this possibility of writing, to use the written medium as a way of inspecting different accounts for their logical consistency, for example, is not a guaranteed outcome of being able to read and write. Rather, the social practices that writing is used for differentially predispose readers and writers to discover or not discover the possibilities made available by the system they have (e.g. Scribner and Cole 1981). In addition, the nature of the system for visually representing language—logographic, syllabic, alphabetic, for example—might also make this discovery more or less easy or difficult, in the same way that different systems of mathematical notation do (although the empirical evidence to warrant this claim has been very difficult to establish).

Third, environments can be changed by the actions of organisms so as to bring into being entirely new objects that were never intended and would not have otherwise existed. Popper (1972) uses the creation of a path through vegetation as an example of this. Paths come into existence through animals initially moving along the lines of least resistance, which are determined jointly by the contours of the terrain and its vegetation along with the predispositions of the animals that move across that terrain. He notes of a path that:

It is not planned—it is an unintended consequence of the need for easy or swift movement. This is how a path is originally made—perhaps even by men—and how language and any other institutions which are useful may arise...In this way, a whole new universe of possibilities or potentialities may arise...(p. 119).

What I want to emphasize here is that, unlike the possibilities that are implicit in counting systems, what has been constructed in this instance is immediately available to the organism—the path is as 'real' in the organism's experience as the terrain and vegetation through which it runs.

At this point, then, the issue becomes clearer. Can we find ways in which social practices can act to create the analogues of 'paths' in human perception, such that those paths not only establish new possibilities and potentialities for a physiological system (the brain) to use, but simultaneously provide the notational system that eases the discovery of those things that are implicit in them? If we can, then we have delineated the self-constituted 'zone of proximal development' that can bootstrap the elaboration of those symbolic cognitive technologies that it is our task to elucidate in accounting for the evolution of human abilities.

Developmental clues

Another set of clues comes from the study of language development by present-day human infants. To see such information as helpful here is not to imply a crass recapitulationism (see, for example, Lock and Peters 1996). Rather, I just want to make the simple point that development is an interactive process. Both *what* an infant learns and *how* this is learned occur in close contact with other human beings. And the actions of these others contribute a massive structuring to the world as-attended-to by the infant. Vygotsky has captured one facet of this structuring process in his conceptualization of the 'zone of proximal development'. Intrinsic to these actions are the 'signs' (words) available for linguistically-mediated behaviour. Within the broad Vygotskyan perspective can be found the seeds of a theory of the relationship between the signs used in interpersonal communication and the character of the social relations within the group who use those signs. Vygotsky's contemporary, Volosinov, puts it thus:

Every sign, as we know, is a construct between socially organized persons in the process of their interaction. Therefore, the forms of signs are conditioned above all by the social organization of the participants involved and also by the immediate conditions of their interaction. ...This is the order that the actual generative process of language follows: *social intercourse is generated...*; *in it verbal communication and interaction are generated*; *and in the latter, forms of speech performances are generated*; *finally, this generative process is reflected in the change of language forms.* (Volosinov 1973, pp. 21, 37).

This way of looking at the issue helps refine it by seeing the elaboration of social structures as providing the substrate that constitutes, *sui generis*, a zone of proximal development that leads language-users on. What I will go on to show, later in this chapter, is how changing relations between people can act to structure each other's perception and attention in new ways, simultaneously bringing into being new things to talk about. In this way, social relations scaffold the elaboration of a linguistic system by providing the requisite structuring principles to recruit the available biology, and, at the same time, also provide the cognitive technology or 'signs' that those biologically-based processes can use (and thereby simultaneously elaborate themselves within the constraints of the developing phenotype).

Comparative clues

A third set of clues comes from attempts to establish the language capabilities of apes (see Ristau 1996). There has been a tendency for this work to be seen as establishing the limits of ape abilities. In this way, such work can highlight particular abilities that human individuals must possess that enable them, as a species, to have transcended the limitations apparent in apes. The dominant cognitive paradigm of contemporary Western psychology tends to favour casting these differences within a model of internal representations and the devices by which these representations are handled. These devices include things like our having a larger working memory capacity (Russell, in press), a greater imitative facility (Tomasello *et al.* 1994), or better cross-modal transfer of information (Ettlinger and Wilson 1990), etc.

But this perspective can be reversed, and we can begin to look at what is going on *outside* the organism, and the role this plays in scaffolding what our brains provide the substrate for. When we do this (see Lock and Colombo 1996, pp. 631–3), then the inherent power of the extrasomatic structures provided by particular human cultural practices becomes apparent. That is, certain modern practices, when conducted with apes as the conversational or interactive partners, can produce *psychological alchemy* —they transmute apes into something beyond what any ape has ever achieved on its own. This is clear evidence of the power of cultural practice. We get apes with what Premack (1980) has called 'upgraded minds'. What these human cultural practices can do with human biology is evidenced in the study of language ontogeny. The difference is that the ways in which we upgrade our children's minds have been created by us, ourselves, and were not handed down to us by some god-like being in any experimental situation (well, as far as we know).

Returning language development to the social

[The human infant] cannot, even theoretically, live an isolated existence;…he is not an independent individual. He lives a common life as one term in a personal relation. Only in the process of development does he learn to achieve a relative independence, and that only by appropriating the techniques of a rational social tradition (Macmurray 1961, p. 50).

In the majority of studies of language acquisition to date, the focus has been predominantly on the individual infant as providing the skills that enable language development to occur. Here I want to redress this by turning to an emphasis on the social nature of these developments. The line I will be following is one that I have elaborated elsewhere (e.g. Lock 1980)—that the communicative acts that infants are engaged in have only an implicit content to begin with, and that, at least in the early stages, development occurs as these contents are realized explicitly. This implicit context exists 'in'—although in a sense also 'beyond'—the ongoing world in which the infant is *jointly* situated interactively with another who is more skilled. What an infant pays attention to and finds of significance in this world is in large part constructed through the actions of that other. Development is thus a *guided reinvention* that is negotiated interactively. Some examples are useful here.

1. Here is a generalization about infants that I have interactive data on (see Lock *et al.* 1989; Lock 1991): At around 6 months of age the majority of things adults do in their interactions with infants serve to set up conditions that enable themselves and their infants to focus their attention on particular things and events in their immediate perceptual world. They do this by, for example, expressing exaggerated surprise at particular noises and events, by emphasizing objects as 'worth looking at' by making them interesting, by jiggling them up-and-down, pointing at them, putting them in piles, etc. The object of the exercise seems to be to coordinate the attention of both parties so that they could sustain a topic as a focus for interaction.

2. Once routines are established that enable the infant to pay sustained attention, around 12–13 months, then adults shift to attempts to specify what is being attended to more precisely, and to being able to direct and re-direct the infant's attention more precisely. They do this by increasing their emphasis on the names of things as well as their properties, and by asking questions such as 'can you show me the x?', 'where's the y?'; etc. My suggestion is that some aspects of the infant's perceptual world are being made more perceptually salient as compared with others in this way, and this can act to provide the conditions whereby implications in the world are transformed into explicit components of it.

3. Once infants begin to 'take over' language from their caretakers, around 18 months, then the other shifts to elaborating on the properties and characteristics of the shared focus of attention, including those beyond the here-and-now, thus accreting further significance to the objects the child perceives. Some examples of this, taken from Lock *et al.* (1989), are concerned with the relationships that can exist between objects, that is, how objects can be regarded as parts of larger wholes (as reflected here by just the mother's speech from particular interactional episodes):
   (a) Show it to Teddy.
   (b) Put it on the saucer.
   (c) Put that bug into the bucket.
   (d) Are you going to get the snake to catch this bubble?

4. Further, this particular mother juggles objects and contexts in even more sophisticated ways, with the result that symbolic play is engineered:
   (e) Would you like a cup of tea?
       Yes, go on, it's a nice little cup.
       You have some. (Child pretends to drink)
       Give it to Teddy.
       Go on, give Teddy a drink. (Child holds cup to Teddy's lips.)
       Here she gets the infant not merely to put two objects in conjunction within the present perceptual world, but to do so in a way which only makes sense through their relation to something that is not immediately present—the 'tea' is imaginary, and must be brought in from absent contexts to inform present action.

It is quite a complicated activity: one object (the cup) is to be related to another (tea), which has to be lifted out of absent contexts (and lifted out of absent objects to be put in this one), and then both the cup and its imaginary contents have to be regarded as a whole and placed in relation to a third, and not just Teddy, but the right part of Teddy—his mouth.

My suggestion is that, by working in the infant's ever-shifting *zone of proximal development*, adults are acting to foreground the implicates of the infant's present abilities and this acts to bootstrap their explication. At root, these interactions are ones in which a coordination is being attempted between two different *Umwelten*,[4] and it is the nature of the attempts at coordination that act to bring the *Umwelt* of the developing infant more towards a commonality with that of the adult. The view being argued here is that the implications of the adult's knowledge of the world are constitutive of her Umwelt, such that she perceives, say, a book as a book, and this in turn implies for her a number of ways of going forward with the interaction. By contrast, a six-month-old infant 'sees' the same object, but 'perceives' it as something to suck, bang, etc., and not something to 'look at' as a book. In the infant's Umwelt, the same physical object is constituted differently from the way her mother constitutes it, both as a perceptual object and in terms of its implications for action.

The point I want to draw out here is that the contributing partners to such interactions are pursuing different projects because they bring different interests and abilities to bear on their supposedly 'shared arena' of interaction. The notion of both interactants being attuned to a common, objective world is not useful here. Rather, the issue is

how the 'objective outside world' in which we observe ourselves and other living things arises out of our subjective (private) universe (our Umwelt), that is to say how the former [the objective] is derived from the latter [the subjective] as an abstraction (T. von Uexküll 1982, p.10).

And this is achieved through, first, the coordination of attention, and its structuring, in interactive situations, and second, by negotiating an increasingly explicit symbolic marking of those coordinates. The fact is that, for humans at least, private universes are structured, from the outset, by their *inter*subjective situation in joint action.

Similarly, interaction can act to give a 'constitutional workout' to abilities that have previously been accorded solely an individual, cognitive status. An example is the ability to analyse constituents into their component parts. This skill has been highlighted as integral to the early development of symbolic abilities in the work of Bates *et al.* (e.g. 1979, 1988). They offer an explanation of the different styles of early language use, the 'expressive' and 'referential' as noted by Nelson (1973), on the basis of a differential reliance by *individual* children on either arbitrary or analysed learning skills:

the 'expressive' child tends to employ acquisition through perception of contiguity, imitating and using unanalysed phrases as means to ends prior to analysis of vehicle-referent relations.

---

[4] I am taking this term from Jacob von Uexküll's use of it:
[The Umwelt] is the world around the animal as the animal sees it, the subjective world as contrasted with the environment. The effects of stimulation appear in this Umwelt as elementary sensations, *Merkzeichen*, which, organized and projected into the object, become meaningful perceptions, conceived by the [infant] as the properties of that object, *Merkmal* (von Uexküll, 1957: xiii).

The 'referential' child is faster at analysis, so that the use of imitated whole forms is short-lived and infrequent. When he does imitate ... he may do so in parallel with and/or following a rapid breakdown into its components and the relationships into which that form can enter. ... Both arbitrary and analysed learning are necessary for rapid and efficient acquisition of language. Nevertheless, individuals may vary in the 'relative' use of one process over the other, and in the timing of analysis with imitation (Bates *et al.* 1979, p. 361).

But, in reality, if one wishes to attribute differential facilities with imitation versus analysis to infants, then one should conceive of those skills as, at least partially, *socially constituted* and not *individually given*. These differential abilities are not based solely in individually-given cognitive operations, but are embedded in the perceptual world of interaction itself. Thus, while from one perspective one might choose, for some purposes, to conceive of infants as having differential amounts of analytic skills which they employ 'on the world', it is equally the case that they have come to live in different socially-constituted perceptual/conceptual worlds, some of which contain more perceptible parts than others (i.e., the examples of interaction given earlier are not typical of all dyads, and part–whole relations are not always so distinctively marked out as in the examples given (see Lock *et al.* 1989). In sum, it is not that infants develop *differently* by the exercise and practice of their individual skills; those skills, and the infants themselves, are *constructed* differently via socially-constitutive interaction (see Lock *et al.* 1989, for further details).

The relevance of this developmental view for language evolution

The claim with respect to language evolution being put forward here is that the initiating communication system used by anatomically modern humans was at least as complex as that found in current one- to two-year-olds and those apes that have been immersed in language programmes (and this is not a new suggestion—see, for example, Bickerton 1990). However, it is not a straightforward task to take these extant exemplars as indicative of the functional characteristics of a primordial system. The major reason for this is that these modern exemplars function within an already-mature communicative environment. This adds the complication that there is a developmental inequality in place between the participants of contemporary communicative acts in which this possibly primordial system is encountered: the human adult participant actually possesses the fully-elaborated system. What this means in practice for the infant is that the immediately apparent benefits of possessing the primordial system are extended beyond the infant's mental horizon. This happens through the adult partner to the communicative act being able, in interaction, to *explicitly* 'point out' what it is the infant *might* mean. A concrete example is useful here in clarification.

At a very general level of analysis, the language abilities of one- to two-year-old infants have a quite limited spatial and temporal extension beyond the infant's immediate 'here-and-now' projects. I have previously described a conversational tactic used by some mothers of young infants as 'context hopping' (e.g. Lock 1991, p. 289). It is this tactic that, I am suggesting, provides the infant with the resources for exploiting the inherent properties of the words they are using to go beyond the here-and-now. An example of context hopping that occurred between a mother exploring a picture book with her 18-month-old son is entailed in the mother's following remark: "Oh look…he's got boots on just like Daddy's".

It seems unlikely that the infant, on his own, would bring Daddy to mind at this point without the word being spoken. Similarly, it is unlikely that the infant, unaided, would abstract out of the picture the similar features that link the pictured boots to Daddy's boots. But the conversational resources the mother is able to bring into their shared here-and-now can very effectively mediate the infant's perception for him. That is, *she* can 'see' similarities without much effort: what she directly sees in the picture is a pair of boots 'like Daddy's'. The shared words are amplified in their signification such that the features of similarity can be interactively foregrounded as a topic. It is this tactic, I am suggesting, that provides the infant with the resources for exploiting the inherent properties of the words they are using to go beyond the 'here-and-now'. What was otherwise *implicit* in the here-and-now is made *explicit*: similarly, what was a *possible* meaning of the indicated object *boot* is assisted in its transition to being an *actual* meaning. Adopting a different terminology, one of the participants in such conversations is able to act in the *zone of proximal development* of the other participant (Vygotsky 1962, 1978). Now, this is clearly not the case for two participants who have abilities at the same level.

For the issue at hand—the initial elaboration of language systems—the problem becomes this—how are participants who are *at the same level* of functioning with a communicative system able to go beyond its constraints? The essential claim being put forward here as a possible solution is twofold. First, the functional elements of the presumed communicative system have immanent potentialities beyond those exploited by the early stages of their use. Second, in particular circumstances, the social characteristics of the communicative process can create their own zone of proximal development. These two facets of the communicative process at hand are being conceived here as the providers of bootstrapping conditions for the elaboration of new abilities which represent the *explication* of properties *implicit* in the potentialities of the initiating system. This re-orientation is such that we can get a handle on how cultural practices can, of themselves and *sui generis*, act as a 'zone of proximal development' for bootstrapping what can be thought about; that is, how implications are constructed as 'explications-in-waiting' that cognition can grab on to.

The same point emerges from the literature on creative problem solving, and how the chance of finding a successful solution can be 'primed' in the way the problem is structured. Thus, for example, the task of joining two hanging ropes that are simultaneously beyond the grasp of an individual with the assistance of a hammer is facilitated if the problem solver sees a pendulum operating beforehand. This alerts the solver to the possibility of using the hammer as a pendulum weight, tying it to one rope so as to set it in a swinging motion that brings it in reach when the other rope is being held. That such possibilities are difficult to grasp without this kind of predisposing 'zone of proximal development' is captured in Piaget's observation on how Darwin developed the concept of evolution:

the two results which seem the most interesting to me are, first, the time that Darwin needed to become aware of ideas which were already implicit in his thought, and, second, the mysterious passage from the implicit to the explicit in the creation of new ideas…One might have believed that this passage concerned only the relationship between thought and action, and that, on the level of thought itself, the passage from 'implicit' schemas...to their reflective explication would be much more rapid. [But]...even in a creator of the greatness of Darwin the passage is far from immediate. This delay establishes...that making things explicit leads to the construction of a structure which is partially new, even though contained virtually in those structures which preceded it (Piaget 1974, p. x).

The role of a 'zone of proximal development' is to enable what Piaget calls here 'reflective explication'.

   At this point, recall that we know something of the power of modern social practices in reconfiguring the demonstrable cognitive abilities of modern apes. We see in the current world the analogous reconfiguration of the cognitive abilities of morphologically modern infants, through their transformation and amplification by the 'cognitive technologies' constituted by symbolically-based communicative systems. A paradigm example that elucidates the interplay of social relations with language in the constitution of abilities is provided, at first sight tangentially, in Elias's (e.g. 1978, 1982) outline of the establishment of modern western practices of politeness.

Elias's account

One interpersonal activity that Elias elucidates concerns blowing one's nose. Elias establishes the historical course of elaborating western practices for dealing with the assorted accumulations of material that periodically inhabit the human nasal passages. At the root of the changes Elias documents in what is considered polite is a hierarchy of actions: blowing the nose; hiding the blowing of it by using a handkerchief; hiding the blowing of it into a handkerchief. But, most importantly, embarrassment is being invented. Embarrassment thus comes to be seen as an emotional state created by the explication into discourse of this hierarchy: For it to be realized, a self-censorious ability has to be established. People have to become able to reflect on their own behaviour—that is, on how they act in company—where previously they had not done so.

   In Elias's view, this kind of change in interpersonal behaviour is not just one of fashion; further,

it does not involve solely changes of 'knowledge' or transformations of 'ideologies', in short, alterations of the content of consciousness, but *changes in the whole human make-up*, within which ideas and habits of thought are only a single sector (Elias 1982, p. 284, emphasis added).

These changes reflect a reorganization and transformation of:

the whole personality throughout all its zones, from the steering of the individual by himself at the more flexible level of consciousness and reflection to that at the more automatic and rigid level of drives and affects (Elias 1982, p. 284).

Elias considers that it is the relationship between the psychological functions controlling an individual's actions that changes during historical time; that it is

these relationships within man between the drives and affects controlled and the built-in controlling agencies, whose structure changes in the course of a civilizing process, in accordance with the changing structure of the relationships between individual human beings, in society at large (Elias 1982, p. 286).

Interaction, discourse, and cognition

How are these changes in the basic structuring of Western psychological structure related to the issues at hand here?

First, we need to remember that the changes in conduct that Elias charts are occurring against a background of a diversifying society. Travel was becoming easier, leading to more and different people meeting each other. Cities were emerging in a contrastive role to that of the countryside, resulting in trade and trade specialization, the establishment of a merchant class, and so on. In general, people were becoming less socially homogeneous, roles were becoming specialized, and so people were sharing less common knowledge among themselves; they had fewer common presuppositions. This had obvious repercussions on the process of communication between fellows. Essentially, it became much harder to make oneself understood. It is likely that this same process is at the root of Armstrong and Katz's (1981) finding of a correlation between the number of basic colour terms in a society's language and its social complexity, and work by Fischer (1966, 1973) on the different structuring of two closely-related Micronesian languages in relation to the social structures of the cultures that use them. In both cases, the more differentiated the social structure, the more differentiated the referential domains marked by words in the language. Thus, in noting below Elias's views with respect to selves and personalities, we might take his specific focus as indicative of changes occurring in other referential domains, changes that are related to changes in social organization. Recall, this is one of the major changes occurring at the point at which the human record begins to show evidence of symbol use.

Second, we need to think about the consequences of these changes with respect to the sort of knowledge a person would need in order to act effectively in such a changing world. Because it was much more difficult to get a message across to another, communication failure could occur much more frequently, making the individual aware of the communication process itself. Further, these changes would provide the individual with many more perspectives on the presentation of his or her self.

Third, language began to code new concepts and to be used more explicitly. On the one hand, the loss of presuppositionality in discourse will force an increasingly elaborated and explicit linguistic coding of communication—people would have been required to make explicit information they had previously left implicit. On the other hand, an increasingly complex society can create all sorts of new situations and experiences among the people whose actions bring it into being—these might come to be expressed in language. Hence, information concerning the presentation of the self would have been available directly to an individual. A society with differentiated roles might well force an awareness upon an individual of the aspects of individuality that those roles are simultaneously constructing. It might eventually provide linguistic concepts for rendering these explicitly. The main point here is that the socially constructed facets of personality will increase, through the explicit realization in discourse, of the number of different perspectives an individual can formulate of his or her self; while, at the same time, this will increase the individual's ability to transcend his or her presupposed, unreflective, non-meta-awareness of his or her self through a richer fabric of communication and concept.

Fourth, Luria and Yudovich (1971) have noted that words have a profound affect on individual psychological functioning:

When he acquires a word, which isolates a particular thing and serves as a signal to a particular action, the child, as he carries out an adult's verbal instruction, is subordinated to this word...By subordinating himself to the adult's verbal orders the child acquires a system of these verbal instructions and gradually begins to utilize them for the regulation of his own behaviour (pp. 13–4).

In this view, through the medium of language, one of the major transitions noted by Elias—from external control of behaviour by threat of punishment to internal control via the self-reflexive censors of shame, guilt, and embarrassment—can be effected; and through these particularly social forms of emotional cognition "people become...sensitive to distinctions which previously scarcely entered consciousness" (Elias 1982, p. 298).

The point is that our personalities, our conceptions of ourselves and others, our emotional experiences, and our views of the world are all explicated from phenomena whose existence is created beyond us in our social worlds. In this view, human conceptual systems are explicated renderings into mental form of human social discourses. These explications have become, initially, salient aspects of the human Umwelt through changes in social relations. They become preserved in cultural practices and the linguistic resources that enable the discourses that sustain these practices. Thus, they are able to act as a 'zone of proximal development' sui generis. And:

I know of no way in which intelligence or mind could arise or could have arisen, other than through the internalization by the individual of social processes of experience and behaviour...And if mind or thought has arisen in this way, then there neither can be nor could have been any mind or thought without language; and the early stages of the development of language must have been prior to the development of mind and thought (Mead 1934, pp. 191–2)

Back to evolution

The prospective summary, then, is that the process of explicating the implicit possibilities of cognitive endowments is contributed to by the potentialities of the various symbol systems that humans use, as well as the nature and structure of the human practices within which these are sustained. It is becoming clearer that (1) *the properties of particular symbol systems* and (2) *the conditions under which they are employed* affect the ease with which humans can use them for particular purposes. Thus changes in social relationships have provided the major resources for the establishment of modern abilities, and these are not solely founded on preadaptive changes in human biology. The *structure of relationships between people and the properties of the discourses and practices they engaged in constituted the conditions that enabled their discovery of the unintended properties of the systems of symbols, social relations, and discourse practices their modes of life constituted*. It is these discoveries that also underlie the evolution of human linguistic abilities—these discoveries, not just the biological kit alone.

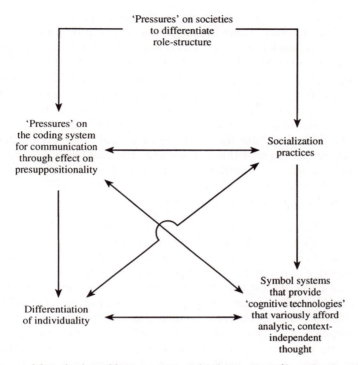

Fig. 17.3. Form and functioning of human communication systems (from Lock and Symes 1996, p. 229).

    The position argued for here is that interaction constructs contexts that language can come to symbolize, thereby providing a cognitive technology that bootstraps the increasing discovery of those 'things' that are implied by what has already been symbolized (e.g. Donald 1991, 1993; Lock and Peters 1996; Olson 1996). The crucial missing link in the pre-Upper Palaeolithic was the lack of the cultural support system of socially-constituted 'pregnant implications' in the perceptual Umwelten of these ancestral humans, such that there was an insufficient basis to exaptively co-opt those biologically-based functions that have come to be regarded as the 'language acquisition device'. There was no naturally constituted 'zone of proximal development' to bootstrap the explicit construction of a symbolic lexicon that benefited from a neurology that predisposed, on the basis of its functional architecture, the duality of patterning found in modern language systems, from the phonetic through to the syntactic. The evidence for the increasing elaboration and complexity of social life in the Upper Palaeolithic is compelling (see, for example, Gamble 1993, pp. 179–202, for a recent review). Rather, the process of elaborating the symbolic support for, and amplification of, cognitive abilities, is embedded in a nexus of influences that feed forward and back to each other. These hypothesized links are portrayed in Fig. 17.3.

    The scenario suggested here is thus close to that argued for by Bickerton (1990) and by Whallon (1989, drawing on Bickerton 1981). It would credit hominids from 40 000 or so years ago back to at least mid-*H. erectus* specimens represented by KNM-ER 3733 at around 700 000 years ago with a vocal communication system that

Bickerton characterizes as *protolanguage*, a "mode of linguistic expression that is quite separate from normal human language and is shared by four cases of speakers: trained apes, children under two; adults who have been deprived of language in their early years, and speakers of pidgin" (Bickerton 1990, p. 122). In Whallon's opinion, such protolanguages would facilitate communication, but could well lack the means for explicitly expressing and reflecting on the temporally and spatially absent world, the *imaginary world enabled at the truly explicit symbolic level*, that is required for elaborating and sustaining the characters of modernity.[5] Thus, communication existed, as did the biological base for its elaboration, and "the social context provides the exaptive process to upgrade this to language. The link between, on the one hand, exploration and the use and knowledge of space, and on the other the scale, depth, and complexity of social life is irrefutable" (Gamble 1993, p. 174).

What that social context does is as follows:

1. It provides for the structuring of attention by embedding objects within cultural practices such that they became different objects in our perception, making available new implications and courses for action directly. For example, given the similarity in the visual systems of chimpanzees and present-day western humans it seems a reasonable assumption that both species 'see' the same physical object when they look at a flat surface supported on 'legs'. But the two species 'perceive' different objects: humans perceive a 'table', and know what and what not to do with it; chimpanzees perceive something to walk and sit on, not a table.

2. It conserves previously elaborated ways of keeping track of implications that have been made explicit: that is, particular symbol systems that have been arrived at. These systems can variously constrain modes of thinking. As an example of what I mean by this, I earlier indicated an analogy with the differences between the Roman and Arabic number systems. The mental operations of multiplication and division are available to users of both systems, but the symbolic tool-kits affect the ease with which these operations can be performed—it is easier to divide 63 by 9 to get 7 than LXIII by IX to get VII. It is even easier to do it on an abacus, but here we are at a further remove in that a technology for manipulating symbols has been introduced. In addition the device—the abacus—can be 'internalized' and used as quickly and as accurately as using it physically, and often faster. In addition, skilled abacus users show very specific enhancements to their mathematical skills: digit memory—forward and backward—increases to 15 digit strings,

---

[5] Elaborating' and 'sustaining' are the important concepts here. It might well be possible to use a communication system that is *not* explicitly elaborated for discussion of an absent world in order to actually convey at least some information about that world. For example, pre-Upper Palaeolithic hominids are implicitly credited here with abilities that give them an advantage over modern apes with respect to understanding what another knows. Thus if A knew that B had been in direction C, then B can implicitly convey that C is not a good direction to go in by resisting A's attempts to go in that direction. What B lacks is the ability to elaborate explicitly in discourse an account or justification as to why A should not go that way. This lack is not crucial in a social group that can rely on a high degree of shared presuppositionality based on common experience. Note also that the approach here departs from that of Noble and Davidson (1996) who explicitly reject the notion of 'protolanguage' on the grounds that languages are symbolic systems by definition, and something either acts as a symbol or it does not: there can be no half measures. While not dissenting from this view, I take it that symbolically-constituted systems can be more or less articulated in what they explicitly code, and that systems with low levels of explicit elaboration can none-the-less be sustained as functional forms of communication that warrant being described as 'protolanguages'.

while for other item lists it remains around the magic number 7 ± 2 (Hatano 1982; Stigler *et al.* 1982).

3. It conserves 'patterns for handling' implications that have been made explicit—what we term 'grammar'. Bickerton (1990), for example, has pointed out that:

Syntax is, to a large extent, a projection of the lexicon, wherein all the sub-categorization frames of verbs and all the grammatical items (and much else) are stored. If the initial lexicon was dramatically limited, then not all of the structures implicit in syntactic principles could immediately be realized. To take an extreme example, if there were no verbs of reporting, and no 'psychological' or 'intentional' verbs, then biclausal structures of the type *he said/thought/believed/ hoped that x had happened/would happen* would be impossible to construct...(pp. 180–1)

In other words, biologically-instantiated possible abilities require a substrate for their actualization. And the emphasis in this chapter shifts that substrate from being some abstract object that is analysed by some 'language acquisition device', as the situation is captured from a cognitive perspective, to one in which the learner is the generator of, and participator in, shared acts of 'making sense'. That is, forms of social being are in process of elaboration, and it is within these social practices and the child's Umwelt that this substrate needs to be located.

Two empirical examples are useful here. First, in a microanalytic study of the emerging use of self words, Budwig (1995) finds a clear relationship between reference, grammatical form, and caregiver's language for children in the age-range 20–32 months in their use of words such as *I*, *me*, and *my* in American English, and *ich* and *man* in German. The use of these words by the children studied was tied in with the notions of self and agency that were established in the course of interacting with caretakers, indicating that the children were picking up subtle cues about agency, and thereby articulating different forms of selfhood that were then reflected in the grammatical uses of self referential words. The caretaker–infant interaction is thus revealed as functioning to delineate a 'problem space' in which 'referential objects'—forms of selfhood and agency—are constructed simultaneously with the vocabulary items that allow these objects to be structurally marked in the child's emerging speech.

Similarly, Bamberg (1996), drawing on Capps and Ochs (1995a, b), takes this tack further in his study of emotional socialization with respect to children's discourses about anger and sadness. What he terms the 'grammars' of being angry and sad, in talking from both the first-person and third-person perspectives, are quite complex in English, and work so as to disentangle the different discursive requirements of handling empathy and blame. Bamberg sets his particular findings into a general framework that sees the development of a linguistic ability to handle 'emotion talk' as 'a process of appropriating the tools necessary to talk meaningfully about the social relationships in which emotions are embedded'. Thus, grammar is set up as "a set of linguistic constructions...directly tied to the discursive purpose to which the particular constructions are put to use":

grammar, if understood correctly, i.e. not as abstract principles of a universalist nature, but as social know-how relevant for the construction of social meaning, plays an integral role in coming to grips with what emotions do and what they are used for in social communicative practices. As such, learning to use the linguistic construction procedures for socially appropriate purposes is deeply embedded in cultural practices (Bamberg 1996, p. 22).

In this view, again, the social and the cognitive are intimately intertwined, and grammar becomes a system used in the service of keeping track of the explications of what otherwise remains implicit in the child's Umwelt.

Now, we need to remember that, developmentally, the grammatical means for differentially handling anger and sadness talk are pregiven in the child's language community—"they have their social existence before they are put to use in social practices" (Bamberg 1996, p. 22). Phylogenetically, this is not the case. But the point here is that the close relationship between social practice and grammatical device established by Bamberg is one where *the latter are instantiated in the former*. That is, in line with Bickerton's point earlier about the relationship between lexical entries and syntax—that the latter is wheeled on to the mental stage to meet the needs of the former—the driving force is the social structure of obligations captured constitutively by words. These words come with a particular set of implications that are unpacked and pointed to by a set of grammatical structures, perhaps structures that are new, but more likely reworked in a bricolage fashion from something older. Thus, as social structures become more complicated, vocabularies and grammars will change. Vocabularies will get larger as there are more things to talk about. Grammars should become more complex in an attempt to signpost explicitly the more complex implications of having, at least, more things to talk about.

Rolfe (1996) has put forward a detailed argument as to how this elaboration is also motivated by the demands of different communicative purposes, thus leading to the bootstrapping of a propositional grammatical system from earlier structural principles. Similarly, the point is reinforced by Bloom's studies (e.g. 1981) on the differential ease of solving problems that are expressed through grammatical devices that are more or less familiar as tactics to speakers of different languages.[6] Like literacy (e.g. Scribner and Cole 1981), neither grammar, symbols, nor social structures are magic bullets, but are predisposers of certain outcomes in interaction with the cultural practices they constitute and support.

Conclusions

...it is precisely the conceptualizing of existing social relations and the formulating of them as symbolic 'tools', e.g. words, that mark the true transition from prehuman ancestor to man [sic]. It was when our ancestors began to gain awareness of the relationships they already recognized in terms of differential behaviour that man emerged (Reynolds 1976, p. 64).

In putting forward the above formulation, the focus on the late emergence of language under the push coming from the changes in social relations that provide, *sui generis*, a 'zone of proximal development', a different way of looking at the biology of

---

[6] Although Bloom's strong claims as to the relationship between grammatical structures available to Chinese and English speakers and their abilities to solve particular problems cast in particular grammatical formats have to be taken cautiously (see, for example, reviews in Lucy 1992, and Lock and Symes 1996), I do not think the view put forward here is an unwarranted interpretation of his findings.

human evolution is constructed. Language is now a species characteristic, but it is not one that was initially selected for. The biological substrates that support it have not been arrived at through their having evolved, but are constructed and reconstructed through an ontogeny that is embedded in a set of social relationships that continuously bootstrap themselves and the resources they conserve, thereby enabling the exaptation or co-option of an existing biology to ever more complex cognitive technologies. But this is not meant to completely de-biologize our views of human nature altogether. Certainly I am socializing human nature, but it is also certainly the case that many aspects of those social relations that contribute to and enable this humanizing process have their bases in biological constraints. Examples that come to mind here concern incest taboos, mate choice (Buss 1994), and social problem-solving (Cosmides 1989). It is precisely such phenomena that we might expect evolutionary processes to constrain and select biases for. But we were not designed for language use.

The consequences of this view are many. Here I draw out two points. *First*, the study of human discourse practices is moved from the fringe of psychological science to its centre, for the processes fundamental to the project of the so-called 'cognitive revolution' are no longer encapsulated within the head of an individual, but distributed in the symbolically-mediated practices that comprise human cultures, distributed between the individual and the social. Bruner (1990) has also argued for this view, though from a different starting point. He reflects analytically on the cognitive science that has been spawned by the cognitive revolution that he played such a role in forming. He deals with the consequences of what he sees as a 'neglect for meaning' in this cognitive science:

There is no question that cognitive science has made a contribution to our understanding of how information is moved about and processed. Nor can there be much doubt on reflection that it has left largely unexplained and even somewhat obscured the very large issues that inspired the cognitive revolution in the first place. So let us return to the question of how to construct a mental science around the concept of meaning and the processes by which meanings are created and negotiated within a community (p. 10).

He accomplishes in this work what Harré (1992) has called 'the second cognitive revolution'. Taking this line does not mean a retreat into subjectivism; an 'Umwelt approach' (Harré 1990) is computable (Bechtel 1993; see also Bechtel and Abrahamsen 1991). Nor does it mean attempting the impossible of comprehending what the world might look like to a bat, for example (Nagel 1974). What it does mean is that a set of approaches to human psychology that have often been argued by their own proponents to be antithetical to a cognitivist stance, and that have been marginalized by the mainstream of cognitive science, are central to the project.

Second, the analysis offered here credits discourse with tremendous powers. Discourse practices are being credited with a central role in the creation of the psychological abilities that underpin discursive practices themselves. 'Cognitive mechanisms', if they exist, are constructed out of an interaction between developmental, maturational, and socio-cultural processes, a constructive process in which the driving engine is a consequence of the changing structures of discourse and social relationships. That is, it is no longer sensible to assume a biologically-given individual with a set of pre-given cognitive abilities that allow information 'to be moved about and processed', nor, for that matter, to use this assumption to legitimate the currently dominant psychological paradigms. Meaningful second-generation cognitive science needs to pursue the Umwelt project; and in doing so it needs to bring a whole new paradigm of work into the mainstream.

References

Arensburg, B., Tillier, A. M., Vandermeersch, B., Duday, H., Schepartz, L., and Rak, Y. (1989). A Middle Palaeolithic human hyoid bone. *Nature*, **338**, 758–60.

Armstrong, D. F. and Katz, S. H. (1981). Brain laterality in signed and spoken language: a synthetic theory of language use. *Sign Language Studies*, **33**, 319–50.

Bamberg, M. (1996). *Language, concepts, and emotions: the role of language in the construction of emotions*. Visiting Scholar Series 6. Department of Psychology, Massey University, Palmerston North, New Zealand.

Bates, E., Benigni, L., Bretherton, I., Camaioni, L., and Volterra, V. (1979). *The emergence of symbols: cognition and communication in infancy*. Academic Press, New York.

Bates, E., Bretherton, I., and Snyder, L. (1988). *From first words to grammar*. Cambridge University Press.

Bechtel, W. (1993). The case for connectionism. *Philosophical Studies* **71**: 119–54.

Bechtel, W. and Abrahamsen, A. (1991). *Connectionism and the mind: an introduction to parallel processing in networks*. Blackwell, Oxford.

Bickerton, D. (1981). *Roots of language*. Karoma, Ann Arbor, MI.

Bickerton, D. (1990). *Language and species*. University of Chicago Press.

Binford, L. R. (1985). Human ancestors: changing views of their behavior. *Journal of Anthropological Archaeology*, **4**, 292–327.

Bloom, A. H. (1981). *The linguistic shaping of thought: a study in the impact of language on thinking in China and the West*. Erlbaum, Hillsdale, NJ.

Bradley, B. and Sampson, C. G. (1986). Analysis by replication of two Acheulian artefact assemblages. In *Stone age prehistory* (ed. G. N. Bailey and P. Callow), pp. 29–45. Cambridge University Press.

Bruner, J. S. (1990). *Acts of meaning*. Harvard University Press, Cambridge, MA.

Budwig, N. (1995). *A developmental–functionalist approach to child language*. Erlbaum, Hillsdale, NJ.

Buss, D. M. (1994). *The evolution of desire: strategies of human mating*. Basic Books, New York.

Campbell, B. G. (1996). An outline of human phylogeny. In *Handbook of human symbolic evolution* (ed. A. J. Lock and C. R. Peters), pp. 31–52. Clarendon Press, Oxford.

Capps, L. and Ochs, E. (1995a). *Constructing panic: the discourse of agoraphobia*. Harvard University Press, Cambridge, MA.

Capps, L. and Ochs, E. (1995b). Out of place: narrative insights into agoraphobia. *Discourse Processes*, **19**, 407–39.

Chase, P. and Dibble, H. (1987). Middle Paleolithic symbolism: a review of current evidence and interpretations. *Journal of Anthropological Archaeology*, **6**, 263–96.

Chomsky, N. (1968). *Language and mind*. Harcourt, New York.

Conkey, M. W. (1996). A history of the interpretation of European 'Palaeolithic art': magic, mythogram, and metaphors for modernity. In *Handbook of human symbolic evolution* (ed. A. J. Lock and C. R. Peters), pp. 288–349. Clarendon Press, Oxford.

Cosmides, L. (1989).The logic of social exchange: has natural selection shaped how humans reason? Studies with the Wason reasoning task. *Cognition*, **31**, 187–296.

Davidson, I. and Noble, W. (1992). Why the first colonization of the Australian region is the earliest evidence of modern human behaviour. *Archaeology in Oceania*, **27**, 135–42.

Davidson, I. and Noble, W. (1993). Tools and language in human evolution. In *Tools, language, and cognition in human evolution* (ed. K. R. Gibson and T. Ingold), pp. 363–88. Cambridge University Press.

de Lumley, H. (1975). Cultural evolution in France in its paleoecological setting during the Middle Pleistocene. In *After the australopithecines* (ed. K. Butzer and G. Isaac), pp. 745–808. Mouton, The Hague.

Dennell, R. (1983). *European economic prehistory: a new approach*. Academic Press, London.

Donald, M. (1991). *Origins of the modern mind: three stages in the evolution of culture and cognition*. Harvard University Press, Cambridge, MA.

Donald, M. (1993). Précis of *Origins of the modern mind:* three stages in the evolution of culture and cognition. *Behavioral and Brain Sciences*, **16**, 737–91.

Elias, N. (1978). *The civilizing process: Vol. I: The history of manners*. Blackwell, Oxford.

Elias, N. (1982). *The civilizing process: Vol. II: Power and civility*. Blackwell, Oxford.

Ettlinger, G. and Wilson, W. A. (1990). Cross-modal performance: behavioral processes, phylogenetic considerations and neural mechanisms. *Behavioral Brain Research*, **40**, 169–92.

Fagan, B. (1989). *People of the earth: an introduction to world prehistory* (6th edn). Scott Foresman, Glenview, IL.

Fischer, J. L. (1966). Syntax and social structure. Truk and Ponape. In *Sociolinguistics: proceedings of the UCLA sociolinguistics conference*, 1964 (ed. W. Bright), pp. 168–87. Mouton, The Hague.

Fischer, J. L. (1973). Communication in primitive systems. In *Handbook of communication* (ed. W. Schramm, I. de Sola Pool, N. Maccoby, E. B. Parker, and F. W. Frey), pp. 313–36. Rand McNally, Chicago.

Freeman, L. (1975). Acheulian sites and stratigraphy in Iberia and the Maghreb. In *After the australopithecines* (ed. K. Butzer and G. Isaac), pp. 661–744. Mouton, The Hague.

Gamble, C. (1986). *The Palaeolithic settlement of Europe*. Cambridge University Press.

Gamble, C. (1993). *Timewalkers: the prehistory of global colonization*. Penguin, London.

Goody, J. (1968). *Literacy in traditional societies*. Cambridge University Press.

Gould, S. J. (1991). Exaptation. *Journal of Social Issues*, **47**, 43–65.

Halverson, J. (1993). Mythos and logos. *Behavioral and Brain Sciences*, **16**, 762.

Harré, R. (1990). Exploring the human Umwelt. In *Harré and his critics: essays in honour of Rom Harré with his commentary on them*, (ed. R. Bhaskar). Blackwell, Oxford.

Harré, R. (1992). Introduction: the second cognitive revolution. *American Behavioral Scientist*, **36**, 5–7.

Hatano, G. (1982). Cognitive consequences of practice in culture-specific procedural skills. *Quarterly Newsletter of the Laboratory of Comparative Human Cognition*, **4**, 15–17.

Holloway, R. (1969). Culture: a human domain. *Current Anthropology*, **10**, 395–412.

Holloway, R. (1996). Evolution of the human brain. In *Handbook of human symbolic evolution* (ed. A. J. Lock and C. R. Peters), pp. 74–108. Clarendon Press, Oxford.

Hublin, J. J. (1985). Human fossils from the north African Middle Pleistocene and the origin of *Homo sapiens*. In *Ancestors: the hard evidence* (ed. E. Delson), pp. 283–8. Alan Liss, New York.

Keller, C. M. (1973). *Montagu Cave in prehistory*. University of California Press, Berkeley, CA.

Laitman, J. and Heimbuch, R. C. (1982). The basicranium of Plio-Pleistecene hominids as an indicator of their upper respiratory system. *American Journal of Physical Anthropology*, **59**, 323–43.

Laitman, J. and Heimbuch, R. C. (1984). The basicranium and upper respiratory system of African *Homo erectus* and early *H. sapiens*. *American Journal of Physical Anthropology*, **63**, 180.

Laitman, J. and Reidenberg, J. S. (1988). Advances in understanding the relationship between the skull base and larynx with comments on the origins of speech. *Human Evolution*, **3**, 99–109.

Laitman, J., Redenberg, J. S., Friedland, D. R., Reidenberg, B. E., and Gannon, P. J. (1992). Neanderthal upper respiratory specializations and their effect upon respiration and speech. *American Journal of Physical Anthropology*, **6**, 129.

Lieberman, P. (1991). *Uniquely human: the evolution of speech, thought, and selfless behavior*. Harvard University Press, Cambridge, MA.

Lindly, J. M. and Clark, G. A. (1990). Symbolism and modern human origins. *Current Anthropology*, **31**, 233–61.

Lock, A. J. (1980). *The guided reinvention of language*. Academic Press, London.

Lock, A. J. (1991). The role of social interaction in early language development. In *Biological and behavioral determinants of language development* (ed. N. Krasnegor, D. Rumbaugh, R. Schiefelbusch, and M. Studdert-Kennedy), pp. 287–300. Erlbaum, Hillsdale, NJ.

Lock, A. J. and Colombo, M. (1996). Cognitive abilities in a comparative perspective. In *Handbook of human symbolic evolution* (ed. A. J. Lock and C. R. Peters), pp. 596–643. Clarendon Press, Oxford.

Lock, A. J. and Peters, C. R. (1996). Ontogeny: symbolic development and symbolic evolution. In *Handbook of human symbolic evolution* (ed. A. J. Lock and C. R. Peters), pp. 371–99. Clarendon Press, Oxford.

Lock, A. J. and Symes, K. (1996). Social relations, communication, and cognition. In *Handbook of human symbolic evolution* (ed. A. J. Lock and C. R. Peters), pp. 204–35. Clarendon Press, Oxford.

Lock, A. J., Service, V., Brito, A., and Chandler, P. (1989). The social structuring of infant cognition. In *Infant development* (ed. G. Bremner and A. Slater), pp. 243–71. Erlbaum, London.

Lucy, J. A. (1992). *Linguistic diversity and thought: a reformulation of the linguistic relativity hypothesis*. Cambridge University Press.

Luria, A. R. and Yudovich, F. A. (1971). *Speech and the development of mental processes in the child*. Penguin, London.

Macmurray, J. (1961). *Persons in relation*. Faber and Faber, London.

Mead, G. H. (1934). *Mind, self, and society*. Chicago University Press.

Nagel, T. (1974). What is it like to be a bat? *Philosophical Review*, **83**, 435–50.

Nelson, K. (1973). Structure and strategy in learning to talk. *Monographs of the Society for Research in Child Development*, **38**, (1 and 2), Serial No. 149.

Noble, W. and Davidson, I. (1996). *Human evolution, language and mind*. Cambridge University Press.

Olson, D. R. (1996). Towards a psychology of literacy: on the relations between speech and writing. *Cognition*, **60**, 83–104.

Peters, C. R. (1996). Tempo and mode of change in the evolution of symbolism (a partial overview). In *Handbook of human symbolic evolution*, (ed. A. J. Lock and C. R. Peters). Clarendon Press, Oxford.

Piaget, J., foreword. In Gruber, H. E. (1974). *Darwin on man: a psychological study of creativity*, pp. ix–xi. Dutton, New York.

Pinker, S. (1994). *The language instinct*. Morrow, New York.

Popper, K. (1972). *Objective knowledge: an evolutionary approach*. Clarendon Press, Oxford.

Potts, R. (1989). Olorgesailie: new excavations and findings in Early and Middle Pleistocene contexts, southern Kenya rift valley. *Journal of Human Evolution*, **18**, 477–84.

Premack, D. (1980). Characteristics of an upgraded mind In *Bericht uber den 32. Kongress der Deutschen Gesellschaft fur Psychologie in Zurich, Vol. 1* (ed. W. Michaelis), pp. 49–70.

Reynolds, V. (1976). *The biology of human action*. Freeman, San Francisco.

Ristau, C. (1996). Animal language and cognition projects. In *Handbook of human symbolic evolution* (ed. A. J. Lock and C. R. Peters), pp. 644–85. Clarendon Press, Oxford.

Rolfe, L. (1996). Theoretical stages in the prehistory of grammar. In *Handbook of human symbolic evolution* (ed. A. J. Lock and C. R. Peters), pp. 776–792. Clarendon Press, Oxford.

Russell, J. (1996). Development and evolution of the symbolic function: the role of working memory. In *Modelling the early human mind* (ed. P. A. Mellars and K. Gibson). McDonald Institute for Archaeological Research, Cambridge.

Scribner, S. and Cole, M. (1981). *The psychology of literacy*. Harvard University Press, Cambridge, MA.

Shipman, P. and Rose, J. (1983). Evidence of butchery and hominid activities at Torralba and Ambrona: an evaluation using microscopic techniques. *Journal of Archaeological Science*, **10**, 465–74.

Stigler, J. W., Barclay, C., and Aiello, P. (1982). Motor and mental abacus skills: a preliminary look. *Quarterly Newsletter of the Laboratory of Comparative Human Cognition*, **4**, 12–4.

Stringer, C. (1985). On Zhoukoudian. *Current Anthropology*, **26**, 235.

Stringer, C. (1989). The origin of early modern humans: a comparison of the European and non-European evidence. In *The human revolution: behavioural and biological perspectives on the origins of modern humans* (ed. P. Mellars and C. Stringer), pp. 232–44. Princeton University Press.

Thieme, H. (1997). Lower Palaeolithic hunting spears from Germany. *Nature*, **385**, 807–10.

Tobias, P. V. (1987). The brain of *Homo habilis*. *Journal of Human Evolution*, **16**, 741–61.

Tobias, P. V. (1991). *Olduvai Gorge*. Cambridge University Press.

Tomasello, M., Savage-Rumbaugh, E. S., and Kruger, A. (1994). Imitative learning of actions on objects by children, chimpanzees, and enculturated chimpanzees. *Child Development*, **64**, 1688–705.

Toth, N. and Schick, K. (1993). Early stone industries and inferences regarding language and cognition. In *Tools, language, and cognition in human evolution* (ed. K. R. Gibson and T. Ingold), pp. 346–62. Cambridge University Press.

Volosinov, V. N. (1973). *Marxism and the philosophy of language*. Harvard University Press, Cambridge, MA.

von Uexkull, T. (1982). Introduction: meaning and science in Jacob von Uexkull's concept of biology. *Semiotica*, **42**, 1–24.

Vygotsky, L. S. (1962). *Thought and language*. MIT Press, Cambridge, MA.

Vygotsky, L. S. (1978). *Mind in society*. Harvard University Press, Cambridge, MA.

Waddell, P. J. and Penny, D. (1996). Evolutionary trees of apes and humans from DNA sequences. In *Handbook of human symbolic evolution* (ed. A. J. Lock and C. R. Peters), pp. 53–73. Clarendon Press, Oxford.

Whallon, R. (1989). Elements of cultural change in the later Palaeolithic. In *The human revolution: behavioural and biological perspectives on the origins of modern humans* (ed. P. Mellars and C. Stringer), 433–54. Edinburgh University Press.

White, R. (1996). On the evolution of human socio-cultural patterns. In *Handbook of human symbolic evolution* (ed. A. J. Lock and C. R. Peters), pp. 239–62. Clarendon Press, Oxford.

Wilkins, W. K. and Wakefield, J. (1995). Brain evolution and neurolinguistic preconditions. *Behavioral and Brain Sciences*, **18**, 161–226.

Wilson, P. J. (1988). *The domestication of the human species*. Yale University Press, New Haven.

Wood, B. (1992). Origin and evolution of the genus *Homo*. *Nature*, **355**, 783–90.

Wynn, T. (1979). The intelligence of later Acheulean hominids. Man, 14, 379–91.

Wynn, T. (1996). The evolution of tools and symbolic behaviour. In *Handbook of human symbolic evolution* (ed. A. J. Lock and C. R. Peters), pp. 263–87. Clarendon Press, Oxford.

Yellen, J. E., Brooks, A. S., Cornelissen, E., Mehlman, M. J., and Stewart, K. (1995). A Middle Stone Age bone industry from Katanda, Upper Semliki Valley, Zaire. Science, **268**, 553–6.

Index